Warman's GLASS

ELLEN TISCHBEIN SCHROY

Wallace-Homestead Book Company
Radnor, Pennsylvania

Copyright © 1992 by Ellen Tischbein Schroy

All Rights Reserved
Published in Radnor, Pennsylvania 19089, by Wallace-Homestead,
a division of Chilton Book Company

Manufactured in the United States of America

Library of Congress Cataloging-in-Publication Data

Schroy, Ellen Tischbein.
    Warman's glass / Ellen Tischbein Schroy.
        p.   cm.—(Encyclopedia of antiques and collectibles)
    ISBN 0-87069-643-2 (pbk.)
    1. Glassware—Collectors and collecting—Catalogs.   I. Title.
  II. Series.
NK5104.S37   1992
748.2'075—dc20   92-50190
                                                   CIP

ON THE COVER. *Back row:* Pattern glass, blue Hobnail water tray, **$115.00;** amethyst candlestick, **$75.00;** lemonade set, amber with hand-painted florals, twig-style basket, c. 1910, **$350.00;** Vallerystahl covered dish, blue milk glass, squirrel finial, **$125.00.** *Middle row:* Heisey basket, **$120.00;** barber bottle, original pewter top, **$95.00;** Pattern glass, vaseline Daisy and Button berry bowl, **$45.00;** Cranberry cruet, **$75.00.** *Front row:* Dark amber flask, **$200.00;** Pattern glass salt shaker, blue, original top, **$20.00;** opalescent striped mustard jar, original top, **$65.00;** Degenhart paperweight, **$75.00;** Pattern glass, dark green rose bowl, **$75.00;** Candlewick shaker, **$10.00.**

2 3 4 5 6 7 8 9 0   1 0 9 8 7 6 5 4

Volumes in the Encyclopedia of Antiques and Collectibles

Harry L. Rinker, Series Editor

Warman's Americana & Collectibles, 5th Edition
  edited by Harry L. Rinker

Warman's Country Antiques & Collectibles
  by Dana N. Morykan and Harry L. Rinker

Warman's English & Continental Pottery & Porcelain, 2nd Edition
  by Susan and Al Bagdade

Warman's Glass
  by Ellen Tischbein Schroy

Warman's Oriental Antiques
  by Gloria and Robert Mascarelli

INTRODUCTION

Warman's Glass offers collectors and dealers in antiques and collectibles information about all the major glass collecting categories in one book. As part of the **Warman's Encyclopedia of Antiques and Collectibles** series, **Warman's Glass** gives readers a wealth of information and price listings, all relating to the colorful world of glass collecting. It also serves as a companion to **Warman's Antiques and Their Prices**.

Warman's Glass includes listings for the antiques marketplace, collectibles marketplace, modern editions, and studio art of contemporary craftsmen. Because this is a "Warman's" book, you will find detailed information relating to the history of a glass type and/or company, reference books, collectors' clubs, and tips to spotting reproductions. Of course, the listings are as detailed as possible. Careful attention has been given to listing correct pattern names, colors, sizes, and other pertinent details.

Warman's Glass covers individual companies, such as Degenhart and Northwood, as well as general glass categories such as Depression Glass and Pattern Glass. Since **Warman's Glass** is a price *guide*, it cannot list every pattern or piece made. Hopefully there will be more volumes utilizing the Warman approach that will cover Pattern glass, Depression glass, etc. Warman's is continually increasing the glass coverage in the Warman price guides as more knowledge and references are found. For over forty years, Warman guides have been the leaders in the antiques and collectibles field, a tradition this and subsequent books will continue.

HISTORY

Historians date early examples of glassware back as far as the third century BC. These early combinations of sand and ash were probably the results of accidental mixing at the edges of a fire. The first attempts at glassmaking are not well documented, but examples of early utilitarian pieces, such as bottles and bowls, have survived. The Egyptians used glass objects and were very fond of small beads and pieces which they used as decorations. Because of the treasures found in the pyramids, historians have been able to document early glassware pieces.

Glass bottles and jars, made from local raw materials, were used to preserve and transport foods. Color variations of these early pieces allow modern science to evaluate what type of sand and other minerals were available to the glassblowers. As the technologies for glassblowing and finally mass production evolved, so did the uses for glass. Utilitarian objects, such as window panes, were followed by production of decorative objects. Scientific use of glass led to advances in many fields. We really don't consider when taking a piece of Corningware out of the freezer and putting in the microwave that it is really a piece of glass and that the ability to use glass in this fashion developed only recently. Glass was first used for storage, only later for cooking.

Glassblowers and manufacturers are credited with many patents for glass techniques as well as manufacturing advances. However, the real credit for attracting collectors to glass must be given to those who constantly strived to develop new colors and shapes.

By adding certain minerals and chemicals, glass changes color and can become stronger or weaker. Certain combinations, such as the one Findlay used for his beautiful onyx ware, created stunning pieces, but the glass was very brittle and as a result few examples survive.

Antique and collectible glassware is like precious gemstones in some ways. Glassware is available in every color and hue of the rainbow. Like precious stones, glass can be engraved, carved, etched, and made into wonderful creations. European glassmakers created masterpieces by engraving crystal objects with detailed portraits and other types of decoration. Cameo glass by Gallé and Daum Nancy were blown and featured carved layers of different colors, much the same way cameo jewelry brooches are created by carving shells. Etched intaglio designs grace cut glass as well as later mass-produced pieces made by companies like Imperial and Fostoria.

Crystal clear glassware was the objective of early blowers as they experimented with different combinations. Cut glass decorators demanded high quality clear leaded glass for their creations.

Experimental color combinations by artists such as Louis Tiffany and Frederick Carder at Steuben resulted in the iridescent hues of Favrile and Aurene glass. Cambridge and Heisey produced vivid translucent colors like Heatherbloom and Flamingo pink. Colors of rich deep blue, amethyst, emerald green, and blood red can also be found.

Glassware has always been manufactured to appeal to the female eye. Brides could choose their trousseau for table settings with specialized serving pieces such as berry bowls, cheese domes, and pickle castors. Today brides can choose from hundreds of crystal patterns, but do not have access to the wide variety of firms that manufactured their grandmother's and great grandmother's glassware.

CARE AND STORING TIPS

Glass is easy to care for and store. Since most glass was produced for utilitarian purposes manufacturers designed their products for heavy use while making them appealing to the eye. Many objects were mass produced. The survival rate is high.

Today's collector often can purchase mint or fine condition examples of most glass, provided they are willing to pay the price. Pieces that show aging, e.g., some gilding removed through washing, also are desirable, since they tend to prove they are not reproductions.

Glassware can be repaired using modern techniques that produce amazing results. Edges with chips can be ground. Price is lowered, but often not significantly. Most importantly, the glass is available for reuse and its beauty can continue to be appreciated.

Take care when purchasing glassware. Examine each piece carefully. Look and feel for wear and imperfections. After purchase, make certain to wrap each piece separately in several layers. Glass will shatter not only when dropped, but also when exposed to changes in temperature. If you purchase a piece, carry it around for several hours, and suddenly go out into the cold air, beware. Don't unwrap it. Allow it to adjust gradually to the change in temperature. Likewise, when you take it back indoors, gently unwrap the piece and allow it to reach room temperature before adding it to your collection. Never wash glassware until it reaches room temperature.

Storing a newly acquired piece in a car trunk for hours is fine. Just do not take it into the house and wash it immediately in cold water. Milk glass of the post World War II era is especially vulnerable to changes in temperature.

Today we know that exposing clear flint glassware to strong sunlight may cause it to chemically react and develop a purple hue. The popular decorating idea of the 1920s through the 1950s of placing shelves of glassware in window frames has proved disastrous for many pieces of glass. What our modern home environment will do to glassware is still not clearly established. Colored glassware hues do not appear to fade, but we are not yet sure what affect artificial light and heat have on glassware.

Most antique and collectible glassware should never see the inside of a dishwasher. The temperatures are too severe and the water pressure too great. Gently hand washing glassware protects the pieces and gives collectors an opportunity to study their collections. Learn the feel of the glassware, take note of the weight and sharpness of the cuttings or pattern. This knowledge will help you spot reproductions and copycats.

When storing antique and collectible glassware, make sure the storage area is sturdy. Shelves should be well secured. One should periodically check that glass objects are not moving slightly because of normal vibrations. Objects should not touch one another. Pieces of packing materials should be used between stacked objects.

ORGANIZATION OF THE BOOK

Listings: I have attempted to make the listings descriptive enough so the specific object can be identified. While most guides limit their descriptions to one line, **Warman's** books contain comprehensive listings. Emphasis has been placed on those items which are actively being sold in the marketplace, but some harder–to–find objects are included in order to demonstrate the market spread. A few categories in this book also appear in **Warman's**

Antiques and Their Prices, and **Warman's Americana and Collectibles.** The listings in **Warman's Glass** expand on these two volumes, creating a new companion volume for the general dealer or specialized collector.

Prices for listings have been obtained from many key sources: dealers, publications, auctions, collectors, and field work. Dealers have been generous with advice; everyone recognizes the need for a guide that is specific and has accurate prices.

Condition is critical in glass collecting. Any conditions which may affect the price have been noted. Whenever possible, examples in good or very good condition have been used as the basis of the prices given.

History: Every collector should know something about the history of his object. We have presented a capsule background for each category. Research in many of the glass collecting categories is ongoing. Collectors are encouraged to continue to learn and share their knowledge about their specific interests. Research of the past decades by such people as Ruth Webb Lee, George and Helen McKearin, Alice Metz, and E. McCamley Belknap has been enhanced by modern researchers such as the late William Heacock.

References: A few general references are listed to encourage collectors to learn more about their objects. Included are author, title, most recent edition, publisher (if published by a small firm or individual, we have indicated "published by author"), and a date of publication. Finding these books may be a bit difficult, but the antiques and collectibles field is blessed with a dedicated core of book dealers who stock these specialized publications. You may find them at flea markets, antiques shows, and through advertisements in leading publications in the field. Many dealers publish annual or semi–annual catalogs. Ask to be put on their mailing lists. Books can go out–of–print quickly, yet many books printed over twenty–five years ago remain the standard work in a field. Also, haunt used book dealers for collectible reference material.

Collectors' Clubs: The large number of collectors' clubs add vitality to the collectibles field. Their publications and conventions produce knowledge which often cannot be found anywhere else. Many of these clubs are short-lived; others are so strong that they have regional and local chapters.

Periodicals: There are several general and specialized periodicals to which the glass collector should subscribe:

Antique Bottle & Glass Collector, PO Box 187, East Greenville, PA 18041.
Antique Glass Quarterly, Rudi Publishing, PO Box 1364, Iowa City, IA 52244.
Antique Week, PO Box 90, Knightstown, IN 46148.
Antiques & Collecting Hobbies, 1006 South Michigan Avenue, Chicago, IL 60605.
Collector News & Antique Reporter, Box 156, Grundy Center, IA 50638.
Glass Collector's Digest, Antique Publications, PO Box 553, Marietta, OH 45750–0553.
Maine Antique Digest, Box 358, Waldoboro, ME 04572.
The Antique Trader Weekly, Box 1050, Dubuque, IA 52001.
The Daze, Depression Glass Daze, Inc., 275 State Road, Box 57, Otisville, MI 48463–0057.

It is impossible to list all the national and regional publications in the antiques and collectibles field. Check your local library for other publications.

Museums: The best way to study a specific field is to see as many documented examples as possible. For this reason, museums with significant collections on display are included. Special attention must be directed to the complex of museums which make up the Smithsonian Institution in Washington, DC. Premier collections of glassware are available for study at several major museums including the Chrysler Museum in Norfolk, VA; the Corning Museum of Glass, Corning, NY; and the Toledo Art Museum, Toledo, OH.

Reproductions: Reproductions are a major concern. Because most are unmarked, the newness of their appearance is often the best clue to uncovering them. Reproduction Alerts appear in the text, read the entire category with them in mind. Glass collectors should also be aware that paper labels have been reproduced. It is unfortunate when these "new" labels find their way into the marketplace, and unforgivable when they are applied to glassware to enhance the price!

Reproductions are only one aspect of the problem; outright fakes are another. Unscrupulous manufacturers make fantasy items which never existed. Reproduction Eyewinker goblets can easily be found, yet the Eyewinker pattern never included a goblet.

Depression glass patterns with an ''*'' indicate that reproductions exist in that pattern; sometimes the entire pattern has been reproduced, other times only a few pieces have been reproduced. Now that importers have started to reproduce the reproductions, collectors must take care when purchasing many of these patterns.

Marks: Antique and collectible glass pieces may have manufacturers marks. Unfortunately, most types of glass are unmarked. It was very difficult to include a mark in a mold. Certain marks, like Heisey's "H" in a diamond, are rather small and can be difficult to find. Some of the acid etched glass marks are also difficult to identify. Careful study of pieces is necessary. Paper labels may have become lost over the years. The dates given on the marks included in this volume are often approximate. Several manufacturers, like Imperial Glass, used several different marks. Marks should be considered as clues, just as style, color, and other characteristics, to the discovery of the maker and date of manufacture.

BUYER'S GUIDE, NOT SELLER'S GUIDE

Warman's Glass is designed to be a buyer's guide to what you would have to pay for an object on the open market from a dealer or collector. **It is not a seller's guide to prices.** If you see one of your possessions in this book and wish to sell it, you should expect to receive approximately 35% to 40% of the value listed. If the object cannot be resold quickly, expect to receive even less. The truth is simple. Knowing to whom to sell an object is worth 50% or more of its value. Buyers are very specialized; dealers work for years to assemble a list of collectors who will pay top dollar for an item. Examine your glass piece as objectively as possible. If it is something from your childhood, try to step back from the personal memories in evaluating its worth.

COMMENTS INVITED

Warman's Glass is a major effort to deal with a complex field. Readers are encouraged to send their comments and suggestions to Ellen T. Schroy, Rinker Enterprises, Inc., 5093 Vera Cruz Road, Emmaus, PA 18049.

STATE OF THE MARKET

Investing in glassware offers opportunities to spend from a few dollars to hundreds of thousands of dollars. A new piece of Fenton glassware can be added to a collection often for $10 or less, while a choice piece of Boston and Sandwich glassware can cost thousands of dollars. Collectors often specialize in a specific pattern or type of glass to provide definition and restraint to what they already have.

Current glass collecting opportunities reflect new areas of interest as well as strongly established older categories. Collectors are continually offered a new rainbow of colors and objects. Modern glass collectibles, such as Fenton, are often purchased with the same zeal as toys. Original boxes are treasured, documentation and advertisements are saved, labels are never removed. Collectors of eighteenth-, nineteenth-, and early twentieth-century glass face different challenges—who made the piece, how was it used, when was it made, etc.

Specialized antiques and collectibles shows concentrating primarily on glass are doing well in the 1990s. Dealers continue to offer high quality glassware. More specialized shows, such as cut glass shows and Depression era glass shows, are drawing more and more collectors. These specialized shows feature a larger variety of patterns and pieces than are found at a general show and expand a collector's horizons. A Depression glass show includes not only the patterns defined as Depression glass, like Miss America, but also fine glassware produced by Heisey, Cambridge, and others. Specialized shows are a wonderful place to experience the myriad of colors available, learn about the shapes, and see the wealth of sizes produced.

General antiques shows of the 1990s must present a balanced approach. Promoters actively try to include dealers who represent the broad market. You will find dealers offering art glass, cut glass, Depression glass, and Pattern glass. General line dealers also offer some glassware items. While general attendance at shows has declined slightly during the past few years due to the recession, glass collecting continues on all levels.

Overall, prices are generally stable, making glassware a favored inventory among dealers. When a particular pattern or type of glassware becomes desirable, dealers offer their best examples. When collecting interest wanes, the glassware is simply packed away until the pattern regains its popularity. It will not tarnish, deteriorate, or be eaten by moths. Few other collecting categories offer this kind of stability.

Glassware dealers maintain a large undisplayed inventory. When a customer wants a specific piece, they can often reach into their reserves and supply it. Few other dealers can do this. It is this type of "customer service" that sets glass dealers apart in the antiques and collectibles field.

Glassware collecting categories that bear watching in the next few years include Northwood, many patterns of Pattern glass, glassware from the 1930 to 1950 period (including patterns made for World War II brides), and studio craftsmen glass.

Buy what you like, use it if you wish, and display it so you can enjoy it.

ACKNOWLEDGMENTS

After ten years as an editor on **Warman's Antiques and Their Prices** and **Warman's Americana and Collectibles** and helping with several other publications, it's time for me to write a price guide covering my favorite thing, glassware. And, like other authors, it is now time to write the hardest page, you know the one, the acknowledgments. To just say thanks to all the wonderful dealers, auctioneers, collectors, and others who have generously shared their collections and assistance, isn't quite enough. Perhaps, "thank you very much for all your kindness and consideration" is better, but still hardly adequate. The antiques and collectibles business is filled with people who gladly share their knowledge and love of their collections.

Thanks to a great boss, Harry L. Rinker, who has shared his unique perspective of the antiques and collectibles field with me for the past ten years. After ten years, it's hard to explain how this working relationship has grown. It's truly an honor to be called a Rinkette. This silly name has real meaning at Rinker Enterprises. It's the name for a wonderful, warm bunch of people who never hesitate to offer a hand and lend a helpful word of encouragement, and who will forever have my thanks.

A special thanks is also extended to Sarah Hamill at Skinner, Inc. and Diane M. Waters at William Doyle Galleries for their assistance in securing some of the excellent photographs included in this book. Thanks also to Bill Jenks for his photos used in the Pattern Glass category. And, of course, a big thanks to all those friends and family members who graciously opened their cupboards and collections to me and allowed their objects to be photographed.

Thanks, too, to Edna Jones and Troy Vozzella for all their encouragement and attention to the details that made the very production of this book a joy. Their fine assistance along with the others at Chilton Book Company enhances all our book projects.

Thanks to a great family for their loving care and support. Their understanding of this effort made it easier and more important. Thanks especially to a dear husband and son, Jeffrey and Mark, who shall forever have special places in my heart.

And, now, dear readers, thanks to you too, for without readers, researchers, collectors, and dealers, this book would be without purpose. Please handle it with care, it's fragile just like the subject matter—glass. And, with your comments and suggestions, it may be able to continue and gleam like a wonderful piece of cut crystal!

Ellen Louise Tischbein Schroy

AUCTION HOUSES

The following auction houses cooperate with Rinker Enterprises, Inc., by providing catalogs of their auctions and price lists. This information is used to prepare **Warman's Antiques and Their Prices**, volumes in the Warman's Encyclopedia of Antiques and Collectibles, such as **Warman's Glass**, and Wallace–Homestead Book Company publications. Their support is most appreciated.

Sanford Alderfer Auction
  Company
501 Fairgrounds Rd.
Hatfield, PA 19440
(215) 368-5477

Ark Antiques
Box 3133
New Haven, CT 06515
(203) 387-3754

Richard A. Bourne Co.,
  Inc.
Corporation St.
P. O. Box 141
Hyannis Port, MA 02647
(508) 775-0797

Butterfield's
220 San Bruno Ave.
San Francisco, CA 94103
(415) 861-7500

Christie's
502 Park Ave.
New York, NY 10022
(212) 546-1000

William Doyle Galleries,
  Inc.
175 E. 87th St.
New York, NY 10128
(212) 427-2730

Early Auction Co.
123 Main St.
Milford, OH 45150
(513) 831-4833

Fine Arts Co. of
  Philadelphia, Inc.
1808 Chestnut St.
Philadelphia, PA 19103
(215) 563-9275

Garth's Auction, Inc.
2690 Stratford Rd.
P. O. Box 369
Delaware, OH 43015
(614) 362-4771 or 369-
  5085

Glass-Works Auctions
P. O. Box 187-102
Jefferson St.
East Greenville, PA 18041
(215) 679-5849

Guerney's
136 East 73rd St.
New York, NY 10021
(212) 794-2280

Hake's Americana and
  Collectibles
P. O. Box 1444
York, PA 17405
(717) 848-1333

Harmer Rooke
  Numismatists, Inc.
3 East 57th St.
New York, NY 10022
(212) 751-4122

Hart Galleries
2311 Westheimer
Houston, TX 77098
(713) 524-2979 or 523-
  7389

Norman C. Heckler &
  Company
Bradford Corner Rd.
Woodstock Valley, CT
  06282
(203) 974-1634

Leslie Hindman, Inc.
215 West Ohio St.
Chicago, IL 60610
(312) 670-0010

James D. Julia, Inc.
P. O. Box 830
Fairfield, ME 04937
(207) 453-7904

Mid-Hudson Auction
  Galleries
One Idlewild Ave.
Cornwall-On-Hudson, NY
  12520
(214) 534-7828

Milwaukee Auction
  Galleries
318 N. Water
Milwaukee, WI 53202
(414) 271-1105

Neal Alford Company
4038 Magazine St.
New Orleans, LA 70115
(504) 899-5329

Nostalgia Publications, Inc.
21 South Lake Dr.
Hackensack, NJ 07601
(201) 488-4536

Pettigrew Auction
  Company
1645 South Tejon St.
Colorado Springs, CO
  80906
(719) 633-7963

David Rago Arts & Crafts
P. O. Box 3592 Station E
Trenton, NJ 08629
(609) 585-2546

Roan Bros. Auction Gallery
R.D. 3, Box 118
Cogan Station, PA 17728
(717) 494-0170

Robert W. Skinner, Inc.
Bolton Gallery
357 Main St.
Bolton, MA 01740
(508) 779-6241

Sotheby's
1334 York Ave.
New York, NY 10021
(212) 606-7000

Western Glass Auctions
1288 W. 11th St., Suite
  #230
Tracy, CA 95376
(209) 832-4527

Woody Auction
Douglass, KS 67039
(316) 746-2694

ABBREVIATIONS

The following are standard abbreviations which are used throughout this volume.

ah	=	applied handle	ls	=	low standard
C	=	century	MIB	=	mint in box
c	=	circa	MOP	=	mother of pearl
cov	=	cover	NE	=	New England
d	=	diameter or depth	No.	=	number
dec	=	decorated	orig	=	original
DQ	=	Diamond Quilted	os	=	orig stopper
emb	=	embossed	pcs	=	pieces
ext.	=	exterior	pr	=	pair
ftd	=	footed	rect	=	rectangular
ground	=	background	sgd	=	signed
h	=	height	sngl	=	single
hp	=	hand painted	SP	=	silver plated
hs	=	high standard	SS	=	Sterling silver
imp	=	impressed	sq	=	square
int.	=	interior	unsgd	=	unsigned
irid	=	iridescent	w	=	width
IVT	=	inverted thumbprint	#	=	numbered
l	=	length			

ABC PLATES

History: The majority of early ABC plates were manufactured in England, imported into the United States, and achieved their greatest popularity from 1780 to 1860. American glassware manufacturers were eager to have glass ABC plates compete in the marketplace. Glass examples could offer another dimension by embossing and/or stippling. The alphabet letters which often surround the rim helped teach a child in the days before formal schooling was available to all.

Glass ABC plates are found in pressed patterns in clear and a wide rainbow of colors. Some designs were based on nursery rhymes, while others reflect the events of the times, like the assassination of President Garfield.

References: Mildred L. and Joseph P. Chalala, *A Collector's Guide to ABC Plates, Mugs, and Things*, Pridemark Press, 1980; Doris Anderson Lechler, *Children's Glass Dishes, China and Furniture Volume II*, Collector Books, 1986, 1990 value update; Margaret and Ken Whitmyer, *Children's Dishes*, Collector Books, 1984.

Milk Glass, "Easter Greetings," gilt letters and beaded edge, floral center, 7" d, $35.00.

5¼" d, Sancho Panza and Dapple, stippled alphabet border	45.00
6" d	
Amber	
Ducks	45.00
Thousand Eye	50.00
Blue	
Dog's head	45.00
Thousand Eye	55.00
Clear	
Barley pattern	45.00
Cane pattern, stippled ground rim with alphabets	30.00
Deer and Tree pattern	50.00
Ding Dong Bell	70.00
Elephant, three figures on howdah waving flag, sgd "R & C" for Ripley & Co	150.00
Emma, girl's head in center, beaded rim, Higbee mark	85.00
Floral bouquet, bow trim	50.00
Garfield, President, profile bust in center, frosted alphabet border	65.00
Hen and chicks	40.00
Starburst center, scalloped rim, New Martinsville	25.00
Star Medallion pattern	40.00
Stork pattern	95.00
Westward Ho pattern	50.00
Cobalt Blue, child's face in center	35.00
Green, Thousand Eye	55.00
Frosted, running rabbit	50.00
Vaseline, Thousand Eye	52.00
6¼" d, clear, frosted center, Christmas Morning, stippled alphabet border	175.00
7" d	
Blue, clock	35.00
Carnival, stork	65.00
Clear, Centennial Exhibition 1776–1876	50.00
Milk Glass, plain center, emb alphabet border, beaded rim	45.00
7¾" d, clear, Arabic and Roman numerals	50.00

ADVERTISING

History: Advertising on glass began with early bottles. Other types of containers, from pickle jars to whiskey bottles, can be found engraved, etched, painted, and labeled. Early manufacturers often used illustrations of the product so that even an illiterate buyer could identify a product. The country store of years past was filled with glass jars which contained advertising and slogans.

Another popular way of advertising was a giveaway or premium. Many types of glassware articles were given away by merchants, manufacturers, and salesmen. Carnival glass was popular with the advertiser because it was durable and it was equally popular with the housewife because it was pretty. Today, carnival glass advertising plates and other forms command a high price.

Usually a collector does not think of glass as a medium when considering advertising collectibles. However, the variety of colors, shapes, and sizes, makes an interesting collection. Many bottles and other types of glass containers have been replaced by plastic containers and the former brown, green, and cobalt blue containers are becoming collectible.

References: Al Bergevin, *Food and Drink Containers and Their Prices*, Wallace–Homestead,

1988; Barbara Edmonson, *Old Advertising Spirits Glasses,* Maverick Publications, 1988; Ralph and Terry Kovel, *Kovels' Advertising Collectibles Price List,* Crown Publishers Inc., 1986; Douglas Congdon–Martin, *Antique Advertising: America for Sale,* Schiffer Publishing, 1991.

Ashtray
    Barber Supplies, William Marvy, clear, red, white, and blue adv, 5" d **15.00**
    Coon Chicken Inn, clear, black bell hop, c1930, 4" w **25.00**
    Dobbs Hats, dark amethyst, hat shape **24.00**
    Goodrich Tire, green, tire shape **45.00**
    Goodyear, amber, tire shape **32.00**
    Grapette Soda, milk glass **35.00**
    Levy's Jewish Rye Bread, milk glass, Art Deco shape, illus of black boy eating bread **65.00**
    Royal Caribbean Cruise Lines, octagonal, clear, blue crown and anchor logo, 4" w **12.00**

Bank, Elsie the Cow, 4½" h, $22.50.

Bank
    Esso, clear, emb "Watch Savings Grow" **15.00**
    Grapette, clear, clown shape **25.00**
    Lincoln Bank, clear, bottle shape, orig top hat, paper label, 9" h **45.00**
    Pittsburgh Paints, clear, log cabin shape, paper label **25.00**
Barber Bottle
    Le Varns Hair Tonic, clear, painted label **70.00**
    T Noonan Barber Supply Co., cobalt blue **50.00**
Basket, John H. Brand Furniture Co. Wilmington, DE, carnival glass, marigold **90.00**
Bath Salts Jar, California Perfume Company, Ariel, white opaque, ribbed, 1903 .... **70.00**

Bowl, carnival glass
    Horlacher, Peacock Tail pattern, purple **85.00**
    Issac Benesch, purple, 6¼" d, Millersburg mark **175.00**
    Ogden Furniture Co., purple **225.00**
    Sterling Furniture Co., purple **245.00**
Bread Plate, Pioneer Flour Mill, San Antonio, clear, pressed glass **45.00**
Calling Card Tray, carnival glass
    Fern Brand Chocolates, purple, turned up sides, 6¼" d **175.00**
    Issac Benesch, Holly Whirl pattern, marigold **100.00**
Candy Dish, Schraft's Chocolates, clear, pressed, 6" sq **25.00**
Ceiling Globe, Pittsburgh Ice Cream, red and black lettering reads "We Serve The Cream of Pittsburgh," milk glass base, 1917 patent **325.00**
Champagne Glass, Compliments of Frederick Bary Co., trumpet shape, cranberry, 22" h **175.00**
Decanter, backbar, Belle of Kentucky, crystal, ribbed, gold letters, orig stopper **100.00**
Dish, Compliments of Pacific Coast Mail Order House, Los Angeles, CA, carnival glass **700.00**
Dispenser
    Hunter's Root Beer, milk glass **45.00**
    Radium Vitalizer, vaseline colored clear glass body, emb letters, cylindrical, metal spigot and lid, 10 x 16" **425.00**
Display Case, counter type, clear
    Dr. West's Toothbrush **375.00**
    Tootsie Rolls, front reads "Pure Delicious Chocolate Candy" **335.00**
Display Jar, clear
    Adam's Pure Chewing Gum, square, thumbprint–type design on stopper, etched label, 11" h, 5" w **135.00**
    American Nut Company, spherical, flattened ball finial on cov, flanged lip, emb label and "Highest Quality Salt Peanuts," 12" h, 10" d **115.00**
    Beich's Candy, clear, sixteen sides, emb lettering, 10" h **50.00**
    Chico's Peanuts, clear glass jar, tin litho lid and base **275.00**
    Compressed Lozenges, H. K. Mulford Co., Phila and Chicago, brown, sq, metal screw top, c1880, 11½" h . **75.00**
    Faultless Wonder Nipples, round, amber frosted glass nipple–shaped cov, emb label, 13" h, 8½" d **800.00**
    Kis–Me Chewing Gum, American Chicle Co, square, chamfered corners, glass stopper, flanged lip, emb "Kiss–Me," paper label **450.00**
    La Palina Cigars, round, knob finial

on cov, emb and paper labels, 7"
h, 6" d 70.00

Lutted's S.P. Cough Drops, cabin
shaped, chimney finial on roof cov,
emb shingle, log, and window designs, emb label and "Genuine Has
'J.L' Stamped On Each Drop," ftd,
7" h, 7¾" l, 5" w 415.00

Peerless Hardwater Soap, spherical,
metal threaded lid, canted, red
stencil–style label on raised band
around 135.00

Planter's Peanut, barrel shaped, peanut finial on cov, emb lettering,
staves, and Mr Peanut characters
10" h 110.00
12" h, 8½" d 225.00

Ramon's Brownie Products, round,
blue lettering and trademark illus
on yellow metal lid, blue "Ramon's
Quality Medicine" label and doctor
illus on jar 125.00

Rexall Drug, spherical, emb script label, no cov, 4½" h, 5" d 145.00

Swift's Toilet Soap, semi ovoid, glass
cov, emb label 175.00

Walla Walla Pepsin Gum, Walla
Walla Gum Co, Knoxville, TN,
square, swirled finial on stopper,
flanged lip, emb label and head
and shoulder Indian wearing head-
dress, 13½" h, 5" w 165.00

Hat, carnival glass
Horlacher, Peacock Tail pattern,
green 90.00
John Brand Furniture, green 45.00
Miller's Furniture, Harrisburg, basket-
weave, marigold 90.00

Ice Cream Dish, Borden's, illus of Elsie
the Cow 15.00

Measure, Birely Soda, clear 10.00

Measuring Cup, Lenkerbrook Farms,
Inc, Pyrex, clear, 8 oz, red letters .. 5.00

Mug, Golden Knight Shaving Soap,
clear, emb letters 15.00

Paperweight
American Card Clothing Co., Worces-
ter, MA, 1882, clear 25.00
Bell System, cobalt blue, bell shape 95.00
Columbia National Bank, clear 12.00
Independent Press Room, Los Ange-
les, clear, rect 15.00
Leeson & Co., Boston, Linen Thread
Importers, clear, black and white
illus, 4⅛" l 50.00
Lehigh Sewer Pipe & Tile Co., Ft
Dodge, IA, clear, 4" l 15.00
Old Bridgeport Double Copper Dis-
tilled Pure Rye Whiskey, Browns-
ville, PA, clear, 3" d 30.00
Osborne Co. Harvesting Machinery,
Auburn, NY, clear 25.00

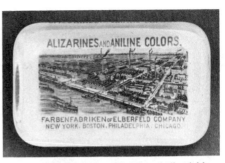

Paperweight, Farbenfabriken of Elberfeld
Company, city view, black illus, red letters, 4 x 2½", $25.00.

Radekar Lumber Co., men working
logs, multicolored scene, milk glass 50.00
Wurtz Auto Garage, Degenhart clear,
mark 55.00

Perfume Bottle, clear
California Perfume Company, Carnation, 1 oz, ribbed, 1923 .... 125.00
Le Golliwogg, de Vigney, Paris,
frosted glass body, painted label,
black puff wig, stopper with figural
Golliwogg head, 3½" h 75.00
Lucky Lindy Perfume, Nipoli Co.,
clear, 1927 .... 25.00
Owl Drug Co., Oil of Sweet Almond
label, 1 oz, cork top 5.00

Plate, Goofus glass, Old Rose Distilling
Co., Chicago, 8¼" d, $65.00.

Plate, carnival glass
Brazier Candles, purple, hand grip, 6"
d 250.00
Campbell & Beesley Co., purple ... 425.00
Davidson Chocolate Society, purple,
6¼" d 235.00
Driebus Parfait Sweets, purple, 6¼" d 235.00
Eagle Furniture, purple 235.00

E. A. Hudson Furniture Co., purple,
7" d, Northwood mark 225.00
Eat Paradise Soda Candies, Season's
Greetings, purple, 6" d 200.00
Fern Brand Chocolates, purple, 6" d   225.00
Gervitz Bros Furniture & Clothing,
purple, 6" d 350.00
Greengard Furniture Co., purple   ... 600.00
Morris N. Smith, purple 250.00
Old Rose Distillery, Grape and Cable
pattern, green, stippled, 9" d 250.00
Roods Chocolate, Pueblo, purple ... 750.00
Spector's Department Store, Heart
and Vine pattern, marigold, 9" d . 325.00
Utah Liquor Co., purple, hand grip,
6" d 300.00
We Use Brocker's, purple, 7" d 500.00
Salt and Pepper Shakers, pr, figural, orig
tops
General Electric, milk glass, early re-
frigerator shape 30.00
Pepsi Cola, clear, bottle shape 45.00
Seltzer Bottle, Zetz 7–Up Bottling Co,
New Orleans, Kaufmann Beverage
Co, clear, red and black label, black
waiter holding tray, 12" h, 4" d 175.00
Sign
Diamond Dyes, diamond shape,
cloth swatches under glass, 10 x
14" 125.00
Magnet Pale Ale, reverse painted,
mirror back, red and silver magnet
center, gold leaf "The Brewery Tad-
caster," oak frame 150.00
Syrup Bottle, Grape Cola, clear, emb,
shield, white enamel label, black let-
ters and details, pewter measure cap,
11" h 350.00
Tumbler
Clark's Teaberry Gum, vaseline 35.00
Drink Ferro–Phos, clear, etched, 4¼"
h 30.00
Moxie, clear, emb 25.00
Small Grain Distilling, Louisville, 4"
h, clear, etched, paneled sides ... 50.00
Wash Board, child size, Carolina Wash-
board, 2 in 1 Junior, clear 35.00
Whiskey Dispenser, Ask For Sanderson's
Whiskey, clear, etched, 15½" h 475.00
Whiskey Shot Glass
A Little Whiskey, Hollinger, Lancas-
ter, PA, script letters 15.00
Always Good, Dan's Rye, Brown &
Daniel, Chicago, IL 20.00
Big Horn Whiskey, Taylor & Williams
Distillery, Louisvlle, KY, c1900 ... 18.00
Blue Rye, John Barth Co, Milwaukee,
IL, c1898 .... 25.00
Drink Old Joel Whiskey, D Felten-
stein, Distributor, St Joseph, MO,
c1902 .... 15.00

John Spengler, Wholesale Liquors,
Kansas City, MO 10.00
Lititz Springs, Straight Rye, Whiskey,
John C Horting, Lititz, PA 25.00
Paul Jones, clear, etched 20.00
The Blochdale, Pennsylvania Pure
White Whiskey, 1912 .... 15.00
Top Knot Whiskey, partridge, cut and
polished 40.00
White Swan Distilling Co, Indianap-
olis, IN, c1915 .... 12.00
Willson & Stevenson, Wholesale Li-
quor Dealers, Hagerstown, MD,
1910 .... 15.00
Wishing You Luck, Sterling Tavern,
Mile and Florence, 2nd & G Sts,
Eureka, CA 20.00

AGATA GLASS

History: Agata glass was patented in January
1887 by Joseph Locke of the New England Glass
Company, Cambridge, Massachusetts.
Agata glass was produced by using a piece of
peachblow glass, coating it with metallic stain,
spattering the surface with alcohol, naptha, or
benzene and firing. The result was a high gloss,
mottled appearance of oil droplets floating on a
watery surface. Shading usually ranged from
opaque pink to dark rose. Pieces are known in a
pastel opaque green. A few pieces have been
found in a satin finish.
Because of the intense heat required for production of this type of glass, and the difficulty of
the technique, it was not manufactured very
long. The few remaining examples of this beautiful type of glass are treasured by collectors and
museums alike.

Reference: John A. Shuman III, *The Collector's
Encyclopedia of American Art Glass*, Collector
Books, 1988, 1991 value update.

Bowl
4" d, green opaque body, mottled border with scalloped gold tracery ... 600.00
5⅜" d, deep rose, crimped rim 650.00
Celery Vase, 6½" h, scalloped sq top,
opaque pink shading to deep rose
body, glossy finish 715.00
Creamer, opaque pink shading to rose
body, applied handle 1,200.00
Cruet, 6" h, pale green opaque bulbous
body, random oil spot dec, applied
handle, acid finish, orig faceted
darker green stopper 550.00
Finger Bowl
4½" d, ruffled rim, opaque pink shading to rose body, pronounced mottling, deep pink lining 800.00

5¼" d, 2⅝" h, crushed raspberry shading to creamy pink body, all over gold mottling, traces of blue mottling 975.00
Juice Tumbler, 3¾" h 825.00
Lemonade Tumbler, 1⅝" d base, 2½" d top, 5⅛" h, New England peachblow shading, pronounced mottling, gold tracery 1,250.00
Pitcher, 6¾" h, crimped rim, opaque pink shading to deep rose body 1,700.00
Plate, 6⅝" d, opaque pink shading to rose body, ribbon candy fluted rim . 875.00
Punch Cup, 3" d, 2¾" h, deep color, oily spots with blue highlights, applied handle with mottling 600.00
Salt Shaker, delicate shading of pink to rose 525.00
Snuff Bottle, 2¾" h, opaque pink shading to rose body, carnelian stopper . 150.00
Spittoon, 5⅜" d, 2¾" h, squatty round body, ruffled and scalloped rim 550.00
Spooner, 3¾" h, green opaque body, mottled upper band and narrow gold band 950.00
Toothpick Holder, bulbous, opaque pink shading to rose body, scalloped rim 800.00

Tumbler, rose, 3¾" h, $675.00.

Tumbler, 3¾" h
  Fine mottling 325.00
  Pronounced mottling, deep color . . . 550.00
Vase
  4¼" h, quatraform, opaque pink shading to rose body, pinched sides, ruffled scalloped rim 695.00
  4½" h, quatraform, flared rim, opaque pink shading to deep rose body, random oil spot dec 880.00
  7¼" h, baluster, opaque pink shading to deep rose body, random oil spot dec, satin finish 1,450.00
Whiskey Taster, 2⅝" h, opaque pink shading to rose body, acid finish . . . 675.00

1932–48

AKRO AGATE GLASS

History: The Akro Agate Company was founded in 1911. Their major product was marbles. In 1914 the owners moved from near Akron, Ohio, to Clarksburg, West Virginia, where they opened a large factory. They continued to produce marbles profitably until after the Depression. In 1930, the competition in the marble business became too great, and Akro Agate Company decided to diversify into other products.

Two of their most successful products were the floral ware lines and children's dishes, first made in 1935. The children's dishes were very popular until after World War II when metal dishes captured the market.

The Akro Agate Company also made special containers for cosmetic firms including the Mexicali cigarette jar, which was originally filled with Pick Wick bath salts, and a special line for Jean Vivaudou Company, Inc. Operations continued successfully until 1948. The factory, a victim of imports, metals, and the increased use of plastics, was sold to the Clarksburg Glass Company in 1951.

Akro Agate glass is a thick-walled type of glass. Many patterns were made in fired–on, opaque, solid, transparent and marbleized colors. Colors include black, blue, cobalt blue, cream, green, pumpkin, white, and yellow. Marbleized combinations are limitless and unusual combinations command the highest prices. An example of an unusual combination is commonly called "Lemonade and Oxblood" and is often found in children's dishes. This yellow background has blood red streaks, and while it is striking in appearance, the name would not be popular with today's mothers.

The Akro Agate Company bought Westite molds after the Westite factory burned in 1936. Westite was known for production of household type fixtures, as well as flower pots, creamers, etc. Westite was made in several colors, but a brown and white marbleized combination was most prevalent, followed by a marbleized green and white combination. The Akro Agate Company began production using these molds and their own striking color combinations.

Many Akro Agate pieces are marked "Made in USA" and often include a mold number. Some pieces also include a small crow in the mark. Westite pieces are marked with a "W" inside a diamond shape.

References: Gene Florence, *The Collector's Encyclopedia of Akro Agate Glassware*, Collector Books, 1975, 1992 value update; Roger and Claudia Hardy, *The Complete Line of the Akro Agate Co.*, published by author, 1992.

Collectors' Club: Akro Agate Art Association, P.O. Box 758, Salem, NH 03079.

Reproduction Alert: Pieces currently reproduced are not marked "Made in USA" and are missing the mold number and crow.

Ashtray
  Ellipsoid, dark jade **6.00**
  Rectangular, turquoise **6.25**
  Square, white opaque, red marbleized swirls **7.50**
Basket, white opaque, orange marbleized swirls, two handles **30.00**
Bell, 5¼" h, pumpkin **50.00**
Bowl
  5" d, emb leaves, white opaque, orange marbleized swirls **35.00**
  6" d, cream opaque, brown marbleized swirls, Westite **20.00**
Cereal Bowl, white opaque, green marbleized swirls **17.50**

Sugar, Concentric Ring, children's dish, yellow, $4.25.

Children's Dishes
  Bowl
    Octagonal, white **8.00**
    Stacked Disc and Panel, large, green **15.00**
  Creamer
    Concentric Ring, blue **10.00**
    Interior Panel, opaque, blue **25.00**
    Interior Stacked Disc and Panel, cobalt blue **40.00**
    Stacked Disc and Panel, pumpkin, 1¼" h **22.50**
  Cup
    Chiquita, green, 1½" h **8.50**
    Concentric Ring, pumpkin, closed handle, 1⅜" **45.00**
    Octagonal
      Blue **10.00**

Orange and white **7.00**
Pumpkin, 1½" h **15.00**
Plain Jane **12.50**
Stippled Band, topaz, 1¼" h **15.00**
Cup and Saucer
  Concentric Ring, azure trans–optic, 1¼" h **25.00**
Interior Panel
  Green opaque **15.00**
  Pumpkin opaque **25.00**
Stippled Band, light topaz, 1½" h **13.00**
Dinner Set, 11 pcs, Stippled Band, azure **100.00**
Pitcher
  Interior Stacked Disc and Panel, transparent green **9.00**
  Octagonal, light blue, 2⅞" h **20.00**
  Stacked Disc, green **5.00**
Plate
  2" d, Concentric Rings, green **4.75**
  3¼" d, Concentric Rings
    Blue **5.00**
    Green **4.75**
  4½" d, Stippled Band, light topaz **6.50**
Saucer
  Interior Panel, opaque, blue, large **4.75**
  Octagonal, lemonade and oxblood **10.00**
Sugar, Octagonal, white opaque, orange marbleized swirls **7.00**
Teapot
  Concentric Rib Opaque, cobalt blue, white lid **30.00**
  Interior Stacked Disc and Panel, azure trans–optic, 2⅜" h **45.00**
Tea Set
  Chiquita, green opaque, 6 pcs ... **65.00**
  Octagonal, opaque green and white, 23 pcs **125.00**
  Trans–Optic, Interior Panel, jade, cov teapot, creamer, cov sugar, four cereal bowls, cups, saucers, and plates, 21 pcs **135.00**
Tumbler
  Interior Stacked Disc and Panel, transparent green **7.50**
  Octagonal, orange opaque **15.00**
Chinese Checkers Set, sixty marbles, Hop Ching wood board, orig box .. **40.00**
Cigarette Box, Mexicali **30.00**
Demitasse Cup and Saucer
  White opaque, orange marbleized swirls **15.00**
  Yellow opaque **12.00**
Flower Pot
  1½" h, opaque green **6.00**
  1¾" h, yellow, ribbed top **7.00**
  2½" h, Banded Dart, aqua **5.00**
  3½" h, Ribs and Flutes, cream **4.00**
  4" h, Stacked Disc, white opaque, blue marbleized swirls **15.00**
  5¼" h, white opaque, brown marbleized swirls, Westite **15.00**

Lamp, white opaque, orange mar-
bleized swirls 175.00
Match Holder, gun shape, white
opaque, green marbleized swirls ... 12.00
Mortar and Pestle, white, hand painted
flowers 10.00
Planter
3" h, Graduated Dart, black, scal-
loped, emb company name and ad-
dress 35.00
6" h, Chiquita, green, oval 4.00
Powder Jar
Apple, pumpkin 165.00
Colonial Lady, blue opaque 75.00
Scottie Dog, blue opaque 75.00
Saucer, 3¼" d, Stippled Band, light topaz 2.00
Smoker Set, white opaque, green marbleized swirls, 5 pcs 30.00
Tiddly Wink Cup, transparent cobalt
blue 6.50
Urn, 3¼" h, white opaque, orange marbleized swirls, ftd 7.50
Vase
4⅜" h, Jean Vivaudou Co, white
opaque, blue marbleized swirls,
emb handles 10.00
8" h, Ribs and Flutes, cobalt blue .. 35.00
8¾" h, Seven Darts, pumpkin 35.00

1883

AMBERINA GLASS

History: Joseph Locke developed Amberina glass
in 1883 for the New England Glass Works. "Amberina," a trade name, describes a transparent
glass which shades from deep ruby to amber
color. It was made by adding powdered gold to
the ingredients for an amber glass batch. A portion of the glass was reheated later to produce
the shading effect. Usually it was the bottom
which was reheated to form the deep red; however, reverse examples have been found. Locke's
July 24, 1883 patent described the base as an
amber glass containing gold, and further claimed
that ruby, violet, and a greenish or bluish tint
may be developed using the process.

Most early Amberina is of flint quality glass,
blown or pattern molded. Patterns include Diamond Quilted, Daisy and Button, Venetian Diamond, Diamond and Star, and Thumbprint.

In addition to the New England Glass Works,
the Mount Washington Glass Company of New
Bedford, Massachusetts, copied the glass in the
1880s and sold it at first under the Amberina
trade name and later as "Rose Amber." It is difficult to distinguish pieces from these two New
England factories. Boston and Sandwich Glass
Works never produced the glass.

Amberina glass also was made in the 1890s
by several Midwest factories, among which was
Hobbs, Brockunier & Co. Trade names included
"Ruby Amber Ware" and "Watermelon." The
Midwest glass shaded from cranberry to amber
and resulted from a thin flashing of cranberry
applied to the reheated portion. This created a
sharp demarkation between the two colors. This
less expensive version caused the death knell for
the New England variety.

In 1884 Edward D. Libbey was assigned the
trade name "Amberina" by the New England
Glass Works. Production occurred in 1900, but
ceased shortly thereafter. In the 1920s Edward
Libbey renewed production at his Toledo, Ohio,
plant for a short period. The glass was of high
quality. Amberina from this era is marked "Libbey" in script on the pontil. A round paper label
with the company logo may also be found.

References: George P. and Helen McKearin,
American Glass, Crown Publishers, 1941; John
A. Shuman III, *The Collector's Encyclopedia of
American Art Glass*, Collector Books, 1988,
1991 value update.

Reproduction Alert: Reproductions abound.
Flashed pieces of Amberina have invaded the
market. Care should be taken when examining a
piece to detect scratches and other defects. True
Amberina glass may shade in color but will be
consistent. Modern reproductions lack the deep
coloration and subtle shading.

**Syrup, Inverted Thumbprint, silver-plated
top, 6¼" d silver-plated tray, James W.
Tufts, quadruple plate, $675.00.**

Bowl
7½" d, Diamond Quilted pattern,
rolled over scalloped edge 185.00
9" d, sq, Daisy and Button pattern .. 250.00
Bowl, cov, 4" d, 5¼" h, swirled ribbing,

thumbprints, Midwestern type coloration 350.00

Butter Dish, cov, 7" d, 5" h, Inverted Thumbprint pattern, amber knob, amber Daisy and Button type pattern tray 300.00

Canoe, 8" l, Daisy and Button pattern, strong color 375.00

Carafe, 7⅛" h, Inverted Thumbprint pattern, reversed color, swirled neck .. 165.00

Celery Vase, 5¾" h, scalloped sq top, pinched paneled sides 135.00

Compote, 8¾" d, Inverted Thumbprint pattern 325.00

Creamer, 4½" h, Hobnail pattern, applied clear reeded handle 175.00

Cruet
   5" h, Coin Spot pattern, faceted cut amber stopper, amber handle 250.00
   5½" h, Diamond Quilted pattern, tricorn rim, faceted cut amber stopper, amber handle 350.00
   6¾" h, 3" d, applied amber handle, orig amber cut faceted stopper, attributed to New England 245.00

Cuspidor, 9" h, 5" d, Swirl pattern, hourglass shape, ruffled rim, gold trim .. 375.00

Finger Bowl
   4¼" d, deep color, attributed to New England Glass Co 275.00
   4½" d, Diamond Quilted pattern, Midwestern type coloration, trefoil rim 125.00

Finger Bowl and Underplate, 5" d x 2½" h bowl, 6¼" d underplate, reverse amberina, Inverted Thumbprint pattern, applied and fired–on enamel blossoms, thistles, Queen Anne's lace, cattails, and ferns, gold rim ... 565.00

Fruit Bowl, 7½" d, 3½" h, sq, ruffled edge, Hobnail pattern 410.00

Lemonade Glass, 5¼" h, Swirl pattern, gold dec, applied handle 245.00

Parfait, 6½" h, ftd, Swirl pattern, gold leaf and bud dec 275.00

Pickle Castor, 11½" h, Hobnail pattern insert, deep color, fancy silver plated frame and cov, Mt Washington 1,100.00

Pitcher
   5¾" h, bulbous, Inverted Thumbprint pattern, applied amber reeded handle, Mt Washington 195.00
   7½" h, inverted swirl, cylindrical neck, amber handle 175.00
   8" h, Inverted Thumbprint pattern, quad spouts, amber handle 185.00
   8½" h, bulbous, Inverted Thumbprint pattern, triangular top, amber reeded handle, Mt Washington ... 225.00

Plate, 7" d, Daisy and Button pattern . 300.00

Punch Cup, 2⅝" d, 2¾" h, Inverted Thumbprint pattern, applied reeded amber handle 115.00

Ramekin, matching underplate, 4¼" d, 2¼" h, slightly ribbed 215.00

Rose Bowl
   5½" d, 5½" h, Diamond Quilted pattern, deep color, pinched tricorn rim, applied amber reeded shell feet, attributed to New England Glass Co 525.00
   9" d, 6½" h, crimped top, Swirl pattern, applied amber feet, attributed to New England Glass Co 325.00

Salt Shaker, elongated Baby Thumbprint pattern, orig top 125.00

Sauce, 5¾" sq, Daisy and Button pattern, fuchsia, scalloped edge 110.00

Spooner, 5" h, Diamond Quilted pattern, pinched scalloped top 140.00

Sugar Shaker, 4" h, globular, Inverted Thumbprint pattern, emb floral and butterfly lid 400.00

Toothpick Holder, 4½" h, Diamond Quilted pattern, fuchsia, triple plated holder with pond lilies and leafy stems 325.00

Vase
   5½" h, 3½" d, three petal top, Inverted Thumbprint pattern, applied amber feet, attributed to New England Glass Co 150.00
   7" h
      Cylindrical, Thumbprint pattern, Midwestern type coloration ruffled rim 125.00
      Lily, ribbed body, attributed to New England Glass Co 375.00
      Trumpet, 3" ruby red top fades to honey amber stem, applied wafer foot, attributed to New England Glass Co 475.00
   10" h, lily, ribbed body, attributed to New England Glass Co 450.00
   10" h, 5⅛" d, cylindrical, Swirl pattern, enameled pink and white flowers, green leaves, gold rim trim, attributed to New England Glass Co, pr 350.00
   10½" h, inverted swirled bulbous body, flared rim, Midwestern type coloration, applied pinched amber rigaree, ftd 175.00
   12" h, trumpet, ribbed body, attributed to New England Glass Co ... 350.00
   12½" h, lily, twelved ribbed body, blue–fuschia folded tricorn rim, applied amber foot, attributed to New England Glass Co 360.00
   23" h, trumpet, ribbed body, knobbed stem, raised circular base, attributed to New England Glass Co ..1,250.00

Water Set, 9" h pitcher, three matching tumblers, 4 pcs 1,150.00

Whimsey, hat, 3¼" d, 2⅜" h, Expanded
Diamond pattern, ground pontil **150.00**
Whiskey Shot Glass, 2½" h, Diamond
Quilted pattern **125.00**

AMBERINA GLASS— PLATED

History: The New England Glass Company, Cambridge, Massachusetts, first made Plated Amberina in 1886; Edward Libbey patented the process for the company in 1889.

Plated Amberina was made by taking a gather of chartreuse or cream opalescent glass, dipping it in Amberina and working the two, often utilizing a mold. The finished product had a deep amber to deep ruby red shading, a fiery opalescent lining, and often vertical ribbing for enhancement. Bases are usually yellow gold. Handles are generally applied, plain amber pieces. Designs ranged from simple forms to complex pieces with collars, feet, gilding, and etching.

Edward Libbey's patent used an opalescent glass which was plated with a gold ruby. The pieces also have a vertical ribbed effect and a wide range of items were made, including creamers, finger bowls, lemonade tumblers, punch cups, toothpick holders, and vases.

The New England Glass Company used paper labels which read "N. E. Glass Co. 1886 Aurora." However, these labels were used infrequently and are rarely found.

Reference: John A. Shuman III, *The Collector's Encyclopedia of American Art Glass,* Collector Books, 1988, 1991 value update.

Reproduction Alert: Examples with rough pontils, inferior linings, and even runny, blurry colors, are appearing on the market.

Bowl, 8" d, 3¼" h, ruffled, vertical ribbing **1,650.00**

Cruet, melon ribbed body, applied handle, faceted stopper, 6¾" h, $3,800.00.

Celery Vase, vertical ribbing **2,600.00**
Cream Pitcher, 2¾" h, 3½" w, bulbous,
vertical ribbing raspberry shading
two–thirds down to golden amber
base, elaborate strap handle, deep oil
spots dec **1,800.00**
Cruet, 6¼" h, deep vertical ribbing, trefoil top, amber handle and faceted
stopper **3,600.00**
Lamp Shade, 14" l, vertical ribbed,
swirled base, fitter ring **4,750.00**
Parfait, vertical ribbing, applied amber
handle, c1886 .... **1,250.00**
Pitcher, 6½" h, vertical ribbing, applied
clear amber handle **4,500.00**
Punch Cup, 2¾" h, vertical ribbing, applied transparent yellow C–scroll handle **1,600.00**
Salt Shaker, vertical ribbing, orig top .. **900.00**
Spooner, 4" h, vertical ribbing, ground
pontil **2,000.00**
Syrup Pitcher, vertical ribbing, orig top,
applied amber handle **5,500.00**
Tumbler, 3¾" h, vertical ribbing **1,850.00**
Vase
3¼" h, bulbous, vertical ribbing,
bluish–white lining **2,500.00**
7¼" h, lily, vertical ribbing, amber
pedestal foot **2,750.00**

ANIMALS

History: It did not take glass manufacturers long to realize that there was a ready market for glass novelties. In the early nineteenth century, walking sticks and witch balls were two dominant forms. As the century ended, glass covered dishes with an animal theme were popular.

In the period between World Wars I and II, glass manufacturers such as Fostoria Glass Company and A. H. Heisey & Company created a number of glass animal figures for the novelty and decorative accessory markets. In the 1950s and early 1960s a second glass animal craze swept America led by companies such as Duncan & Miller Glass Company and New Martinsville–Viking Glass Company. A third craze struck in the early 1980s when companies such as Boyd Crystal Art Glass, Guernsey Glass, Pisello Art Glass, and Summit Art Glass began offering the same animal figure in a wide variety of collectible glass colors, with some colors in limited production.

There are two major approaches to glass animal collecting: (a) animal type and (b) manufacturer. Most collectors concentrate on one or more manufacturer, grouping their collections accordingly.

References: Everett Grist, *Covered Animal Dishes,* Collector Books, 1988, 1991 value update; Frank L. Hahn and Paul Kikeli, *Collector's Guide to Heisey and Heisey By Imperial Glass Animals*, Golden Era Publications, 1991; Evelyn Zemel, *American Glass Animals A to Z*, A to Z Productions, 1978.

Price Note: Prices are for animal figures in clear (crystal) glass unless otherwise noted.

Angelfish, Heisey, clear 110.00
Bear, Mosser Glass Co, solid, sitting
    Autumn Amber 40.00
    Tawny 10.00
    Violet D'Orr 24.00
Bull, Heisey, clear, 4" h 1,100.00
Cat, Mosser Glass Co, sitting, 3" h
    Chocolate 6.00
    Heirloom Pink 6.00
Doe
    Fostoria, blue, 4½" h 35.00
    Tiffin Glass, clear, lily pad base 125.00
Dog
    German Shepherd, New Martinsville, amethyst, frosted base, 5⅛", 1937–50 . . . . 135.00
    Scottie, milk glass, 6" l, sitting, L. E. Smith 80.00
    Skippy, Boyd Crystal Art Glass, sitting
        Crown Tuscan 10.00
        Pippin Green 7.50
Donkey
    Duncan Miller, clear 165.00
    Heisey, clear 240.00
Dove, Duncan Miller, clear 165.00
Duck, Boyd's Crystal Art Glass Co
    Debbie, introduced July 1981
        English Yew 5.00
        Mardi Gras 6.00
        Snow 5.00
    Ducklings, introduced Sept 1981
        Crown Tuscan 2.50
        Furr Green 3.00
        Golden Delight 2.50
Eagle, Cambridge, clear, 6" h, bookend 70.00
Elephant
    Bob Henry Glass Co, Bimbah, c1980, 4" h
        Autumn Amber 35.00
        Petunia, carnival 65.00
        Snowy Pine 20.00
    New Martinsville, clear, matched pr 175.00
Giraffe, Heisey, clear, head turned, 11" h 175.00
Goose
    Duncan Miller, clear, plump 230.00
    Heisey, Mallard, clear, wings half up, 4½" h 85.00
Horse
    Fostoria, clear, rearing 50.00
    Heisey
        Clydesdale, clear 400.00
        Plug, Sparky
            Amber, 4¼" h 575.00

Clear 85.00
    McKee, milk glass, base sgd "McKee" 300.00
Mouse, Pee Gee Glass Co, boy and girl mouse, 3" h
    Mellow Yellow 12.00
    White Delight 11.00
    Wild Cherry 12.50
Pelican, Fostoria, clear, 3" sq base, 4½" w, 4½" h, c1938–44 . . . . 95.00
Pheasant, ring neck
    Heisey, clear 95.00
    Paden City, light blue, head turned, 2½" w, 2¾" d base, 12" l, 7" h . . 115.00
Polar Bear, 2" h, wisteria, etched signature "Maleris" and orig paper label 100.00
Pony
    Boyd Crystal Art Glass Co, Joey, introduced March 1980
        Candy Swirl 15.00
        Chocolate 30.00
        Persimmon 25.00
    Heisey, clear, 3" l, 5" h, c1940–52 . 100.00
    Imperial, Heisey mold
        Caramel Slag 35.00
        Clear, c1964 . . . . 45.00
    New Martinsville, clear, long legs, oval base, 4¼" l, 12" h 100.00
    Paden City, clear, 5½" l base, 12" h 60.00
Pouter Pigeon, bookends, pr
    Cambridge, clear, 5" l, 6" h 150.00
    Paden City, clear, 3¾" l, 6½" h 90.00
Rocking Horse, Guernsey Glass Co, Rocky, reproduction of 1915 Cambridge candy container, 4¼" l, 13" h
    Carousel Slag 12.00
    Hi–O–Silver 12.50
    Holly Berry 10.00

Rooster, clear, 8" h, 5¾" l base, $45.00.

Rooster, Heisey, clear, fighting stance, 8½" h, 1940–46 . . . . 150.00
Sea Horse, Fostoria, clear, 8" h, 1938–44 . . . . 90.00
Seal, Fostoria, lilac, 3¼" sq base, 3¾" h 95.00
Shark, Baccarat, clear 110.00

Sparrow, Heisey, clear, 4" l, 2½" h,
   1942–45 .... **75.00**
Star Fish, New Martinsville, clear, 6¼"
   l, 7¾" h **35.00**
Swan
   Duncan and Miller
      Clear, spread wings, 12" w, 11" h **35.00**
      Ruby, 12" h **50.00**
   Heisey, clear, mother and two cyg-
      nets, 7" h, 1947–49, 3 pcs **600.00**
   Tiger, New Martinsville, clear, pr **300.00**
   Wild Boar, Baccarat, clear **145.00**

After 1929

APPALACHIAN GLASSWARE MANUFACTURERS

History: The American Appalachians have been home to some interesting glass manufacturers. Collectors are now beginning to appreciate and seek out products by these makers. Although some of these companies were contemporaries to Depression glassware makers, their wares are less known and have not yet been as carefully documented.

Glass manufacturers have historically been the most reluctant to mark and document their work. The nature of the creation of glass often prohibits a molded mark, and paper labels soon are lost. Further confusion is due in part to the fact that workers moved from company to company, taking their particular skills and favorite designs to each new venture.

References: Anne Geffken Pullin, *Glass Signatures, Trademarks, and Trade Names From The Seventeenth To The Twentieth Century,* Wallace–Homestead Book Company, 1986; Hazel Marie Weatherman, *Colored Glassware Of The Depression Era, Book 2,* Glassbooks, Inc., 1982.

Periodical: *The Daze,* Box 57, Otisville, MI 48463.

Museum: Blenko Glass Company Factory Museum, Milton, West Virginia.

Additional Listings: See specific companies for other Appalachian Glassware listings, such as Morgantown, New Martinsville Glass, Paden City, L. E. Smith, Westmoreland Glass Company.

BLENKO GLASS COMPANY

History: Blenko Glass Company, located in Milton, West Virginia, was founded in 1922 by Brit-

ish glassmaker William J. Blenko. He originally made stained glass for church windows, but since 1929 has made decorative household glass and glass building slabs. Blenko provided the blown faceted glass windows for the Air Force Academy Chapel in Colorado Springs, Colorado.

Blenko glassware is handmade and only marked with paper labels. Tall pieces, ranging from 18 to 28 inches, are specialities of this manufacturer. Vibrant colors and heavy walls are predominate with the clean modern lines of most pieces.

Ashtray, 8" l, freeform, amethyst **10.00**
Bowl
   3" d, 4" h, amber, scalloped edge .. **10.00**
   6¼" d, tangerine, turned in edge ... **12.00**
   6½" d, amber, scalloped edge, heavy
      base **15.00**
Compote
   5¾" d, 6" h, red bowl shades to gold,
      gold stem and foot **15.00**
   10" d, 5½" h, amber, scalloped edge **25.00**
Creamer, red **18.00**
Decanter
   10" h, amethyst, orig amethyst stop-
      per **20.00**
   15½" h, clear, 6" h pointed stopper . **25.00**
Pitcher, 6½" h, clear, bulbous, applied
   handle **20.00**
Sand Glass, 25 minutes, 19" h, clear,
   wood case **40.00**
Snowman, red top hat **20.00**
Tankard, 9" h, gold, applied handle .. **18.00**
Vase
   5" h, Rosettes pattern, cobalt blue .. **60.00**
   8½" h, Florette pattern, flared, clear **35.00**
   11" h, Crackle, green, flip **50.00**
   25" h, Crackle, avocado, tapered
      neck, scalloped edge **35.00**
Water Set, 10" h pitcher, dark amber,
   random small indentation in body, six
   6" h tumblers, 7 pcs **65.00**

BRYCE BROTHERS COMPANY

History: Bryce Brothers Company was located in Mt Pleasant, PA. It was incorporated in 1896 and manufactured hand blown stemware for hotel use as well as home use. Their designs included etched, engraved, and decorated table wares. Accessory items such as baskets and vases were added. Colored glasswares were added in the early 1920s and reflected popular colors of the times, including amber, amberosa, amethyst, blue, canary, green, and ruby. Some iridescent shades were also made. During the late 1920s, dark blue, light blue, and pink were added to the lines. Aurene colored wares and black wares were added in the 1930s. Colored stems were used with crystal to create interesting color combinations. In 1965, Bryce Brothers Company was bought by Lenox Corporation.

Carleton pattern, crystal
Goblet	10.00
Sherbet	10.00

El Rancho pattern
Goblet, emerald green, 12 oz	7.00
Sherbet, emerald green, 6 oz	6.00
Tumbler, yellow, ftd, 5½" h	7.00

Future pattern, Carulean Aqua, tumbler, ftd	4.00

Modern pattern, Smoke
Juice Tumbler, ftd	4.00
Sherbet	4.00

Silhouette pattern, Carulean Aqua, designed for Eva Zeisel, dessert	4.00

Central Glass Works, Chippendale pattern, child's candlestick, clear, marked in mold, 4¼" h, $15.00.

CENTRAL GLASS WORKS

History: Central Glass Works, Wheeling, West Virginia, was established as a cooperative in 1863 by workmen from J. H. Hobbs, Brockunier and Company. It failed shortly thereafter and was reorganized as a stock company in 1867. Production continued until 1939.

Early goods were bottles, lamps, and barware. Around 1900, production began of crystal and decorated tablewares, as well as barware and tumblers for homes and famous hotels. In 1919 Central Glass acquired the molds for Benjamin W. Jacob's very successful Chippendale pattern. The trademark, Krys-Tol (and sometimes the patent date) is marked in the mold. Chippendale was made in more than three hundred forms and was widely distributed. It achieved such great popularity in England that molds were sent to an English firm in 1933.

Central Glass produced a large line of optic glassware, as well as selling blanks to decorating companies. Several etched patterns were also popular.

Bowl
9" d, Frances pattern, orchid	15.00
11½" d, Balda Lavender pattern, rolled edge	45.00
Butter Dish, cov, Chippendale pattern	18.00
Champagne	22.00

Console Set, bowl and candlesticks
Memphis pattern	45.00
Zoricor pattern	48.00

Cordial Set, decanter, six stemmed cordials, Balda Lavender pattern	325.00
Creamer and Sugar, Chippendale pattern	25.00

Goblet
Acorn pattern	12.00
Balda Lavender pattern	27.00
Frances pattern	14.00
Hester pattern	14.00
Sheila pattern	13.50
Veninga pattern	14.00

Hair Receiver, cov, Chippendale pattern	12.00

Pitcher, water
Acorn pattern	17.50
Balda Lavender pattern	300.00
Ring Holder, Chippendale pattern	12.00
Sugar, cov, Frances pattern, green	8.50
Tumbler, Hester pattern	9.00
Tumble–Up, Thistle etching	15.00

Wine
Balda Lavender pattern	24.00
Chippendale pattern	7.50

DUNBAR GLASS COMPANY

History: Dunbar Flint Glass Corporation, began production in Dunbar, West Virginia, in 1938, by making lamp chimneys. By the time of the Depression, the company had achieved wide success making a variety of blown and pressed tableware. The company closed in 1953.

The colors produced by Dunbar were vibrant, and pieces can sometimes be dated by their color. Rose pink and Bermuda green were the colors of choice in the 1920s. By the 1930s, Stiegel green, cobalt blue, and ruby were predominate. By 1936, amethyst and topaz, as well as blue and ruby luster were the colors of choice. Pieces were further decorated with gold designs and the Rambler Rose border was the most popular.

Dunbar is well-known for thin walled glassware. Their fine reputation was also enhanced by the quality and quantity of refreshment sets, liquor services, and cocktail sets that they produced.

Beverage Set, pitcher, six tumblers
Aramis	50.00
Athos	35.00
Barbra, pink	50.00
Poinsettia	40.00
Porthos	38.00
Bon Bon Box, cov, Rambler Rose	20.00

Cake Stand, ftd, rose pink, gold inlaid dec	**18.00**
Candy Jar, pear shape	**10.00**
Cheese and Cracker Server, green, gold inlaid dec	**18.00**
Ice Bucket, crystal, silver plated handle and tongs	**15.00**
Liquor Set, bottle, six cordials, Meeny	**35.00**
Mayonnaise Set, bowl, underplate, orig spoon	
Decalomania	**15.00**
Rambler Rose	**17.50**
Relish, Rambler Rose, 11" l, four sections	**18.00**
Sandwich Tray, Rambler Rose	**16.00**
Tumble–Up	
Modernist cutting	**15.00**
Rambler Rose, rose pink	**25.00**
Vase	
6½" h, Rambler Rose, rose pink	**12.00**
8" h, grapes dec	**9.00**

Syrup, Pilgrim Glass, crackle, applied clear handle, $5.00.

PILGRIM GLASS COMPANY

History: The Pilgrim Glass Company was located in Ceredo, West Virginia. The firm produced hand blown colored wares during the 1970s. Robert Moretti was the chief designer and responsible for the paperweight line.

Pilgrim Glass is found with two distinctive marks, including silvered paper labels.

Cruet, 7" h, cranberry, applied clear handle, clear stopper	**25.00**
Jack In The Pulpit Vase, 12½" h, green irid, yellow and orange stripes, sgd "B Caldwell"	**75.00**
Paperweight, 4½" d, clear, blue flower, wine swirls, sgd "Allesandro Moretti"	**40.00**
Pitcher, 7½" h, ruby, crackle, waisted, applied clear handle	**18.00**
Plate, 12" d, Christmas, Della Robia design, clear	**20.00**

Vase	
5" h, white, cranberry streaks, fluted top, clear base	**15.00**
8" h, bud, ruby, clear ball shaped base	**12.00**

SENECA GLASS COMPANY

History: Seneca Glass Company, Morgantown, West Virginia, was founded in 1891 by a group of immigrants from the Black Forest countryside of Germany. Although the first site was the former Fostoria Glass Company plant, in Fostoria, Ohio, the company was chartered in West Virginia. In 1896, Seneca moved to Morgantown and began production of fine blown and cut crystal.

During the Depression era, Seneca Glass Company introduced a variety of colors, but was widely known for its rock crystal production. Seneca currently produces plain and cut goblets, sherbets, wine glasses, and other table wares. Colored casual glassware, speciality Christmas items, and an extensive series of bells, rounds out current production.

Champagne	
Ester	**7.50**
Festus	**7.50**
Naomi	**7.50**
Cocktail	
Driftwood, ruby	**5.00**
Naomi	**8.00**
Finger Bowl, Festus	**7.00**
Goblet	
Anais	**7.00**
Asteric, cut, crystal	**9.00**
Brittany, cut, crystal	**22.00**
Candlewick	**8.50**
Estes	**9.00**
Driftwood	
Amber	**3.00**
Avocado Green	**3.00**
Emerald Green	**4.00**
Ruby	**5.00**
Fashionables, avocado green	**4.50**
Germana	**9.00**
Images, clear	**4.00**
High Ball	
Chalice, cut, crystal	**25.00**
Driftwood	
Avocado Green	**3.00**
Ruby	**5.00**
Iced Tea Tumbler	
Driftwood	
Avocado Green	**3.00**
Emerald Green	**4.00**
Fashionables, avocado green	**5.00**
Juice Pitcher, Driftwood emerald green	**30.00**
Juice Tumbler, Driftwood	
Amber	**3.00**
Brown	**3.00**
Emerald Green	**4.00**
Ruby	**5.00**

Old Fashioned, Chalice, cut, crystal ..	**25.00**
Parfait	
Festus	**9.00**
Naomi	**10.00**
Sherbet	
Allegheny	**5.00**
Asteric, cut, crystal	**6.00**
Candlewick	**6.50**
Ester	**6.50**
Tumbler	
Alleghany pattern, clear, black scalloped foot	
3½" h, 10 oz	**12.00**
4¼" h, 14 oz	**12.00**
Driftwood, decorated on foot	
Amber	**3.00**
Avocado Green	**3.00**
Emerald Green	**4.00**
Images, decorated on foot	**4.00**
Wine	
Brittany, cut, crystal	**22.00**
Dorchester, cut, crystal	**30.00**
Driftwood, ftd, ruby	**9.00**
Naomi	**12.00**

ARCHITECTURAL ELEMENTS

History: Architectural elements are those items which have been removed or salvaged from buildings, ships, or gardens. Many are handcrafted. Windows, ornaments, and newel post finials are examples of architectural elements found in glass. Part of their desirability is due to the fact that it would be extremely costly to duplicate the items today.

The current trend of preservation and recycling architectural elements has led to the establishment and growth of organized salvage operations who specialize in removal and resale of elements. Special auctions are now held to sell architectural elements from churches, mansions, office buildings, etc. Today's decorators often design an entire room around one architectural element, such as a stained glass window, or use several items as key accent pieces.

References: Ronald S. Barlow (Comp.), *Victorian Houseware: Hardware and Kitchenware*, Windmill Publishing Co., 1991; Alan Robertson, *Architectural Antiques*, Chronicle Books, 1987; Margaret and Kenn Whitmeyer, *Bedroom & Bathroom Glassware of the Depression Years*, Collector Books, 1990, 1992 value update.

Cabinet Knob	
Floral emb, center hole to accommodate screw	**5.00**
Hexagonal, geometric, metal screw	
Large	
Amber	**5.00**

Black	**7.00**
Crystal	**3.50**
Green	**4.00**
Milk Glass	**3.50**
Pink	**4.00**
Medium	
Amber	**4.50**
Black	**6.50**
Crystal	**3.00**
Green	**3.50**
Lavender	**6.50**
Milk Glass	**3.50**
Pink	**3.50**
Small	
Amber	**4.00**
Blue	**5.00**
Crystal	**2.00**
Green	**3.00**
Milk Glass	**3.00**
Pink	**3.00**
Onion shape, flush mounted, jadite .	**7.50**
Round, medium, flush mounted or center metal screw	
Amber	**5.00**
Black	**6.00**
Crystal	**3.50**
Green	**4.00**
Milk Glass	**3.50**
Pink	**4.00**

Tiebacks, opalescent glass, six–petal flower, 4½" d, pr, $100.00.

Clothes Hook, short hook, pink, c1930	**9.00**
Curtain Tieback, pr	
Amberina Glass, orig pewter shanks, New England Glass Works	**150.00**
Mercury Glass, grape dec, 2½" d ...	**35.00**
Opalescent Glass, attributed to Sandwich, large, petaled flower design, orig pewter shanks	**100.00**
Door Knobs, pr glass knob, metal mountings and shaft	
Amber, deep color, octagonal	**80.00**
Crystal, oval, cut design	**30.00**
Jadite, hexagonal	**95.00**
Topaz, center design, hexagonal ...	**85.00**
Doors, pr, 89" h, 21" w, stained and painted glass, finches and flowers, Renaissance style fretwork border, French, 20th C	**2,500.00**

Drawer Pull, set of 6
  Opalescent, fiery, hexagonal, attrib-
  uted to Sandwich **200.00**
  Vaseline, round, rayed flower design **185.00**
Drawer Pull, single
  Anchor Shape, center flush mounted
  screw
    Amber **8.50**
    Crystal **4.00**
    Green **7.50**
    Milk Glass **9.00**
    Pink **7.50**
  Rounded or faceted ends, metal
  screws
    Amber **12.00**
    Crystal **6.00**
    Green **10.00**
    Lavender **18.00**
    Pink **10.00**
Fanlight, 52" w, 26" h, Federal, leaded
  glass panes, hinged wooden fan
  shaped molding, mullioned glazed
  panels, beaded swags design, New
  England, c1810 .... **3,200.00**
Hand Towel Holder, double clear glass
  rods, metal mounting bracket
    Blue **35.00**
    Jadite **32.50**
    Milk glass, white **10.00**
    Pink **30.00**
Newel Post Knob
  6½" h, double cut overlay, white cut
  to cranberry, stars and circle dec,
  several small nicks **600.00**
  8¼" h, pressed glass, electric blue,
  hobbed pineapple form, brass base,
  c1840–60 .... **165.00**
Panel, leaded
  75" h, 7" w, Frank Lloyd Wright,
  c1913, asymmetrical, clear, white,
  and red glass, architectural rigging
  motif, executed by Temple Art
  Glass Co for Francis W Little
  House, Wayzata, MN **6,600.00**
  96" h, 20" w, Prairie School, c1910,
  rect panel of textured, rippled, and
  opaque glass, turquoise, white, and
  avocado, clear glass ground, stylized flowering plant motif, set of six
  panels **6,000.00**
Soap Dish, wall mounted, transparent
  blue, c1940 .... **10.00**
Toilet Paper Holder, clear glass arms,
  glass rod **15.00**
Toothbrush Holder, wall mounted,
  opaque blue glass, slots for five tooth-
  brushes, central well for toothpaste
  tube **15.00**
Towel Bar
  Clear glass, one piece, curved ends,
  metal mounting brackets
    Blue **25.00**

Jadite **20.00**
  Milk glass, white **8.00**
Jadite glass holders, clear glass towel
  rod **8.50**
Pink glass, faceted balls, clear glass
  towel rod **10.00**
Transom Window, 9" h, 30¾" l, leaded,
  finely plated, dusty pink and deep
  purple wisteria blossoms, green
  leaves, mottled lavender branches,
  twilight ground, marked "Tiffany Studios," oak frame **2,750.00**
Window, leaded
  21½" h, 44½" w, Tiffany, central
  monogram medallion of orig company "Louis C Tiffany and Associated Artists," multicolored floral
  rectilinear panel with ripple glass
  and jewels, aqua–blue mottled
  glass border, mounted in window
  frame, 1878–82, removed from
  Bishop's House and Chancery Office, Burlington, VT, in 1977, includes copies of letters of authentication and appraisal **3,400.00**
  22" sq, Tiffany, bordered medallions
  with swirled, rippled, confetti, opalescent glass, and jewels, unsigned,
  mounted in window frames, removed from Bishop's House and
  Chancery Office, Burlington, VT, in
  1977, includes copies of letters of
  authentication and appraisal, pr . **1,700.00**
  29" h, 27½" w, Tiffany, central tiny
  white blossoms radiating towards
  large mottled brown and white pebbled blossoms, pink and green sta-
  mens, amber glass surround, geometric green glass border **18,000.00**
  30½" h, 13¼" w, Gothic interlocking
  arch motif, etched design inside
  arched sections, beveled orig frame **250.00**
  36" h, 36" w, blue grapes, green
  leaves, blue scrolls, opal red ribbon, amber ground, blue pane border, orig wood frame **575.00**
Window, stained
  13¼" h, 43½" l, scenic, hand painted
  outside layer of winding road with
  cottages, stone walls, and fences,
  sailboats and flamingos on river,
  mountain in background, deeper
  layer of multicolored dicroic glass,
  representing brilliant sky from day-
  break through sunset, twenty–four
  mottled green and red favrile glass
  leaded segments border, wooden
  frame, attributed to Tiffany Studios
  Workshop **4,200.00**
  39" h, 34" w, arched, jeweled navy
  border framing abstract amber and

white mosaic design, faceted circles, arched wooden frame, c1900 **450.00**
96" h, designed and executed by Alice D Laughlin, Glouester, MA, divided into eight panels depicting scenes of medieval clergy, surrounded by multicolored foliate border **900.00**

BACCARAT GLASS

History: The Sainte–Anne glassworks at Baccarat in the Voges, France, was founded in 1764 and produced utilitarian soda glass. In 1816 Aime–Gabriel d'Artiques purchased the glassworks, and a Royal Warrant was issued in 1817 for the opening of Verrerie de Vonuché Baccarat. The firm concentrated on lead crystal glass products. In 1824 a limited company was created.

From 1823 to 1857 Baccarat and Saint–Louis glassworks had a commercial agreement and used the same outlets. No merger occurred. Baccarat began the production of paperweights in 1846. In the late 19th century the firm achieved an international reputation for cut glass table services, chandeliers, display vases and centerpieces, and sculptures. Products eventually included all forms of glassware. The firm still is active today.

Manufacturer/Distributor: Baccarat Inc., 625 Madison Ave., New York, NY 10022.

Animal, Polar Bear, crystal, sgd **125.00**
Ashtray, 4½" d, Pinwheel, sgd **85.00**
Atomizer, 5" h, 3½" l, oval, etched crystal body, metal chrome top, marked **85.00**
Beverage Set, 9¾" h pitcher, six 2½" d, 4¾" h tumblers, 11½" d tray, Rose Tiente, marked **600.00**
Biscuit Jar, cov, 6" h, crystal, etched ground, cranberry flowers, leaves, and vines, marked inside lid **400.00**
Bookends, pr, 12" h, crystal, serpentine tube on molded rocky form base, etched "Baccarat, France" **150.00**
Bowl
5½" d, crystal, etched leaf ground, cameo cut chartreuse floral dec .. **75.00**
8" d, Rose Tiente, scalloped, ftd, sgd **110.00**
Brandy Snifters, crystal, gilded foliate cartouche, monogrammed N, set of 12 .... **275.00**
Calling Card Holder, 5½" h, opaline, fan shape, pedestal base, relief butterflies, trees, and flowers, sgd **165.00**
Candelabra, pr, 16" h, crystal, ormolu mounts, early 19th C **1,800.00**
Candlesticks, pr
10¾" h, Eiffel Tower pattern, Rose Tiente **225.00**

14½" h, baluster form, crystal, spiral, dome base, 19th C **200.00**
Celery Tray, 9½" l, 3½" w, Rose Tiente **50.00**
Champagne Bucket, 9¼" h, tapering cylinder, rect stop fluted molded sides, stamped "Baccarat, France" . **400.00**
Chandelier, 32" w, 25" h, crystal, four branches, baluster column, 20th C, wired for electricity **825.00**
Cigarette Lighter, Rose Tiente, silver plated top **125.00**
Cologne Bottle
5½" h, Rose Tiente, Diamond Point Swirl, orig stopper **90.00**
8" h, 3¼" d, Rose Tiente, pinwheel . **85.00**
Compote, 4½" h, Rose Tiente, Swirl pattern **75.00**
Console Bowl, 14" d, 3½" h, wide flattened rim, narrow knopped foot, etched "Baccarat, France" **500.00**
Decanter
9¾" h, Rose Tiente, orig stopper ... **115.00**
14" h, crystal, amphora style, lightly ribbed, collared stem, domed foot, conforming stopper, factory acid stamped mark **250.00**
Dish, oval, 3½" w, 9½" l, Rose Tiente **75.00**
Dresser Set
5 pcs, Art Deco, amberina, swirl, brass rack with beveled mirror, marked **650.00**
16 pcs, crystal, shaped rect molded glass case, all over gilt vermicule pattern, removable gilt metal frame, six scent bottles with metal hinged cov, four gilt molded toilette bottles with stoppers, c1875 ..... **425.00**
Epergne, 14" h, crystal, twig and floriform silver plated mounts supporting fluted glass bowl and vase, c1900 .. **300.00**
Fairy Lamp
3⅞" h, shaded white to clear **275.00**
5½" h, 4½" d, Rose Tiente, sunburst, matching base **245.00**
Jar, cov, 6" h, 3¼" d, sapphire blue, swirl, marked **75.00**
Finger Bowl, 4¾" d bowl, 6¼" d underplate, ruby, medallions and flowers, gold dec **325.00**
Goblet
Perfection pattern **38.00**
Vintage pattern, cone shaped amber bowl, etched grape design, cut stem and base, set of six **115.00**
Jewelry Box, cov, 4" d, 2¾" h, hinged lid, Button and Bow pattern, sapphire blue, brass fittings **125.00**
Liquor Bottle, 10⅛" h, 3½" d, lime green, gold flowers and leaves dec, three petal top, clear bubble stopper with gold dec, clear pedestal base, orig paper label **125.00**

Perfume Atomizer, amberina, 6″ h, $50.00.

Mustard, cov, 3″ d, 5″ h, Rose Tiente, swirl 75.00
Perfume Bottle
    4¼″ h, 1½″ d, Rose Tiente, swirl, marked 65.00
    5½″ h, amberina, Shell pattern, orig stopper 65.00
Pitcher
    9¼″ h, Rose Tiente, Helical Twist pattern 275.00
    15″ h, tankard, deeply etched full length portrait of Napoleon in oval, wide ribbed base 400.00
Powder Jar, cov, 3½″ d, 4¼″ h, Rose Tiente, swirl, marked 100.00
Rose Bowl, 3″ d, cranberry, lace enamel dec 150.00
Scent Bottle, 3½″ h, Art Deco, Toujours Fidele, c1930 .... 65.00
Sweetmeat Jar, cov, cranberry colored strawberries, blossoms, and leaves, cut back to clear ground of ferns, silver plated cov and handle, sgd 350.00
Toothpick Holder, 2½″ h, scalloped, Rose Tiente 100.00
Tray, 9″ w, 13″ l, Rose Tiente 125.00
Tumble–Up, carafe and tumbler, Rose Tiente, Swirl pattern 200.00
Tumbler, 3½″ h, Rose Tiente, marked . 55.00
Vase
    8¼″ h, bamboo stalk form, relief molded leaf sprig at side, coiled snake around base, enameled and gilt insects, early 20th C, sgd 500.00
    9¼″ h, ovoid, crystal, large thumbprint design, acid stamped factory mark 190.00
    12″ h, expanding circular section on short foot, opaline, pale yellow enameled hummingbird, butterfly, and summer blossoms, border of pink thistle blossoms and gilt

leaves, marked "Baccarat le 26 Septembre 1860″ **1,000.00**
13″ h, crystal, molded, fish breaking waves, Japanese taste, gilt bronze mounting **2,700.00**
Wine
    D'Assas pattern, crystal **50.00**
    Perfection pattern, crystal **45.00**
Wine Coolers, pr, 9½″ h, crystal, tapered oct base, applied gilt bronze collar, loop handles **1,700.00**

BARBER BOTTLES

History: Barber bottles, colorful glass bottles found on shelves and counters in barber shops, held the liquids barbers used daily. A specific liquid was kept in a specific bottle which the barber knew by color, design, or lettering.

The bulk liquids were kept in utilitarian containers under the counter or in a storage room. Some barber bottles indicated the name of the product, like "Bay Rum," while others were more decorative.

Barber bottles are found in many types of glass: art glass with varied decoration, pattern glass, and commercially prepared and labeled bottles.

References: Richard Holiner, *Collecting Barber Bottles*, Collector Books, 1986; Ralph & Terry Kovel, *The Kovels' Bottle Price List, Eighth Edition* Crown Publishers, Inc. 1987; Philip L. Krumholz, *Value Guide For Barberiana & Shaving Collectibles*, Ad Libs Publishing Co., 1988.

5″ h, cut glass, hobstar base, pewter top   75.00
6½″ h, clear, ribbed, decorated band around center, gold trim, raised enamel dot pattern, pontil 65.00
6¾″ h, amethyst, white enameled flowers, orange dot pattern, pontil 95.00

Cranberry, opalescent, 7¼″ h, $150.00.

6¾" h, 3½", cranberry, rings of hobnails on neck **175.00**

7" h

Clear, recessed paper label **45.00**

Opalescent

Blue, Stars and Stripes pattern, ground pontil **200.00**

Cranberry, Daisy and Fern pattern, melon base, rolled lip, pr **275.00**

7¼" h

Amber, Coin Spot pattern, melon ribbed, rolled lip, smooth base ... **85.00**

Canary, Hobnail pattern, three pouring rings, round lip, smooth base . **75.00**

7½" h

Iridescent, Loetz type, crackled green over cobalt blue, blown, ground pontil, c1900 .... **250.00**

Opalescent

Blue, Daisy and Fern pattern, rolled lip, ground pontil **150.00**

Cranberry, Stripes, rolled lip, ground pontil **125.00**

7¾" h, amethyst, enameled flowers ... **160.00**

8" h

Amethyst, enameled floral dec, blown, open pontil **250.00**

Blue, horizontal brown band design, applied white enamel floral pattern, sheared lip, exposed pontil **115.00**

Clambroth, emb "Water" in red letters across front, porcelain stopper **45.00**

Loetz, irid purple streaks, sheared mouth, smooth base, 1870 ...... **175.00**

Mary Gregory, cobalt blue, white enameled dec

Hunter with bird on hand, gold trim, blown **185.00**

Woman holding a bird, gold trim, blown **175.00**

Young girl with tennis racquet, cobalt blue, gold trim **375.00**

Opaque, clambroth type white body, tapering cone shape, "Water" emb in red, orig porcelain stopper **65.00**

8¼" h, spatter, light blue and white, polished mouth and base **200.00**

8¼" h, 3" w, opalescent, cranberry, sq, white opalescent feathers **275.00**

8⅜" h, opalescent, Spanish Lace pattern, cranberry, rolled lip, polished pontil **125.00**

8½" h, cobalt blue, bell shape, raised white and orange enameled flowers, sheared lip, exposed pontil **75.00**

9" h, milk glass, hand painted, "Bay Rum", pink and white flowers, green leaves, pastel ground, rolled lip, pontil **145.00**

9¼" h, opalescent, Waffle pattern, light blue, rolled lip **120.00**

11" h, frosted ground, hand painted gold

medallion, raised enamels, blue highlights, gold lip, pontil **75.00**

BASKETS

History: Glass baskets have been made by glassblowers for centuries. Their popularity lead to wonderful creations of art glass with thorny handles, as well as plain baskets with simple designs. Cut glass baskets have often enjoyed a special place because of their beauty. Pressed glass patterns often also included a basket form to match the compotes and stemware lines.

Unlike their popular natural material counterpart, glass baskets were not made for gathering eggs or going to market, but to hold delicate candies, potpourri, or flowers. Special baskets were made to hold sugar or jelly, while others were made to hold spoons. Small baskets were often included on an elegantly decorated table to hold salt or almonds at each place setting. Larger, usually more ornate, baskets were used as centerpieces to hold fruit and/or flowers. Truly elegant table decorations were treasured and often special pieces were used only for specific functions. One served pickles from pickle castors, almonds from baskets, and so on.

Manufacturers of glass baskets include Heisey, Cambridge, Tiffany, and other well-known names. Examples are found in almost every color and generally have applied non–movable handles.

Reference: John Mebane, *Collecting Brides' Baskets And Other Glass Fancies,* Wallace–Homestead, 1976.

4½" h, Massachusetts pattern, US Glass Co, clear, clear applied handle **50.00**

4½" h, 3¾" w, satin, mother of pearl, herringbone, deep pink ruffled edge, pink shaded ground, white int., applied clear thorny handle **435.00**

5" d, opaline, ruffled, applied clear handle **45.00**

5" h, Octagon, Heisey, flamingo **75.00**

5½" d, 8" h, Brilliant Period cut glass, Berlyn pattern, Quaker City Glass Co, applied twisted handle, three step pedestal base **375.00**

6" h, two handles

Diane, Cambridge, crystal, ftd **20.00**

Gloria, Cambridge, pink, c1935 .. **24.00**

Wildflower, Cambridge, crystal, etched design, ftd **20.00**

6" h, 4¾" d, end of day pink, brown, and white spatter, white lining, ruffled edge, applied clear thorny handle .. **165.00**

6½" d, Brilliant Period cut glass, intaglio cutting, applied twisted handle **150.00**

6½" h, 3⅞" d, end of day lavender, pink, and white spatter overlay, white lining, emb raindrop pattern, ruffled edge, cobalt blue twisted handle, Czechoslovakian 80.00

6¾" h, creamy opaque body, applied pink flowers, applied vaseline twist handle 200.00

6¾" h, 5" d, Hobnail pattern, yellow opaque body, crimped edge, applied clear thorn handle 185.00

6¾" h, 5¼" d, end of day gold, white, and pink spatter overlay, white lining, emb swirl ribbed body, ruffled edge, clear briar handle 165.00

7" h
Decagon, Cambridge, cobalt blue, c1930 .... 25.00
Hobnail pattern, white body, rose lining 95.00
Portland pattern, Portland Glass Co, clear, applied pressed clear leafy handle 85.00
Reverse 44 pattern, US Glass Co, clear, gold trim, applied reeded handle, ... 125.00

7" h, 4½" d, cranberry, clear foot, foliate band and handle 175.00

7" h, 6¾" l, 5¾" w, vaseline opalescent, Diamond Quilted pattern, applied pink flowers and clear leaves, applied clear twisted thorn handle 200.00

7" h, 9" d, American pattern, Fostoria, clear, reeded handle 60.00

7¼" h, 5¼" d, orange, clear rigaree, applied crystal leaves, applied clear handle 175.00

7½" h
Cabbage Leaf, pink overlay, yellow lining, applied clear thorn handle 190.00
Lariat, Heisey, crystal, bonbon type . 65.00

7½" h, 4½" d, end of day blue, brown, and white spatter overlay, white lining, ruffled edge, applied clear twisted thorny handle 165.00

7½" h, 4¾" d, pink candy stripe swirl overlay, white lining, ruffled edge, applied clear twisted thorny handle ... 165.00

7½" h, 5¼" d, oxblood red and opaline swirled body, gold aventurine splotches, gold enamel dec, thick crystal casing, crystal handle 285.00

7¾" h, 7" w, satin, mother of pearl, diamond quilted, deep gold, melon ribbed body, sq crimped top, sq spatter handle, Mt Washington, c1880 .. 785.00

8" d, creamy opaque body, rose lining, amber edged ruffled rim, twist handle 165.00

8" h, 6" d, Diamond Quilted pattern, opalescent vaseline shading to pink, applied pink handle 160.00

8" h, 11" d, Brilliant period cut glass, Harvard pattern, hobstars and prisms 475.00

8" d, 11¾" d, Brilliant Period cut glass, Panel pattern, hobstars and elongated vesicas, flaring scalloped and serrated rim, pointed overall notched handle, sgd "Hawkes" 5,000.00

8½" h
Caramel shading to apricot, clear edge, applied clear thorn handle . 275.00
Opaque white, pink scallops, applied clear handle, Stevens and Williams 225.00

8½" h, 7½" l, 4½" w, deep royal blue shading to lighter blue, two applied white opaline flowers and clear leaves, applied clear twisted thorn handle 235.00

8¾" h, 5" d, opalescent light vaseline, green edge, thorny nubs, applied clear handle 185.00

Spatter, maroon, turquoise, gold, green, and pink, white lining, applied clear twisted thorn handle, 5½" sq, 5" h, $150.00.

9" h, peachblow, amber ruffle, petal feet, applied amber thorn handle ... 190.00

9" h, 5½" w, apricot to pink opalescent, pedestal rose bowl shape, vertical ribbed interior, applied clear leaves, stems, and vine, applied twisted thorn handle, c1880 .... 265.00

9½" h, cranberry, ruffled, clear petal feet, applied clear thorn handle 200.00

10" d, Snail pattern, George Duncan & Sons, clear, pewter handle, cake type 95.00

11" h, Cleo, Cambridge Glass, amber, two side handles 30.00

11½" h, Illinois pattern, clear, applied clear handle 100.00

12" h, Cabbage Rose pattern, clear, applied clear handle 100.00

12" h, 15" l, Broken Column pattern, clear, applied clear handle 125.00

BLACK GLASS

History: Black glass was one of the colors made during early glass production as far back as 1600. These early bottles were of a thick body and were primarily used for fermenting types of liquids, where the glass walls had to withstand pressures of the fermenting ale or wine. The Bohemians developed an opaque black glass which they used as a base for gold matte decorations, often of an Oriental taste. Other European glassware manufacturers, including the English, produced black glass items, however its popularity was always limited.

American production of black glass dates back to Deming Jarvis when he was at the Boston and Sandwich Glass Company circa 1865. His ingredients included manganese and even powdered charcoal. While developing glass with greater strengths and other desirable properties, glassblowers noticed that the more manganese they added, the darker the purple glass became. Some early "black" glass pieces may actually be very dark purple or even very dark green. Other 19th-century glass houses, like Atterbury, Dalzell, and Gilmore, produced lamps, bottles, and other items of black glass.

In 1915 Westmoreland Specialty Company introduced a black glass line, and this "new" color was quickly copied by Duncan and Miller as well as Northwood, Fenton, and Cambridge. Fostoria was one of the last of the major manufacturers to get involved when they began production in 1924 and by that time, demand was beginning to fail. United States Glass Company became the leading exponent of black glass during the 1920s and continued to hold this lead until around 1926.

Popularity of black glass became greater again in 1929 with the introduction of black stemmed wares. Morgantown Glass Works lead the way, quickly followed by Fostoria and Central Glass Works. Black tableware sets were introduced during this period. Shapes reflected the design attitudes of the times and square plates and square footed stemware created a bold statement.

By 1932 sales began to drop off again, as they did for most handmade glass. Cambridge continued its ebony line until 1939. Raw ingredient shortages caused by World War II seriously affected the colored glassware industry and almost no black glass was produced again until 1949. Westmoreland issued black variety items. Again, some of the major glassmakers, (Fostoria, Cambridge, and Viking) entered the field. Smaller manufacuters like Boyd and Degenhart joined the marketplace. A large percentage of the black glass offered in today's marketplace comes from the last surge which lasted into the mid 1950s.

References: Margaret James, *Black Glass, An Il-* lustrated *Price Guide,* Collector Books, 1981; Marlena Toohey, *A Collector's Guide To Black Glass,* Antique Publications, 1988.

Ashtray, 4" d	
Cloverleaf pattern, Hazel Atlas, 1930–36, match holder center . . .	**65.00**
Square, Hazel Atlas	**5.00**
Basket, 5" h, emb and basketweave bands, two handles	**30.00**
Batter Set, batter jug and syrup, clear body, black cov and tray, Paden City, 1936	**60.00**
Berry Bowl	
Orchid pattern, Paden City, early 1930s, 8½" d, two handles	**75.00**
Ribbon pattern, Hazel Atlas, c1930 .	**25.00**
Bonbon, cov, Flower Garden with Butterflies pattern, US Glass, late 1920s, 6⅝" d	**225.00**
Bookends, pr	
Horse, L. E. Smith, 1950s	**50.00**
Scottie Dog, 6½" h, Imperial, frosted, 1979, made for National Cambridge Collectors Inc	**50.00**
Bowl, 7½" d, Alternating Flute and Panel, Imperial, c1930	**40.00**
Butter Dish, cov, Dawn, Heisey, rect .	**110.00**

Candlestick, Fostoria, 4" h, $35.00.

Candlestick	
3" h, Oak Leaf pattern, Fostoria, pr .	**85.00**
4" h, opaque, wafer foot, three knobs on stem, etched "Italia," Venini paper label	**125.00**
Candy Dish, cov	
Orchid pattern, Paden City, early 1930s, 6½" h, sq	**90.00**
Ovide pattern, Hazel Atlas, 1930–35	**37.50**
Celery Tray	
Lodestar, Dawn, Heisey	**50.00**
Viking, clear swan handle, oval	**60.00**
Cereal Bowl	
4⅞" d, Orchid pattern, Paden City, early 1930s	**30.00**

5" d, Diamond Quilted pattern, Imperial, early 1930s **12.50**

Cheese and Cracker, 10" w, 5⅜" h, ftd, Flower Garden with Butterflies pattern, US Glass, late 1920s **325.00**

Cigarette Box, cov, 4⅜" l, Flower Garden with Butterflies pattern, US Glass, late 1920s **125.00**

Compote
3¼" h, Orchid pattern, Paden City, early 1930s **32.00**
6½" h, Co–Operative Glass Co, c1924 .... **35.00**
7" h, Flower Garden with Butterflies pattern, US Glass, late 1920s **175.00**

Console Bowl
8½" d, Flower Garden with Butterflies pattern, US Glass, late 1920s **150.00**
10½" d, rolled edge, Diamond Quilted pattern, Imperial, early 1930s **45.00**

Cordial Decanter, 12 oz, ball shape, applied clear handle, clear stopper, Cambridge, Farber Bros metal holder, c1933 .... **90.00**

Creamer
Cloverleaf pattern, Hazel Atlas, 1930–36, 3⅜" h, ftd **17.50**
Diamond Quilted pattern, Imperial, early 1930s **15.00**
Mt Pleasant **18.00**
Orchid pattern, Paden City, early 1930s **42.00**

Cream Soup Bowl, 4¾" d, Diamond Quilted pattern, Imperial, early 1930s **15.00**

Cup and Saucer
Cloverleaf pattern, Hazel Atlas, 1930–1936 .... **19.00**
Diamond Quilted pattern, Imperial, early 1930s **18.00**

Flower Pot, 3"h, L. E. Smith, c1930 .. **15.00**

Ice Bucket
Diamond Quilted pattern, Imperial, early 1930s **85.00**
Orchid pattern, Paden City, early 1930s **90.00**
Tally Ho pattern, Cambridge, Farber Bros chrominum plated frame and handle, c1935, 5½" h **75.00**

Mayonnaise, silver dec, L. E. Smith ... **15.00**

Nappy, handle
4½" d, Dawn, Heisey **35.00**
5½" d, Diamond Quilted pattern, Imperial, early 1930s **15.00**

Orange Bowl, 11" d, ftd, Flower Garden with Butterflies pattern, US Glass, late 1920s **215.00**

Place Card Holder, 2½" h, Fostoria ... **30.00**

Plate
6" d
Cloverleaf pattern, Hazel Atlas, 1930–36 .... **13.75**

Diamond Quilted pattern, Imperial, early 1930s **5.00**
8" d
Cloverleaf pattern, Hazel Atlas, 1930–36 .... **30.00**
Diamond Quilted pattern, Imperial, early 1930s **12.00**
Mt Pleasant **14.00**
Ribbon pattern, Hazel Atlas, c1930 **12.00**
8½" d, sq, Orchid pattern, Paden City, early 1930s **40.00**
10" d, Flower Garden with Butterflies pattern, US Glass, late 1920s **100.00**
10½" d, grill, Cloverleaf pattern, Hazel Atlas, 1930–36 .... **15.00**
12" d, Cloverleaf pattern, Hazel Atlas, 1930–1936 .... **12.00**

Relish, divided, Lodestar, Dawn, Heisey **60.00**

Salt and Pepper Shakers, pr
Cloverleaf pattern, Hazel Atlas, 1930–36 .... **75.00**
Ovide pattern, Hazel Atlas, 1930–35 **25.00**
Ribbon pattern, Hazel Atlas, c1930 . **40.00**

Sandwich Server, center handle
Diamond Quilted pattern, Imperial, early 1930s **40.00**
Flower Garden with Butterflies pattern, US Glass, late 1920s **100.00**
Orchid pattern, Paden City, early 1930s **60.00**

Sherbet
Cloverleaf pattern, Hazel Atlas, 1930–1936 .... **17.00**
Diamond Quilted pattern, Imperial, early 1930s **12.50**
Ovoid pattern, Hazel Atlas, 1930–35 **7.50**

Sugar, cov
Cloverleaf pattern, Hazel Atlas, 1930–1936 .... **12.00**
Diamond Quilted pattern, Imperial, early 1930s **15.00**
Orchid pattern, Paden City, early 1930s **50.00**

Sweet Pea Vase, 7" h, 8½" d, Cambridge, c1922 .... **55.00**

Tumbler, Town & Country, Heisey **30.00**

Vase
6" h, fan, dolphin handles, Fenton, c1927 .... **55.00**
6¼" h, cupped, Flower Garden with Butterflies pattern, US Glass, late 1920s **145.00**
7¾" h, flared top, silver deposit dec, Diamond Glass Ware Co, c1939 . **45.00**
8" h, Tut, Fostoria **50.00**
10" h, Orchid pattern, Paden City, early 1930s **90.00**
10½" h, floral dec, satin, Tiffin Glass **95.00**

Wall Pocket, 9" l, Flower Garden with Butterflies pattern, US Glass, late 1920s **295.00**

BLOWN THREE MOLD

History: The Jamestown colony in Virginia introduced glassmaking into America. The artisans used a "free blown" method.

Blowing molten glass into molds was not introduced into America until the early 1800s. Blown three mold glass used a predesigned mold that consisted of two, three, or more hinged parts. The glassmaker placed a quantity of molten glass on the tip of a rod or tube, inserted it into the mold, blew air into the tube, waited until the glass cooled, and removed the finished product. The three part mold is the most common and lends its name to this entire category.

Impressed decorations on blown mold glass usually are reversed (what is raised or convex on the outside will be concave on the inside). This is useful in identifying the blown form.

By 1850 American-made glassware was in relatively common usage. The increased demand led to large factories and the creation of a technology which eliminated the smaller companies.

Collectors should be aware that reproductions of blown mold glass are offered widely in the marketplace. Some reproductions are specially produced for museums and gift shops. While many are marked, most are not. Modern artists have kept the craft of blown molded glassware alive—collectors should learn to recognize the characteristics of new glass.

Reference: George S. and Helen McKearin, *American Glass*, reprint, Crown Publishers, 1941, 1948.

Collectors' Club: National Early American Glass Club, 7417 Allison Street, Hyattsville, MD 20784.

Additional Listings: Early American Glass and Stiegel–Type.

Basket, pontil, solid applied handle
   3⅛" d, 3½" h, cobalt blue, plain base,
     gold rib dec traces **110.00**

Tumbler, McKearin GII–18, 3⅜" h, $175.00.

   4" d, 4½" h, clear, rayed base **275.00**
Bottle, 6⅞" h, olive green, pint, undamaged, McKearin GIII–16 .... **550.00**
Bowl
   4¼" d, 1¾" h, clear, straight sided,
   sixteen diamond base, pontil, outwardly folded rim **210.00**
   5" d, 1⅝" h, clear, rounded sides,
   rayed base, pontil, outwardly folded rim **155.00**
   5" d, 2⅛" h, clear, slightly rounded
   sides, rayed base, pontil **375.00**
   6" d, 1¾" h, clear, straight slanting
   sides, sixteen diamond base, pontil, outwardly folded rim **130.00**
   6¼" d
     Clear, rayed base, slanted sides,
     pontil, folded rim **175.00**
     Clear, twelve diamond base, pontil,
     folded rim **185.00**
   6⅜" d, 5¾" h, clear, folded rim, sixteen diamond base, pontil, ftd, tilts
   to one side, McKearin GII–18 ...**4,800.00**
Carafe, 9¼" h, dark yellow–green, rayed base, deep pontil **2,300.00**
Creamer
   2⅞" h, clear, fifteen diamond base,
   pontil, applied ribbed handle, tip
   missing **100.00**
   3¼" h, clear, ringed base, formed
   mouth and spout, applied solid
   handle with curled end **375.00**
Cruet
   Clear, 5⅜" h, plain base, pontil,
   formed pouring lip, McKearin GII–28 .... **45.00**
   Sapphire blue, rayed base, pontil,
   molded neck rings, orig solid tam
   stopper **450.00**
Cup Plate, 3⅞" d, clear, folded rim, rayed base, pontil, McKearin GII–1 . **550.00**
Decanter
   Clear
     Pint, square, chamfered corners,
     plain base, pontil, pressed stopper **235.00**
     Quart, fourteen diamond base,
     pontil, three applied double
     pouring rings, orig acorn stopper **425.00**
     Quarter pint, rayed base, pontil,
     orig ribbed solid stopper **300.00**
   Pale yellow–green, quart, rayed base,
   pontil, flanged lip **800.00**
Dish
   5" d, clear **325.00**
   5¾" d, 1⅞" h, clear, rayed base, pontil, folded rim **185.00**
   6⅜" d, clear, folded rim, rayed base,
   iron pontil **90.00**
   7" d, clear **475.00**
Flip, clear, 5⅝" h, 4⅝" d, eighteen diamond base **130.00**

Hat
Clear
2⅛" h, fifteen diamond base, pontil, folded rim **275.00**
2¼" h, swirled rayed base, pontil, folded rim **110.00**
Sapphire blue, 2⅝" h, 2¼" d, folded rim, ringed and pontil base **850.00**
Inkwell
McKearin GII, olive green **120.00**
McKearin GII–18, 2⅝" d, 2" h, olive green **120.00**
McKearin GIII, olive green **160.00**
Lamp
Fluid, 6½" h, clear, double paw pressed base, orig brass collar, marked "BTM font/Mt Vernon Works," McKearin GI–30 .... **800.00**
Sparking, clear, blown three mold stopper mold, applied handle, orig tin and cork burner, McKearin 110–4 .... **575.00**
Miniature, decanter, 3½" h, clear, McKearin GIII–12, ground upper rim **125.00**
Mustard
3⅞" h, clear, flanged lip, iron pontil   **25.00**
5" h, clear, solid sheared ball finial, flanged, folded lip, pontil, orig matching cov **120.00**
5¼" h, clear, plain base, pontil, orig pressed finial finish hollow blown cov, McKearin GI–24 .... **85.00**
Pitcher
3¾" h, clear, bulbous shape, fifteen diamond base, pontil, solid applied handle **275.00**
7" h, clear, rayed base, pontil, manipulated mouth, hollow applied handle **230.00**
8½" h, clear, tool mark at lower part of applied handle **250.00**
8¾" h, clear, McKearin GV–17 .... **400.00**
10¼" h, clear, pillar molded **200.00**
Plate, 5⅜" d, clear, plain base, pontil, folded rim **150.00**
Salt, master
Clear, hollow stem and base, pontil **575.00**
Purple blue, 2¼" h, rayed and ringed base, pontil **750.00**
Sapphire blue, 2½" h, rayed base, pontil, galleried rim **1,600.00**
Salt Shaker
4⅝" h, clear, pontil base, orig metal cap **65.00**
5" h, clear, sheared lip, orig metal cap and pontil **70.00**
Toddy Plate, 4¼" d, clear, rayed base, pontil, folded rim **260.00**
Toilet Bottle
Clear, rayed base, pontil, tam stopper **550.00**
Cobalt Blue, plain base, pontil matching stopper, McKearin GI–7 ..... **350.00**

Sapphire Blue, plain base, pontil, flanged folded lip **170.00**
Violet, 6¾" h, smooth base, flanged lip, orig tam stopper **650.00**
Yellow–Green, 6⅝" h, tapering ovoid shape, plain base, pontil, orig matching stopper, McKearin GI–3, type–II **2,600.00**
Tumbler
3⅛" h, clear, ringed base, pontil, inwardly folded lip **220.00**
3¼" h, clear, barrel shape, rayed base, pontil **325.00**
3½" h, clear, barrel shape, rayed base, plain sheared lip, pontil **375.00**
3⅜" h, clear, ringed base, pontil, Sandwich Glass Co **275.00**
Vinegar Bottle, 6¾" h, sapphire blue, McKearin GI– **250.00**
Whimsey, hat, cobalt blue, similar to McKearin GIII–6 .... **750.00**
Whiskey Taster, 1⅝" h, clear, ringed base, pontil **185.00**
Whiskey Tumbler
2⅝" h, clear, barrel shape, sixteen diamond base, pontil **210.00**
2¾" h, clear, plain base, pontil **275.00**

BOHEMIAN GLASS

History: The once independent country of Bohemia, now a part of Czechoslovakia, produced a variety of fine glassware: etched, cut, overlay, and colored. Glass production has been recorded as early as the 14th and 15th centuries. Wheel cutting techniques were practiced in the 16th century. By the mid 19th century, coal replaced wood as fuel and many new factories sprang up. Beautiful examples of exquisite cutting and engraved portraits were skillfully crafted. Bohemian glassware was first imported into America in the early 1820s and continues today.

Bohemia is known for its "flashed" glass that was produced in the familiar ruby color, as well as amber, green, blue, and black. Common patterns include "Deer and Castle," "Deer and Pine Tree," and "Vintage."

Most of the Bohemian glass encountered in today's market is of the 1875–1900 period. Bohemian glassware was carried around the world by travelers and salesmen. Engravers often decorated pieces to fill the demand of this group of eager buyers and tailored their decorations to fit the tastes and desires of the buyers. Bohemian–type glass also was made in England, Switzerland, and Germany.

Reference: Brigitte Klesse and Hans Mayr, *European Glass from 1500–1800, The Ernesto Wolf Collection*, Kremayr & Scheriau, 1987.

Reproduction Alert.

Beaker
4⅛" h, amber flash, three panels, engraved named scenes of Prague, flaring base, mid 19th C **300.00**
4½" h
Blue and white overlay, arched panels with gilt ivy and stylized foliage on oval white overlay, flaring base, mid 19th C **225.00**
Blue and white overlay, multicolored spring floral bouquet on oval white overlay, gilt foliage, arched panels, mid to late 19th C **250.00**
Clear, continuous hunters in landscape, band of flowering branches **350.00**
4⅝" h, waisted cylindrical, multicolored enameled morning glories between cut roundels, pink overlay, white ground **600.00**
4¾" h
Green flashed, circular and oval cut windows, multicolored enameled flowers, gilt lines **200.00**
White overlay, multicolored enameled peasant girl, oval cartouche edged with gilt ivy, loose bouquet of flowers on reverse **450.00**
5" h, pink flashed, opaline, cut stylized leaves and drapery, enamel and gilt flowering branches, flaring base, late 19th C **465.00**
5⅛", blue and white overlay, rect panel engraved with stag landscape, oval roundels, named scenes, gilt highlights, late 19th C **300.00**
5¼" h, white on amethyst overlay, quatrefoil and circular cut windows, painted trailing roses **225.00**

Covered Goblet, Egyptian motif of pyramids, sphinx, and palm trees, ruby ground, etching with yellow wash, $185.00.

5½" h
Amber and ruby flashed, alternating panels engraved with cornucopia, flowers, beehive, and urn, cut panels, scalloped foot **200.00**
Amber flashed, engraved, animals and building, C scroll panels, flared foot, c1860 .... **100.00**
Bowl, 3" d, 1¾" h, Lithyalin, three rows of honeycomb cutting, mottled brown, designed to simulate polished agate, Frederich Eggermann, c1835 . **385.00**
Box, cov
3½" d, domed lid, ruby flashed, Vintage pattern, engraved clear and frosted grape clusters and vines, gilt brass fittings **165.00**
3¾" d, domed hinged lid, ruby flashed, engraved clear and frosted buildings, scrolling foliate bands, brass fittings **185.00**
Celery Tray, ruby flashed, Deer and Castle pattern, clear and frosted **100.00**
Compote, 9½" d, 6½" h, amber flashed, Deer and Castle pattern, engraved clear and frosted animals, castle, and trees **175.00**
Decanter, 8¼" h, octagonal, triple ringed neck, windows engraved with named scenes of Prague on alternating pink and blue flash, yellow flash ground, enameled black foliage **950.00**
Flip Glass, 6" h, 6" d, clear, cut, engraved forest scene with fox and birds **125.00**
Goblet
5½" h, ruby, engraved stag, rocky landscape, enameled stylized foliage and flowers, flaring base **200.00**
5¾" h, paneled, ruby flash roundels, engraved named scenes, white enamel flowers, flaring foot **185.00**
6¼" h, Annagelb, hexagonal bowl, raised enameled bosses, gilt named scenes, conforming knop and petal base **420.00**
Jar, cov, 7" h, barrel shape, bands of clear engraving, red satin discs, barrel finial **150.00**
Mantel Lusters, pr, 6½" d, 12¼" h, cranberry cut overlay, cut scalloped tops, white overlay panels, multicolored flowers, all over gold flowers and scrolls, clear cut prisms **1,000.00**
Mug, 6" h, ruby flashed, engraved castle and trees, applied clear handle, sgd "Volmer 1893" **120.00**
Perfume Bottle, 7" h, ruby flashed, Deer and Castle pattern, clear and frosted, gold dec **125.00**
Pickle Jar, cov, 6" h, ruby flashed, Deer and Castle pattern, clear and frosted **75.00**
Powder Box, cov, 4¼" d, round, straight

sides, flat top, ruby flashed, etched cov with leaping stag, forest setting, landscape and birds on sides, clear base **140.00**
Stein
4½" h, 2¾" d, ruby flashed, engraved dog and deer in forest, "Souvenir de Luchon" on front, pewter mounts **250.00**
6½" h, 3" d, ruby flashed, engraved cathedral panels, leaves, and scrolls, pewter mounts, ruby inset lid **310.00**
Sugar Shaker, ruby flashed, Bird and Castle pattern, clear and frosted **85.00**
Teapot, 11" w, cranberry cut to clear, panels of flowers, gilt spout and handle **200.00**
Tumbler, 4¼" h, engraved scene, early 19th C **175.00**
Vase
5" h, deep green glass, faceted foot, molded Bacchanalian dancing woman in foliage, c1930 .... **150.00**
6⅛" h, waisted cylindrical, cut oval panels engraved with symbols of Prosperity, amber flash reserved on amethyst ground, all over flowering branches engraving **450.00**
11" h, gold rose dec, late 19th C ... **195.00**

BOTTLES

History: Cosmetic bottles held special creams, oils, and cosmetics designed to enhance the beauty of the user. Some also claimed, especially on their colorful labels, to cure or provide relief from common ailments.

A number of household items, e.g. cleaning fluids and polishes, required glass storage containers. Many are collected for their fine lithograph labels. Others are collected because of the rainbow of colors in which they were manufactured.

Medicine bottles contained "medicines" of all kinds, from bitters to elixirs and promised to cure everything from snake bites to serious illnesses. These small bottles make very interesting collectibles as their claims rival the best of today's Madison Avenue advertising executives.

Mineral water bottles contained water from a natural spring. Spring water was favored by health conscious people between the 1850s and 1900s.

Nursing bottles, used to feed the young and sickly, were a great help to the housewife because of graduated measures, replaceable nipples, and the ease of cleaning, sterilizing, and reuse.

Soda bottles, beer bottles, and other popular drink bottles carried our favorite beverages from the manufacturer to store or distributor shelves. Painted labels and a myriad of colors attract today's collectors.

References: Ralph and Terry Kovel, *The Kovels' Bottle Price List, Eighth Edition,* Crown Publishers, Inc., 1987; Jim Megura, *The Official Price Guide to Bottles, Eleventh Edition,* House of Collectibles, 1991; Carlo and Dorothy Sellari, *The Standard Old Bottle Price Guide,* Collector Books, 1989.

Periodicals: *Antique Bottle And Glass Collector,* P. O. Box 187, East Greenville, PA 18041; *Bottles and Extras,* Box 154, Happy Camp, CA 96039.

Collectors' Club: Federation of Historical Bottles Collectors, 14521 Atlantic, Riverdale, IL 60627.

Museum: National Bottle Museum, Ballston Spa, NY.

BEER BOTTLES

Embossed
Buffalo Brewing Co, Sacramento, CA, emb buffalo jumping through horseshoe, amber, blob top, 12" h ... **18.00**
Callie & Co Limited, emb dog's head, St Helens below center, dark green, ring type blob top, 8¼" h **15.00**
Chattachoochee Brewing Co, Brownsville, AL, aqua, 9½" h **8.00**
Cumberland Brew Co, Cumberland, MD, amber **8.00**
Excelsior, aqua, 9¼" h **15.00**
Germania Brewing Co, aqua, 7½" h **12.00**
Hand Brew Co, Pawtucket, RI, aqua **12.00**
Hinckel Brew Co, Albany, Boston, Manchester, fancy, amber, blob top **15.00**
Iroquis, Buffalo, Indian head, amber **10.00**
McCormick Brewery, 1897, Boston, clear **10.00**
National Brewing Co, Baltimore, eagle, amber, blob top **17.50**
Piel Bros, East New York Brewery, fancy logo, aqua **15.00**
Royal Ruby, ABM, 9½" h **18.00**
Trommer's Evergreen Brewery, aqua **7.50**
Painted Label
Augusta Brewing Co, Augusta, CA, aqua, 7" h **12.00**
Camden City Brewery, amber, 9" h . **9.00**
Cock n' Bull Ginger Beer, crown top, 7" h **4.00**
Gutsch Brew, red, 8½" h **15.00**
Rolling Rock Extra Pale, blue and white label, green bottle, unopened **15.00**
Schlitz Brewing Co, amber, 9½" h .. **8.00**
Paper Label
Central Brand Extra Lager Beer, aqua, 9¼" h **5.00**
Cooks 500 Ale, aqua, 9½" h **3.50**

Diamond Jim's Beer, aqua, 9¼" h .. **5.00**
Grand Prize Beer, Gulf Brewing Co,
  Houston, clear, crown top, 9" h .. **7.50**
Mineral Spring Beer, aqua, 9" h **5.00**
Pabst Extract, amber, two labels **8.00**
Schells Beer, Schells Brewing Co, am-
  ber, 9½" h **3.50**
Southern Brewing Co, machine
  made, green, 9½" h **2.50**

Bitters, Rohrer's Bitters Expectoral Wild Cherry Tonic, Lancaster, PA, brown, square tapering sides, emb rope edging, dec, and lettering, ¾ quart, $80.00.

BITTERS BOTTLES

Abbott's Bitters, amber, 8" h **8.00**
African Stomach Bitters, amber, 9½" h **40.00**
Angostura Bark Bitters, amber, 7" h ... **90.00**
Atwood's Quinine Tonic, aqua **35.00**
Barto's Great Gun Bitters, "Reading,
  Pa." in center circle, cannon shop
  bottle, olive amber, 11" h, 3¼" d ... **785.00**
Bender's Bitters, aqua **50.00**
Bird Bitters, Phila, PA, clear **75.00**
Brown's Celebrated Indian Herb Bitters,
  Indian queen, yellow, rolled mouth,
  12" h **750.00**
Calabash Bitters, aqua **75.00**
Castilian Bitters, light honey amber ... **100.00**
Catawba Wine Bitters, cluster of grapes
  in front and back, green, 9" h **65.00**
Clarke's Compound Mandrake Bitters,
  aqua, applied top, smooth base,
  1865–75, 7½" h **55.00**
Clayton's & Russell's Bitters, "Cele-
  brated Stomach Bitters," sq **68.00**
Climax Bitters, pale gold amber **75.00**
Columbo Peptic Bitters, amber **30.00**
Constitution Bitters, deep amethyst,
  sloping collared mouth, 9⅛" h **725.00**

Dandelion Bitters, rect bottle, clear, amber, tapered top, 8" h **32.00**
Doyle's Hop Bitters, amber, sloping collared mouth, 9⅜" h **25.00**
Drake's Plantation, cabin shape, six
  logs, olive amber **140.00**
Dr Geo Pierce's Indian Restorative Bitters, Lowell, MA, aqua, applied top,
  open pontil, 1857–60, 7⅞" h **135.00**
Dr Gilbert's Rock and Rye Bitters, blue–
  green **100.00**
Dr Petzolds Genuine German Bitters,
  amber, applied top, smooth base,
  1884–90, 10¼" h **120.00**
Dr Renz's Herb Bitters, olive, amber
  tones, applied top, smooth base,
  1862–74, 9⅞" h **160.00**
Dr Soule Hop Bitters, hop and leaf mo-
  tif, black–red, applied top, smooth
  base, 1872–82, 9⅛" h **230.00**
Dr Von Hopfs, Chamberlain & Co, Des
  Moines, IA, Curacoa bitters, amber,
  tooled top, smooth base, 1890–1900,
  8" h **70.00**
Eagle Aromatic Bitters, amber **25.00**
Emerson Excelsior Botanic Bitters, "E.H.
  Burns, Augusta, ME," amber, 9" h .. **75.00**
English Female Bitters, clear **70.00**
Excelsior Aromatic Bitters, smoky amber **100.00**
Ferro Quina, Stomach Bitters, Blood
  Maker, Dogliani Italia, D.P. Rossi,
  1400 Dupont Str. S.F., Sole Agent,
  USA and Canada, amber, tooled top,
  smooth base, 1895–1909, 9" h **80.00**
Globe, The, Tonic Bitters, amber, slop-
  ing collared mouth, 10" h **65.00**
Goff's Bitters, H on bottom, clear and
  amber, 5¾" h **25.00**
Hall's Bitters, amber, applied top,
  smooth base, 1875–85, 3" h **170.00**
Hart's Star Bitters, Philadelphia, PA ... **175.00**
Hentz's Curative Bitters, pale green ... **100.00**
Holtzermann's Patent Stomach Bitters,
  rect cabin, yellow–amber, sloping
  collared mouth, 9½" h **425.00**
Hutching's Dyspepsia Bitters, aqua,
  sloping collared mouth, 8⅜" h **75.00**
John Moffit, Phoenix Bitters, NY, olive
  amber, eight sided, round collar pontil, 6⅜" h **2,500.00**
Kimball's Jaundice Bitters, golden amber, sloping collared mouth, iron pontil, 7" h **150.00**
King Solomon's Bitters, amber **150.00**
Lorimer's Juniper Bitters, sq, blue–
  green, 9½" h **60.00**
McKeever's Army Bitters, on shoulder,
  drum shaped bottom, cannonballs
  stacked on top, tapered top, amber,
  10¼" h **600.00**
Night Cap Bitters, clear, three sided .. **80.00**
Old Homestead Wild Cherry Bitters, sq

cabin, deep golden amber, sloping collared mouth, 9½" h 150.00
Oregon Grape Root Bitters, round, clear, 9¾" h 48.00
Phoenix Bitters, olive amber, rolled mouth, 5⅛" h 250.00
Porter's, Dr, Medicated Stomach Bitters 70.00
Radium Bitters, rect, clear 35.00
Rothenberg, S.B., Sole Agent, U.S., gin shape, milk glass, applied collared mouth, 9" h 100.00
Sazerac Aromatic Bitters, lady's leg, milk glass, applied mouth, 12¼" h . 275.00
Seaworth Bitters, lighthouse shape 275.00
Suffolk Bitters, pig, yellow–amber, double collared mouth, 10" h 325.00
Sunny Castle Stomach Bitters, light amber 60.00
Toneco Stomach Bitters, "Appetizer & Tonic," clear, sq 60.00
Traveller's Bitters, man standing with cane, oval, amber, 1834–1870, 10½" h 260.00
Turkish Bitters, amber 75.00
Uncle Tom's Bitters, light amber 75.00
Von Humboldt's Stomach Bitters, sq, amber 80.00
Willards' Golden Seal Bitters, aqua, tooled top, smooth base, 1880–92, 7½" h 50.00

COSMETIC BOTTLES

Boswell & Warner's Colorific, rect, cobalt blue, indented panels, tooled sq lip, c1880, 5½" h 85.00
De Vry's Dandero–Off Hair Tonic, clear, 6½" h 10.00
Hind's Honey and Almond Cream, 5½" h 7.50
Hyacinthia Toilet Hair Dressing, rect, crude applied lip, open pontil, aqua, 6" h 22.00
Kranks Cold Cream, milk glass, screw top, 2¾" h 4.00
Pompeian Massage Cream, amethyst, 2¾" h 4.00
Van Buskirb's, aqua, 5" h 3.00
Violet's Dulce Vanishing Cream, eight panels, 2½" h 15.00

FOOD BOTTLES

Baking Powder, Eddy's, tin top 12.00
Banana Flavor, Herberlings, paper label, 8" h 8.00
Catsup
 Curtis Brothers, clear, blue label . . . 10.00
 Quickshank, paper label 4.00
Coffee, Sunshine, oval shape, zinc lid 5.00
Ginger, Sanford's, label 10.00

Grape Juice, Bass Islands, 5" h 5.00
Honey, Land of Lakes, honeycomb, metal cap 8.00
Horseradish
 E. T. Caldren, aqua, paper label 8.00
 Heinz Nobel & Co, emb, two anchors, horse head on lid, 1873, 5" h 275.00
Lemonade, G. Foster Clark & Co, Eiffel Tower, 2¾" h 10.00
Lemon Extract, Louis & Company 10.00
Olive, Chef, 5" h 5.00
Peanut
 Nut House, emb house, bulb shape 170.00
 Squirrel Brand Salted Nuts, emb squirrel, 13" h 110.00
Peanut Butter, Bennett Hubba, 5" 12.00
Pepper Sauce, cathedral, six panels, blue–green, applied ring lip, open pontil base, c1850, 8⅞" h 350.00
Pickle
 Cathedral, aqua, rolled lip, smooth base, America, 1870–80, 9¼" h . 75.00
 J. McCollick & Co, NY, bluish–aqua, beaded bands, paneled shoulder, emb, applied ring lip, iron pontil base, c1850, 11½" h 900.00
 Shaker Brand, olive–yellow 325.00
 Skilton Foote & Co, yellow–amber, lighthouse shape, 11⅜" h 130.00
Vinegar
 Weso Biko Company Cider Vinegar, jug shape 40.00
 Whitehouse, jug type, 10" h 20.00
Yogurt, Yami, Pellissier Dairy Farms, round, red, metal foil lid, 8 oz 5.00

HOUSEHOLD BOTTLES

Alma Polish, aqua, name emb on shoulder, marked "M & Co" on base, 5" h 5.00
EZ Stove Polish, aqua, 6" h 12.00
Golden Key Ammonia, paper label, 8" h 3.50
Gordon's Chafola Furniture Polish, emb, open pontil 150.00
Jennings Blueing, aqua, blob top, 7" h 5.00
Lake Shore See Co, aqua, 5¾" h 6.00
Osborn's Liquid Polish, round, open pontil, amber 325.00
Parson's Ammonia, aqua, 1882 . . . . . . 18.00
Sanford's Library Paste, amber, emb label, pint 17.50
Standard Oil Co, clear, orig label, 6" h 6.00

INK BOTTLES

Bertinguiot, medium olive–green, sheared top, open pontil, 2" h 275.00
Billing & Co, Banker's Writing Ink, aqua, "B" in center, 2" h 15.00

Ink, light teal, umbrella style, octagonal base, open pontil, 2¼" h, $40.00.

Carter's
Black Writing Fluid, yellow–amber, wide beveled corner, double collared mouth, label, 9¼" h 190.00
Cathedral, cobalt blue, hexagonal, 9¾" h 55.00
Cone, turquoise blue, tooled top, smooth base, 2½" h 110.00
E. Waters/Troy, NY, aquamarine, cylindrical, applied flared mouth, 2¼" h . 275.00
Farley's, yellow–amber, octagonal, sheared mouth, 1¾" h 550.00
Harrison's Columbian Ink, aquamarine, twelve sided, applied flared mouth, 5⅞" h 120.00
Hover, Philadelphia, medium green, cylindrical, applied mouth with spout, 9¼" h 130.00
Inverted Funnel, cobalt blue, open pontil, 2" h 140.00
J. A. Williamson Chemist, blue–green, cylindrical, applied mouth with spout, 9⅝" h 120.00
J. K. Palmer/Chemist/Boston, olive–amber, cylindrical, applied mouth with spout, 9¼" h 270.00
Lake's, aqua, cone, 2½" h 15.00
Maynard & Noyes, olive–amber, three part mold, sloping collared mouth with spout, label, 8" h 100.00
Pitkin Ink, Keene, dark aqua, open pontil, 1¾" h 150.00
S M Bixby & Co NY, aquamarine, fluted dome, nine sided, tooled mouth, 1⅞" h 100.00
S. O. Dunbar Taunton, aquamarine, eight sided umbrella shape, rolled mouth, 2⅜" h 70.00
Shepard & Allen's Writing Fluid, golden amber, cylindrical, red label, 6⅜" h 85.00
T & M, light sapphire blue, rolled lip, open pontil, 2½" h 70.00
Umbrella, dark aqua, applied top, sticky pontil, 2⅞" h 50.00
Wood's Black Ink, Portland, ME, aqua, tapered, ring top, 2½" h 25.00

MEDICINE BOTTLES

Amaryllis Val Schmidt & Co, Chemists, San Francisco, cobalt blue, tooled top, 1880–90, 5¾" h 130.00
American Drug Store N.O., tapered top, amber, 9¼" h 50.00
Barber Medicine Co, Kansas City, MO, aqua, label, 7½" h 20.00
Bennet's Magic Cure, sq, beveled edges, deep blue, applied sq collar lip, smooth base, 1865–75, 5⅛" h . 375.00
C & B/S F, dark aqua, applied top, smooth base, 6¼" h, 1865–75 ..... 75.00
Chief Tonic, clear, tooled top, smooth base, 1893–1905, 9¾" h 175.00
Chlorate Potassique, pontil, clear, painted brown, 6½" h 20.00
Crane & Brigham, San Francisco, dark aqua, applied top, smooth base, 8⅞" h 50.00
Dr Henley's Celery, Beef and Iron, C B & I Extract Co, amber, tooled top, smooth base, 1884–94, 9½" h 110.00
Dr J. A. Sherman's Rupture Curative Compound, rect, indented panels, cobalt blue, blue striations, tooled, applied sq collar, smooth base, 1870–80, 8¼" h 1,000.00

Medicine, O'Rourke & Hurley, Little Falls, NY, cobalt blue, 4⅛" h, $12.00.

E. A. Burkhout's Dutch Liniment, Prepared At Mechanicville, Saratoga Co, NY, pontil, aqua, 5¼" h 150.00
J. A. Gilka, two men with club and crown, black, 9" h 25.00
Girolamo Pagliano, vertical letters, rect, beveled corners, apple green, 4⅜" h 25.00
Gra Car Certosa of Pavia, aqua, 9½" h 20.00
Granular Citrate of Magnesia, kite with letter inside, ring top, cobalt, 8" h .. 30.00
G. W. House Clemens Indian Tonic, ring top, aqua, 5" h 100.00
Hop–Cel Company, San Francisco, Nerve, Blood & Brain Tonic, amber, tooled top, smooth base, 1890–1910, 9" h 25.00
John J Smith, Louisville, KY, round, deep

green, sloping collared mouth, scarred base, 5¾" h 175.00

Kobole Tonic Med Co, Chicago, IL, milk glass, 8½" h 35.00

Levarn's Hair Tonic and Dandruff Cure, Granville, NY, clear, tooled top, black and white label under glass, 7½" h . 60.00

O. K. Plantation, triangular, amber, 11" h 200.00

Phillips Emulsion, (N backwards), amber, 9½" h 30.00

Pine Tree Tar Cordial, Phila, tree and patent 1859 on one panel, L.Q.G. Wisharts on other, blob top, green, 8" h 50.00

Reed & Carnrick, NY, dark blue, 6¼" h 25.00

Ricin, The P. S. Co. Inc., Phila, PA, emerald green, tooled top, smooth base, 1890–1900, 3½" h 60.00

Roshton & Aspinwall, New York, Compound Chlorine Tooth Wash on back, flared top, pontil, golden olive, 6" h 250.00

Rushton Clark & Co., Chemist's New York, aqua, applied top, open pontil, 9½" h 95.00

Smith's Green Mountain Renovator, rect, beveled edges, olive–amber, applied double ring lip, pontil base, c1850, 7" h .....:............. 675.00

Sun Drug Co, Los Angeles, CA, light amber, tooled top, smooth base, winged mortar and pestle motif, 1890–1905, 5¾" h 170.00

Teissier Prevos A Paris, graphite pontil, blue, 7½" h 70.00

True Daff's Elixir, rect, beveled edges, yellow–green, applied ring lip, ball pontil base, England, 1830–50, 4⅞" h 350.00

Warner's Safe Cure, oval shape, golden amber, applied lip, smooth base, 1870–90, 8½" h 175.00

Whitwell's Liquid Improved Opodeloc, cylindrical, clear, emb, sloping flanged lip, pontil, two part mold, 4⅝" h 100.00

MILK BOTTLES

Capital Dairy, North Dartmouth, MA, quart, round, clear, emb, capital dome emb on front slug plate 15.00

Firestone Farms, Columbiana, OH, one half pint, round, clear, emb, Firestone emblem emb in slug plate 25.00

Gettysburg Ice and Storage Co, Gettysburg, PA, quart, round, clear, emb name 10.00

University of Connecticut, Storrs, CT, one half pint, round, clear, emb name 7.50

White Springs Farm Dairy, Geneva, quart, orange pyro 10.00

MINERAL BOTTLES OR SPRING WATER BOTTLES

American Kissinger Water, aqua, pint . 50.00

Artesian Water, round, golden chocolate–amber, twelve paneled base, iron pontil, 1850–60, pint 450.00

Boardman, J & Co, cobalt blue 50.00

B. R. Lippincott & Co, Stockton Superior, Mineral Water, Union Glass Works, cobalt blue, applied top, iron pontil, 1852–58, 7⅜" h 425.00

Buffalo Mineral Water Springs Natures, Materia Medica Trade Mark, yellow, lady sitting on stool motif, 10½" h .. 120.00

Champlain Spring, Alkaline Chaalybeate, Highgate, VT, round, deep green, applied collar lip, c1870, quart 160.00

Chase & Co, Mineral Water, San Francisco, CA, green, applied top, iron pontil, 7⅜" h 45.00

Crystal Spring Water, Saratoga, NY, horseshoe shape, green, quart, 9½" h .. 85.00

Distilled Soda Water Co of Alaska, aqua, mug shape base, tooled top, smooth base, 7¼" h 325.00

E. L. Billing's Sac City Geyser Soda, sapphire blue, applied top, smooth base, 7¼" h 160.00

E. M. Keane Ale, round, golden amber, applied lip, c1870, 9⅛" h 600.00

F. & L. Schaum Baltimore Glass Works, round, olive–green, rect slug plate reverse, iron pontil, 1850–60, 7⅛" h . 375.00

Geyser Springs, emerald green, 7⅝" h 550.00

Indian Spring, aqua, emb Indian head, 10½" h 15.00

Lancaster Glass Works, round, sapphire blue, applied blob lip, iron pontil, 1850–60, 7" h 110.00

Lynde & Putnam, Mineral Waters, San Francisco Cala, Union Glass Works, Philada, teal blue, applied top, iron pontil, 7½" h 95.00

Middletown Mineral Spring Co, round, emerald green, applied tapered lip, orig label, c1870 .... 425.00

Mills' Seltzer Springs, aqua, applied top, smooth base, 7½" h 70.00

Napa Soda–Natural Mineral Water, T A W, dark blue–green, applied top, smooth base, 7¼" h 80.00

Round Lake Mineral Water, red–amber, 9¼" h 750.00

Roussel's Mineral Water, dark blue–green, applied top, iron pontil, 1847–55, 7¼" h 70.00

Rutherford's Premium Mineral Water, ground pontil, dark olive, 7½" h ... 60.00

San Francisco Glass Works, tapered neck, blob top, sea green, 6⅞" h ... 15.00

Saratoga Seltzer Water, cylinder shape,

teal blue–green, applied ring lip, c1890, 7½" h **85.00**

Veronica Mineral Water, amber, sq ... **8.00**

Vichy Water Cullums Spring, Choctaw Co, AL, dark olive, 7¼" h **35.00**

Witter Medical Spring Co, amber, 9½" h **8.00**

Wm. W. Lappeus, Premium Soda or Mineral Water, Albany, ten sided, blue, blob top, iron pontil base, 1850–60, 7" h **725.00**

Ziegler's Soda Works, Tucson, AZ, aqua, mug shape base, tooled top, 6½" h **140.00**

Nursing, clear, 7¾" l, c1830, $250.00.

NURSING BOTTLES

Baby's Delight **45.00**

Empire Nursing Bottle, bent neck, emb name, 6½" h **50.00**

Happy Baby, baby outline, big letters, 8 oz **5.00**

Hygenic Feeder, emb, open on both ends **30.00**

Manx Feeding Bottle, bulbous, clear, tooled sq collar, emb "Patent July 4, 1876," 3" h **200.00**

Marguerite Feeding Bottle, inside screw, daisy on top **32.00**

Mother's Comfort, clear, turtle type ... **20.00**

Sweet Babee Nurser, clear, emb "Easy Clean, Pat'd May 3, 1910" **12.00**

Teddy's Pet, Peaceful Nights, clear, emb, turtle shape, 4 oz **70.00**

POISON BOTTLES

A. Chester Baker, Boston, cobalt blue, emb **45.00**

Carbolic Acid, ring top, cobalt blue, poison crosses all around, 5" h **15.00**

Durfee Embalming Fluid Co, amethyst, 8¾" h **25.00**

Finlay Dicks & Co, New Orleans, LA, Dicks Ant Destroyer **30.00**

Ikey Einstein Poison, rect, ring top, clear, 3¾" h **25.00**

JTM & Co, three cornered, "Poison" on one side, ring top, amber, 10" h **80.00**

Kilner Bros, round, fluted panels, topaz, emb "POISON" on two shoulders, 1900, 8¾" h **75.00**

Lin Saponis, green, 6¾" h **20.00**

Liq Morph Hydrochl Poison, cobalt blue, label, 4½" h **40.00**

Melvin & Badger Apothecaries, Boston, MA, irregular hexagon, cobalt blue, 6" h **30.00**

Norwich, IGA, cobalt blue, 8" h **75.00**

Owl Poison Ammonia, three cornered, cobalt blue, label, 5¼" h **25.00**

Spirits, silver, milk glass, 9" h **20.00**

Tinct Opii, poison on base, cobalt blue, 7" h **40.00**

Trioloids Poison, triangular, blue, c1900, 3⁵⁄₁₆" h **25.00**

Victory Chemical Co, Quick Death Insecticide, 148 Fairmount Ave, Phila, PA, 8 oz, clear, 7" h **12.00**

SODA BOTTLES

Bacon's Soda Works, light green, blob top, 7" h **9.50**

Dr Pepper, light green, emb mark, 12" h **6.00**

Geyser Soda Springs, dark aqua, blob top, 7" h **7.50**

Italian Soda Water Manufacturing, San Francisco, dark green applied top, 7½" h **15.00**

Ross Royal Belfast Ginger Ale, green, diamond shape paper label, 10" h .. **5.00**

Wilson's Soda Works, aqua, 8" h **5.00**

WHISKEY, EARLY

A. M. Bininger & Co, golden amber, bulbous shape, rolled lip, smooth base, handle, emb "A. M. Bininger & Co/No 19 Broad St, NY," c1865, 8⅞" h **750.00**

Casper's Whiskey Made By Honest North Carolina People, blue, round, tooled tapered lip, c1870–80, 12" h **425.00**

Diamond Club, round, medium blue–green, applied tapered ring lip, iron pontil, 1850–60, 9⁷⁄₁₆" h **200.00**

E. G. Booz's Old Cabin, Philadelphia, amber, 1840 .... **65.00**

Flora Temple Harness Trot, horse, topaz–olive, applied ring lip and handle, smooth base, c1880, 8½" h ... **85.00**

Ginter Co. Importers, deep yellow–green, 1860–80, 11" h **65.00**

Hodico, Hollenbach, Dietrick & Co, Reading, PA, amber, 11⅛" h **45.00**

Jesse Moore, dark red–amber **50.00**

N. B. Dursley, deep olive–amber, sq, 1783 .... **525.00**

Old Joe Gideon, amber, half pint **15.00**

Oxford Rye Whiskey, c1880, 11½"h ..   **20.00**
Phoenix Old Bourbon, honey amber,
   bird and coffin, pint **120.00**
Pride of Kentucky, yellow–amber **750.00**
Sour Mash 1867, amber, barrel shape,
   8¼" h **25.00**
Spruance Stanley & Co, San Francisco,
   tooled top, 1868 ....   **25.00**
Turner Brothers, olive–green, sq, 1860–
   1900, 9¾" h **65.00**

BREAD PLATES

History: Beginning in the mid–1880s, special trays or platters were made for serving bread and rolls. Designated by collectors as "bread plates," these small trays or platters can be found in porcelain, glass (especially pattern glass), and metals.

Bread plates often were part of a china or glass set. However, many glass companies made special plates which honored national heroes, commemorated historical or special events, offered a moral maxim, or supported a religious attitude. The theme on the plate could be either in a horizontal or vertical format. The favorite shape for these plates is oval, with a common length being ten inches.

Reference: Anna Maude Stuart, *Bread Plates And Platters*, published by author, 1965.

Lord's Supper, clear, frosted grape leaf border, 10⅞ x 7", $70.00.

Actress, clear, Miss Neilson center, 9"
   w, 13" l **80.00**
Aurora, ruby stained, round, large star
   in center, 10" d **35.00**
Baltimore, clear, 12½" d **70.00**
Basketweave, amber **35.00**
Beaded Loop, clear **30.00**
Butterfly and Fan, clear **45.00**
Canadian, clear, 10" l **55.00**
Continental, clear, c1870, 11¾" l **90.00**
Crying Baby, clear **50.00**
Cupid and Venus, amber **75.00**

Daisy and Button, apple green, 13" l ..   **60.00**
Deer and Pine Tree, blue, oblong **100.00**
Double Vine **45.00**
Egyptian, clear, Mormon Temple **300.00**
Fern, clear **35.00**
Finecut and Panel, amber, 13" l **45.00**
Frosted Lion, clear and frosted, round,
   Cable border, 10½" d **75.00**
Garden of Eden, clear **30.00**
Grace, clear **60.00**
Historical
   Garfield Memorial, clear **40.00**
   Grant, clear **45.00**
   Liberty and Freedom, clear **65.00**
   McKinley, clear, oval **50.00**
   Three Presidents, clear, frosted center   **85.00**
Horseshoe, clear, double horseshoe
   handles, 14" l, 10" w **65.00**
Iowa, clear, motto **80.00**
Lion, frosted and clear, lion handles,
   GUTDODB, 12" l **125.00**
Minerva, clear **60.00**
Moon and Star, clear, rect **45.00**
Motto
   A Pleasure To..., clear **40.00**
   Be Industrious, clear, handles, oval,
     12" l, 8¼" w **50.00**
   Faith, Hope, and Charity, clear, plain
     center, emb "Patd Nov 23, 1875"   **30.00**
One Hundred One, clear, farm imple-
   ment center, 11" d **75.00**
Palmette, clear, handles, 9" d **30.00**
Polar Bear, frosted and clear **150.00**
Queen Anne, clear **50.00**
Rock of Ages, clear and opalescent,
   colored and clear combinations,
   c1870, 12⅞" l **175.00**
Royal Lady, vaseline **135.00**
Scroll with Flowers, clear **25.00**
Shell and Tassel, clear, round **60.00**
Swan with Flowers, clear **35.00**
Tennessee, clear, colored jewels **75.00**
Three Graces, clear **45.00**
US Coin, clear, frosted coins **300.00**
Westward Ho, frosted and clear, oval .   **180.00**
Wheat and Barley, clear **25.00**

BRIDE'S BASKETS

History: Bride's Baskets are one of the wonderful types of antiques that have evolved into an exciting collecting area from rather plain beginnings. The term "Bride's Basket" was first used around 1920. Until that time, the bowls were described by their makers according to the intended use, e.g. berry or fruit bowls. The practice of serving berries and cream was popular during the end of the 18th century into the beginning of the 19th century. Berry sets consisting of a master bowl and matching serving bowls were "necessities" of a household. Berry bowls were made in most glass types of the period, including vividly colored glass, cut glass, and even pressed glass. By adding a metal frame, or standard, usually with a bail handle, a simple berry bowl became a basket. Ornate silver plated holders enhanced the beauty of the glassware and were added by companies such as Pairpoint and Wilcox. These bowls were a popular wedding gift in the 1880–1910 era, hence, the name of "bride's basket."

The name "bride's basket" is now well known and although not as popular now as in the post World War I period, bride's baskets are still collected. Art glass bowls with original silver plated holders can command high prices.

Over the years, bowls and bases became separated and married pieces resulted. When the base has been lost, the bowl is sold separately.

Reference: John Mebane, *Collecting Bride's Baskets And Other Glass Fancies,* Wallace–Homestead, 1976.

Reproduction Alert: The glass bowls have been reproduced.

Note: Items listed have a silver-plated holder unless otherwise noted.

Mt. Washington, cameo glass, squared crimped edge, white cased to rose-red, cameo cut winged griffins, floral bouquets and swags, silver-plated metal frame marked "Pairpoint," leaf and berry embellished handle, 10½" h, 8" sq bowl, $825.00. Photograph courtesy of Skinner, Inc.

8" d, 10½" h, sq crimped edge bowl, white cased to rose–red, cameo cut winged griffins, floral bouquets and swags, fitted silver plated metal frame with leaf and berry embellished handle, Mt Washington Glass Co bowl, framed marked "Pairpoint" **825.00**

8" d, 10½" h, Loetz type glass, irid gold, blue, and purple, recessed indenta-

tions, ruffled, ground pontil, ftd metal stand **315.00**

8" d, 11" h, spatter, cream spatter on cranberry body, closely crimped top, silver plated holder, bail handle with applied flowers and leaves dec, holder marked "Tufts" **315.00**

9" d, peachblow, shiny finish, amber applied rim, silver plated holder marked "Wilcox" **175.00**

9" d, 4" h bowl, 11½" h overall, Mt Washington, flint, deep fuchsia, all over printed process flowers and leaves, fancy silver holder with rosebud finial sgd "Pairpoint" **675.00**

9" d, 12" h, Mt Washington, Rose Amber, Coin Spot pattern, deep color, fancy silver plated Pairpoint stand .. **875.00**

9¼" d, opalescent, blue, crimped rim, reticulated silver plated holder marked "Wallingford, Biggins & Rodgers Co" **195.00**

9½" d
Pigeon Blood, enamel floral dec, silver plated holder **200.00**
Satin, blue ground with moire type pattern, MOP lining, silver plated holder with applied strawberries and leaves, marked "Simpson, Hall, Miller Co." **350.00**

10" sq, custard, melon ribbed bowl, enameled daisies, applied rubena crystal rim, twisted and beaded handle, ftd emb silver plated frame, marked "Wilcox" **425.00**

10⅜" d, spangle, multicolored, ruby, cranberry, and green, ivory and yellow base, silver flecks **115.00**

10½" d, Hobnail pattern, pink, enameled flowers, ruffled rim, reticulated silver plate frame **235.00**

10½" d, 23½" h, Burmese, acid finish, deep ruffled top, enameled yellow spider chrysanthemums, ornate silver plated standard with three cherubs, ball feet **1,600.00**

11" d, 4½" h bowl, 11½" h overall Crown Milano, tricorn bowl, tightly ruffled, six large pansies, purple and orange tracery medallions, pale yellow interior, orig tricorn ftd stand sgd "Pairpoint" **2,950.00**

11" h
Cased, pink exterior, peachblow lining, gold stylized flowers, ornate silver plated holder with aquatic marine life motif, marked "Pairpoint Mfg Co." **800.00**
Peachblow, crimped undulating rim, enameled white flowers, yellow centers, gold–tan branches, ornate silver plate stand **550.00**

11¼" h, satin, emerald green, shaded light to dark bowl, enameled dec, ornate ftd silver plate frame **285.00**

11½" h, sapphire blue bowl, applied ruffled rim, gold tracery and courting scene dec, ornate ftd Meriden stand **300.00**

13½" h, robin's egg blue shaded to white, scalloped rim, applied frosted ribbon, frosted Optic Petal pattern, silver plate base, engraved griffins, butterflies, and bees, cupola in center with leaves and berries on sides, full figural swan inside, figural lilies and berries on handle, marked "Reed & Barton" **250.00**

BRISTOL GLASS

History: Bristol glass is a designation given to a semi–opaque glass, usually decorated with enamel and cased with another color.

Initially the term referred only to glass made in Bristol, England, in the 17th and 18th centuries. By the Victorian era firms on the Continent and in America copied the glass and its forms.

Glass forms commonly found in Bristol glass include cologne bottles, perfume bottles, scent bottles, decanters, finger bowls, and all types of small boxes.

Reference: Charles R. Hajdamach, *British Glass, 1800–1914*, Antique Collectors' Club, 1991.

Biscuit Jar, cov

4⅝" d, 6" h, light gray body, enameled white, pink, and blue flowers, green leaves, gold stems, silver plated rim, cov, and handle **135.00**

5" d, 7½" h, apple green body, enameled green and yellow flowers and plants, silver plate rim, cov, handle, and base, figural strawberry finial **175.00**

Box, hinged cov

1⅝" l, 1" h, turquoise body, gold dec **100.00**

5¾" l, 3⅝" h, egg shape, white body, pink, cream, blue, and yellow floral dec **215.00**

Compote, fluted, white body, hand painted cat scene, metal base **75.00**

Creamer and Sugar, cov, white body, multicolored floral dec **60.00**

Decanter, 11½" h, rose shading to deep rose body, purple flowers, gilt butterfly on neck, applied handle, marbleized rose and white stopper **115.00**

Dresser Bottle, scalloped tulip stopper

8¼" h, 2¾" d, blue body, white enameled dec, gold trim, matching blue stopper with white dots **100.00**

9¼" h, 3¼" d, apple green body, matching stopper, reeded gold trimmed green handles **100.00**

11¼" h, 3½" d, white body, green and brown leaves and ferns, blue flowers with gold trim, matching stopper with gold trim **110.00**

Dresser Tray, 11" l, 7¾" w, rect, turquoise body, lacy gold band, gold and yellow flowers and leaves **125.00**

Egg Cup, white body, gold bands **18.50**

Goblet, 10¾" h, pedestal base, blue body, polychrome enamel floral dec, gilt trim **80.00**

Lamp, 13¼" h, oil, blue body, enameled white egret, multicolored flowers and foliage, brass fittings, black base ... **300.00**

Mantel Lusters, 15⅝" h, 6¼" d, pink overlay, white lining, blue, yellow, and white flowers, gold trim, prisms, pr **850.00**

Pitcher

2¼" h, 3¼" d, turquoise body, gold band, enameled yellow flowers and leaves, applied turquoise handle . **60.00**

8¼" h, light green body, enameled bird and flowers, applied clear handle **65.00**

Plate, 14½" d, white body, hand painted, lavender and ochre French lilacs, green leaves **75.00**

Ring Box, cov, 1¾" h, 1¾" d, turquoise body, gold flowers and leaves **45.00**

Rose Bowl, 4⅛" h, 3¼" d, turquoise body, gold rope garlands and tassels, white outlines, four crimp top **75.00**

Salt, 2⅜" d, light gray body, enameled herons and foliage, silver plated rim and handle **45.00**

Sweetmeat Jar, cov

3" d, 5½" h, deep pink body, enameled flying duck, leaves, and blue flowers, white lining, SP top, rim, and bail handle **115.00**

Vase, shaded light pink to dark pink ground, painted enamel dec, 8½" h, $50.00.

5½" d, 4½" h, green body, garlands
of flowers and butterflies, silver
plated top and bail **125.00**
Tumbler, 6¾" h, 2¾" d, turquoise body,
gold and white rope garlands, gold
foot **70.00**
Vase
2" h, 1¼" d, turquoise body, gold
bands, enameled yellow flowers
and leaves, pr **70.00**
8½" h, white body, enameled flower
and leaf dec, ruffled top, ram's
head handles, English **65.00**
9" h, white body, portrait of young
boy and girl, pr **150.00**
9⅝" h, white body, hand painted,
flowers, gold trim, raised enameling, pr **100.00**
10" h, blue body, cut out base,
enamel floral dec, pr **110.00**
13" h, pink body, gold, blue, and
white dec, pr **120.00**
17" h, 7" w, white body, American
cattle dec, artist sgd, pr **235.00**
17½" h, baluster, ftd, cut scalloped
top, creamy opaque body, enameled mill scene, enameled pink floral border, gold trim, pr **300.00**

BURMESE GLASS

History: Burmese glass is a translucent art glass
originated by Frederick Shirley and manufactured
by the Mount Washington Glass Co., New Bedford, Massachusetts, from 1885 to c1891.

Burmese glass shades from a soft lemon to a
salmon pink. Uranium was used to attain the
yellow color and gold was added to the batch so
that on reheating one end turned pink. Upon
reheating again, the edges would revert to the
yellow coloring. A yellow top edge is a common
indicator that the glassworker reheated the piece
at least twice. The blending of the colors was so
gradual that it is often difficult to determine
where one color ends and the other begins.

Although some of the glass has a natural surface that is glossy, most of it is acid finished,
resulting in a velvet–type finish. The majority of
the items were free blown, but some were blown
molded in a ribbed, hobnail, or diamond quilted
design. Glass finishing techniques of the glassworkers resulted in ruffled edges, turned down
rims, and even included the application of stems,
leaves, and flowers. Hand painted enameled
decorations include insects, fish, birds, Egyptian
motifs, flowers, leaves, and even poetic verses.
Artists such as Albert Steffin, Frank Guba, Adolf
Frederick, and Timothy Canty often signed their
works. Paper labels were also used to mark Burmese objects.

American–made Burmese is quite thin, fragile,
and brittle. The only English factory licensed to
make Burmese was Thos. Webb & Sons. Out of
deference to Queen Victoria, they called their
wares "Queen's Burmese."

Reference: John A. Shuman III, *The Collector's
Encyclopedia of American Art Glass,* Collector
Books, 1988, 1991 Value Update.

Museums: New Bedford Glass Museum, New
Bedford, MA; The Chrysler Museum, Norfolk,
VA; The Corning Museum of Glass, Corning, NY;
The Toledo Museum of Art, Toledo, OH.

Reproduction Alert: Reproductions abound in
almost every form. Since uranium can no longer
be used, some of the reproductions are easy to
spot. In the 1950s Gunderson produced many
pieces in imitation of Burmese.

Bon Bon, 2" d, acid finish, tricorn, Mt
Washington **300.00**
Bowl
5" l, 4½" w, 2" h, rect top, very deep
color, very thin walls, Mt Washington, c1880 .... **425.00**
6¼" d, 3¾" h, floral dec, applied glass
rim, marked "Thos Webb" **1,100.00**
7¼" d, 6" h, six ruffles, three pulled
edges, three applied shell reeded
feet, large applied berry over pontil, very deep pink shading, Mt
Washington **1,500.00**
Celery, 6" h, 4" w flaring top, acid finish,
2½" h fluted silver plated base sgd
"Wm Rogers Mfg Co, Hartford, CT,
#1300," Mt Washington **1,500.00**
Champagne Glass, 5½" h, raspberry
shading to yellow, circular base, two
handles **250.00**
Creamer
3" h, acid finish, crimped rim **325.00**
5½" h, acid finish, crimped rim **275.00**
Cruet, ribbed, acid finish, hollow blown
ribbed stopper, Mt Washington **1,100.00**
Cup and Saucer, shiny finish, applied
handle **325.00**
Dish, 5" d, ¾" h, shiny finish, deep col-
or, Mt Washington **175.00**
Epergne, 9½" h, acid finish, two unde-
corated fairy lamps with sgd Clarke
bases, two bud vases, center metal
standard holding upright vase, silver
plated stand, Webb **1,500.00**
Fairy Lamp
8½" h, 8" w metal base, pyramid
shade, prunus blossom dec, sgd
clear glass candle cup, twin Burmese dec bud vases, metal base
stamped "Clarke's Patent Fairy
Lamp" **2,750.00**
9½" h, dome shaped shade, urn

shaped base, double prunus blossoms dec, sgd Clarke candle cup
and candle cup holder **950.00**
Hat
  1¼" h, shiny finish, Pairpoint, c1930 **450.00**
  3" h, 4" w brim, diamond quilted pattern, Gundersen **365.00**
Jack-In-The-Pulpit
  9½" h, acid finish, crimped rim, Mt
  Washington paper label, pr **700.00**
  10" h, 4¼" w top, deep color, yellow
  edge, Mt Washington, c1880 .... **725.00**
  12" h, enamel floral dec, crimped fold
  over rim **700.00**
Jar, 3" h, 2⅝" d, acid finish, rich coloring, brown leaves, blue and white
  enameled flowers, star shaped top,
  unsgd, Webb **300.00**
Lamp Shade, gas light, 5" l, Mt Washington
  Acid Finish **250.00**
  Satin Finish **295.00**
Lemonade Set, tankard pitcher, six
  matching tumblers, acid finish, deep
  pink to yellow, applied Burmese handle, Mt Washington **2,250.00**
Lemonade Tumbler, 5" h, shiny finish,
  applied handle **225.00**
Mustard Pot, barrel shaped, vertical
  ribs, shiny metal collar, hinged lid inscribed "1334," Mt Washington **285.00**
Perfume Bottle, 5¼" h, shiny finish,
  branches and pine cone dec, hallmarked monogrammed sterling silver
  cap **750.00**
Pin Jar, cov, 2¾" h, 4" d, unfired finish,
  tomato shape, melon ribbed, shaded
  green ground, large purple and white
  chrysanthemums, green leaves, fancy
  silver plated cov, Mt Washington ... **265.00**
Pitcher
  5¼" h, 3¼" w, acid finish, petticoat
  shape, deep color, applied loop
  handle, Mt Washington **875.00**
  9" h, acid finish, tankard, rural scene
  and florals, Longfellow verse, Mt
  Washington **3,250.00**
Plate
  6" d, acid finish **100.00**
  9" d, acid finish, Gundersen **650.00**
  9¾" d, acid finish, deep salmon pink
  shading to yellow, Mt Washington,
  c1880 .... **375.00**
Relish Dish, 3" h, 5¾" d, 6½" h x 8" w
  silver plated tray, twin hat shaped
  bowls, pastel yellow crown, shading
  to blushed rolled rim, three butterflies and dragonfly dec on each, flattened brim with brilliant golden laden
  bittersweet blossoms, figural calla
  lily handle on silver plated handle,
  Webb **1,450.00**

**Salt and Pepper Shakers, pr, Mount Wash-
ington, silver plated Tufts holder, 7½" h,
4¾" w, $525.00.**

Rose Bowl
  2¼" h, 2½" d, acid finish, eight crimp
  top, salmon pink evenly shaded to
  yellow, five petal lavender flowers,
  green and brown foliage dec, Webb **300.00**
  3" h, acid finish, floral dec **275.00**
Rose Jar, cov, 5¼" h, floral dec, Mt
  Washington **400.00**
Salt, 2¾" d, acid finish, bittersweet colored blossoms, gold branches, Webb **450.00**
Scent Bottle, 4⅞" l, 1¼" w at shoulder,
  lay down type, shading from blush at
  shoulder to soft yellow point, mistletoe leaves, white berries dec, sterling
  screw on top hallmarked "CM," rampant lion, "N" and anchor, attributed
  to Webb **1,250.00**
Sugar Shaker, deep salmon shading to
  yellow, all over beaded white and
  blue flowers, orig top, Timothy Canty
  style dec, Mt Washington **1,300.00**
Sweetmeat Jar, cov, 7" h, acid finish,
  cylindrical, bittersweet and gold foliage, silver plated collar, lid, and bail
  handle, Webb, sgd **475.00**
Syrup, 4⅝" h, shiny finish, enameled
  daisy and vine dec, applied handle
  with additional gold dec **550.00**
Toothpick Holder
  2½" h, acid finish, cylindrical, trefoil
  top, floral dec, Optic Diamond
  Quilted pattern, Mt Washington .. **425.00**
  2¾" h, acid finish, cylindrical,
  crimped top, Optic Diamond
  Quilted pattern, Mt Washington,
  orig paper label **500.00**
Tumbler
  3" h, acid finish, faint dec of palm
  trees **75.00**
  3¾" h, two rose buds on foliate
  branch, Mt Washington **885.00**

Vase, inverted bell shape with flared scalloped and pinched rim, scalloped pedestal base, acid finish, unmarked, $425.00.

Vase
3" h
   Acid finish, bulbous, tricorn, fold
   over rim 250.00
   Queen's, leaf and berry dec, fold
   in petal rim, marked "Queen's
   Burmese" 300.00
3½" h, acid finish, petal top, sgd
   "Queen's Burmese" 325.00
3¾" h, 2½" d, acid finish, ruffled,
   acorns, green and brown leaves,
   unsgd, Webb 300.00
3¾" h, 3¼" d, acid finish, bulbous,
   collared six pentagon top, salmon
   pink evenly shaded to yellow, five
   petal lavender flowers, green and
   brown foliage, Webb 325.00
4" h, acid finish, fluted base, ruffled
   rim 325.00
4¼" h, 2⅝" d, acid finish, closely ruffled flared top, lavender five petal
   flowers, green and brown leaves,
   unsgd, Webb 325.00
5" h, acid finish, ftd, ruffled top 225.00
5½" h, acid finish, bulbous, flared
   rim, deep color, Mt Washington .. 550.00
6" h, shiny finish, bulbous, Mt Washington 350.00
6" h, 7" d, flaring rim, bulbous base,
   lightly ruffled, glossy finish, Pairpoint, c1920 .... 625.00
7" h, 5¾" d, cov, two delicate applied
   handles, finial shaped lid, Mt
   Washington 785.00
8" h, lily, forget–me–nots dec, coral
   detailing stripes around base and
   rim, Mt Washington 1,285.00
8" h, 6¼" d, Burns Auld Lang Syne
   verse in black enamel, framed by
   grapevine, bunch of purple grapes,
   autumn leaves, Mt Washington ..3,450.00
8½" h, 4" d, acid finish, red buds,
   green and brown leaves, yellow
   wafer foot, Webb 700.00
9" h, tapering ovoid, hand painted
   dec of four swallows in flight, white

enamel beaded border, orig labels
"Mt. W. G. Co Burmese pat'd Dec.
15, 1885," matched pr **3,300.00**
9½" h, acid finish, lily, Tappan, Gundersen, c1940 .... 375.00
9¾" h, 4½" d, lily, ruffled top, Mt
   Washington 625.00
10" h, 4¼" d, acid finish, lily, reheated yellow top edge, Mt Washington 375.00
10" h, 5" d, shiny finish, trumpet,
   scalloped top, deep color, Pairpoint, c1920 .... 625.00
10¼" h, 5½" w at shoulder, acid finish, gourd shape, deep color, Mt
   Washington 975.00
12" h, acid finish, trumpet, tricorn rim 375.00
12" h, 7" d base, bulbous, all over
   enameled and painted bouquets of
   yellow, white, and purple asters,
   leaves, and vines, deep yellow with
   pink shading 3/5 to base, decoration attributed to Albert Steffin, Mt
   Washington 1,850.00
Whiskey Glass, 2¾" h, shiny finish, Optic Diamond Quilted pattern, Mt
   Washington 385.00

After 1920

CAMBRIDGE GLASS

History: Cambridge Glass Company, Cambridge, Ohio, was incorporated in 1901. Initially the company made clear tableware, later expanding into colored, etched, and engraved glass. Over 40 different hues were produced in blown and pressed glass.

   The Cambridge, Ohio area was successful because a good supply of natural gas and silica sand were available. The National Glass Company brought much talent to the area, particularly Arthur J. Bennett, who managed the new factory. Under his supervision, the first piece of crystal glassware, a water pitcher, was produced in May of 1902 by the new firm. When the National Glass Company developed financial difficulties in 1907, Mr. Bennett recognized the potential and refinanced the company. By 1910 the company had expanded and opened another plant in Byesville, Ohio. It continued operations until 1917 when it closed and all employees were transferred to the plant at Cambridge. With the addition of these talented employees and new capital investments, the Cambridge Glass Company grew. All products were handmade. Over 5,000 molds were used to create the complete line of patterns offered.

One of the distinctive characteristics of Cambridge glassware are the jewel-like colors. Transparent colors include: amber, amethyst, apple green, Carmen (brilliant ruby red), cinnamon, crystal, Dianthus (light transparent pink), Eleanor Blue (dark blue), emerald, forest green, Gold Krystol (gold tint), Heatherbloom (delicate orchid), LaRosa (light pastel pink), Mandarin Gold (very light golden yellow), mocha, Moonlight (pastel blue), peach–blo (light pink), pistachio (pastel green), Ritz Blue (bright blue), Royal Blue, Smoke, and Willow Blue. Opaque colors include: Azure Blue (dark blue), Blue Milk (light blue), Coral (flesh-like orange–pink), Crown Tuscan (flesh-like pink), Ebon (satin finish black), Ebony (black), Heliotrope (purple), Ivory (light cream), Jade (blue–green), Milk (white), Opal (pearly), Pearl Green (glossy green), Pomona Green (light green), Primrose (opaque yellow), Turquoise, and Violet (light purple). Shaded transparent colors include: Amberina, Mardi Gras (crystal body with assorted color flecks), Rubina, (later called Sunset), Tomato (yellow green at top, blending to red and yellow green at base), and Varitone (Moonlight, LaRosa, Mocha, and Pistachio).

Five different marks were employed during the production years, but not every piece was marked. A paper sticker was used from 1935 to 1954.

The plant closed in 1954. Some of the molds were later sold to the Imperial Glass Company, Bellaire, Ohio.

The National Cambridge Collectors, Inc. deserve a great deal of credit for the work they do. Incorporated in 1973, they are a non–profit education organization devoted to the preservation and collection of Cambridge Glass Company wares. They established a permanent museum in 1982. Another valued contribution by this group are the excellent reference books they have produced. They contain the patterns, etchings, and even color comparisions.

References: National Cambridge Collectors, Inc., *The Cambridge Glass Co., Cambridge, Ohio* (reprint of 1930 catalog and supplements through 1934), Collector Books, 1976, 1990 value update; National Cambridge Collectors, Inc., *The Cambridge Glass Co., Cambridge, Ohio, 1949 Thru 1953* (catalog reprint), Collector Books, 1976, 1990 value update; National Cambridge Collectors, Inc., *Colors In Cambridge Glass*, Collector Books, 1984, 1991 value update; Mark Nye, *Cambridge Stemware*, published by author, 1985.

Collectors' Club: National Cambridge Collectors, Inc., P.O. Box 416, Cambridge, OH 43725.

Compote, amber, 7" h, 7½" d, $15.00.

FLOWER HOLDERS, FIGURAL

Bashful Charlotte
Cinnamon, frosted, 11" h	300.00
Crystal, 6½" h	85.00
Peach–Blo, frosted, 11" h	200.00

Draped Lady, flower frog
Amber, 13" h	225.00
Crystal, 8½" h	70.00
Frosted, clear 8¾" h	75.00
Green, 13" h	250.00
Heron, crystal, 9" h	95.00

Mandolin Lady, 9" h
Crystal	200.00
Green	275.00
Rose Lady, amber, 8½" h	250.00

Two Kids, 8¾" h
Crystal	150.00
Green	200.00
Peach–Blo	225.00

PATTERNS

Apple Blossom
Ashtray, ftd, yellow, #1314	20.00
Baker, 10" d, crystal	19.00
Basket, two handles, pink	18.00

Bowl, 6" d
Amber	15.00
Blue	14.50
Green	15.00
Butter, cov, yellow	115.00
Candy Box, cov, crystal	32.00
Cheese and Cracker, amber	37.50
Console Bowl, 12½" d, clear	19.00
Creamer and Sugar, ftd, tall, yellow	42.00
Cream Soup, liner plate, amber	25.00
Cup and Saucer, yellow	22.00
Fruit Dish, liner, sq, amber	10.00
Ice Bucket, crystal	35.00
Mayonnaise, liner, ladle, amber	40.00

Pitcher
50 oz, ftd, crystal	60.00

64 oz, flat, pink	135.00
67 oz, loop handle, amber	210.00
80 oz, ball, blue	195.00
Oyster Cocktail, pink	18.00

Plate

6" d, crystal	5.00
7½" d, amber	12.00
8½" d, pink	12.00
9½" d, blue	42.00
10" d, grill, crystal	15.00
Platter, 11½" l, blue	37.50
Salt and Pepper Shakers, pr, crystal	30.00

Sandwich Plate, center handle, 11" d,

blue	40.00
Sherbet, crystal, gold trim	17.00

Tumbler, crystal

Flat	20.00
Footed, 12 oz	32.00

Vase

6" h, yellow	40.00
12" h, keyhole base, blue	60.00

Caprice

Ashtray

Blue, shell, ftd	8.00
Crystal	7.00
Bitter Bottle, crystal	50.00
Bon Bon, green, 6" d, sq	45.00

Bowl, blue

7" d, divided, two handles	30.00
8" d, four feet	50.00
Cake Plate, 13" d, ftd, crystal	65.00

Candlesticks, pr

#67, crystal	15.00
#70, crystal	50.00
Triple level, crystal	55.00
Candy, cov, blue, three toes	115.00
Celery Tray, 8½" l, three parts, crystal	18.00
Champagne, crystal	20.00

Cigarette Box, cov

Blue, 3½" l, 2¼" w	27.00
Crystal, small	16.00
Milk Glass, white, ftd	70.00
Cigarette Holder, 3" h, triangular, blue	25.00
Coaster, 3½" d, blue	20.00
Cocktail, crystal	18.00

Cordial

Blue	60.00
Crystal	32.00
Creamer, tall, crystal	7.00
Cup and Saucer, crystal	17.00
Decanter, stopper, crystal	60.00
Goblet, pale pink, 9 oz	35.00
Iced Tea Tumbler, crystal	12.50
Lemon Plate, 6½" d, blue	15.00
Marmalade, cov, blue	75.00
Mayonnaise, ftd, #105, blue	38.00
Mustard, cov, blue	40.00
Oyster Cocktail, crystal	12.00
Pickle, 9" d, blue	24.00
Pitcher, ball, 32 oz, crystal	60.00

Plate

6½" d, crystal	7.50

8½" d, blue	20.00
9½" d, crystal	30.00
17" d, flat, blue	140.00
Relish, three parts, crystal	22.00
Rose Bowl, blue, 8" d, four toes	175.00
Salad Dressing Server, two spoons, blue, #112	135.00

Salt and Pepper Shakers, pr

Ball shape, blue	48.00
Egg shape, crystal	35.00
Individual size, flat, crystal	20.00
Sherbet, tall, crystal	14.00
Sugar, blue	17.50
Torte Plate, 14" d, crystal	30.00
Tumbler, ftd, 5¼", crystal	14.00
Vase, cornucopia shape, blue	85.00
Wine, blue	59.00

Carmen

Brandy Snifter, 20 oz	42.00
Compote, 7", nude stem	150.00
Decanter Set, amber decanter with six matching whiskey glasses	45.00

Chantilly

Bon Bon, ftd	17.50
Bowl, 10" d, flared	25.00
Butter, cov	145.00
Candlesticks, pr, 6" h, three lite	65.00
Candy Dish, cov, sterling knob	70.00
Creamer and Sugar, sterling base	50.00
Cocktail Shaker, metal top	95.00
Compote, 5", Stem #3625	30.00
Cup and Saucer, Martha blank, silver overlay	165.00
Goblet, 7¾" h, Stem #3625	20.00
Hurricane Lamp, keyhole base, prisms	95.00
Mayonnaise, liner, orig ladle	32.00

Plate

6½" d	7.50
8" d	14.00
10½" d	35.00
Salt and Pepper Shakers, pr	30.00

Sherbet, Crown Tuscan, white, $38.00.

Torte Plate, 14" d 30.00
Tumbler, 10 oz, ftd 18.00
Vase
   8" h 60.00
   10" h, bud 24.00
Wine, 5½" h, Stem #3635 .... 25.00

Crown Tuscan
Bowl, ftd, #3400 line, 11¼" sq 58.00
Candlesticks, pr
   Dolphin, two light 245.00
   Keyhole, two light 120.00
Candy Dish, cov, gold trim, three part 48.00
Cigarette Box, large 35.00
Compote, seashell, 6" h, gold trim .. 65.00
Cornucopia, 9½" l 88.00
Shell Bowl, 3 ftd, 11" d 75.00

Deco
Asparagus Plate, crystal 20.00
Console Bowl, Heron flower frog,
   ebony flip bowl 135.00
Cruet, 7¾" h, green 75.00

Diane
Bowl
   5" d 20.00
   11" d, two handles 35.00
   12" l, oval, ftd, 3400/160 .... 50.00
Candlesticks, pr, 6" h, 3900/74 .... 75.00
Candy Dish, cov, ftd, crystal 90.00
Cigarette Urn 35.00
Cocktail Shaker, glass top 95.00
Compote, tall 90.00
Creamer and Sugar, individual size . 30.00
Cup 17.50
Ice Bucket, chrome handle 65.00
Martini Pitcher 300.00
Plate
   6" w, square 6.00
   8" d 8.50
   10½" d 45.00
Relish, etched 45.00
Saucer 6.50
Seafood Cocktail, orig icer insert ... 47.00
Sherbet, low 17.50
Tumbler, 8 oz, ftd 24.00
Vase, 5" d, globe 25.00

Elaine, crystal
Basket, 6" h 17.50
Bon Bon 14.00
Bowl, 11" d 24.00
Candlesticks, pr, 5" h 35.00
Cocktail Shaker, metal top 85.00
Compote, Gadroon cutting 58.00
Creamer 12.00
Cup 17.50
Hurricane Lamp, candlestick base .. 65.00
Juice Tumbler, ftd 18.00
Mayonnaise, liner, divided bowl, two
   ladles 35.00
Pitcher, ball 80.00
Plate
   6½" d 7.50
   8" d 12.50

10½" d 35.00
Salt and Pepper Shakers, pr 30.00
Saucer 3.50
Sugar 12.00
Tumbler, ftd 17.50
Wine 24.00

Everglades, crystal
Basket, 7½" h, two handles 42.00
Bowl, four toes
   10" d 40.00
   12" d 50.00
Candlesticks, pr, two lite 75.00
Relish Tray, three part, two handles,
   10" l 45.00

Gloria
Bon Bon, 5½" d, crystal 12.50
Bowl
   6" d, yellow 20.00
   11" d, two handles, crystal 28.00
Candy Box, cov, ftd, crystal 35.00
Cocktail Shaker, crystal 65.00
Compote, 3½" d, ftd, pink 30.00
Cordial Decanter, upright "S" shape,
   four matching cordials, assorted
   colors, Farberware holders 100.00
Creamer and Sugar, amethyst, silver
   overlay 145.00
Cup, yellow 17.50
Ice Bucket, chrome handle, pink ... 65.00
Plate
   6" d, crystal 6.00
   8½" d, yellow 18.50
   9½" d, pink 25.00
Relish, etched 45.00
Saucer 3.50
Sherbet, low 17.50
Tumbler, 8 oz, ftd, pink 24.00
Vase, 12" d, sq top, yellow 55.00

Mt Vernon
Candlesticks, pr, 4" h, crystal 35.00
Decanter, orig stopper, crystal
   Large 70.00
   Small 55.00
Goblet, crystal 9.00
Plate, 8" d, crystal 8.00
Vase, 6½" h, ftd, crystal 35.00

Nude Stem
Brandy
   Amber 125.00
   Carmen 165.00
   Cobalt Blue 165.00
Cocktail, amber 95.00
Compote, Carmen, flared 175.00
Goblet, 9" h
   Amethyst 135.00
   Crystal 110.00
Ivy Ball, 9½", purple 225.00

Rosepoint, crystal
Basket, two handles, gold trim 55.00
Bowl
   5" d, two handles 25.00
   13" d, 2¼" h 90.00

Candlestick, Mt. Vernon, clear, dolphin pedestal, 9½" h, $55.00.

Butter, cov, round	200.00
Cake Plate, 11" d, two handles	65.00
Candlesticks, pr	
2⅝" h	30.00
6" h, keyhole, two light	35.00
7¼" h	43.00
Candy Dish, 3 part	85.00
Celery, 11" l	50.00
Champagne	25.00
Cocktails, #3121	36.00
Compote, scalloped edge	45.00
Corn Dish	55.00
Creamer and Sugar, individual size	45.00
Cruet, oil, orig stopper, ftd	225.00
Cup and Saucer	45.00
Goblet, 10 oz	25.00
Ice Tub	115.00
Juice Tumbler, 3 ftd	40.00
Lemon Box, cov	170.00
Mayonnaise, orig spoon	60.00
Old Fashioned	85.00
Pickle Dish	60.00
Plate	
6" d, two handles	17.00
8" d	18.50
10½" d	95.00
12½" d, ftd	70.00
Relish	
8" l, 3 part	38.00
12" l, 3 part, four small feet	100.00
Salad Bowl, 10½" d, round	75.00
Salt and Pepper Shakers, pr	68.00
Tumbler, ftd, 10 oz	24.00
Vase	
5" h, globe shape	55.00
6" h	50.00
10" h, cornucopia	115.00
Wine	62.00
Tally Ho	
Goblet, 14 oz	
Amber	15.00
Catawaba Crystal	32.00

Emerald Green	20.00
Mug, Carmen	38.00
Plate, 9½" d, Carmen, dinner	28.00
Tuxedo	
Bridge Set, 5 pcs, optic	65.00
Decanter Set, ball shape, 32 oz, emerald green, two 2½ oz tumblers	35.00
Goblet, crystal and carmen	10.00
Tumbler, 12 oz, crystal and carmen	10.00
Wild Flower, crystal	
Basket, 6" h, two handles	24.00
Bowl, 10" d, flared	30.00
Candy Dish, cov, gold trim	68.00
Celery/Relish, five parts	90.00
Champagne	30.00
Corn Dish	50.00
Creamer	14.00
Cup and Saucer	20.00
Goblet	32.00
Hurricane Lamp, keyhole base, prisms	120.00
Juice Tumbler	14.00
Pitcher, ball	95.00
Plate	
6½" d	7.50
8" d	12.00
10½" d	40.00
11" d, two handles	65.00
Sugar	14.00
Tumbler, 10 oz	15.00
Vase, 11" h, ftd	37.50

1921

CAMEO GLASS

History: Cameo glass is a form of cased glass. A shell of glass was prepared; then one or more layers of glass of a different color(s) was faced to the first. A design was then cut through the outer layer(s) leaving the inner layer(s) exposed.

This type of art glass originated in Alexandria, Egypt, 100–200 A.D. The oldest and most famous example of cameo glass is the Barberini or Portland vase which was found near Rome in 1582. It contained the ashes of Emperor Alexander Serverus who was assassinated in 235 A.D.

Emile Gallé is probably one of the best known artists of cameo glass. He established a factory at Nancy, France, in 1884. Although much of the glass bears his signature, he was primarily the designer. On many pieces, assistants did the actual work, even signing his name. Glass made after his death in 1904 has a star before the name Gallé. Other makers of French cameo glass include D'Argental, Daum Nancy, LeGras, and Delatte. The French cameo glass makers produced some of the most beautiful examples found in today's antique and collectible glass market.

English cameo does not have as many layers of glass (colors) and cuttings as do French pieces. The outer layer is usually white, and cuttings are very fine and delicate. Most pieces are not signed. The best known makers are Thomas Webb & Sons and Stevens and Williams.

References: Victor Arwas, *Glass Art Nouveau to Art Deco*, Rizzoli International Publications, Inc., 1977; Ray and Lee Grover, *English Cameo Glass*, Crown Publishers, Inc., 1980; Charles R. Hajdamach, *British Glass, 1800–1914*, Antique Collectors' Club, 1991; Tim Newark, *Emile Galle*, The Apple Press, 1989; Albert C. Revi, *Nineteenth Century Glass*, reprint, Schiffer Publishing, Ltd., 1981; John A. Shuman III, *The Collector's Encyclopedia of American Art Glass*, Collector Books, 1988, 1991 value update; Wolf Ueker, *Art Nouveau and Art Deco Lamps and Candlesticks*, Abbeville Press, 1986.

Additional Listings: See Daum Nancy, and Gallé, as well as other makers.

Lamp, Degue, raspberry rose color layered in burgundy, Egyptian desert motif of camel and robed figure at riverside, palm trees, and mountain view on base and shade, both sgd "Degue" in cameo, sockets above and below wrought metal mount, 14½" h, $3,300.00. Photograph courtesy of Skinner, Inc.

AMERICAN

Mount Washington Glass Company
Bride's Basket, 10½" h, 8" sq bowl, sq crimped bowl, white cased to rose–red, cameo cut winged grif-

fins, floral bouquets, and swags, silver plated metal stand with leaf and berry embellished handle marked "Pairpoint" **825.00**
Lamp, 17¼" h, oil type, rose ground, cameo cut opaque white birds, leaves, and designs, wrought iron base, orig Meridan burner and reservoir **1,200.00**
Lamp Base, 8" d cameo base, pink ground, white overlay acid etched with ornate urn and bird design, brass and gilt metal lamp fittings . **375.00**
New England Glass Company
Lamp, fluid, 10¾" h, 8" d, white ground, cameo cut pink birds and flowers, iron base, brass font **300.00**
Louis C. Tiffany
Vase
8½" h, ovoid, pearly irid ground, cameo cut and carved, white calla lilies, lime green leaves and insects, inscribed "L. C. T. X1175," c1892–1928 .... **5,500.00**
17⅞" h, slender trumpet, bulbous neck, brilliant blue irid ground, cameo cut and carved trailing green stems and leaves, circular white etched blossom frieze, inscribed "L. C. Tiffany Favrile 7209J," c1915 .... **6,500.00**

ENGLISH

Frederick Carder
Bowl, 11½" d, heavy walls, shallow, frosted colorless crystal ground, brilliant cobalt blue overlay, cameo cut and carved intricate repeating design of chyrsanthemum blossoms, buds, and leafy stems, sgd in script at edge "F. Carder" **2,800.00**
Dolce Relievo
Vase, 5" h, Diamond Quilted pattern, blue mother–of–pearl ground, cameo cut low relief white medial band of apple blossoms **1,800.00**
Stevens and Williams
Lamp, 8" h, yellow ground, cameo cut red fuchsias and leaves, sgd . **2,500.00**
Perfume Bottle, 4" h, bulbous, red ground, carved white trailing fuchsias, hinged spherical silvered metal cap, c1900 .... **395.00**
Vase
4" h, barrel, bright blue ground, white overlay, cameo cut ferns, grasses, and whild thistle, sod border, circular trademark on base reads "Stevens & Williams Art Glass" **1,200.00**
5⅝" h, baluster, translucent lime

green ground, cameo cut and etched pendent dogwood blossoms, flowering rose bushes, lower section with reserved arched frieze of alternation blossoms and squares, similar to frieze on waisted neck **2,750.00**

Unknown Maker

Biscuit Jar, cov, 6½" h, 5½" d, frosted vaseline ground, opaque white carved berries and leaves, silver plated top, rim, and handle **2,000.00**

Bowl, 8¼" d, 4" h, frosted blue ground, carved opaque white flowers, leaves, and branches **2,490.00**

Perfume Bottle

3¼" h, yellow ground, white overlay, cameo cut and carved floral motif, hallmarked silver rim, hinged ball cov, glass stopper missing, slight dents in cov **900.00**

5¼" h, spherical, bright blue ground, white overlay, cameo cut and carved wildflower blossoms and grasses, linear borders, matching darker blue stopper, unsgd **1,760.00**

Rose Bowl, 3" d, brown ground, cameo cut white morning glories . **375.00**

Sweetmeat Jar, cov, 3" h, 4¾" d, frosted deep cranberry ground, carved opaque white apple blossoms and leaves, silver plated top, rim, and handle **1,000.00**

Vase

4½" h, baluster, citron ground, cameo cut and carved white lilac sprays, lotus trim at neck **400.00**

5" h

Baluster shape, robin's egg blue cased in opal glass, white cameo enamel leaves and buds **200.00**

Flared ringed ovoid, yellow ground, white overlay, cameo cut and carved African violet blossoms, buds, and leafy stems **800.00**

6" h, baluster, blue ground, white overlay, trumpet vine blossoms, buds, and turning leaves, linear borders, small carbon speck at top **800.00**

6½" h, 3⅝" d, frosted vaseline ground, carved opaque white flowers and leaves, carved top and base bands, white butterfly on back **1,400.00**

8¼" h, 5" l, 2¾" w, bud, orig gilt mount, crimson inverted teardrop shaped ground, white leafed poppy, fully opened blossom and bud, wheat stalk, graceful oak stalk sweeps across back, two white rings just above holder, holder held between paws of rampant lion, burnished gold polish on lion, shield, and shaped platform base, base sgd "England," "56," "1704," "EP," and unidentified maker's stamp **1,835.00**

8¾" h, elongated bulbed form, bright turquoise blue ground, blue–white overlay, cameo cut and finely hand carved jasmine blossoms, buds, and leafy branches, unsgd **2,420.00**

8¾" h, gourd, yellow ground, white overlay, cameo cut passion flower blossoms, buds, and leafy vines, tiny insect below double linear border, unsgd **1,100.00**

Thomas Webb & Sons

Cologne Bottle, 7½" h, bulbous, pastel yellow ground, white overlay hand carved florabunda roses, buds, leaves, thorny branches, and butterfly, leaf spike border, matching glass stopper with rose bud and leaf dec, Webb four sided medallion on base **4,600.00**

Compote, 10" d, 4" h, blue ground, cameo cut pink and white flowers, sgd **1,800.00**

Inkwell, 3½" d, 4" h, frosted amber ground, cameo cut bluish–white flowers, sterling silver hinged top, sgd **1,000.00**

Rose Bowl, lime green ground, heavy cameo carved raspberries and leaves, butterfly on reverse **1,450.00**

Scent Bottle, 4" h, frosted blue ground, cameo cut white irises, Gorham sterling silver hinged top, sgd **800.00**

Vase

4⅛" h, frosted raspberry red ground, cameo cut white flowers, sgd **725.00**

4½" h, 3½" w, ivory ground, cameo carved sprays of flowers, five carved feathers, nutmeg stain, crimped top, sgd **1,275.00**

George Woodall

Vase

8¼" h, oval, yellow ground, white overlay, cameo cut and carved palm like grasses, matching geometric borders, sgd "Geo. Woodall" at lower left of plant stalk **3,350.00**

11⅞" h, 6" d, baluster shape, everted lip, very deeply carved, three white dancing girls with outstretched arms, dark brown ground, foliage carved around neck and upper section. attributed to Woodall **4,750.00**

FRENCH

D'Argental
Bowl, 3½" d, 3½" h, soft pink translucent frosted ground, navy blue and soft yellow overlay, cameo cut and carved, rowboat moored at shore, hills and tree landscape, sgd in cameo **575.00**
Box, cov
5¼" d, 4¼" h, round, branch with flowers covers lid, matching band around center of base **850.00**
6⅞" d, compressed sperical form, yellow ground, mauve overlay, cameo carved roses, lid with central knop sgd in cameo **1,100.00**
Center Bowl, 8¾" d, double conical contour, wide everted mouth, frosted ground, pale and dark burgundy overlay, cameo cut orchid blossoms and leaves, sgd in cameo "D'Argental" with croix de Lorraine, c1900 ....**2,200.00**
Lamp, table, 20" h, conical domed shade, amber ground, deep red overlay, birds and butterfly among pine branches, shade supported by gilt metal arms, inverted baluster standard base, shaded amber ground, deep red overlay, acid cut continuous mountain landscape

Perfume Burner, D'Argental, bell form, honey–amber, overlaid shades of orange and brown, blossoms, birds, and leafy stems, sgd "D'Argental" in cameo, gilt metal rim and cap impressed "Lampberger Made in France," 6½" h, $660.00. Photograph courtesy of Skinner, Inc.

with lake, large pine trees, jagged mountains silhouetted against sky, polished dark red spreading circular foot and waisted neck, base sgd in cameo "d'Argental," c1900 ....**16,500.00**
Perfume Bottle, 5¼" h, lime green ground, light and dark burgundy overlay, cameo carved flowers, buds, and leaves, carved signature, gold washed metal top sgd "Le Parisien" **1,150.00**
Perfume Burner, 6½" h, bell shape, honey amber bottle base, orange and shaded brown overlay, cameo cut and carved blossoms, birds, and leafy stems, sgd in camo, gilt metal rim and cap imp "Lampeberger Made in France" **660.00**
Vase
5" h, cameo carved rocky shore with lighthouse, three colors, sgd **675.00**
5½" h, frosted ground, cameo carved red foliage **650.00**
7" h, cameo carved brown and orange, cottage in foreground, castle on hill in distance **785.00**
7¼" h, light amber ground, brown overlay, cameo cut and carved, pine cones and mushrooms, outer layer polished **950.00**
11¾" h, oval, mottled and shaded fiery amber ground, amber, orange, and brown overlay, cameo cut and wheel carved in broad mountainous landscape scene, center on distant castle, sgd "Spesbourg/Sites d'Alsace," and "D'Argental" **1,300.00**
12" h, cameo cut and carved, three scenes, one with man in middle of lake, second with man in boat coming to shore, and third boat at lake's edge, each scene in window like cutting, triangular cut to clear dec ....,......**5,200.00**

A. Delatte
Vase, 8½" h, ovoid, ftd, bright yellow cased in clear ground, enameled flesh tones and black, partly draped maiden playing harp, flanked by nude dancing maidens, sgd in enamel "A Delatte Nancy" **800.00**

De Vez
Vase, 4¾" h, baluster, opaline ground cased in pink and green overlay, cameo carved house on tree lined lake, sgd in cameo **500.00**

Legras
Vase
6⅝" h, shaped rect, etched and enameled, orange, green, and

brown riverbank scene, sgd "Legras" **400.00**

7⅛" h, cylinder, U form rim, spreading circular base, pale pink ground, white, lime, and dark green overlay, cameo carved trees along riverbank, sgd in cameo **700.00**

10¼" h, modified trumpet shape, deep red leaves and cherries, semi–martele frosted ground, sgd in cameo **500.00**

11¾" h, single layer acid–cut crystal ground, maroon enameled leaves **515.00**

12⅜" h, baluster, frosted ground, etched and enameled orchid dec, sgd "Legras" **385.00**

Le Verre Francais

Atomizer, 5½" h, pear form, clear ground, mottled orange to blue overlay, cameo carved leaves, twisting vines, and loose berries, sgd "Le Verre Francais" **450.00**

Lamp, boudoir

14¼" h, bright mottled pink, overlaid in amethyst and burgundy, cameo cut Art Deco stylized sunflower motif, wrought metal fittings, shade and base illuminate, shade sgd on side **3,025.00**

15" h, 9⅛" d raising peaked shade with flaring rim, striped pink and white ground, purple overlay, cameo carved starburst blossoms, candy cane mark, later engraved "Le Verre Francais" **5,725.00**

Night Light, shade engraved "Le Verre Francais"

5¾" h, peaked form, yellow and blue mottled ground, red and blue overlay, cameo carved columbine, wrought iron base with three leaf form feet **2,400.00**

6" h, cylindrical, domed top, orange ground, reddish brown overlay, cameo carved stylized hanging trumpet blossoms, tripod wrought iron base **1,350.00**

8" h, conical, mottled yellow and orange ground, orange shading to blue overlay, cameo carved blossoms, wrought iron base with three leaf form feet, unsigned **1,100.00**

11" h, bullet form, mottled yellow ground, red shading to blue overlay, cameo carved stylized poinsettia, circular wrought iron base **1,320.00**

Vase

2¾" h, cabinet, cylinder, bulbous rim, yellow ground, brown shaded to mottled red overlay, cameo carved horizontal band of cats in different poses, engraved "Le Verre Francais" **1,100.00**

6⅛" h, bulbous, circular foot, yellow ground, mottled brown shaded to orange overlay, cameo carved foliage and stylized blossoms, sgd "Le Verre Francais," stamped "France" **800.00**

6¼" h, coupe form, knopped stem, circular foot, aqua blue shading to yellow ground, burgundy shading to red overlay, cameo carved orchids, engraved "Le Verre Francais" **600.00**

9½" h, spherical, mottled yellow and white with aqua highlights, overlaid in orange, cameo cut Art Deco symmetrical mushroom forms, sgd "Le Verre Francais" . **990.00**

10" h, baluster, knopped circular foot, orange ground, purple overlay, cameo carved pair of swans, engraved "Le Verre Francais," stamped "France" **1,320.00**

10¼" h, cylinder, circular black glass foot, mottled pink ground, lavender overlay, cameo carved overlapping leaves and rosettes, foot etched "France" **1,550.00**

11" h, waisted cylinder, cushion foot, yellow ground, burgundy shading to red overlay, cameo carved stylized poppies, engraved "Le Verre Francais" and "France" **600.00**

11½" h, flared cylinder, knopped circular foot, yellow ground, dark brown shaded to orange overlay, cameo carved sunflowers, sgd "Le Verre Francais," etched "France" **2,200.00**

12½" h, trumpet form, inverted rim, spreading foot, bright yellow ground, orange shading to blue overlay, cameo carved pendant vines and pomegranate fruit, engraved "Le Verre Francais" **1,765.00**

16¾" h, elongated, mottled off–white overlaid in red, orange, and blue shading to blue, acid cut repeating Art Deco stylized poppies, sgd "Le Verre Francais" **1,650.00**

17⅜" h, coupe form, tangerine ground, burgundy shaded to red overlay, cameo carved slender stems and stylized clustered blossoms, engraved "Le Verre Francais," acid stamped "France" . **2,310.00**

17½" h, baluster, cushion foot,

cream and orange mottled ground, purple overlay, cameo carved pendant leaves and berries, engraved "le Verre Francais," stamped France" **1,320.00**

17¾" h, inverted pear shape, cushion foot, bright yellow ground, blue shaded to orange overlay, cameo carved stylized blossoms, engraved "Le Verre Francais" . .**1,450.00**

19⅜" h, ovoid, everted rim, knopped cushion foot, mottled pink ground, burgundy shaded to orange overlay, cameo carved foxgloves, sgd "Le Verre Francais" **1,775.00**

19¾" h, swelled cylinder, everted rim, cushion foot, mottled yellow and orange ground, green shaded to purple overlay, cameo carved stylized blossoms, candy cane mark **2,860.00**

21½" h, baluster, mottled pink and white overlaid in shades of amethyst, orange highlights, cameo cut Art Deco repeating blossoms, cameo engraved "Le Verre Francais" and "Charder" **2,200.00**

J. Mabut
Rose Bowl, 5¼" h, pinched top, leaf tip form inverted rim, frosted ground, cut and enameled green holly branches and red berries, gilt trim, sgd in gilt "A La Paix/J Mabut/34 avenue de l'opera Paris Modele depose," c1900 . . . . **825.00**

Michel
Vase, 10¼" h, 5¼" d, deep blue on orange on yellow, sailing ship on one side, lighthouse on obverse, flower border **1,220.00**

Muller Freres
Lamp, table, 14¾" h, domed cameo shade, mottled orange body, brown overlay, carved leates and berries on tendrilling vines, sgd in cameo, openwork wrought iron four arm base, curling vine motif **3,850.00**

Vase
5⅞" h, ovoid, everted rim, opalescent body, molded with spiky artichoke leaves from shoulder, molded sgd **130.00**

7¾" h, ovoid, mottled, orange and blue–back int. dec, polished mark **330.00**

8¼" h, ovoid, everted rim, salmon body, pink and burgandy overlay, cameo carved roses and thorny stems, sgd in cameo . . . **2,200.00**

9" h, Art Deco style, colorless, internal dec of silver speckeled in-

clusions, orange, green, and blue swirls and striations, sgd on base rim "Muller Fres Luneville" **525.00**

13" h, oviform, waisted neck, yellow walls overlaid in green and puorple, etched floral sprays and circular leaves, sgd "Muller Fres/Luneville" in cameo **5,250.00**

14¼" h, slender baluster, rim folded back at sides to form handles, orange body, brown overlay, cameo carved trees and mountains scene, sgd in cameo "Muller Fres., Luneville" **1,980.00**

16¼" h, frosted colorless body with blue, green, and yellow flecks, red and dark maroon overlay, cameo cut and wheel finished, iris blossoms, stems, and spiked leaves, sgd "Muller Fres Luneville" at side **1,850.00**

Richard
Vase, 6" h, orange ground, cameo carved dark brown flowers and leaves, sgd **525.00**

Unknown Maker
Flower Pot, 7¼" h, Art Deco, heavy walls, colorless flared pot, acid etched repeating deeply carved curvilinear design **300.00**

Verrerie D'Art, De Lorraine
Vase
3" h, textured ground, amethyst to clear orchids, marked on base . **850.00**

6¼" h, purple and mottled clear glass ground, acid cut foliate designs, sgd "C. Vessiere Nancy" at side **200.00**

CAMPHOR GLASS

History: Camphor glass derives its name from its color. Most pieces have a cloudy white appearance similar to gum camphor; the remainder has a pale colored tint. Camphor glass is made by treating the glass with hydrofluoric acid vapors.

Other similar types of opaque glassware exist and there is confusion between camphor, clambroth, Bristol, and opaline. All are made through similar manufacturing techniques and have similar characteristics. As glass collecting changes through the years, terms such as camphor and clambroth are giving way to opaline or opaque, which may not be quite as descriptive, but are more meaningful to modern collectors.

Biscuit Jar, cov, white body, brass fittings **60.00**

Bookends, pr, 7" h, horse heads, white body **80.00**

Bottle, 6½" h, orig stopper **35.00**

Bowl, 7½" d, 3½" h, white body, flared,
scalloped rim, ftd 75.00
Box, cov, 5" d, hand painted holly spray
dec, hinged lid 85.00
Creamer, 3¾" h, souvenir 25.00
Goblet, 7" h, butterscotch bowl, gold
dec, blue ring, red jewels 90.00
Hair Receiver, white body, gold scroll
dec 50.00
Lemonade Set, pitcher and eight tumblers, white body, applied white handle 150.00
Mustard, cov, Wild Rose and Bowknot,
white body, rose trim 40.00
Plate, white body, hand painted
6½" d, Easter Greeting 25.00
7¼" d, owl 28.00
Powder Jar, cov, sq, blue body, bird finial, c1920 .... 60.00

Candlesticks, pr, vaseline, 7" h, $55.00.

Ring Tree, 4½" h, white body 15.00
Rose Bowl, white body, hand painted,
blue forget-me-nots, gold trim 45.00
Salt and Pepper Shakers, pr, 3½" h,
white body, hand holding torch, orig
tops, c1876 .... 75.00
Scent Bottle, 8" h, white body, gold
scrolling dec 45.00
Shoe, 5" l, lady's, white body, Libbey
Glass, World's Fair, 1893 .... 50.00
Sugar Shaker, 3½" h, tinted yellow
ground, pressed leaf dec, silver plated
top 55.00
Toothpick Holder
Bucket shape 35.00
Swirled, ruffled rim 30.00
Tray, 8" w, 10½" l, Wild Rose and
Bowknot, white body, rose trim 30.00
Vase
8" h, fan shape, clear leaf design and
trim 85.00
10½" h, Grecian shape, double han-
dles, clear base 115.00

CANDLEWICK

History: Candlewick, Imperial Glass Corp.'s No.
400 pattern introduced in 1936, was made con-
tinuously until October 1982 when Imperial de-
clared bankruptcy. In 1984 Imperial was sold to
Lancaster–Colony Corp. and Consolidated Stores
International, Inc. Imperial's assets, including inventory, molds, buildings, and equipment were
liquidated in 1985.

Imperial's Candlewick molds were bought by
various groups, companies, and individuals. Approximately 200 molds were purchased by Mirror Images, Lansing, Michigan. Eighteen small
molds were bought by Boyd Crystal Art Glass,
Cambridge, Ohio. Sadly, the location of some
Candlewick molds is unknown.

Candlewick is characterized by the crystal–
drop beading used around the edge of many
pieces; around the foot of tumblers, shakers, and
other items; in the stems of glasses, compotes,
cake and cheese stands; on the handles of cups,
pitchers, bowls, and serving pieces; on stoppers
and finials; and on the handles of ladles, forks,
and spoons. The beading is small on some
pieces, while on others it is larger and heavier.

A large variety of pieces were produced in the
Candlewick pattern. Over 650 items and sets are
known. Shapes include round, oval, oblong,
heart, and square. Imperial added or discontinued items according to popularity and demand.
The largest assortment of pieces and sets were
made during the late 1940s and early 1950s.

Candlewick was produced mostly in crystal.
Viennese Blue (pale blue, 1937–38), Ritz Blue
(cobalt, 1938–41), and Ruby Red (red, 1937–41)
were made. Other colors that have been found
include amber, black, emerald green, lavender,
pink, and light yellow. From 1977 to 1980, four
items of 3400 Candlewick stemware were made
in solid colors of Ultra Blue, Nut Brown, Verde
Green, and Sunshine Yellow. Solid black stemware was made on an experimental basis at the
same time.

Other decorations on Candlewick include silver overlay, gold encrustations, cuttings, etchings, and hand–painted designs. Pieces have
been found with fired–on gold, red, blue, and
green beading. Other companies encased Candlewick pieces in silver, chrome, brass, and
wood.

Collectors should take time and learn the characteristics, shapes, and types of Imperial pieces
made. Many items have been made that are similar to Candlewick and are often mixed with or
labeled Candlewick at shops and shows. Learn
to identify "look-alikes." Beware!

References: National Imperial Glass Collector's
Society, *Imperial Glass Catalog Reprint*, Antique
Publications, 1991; Virginia R. Scott, *The Col-
lector's Guide to Imperial Candlewick, 2nd Edi-*

tion, privately printed, (available from the author), 1987; Mary M. Wetzel, *Candlewick, The Jewel of Imperial,* 2nd Edition, 1986.

Periodical: *The National Candlewick Collector Newsletter,* 275 Milledge Terrace, Athens, GA 30606.

Museum: Bellaire Museum, Bellaire, OH 43906.

Reproduction Alert: Six-inch baskets in pink and Alexandrite and a pink four-piece child's set (consisting of a demitasse cup and saucer, 6" plate, and 5" nappy) have been made by Viking Glass Co., New Martinsville, Ohio, for Mirror Images, Lansing, Michigan. In 1987 Viking made clear plates, bowls, cups, saucers, large and small flat–base sugars and creamers (400/30 and 400/122), and 6½" trays (400/29) for Mirror Images. These pieces have ground bottoms and are somewhat heavier than original Candlewick pieces. They are not marked.

Light green Candlewick items have recently appeared. The origin of these items is not presently known.

Boyd Crystal Art Glass, Cambridge, Ohio, has used Candlewick molds to make items in various slag and clear colors. All Boyd molds have been marked with a B in a diamond trademark.

In late 1990 Dalzell–Viking Corporation, New Martinsville, WV, began making a five-piece place setting (6" plate, 8½" plate, 10" dinner plate, cup and saucer) in Crystal, Black, Cobalt, Evergreen, and Ruby Red. Retail price is $75 to $95 a place setting. The 1991 Dalzell–Viking price list also includes a 5" and 6" two-handled bowl, 7" and 8" two-handled tray, and 10" five-part relish dish in Crystal. These new pieces are quite heavy when compared to period Candlewick, have ground bottoms, and etched "Dalzell" on the center base rim.

Ashtray
4¼" l, oblong, large beads, 400/134/	
1	**5.00**
6" d, round, large beads, 400/150	
Cobalt blue	**10.00**
Crystal	**6.00**
Lavender	**12.00**
Pink	**8.00**
6½" d, eagle, frosted, 1776/1	**50.00**
Ashtray Set, nested, 4", 5", 6", three piece set	
All crystal, 400/450	**17.50**
Blue, yellow, and pink, 400/550 ...	**26.50**
Red, white, and blue, patriotic, 400/ 550	**125.00**
Atomizer	
400/96 shaker with atomizer top made by De Vilbiss	
Amber	**95.00**
Amethyst	**100.00**
Green	**90.00**

400/167 shaker bottoms, aqua and amethyst	**95.00**
400/247 shaker bottoms, aqua and amethyst	**95.00**
Banana Stand, 11" d plate, two sides turned up, four bead stem, 400/103E	**500.00**
Basket, applied handle	
6½" h, turned up sides, 400/40/0 ...	**27.50**
11" h, 400/73/0	**95.00**
Bon Bon, 6" d, beaded edge, heart shaped, curved over center handle, 400/51T	
Crystal	**22.50**
Light blue	**35.00**
Ruby red with crystal handle, ...	**95.00**
Bouillion, liner, #126	**50.00**
Bowl, beaded edge	
8½" d, two handles, 400/72B	**16.00**
9" d, square crimped, four ball toes, 400/72SC	
Black	**125.00**
Crystal	**30.00**
Light blue	**55.00**
Red	**125.00**
10½" d, 400/75	**30.00**
14" d, belled, large beads on sides, 400/104B	**55.00**
Buffet Set	
400/92D, 14" d plate, two pc set ...	**50.00**
400/166B, 5½" d cheese compote, plain stem	**50.00**
400/9266B	**50.00**
Butter Dish, cov	
California, 6¾ x 4", 400/276	
Beaded top, c1960	**85.00**
Plain top, c1951	**95.00**
Rect, ¼ lb, graduated beads on cov, 400/161	**23.00**
Round, 5½" d, two bead finial, 400/ 144	**25.00**
Cake Stand/Plate	
10" d, domed foot, wedge marked plate, 400/67D	**55.00**
11" d, three bead stem, 400/103D ..	**57.50**
14" d, round, birthday cake plate, 72 candle holes, 400/160	**250.00**
Canape Set, 400/36	**18.00**
Candleholder	
3½" h	
Domed foot, small beads, round handle, 400/81	**20.00**
Rolled saucer, small beads, 400/ 79R	**10.50**
5" h, round bowl with beaded or fluted insert vase, 400/40CV	**55.00**
5½" h, ftd, three sections arched beads on stem, 400/224	**35.00**
6½" h, three bead stem	
400/175	**50.00**
400/1752, prisms	**70.00**
9" h, oval beaded base, three candle cups, 400/115	**50.00**

Candy Dish, cov

5½" h, box, two bead finial, 400/59   **25.00**

6½" h, round bowl, sq cov, two bead finial, 400/245 ....   **75.00**

7" h, two bead finial, three partitions, 400/110 ....   **45.00**

Celery Tray, 13½" l, oval, two curved open handles, 400/105 ....   **27.50**

Champagne, 3400 Line, flared bell top, four graduated beads in stem, tall, 5 oz **12.50**

Cheese and Cracker Set, 400/151 cheese compote, 400/145D 11½" d handled plate, two pc set 400/145 ..   **50.00**

Cheese, Toast or Butter Plate, 7¾" d, cupped edge, domed cov, bubble knob, 400/123 ....   **95.00**

Cigarette Set, frosted crystal, 6½" d 1776/eagle ashtray, 3" h cigarette jar, small beads, two pc set **65.00**

Clock, 4" h, beaded edge **100.00**

Coaster, 3½" d, round, spoon rest, 400/226 ....   **10.00**

Cocktail, 400/190 Line, bell shaped bowl, hollow trumpet shaped stem, beaded around foot, crystal, 4 oz ..   **16.50**

Cocktail Set, 6" d plate, 2½" off–center indent, 400/39; one bead cocktail glass; set, 400/97 ....   **25.00**

Compote, beaded edge, ftd

5" d, three sections, arched beads in stem, 400/220 ....   **35.00**

8" d, 4 bead stem, 400/48F **65.00**

9" d

Domed foot, large bead stem, ribbed, 400/67B **75.00**

Flat foot, plain or crimped beaded edge, 400/67B **65.00**

Console Set, bowl and pr candleholders

12" d float bowl, 92F, cupped edge, 2–light candleholders, 400/100; set 400/920F **75.00**

13" d mushroom bowl, 400/92L on 400/127B 7½" d base, 6" h ftd urn candleholders, 400/129R; set 400/136 ....   **120.00**

Cordial, 1 oz, crystal

3400 Line, flared bell top, four graduated beads in stem **25.00**

4000 Line **25.00**

Cordial Bottle, 15 oz, beaded foot, handle, three bead stopper, 400/82

Crystal **125.00**

Crystal with red stopper and base ..   **250.00**

Creamer and Sugar Set, ftd, beaded foot, plain handles, c1937, 400/31

Crystal **35.00**

Light blue **55.00**

Cup and Saucer

After Dinner, small, slender, 4½" d beaded saucer, two pc set 400/77   **18.50**

Coffee, slender, beaded handle, 400/

37, saucer, 400/35, two pc set 400/37 ....   **10.00**

Tea, round, beaded handle, 400/35, beaded saucer, 400/35, two pc set 400/35 ....   **9.50**

Deviled Egg Tray, 11½" d, twelve indentations, heart shaped center handle, 400/154 ....   **80.00**

Dresser Set, round mirrored tray, 400/151, powder jar, beaded base, three bead cov, two round perfume bottles, beaded base, four bead stoppers, made for I Rice Co, 1940s, four pc set   **150.00**

Epergne Set, 9" d ftd crimped bowl, one bead stem, 400/196, 7¾" h two bead peg vase, set 400/196 ....   **145.00**

Floating Garden Bowl, 11" d, 400/75F   **35.00**

Goblet, crystal

400/190 Line, bell shaped bowl, hollow trumpet shaped stem, beaded around foot, 10 oz **16.50**

3400 Line, flared bell top, four graduated beads in stem, 9 oz **15.00**

Iced Tea Tumbler

400/18, domed beaded foot, rounded top, 12 oz **22.50**

400/19, beaded base, straight sides, 12 oz **12.00**

3400 Line, flared bell top, one bead stem, crystal, 12 oz **15.00**

Jam Set

Two pieces, 400/2989 ....   **85.00**

Five pieces, two 400/89 cov marmalade jars, three bead ladles, 400/159 oval tray; five pc set 400/1589   **75.00**

Jelly Compote, 6" d, divided, beaded edge, 400/52 ....   **15.00**

Juice Tumbler, 400/19, beaded base, straight sides, 5 oz **8.00**

Lamp, hurricane, 3½" d saucer candleholder, 400/79R, 9" h chimney, 400/152R

Two pc set, 400/79 ....   **50.00**

Three pc set, 400/79R, 400/152 Candlewick adapter, 400/152R **70.00**

Marmalade, cov, spoon, $25.00.

Lemon Dish, 10½" l, three partitions .. **37.00**
Lemon Tray, 5½" d plate, center handle
  of three sections of arched beads,
  large bead on top, 400/221 .... **25.00**
Marmalade Jar, round, beaded edge
  cover, two bead finial, 400/89 ..... **25.00**
Marmalade Ladle, 4¾" l, small bowl,
  three bead handle, 400/130 .... **6.00**
Marmalade Set, 400/19 old-fashioned
  tumbler, beaded notched cov, two
  bead finial, 400/130 ladle, set, 400/
  1989 .... **35.00**
Mayonnaise Set, 7" d beaded plate, 400/
  23D, 5" d heart shaped bowl, 400/49/
  1, three bead ladle, 400/165, set,
  400/49 .... **30.00**
Mint Tray
  8" l, handle, 400/149/D **25.00**
  9" d, heart shaped center handle, 400/
  149 .... **25.00**
Mirror, domed beaded glass base, brass
  holder and frame, two sided mirror
  flips on hinges, maker unknown **65.00**
Mustard Jar, beaded foot, notched
  beaded cover, two bead finial, 3½" l
  glass spoon, shell bowl, fleur–de–lis
  handle, three pc set, 400/156 ...... **30.00**
Nappy, 6" d, beaded edge, 400/3F ... **9.50**
Old-Fashioned   Tumbler,   400/19,
  beaded base, straight sides 7 oz **15.00**
Oil and Vinegar Set, two 400/164 and
  400/166 cruets, beaded foot, 400/29
  7" l kidney shaped tray, three pc set
  400/2946 .... **85.00**
Parfait, 3400 Line, flared bell top, one
  bead stem **30.00**
Pastry Tray, 11½" l, beaded plate, heart
  shaped center handle, 400/68D **30.00**
Pickle, 8½" l, oval, 400/58 .... **17.00**
Pitcher
  Manhattan, beaded foot, plain handle, 400/18
    40 oz **110.00**
    80 oz **145.00**
  Water, 80 oz, beaded question mark
  handle, ice lip **95.00**
Plate, beaded edge
  6" d, bread and butter, 400/1D **6.00**
  8½" d, salad–dessert, 400/5D **8.00**
  9" d, luncheon, 400/7D **12.00**
  10" d, two handles, crimped, 400/
  72C **25.00**
  10½" d, dinner, 400/10D **22.50**
  12" d, two open handles, 400/145D **30.00**
Platter, 14" l **85.00**
Punch Set
  11 pcs, cov family punch jar, domed
  beaded foot, notched two bead
  cov, 400/139, small 400/139 ladle,
  eight 400/77 demi–cups, 400/139/
  77 set **225.00**
  15 pcs, six quart, 400/20 bowl, 400/

128B base, 400/91 ladle, twelve
  400/37 cups, question mark handle **250.00**
Relish and Dressing Set, 10½" d round
  four partition relish, 400/112, 400/89
  cov jar fits center well, long three
  beads ladle, c1941, four pc set **75.00**
Relish Dish, beaded edge
  6½" l, two sections, two tab handles,
  400/54 .... **10.00**
  8½" l, oval, two sections, 400/57 .. **15.00**
  10½" l
    2 sections, two tab handles, 400/
    256 .... **22.00**
    3 sections, two tab handles, also
    called "Butter 'n Jam" (center
    holds stick of butter), 400/262 . **45.00**
  12" l, rect, three sections one side,
  long section on other, tab handle
  each end, 400/215 .... **50.00**
Salad Fork and Spoon, #701 .... **24.00**

Salad, clear, crescent shape, $45.00.

Salad Set, 10½" d beaded bowl, 400/
  75B, 13" d cupped edge plate, 400/
  75V, fork and spoon set, 400/75, 400/
  75 set **65.00**
Salt and Pepper Shakers, pr, beaded foot
  Bulbous,   9   beads,   plastic   tops,
  c1941, 400/96 .... **15.00**
  Individual, chrome tops, 400/109 .. **10.00**
  Round
    400/96, 8 beads, chrome tops ... **10.00**
    400/116, one bead stem, plastic or
    metal tops, c1941 .... **60.00**
    400/190, trumpet foot, chrome tops **32.50**
Sauce Boat Set, oval handled gravy
  boat, 9" l oval plate with indent, 400/
  169 .... **85.00**
Seafood, matching icer, 400/190 Line,
  bell shaped bowl, hollow trumpet
  shaped stem, beaded around foot,
  crystal **35.00**
Sherbet, 5 oz
  400/19, beaded base, straight sides,
  low **8.00**
  400/190 Line, bell shaped bowl, hol-

low trumpet shaped stem, beaded
around foot **12.50**
3400 Line, flared bell top
  Low, one bead stem **10.50**
  Tall, four graduated beads in stem   **12.50**
Tid–Bit Server, two tier, 7½" d and 10½"
d plates joined with metal rod, round
handle at top, 400/2701
  Crystal **50.00**
  Emerald green **450.00**
Tid–Bit Set, nested, heart shaped, 4½",
5½", 6½", beaded edges, 400/750,
three pc set **30.00**
Torte Plate, 17" d, beaded edge, flat or
cupped edge, 400/20V **40.00**
Tray, 9½" l, oval, ribbed, two handles   **35.00**
Tumbler
  400/18, domed beaded foot, rounded
  top
    Dessert, 6 oz **25.00**
    Water, 9 oz **20.00**
  400/19, beaded base, straight sides,
  10 oz **10.00**
Vase
  3¾" h, bud, beaded foot, ball,
  crimped top, 400/25 . . . .   **20.00**
  5¾" h, bud, beaded foot, tapered
  large beads, crimped top, 400/107   **25.00**
  7" h, rolled beaded top, solid glass
  arched handles with small bead
  edging, flat foot, 400/87R **35.00**
  8" h
    Crimped beaded top, graduated
    beads down sides, 400/87C . . .   **22.50**
    Fan shaped, beaded top, solid glass
    arched handles with small bead
    edging, flat foot, 400/87F **25.00**
  8½" h, bud, beaded foot, ball
    Narrowed top slants, applied han-
    dle, 400/227 . . . .   **85.00**
    Trumpet shaped top, crimped, 400/
    28C **35.00**
Wine
  400/190 Line, bell shaped bowl, hollow trumpet shaped stem, beaded
  around foot, 5 oz **17.50**
  3400 Line, flared bell top, four grad-
  uated beads in stem, 4 oz **20.00**

CARNIVAL GLASS

History: Carnival glass, an American invention,
is colored pressed glass with a fired-on iridescent
finish. It was first manufactured about 1905 and
was immensely popular both in America and
abroad. Over 1,000 different patterns have been
identified. Production of old carnival glass patterns ended in 1930.

Most of the popular patterns of carnival glass
were produced by five companies—Dugan, Fenton, Imperial, Millersburg, and Northwood.

Northwood patterns frequently are found with
the "N" trademark. Dugan used a diamond
trademark on several patterns.

In carnival glass, color is the most important
factor in pricing. The color of a piece is deter-
mined by holding the piece to the light and looking through it.

References: Bill Edwards, *The Standard Encyclopedia of Carnival Glass, Revised Third Edition,*
Collector Books, 1991; Marion T. Hartung, *First
Book of Carnival Glass to Tenth Book of Carnival
Glass* [series of 10 books], published by author,
1968 to 1982; Tom and Sharon Mordini, *Carnival Glass Auction Prices,* printed by authors,
1992; Thomas E. Sprain, *Carnival Glass Tumblers, New and Reproduced,* published by author, 1984.

Collectors' Clubs: American Carnival Glass As-
sociation, P. O. Box 235, Littlestown, PA 17340;
Collectible Carnival Glass Association, 2360 N.
Old SR 9, Columbus, IN 47203; Heart of Amer-
ica Carnival Glass Association, 3048 Tamarak
Drive, Manhattan, KS 66502; International Car-
nival Glass Association, Inc., RR 1, Box 14,
Mentone, IN 46539; New England Carnival
Glass Club, 12 Sherwood Road, West Hartford,
CT 06117.

Acanthus, Imperial
  Bowl
    7" d, green **25.00**
    8" or 9" d
      Marigold **65.00**
      Purple **60.00**
      Smoky **72.00**
  Plate, 10" d, marigold **150.00**
Acorn, Fenton
  Bowl
    5" d, blue, ribbon candy rim **60.00**
    7" d, ruffled, aqua **75.00**
  Ice Cream Bowl, green **70.00**
Acorn Burrs, Northwood
  Berry Set, master and six sauces
    Marigold **215.00**
    Purple **365.00**
  Butter Dish, cov
    Marigold **125.00**
    Purple **225.00**
  Creamer
    Dark **100.00**
    Marigold **55.00**
  Punch Cup
    Ice Blue **85.00**
    Marigold **20.00**
    Purple **25.00**
  Sauce, 5" d
    Marigold **30.00**
    Pastel **60.00**
  Spooner, marigold **75.00**
  Tumbler
    Green **55.00**

Marigold	45.00
Purple	55.00

Apple Blossom, Dugan
Bowl, 7½" d

Marigold	25.00
Peach Opal	125.00
Plate, 8¾" d, green	125.00

Apple Blossom Twigs, Dugan

Bowl, three in one edge, peach opal	85.00
Plate, marigold	75.00

Beaded Cable, Northwood

Candy Dish, ftd, marigold	45.00
Rose Bowl, aqua opal	285.00

Blackberry, Fenton

Compote, small, blue	60.00
Hat, marigold	40.00

Blackberry Spray, Fenton

Bon Bon, green	50.00
Compote, marigold	38.00
Hat, marigold	40.00

Butterfly and Berry, Fenton

Berry Set, master and six sauces, marigold	200.00
Bowl, 8" to 9" d, ftd	
Blue	70.00
Marigold	65.00
Butter Dish, cov, green	195.00
Sauce Dish	
Marigold	24.00
Purple	85.00
Table Set, 4 pcs, marigold	225.00
Tumbler	
Blue	36.00
Marigold	18.00
Vase, 6" h, marigold	35.00
Water Set	
7 pcs, blue	510.00
7 pcs, marigold	350.00
11 pcs, marigold	450.00

Butterfly and Fern, Millersburg

Pitcher, water, marigold	70.00
Tumbler, aqua	50.00

Carolina Dogwood, Westmoreland

Bowl, peach opal, piecrust edge	115.00
Plate, white, irid	300.00

Circle Scroll, Dugan

Butter Dish, cov, marigold	215.00
Compote, amethyst	125.00
Spooner, marigold	150.00
Whimsey, 7" h, purple	90.00

Coin Dot, Northwood
Bowl, 7" d

Green	30.00
Marigold	38.00
Purple	27.50
Pitcher, marigold	165.00
Rose Bowl	
Green	50.00
Marigold	42.50
Tumbler, marigold	48.00

Dahlia, Dugan or Diamond Glass Co.

Bowl, 10" d, ftd, white	195.00
Butter Dish, cov, marigold	150.00
Creamer	
Purple	125.00
White	125.00
Pitcher, purple	650.00
Sauce	
Marigold	40.00
Purple	45.00
Tumbler	
Marigold	120.00
Purple	185.00
White	175.00

Dandelion, Northwood
Mug

Marigold	285.00
Purple	275.00
Pitcher, marigold	375.00
Tumbler	
Green	95.00
Ice Blue	185.00
Marigold	45.00
White	145.00

Left to right: Beaded Cable, rose bowl, Northwood, blue, ftd, $45.00; Dandelion, pitcher, Northwood, green, $575.00; Fashion, creamer, Imperial, dark, $90.00.

Daisy and Plume, bowl, ftd, peach opal 100.00
Diamond Ring, Imperial
  Bowl, berry, 5" d, amethyst 48.00
  Fruit Bowl, 9" d, marigold 40.00
Dragon and Lotus, Fenton
  Bowl, 7" to 9" d, three ftd
    Green 70.00
    Marigold 45.00
    Purple 90.00
  Ice Cream Bowl, 9" d, collared base
    Blue 55.00
    Marigold 50.00
Dutch Twins, Unknown Maker
  Ashtray, marigold 25.00
  Dresser Set, 5 pcs, marigold 210.00
Fern Panels, Northwood, hat, marigold 30.00
Floral and Grape, Fenton
  Pitcher, water, blue 135.00
  Tumbler, marigold 30.00
Fluffy Peacock, Fenton
  Pitcher, water, blue 135.00
  Tumbler, marigold 45.00
  Water Set, 7 pcs, blue 800.00
Flute, Imperial, bowl, 9" d, marigold . 17.50
Flute, Millersburg, vase, 9" h, amethyst 82.00
Golden Grape, Dugan
  Bowl, 7" d, marigold 35.00
  Rose Bowl, collar base, marigold ... 55.00
Good Luck, Northwood
  Bowl, ruffled
    Green, basketweave back 300.00
    Marigold, basketweave back 125.00
    Purple, ribbed back 165.00
  Plate, 9" d, purple 300.00
Grape, Imperial
  Bowl, 4¾" d, marigold 13.00
  Tray, center handle, marigold 27.50
  Water Set, 7 pcs, marigold 200.00
Grape and Cable, Fenton and North-
wood
  Banana Boat
    Blue 325.00
    Green 275.00
    Marigold 145.00
    Purple 225.00
  Bon Bon, two handles
    Blue 60.00
    Green 45.00
    Marigold 35.00
  Bowl, 8" to 9" d, spatula ftd, ruffled
    Green 70.00
    Marigold 70.00
    Purple 65.00
  Butter Dish, cov
    Blue 200.00
    Green 175.00
    Marigold 175.00
    Purple 185.00
  Candlesticks, pr
    Green 172.00
    Marigold 160.00
    Purple 275.00

  Cologne Bottle
    Marigold 145.00
    Purple 175.00
  Cup and Saucer
    Green 365.00
    Purple 445.00
  Dresser Tray
    Green 250.00
    Marigold 110.00
    Purple 175.00
  Hatpin Holder, 7" h
    Green 215.00
    Marigold 200.00
    Purple 230.00
  Perfume Bottle, marigold 325.00
  Pin Tray
    Green 90.00
    Purple 100.00
  Plate, 9" d
    Marigold 90.00
    Purple, sgd "Northwood" 100.00
  Powder Jar, cov
    Green 100.00
    Marigold 65.00
    Purple 115.00
  Punch Bowl, matching base
    Green 600.00
    Marigold 250.00
    Purple 420.00
  Punch Cup
    Green 35.00
    Ice Blue 65.00
    Marigold 24.50
  Sauce
    Marigold 35.00
    Purple 38.00
  Spooner
    Green 90.00
    Marigold 95.00
  Sugar, cov
    Green 115.00
    Marigold 95.00
    Purple 90.00
  Sweetmeat, cov, purple 200.00
  Tumbler
    Green 45.00
    Marigold 35.00
    Purple 37.50
  Water Set, 7 pcs, purple 400.00
  Whiskey Shot Glass
    Marigold 30.00
    Purple 135.00
Grape Arbor, Northwood
  Hat, blue 80.00
  Pitcher, water, white 475.00
  Tumbler, ice blue 140.00
Grapevine Lattice, Dugan
  Bowl, 7" d, ruffled, marigold 28.00
  Plate, 6" d, white 80.00
  Tumbler, purple 35.00
Greek Key, Northwood
  Bowl, green 75.00

Pitcher, water, green 700.00
Tumbler, purple 75.00
Hearts and Flowers, Fenton
Bowl, 8" d, blue, piecrust rim 425.00
Compote, white 150.00
Plate, marigold 300.00
Heavy Iris, Dugan
Pitcher, water, tankard
Marigold 110.00
Peach Opal 1,000.00
Tumbler, white 175.00
Water set, 9 pcs, marigold 610.00
Holly and Berry, bowl, amber/blue ... 125.00
Kittens, Fenton
Bowl, cereal, blue 200.00
Cup and Saucer, marigold 225.00
Dish, marigold 80.00
Plate, 4½" d, marigold 150.00
Toothpick Holder, blue 300.00
Leaf and Beads, Northwood
Candy Dish, ftd, green 75.00
Nut Bowl, purple 65.00
Rose bowl
Aqua opal 235.00
Marigold 65.00
Leaf Tiers, Unknown Maker
Bowl, 5" d, ftd, marigold 25.00
Creamer, marigold 45.00
Lamp Shade, marigold 90.00
Tumbler, marigold 70.00
Lion, Fenton
Bowl
5" d, marigold 110.00
7" d
Blue 300.00
Marigold 115.00
Plate, 7" d, marigold 575.00
Little Fishes, Fenton
Bowl
6" d, three ftd
Marigold 50.00
Purple 145.00
8" to 9" d, three ftd
Blue 190.00
Marigold 145.00
Sauce, 5" d, ftd, aqua 200.00
Little Flowers, Fenton
Berry Set, master bowl, three sauce
dishes
Blue 95.00
Green 235.00
Bowl
5" d
Aqua 100.00
Blue 40.00
Green 25.00
8" to 9" d
Blue 90.00
Purple 85.00
10" d, purple 75.00
Nut Bowl, marigold 75.00
Plate, 6" d, marigold 165.00

Little Stars, Millersburg
Bowl
7" d, marigold, fluted 115.00
8" d, purple, ruffled 135.00
Ice Cream Bowl, 8" d, marigold 115.00
Lotus & Grape, Fenton
Bon Bon, two handles
Blue 45.00
Celeste Blue 315.00
Green 65.00
Marigold 45.00
Bowl
5" d, ftd
Blue 45.00
Green 75.00
Marigold 48.00
9" d, green 100.00
Plate, 9" d, blue 600.00
Louisa, Westmoreland
Bowl, 8" to 9" d, three ftd
Green 48.00
Marigold 50.00
Peach Opalescent 475.00
Nut Bowl, ftd
Green 48.00
Marigold 30.00
Purple 35.00
Plate, 9½" d, ftd
Marigold 150.00
Teal Blue 100.00
Rose Bowl, ftd
Green 70.00
Lavender 75.00
Marigold 35.00
Purple 65.00
Salt and Pepper Shakers, pr, marigold 35.00
Lustre Flute, Northwood
Breakfast Set, creamer and sugar, in-
dividual size
Green 85.00
Marigold 50.00
Creamer, green 48.00
Hat, fluted, 5" d
Green 35.00
Marigold 30.00
Nappy
Green 32.00
Marigold 30.00
Punch Cup, green 16.00
Sugar, open, two handles
Green 30.00
Marigold 32.00
Tumbler, marigold 25.00
Lustre Rose, Imperial
Bowl
7" d, stippled
Marigold 45.00
Vaseline 75.00
8" to 9" d, three ftd
Amber 75.00
Blue 85.00
Clambroth 35.00

Green	45.00
Marigold	35.00
Butter Dish, cov, marigold	50.00
Creamer and Sugar, marigold	40.00

Fernery

Amber	75.00
Blue	80.00
Marigold	38.00
Purple	90.00
Smoky	70.00

Pitcher, water

Clambroth	70.00
Marigold	55.00

Plate, 9" d

Amber	85.00
Marigold	55.00
Purple	90.00

Rose Bowl

Amber	85.00
Green	48.00

Sauce Dish

Green	25.00
Marigold	12.00

Spooner

Amber	50.00
Green	40.00
Marigold	35.00
Purple	30.00

Sugar, cov

Amber	75.00
Marigold	50.00

Tumbler

Green	35.00
Marigold	18.00
Purple	35.00
Water Set, 7 pcs, marigold	250.00

Maple Leaf, Dugan

Berry Set, master bowl, five sauces,

marigold	75.00

Bowl, 6" d

Marigold	15.00
Purple	20.00
Butter Dish, cov, blue	85.00

Creamer

Blue	60.00
Marigold	45.00
Purple	60.00
Pitcher, water, purple	175.00

Spooner

Marigold	45.00
Purple	50.00

Sugar, cov

Marigold	50.00
Purple	60.00

Tumbler

Blue	45.00
Clambroth	75.00
Marigold	25.00
Purple	35.00

Marilyn, Millersburg

Pitcher, water

Green	675.00
Purple	725.00

Tumbler

Green	325.00
Marigold	165.00
Purple	115.00

Memphis, Northwood

Fruit Bowl on stand, ice blue	1,950.00

Punch Bowl, 11½" d, base, 2 pcs

Marigold	195.00
Purple	300.00

Punch Cup

Green	35.00
Ice Blue	60.00
Ice Green	70.00
Marigold	25.00
Purple	30.00
White	55.00

Milady, Fenton

Pitcher, water, tankard

Blue	750.00
Marigold	475.00

Tumbler

Blue	65.00
Marigold	75.00

 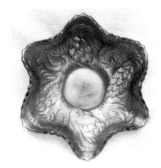 

Left to right: Fisherman's Mug, marigold, $235.00; Pine Cone, dish, Fenton, marigold, hexagonal ruffle, 6⅛" d, $25.00; Heavy Iris, tumbler, Dugan, $65.00.

Purple	**125.00**

Nippon, Northwood
Bowl, 8" to 9" d

Ice Blue	**175.00**
Ice Green	**150.00**
Marigold	**50.00**
Purple	**145.00**
White, fluted	**155.00**

Plate, 9" d

Marigold	**355.00**
White	**575.00**

Octagon, Imperial

Bowl, 10" sq, green	**48.00**
Butter Dish, cov, marigold	**110.00**
Compote, jelly, green	**75.00**
Decanter, marigold	**80.00**

Pitcher, water, 8" h

Marigold	**80.00**
Purple	**450.00**
Spooner, marigold	**48.00**

Table Set, cov butter dish, creamer,
cov sugar, and spooner, marigold . **225.00**
Tumbler

Green	**80.00**
Marigold	**27.50**
Purple	**75.00**

Wine

Marigold	**35.00**
Purple	**50.00**

Ohio Star, Millersburg

Compote, marigold	**525.00**

Vase

Marigold	**300.00**
Purple	**725.00**

Open Rose, Imperial
Berry Set, master bowl, six sauces,
marigold **85.00**
Bowl

5" d, marigold	**18.00**

7" d, ftd

Green	**40.00**
Marigold	**35.00**
Purple	**45.00**

8" to 9" d

Amber	**25.00**
Aqua	**55.00**
Green	**42.00**
Marigold	**30.00**
Purple	**45.00**
Smoky	**65.00**

Plate, 9" d

Amber	**150.00**
Clambroth	**115.00**
Green	**70.00**
Marigold	**55.00**
Purple	**165.00**

Rose Bowl

Amber	**60.00**
Green	**50.00**
Purple	**325.00**
Tumbler, marigold	**20.00**
Vase, marigold	**45.00**

Orange Tree, Fenton
Bowl

5½" d, ftd, purple	**55.00**

8" to 9" d

Amber	**60.00**
Blue	**60.00**
Green	**65.00**
Marigold	**35.00**
Purple	**75.00**

10" d, three ftd

Blue	**160.00**
Green	**265.00**
Marigold	**85.00**
White	**175.00**

Breakfast Set, individual size creamer
and cov sugar

Blue	**125.00**
Marigold	**85.00**
Purple	**100.00**

Compote, 5" d

Blue	**65.00**
Green	**65.00**
Marigold	**25.00**

Creamer, ftd

Blue	**50.00**
Marigold	**35.00**
White	**50.00**

Goblet

Aqua	**100.00**
Blue	**60.00**
Green	**125.00**
Marigold	**20.00**

Hatpin Holder

Blue	**195.00**
Green	**355.00**
Marigold	**135.00**
Purple	**165.00**

Loving Cup

Blue	**220.00**
Green	**200.00**
Marigold	**135.00**
Purple	**175.00**
White	**200.00**

Mug

Amber	**125.00**
Blue	**50.00**
Marigold	**35.00**
Purple	**90.00**

Pitcher, water

Blue	**325.00**
Marigold	**235.00**
White	**395.00**

Plate, 9" d

Blue	**260.00**
Clambroth	**150.00**
Green	**265.00**
Marigold	**135.00**

Powder Jar, cov

Blue	**60.00**
Green	**365.00**
Marigold	**60.00**
Purple	**75.00**

Punch Cup
Blue	30.00
Marigold	20.00
Purple	25.00

Punch Set, 9 pcs, blue 465.00

Rose Bowl
Blue	65.00
Marigold	45.00
Purple	95.00

Sauce Dish, ftd
Blue	32.00
Marigold	20.00

Shaving Mug
Amber	125.00
Blue	60.00
Marigold	35.00
Purple	95.00

Sugar, cov
Blue	60.00
Marigold	35.00
White	50.00

Tumbler
Blue	50.00
Marigold	48.00
White	95.00

Water Set, 8 pcs, blue 500.00

Wine
Blue	40.00
Green	165.00
Marigold	24.00

Panther, Fenton
Bowl, berry, marigold	25.00
Bowl, centerpiece, marigold	600.00
Bowl, ruffled, 9" d, claw ftd, blue ..	250.00

Peach, Northwood
Berry Set, master bowl, four sauces, white	400.00
Table Set, cov butter, creamer, cov sugar, spooner, white	575.00
Tumbler, blue	65.00

Peacock and Grape, Fenton
Bowl, 8" d, ruffled, violet	65.00
Bowl, 9" d, collared base, blue	60.00
Plate, 9" d, ftd, marigold	180.00

Peacock and Urn, Millersburg
Berry Set, master bowl, five sauces, purple	750.00
Compote, 5½ x 5", aqua	325.00
Goblet, marigold	75.00
Ice Cream Bowl, master, stippled, ice blue	800.00
Plate, 9" d, marigold	165.00
Sauce, blue	125.00

Peacock at the Fountain, Northwood
Bowl, berry, master, marigold	90.00
Compote, blue	500.00
Creamer, purple	90.00
Orange Bowl, ftd, lavender	325.00
Punch Set, 6 pcs, marigold	500.00
Spooner, purple	80.00
Tumbler, purple	48.00

Peacocks on the Fence, Northwood
Bowl, ruffled, ribbed back
Marigold	185.00
Purple, piecrust rim	335.00
White, very irid	875.00
Plate, 9" d, ice green	325.00

Persian Medallion, Fenton
Bon Bon, two handles, aqua	100.00
Bowl, scalloped edge, marigold	35.00
Compote, 6¼" h, blue, flared top ..	70.00
Fruit Bowl, 10" d, three feet, int. Persian Medallion, ext. Grape and Cable pattern, blue	160.00
Plate, 6½" d, blue	60.00

Polo, Unknown Maker, ashtray, marigold 25.00

Rose Show, Northwood
Bowl, marigold	275.00
Plate, pastel	475.00

Sailboat, Fenton
Bowl, 4" d, marigold	40.00
Wine, marigold	15.00

Seacoast, Millersburg
Pin Tray, green 275.00

Singing Birds, Northwood
Mug
Cobalt Blue	195.00
Purple	95.00

Smooth Rays, Westmoreland
Bowl, 8" d, dome base
Marigold	30.00
Primrose	68.00
Compote, green	75.00

Springtime, Northwood
Butter Dish, cov, purple	210.00
Creamer, marigold	125.00
Spooner, marigold	120.00
Sugar, cov, amethyst	200.00

Stag & Holly, Fenton
Bowl, marigold	75.00
Plate, amethyst	200.00
Rose Bowl, ftd, green	400.00

Star of David and Bows, Northwood, bowl, 7" d, amethyst, ftd 75.00

Stippled Rays, Northwood
Bon Bon, blue	40.00
Creamer and Sugar, marigold	65.00
Plate, 7" d, amethyst	45.00

Swirl Hobnail, Millersburg
Rose Bowl, scalloped rim
Marigold	225.00
Purple	250.00
Spittoon, marigold	575.00

Three Fruit, Northwood
Bowl, 9" d, fluted, purple, marked .	70.00
Bon Bon, marigold	50.00
Plate, stippled, green	125.00

Tree of Life, Imperial
Basket, marigold	40.00
Perfume Bottle, marigold	45.00
Plate, 8" d, marigold	27.00
Tumbler, marigold	24.00

Triplets, Dugan

Bowl, 7" d, scalloped, marigold	**35.00**
Compote, marigold	**30.00**
Hat, amethyst	**40.00**

Trout and Fly, Millersburg

Bowl, 8¾" d, oval, marigold	**315.00**
Bowl, 8¾" d, round	
Green	**450.00**
Marigold	**325.00**

Vintage, Fenton

Card Tray, marigold	**40.00**
Cup, green	**35.00**
Epergne, amethyst	**100.00**
Fernery, blue	**45.00**
Plate, 11" d, ruffled, marigold	**150.00**

Wild Rose, Northwood, bowl, green .. **45.00**

Wishbone, Northwood

Bowl, 10" d	
Amethyst	**85.00**
Marigold, dark	**65.00**
Tumbler, green	**125.00**

Wreath of Roses, Dugan

Rose Bowl, marigold	**45.00**
Spittoon, amber	**160.00**

Wreathed Cherry, Dugan

Bowl, berry, master, purple	**125.00**
Bowl, berry, individual, purple	**40.00**
Creamer, marigold	**65.00**
Toothpick Holder, amethyst	**150.00**
Tumbler, white	**150.00**

Zipper Loop, Imperial, lamp, oil, 8" h, smoke irid, small base chip **450.00**

CHILDREN'S TOY DISHES

History: Dishes made for children often served a dual purpose—playthings and a means of learning social graces. Dish sets came in two sizes. The first was for actual use by the child when entertaining her friends. The second, a smaller size than the first, was for use with dolls.

Children's dish sets often were made as a sideline to a major manufacturing line either as a complement to the family service or as a way to use up the last of the day's batch of materials.

Children's toy dishes were made by many of the major manufacturers, such as Cambridge, Akro Agate, Jeannette Glass Co., and Hazel Atlas. Collectors prefer complete sets and mint pieces, sometimes this is difficult to achieve because the pieces were toys and enjoyed by children of years ago.

Children's toy dishes are commonly sold in combinations such as berry sets, table sets, and water sets. Due to the small size of the items, the display desirability of a grouping of pieces has increased their value.

References: Doris Lechler, *Children's Glass Dishes, China and Furniture*, Collector Books, 1983, 1991 value update; Doris Lechler, *Children's Glass Dishes, China, Furniture, Volume II*, Collector Books, 1986, 1990 value update; Doris Lechler, *English Toy China*, Antique Publications, 1989; Doris Lechler, *French and German Dolls, Dishes, and Accessories*, Antique Publications, 1991; Doris Lechler, *Toy Glass*, Antique Publications, 1989; Lorraine May Punchard, *Child's Play*, published by author, 1982; Margaret & Kenn Whitmyer, *Children's Dishes*, Collector Books, 1984.

AKRO AGATE

Creamer

Interior Panel, opaque, blue	**25.00**
Concentric Ring, opaque, light blue, small	**9.00**

Cup

Chiquita, lavender	**25.00**
Concentric Ring, pumpkin, closed handle, 1⅜" d	**45.00**

Cup and Saucer, Interior Panel, jade .. **20.00**

Dinner Set, 11 pcs, Stippled Band, azure **100.00**

Pitcher, Octagonal, dark blue, open handle, 2⅞" h **20.00**

Plate, Concentric Rib, opaque, dark blue **6.00**

Saucer

Interior Panel, opaque, blue, large ..	**4.75**
Octagonal, white, closed handle, large	**2.75**

Tea Set

13 pcs, Raised Daisy, orig box	**210.00**
23 pcs, Octagonal, opaque green and white	**125.00**

Teapot, Concentric Rib, opaque, cobalt blue, white lid **30.00**

Tumbler, Octagonal, cream **10.00**

Water Service, Stippled Band, amber, pitcher and six tumblers **65.00**

DEPRESSION GLASS

Creamer

Cherry Blossom, Jeannette Glass Co., 1930–39	
Delphite	**35.00**
Pink	**30.00**
Doric and Pansy, Jeannette Glass Co., 1937–38	
Pink	**25.00**
Teal	**32.00**
Laurel, McKee Glass Co., 1930s	
French Ivory, red decorated rim ..	**30.00**
Jade Green	**30.00**
Opaque	
Plain	**20.00**
Scottie dog decal	**45.00**
Moderntone, Little Hostess, Hazel Atlas, fired–on color	**5.50**

Cup

Cherry Blossom, Jeannette Glass Co.,
1930–39
Delphite	30.00
Pink	24.00

Doric and Pansy, Jeannette Glass Co.,
1937–38
Pink	20.00
Teal	30.00

Homespun, Jeannette Glass Co.,
1939–49
Crystal	15.00
Pink	20.00

Laurel, McKee Glass Co., 1930s
French Ivory, red decorated rim ..	18.00
Jade Green	17.50
Opaque	
Plain	15.00
Scottie dog decal	30.00

Moderntone, Little Hostess, Hazel At-
las, fired–on color | 4.50

Plate

Cherry Blossom, Jeannette Glass Co.,
1930–39, 6″ d
Delphite	9.50
Pink	6.00

Doric and Pansy, Jeannette Glass Co.,
1937–38
Pink	5.00
Teal	7.50

Homespun, Jeannette Glass Co.,
1939–49
Crystal	7.50
Pink	10.00

Laurel, McKee Glass Co., 1930s
French Ivory, red decorated rim ..	12.00
Jade Green	10.00
Opaque	
Plain	7.00
Scottie dog decal	20.00

Moderntone, Little Hostess, Hazel At-
las, fired–on color, 5¼″ d .... | 5.50

Saucer

Cherry Blossom, Jeannette Glass Co.,
1930–39
Delphite	7.50
Pink	6.00

**Sugar, open, teal, Doric & Pansy, 2½″ h,
3¼″ w, $30.00.**

Doric and Pansy, Jeannette Glass Co.,
1937–38
Pink	3.00
Teal	4.50

Homespun, Jeannette Glass Co.,
1939–49
Crystal	5.00
Pink	7.00

Laurel, McKee Glass Co., 1930s
French Ivory, red decorated rim ..	7.00
Jade Green	6.50
Opaque	
Plain	5.00
Scottie dog decal	20.00

Moderntone, Little Hostess, Hazel At-
las, fired–on color | 1.50

Sugar, cov

Cherry Blossom, Jeannette Glass Co.,
1930–39
Delphite	30.00
Pink	25.00

Doric and Pansy, Jeannette Glass Co.,
1937–38
Pink	25.00
Teal	32.00

Laurel, McKee Glass Co., 1930s
French Ivory, red decorated rim ..	30.00
Jade Green	28.00
Opaque	
Plain	20.00
Scottie dog decal	40.00

Moderntone, Little Hostess, Hazel At-
las, fired–on color | 5.50

Table Set, Sweetheart, 4 pcs .... | 85.00

Teapot, cov

Homespun, Jeannette Glass Co.,
1939–49, pink .... | 75.00

Moderntone, Little Hostess, Hazel At-
las, brown base, lemon yellow lid | 135.00

Tea Set

12 pcs

Homespun, Jeannette Glass Co.,
1939–49, pink, mint in orig box | 225.00

Moderntone, Little Hostess, Hazel
Atlas, pastel pink, green, blue,
and yellow, saucer and sugar
missing .... | 40.00

14 pcs, orig box

Cherry Blossom, Jeannette Glass
Co., 1930–39
Delphite	260.00
Pink	225.00

Doric and Pansy, Pretty Polly Party
Dishes, Jeannette Glass Co.,
1937–38
Pink	185.00
Teal	250.00

Laurel, McKee Glass Co., 1930s
French Ivory, red decorated rim	245.00
Jade Green	225.00
Opaque	
Plain	150.00

Scottie dog decal **400.00**
16 pcs, Moderntone, Little Hostess,
Hazel Atlas, gray, rust, gold, and
turquoise, orig box **160.00**

MILK GLASS

Butter, cov
Versailles, emb roses, raised scal-
loped draping, blue trim, Dither-
idge, c1900 .... **150.00**
Wild Rose **50.00**
Creamer, Wild Rose **65.00**
Cup, Nursery Rhyme **20.00**
Ice Cream Platter, White Rose **60.00**
Mug, Gooseberry, 1⅞" **30.00**
Punch Bowl Set, White Rose, lemon
stain, punch bowl, six cups **200.00**
Punch Cup
Nursery Rhyme **25.00**
Wild Rose **15.00**
Spooner, Wild Rose **45.00**
Stein, Monk, rings on top **25.00**
Table Set, Thumbelina, cov butter, crea-
mer, and cov sugar **50.00**

Castor Set, Gothic Arches, clear, silver-plated base, $165.00.

PATTERN GLASS

Berry Bowl
Fine Cut X
Individual **18.00**
Master **30.00**
Flute **5.00**
Lacy Daisy **7.00**
Pattee Cross, individual **12.00**
Butter Dish, cov
Alabama **200.00**
Amazon **50.00**
Austrian, canary **200.00**
Button Arches, ruby stained, enamel
flowers, souvenir **165.00**
Doyle's 500, amber **100.00**

Drum **115.00**
Hobnail, thumbprint base, blue **100.00**
Liberty Bell **150.00**
Lion Head **175.00**
Mardi Gras, 4¼" h **125.00**
Michigan, 5¼" d, 3¾" h, rose stain . **185.00**
Pennsylvania, dark green **100.00**
Stippled Forget–Me–Not **90.00**
Tulip and Honeycomb **35.00**
Wee Branches, alphabet base **110.00**
Cake Stand
Fine Cut and Fan **35.00**
Hawaiian Lei **35.00**
Palm Leaf Fan **35.00**
Rexford **30.00**
Ribbon Candy, green, 6½" d, 3½" h **45.00**
Candlesticks, pr
Moonlight Blue **20.00**
Star, Cambridge Glass, light blue ... **25.00**
Castor Set, American Shield, four bottles **125.00**
Condiment Set, Hickman, open salt,
pepper shaker, cruet, and leaf shaped
tray **65.00**
Creamer
Alabama **60.00**
Amazon, pedestal **25.00**
Austrian, canary, Greentown, 3¼" h,
2⅛" d **75.00**
Buzz Saw **15.00**
Dewdrop **30.00**
Drum **65.00**
Fernland **15.00**
Flat Diamond & Sunburst **12.00**
Grapevine with Ovals **40.00**
Hawaiian Lei **10.00**
Hobnail with Thumbprint base, am-
ber **40.00**
Liberty Bell **65.00**
Lion Head **100.00**
Mardi Gras, ruby stain, 2⅞" h **75.00**
Michigan, clear, gold trim **55.00**
Nursery Rhyme **30.00**
Pennsylvania **30.00**
Pert **55.00**
Stippled Forget–Me–Not **80.00**
Tappan
Amethyst **35.00**
Clear **10.00**
Twin Snowshoes **18.00**
Twist, opalescent, blue **80.00**
Wee Branches **80.00**
Whirligig **18.00**
Cruet, English Hobnail, green **25.00**
Cup and Saucer, Lion Head **80.00**
Goblet, Vine, cobalt blue **60.00**
Honey Jug, Mardi Gras, ruby stain, 2½"
h **85.00**
Horseradish Dish, Menagerie, bear ... **120.00**
Ice Cream Platter, ABC **125.00**
Lemonade Pitcher, Lily of the Valley .. **125.00**
Mug
Austrian **45.00**

Fighting Cats	25.00
Grapevine	20.00
Heron	10.00
Hobnail, cranberry rim	35.00
Liberty Bell, emb "1776–1876" between two bells, 2" h	200.00
Michigan	45.00
Old Butterfly	30.00
Stippled Forget–Me–Not	60.00
Wee Branches	20.00
Nappy, Michigan	50.00

Pitcher

Colonial	15.00
Hobb's Hobnail	45.00
Michigan, rose stain	50.00
Nursery Rhyme	100.00
Oval Star, Northwood, gold trim	40.00
Pattee Cross, gold trim	48.00
Waffle and Button	30.00
Plate, Wee Branches	48.00

Punch Bowl

Nursery Rhyme	35.00
Thumbelina	30.00
Whirligig	18.00

Punch Bowl Set, punch bowl, six cups

Flattened Diamond and Sunburst	68.00
Nursery Rhyme	150.00
Star Arches	75.00
Tulip and Honeycomb	75.00

Punch Cup

Inverted Strawberry, Cambridge	16.00
Wheat Sheaf	8.00
Rose Bowl, Mardi Gras, 2" h, 2½" d	25.00
Sauce, Flute	6.00
Saucer, Puss in Boot	22.50

Spooner

Amazon, pedestal, sawtooth rim	30.00
Austrian, canary	90.00
Colonial, green, Cambridge	20.00
Diamond and Panels	18.00
Doyle's 500, amber	35.00
Hawaiian Lei	20.00
Lion Head	90.00
Mardi Gras, ruby stain	75.00
Menagerie Fish, amber	145.00
Michigan, rose stain	120.00
Pennsylvania	15.00
Stippled Forget–Me–Not	80.00
Tulip and Honeycomb	18.00
Twist, opalescent, vaseline	75.00
Whirligig	18.00

Sugar, cov

Alabama	90.00
Amazon, pedestal	30.00
Austrian, canary	148.00
Beaded Swirl	35.00
Colonial, Cambridge	40.00
Drum	60.00
Fernland	18.00
Hawaiian Lei	30.00
Liberty Bell	135.00
Lion Head	125.00

Mardi Gras, ruby stain	85.00
Menagerie, blue	275.00
Michigan, clear, gold trim	50.00
Nursery Rhyme	45.00
Stippled Forget–Me–Not	100.00
Tappan, amethyst	45.00
Tulip & Honeycomb	24.00

Table Set, cov butter dish, creamer, sugar, and spooner

Arrowhead in Oval	75.00
Bead & Scroll	325.00
Beaded Swirl	110.00
Colonial, Cambridge	100.00
Duncan and Miller #42	350.00
Hawaiian Lei	135.00
Lion Head	500.00
Menagerie, blue	420.00
Nursery Rhyme	250.00
Oval Star	65.00
Pennsylvania, excellent gold	285.00
Sweetheart, Cambridge	85.00
Twist, white opal	600.00
Tray, Doyle's 500, amber	50.00

Tumbler

Michigan	10.00
Nursery Rhyme	15.00
Pattee Cross	8.00
Sandwich Ten Panel, sapphire blue	135.00
Water Set, Nursery Rhyme, pitcher and six tumblers	225.00

CONSOLIDATED GLASS COMPANY

History: The Consolidated Lamp and Glass Company resulted from the 1893 merger of the Wallace and McAfee Company, glass and lamp jobbers of Pittsburgh, and the Fostoria Shade & Lamp Company of Fostoria, Ohio. When the Fostoria, Ohio, plant burned down in 1895, Corapolis, Pennsylvania, donated a seven-acre tract of land near the center of town for a new factory. In 1911 the company was the largest lamp, globe, and shade works in the United States, employing over 400 workers.

In 1925 Reuben Haley, owner of an independent design firm, convinced John Lewis, president of Consolidated, to enter the giftware field utilizing a series of designs inspired by the 1925 Paris Exposition Internationale des Arts Decoratifs et Industriels Modernes and the work of Rene Lalique. Initially, the glass was marketed by Howard Selden through his showroom at 225 Fifth Avenue, New York, New York. The first two lines were Catalonian and Martele.

Additional patterns were added in the late 1920s: Florentine (January 1927), Chintz (January 1927), Ruba Rombic (January 1928), and Line 700 (January 1929). On April 2, 1932, Consolidated closed it doors. Kenneth Harley moved thirty–five to forty molds to Phoenix. In March 1936 Consolidated reopened under new management. The "Harley" molds were returned. During this period the famous Dancing Nymph line, based on an 8" salad plate in the 1926 Martele series, was introduced.

In August 1962 Consolidated was sold to Dietz Brothers. A major fire damaged the plant during a 1963 labor dispute. In 1964 the company closed its doors for good.

References: Ann Gilbert McDonald, *Evolution of the Night Lamp*, Wallace–Homestead Book Co., 1979; Jack D. Wilson, *Phoenix & Consolidated Art Glass, 1926–1980*, Antique Publications, 1989.

Almond Dish, Ruba Rombic, smoky topaz, 3"l	225.00
Ashtray, Santa Maria, green wash	200.00
Berry Bowl, 8" d, Cross–Cross, cranberry opalescent	165.00
Biscuit Jar, Florette, light green, satin	200.00
Boat, Love Birds, 13" l, frosted and clear	350.00
Bon Bon, Ruba Rombic, 6" d, smoky topaz	110.00
Bowl	
Coronation, Martelle, 5½" d, flared, blue	65.00
Dance of the Nudes, 8" d, dark blue wash	350.00
Ruba Rombic, smoky topaz	
8" d, cupped	400.00
9" d, flared	450.00
Box, cov, 7" l, 5" w, Martele line, Fruit and Leaf pattern, scalloped edge	65.00
Butter Dish, cov	
Cone, cased pink satin, c1894–1920	95.00
Cosmos, 7½" d	170.00
Candlesticks, pr	
Martele line, Hummingbird pattern, pedestal base, oval body, jade green, 6¾" h	225.00

Condiment Set, Coreopsis, blue, pink, and green, 6½" h, $325.00.

Ruba Rombic, smoky topaz	200.00
Cologne Bottle, 4½" h, Cosmos, orig stopper	100.00
Condiment Set, Florette, light blue cased glass	125.00
Console Bowl, Cockatoo, blue, frosted highlights	250.00
Creamer, Cosmos	150.00
Creamer and Sugar, Ruba Rombic, sunshine yellow	200.00
Cruet, Guttate, cased pink, orig stopper	300.00
Cup and Saucer, Dance of the Nudes, ruby flashed	250.00
Decanter, Ruba Rombic, jungle green	650.00
Goblet	
Martelli Russet Yellow Fruits, 9 oz	30.00
Spanish, green, 4½" h	15.00
Iced Tea Tumbler, Catalonian, 5½" h, purple wash, flat	12.00
Jug, Catalonian, lavender	100.00
Lamp	
Blackberry, 18" h, green wash	600.00
Cockatoo, blue, bittersweet, tan, and white	275.00
Dogwood, brown stain, off white flowers, socket missing	120.00
Florette, cased pink kerosene font, clear base	415.00
Love Birds, crystal, gold wash on birds	350.00
Miniature Lamp	
7" h, Cosmos, fish net ground	350.00
9" h, Cosmos, pink, yellow, and blue dec, electrified	75.00
Night Light, Santa Maria, block	450.00
Pickle Castor, Cosmos, pink band, ftd, ornate silver plated frame	400.00
Pitcher	
5" h, Cosmos	170.00
9½" h, 7¼" d, pink cased glass, molded drapery design, beading on neck, applied clear handle, c1920	250.00
Plate	
Dance of the Nudes	
8" d, luncheon	
Light Blue, frosted	250.00
Ruby Flashed	175.00
10" d, green wash	250.00
Martelli, Orchid, pink, birds and flowers, 12" d	95.00
Platter, Dance of the Nudes, Palace	
Dark Blue Wash	1,000.00
Clear	400.00
Puff Box, cov, Love Bird, blue	125.00
Salt and Pepper Shakers, pr	
Cone	
Green	70.00
Pink	75.00
Cosmos	185.00
Guttate	
Green	80.00
Pink satin	100.00

Sauce, Criss–Cross, cranberry opalescent 55.00
Snack Set, Martele Fruits, pink 35.00
Spooner
    Cosmos, pink flowers 130.00
    Criss–Cross, cranberry opalescent .. 65.00
    Florette, pink cased, metal rim and handles 75.00
Sugar, cov
    Cosmos 175.00
    Guttate, cased pink 115.00
Sugar, open, Ruba Rombic, cased golden amber shading to yellow 50.00
Sugar Shaker
    Cone, cased blue, orig top, c1894– 1920 .... 125.00
    Guttate, orig pewter top
        Cased pink 195.00
        Cranberry 425.00
Sundae, Martelli Russet Yellow Fruits . 30.00

Syrup Pitcher, Cosmos glass, 6½″ h, $120.00.

Syrup, Cosmos, silver plated lid 200.00
Toilet Bottle, Ruba Rombic, jade, cased 650.00
Toothpick Holder
    Florette, pink cased 65.00
    Guttate, cranberry 175.00
Tumbler
    Catalonian, yellow 22.00
    Cosmos 85.00
    Guttate, pink satin 50.00
    Katydid, clambroth, rare, unlisted color 150.00
    Martelli Russet Yellow Fruits, 5¾″ h, ftd 30.00
Vase
    Bird of Paradise, rect 300.00
    Catalonian, fan, blue, lavender, and green wash 100.00
    Coronation, 8″ h, blue, cased 450.00
    Dance of the Nudes, ruby flashed
        Crimped 250.00
        Fan 250.00
    Florentine Etch
        4½″ h, brown 250.00

7″ h
    Coffee brown 550.00
    Sterling silver edges 450.00
8½″ h, green, collar 325.00
12″ h, green 375.00
Katydid, fan, custard glass, frosted highlights 200.00
Line 700, 6½″ h, frosted lining 150.00
Owl, yellow cased, #2756 .... 165.00
Spanish, fan, green
    6½″ h 20.00
    7½″ h 25.00
Tropical Fish, blue fish, custard ground 300.00
Wild Geese, 9½″ h oval, blue geese, white ground 250.00
Violet Vase, Catalonian, 3½″ h, amethyst 50.00

CONTEMPORARY COLLECTOR GLASSES

History: Contemporary collector glasses date back to the movie premier of *Snow White and the Seven Dwarfs* in December of 1937. Libbey Glass and Walt Disney designed tumblers with a safety edge and sold the glasses through variety stores and through local dairies. The glasses were popular with the public and today collector glasses can be found with almost every Disney character and movie theme. In 1953 Welches began to use decorated tumblers as jelly containers and featured Howdy Doody and his characters. These glasses were eagerly received and Welches soon added other cartoon characters, like Mr. Magoo, to the designs. In the late 1960s, fast food restaurants started to use tumblers as advertising premiums. Soft drink manufacturers like Coke and Pepsi saw the advertising potential and helped develop marketing plans around the characters and soft drink products.

Contemporary collector glasses are usually produced in series and it is important to collectors to assemble all the different color variations and items in a series.

Care should be taken when using these tumblers as several early examples were decorated with a lead based paint. Collectors should try to purchase examples with brightly colored decorations, and avoid faded examples. Because these bright tumblers were made in huge quantities, collectors may be able to find very good to excellent examples.

References: Myles Bader and John Hervey, *Hervey & Bader Collectors' Guide To Glass Collecting,* published by authors, 1988; Mark E. Chase and Michael Kelly, *Contemporary Fast–Food and Drinking Glass Collectibles,* Wallace–Homestead, 1988; John Hervey, *Collector's Guide To Cartoon & Promotional Drinking*

Glasses, L–W Book Sales, 1990; Carol and Gene Markowski, *Tomart's Price Guide To Character & Promotional Glasses*, Wallace–Homestead, 1990.

Alice In Wonderland, Queen of Hearts and Rabbit 20.00
American Greeting Corp
Christmas is a gift of love 3.00
Holly Hobbie, Coke, Happiness is... 3.00
Aquaman 10.00
Batman, Super Series, 1976 .... 12.00
Betty Boop, King Features Syndicate, 1988 .... 7.50
Bianca, Disney Rescuers, Pepsi 8.00
Bicentennial Collection, Red Steer Restaurant, 1976
Cataldo Mission 5.00
Oregon Trail 5.00
Silver City 5.00
Bozo The Clown, 1950s 7.50
Brutus and Nero, Disney Rescuers, Pepsi 10.00
Burger Chef, Endangered Species Collector, Bald Eagle, 1978 .... 5.00
Burger King, King Series, 1978 .... 4.00
Capt Cook, McDonalds, 12 oz, thick base 10.00
Cinderella, 1950, Cinderella attending to stepsisters 7.00
Coca–Cola
Atlanta, mug 5.00
Calendar Girl, 1927 type 3.00
Dairy Queen, "Scrumpdillyishus" .. 7.50
Drink, flared, syrup line, engraved "Drink/5 cents" 75.00
Drink Coca–Cola
Canadian, registered trademark .. 6.50
Stained Glass Style, Drink Coca–Cola 3.00
Enjoy Coke, 1970 .... 2.50
Jack In The Box, Tiffany style 4.00
Philadelphia, bell shaped glass, gold letters 8.50
Spartanburg, bell shaped glass, white letters 5.00
West Point–La Grange, bell shaped glass, white letters 7.00
Davy Crockett
5" h, frosted white, dark brown portrait on both sides, Ritchey's Milk adv, mid 1950s 35.00
5¼" h, clear, two printed scenes, yellow, dark brown, and green, "Davy Crockett 1786–1836," mid 1950s 18.00
Domino's Pizza, Avoid The Noid, 1988, beach scene 2.00
Elsie The Cow, Borden's, dutch costume 10.00
Empire Strikes Back 3.00
Flash 10.00
Hawaii, McDonalds 6.00
Hershey's Milk Chocolate Kiss 4.00

Hopalong Cassidy, 5" h, milk glass, message in black letters, raised "Hoppy" on bottom, early 1950s 25.00
Jungle Book, Pepsi
Baloo 25.00
King Louie, Canadian 27.50
Kentucky Derby
1973 .... 10.00
1980 .... 8.00
1981 .... 7.00
1984 .... 6.00
1990 .... 3.00
Lady and the Tramp, Jock 15.00
Libbey Classics
Gulliver's Travels 8.00
Robin Hood 12.00
Treasure Island 10.00
Looney Tunes, seven different designs . 3.00
M*A*S*H, Hawkeye and Honeycut ... 10.00
Mr. Magoo, Welch Jelly, 1962 .... 7.00
Norman Rockwell, illustrator
Arby and Pepsi, 1979, winter scene 3.00
Country Time Lemonade, Saturday Evening scene, Grandpa's Girl ... 5.00
Patriots Of The American Revolution, Coca–Cola, 1976
George Washington 6.00
Patrick Henry 4.50
Penny, Disney Rescuers, Pepsi 7.00
Peter Pan, Canadian 10.00
Pierre The Bear, 1977, summer 4.00
Pizza Time Theater, Chuck E. Cheese . 5.00
Popeye, 1936 copyright, Popeye and Olive Oil 35.00
Return of the Jedi 2.00
Robin, Super Series, 1976 .... 6.00
Ronald McDonald, McDonalds, 12 oz, thick base 10.00
Seven Up
7–11, filigree design, smoke colored glass 10.00
7–Up, beach chairs 4.00
Uncola, upside down bell shape ... 2.00
Shazam 10.00
Sleeping Beauty, 1958 .... 10.00
Smurfs, Hardee's .... .50
Snow White and the Seven Dwarfs, Musical Note Series, 1938, 4¼" h 15.00
Star Trek, Taco Bell, four different designs 5.00
Star Wars, four different designs 3.00
Supergirl 15.00
Superman 10.00
Walt Disney Souvenir Set, Mickey 7.50
Wonder Woman 10.00

CORALENE

History: Coralene is a glass or china object which has the design painted on the surface of the piece and tiny glass colorless beads applied with a fixative. The piece is placed in a muffle which fixes the enamel and sets the beads. The design and technique were named coralene by Mt. Washington Glass, believed to be the originator of American coralene decoration.

Several American and English companies made glass coralene in the 1880s. Seaweed or coral was the most common design. Other motifs were ' Wheat Sheaf'' and "Fleur-de-Lis.'' Most of the base glass was satin finished.

Reproduction Alert: Reproductions are on the market, some using an old glass base. The beaded decoration on new coralene has been glued and can be scraped off.

Tumbler, satin glass, shaded medium pink to light pink, cased white, gold rim and dec, 3¾" h, $225.00.

Bowl
  4½" d, blue ground, flowers and
    leaves, silver plated holder 150.00
  5½" d
    Peachblow, ruffled, yellow cora-
      lene seaweed dec 185.00
    Satin, blue ground, MOP, herring-
      bone, pink coralene seaweed
      dec, crimped top, applied glass
      rim 625.00
  Pickle Castor, Diamond Quilted pattern
    rubina insert, white coralene flowers
    and dot pattern, ornate Tufts frame,
    braided handle 245.00
  Pitcher
    5¼" h, cased white ground, bright
      pink lining, gold seaweed coralene,
      applied amber reeded handle 220.00
    6¼" h, shaded yellow ground, white
      lining, coralene seaweed dec 350.00
    7¾" h, sq mouth, shaded pink satin
      ground, yellow coralene seaweed
      dec, applied frosted handle,
      Hobbs, Brockunier & Co. 750.00
  Sweetmeat, blue ground, flowers and
    leaves, silver plated holder 400.00
  Toothpick Holder, 2½" h, sq raised rim,

bulbous body, glossy peachblow
ground, opaque lining, yellow seaweed coralene dec 275.00
Tumbler, white satin ground, acorns and
leaves outlined in coralene 35.00
Vase
  4½" h, 3⅜" d, Diamond Quilted pat-
    tern, shaded pink, yellow beaded
    coralene stars in centers of dia-
    monds, white enameled beading
    around to edge 495.00
  5⅜" h, golden yellow snowflake MOP
    satin ground, white lining, yellow
    wheat coralene dec 500.00
  5½" h, 4" d, shaded pink snowflake
    MOP satin glass ground, white lin-
    ing, white enameled dot beading
    around top, wheat coralene dec .. 550.00
  7½" h
    Blue ground, bulbous, yellow cor-
      alene seaweed dec 250.00
    Peachblow ground, yellow cora-
      lene seaweed dec 375.00
    Yellow to white ground, yellow
      coralene seaweed dec 200.00
  7¾" h, 4¾" d, pink and green striped
    satin ground, off white lining,
    heavy yellow beaded coralene ... 475.00
  8" h, 5" d, satin ground, alternating
    pink, white, and green stripes at top
    which shade to white, yellow cor-
    alane beading 500.00
  10½" h, Diamond Quilted pattern,
    MOP satin shaded pink ground,
    yellow wheat coralene 1,100.00

CRANBERRY GLASS

History: Cranberry glass is transparent and named for its color, achieved by adding powdered gold to a molten batch of amber glass which then is reheated at a low temperature to develop the cranberry or ruby color. The glass color first appeared in the last half of the 17th century, but was not made in American glass factories until the last half of the 19th century.

Cranberry glass was blown, mold blown, or pressed. Examples often are decorated with gold or enamel. Less expensive cranberry glass was made by substituting copper for gold and can be identified by its bluish–purple tint.

References: Charles R. Hajdamach, *British Glass, 1800–1914*, Antique Collectors' Club, 1991; William Heacock and William Gamble, *Encyclopedia Of Victorian Colored Pattern Glass: Book 9, Cranberry Opalescent from A to Z*, Antique Publications, 1987.

Additional Listings: See specific categories such as Baskets, Bride's Baskets, Cruets, Jack–in–the–Pulpit Vases, etc.

Reproduction Alert: Reproductions abound. These pieces are heavier, off–color, and lack the quality of older examples.

Barber Bottle, 7" h, Inverted Thumbprint pattern, porcelain top 85.00
Bottle, 10¼" h, 4" d, blue and enameled white flowers, gold and silver leaves, clear bubble stopper with engraved flowers 165.00
Box, cov, hinged, round
   3½ x 3½", gold band with pink and blue flowers, leaves, center with pink, blue and white flowers 210.00
   3¾ x 2⅞", enameled pink and white flowers, green leaves 200.00
   4¼ x 4¼", clusters of white flowers and leaves, two multicolored birds 250.00
Celery Vase, Leaf Mold, Northwood .. 135.00
Chalice, cov, 16" h, enamel portrait of girl, gold trim 195.00
Condiment Set, 5½" h, 5" d, open salt, pepper shaker, and mustard pot, silver plated holder 175.00
Creamer
   3⅝" h, two bands, enameled white dots and flower dec, applied clear handle 100.00
   5" h, 4¼" w, deep color, Inverted Thumbprint pattern, sq top, flower with deep blue center and four applied amber leaves on branch dec, applied deep amber thorn handle 335.00
Cruet
   7½" h, enameled white flowers and leaves, applied clear handle, clear bubble stopper 175.00
   8¾" h, flattened bulbous vessel, pewter casing, figural cherub pewter stopper 220.00
   9½" h, engraved flowers and leaves, applied clear handle and wafer foot, clear cut faceted stopper 195.00

Pickle Castor, melon shape, four mold, plated frame marked "WR/New York/ 482," 10" h, $225.00.

13" h, three petal top, engraved flowers and leaves, applied clear handle and pedestal base, clear bubble stopper 235.00
Decanter, 11" h, 3⅞" d, three petal top, gold basket and scrolls dec, clear foot, handle, and bubble stopper ... 175.00
Ewer, 9½" h, gold leaves, white enamel outlines, flowers, and branches, applied clear handle 165.00
Lamp, hanging, hall type, 9" h, 6" d, Inverted Thumbprint pattern, deep coloring, orig chains, ceiling cap ... 300.00
Lamp Shade, 7¾" l, 4¾" fitter ring, Hobnail pattern, ruffled rim 100.00
Lemonade Set, 10¾" h pitcher, six matching glasses, 13¾" d undertray, polychrome floral dec, applied angular amber handles, attributed to Mt Washington, minor imperfections ... 665.00
Jewel Box, 6" h, round, lid with enamel white slate roof, turret, and doves, blue enamel flowers, brass ring handles and ball feet 400.00
Marmalade Jar, cov, Inverted Thumbprint pattern, wild rose and fern enamel dec, silver plated top, fleur–de–lis finial 150.00
Perfume Bottle
   2¼" d, 5¾" h, sanded enameled gold leaves, white enameled white flowers, clear ball stopper, gold trim .. 150.00
   3⅜" l, ¾" oval, lacy filigree openwork ormolu, gilt collar, engraved, hinged lid, inner stopper, attached chains and finger ring 235.00
Pickle Castor
   Coin Spot pattern, enamel dec, silver plated holder 225.00
   Inverted Thumbprint pattern, double, enameled gold florals and scroll, Moser style, ornate ftd Wilcox frame and cov, braided handle, resilvered 400.00
   Ribbed, enameled flowers, silver plated holder and tongs 275.00
   Swirl, ornate silver plated holder ... 225.00
Pitcher
   2⅝" h, bulbous, round mouth, applied clear handle, enameled green and white leaves, small yellow leaves, gold bands, applied red jewels 125.00
   6½" h, 4¼" d, bulbous, round mouth, Inverted Thumbprint pattern, applied clear handle 145.00
   7⅜" h, bulbous, round mouth, applied clear rope and braided handle 250.00
Salt, master
   2¼ x 2⅛", Optic pattern, applied clear wishbone feet 65.00
   3¾ x 1¾", applied clear shell trim,

fluted silver plated holder, orig
  spoon 100.00
Sugar Shaker, 5¾" h, paneled, silver
  plated top 85.00
Syrup, Baby Inverted Thumbprint pattern, applied clear handle, pewter lid 125.00
Toothpick Holder, Fraizer pattern 85.00
Tumble–Up, carafe and tumbler, Inverted Thumbprint pattern 95.00
Tumbler
  3½" h, Inverted Thumbprint pattern . 45.00
  3¾" h, gold top band, enameled pink
    and white flowers, green leaves,
    gold scrolls 60.00
Vase
  3" h, 2¼" d, enameled white scrolls
    and dots, gold trim 40.00
  4⅝" h, 2⅝" h, Inverted Thumbprint
    pattern, applied crystal icicles 250.00
  4¾" h, 1⅞" d, lacy gold foliage dec,
    small green and white flowers,
    clear wafer foot, pr 110.00
  4¾" h, 3¾" d, emb Fleurette pattern,
    ground pontil, pr 175.00
  5" h, 2½" d, enameled green, yellow,
    and white oak leaves and acorns,
    lacy gold foliage 225.00
  9¼" h, 3½" d, enameled white daisies
    and leaves, pr 235.00
  9⅜" h, 3¾" d, enameled white daisies
    and leaves, pr 225.00
  10½" h, 5½" d, gold scrolls and
    leaves, small blue and white flow-
    ers, pedestal base 225.00

1892

CROWN MILANO

History: Crown Milano is an American art glass
produced by the Mt. Washington Glass Works,
New Bedford, Massachusetts. The original patent
was issued in 1886 to Frederick Shirley and Albert Steffin.

Normally it is an opaque white satin glass finished with light beige or ivory color ground embellished with fancy florals, decorations, and
elaborate heavy raised gold. When marked,
pieces carry an entwined CM with crown in purple enamel on the base. Sometimes paper labels
were used. The silver-plated mounts often have
"MW" impressed or a Pairpoint mark as both
Mt. Washington and Pairpoint supplied mountings.

Reference: John A. Shuman III, *The Collector's
Encyclopedia of American Art Glass,* Collector
Books, 1988, 1991 value update.

Museum: New Bedford Glass Museum, New
Bedford, MA.

**Vase, double bulbed elongated form, this-
tle motif, pink seed blossoms, elaborate
green, brown, and white leaf designs,
unsgd, 13¾" h, $1,210.00.**

Biscuit Jar, cov
  5½" h, squatty, round, opal ground,
    all over hand painted rose blos-
    soms, buds, leaves, and thorny
    stems, gold outlines, silver plated
    rim, bail, and cover imp "MW,"
    purple "CM" and crown mark ... 200.00
  6" h, painted Burmese ground, all
    over bamboo design, green, gold
    and brown enamel, ornate silver
    hardware 1,150.00
  6½" h, hobnail molded opal ground,
    hand painted, enameled, and ap-
    plied sea creature, red and yellow
    glass beads and gold outlines, silver
    plated rim, bail, and floral "MW"
    cover, applied butterfly, purple
    "CM," applied butterfly, purple
    "CM" mark 900.00
  7½" d, 5" h, pink and white enamel
    outlined blossoms, leaves, and
    thorny stems, opal jar, silver plated
    rim, bail, and butterfly mounted
    cov, base and cov sgd 880.00
Bride's Basket
  9" d, 4" h, multicolored roses, asters,
    and pansies, lusterless white
    ground, tricorn, folded and cut rim
    bowl, silver plated mounting, black
    crown mark, worn 500.00
  11" d, 11½" h, tricorn, tightly ruffled,
    six large pansies, purple and orange

tracery medallions, pale yellow interior, orig tricorn ftd stand sgd "Pairpoint" **2,950.00**

Bride's Bowl, 10" d, 2¾" h, eighty crimps, painted Burmese ground, four medallions of bouquets of pansies, leaves, and stems, gold scrolls, four single pansies **875.00**

Cracker Jar, autumn foliage, blue and purple berries and blossoms, beige gray traceries, silver plated cov, stamped "MW 537" **1,100.00**

Creamer and Sugar, 4½" h, opal ground, floral dec, applied reeded handles, purple "CM" and crown mark **200.00**

Cup and Saucer, glossy finish, slight vertical ribbing, all over tulip, rose, and cornflower dec, gold edges and highlights, applied handles with scrolls, numbered **785.00**

Ewer

11½" h, yellow shaded body, all over white enameled blossom clusters, connected by delicate raised gold leaves and vines, applied twisted handle, sgd **1,430.00**

12" h, white neck and body, background shadow dec of sepia colored scrolls and florals, spout with raised gold dec, abstract dec, twisted handled with brushed gold highlights, hundreds of individual dots (dark blue, light blue, rust, coral, pink, yellow, green, black, and gold) form stylized florals and geometric designs **1,750.00**

Jar, cov

4" h, squatty, star molded, custard colored, apricot chrysanthemums and jeweled starfish, silver plated rim, bail handle, and floral cov, imp "M.W. 4417" **660.00**

5¾" h, melon ribbed bowl, enamel dec, applied gold bead dec, silver plated rim, bail and crab motif cov, one bead missing, worn silver ... **550.00**

6¾" h, melon ribbed bowl, blue body, gold enhanced floral dec, silver plated rim and raised cov, unsgd **330.00**

10½" h, molded floral ground, pink, green, and white blossoms and broad leaves, elaborate silver plated Rogers Bros handled frame, some corrosion on stand **1,320.00**

Jardiniere, 6" h, 8" d, blue, yellow, and pink chrysanthemum blossoms, shiny pink ground, scrolling gilt borders, blue crown mark, numbered **385.00**

Pitcher, 12" h, hand painted, portrait of costumed couple in center, attributed to Frank Guba, scrolled gilt borders,

applied rope twist handle, red crown and wreath mark **660.00**

Rose Bowl

4¼" h, swirled gold enamel stylized sq floral, yellow shaded opal ground, unsigned **225.00**

4½" h, 5" d, shaded Burmese yellow to soft brown ground, purple, pink, and yellow orchids, green and brown foliage, sgd and numbered in purple **450.00**

Rose Jar, 8½" h, raised bulbed rim, molded stylized borders, eight–ribbed oval body, hand painted roses, gold dec, unsigned **500.00**

Salt and Pepper Shakers, pr, shiny finish, pink florals, gold stripes **225.00**

Sugar Shaker, 6" h, 2½" d, vertical ribs, sky–blue to white ground, stylized daisy blossoms and wispy branches, pewter top, Mount Washington **435.00**

Syrup, melon ribbed body, pale lime green ground, oak branch laden with leaves, autumn hues, raised gold outlines, dark oxidation on silver plated lid and repousse collar, attributed to Mount Washington **985.00**

Tumbler, 3¾" h, shiny finish, gold bow and swag enameling, red wreath mark, pr **500.00**

Vase, frosted body, burgundy rim, colorful autumn leaf and berry dec, 11½" h, $1,870.00. Photograph courtesy of Skinner, Inc.

Vase

4" h, amber and umber organic swirls, beaded pinwheel dec, ribbed and swirled lusterless ground, black crown and CM mark **525.00**

4½" h, 4¼" d, jeweled, gilt enameled apple blossoms, gold beaded dec, two applied handles, orig paper label on base, three beads missing . **665.00**

5½" h, squatty, pastel yellow body, gold outlined pink and lavender orchid blossoms, applied ribbed handles, sgd **990.00**

6" h, onion shape, twenty four molded swirls, narrow neck, four turned down folds, flower like mouth, four large fern leaves and shadow of buff colored fern leaves, white int., attached silver plated stand **385.00**

6¼" h, 3½" d, cylindrical, flaring ruffled top, pale blue body, blue traceries of wild roses, nine heavily raised gold wild roses, buds, stems, thorns, and branches, numbered on base **400.00**

8½" h

Ribbed oval, bulbed molded border motif, hand painted pink rose blossoms, unsgd **1,100.00**

Ribbed, yellow–amber body, autumn oak leaves and acorns, gold outlines, unsgd **1,540.00**

9" h, egg shape, all over fern dec, gold floral medallions, paper label **500.00**

9¾" h, extended thin neck, bulbous base, pink tinted body, raised gold and blue enameled pansy dec, one sgd, pr **1,870.00**

10½" h

Blackberry, green, brown, and gilt enamel blossoms, leaves, and berries, creamy yellow ground, unsgd **385.00**

Dragons, gilt enameled green and brown scrolling designs, winged dragons, shaded yellow lusterless body **2,530.00**

12¼" h, gilt enameled pink, green, and blue thistle dec, creamy lusterless ground, unsigned **1,450.00**

13½" h, gilt and silvered enameled Figi chrysanthemum dec, applied swirled thorny handle, shiny opal ground, red wreath and crown mark **770.00**

13¾" h, double bulbed elongated shape, pink seed thistle blossoms, green, brown, and white leaf dec, unsgd **1,210.00**

14½" h, white, yellow, amber, and brown cymbidium orchids, Burmese colored ground, unsgd **2,310.00**

CRUETS

History: Cruets are small glass bottles used to hold oil, vinegar, wine, and other liquids for use on the table or serving buffet. The high point of cruet use was during the Victorian era when a myriad of glass manufacturers made cruets in a wide assortment of patterns, colors, and sizes. All cruets had stoppers; most had handles. Cruets also have pouring lips or spouts. Perfume bottles, often the same size, do not have pouring lips.

Pattern glass manufacturers included cruets as part of their patterns. Later depression era manufacturers also included cruets in their lines, often offering different sizes for assorted purposes.

References: Dean L Murray, *More Cruets Only*, Killgore Graphics, Inc., 1973; William Heacock, *Encyclopedia of Victorian Colored Pattern Glass: Book 6, Oil Cruets From A To Z*, Antique Publications, 1981.

Additional Listings: Pattern Glass and specific glass categories such as Amberina, Cranberry, and Satin.

Amber, Cambridge, 4½" h, $18.00.

3" h, amberina, ball shape, tiny Inverted Thumbprint pattern, polished pontil, orig stopper **200.00**

4½" h, spatter, red and white spatter, white ground, tricorn top, applied clear handle **145.00**

5" h, satin, Diamond Quilted pattern, MOP, pink ground, applied clear thorn handle, orig clear stopper **575.00**

5¾" h

Amberina, Inverted Thumbprint pattern, applied amber handle, orig amber stopper, Mt Washington ... **325.00**

Esther pattern, emerald green, gold dec, orig stopper **150.00**

6" h, rose amber Inverted Thumbprint pattern, applied amber handle, faceted amber stopper **250.00**

6" h, 3½" w, cranberry, blown mold diamond quilted pattern, lightly ribbed, applied crystal handle, clear cut crystal stopper **125.00**

6½" h, peachblow, mahogany shading

to cherry red to cream, white lining, trefoil top, Wheeling 1,285.00
7" h Peachblow, acid finish, enameled fish, water lilies and cattails, gold outlines, applied amber handle, orig faceted amber stopper 1,200.00
Satin, yellow, raised diamond quilted pattern, applied frosted handle, faceted clear stopper 250.00
7" h, 3½" d, amberina, Inverted Thumbprint pattern, three petal top, applied amber handle, orig amber faceted cut stopper 200.00
7" h, 4" w, spangled, cranberry shading to clear, all over white spatter, silver flecks, enameled blue top band with white geometric design, applied clear handle, orig stopper, attributed to Hobbs, Brockunier Co 225.00
7¼" h, 3¼" d, sapphire blue, bulbous, round mouth, white enameled wreaths, scrolls, and dots, applied blue handle, orig blue ball stopper with matching enamel dec 125.00
8" h, 3⅛" d, amber, three petal top, blue enameled daisies, gold leaves, applied amber handle, amber ball stopper 110.00
8" h, 4" d, amber, four dimpled sides, gold trim, applied sapphire blue handle, sapphire blue bubble stopper .. 125.00
8¾" h, 3" d, sapphire blue, four petal top, emb swirls, applied fancy crystal handle, clear bubble stopper 90.00
9¼" h, 4½" d, amber, engraved butterfly and ferns, star cut base, applied blue handle, blue cut faceted stopper ... 200.00
9¾" h, 4⅞" d, teal blue, engraved ferns, star cut base, applied clear rope handle, clear cut faceted stopper 175.00
11" h, 3⅞" d, cranberry, three petal top, gold basket and scrolls dec, clear foot, handle, and bubble stopper ... 175.00

CUP PLATES

History: Many early cups and saucers were handleless, with deep saucers. The hot liquid was poured into the saucer and sipped from it. This necessitated another plate for the cup, the "cup plate."

The first cup plates made of pottery were of the Staffordshire variety. In the mid–1830s to the 1840s, glass cup plates were favored. Boston and Sandwich Glass Company was one of the main contributors to the lacy glass type.

It is extremely difficult to find glass cup plates in outstanding (mint) condition. Collectors expect some marks of usage, such as slight rim roughness, minor chipping (best if under the rim),

and in rarer patterns a portion of a scallop missing. Condition can detract from the value, but the color may drastically increase it. Most cup plates were made of clear glass, but many deeply colored green, blue, and purple cup plates are known, as well as some opaque white and colored cup plates.

Reference: Ruth Webb Lee and James H. Rose, *American Glass Cup Plates*, published by author, 1948, reprinted by Charles E. Tuttle Co., Inc. in 1985.

Notes: The numbers used are from the Lee–Rose book in which all plates are illustrated.

Prices are based on plates in "average" condition, and clear unless otherwise noted.

LR–82, Acorn & Leaves, silver opaque blue, fiery opalescent, $500.00.

Lee–Rose 2, 3⅝" d, amber, blown, eighteen ribs, midwestern origin 1,100.00
Lee–Rose 4–A, 4⅛" d, clear, swirled red and white latticinio, gold flecks in rim, attributed to Nicholas Lutz, Sandwich 150.00
Lee–Rose 10, 3⅜" d, clear, plain rim, New England 55.00
Lee–Rose 11, 2¹³⁄₁₆" d, clear, plain rim, New England origin, small shallow rim chips and roughness 60.00
Lee–Rose 13, 3¾" d, deep blue, A–type mold, plain rim, New England origin 60.00
Lee–Rose 21, 3⁷⁄₁₆" d, clear, 15 scallops with shelves rim, stars between shoulder fans, strawberry diamond center, New England origin, minor rim roughness 80.00
Lee–Rose 22–A, 3⁷⁄₁₆" d, clear, 15 scallops with shelves, circles between shoulder fans, six pointed star center, New England or Sandwich origin ... 85.00
Lee–Rose 22–B, 3⁷⁄₁₆" d, clear, 18 scallops with shelves, circles between shoulder fans, six pointed star center, pontil, New England origin, slight roughness 80.00

Lee–Rose 26, 3⁹⁄₁₆″ d, clear, 15 even scallops, eleven lance points center, attributed to Sandwich or New England Glass Co **150.00**

Lee–Rose 28, 3¼″ d, clear, 17 even scallops, twelve lance points, New England or Sandwich origin **30.00**

Lee–Rose 36, 3¼″ d, opal opaque, 17 even scallops, seven–stalk sheaf with rounded points, rosettes in spandrels between eight central leaves, New England origin **475.00**

Lee–Rose 37, 3¼″ d, opalescent, 17 even scallops, seven–stalk sheaf with rounded points, attributed to Sandwich or New England Glass Co, two heat checks in rim, light roughness . **150.00**

Lee–Rose 41–A, 3³⁄₁₆″ d, clear, 17 even scallops, six–stalk sheaf, radial lines dividing cross–hatched band, New England or Sandwich origin, minor roughness, near mint **190.00**

Lee–Rose 45, 3⁹⁄₁₆″ d, pale opalescent, 19 even scallops, rope top and bottom, wide cap ring, attributed to Sandwich or New England Glass Co, mold overfill, slag deposit near center **100.00**

Lee–Rose 46, 3½″ d, lavender, 15 even scallops, geometric shoulder design, strawberry diamond pattern, eastern origin **125.00**

Lee–Rose 51, 3¾″ d, clear, pontil, 15 scallops with points between, stippled center background, New England origin, moderate rim roughness, few shallow flakes **175.00**

Lee–Rose 52, 3¾″ d, opalescent, 15 scallops with points between, stippled, eastern origin **200.00**

Lee–Rose 58, 3⅜″ d, cloudy, unlisted color, plain rope, band of radial lines on inner and outer edge of underside of shoulder, bull's eyes on plain band, waffle center, eastern origin **275.00**

Lee–Rose 60, 3⅜″ d, clear, plain rope, cross–hatched background on underside of shoulder, eastern origin **200.00**

Lee–Rose 61, 3⅜″ d, opalescent, 48 even scallops, waffle center, attributed to New England Glass Co **250.00**

Lee–Rose 70, 3⁷⁄₁₆″ d, clear, plain rope, midwestern origin **125.00**

Lee–Rose 75–A, 3¹³⁄₁₆″ d, clear, rope rim top and bottom, strawberry diamond between border sheaves, attributed to New England Glass Co, one tiny rim flake **70.00**

Lee–Rose 79, 3¾″ d, pink tint, rope top and bottom, rope table ring with tiny feet, New England origin **50.00**

Lee–Rose 80, 3¾″ d, opalescent, rope top and bottom, plain table ring, New England origin **250.00**

Lee–Rose 81, 3¾″ d, fiery red opalescent, rope top and bottom, rope table ring with tiny feet, New England origin **350.00**

Lee–Rose 82, 3⅝″ d, clear, plain rim, five–pointed star center, attributed to New England
Opalescent, normal rim roughness .. **400.00**
Opaque blue **275.00**

Lee–Rose 88, 3¹¹⁄₁₆″ d, deep opalescent opaque, rope top, shoulder baskets, pinwheel with stars center, attributed to Sandwich or New England Glass Co, two minute flakes under rim ... **175.00**

Lee–Rose 95, 3⅝″ d, opal opaque, ten sided, rope top and bottom, New England origin, tiny under rim nick **150.00**

Lee–Rose 100, 3¼″ d, clear, plain rim, stippled background, attributed to Philadelphia area, unseen flake under rim, normal mold roughness **75.00**

Lee–Rose 107, 3⅜″ d, clear, plain rim, attributed to Philadelphia area, slight underfill, trace of mold roughness .. **50.00**

Lee–Rose 120, 3¹⁄₁₆″ d, clear, lacy, 30 even scallops, stippled, midwestern origin **165.00**

Lee–Rose 121, 3¹⁄₁₆″ d, clear, lacy, porthole shoulder pattern, stippled, midwestern origin, slight rim roughness, two minor nicks, mold overfill **100.00**

Lee–Rose 135, 3⁷⁄₁₆″ d, clear, 24 bull's eyes, points between, peacock feather pattern, midwestern origin .. **75.00**

Lee–Rose 148–C, 2⅞″ d, clear, 17 scallops, points between, one point and one scallop missing, midwestern origin **75.00**

Lee–Rose 150–B, 2¹⁵⁄₁₆″ d, clear, plain rim, rope on bottom, midwestern origin **50.00**

Lee–Rose 163, 3¼″ d, light green, 34 scallops, radial lines beneath, irregular stippling, midwestern origin **65.00**

Lee–Rose 179, 3⁷⁄₁₆″ d, lavender, 10 scallops, rope top and bottom, attributed to Philadelphia area **125.00**

Lee–Rose 183–B, 3½″ d, deep blue, octagonal rim, 7 scallops between corners, midwestern origin **90.00**

Lee–Rose 200, 3⅛″ d, clear, 96 sawtooth scallops, midwestern origin ... **35.00**

Lee–Rose 215, 3⅝″ d, clear, Scotch Plaid, 60 even scallops, Curling, Ft Pitt Glass Works, minor rim roughness **100.00**

Lee–Rose 225–A, 3½″ d, clear, 12 large scallops, 4 small scallops between, attributed to Philadelphia area **50.00**

Lee–Rose 242–A, 3½″ d, black amethyst, lacy, 60 even scallops, eastern origin, mold underfill and overfill .. **650.00**

Lee–Rose 247, 3⁷⁄₁₆" d, emerald green, lacy, twelve sided, 60 scallops, attributed to Sandwich or New England Glass Co, small chip on one scallop **750.00**

Lee–Rose 253, 3⁹⁄₁₆" d, bluish–green, Roman Rosette, 8 large serrated scallops, points between, midwestern origin, two very small rim nicks **300.00**

Lee–Rose 255, 3⅝" d, amethyst tint, 24 bold scallops, divided by pairs of small scallops, Sandwich origin **20.00**

Lee–Rose 258, 3⅜" d, cloudy, 76 even scallops, attributed to Sandwich, minute rim roughness **70.00**

Lee–Rose 259, 3⁷⁄₁₆" d, clear, 12 large stippled scallops, points between, eastern origin, small chip on one point and one scallop, normal mold roughness **85.00**

Lee–Rose 276, 3⁷⁄₁₆" d, blue, lacy, 55 even scallops, arcs of central quadrants outlined in heavy dots, dots in centers of central diamond–shaped figures, coarse rope table ring, Boston and Sandwich Glass Co, slight opalescent bloom **325.00**

Lee–Rose 279, 2⅞" d, clear, lacy, 24 scallops, points between, rope band on shoulder, eastern origin
Light green, two chipped scallops .. **250.00**
Olive green, unlisted color, several small rim nicks **90.00**

Lee–Rose 284, 3³⁄₁₆" d, clear, 24 large bull's eyes divided by points, Philadelphia origin, one shallow chip, minute rim roughness **250.00**

Lee–Rose 291, 3" d, 62 even scallops, stippled shoulder and center background, unknown origin
Amethyst **300.00**
Medium blue, minor rim nicks **200.00**

Lee–Rose 310–B, 3⁷⁄₁₆" d, opalescent, 63 even scallops, attributed to Philadelphia area, some rim roughness .. **85.00**

Lee–Rose 311, 3⅝" d, amber stain on center design and border triangles, 23 bold scallops, pairs of smaller scallops between, Sandwich origin, 2 scallops missing **300.00**

Lee–Rose 319, 3⁵⁄₁₆" d, clear, 66 even scallops, unknown origin, one scallop missing, five have small flakes, normal mold roughness **100.00**

Lee–Rose 343–B, 3⁷⁄₁₆" d, clear, plain, dotted below, fire polished, attributed to Philadelphia area **45.00**

Lee–Rose 347, 3¾" d, yellow, 65 even scallops, unknown origin **115.00**

Lee–Rose 383, 3⅞" d, electric blue, unlisted color, 40 points, curved shoul-

der lines form six complete squares, eastern origin, minor roughness **50.00**

Lee–Rose 388, 3⁵⁄₁₆" d, opaque white, plain rim, central star, attributed to Philadelphia area **35.00**

Lee–Rose 399, 3⁵⁄₁₆" d, clear, eastern origin, normal mold roughness **60.00**

Lee–Rose 412, 3³⁄₁₆" d, clear, ten sided, star center, Sandwich origin **95.00**

Lee–Rose 425, 3⅜" d, deep amethyst, unlisted color, 9 large scallops with hearts between, three round dots on each scallop, strawberry diamond band, eastern origin, trace of mold roughness **1,600.00**

Lee–Rose 430, 3⅜" d, clear, 9 large scallops, hearts between, diamond diapering between shoulder hearts, eastern origin **75.00**

Lee–Rose 433, 4⅛" d, clear, 11 large scallops, hearts between, unknown origin, two chips, mold roughness .. **75.00**

Lee–Rose 440–B, 3½" d, 24 large scallops, two smaller scallops between, Valentine center, attributed to Sandwich
Cobalt blue, unlisted color, minor rim nicks **150.00**
Gray–blue, nine scallops flaked, one missing **100.00**

Lee–Rose 445, 3⁷⁄₁₆" d, 24 bull's eyes, points between, midwestern origin
Clear, two rim chips, minor roughness **70.00**
Cloudy, four bull's eyes missing, five chips, mold roughness **265.00**

Lee–Rose 455, 3⅞" d, opalescent, 48 even scallops, twelve hearts on shoulder, Sandwich origin **265.00**

Lee–Rose 459–M, 3¾" d, jade opaque, 43 even scallops, twelve hearts on shoulder, Sandwich origin, near mint **450.00**

Lee–Rose 465–F, 3⅜" d, violet blue, 63 even scallops, thirteen hearts on shoulder, Sandwich origin, one scallop missing, 5 tipped **130.00**

Lee–Rose 465–J, 3½" d, opalescent, 48 even scallops, thirteen hearts on shoulder, Sandwich origin, minor rim nicks **40.00**

Lee–Rose 510, 3" d, peacock blue, 22 scallops, points between, eighteen rays in central sunburst, eastern origin, attributed to Sandwich, minor rim nicks **200.00**

Lee–Rose 516, 3¼" d, amethyst, 66 even scallops, twenty rays in central sunburst, attributed to Sandwich, rim chip on underside, surface spalls, rim roughness **425.00**

Lee–Rose 562, 3⁷⁄₁₆" d, clear, Henry Clay, 18 large scallops, two smaller scallops between, Sandwich origin . **75.00**

Lee–Rose 565–B, sapphire blue, unlisted color, Henry Clay, 51 even scallops, four shields on shoulder, unsymmetrically placed pomegranates in lower left cornucopias, Sandwich origin, several minor rim nicks **70.00**

Lee–Rose 568, 3⁷⁄₁₆″ d, clear, Harrison, 67 even scallops, swags and blank lozenges on shoulder, attributed to Sandwich, one scallop tipped, mold roughness **50.00**

Lee–Rose 576, 3⁹⁄₁₆″ d, medium blue, Victoria, 25 large scallops, two smaller scallops between, Sandwich origin **85.00**

Lee–Rose 580, 3¾″ d, clear, Victoria and Albert, 56 even scallops, English origin **250.00**

Lee–Rose 580–B, 3¾″ d, clear, 58 even scallops, English origin, underfill covering 1½ of rim **275.00**

Lee–Rose 582, 3¾″ d, medium blue, Jenny Lind, 56 even scallops, English origin **2,800.00**

Lee–Rose 586–B, 3⁷⁄₁₆″ d, clear, Ringgold, Palo Alto, stippled ground, small letters, Philadelphia area, 1847–48, trace of mold roughness . .   **650.00**

Lee–Rose 595, 3¼″ d, amber, unlisted color, attributed to Sandwich, three small mold spalls, one scallop missing, six scallops tipped, one spall on underside, average mold roughness .   **265.00**

Lee–Rose 605–A, 3½″ d, clear, octagonal, 7 scallops between corners, ship, stippled and plain rope rigging, three scallops lightly tipped **275.00**

Lee–Rose 610–A, 3⁵⁄₈″ d, yellow tint, unlisted color, 23 bold scallops, two smaller scallops between, ship, minor rim nicks **25.00**

Lee–Rose 615–A, 3³⁄₈″ d, clear, Constitution, 25 scallops, points between, unknown origin **650.00**

Lee–Rose 635, 3⁷⁄₁₆″ d, medium green, unlisted color, Maid of the Mist, plain rim, large circles on shoulder, small rim chips **700.00**

Lee–Rose 643, 3⁹⁄₁₆″ d, clear, Bunker Hill Monument, 53 even scallops, drape pattern shoulder, Sandwich origin **35.00**

Lee–Rose 650, 3¹¹⁄₁₆″ d, pale blue, eagle, rope top and bottom, New England origin, slight mold underfill to edge **425.00**

Lee–Rose 653, 3″ d, clear, plain rim, acorns on shoulder, central eagle in laurel wreath, attributed to midwestern area, large chip **125.00**

Lee–Rose 668, 3¹⁄₁₆″ d, clear, 56 even scallops, sawtooth design around

central eagle, attributed to midwestern area **100.00**

Lee–Rose 672, opalescent, eagle, minor rim nicks, small heat check on the edge **50.00**

Lee–Rose 676, 3¹¹⁄₁₆″ d, clear, 60 even scallops, "Fort Pitt" in banner held by central eagle, Curling, Ft Pitt Glass Works **65.00**

Lee–Rose 691, 3³⁄₁₆″ d, clear, 24 large beads with reels between, lyre center, midwestern origin, mold roughness .   **175.00**

Lee–Rose 691–A, 3³⁄₁₆″ d, clear, 42 even scallops, lyre center, midwestern origin, normal mold roughness **450.00**

Lee–Rose 695, 3″ d, clear, 42 even scallops, nine–bee beehive, midwestern origin, two scallops tipped, normal mold roughness **125.00**

CUSTARD GLASS

History: Custard glass was developed in England in the early 1880s. Harry Northwood made the first American custard glass at his Indiana, Pennsylvania, factory in 1898.

From 1898 until 1915, many manufacturers produced custard glass patterns, e.g., Dugan Glass, Fenton, A. H. Heisey Glass Co., Jefferson Glass, Northwood, Tarentum Glass, and U.S. Glass. Cambridge and McKee continued the production of custard glass into the Depression.

The ivory or creamy yellow custard color is achieved by adding uranium salts to the molten hot glass. The chemical content makes the glass glow when held under a black light. The higher the amount of uranium, the more luminous the color. Northwood's custard glass has the smallest amount of uranium, creating an ivory color; Heisey used more, creating a deep yellow color.

Custard glass was made in patterned tableware pieces. It also was made as souvenir items and novelty pieces. Souvenir pieces are marked with place names or hand painted decorations, e.g., flowers. Patterns of custard glass often were highlighted in gold, enamel colors, and stains.

References: William Heacock, *Encyclopedia Of Victorian Colored Pattern Glass, Book IV: Custard Glass From A to Z*, Peacock Publications, 1980; William Heacock, James Measell and Berry Wiggins, *Harry Northwood: The Early Years 1881–1900*, Antique Publications, 1990.

Reproduction Alert: L. G. Wright Glass Co. has reproduced pieces in the Argonaut Shell and Grape and Cable patterns. It also introduced new patterns, such as Floral and Grape and Vintage Band. Mosser reproduced toothpicks in Argonaut Shell, Chrysanthemum Sprig, and Inverted Fan & Feather.

Banana Boat
  Geneva, Northwood, green trim **135.00**
  Grape & Thumbprint, Northwood .. **375.00**
  Maple Leaf, Northwood **200.00**
Berry Bowl, master
  Argonaut Shell, Northwood, dec,
    oval, marked "Northwood" **245.00**
  Beaded Circle, Northwood **185.00**
  Cherry & Scale, Fenton **115.00**
  Chrysanthemum Sprig, Northwood,
    dec **195.00**
  Diamond with Peg, Jefferson **225.00**
  Everglades, Northwood **200.00**
  Fan, Dugan **135.00**
  Geneva, Northwood, green trim, 8½"
    l oval **95.00**
  Georgia Gem, Tarentum, dec **72.00**
  Inverted Fan & Feather, Northwood . **225.00**
  Louis XV, Northwood, gold trim **135.00**
  Maple Leaf, Northwood **250.00**
  Ring Band, Heisey **115.00**
  Victoria, Tarentum **165.00**
  Winged Scroll, Heisey **175.00**
Berry Set
  Argonaut Shell, Northwood, master
    and six sauces, seven pcs **525.00**
  Chrysanthemum Sprig, Northwood,
    11" oval unsigned master, six indi-
    viduals sgd "Northwood" script,
    seven pcs **675.00**
  Everglades, Northwood, master and
    six sauces, seven pcs **725.00**
  Grape and Gothic Arches, North-
    wood, master and six sauces **495.00**
  Intaglio, Northwood, 9" master, five
    pcs **400.00**
  Victoria, Tarentum, master and six
    sauces **625.00**
Bowl
  Chrysanthemum Sprig, Northwood,
    10½" d **135.00**
  Delaware, US Glass, 5½" d **48.00**
  Grape and Cable, Northwood, 7½" d,
    basketweave exterior, nutmeg stain **50.00**
Butter, cov
  Argonaut Shell, Northwood **250.00**
  Beaded Circle, Northwood **275.00**
  Cherry & Scale, Fenton **225.00**
  Chrysanthemum Sprig, Northwood,
    6" h **275.00**
  Everglades, Northwood **375.00**
  Fan, Dugan **215.00**
  Geneva, Northwood, green and red
    trim **135.00**
  Georgia Gem, Tarentum, enamel dec **135.00**
  Grape and Cable, Northwood **225.00**
  Intaglio, Northwood **175.00**
  Inverted Fan & Feather, Northwood . **325.00**
  Louis XV, Northwood **120.00**
  Maple Leaf, Northwood **200.00**
  Ribbed Drape, Jefferson **265.00**
  Ring Band, Heisey **185.00**

Victoria, Tarentum **280.00**
Wild Bouquet, Northwood **325.00**
Winged Scroll, Heisey **175.00**
Calling Card Tray, Vermont, US Glass,
  7½" d **100.00**
Celery
  Chrysanthemum Sprig, Northwood . **550.00**
  Georgia Gem, Tarentum **175.00**
  Ivorina Verda, Heisey **285.00**
  Ring Band, Heisey **300.00**
  Victoria, Tarentum, gold trim **250.00**
Cigarette Jar, Ivorina Verda, Heisey ... **150.00**
Cologne Bottle
  Ivorina Verde, Heisey **240.00**
  Northwood Grape, Northwood, nut-
    meg stain, orig stopper, marked
    "N" **400.00**
Compote, Intaglio, Northwood, ftd
  7½" d **200.00**
  9" d **365.00**
Condiment Set
  Chrysanthemum Sprig, Northwood,
    cruet, pr salt and pepper shakers,
    tray **1,150.00**
  Creased Bale, Dithridge, four pcs ... **180.00**
  Ring Band, Heisey, jelly compote,
    toothpick, pr salt and pepper shak-
    ers, tray **450.00**
Condiment Tray
  Chrysanthemum Sprig, Northwood . **600.00**
  Ring Band, Heisey **95.00**
Cracker Jar, cov, Grape & Cable, North-
  wood, two handles **600.00**
Creamer
  Argonaut Shell, Northwood **100.00**
  Beaded Circle, Northwood **125.00**
  Cherry & Scale, Fenton **110.00**
  Chrysanthemum Sprig, Northwood,
    blue body, gold dec **385.00**
  Delaware, US Glass, rose dec **65.00**
  Diamond with Peg, Jefferson **75.00**
  Fan, Dugan **95.00**
  Fluted Scrolls, Heisey **65.00**
  Georgia Gem, Tarentum, breakfast
    size **35.00**
  Grape and Cable, Northwood **100.00**
  Heart with Thumbprint, Tarentum .. **80.00**
  Intaglio, Northwood **100.00**
  Inverted Fan & Feather, Northwood . **135.00**
  Jackson, Northwood **65.00**
  Jefferson Optic, Jefferson **125.00**
  Louis XV, Northwood **75.00**
  Maple Leaf, Northwood **100.00**
  Northwood Grape, Northwood, nut-
    meg stain **100.00**
  Ribbed Drape, Jefferson **115.00**
  Ring Band, Heisey **95.00**
  Vermont, US Glass Co **95.00**
  Victoria, Tarentum **95.00**
  Wild Bouquet, Northwood **130.00**
  Winged Scroll, Heisey **65.00**

Cruet
Argonaut Shell, Northwood, orig stopper 425.00
Chrysanthemum Sprig, Northwood, clear stopper, goofus type gold dec 60.00
Georgia Gem, Tarentum, orig stopper 250.00
Intaglio, Northwood, green dec 400.00
Inverted Fan & Feather, Northwood . 600.00
Louis XV, Northwood 250.00
Maple Leaf, Northwood 900.00
Ribbed Drape, Jefferson 350.00
Ring Band, Heisey 300.00
Wild Bouquet, Northwood, enamel dec 550.00
Winged Scroll, Heisey 185.00
Custard Cup, Winged Scroll, Heisey .. 50.00
Dresser Tray
Northwood Grape, Northwood 225.00
Winged Scroll, Heisey, hand painted dec 165.00
Ferner, Grape & Cable, Northwood, 7½" d, ftd 150.00
Goblet
Beaded Swag, Heisey 50.00
Grape and Gothic Arches, Northwood, nutmeg stain 65.00
Hair Receiver
Georgia Gem, Tarentum, souvenir .. 45.00
Winged Scroll, Heisey 125.00
Humidor, Winged Scroll, Heisey 175.00
Ice Cream Bowl, individual size
Fan, Dugan 45.00
Peacock & Urn, Northwood 35.00

Jelly Compote, Chrysanthemum Sprig, Northwood, 5" h, $75.00.

Jelly Compote
Argonaut Shell, Northwood 160.00
Beaded Circle, Northwood 350.00
Chyrsanthemum Sprig, Northwood . 75.00
Geneva, Northwood 95.00
Intaglio, Northwood, green trim 100.00
Inverted Fan & Feather, Northwood . 315.00
Maple Leaf, Northwood 375.00
Ribbed Drape, Jefferson 175.00

Ring Band, Heisey 172.00
Match Holder, Winged Scroll, Heisey . 165.00
Mug
Diamond with Peg, Jefferson, souvenir 48.00
Punty Band, Heisey 50.00
Ring Band, Heisey, souvenir 45.00
Napkin Ring, Diamond with Peg, Jefferson, souvenir 150.00
Nappy
Northwood Grape, Northwood 50.00
Prayer Rug, Imperial, 6" d 50.00
Winged Scroll, Heisey 50.00
Olive Dish, Winged Scroll, Heisey ... 45.00
Pickle Dish
Beaded Swag, Heisey 250.00
Vermont, US Glass 35.00
Pin Tray
Chrysanthemum Sprig, Northwood . 50.00
Delaware, US Glass, rose dec 40.00
Grape & Thumbprint, Northwood .. 135.00
Ivorina Verde, Heisey 190.00
Pitcher, water
Argonaut Shell, Northwood 300.00
Beaded Circle, Northwood 425.00
Cherry and Scale, Fenton 325.00
Chrysanthemum Sprig, Northwood . 375.00
Diamond with Peg, Jefferson, 7½" h, tankard 250.00
Everglades, Northwood 600.00
Fan, Dugan 260.00
Georgia Gem, Tarentum, gold dec . 315.00
Intaglio, Northwood, gold and green 350.00
Inverted Fan and Feather, Northwood 400.00
Louis XV, Northwood 225.00
Maple Leaf, Northwood 345.00
Ribbed Drape, Jefferson 265.00
Ring Band, Heisey 235.00
Vermont, US Glass 250.00
Victoria, Tarentum 350.00
Winged Scroll, Heisey, tankard 235.00
Plate
Grape & Cable, Northwood, 8" d .. 70.00
Prayer Rug, Imperial, 7½" d 20.00
Three Fruits, Northwood, 7½" d 22.00
Powder Jar, cov
Georgia Gem, Tarentum, souvenir .. 55.00
Ivorina Verde, Heisey 50.00
Punch Bowl, matching base, Grape & Cable, Northwood 800.00
Punch Cup
Diamond with Peg, Jefferson 60.00
Grape & Cable, Northwood 48.00
Inverted Fan and Feather, Northwood 250.00
Ring Band, Heisey 60.00
Ring Tree, Delaware, US Glass, 4" h .. 50.00
Rose Bowl, Grape and Gothic Arches, Northwood 75.00
Salt and Pepper Shakers, pr, orig tops
Argonaut Shell, Northwood 350.00
Beaded Circle, Northwood 255.00
Carnelian, Northwood 450.00

Chrysanthemum Sprig, Northwood . 250.00
Diamond with Peg, Jefferson 95.00
Fluted Scrolls, Heisey 125.00
Fluted Scrolls with Flower Band,
   Northwood 130.00
Geneva, Northwood 175.00
Georgia Gem, Tarentum 80.00
Heart, Northwood 160.00
Intaglio, Northwood 165.00
Inverted Fan & Feather, Northwood . 450.00
Louis XV, Northwood 215.00
Maple Leaf, Northwood 500.00
Punty Band, Heisey 185.00
Ribbed Drape, Jefferson 175.00
Ring Band, Heisey 115.00
Trailing Vine, Couderspot Glass 150.00
Winged Scroll, Heisey 175.00
Salt, open, Chrysanthemum Sprig,
   Northwood 100.00
Sauce Dish
   Argonaut Shell, Northwood, 5⅛" l,
      3½" w, 3⅛" h, oval, gold and green
      trim, marked "Northwood" 45.00
   Beaded Circle, Northwood 55.00
   Beaded Swag, Heisey, souvenir 70.00
   Cane Insert, Tarentum 30.00
   Chrysanthemum Sprig, Northwood . 75.00
   Delaware, US Glass, rose dec 45.00
   Diamond with Peg, Jefferson 35.00
   Everglades, Northwood 65.00
   Fan, Dugan 40.00
   Geneva, Northwood, oval 35.00
   Georgia Gem, Tarentum 30.00
   Intaglio, Northwood 35.00
   Inverted Fan & Feather, Northwood . 50.00
   Jefferson Optic, Jefferson, gold dec . 15.00
   Louis XV, Northwood, gold trim 40.00
   Maple Leaf, Northwood 80.00
   Peacock and Urn, Northwood 40.00
   Ribbed Drape, Jefferson 42.50
   Ring Band, Heisey, gold and rose dec,
      marked 40.00
   Victoria, Tarentum 50.00
   Wild Bouquet, Northwood 50.00
   Winged Scroll, Heisey, 4½" d 35.00
Spooner
   Argonaut Shell, Northwood 110.00
   Beaded Circle, Northwood 120.00
   Chrysanthemum Sprig, Northwood,
      blue body, gold trim 220.00
   Diamond with Peg, Jefferson 95.00
   Everglades, Northwood 135.00
   Fan, Dugan 75.00
   Geneva, Northwood 50.00
   Georgia Gem, Tarentum, floral dec . 60.00
   Grape and Cable, Northwood, nut-
      meg stain 95.00
   Intaglio, Northwood 85.00
   Inverted Fan & Feather, Northwood . 115.00
   Louis XV, Northwood 60.00
   Maple Leaf, Northwood 85.00
   Ribbed Drape, Jefferson 65.00

Ring Band, Heisey 90.00
Trailing Vine, Couderspot Glass, blue
   body 65.00
Victoria, Tarentum 60.00
Wild Bouquet, Northwood 70.00
Winged Scroll, Heisey 65.00
Sugar, cov
   Argonaut Shell, Northwood 160.00
   Beaded Circle, Northwood 175.00
   Cherry & Scale, Fenton 125.00
   Chrysanthemum Sprig, Northwood,
      blue body, gold dec 325.00
   Diamond with Peg, Jefferson 100.00
   Everglades, Northwood 150.00
   Fan, Dugan 95.00
   Fluted Scrolls, Heisey 150.00
   Geneva, Northwood 155.00
   Georgia Gem, Tarentum, floral dec . 120.00
   Heart and Thumbprint, Tarentum, in-
      dividual 75.00
   Intaglio, Northwood 115.00
   Inverted Fan & Feather, Northwood . 175.00
   Jefferson Optic, Jefferson 140.00
   Louis XV, Northwood, gold dec 90.00
   Ribbed Drape, Jefferson 145.00
   Ring Band, Heisey, 6½" h, 4" d, red
      roses, green leaves, gold trim,
      marked 118.00
   Victoria, Tarentum 175.00
   Winged Scroll, Heisey 160.00
Syrup, orig top
   Geneva, Northwood 250.00
   Ring Band, Heisey 300.00
   Winged Scroll, Heisey 350.00
Toothpick Holder
   Argonaut Shell, Northwood 275.00
   Chrysanthemum Sprig, Northwood,
      blue body, gold trim 300.00
   Diamond with Peg, Jefferson 65.00
   Georgia Gem, Tarentum, souvenir . . 40.00
   Inverted Fan & Feather, Northwood . 350.00
   Maple Leaf, Northwood 550.00
   Punty Band, Heisey, souvenir 65.00
   Ribbed Drape, Jefferson 150.00
   Ring Band, Heisey, souvenir 45.00
   Vermont, US Glass, green dec 135.00
   Wild Bouquet, Northwood, blue
      body, enameled dec 100.00
   Winged Scroll, Heisey 100.00
Tumbler
   Argonaut Shell, Northwood 85.00
   Cherry & Scale, Fenton 40.00
   Chrysanthemum Sprig, Northwood,
      set of six 300.00
   Delaware, US Glass, green dec 50.00
   Diamond with Peg, Jefferson 45.00
   Fan, Dugan 50.00
   Fluted Scrolls, Heisey 40.00
   Geneva, Northwood, 3⅞" h, 3" d
      Gold trim, green custard ground . 60.00
      Red and green trim 50.00
   Georgia Gem, Tarentum 48.50

Grape and Cable, Northwood, nutmeg stain	60.00
Grape and Gothic Arches, Northwood, gold, carnival finish	55.00
Intaglio, Northwood, green trim	40.00
Inverted Fan and Feather, Northwood	100.00
Jackson, Northwood	30.00
Louis XV, Northwood, gold trim	55.00
Maple Leaf, Northwood	90.00
Prayer Rug, Imperial	80.00
Punty Band, Heisey, souvenir	35.00
Ribbed Drape, Jefferson	75.00
Ring Band, Heisey	65.00
Vermont, US Glass, blue dec	55.00
Victoria, Tarentum	65.00
Wild Bouquet, Northwood	25.00
Winged Scroll, Heisey	65.00

Vase

Diamond Peg, Jefferson Glass Co	
6" h, souvenir	65.00
8" h	100.00
Grape and Cable, Northwood, 3½" h	48.00
Grape Arbor, Northwood, nutmeg stain	65.00
Prayer Rug, Imperial	50.00
Winged Scroll, Heisey, 9" h	185.00
Whimsey, hat, Ring Band, Heisey	275.00
Whiskey Shot Glass, Diamond Peg, Jefferson, souvenir	48.00

Wine

Beaded Swag, Heisey, advertising	75.00
Diamond with Peg, Jefferson	45.00
Punty Band, Heisey, souvenir	50.00

CUT GLASS, AMERICAN

History: Glass is cut by the process of grinding decoration into the glass by means of abrasive–carrying metal wheels or stone wheels. A very ancient craft, it was revived in 1600 by Bohemians and spread through Europe, to Great Britain, and to America.

American cut glass came of age at the Centennial Exposition in 1876 and the World Columbian Exposition in 1893. The American public recognized American cut glass to be exceptional in quality and workmanship. America's most significant output of this high quality glass occurred from 1880 to 1917, a period now known as the "Brilliant Period."

The Early Period was from 1765 to 1829 and is rare. Designs of this period reflect the influence of English and Irish cut glass. Motifs include prisms, flutes, single star, diamonds, and a simple form of the strawberry diamond. The Middle Period from 1830 to 1870 produced simple, typically American designs in reaction to European patterns. Flute cuttings, engraved fine lines, etch-

ing, engraved historical scenes and cut colored glass were predominate. Brilliant Period patterns are much more complex and usually cut deeper into the blank. Motifs include prisms, notched prisms, hobstars, curved miter splits, fans, and pin wheels, as well as stars and blocks and many design components of the earlier periods.

All cut glass blanks were hand blown until 1902. The H. C. Fry Glass Company of Rochester, Pennsylvania, produced the first pressed blanks in 1902.

About the 1890s some companies began adding an acid–etched "signature" to their glass. This signature may be the actual company name, its logo, or chosen symbol. Today, signed pieces can command a premium over unsigned pieces since the signature clearly establishes the origin. Signatures are often rather pale and may be difficult to find.

However, caution should be exercised in regard to signature identification. Objects with forged signatures have been in existence for some time. To check for authenticity, run your finger tip or finger nail lightly over the area with the signature. As a general rule, a genuine signature cannot be felt; a forged signature exhibits a raised surface.

Many companies never used the acid–etched signature on the glass and may or may not have affixed paper labels to the items originally. Dorflinger Glass and the Meriden Glass Co. made cut glass of the highest quality, yet never acid–etched a signature on the glass. Furthermore, cut glass made before the 1890s was not signed. Many of these polished items, cut on blown blanks, were of excellent quality and often won awards at exhibitions.

Consequently, if collectors restrict themselves to signed pieces only, many beautiful pieces of the highest quality glass and workmanship will be missed.

References: Bill and Louise Boggess, *Collecting American Brilliant Cut Glass 1876–1916*, Schiffer Publishing, Ltd., 1992; City of Corning, New York, Centennial, *Corning, N. Y., 1891, Illustrated*, Corning–Painted Post Historical Society, 1990; E. S. Farrar & J. S. Spillman, *The Complete Cut & Engraved Glass Of Corning*, Crown Publishers [Corning Museum of Glass monograph], 1979; John Feller, *Dorflinger: America's Finest Glass, 1852–1921*, Antique Publications, 1988; J. Michael Pearson, *Encyclopedia Of American Cut & Engraved Glass*, Volumes I to III, published by author, 1975; Albert C. Revi, *American Cut & Engraved Glass*, Thomas Nelson, Inc., 1965; Martha Louise Swan, *American and Engraved Glass*, Wallace–Homestead, 1986; H. Weiner & F. Lipkowitz, *Rarities In American Cut Glass*, Collectors House of Books, 1975.

Periodicals: *Antique Glass Quarterly*, Rudi Publishing, P. O. Box 1364, Iowa City, IA 52244;

Glass Collector's Digest, Antique Publications, P. O. Box 553, Mariette, OH 45750–0553.

Collectors' Club: American Cut Glass Association, 3228 South Blvd, Suite 271, P. O. Box 1775, Edmond, OK 73013.

Museums: High Museum of Art, Atlanta, GA; Historical Glass Museum, Redlands, CA; Huntington Galleries, Huntington, WV; Lightner Museum, St. Augustine, FL; The Chrysler Museum, Norfolk VA; The Corning Museum of Glass, Corning, NY; The Toledo Museum Of Art, Toledo, OH.

Serving Plate, Kensington pattern, Hawkes, centrally sgd, American Brilliant period, 13" d, $715.00. Photograph courtesy of Skinner, Inc.

Ambrosia Bowl, 12" d, 10¼" h, panel
 and cut fruit design **140.00**
Atomizer
 4" h, 2½" sq, Harvard pattern, gold
  washed top **125.00**
 6½" h, all over cutting, marked
  "DeVilbiss," Brilliant Period **125.00**
 8" h, 2½" sq x 4" h cut glass perfume
  bottle, Harvard pattern, gold
  washed atomizer **100.00**
Banana Bowl, 11" d, 6½" h, Harvard
 pattern, hobstar bottom **210.00**
Basket, 11" h, 8" l, Harvard, hobstars
 and prism cut **475.00**
Bell
 5¾" h, dinner size, hobstars, fans,
  strawberry diamond **255.00**
 6¾" h, strawberry diamond and fan
  sharply cut, pattern cut on knob at
  end of stem as well **550.00**
Berry Set
 Cluster pattern, master bowl and six
  sauces, hobnail, hobstar, star,
  strawberry diamond, Eggington,
  seven pcs **495.00**
 Regis pattern, master bowl, eleven

sauces, sgd "Libbey" with saber,
 twelve pcs **550.00**
Bishop's Hat Bowl, 12" d, 5" h, intaglio
 diamond point cut, sgd "Tuthill" ... **275.00**
Bon Bon, 8" d, 2" h, Broadway pattern,
 Huntly, minor flakes **125.00**
Bone Dish, 7 x 5", Russian pattern, crescent shape, set of 4 .... **355.00**
Bowl
 5" d, cross–cut diamond and fan, pr **70.00**
 7" d, sq, Russian pattern, rayed center **605.00**
 7" d, 2" h
  Figured blank, hobstars and fans . **75.00**
  Grecian, sgd "Hawkes" **625.00**
 8" d, hobstars and cut arches **235.00**
 8" d, 2" h, cross–cut diamond and fan **60.00**
 8" d, 3" h, Iris, sgd "Hawkes Gravic" **250.00**
 8" d, 4" h, Ellsmere pattern, sgd "Libbey" **600.00**
 8¼" d, border of hobstars with floral
  panels **110.00**
 9" d
  Band of hobstars, starred hobs, triple sq rim, minute rim chips ... **250.00**
  Geometrical pattern, hobstars,
   flared fans, strawberry diamonds
   and deep miters, sgd "Roden
   Bros" **275.00**
  Hobstars, cross–hatching, notched
   prism, sgd "Libbey" with saber **220.00**
  Palm pattern, five sided, Taylor
   Bros **450.00**
  Russian pattern, cane, feather, and
   hobstars **140.00**
 9" d, 4" h, Prima Donna pattern, sgd
  "Clark" **375.00**
 9" d, 4½" h, Alhambra pattern **770.00**
 9¼" d, 2¾" h, cut glass, heavy blank,
  deep cross miter and hobstar cutting, Sinclaire, central S wreath
  mark, minor damage **165.00**
 10" d
  Kohinoor pattern, blown–out type
   blank, swirled pattern design,
   sgd "Hawkes" **1,250.00**
  Primrose pattern, intaglio, sgd
   "Hawkes" **200.00**
 10" d, 4" h, Nautilus pattern, blown
  blank, sgd "Hawkes" **2,400.00**
 10" d, 4½" h
  Chrysanthemum pattern, wood polished, sgd "Hawkes" **650.00**
  Venetian, wood polished, sgd
   "Hawkes" **500.00**
 10" l, 6½" w, 3" h, rect, Snowflake
  and Holly pattern, rim chips, sgd
  "Sinclaire" **275.00**
 10" l, 8" h, Sultana, folded–in sides,
  Dorflinger **525.00**
 18" l, 11½" w, rect, intaglio rose cutting, hobstar bottom, sgd "Sinclaire" **165.00**

Box
5" l, 3" h, intaglio pears and cherries, sgd "Heisey" 110.00
6" l, 5" w, round, green cased to clear, sterling silver repousse lid, hobstar base, vertical punties and prism columns 500.00
8" d, hinged, round, Florence hobstar lid, miter cut sides 320.00
Bread Tray
11" l, 5" w, hobstars, sgd "Clark" .. 275.00
12" d, 4" h, fold–over rim, floral cut, Pairpoint 200.00
13" l, Holly and Snowflake pattern, Sinclaire 605.00
13¾ x 6¼", hobstars and cane, rim flake 250.00
Butter, cov
5" h, 7" d plate, Russian and floral . 385.00
5" h, 8" d plate
Hobstar chain cut on figured blank 325.00
Hobstars and fans, sgd "Libbey" . 425.00
Butter Pat
Cypress, Laurel 32.00
Hobstars, well cut 30.00
Candlesticks, pr
8" h
Hollow teardrop stems, rayed bases, hobstars, hobnail, and diamonds 975.00
Teardrop stems, floral and Harvard 250.00
9½" h, teardrop stem, hobstar base, hobstars 230.00
11" h, teardrop stem, notched prisms, 24 point hobstar base 600.00
11½" h, large air trap base, floral cut 470.00
12" h, Adelaide pattern, amber, Pairpoint 250.00
14" h, teardrop stems, cut and engraved, sgd "Sinclaire" 325.00
Candy Basket, 3¾" h, engraved florals, Hawkes, sterling silver rim and handle 85.00
Canoe
2" l, Harvard pattern 70.00
11¼" l, Harvard pattern sides, hobstar base 175.00
11½" l, Brilliant Period 250.00
13½" l, 4½" w, floral and leaves ... 75.00
Carafe
Harvard pattern 160.00
Hobstars and notched prisms 110.00
Wedgemere pattern, 9" h, Libbey ..1,000.00
Casserole, cov, 8½ x 7" h, Palm pattern, sgd "Taylor Bros" 1,300.00
Celery Tray
11" l, hobstars, double miters, strawberry diamond on blown blank .. 150.00
11" l, 4½" w, hobstars, flashed fans, strawberry diamond, Unger Bros . 145.00
11"l, 5" w, floral and Harvard pattern, double X–vesicas 110.00

11½" l, 5" w, hobstars, cross hatch, and notched prisms on figured blank 60.00
12" l, hobstars, flashed double vesicas, sgd "Alford" 250.00
12" l 4" w, intaglio cut, Libbey pattern 165.00
Chalice, 12" h, 4½" d, butterflies and flowers, facet cut knob near base, pattern cut base 375.00
Champagne
Double teardrop stems, strawberry diamonds and fans, set of six 300.00
Flared bowls, delicate stems, hobstar chain and bases, set of nine 450.00
Kalana Lily pattern, stemmed, Dorflinger 50.00
Monarch pattern, saucer style, set of twelve 1,200.00
Rayed Button Russian pattern, Russian bases, tumbler type, set of six 480.00
Russian pattern, knobbed stem, rayed star base, set of twelve 660.00
Champagne Bucket, 7 x 7", sgd "Hoare" 350.00
Champagne Pitcher
12" h, Russian pattern, applied angular notched handle 1,250.00
12½" h
Cane pattern, other cutting, sterling silver rim 400.00
Hobstars, fan, and strawberry diamond, 24 point hobstar base, triple notched handle 375.00
14½" h, hobstars and canes 430.00
Cheese and Cracker Dish, Double Lozenge pattern 275.00
Cheese Dish, cov
6" h dome, 9" d plate, cobalt blue cut to clear, bull's eye and panel, large miter splits on bottom of plate ... 200.00
8" h, 10½" d plate, swirling pattern serving plate, matching high dome cov, faceted knob top, Brilliant Period, flat edge chip, minor wear .. 550.00
Cigarette Holder, 4" l,¾" w, nailhead diamond, strawberry diamond, fans, and honeycomb 630.00
Claret Jug, 12" h, lapidary ring neck, hobstars and fan, faceted stopper ... 165.00
Cocktail Shaker, strawberry diamond and fan, sterling silver top, sgd "Hawkes" 275.00
Cologne Bottle
5" h, bulbous, strawberry diamond, fans, and hobstars 150.00
5½" h, Russian pattern, chip on top 715.00
6" h, Hob and Lace pattern, green cased to clear, pattern cut stopper, Dorflinger 600.00
6¼" h, sq, red cut to clear, Octagon Diamond pattern, horizontal

stepped shoulder, matching starred
stopper, chips at inner stopper edge **550.00**
7″ h, bulbous, green cut to clear, all
over cutting, faceted stopper, Bril-
liant Period **245.00**
7″ h, 3½″ d base, bulbous, Cane pat-
tern, long slim flute cut neck,
pointed stopper **125.00**
7½″ h, 2¾″ d, Parisian pattern, sq
shape, Dorflinger, pr **620.00**
Compote
6″ d, 9″ h, Ribbon Star pattern, rayed
foot **275.00**
7″ d, 5″ h, hobstars, rayed foot, sgd
"Maple City" **150.00**
7½″ d, green, fold–down rim, St Louis
diamond, 4″ h pedestal base, sgd
"Hawkes" **85.00**
8″ h, daisies and leaves **80.00**
8½″ d, 7″ h, two notch cut handles,
hobstar base, teardrop stem, hob-
stars **400.00**
9″ d, 9″ h
Basketweave, air trap stem **715.00**
Teardrop stem, hobstars and dia-
monds **275.00**
9½″ h, hollow stem, cut star base,
Brilliant Period, pr **310.00**
9¾″ h, cov, Arcadia pattern, sgd "Ber-
gen" **1,850.00**
10″ d, 14″ h, Design #100, notch cut
teardrop stems, hobstar base, El-
mira, pr **2,700.00**
Console Set
12″ d ftd bowl with wide flat rim, pr
9⅛″ h baluster form candlesticks,
cross–hatched diamond and flute
cutting, three pcs **600.00**
14″ d center plate, pr candlesticks and
bowl, amber, cut dec, Sinclaire, S
wreath mark **325.00**
Cookie Jar, cov
Hobstars, fans, double "X" cut vesicas, strawberry diamond, curved–
in sides, matching pattern cut glass
lid rests in sterling silver rim **800.00**
Hobstars, strawberry diamond, cane,
and fans, pattern cut glass lid **900.00**
Cordial, cut, engraved, faceted stem,
sgd "Hawkes" **65.00**
Cordial Set, 9″ h ring necked decanter,
orig stopper, eight 4″ h cordial
glasses, green cut to clear, Flute pat-
tern, Dorflinger, nine pcs **900.00**
Cracker Jar, cov, 7″ d, floral cut, silver
plate lid and bail handle, Pairpoint . **275.00**
Creamer, 4″ h, prism and punties **65.00**
Creamer and Sugar
Clear Button Russian pattern, hobstar
bases, cut creamer handle, cov
sugar with wafer foot, pattern cut
lid **800.00**

Hobstar clusters, blown blanks, El-
mira **275.00**
Hobstars and fans, figured blanks,
plain handles **90.00**
Hobstars, fans, and strawberry dia-
monds, notched handles **145.00**
Hobstars, nailhead, and fan, triple cut
handles, 4″ h, pr **250.00**
Intaglio fruit and geometric cutting . **75.00**
Pedestal, 7″ h cov sugar, pinwheel,
hobstar, fans, rayed bases **975.00**
Cream Pitcher, 5¼″ h, bulbous, notched
fluted rim, Persian, clear hobstar cen-
ter, triple notched handles **150.00**
Cruet
6″ h, Chrysanthemum pattern, tri–
pour spout, cut handle and stopper,
sgd "Hawkes" **350.00**
7″ h, Butterfly and Daisy pattern, Pair-
point **85.00**
9½″ h, Alhambra pattern, honeycomb
handle, tall pyramidal shape **675.00**
Decanter
7″ h, Lotus pattern, ship's, pattern cut
stopper, Egginton **380.00**
10″ h, bulbous, hobstars and straw-
berry diamonds **275.00**
11″ h, Argand pattern, sterling silver
flip–top lid and handle, Hoare . . . **700.00**
12″ h, Russian and Pillar pattern,
matching cut stopper **1,100.00**
12½″ h, rib molded hollow handle
pitcher, polished wheel cutting, silver capped stopper, imp "Tiffany &
Co Makers Sterling" **420.00**
13″ h, Russian pattern, ftd, triple
notched handle, scalloped base,
faceted stopper **715.00**
13½″ h, Brazilian pattern, heavy
blank, bulbous, wood polished,
Hawkes **650.00**
Dish, 10 x 7″, Russian pattern, hobstar
button variant, heart shape **220.00**
Door Knob, facet cut **25.00**
Dresser Tray, 12″ l, 8″ w, hobstar and
diamond with fan border **322.50**
Egg Nog Bowl, 12″ d, 9½″ h, pinwheel
cut, two pcs **310.00**
Fernery, 8″ d, hobstar and fan, three ftd **80.00**
Finger Bowl, underplate
Russian pattern, set of six **330.00**
Strawberry diamond and fan, set of
four **200.00**
Flask, 6″ l, 3½″ w, lady's, cross–cut dia-
mond, strawberry diamond and fan,
sterling silver lid **180.00**
Flower Center
5½″ d, 4¼″ h, hobstars with strawberry diamond points and fans, 16
point rayed base, blue and notch
cut neck **295.00**

6" d, 5" h, hobstars, flashed fans, hobstar chain and base **300.00**

10" d, 7½" h, hobstars in diamond shaped fields, fans, strawberry diamond, honeycomb neck **775.00**

9" h, step–cut and scalloped rim, 48 point hobstar base **750.00**

10" d, hobstars, fan, and diamond, horizontal step–cut neck, scalloped rim, large hobstar base **600.00**

12" d, 7¾" h, etched and wheel cut motif, honeycomb flared neck, some wear **500.00**

14½" d, 8¾" h, monumental blank, hobstar, fan, fine cut, and cane cutting, horizontal stepped neck, minor roughness **1,540.00**

Flower Pot, 6" h, 6" d, hobstars and fans, pyramidal starred fields **775.00**

Glove Box, cov, 11" l, 4" w, Harvard border around intaglio cut floral, hinged lid, silver fittings **750.00**

Goblet, water

Clear Button Russian pattern, facet cut teardrop stem, rayed base **125.00**

Double lozenge **110.00**

Double teardrop stems, 6½" h, 3½" d, strawberry diamond and fans, wood polished, set of twelve **780.00**

Double teardrop stems, hobstar bases, cane, hobstars, fans, and strawberry diamonds **1,400.00**

Rayed Button Russian, 6" h, teardrop stems, sgd "Hawkes," set of nine **1,170.00**

Russian pattern, knobbed stem, rayed star base, set of 15 .... **1,240.00**

Hair Receiver

4" d, 3 " h, floral and leaves, rayed base, engraved sterling silver top . **75.00**

5" d, 3½" h, Harvard pattern **150.00**

Humidor, cov

6¾" h, all over notched prism, glass lid **350.00**

7½" h, Middlesex, hollow stopper, lid to hold sponge, Dorflinger **475.00**

9" h

Monarch pattern, matching cut glass lid with hollow for sponge, hobstar base, Hoare **625.00**

Hobstars, beaded split vesicas, hobstar base, matching cut glass lid with hollow for sponge, ... **550.00**

Ice Bucket

6" d, Jewel pattern, hobstar bases, two handles, 8½" d underplate, Clark . **525.00**

6" d, 6" h, hobstar and cross–cut panels, tab handles **350.00**

7" d, 5½" h, Harvard pattern, tab handles **440.00**

7" d, 8" d underplate, hobstars and notched prisms, double handles .. **935.00**

Ice Cream Set

7 pcs, 13" l, 8" w tray with curved ends, six 5" sq bowls, Rayed Button Russian pattern **1,100.00**

11 pcs, tray and ten plates, Pineapple and Fan pattern **300.00**

Ice Cream Tray

10" l, oval, scalloped rim, rings of hobstars surrounded by clear band, sgd "Taylor & TB" **577.50**

12½" l, 7⅝" w, 2¼" h, twenty–two hobstar clusters, scalloped sawtooth rim, Brilliant Period **195.00**

14" l, 7" w, Nelson pattern variation, all over cutting, sgd "Fry" **270.00**

14" l, 10" w, Devonshire pattern, sgd "Hawkes" **925.00**

14¼" l, 7¼" w, Rose Combination pattern, Irving, clear blank **475.00**

Jar, cov

1¾" sq, prism and cane, rayed base, sterling silver repousse lid, marked "Unger Bros" **75.00**

5" d, emerald green cut to clear, hobstar, cross–cut diamond and fan, green star cut knob **145.00**

6" h, Holland pattern, hobstar lid, sgd "Hawkes" **300.00**

9" h, 7" d, Hobstar and Oval, cylindrical jar, rose dec flared silver rim, Brilliant Period, small chip at base edge **750.00**

Ketchup Bottle

6½" h, Ramona pattern, Pairpoint .. **450.00**

8½" h, hobstars **240.00**

Knife Rest

3½" l, dumbbell shape, all over cutting, Brilliant Period **25.00**

4" l

Facet panel cut, orig box, pr **100.00**

Notched prism ball ends and bar . **38.00**

4½" h, all over strawberry diamond and miter **75.00**

4½" l, faceted ball ends, serrated bar **40.00**

4¾" h, nailhead diamonds and strawberry diamonds **85.00**

5" l, faceted ball ends, panel cut bar **45.00**

Lamp

Boudoir, 13" h, 6½" d, mushroom shade, St Louis Diamond neck, notched prism and hobstars, flashed fans **400.00**

Hanging Globe, 12" d, cross–cut diamond and fan, 20" to top of brass finial, orig brass chain and mounting fixture **475.00**

Kerosene, 7" h to top of chimney, geometric pattern **425.00**

Table

18" h, mushroom shade, hobstars, cane vesicas, fans, pr **4,300.00**

21" h, 12" d shade, La Rabida pattern, double light, Straus **3,200.00**
22½" h, Sultan's hat shade, Harvard and late floral cuttings **500.00**
27" h, pointed top, Harvard pattern, hobstars **2,750.00**
31" h, predominately pinwheel cutting with hobstar and fan cutting, "street light" style, mushroom cap, four teardrop balls, horizontally stepped flared base, Brilliant Period **26,400.00**
Lamp Shade, 7½" h, 7" w, Hobstar Button Russian pattern **225.00**
Loving Cup, 5½" h, sterling silver rim, monogrammed, dated 1900 .... **400.00**
Mayonnaise Set
Two pieces, bowl and matching underplate
Prism and hobstars **190.00**
Punties, flashed pinwheel **135.00**
Hobstars, cane, and strawberry diamond on blown blanks **275.00**
Three pieces, bowl, cov, underplate, bull's eye and flashed pinwheel, three pcs **145.00**
Medicine Bottle, globe shape, Clear Button Russian pattern, matching cut top **625.00**
Milk Pitcher
5" h, tankard, hobstars and notched rim, sgd "Dorflinger" **150.00**
6" h,
Floral, hobstars, and cane **255.00**
Hobstars and fans **200.00**
7¼" h, red cut to clear, cross–hatching and fan cutting, bulbous body, Brilliant Period, numerous small body chips **1,300.00**
8" h, Brilliant Period cutting, sgd "Clark" **200.00**
Mug, 4" h, Tyrone pattern, handle, Pairpoint **235.00**
Mustard, cov, 3½" h, underplate, panel and notched prism, sgd "Maple City Glass" **220.00**
Napkin Ring, hobstars and bow tie fans **85.00**
Nappy
5" d, hobstars and cross–cut diamond, handle **35.00**
5½" d, floral and cane, notched handle **45.00**
6" d
Cane and cross–hatching, two handles **125.00**
Figured blank, hobstar cluster, no handle **50.00**
Harvard pattern, handle
Engraved "Good Wishes" **200.00**
No engraving, loop style handle **175.00**
Hobstars and other cutting, single handle **125.00**

Primrose and Hobstars, sgd "Tuthill" **150.00**
Russian pattern, notched handle .. **90.00**
6¾" l, 6¼" w, five pointed star shape, intricate cutting, Brilliant Period .. **110.00**
7½" w, hobstars, feathered leaves, other cutting, scalloped and serrated rim, double thumbprint handle **95.00**
7½" l, 6½" w, ring handle, Brilliant Period **75.00**
9" d, cane vesicas center surrounded by hobstars and further cane cutting, scalloped and serrated rim, two handles **425.00**
Orange Bowl
9¾ x 6¾ x 3¾", hobstars and strawberry diamond **180.00**
10" d, pinwheel, notched prism and hobstar in vesicas **165.00**
Paste Pot, vertical notched prisms, crossing miters **170.00**
Pastry Tray, 9" d, 7" h, floral, handle .. **90.00**
Perfume Bottle
3½" l, pistol shape, sterling silver fittings **230.00**
5½" h, 3" d, six sided, alternating panels of Harvard pattern and engraved florals, rayed base, matching faceted stopper **150.00**
5¾" h, three panels Harvard and three panels floral **125.00**
6½" h
Bulbous, all over cutting, orig stopper, Brilliant Period **200.00**
Cranberry, Art Deco style deeply cut opposing triangles and cross–hatching, tall stopper **145.00**
7" l, oval cut column, hinged sterling silver cov with polychrome portrait center **220.00**
Petit Four Stand, 7½" d, 5" h, hobstars alternating with fields of cane and diamond, pedestal base, hobstar bottom **225.00**
Picture Frame, 4¾ x 6¾", heavy cut corners with florals on each panel, pr .. **250.00**
Planter, 12" l, 4" w, 4" h, close notched rim, all over cutting, 3½" d sunflowers, hobstar center, small rayed flowers, heavy detailed ferns, cut rayed base, American Brilliant Period **345.00**
Plate
6" d, Gothic pattern, Baker **65.00**
7" d
Gladys pattern, Hawkes **115.00**
Gloria pattern, Libbey **165.00**
Grecian pattern, Hawkes **750.00**
Hindoo pattern, Hoare **115.00**
Hunt pattern, 16 point hobstars, fans, prisms radiants **100.00**
Lace pattern, Hawkes **330.00**

10" d
  Corinthian pattern, Libbey **285.00**
  Hobstar rim band, 32 point hobstar
    center **160.00**
  Rosaceae pattern, sgd "Tuthill" ..**1,000.00**
  Vintage intaglio, sgd "Tuthill" ... **660.00**
Powder Box, cov
  4½" d, silver thread, vintage and flo-
    ral, cross–cut diamond, sgd "Sin-
    claire" **330.00**
  5" d, 3" h, Harvard pattern **150.00**

Punch Bowl on Stand, American Brilliant period, $500.00. Photograph courtesy of William Doyle Galleries.

Punch Bowl
  One piece, 14" d
    Dauntless pattern, sgd "Bergen" . **575.00**
    Hobstar chain, notched prisms,
      zipper, mitered panels, sgd
      "Clark" **1,210.00**
  Two piece
    9" d, 10" h, hobstars and pinwheels **400.00**
    12" d, 8" h, strawberry diamond and
      hearts **550.00**
    12" d, 9" h, Colonial pattern, Dorflin-
      ger **550.00**
    12" d, 11½" h, Temple pattern, sgd
      "Maple City" **1,000.00**
    12" d, 13" h, Arcadia pattern, ped-
      estal **1,100.00**
  Punch Bowl Set, 16" d, 14½" h, Ribbon
    Star pattern, matching pedestal base,
    ten cups, twelve pcs **3,200.00**
Punch Cup
  Cranberry cut to clear, cross–cut dia-
    mond, clear handle, 2½" h **80.00**
  Hobstars, pedestal, handle **75.00**
  Monarch pattern, set of ten **300.00**
Punch Ladle
  11½" l, silver plated emb shell bowl,
    cut and notched prism handle ... **150.00**
  14" l, 5¼" w, Harvard pattern handle,

ornate Pairpoint silver plate stem
  and double spout bowl **325.00**
15" l
  Hobstars, strawberry diamond, and
    fans in teardrop handle, sgd
    "Bergen" **400.00**
  Notched prism, hobstars, and fan
    handle, Wallace sterling silver
    twisted handle and scroll en-
    graved bowl, dated 1902 ...... **300.00**
  17" l, double pouring spout, hobstars
    and notched prisms, sgd "Meri-
    den" **500.00**
Ramekin, matching underplate, ruby
  cased to clear, Clear Button Russian
  pattern **600.00**
Relish
  6" l, pinwheel, hobstars, fans, and
    prisms **65.00**
  7½" l, 5½" w, flat, oval, Vintage pat-
    tern, hobstar gallery, sgd "Tuthill" **275.00**
  8" l, 3½" w, hobstars **35.00**
  13" l, leaf shape, Clear Button Russian
    pattern **315.00**
Rose Bowl
  5" d, all over geometric engraving,
    American, blown blank **180.00**
  5" h, Brilliant Period, free form, tri-
    angular, all over floral engraving,
    engraved rim band, sgd "Libbey" **300.00**
  6" d, Russian pattern **450.00**
  6" h, 5½" d, vesica, fan, and cross—
    cut diamonds **400.00**
  6" h, 7" w, fan, cane, and prisms ... **310.00**
  7" h
    Brunswick pattern, pedestal, sgd
      "Hawkes" **1,025.00**
    Clear Button Russian pattern **525.00**
    9" h, Queens pattern, Hawkes **1,400.00**
Rum Jug, 7½" h, all over notched prism **325.00**
Rouge Jar, cov, 1¾" w, sq, cut panels,
  engraved sterling silver tops, pr **75.00**
Salad Bowl and Underplate
  10" d, 6" h bowl, 11½" d underplate,
    Spillane (Trefoil & Rosette) pattern,
    cross–cut vesicas, notched prism,
    hobstars and fans, sgd "Libbey" . **2,200.00**
  10" d, 7" h, strawberry diamonds, un-
    derplate, minute nicks **300.00**
Salad Serving Utensil
  Fork and Spoon, silver plated, cross–
    cut diamond glass handles **300.00**
  Server, strawberry diamonds, silver
    plate trim, Gorham **250.00**
Salt, open
  Feather **14.00**
  Notched prism, set of 6 .... **65.00**
Salt Shaker
  Garland pattern, 4" h, green, sterling
    silver lid **55.00**
  Notched prism columns **25.00**
Scent Bottle, lay down type, 5¼" l, cran-

berry, ten panel, ornate engraved silver ends, one with screw on lid, other end hinged **195.00**

Serving Plate, 13" d, Kensington pattern, center sgd, "Hawkes," Brilliant Period **715.00**

Sherbet, sgd "Eggington," Brilliant Period **45.00**

Spittoon, lady's, 7½" h, 4½" d, fold-over rim, floral cut, Pairpoint **330.00**

Spoon Basket, 4" w, 8" l, flat, Lotus pattern, Eggington **80.00**

Spooner, 5½" h, elongated hobstars, deep vesicas and cane diamonds, large hobstar base, sawtooth rim, Brilliant Period **165.00**

Stemware, Russian pattern, Brilliant Period, eight juice tumblers, eight liquors, nine sherries, fourteen wines, fifteen water glasses, some chips and polished rims, wear roughness, set of fifty four pcs **2,500.00**

String Holder, notched prisms, ornate pierced Gorham sterling silver top .. **150.00**

Sugar Cube Tray, 9" l, cane **75.00**

Sugar Shaker

  Emerald green cut to clear, cane and fan, marked "Sterling" floral repousse top **415.00**

  Hobstars, diamond, cane, and other cuttings, sterling silver top **165.00**

Syrup Pitcher

  Fancy vertical notched prisms, silver plated hinged lid and handle, 4" h, **70.00**

  Large hobstars, vesicas, and fans, Brilliant Period **150.00**

  Russian pattern, hinged silver plate top, cut handle **770.00**

  Strawberry diamond and fan, sterling silver top **120.00**

Tankard Pitcher

  8" h, sunburst, hobstar bands, rayed base, sgd "Libbey" **275.00**

  8½" h, Brunswick pattern, sgd "Hawkes" **500.00**

  9" h, Orpheus pattern, pattern cut handle, sgd "Hawkes" **1,250.00**

  9½" h, Cane pattern, notched handle **225.00**

  10" h, vertical notched prism, rayed base, double notched handle, sterling silver collar, narrow repousse band **200.00**

  11" h, 5" d, hobstar and ovals filled with cane and nailhead diamond, hobstar base **350.00**

  11½" h, cane and hobstar cut, 24 point hobstar base **275.00**

  12" h, Snowflake pattern, sgd "Libbey" in circle **1,072.00**

  12½" h, Alhambra (Greek Key) pattern, wide sterling silver top and lip, Meriden Cut Glass Co. **1,850.00**

Tantalus, two 9½ x 3" sq bottles, honeycomb and engraved florals, 13" h frame, quadruple plate on copper frame, sgd "Hawkes" on frame and bottles **250.00**

Toothbrush Holder, cane **140.00**

Toothpick Holder

  2½" h, prism cut **35.00**

  2⅝" h, 1⅝" d, light amber, squared tulip shape holder, cut scalloped top, diamond cut sides, sq foot with cut diamonds **60.00**

  3" h, pedestal, hobstars **90.00**

Tray

  9½" l, 6" w, rect, Persian pattern ... **220.00**

  12" l

    Corinthian pattern, sgd "Libbey" . **625.00**

    Hobstars, cane, and strawberry diamonds **300.00**

    Pinwheels, hobstars, and floral ... **110.00**

  13" l, Alhambra pattern **1,300.00**

  13" l, 8½" w, rect, handled, sunbursts and leaves **250.00**

  13½" l, 13½" w, oak leaf shape, flashed fancy notched prisms, vesicas, cane Pitkins and Brooks **1,025.00**

  14" l, Kohinoor pattern surrounding intaglio cut medallions, hobstar center, cane, and vesicas **2,000.00**

  14½" l, 8" w, Cane Hob Diamond pattern, rect, handles, one cane tooth chipped at edge **150.00**

  15" l, hobstars, cane, and central feather, sgd "Libbey" with saber . **605.00**

  16" l, 11" w, cut in bows and feather design, sgd "Sinclaire" **210.00**

  18" l, oval, Carolyn pattern, thick heavy blank, well cut, Hoare **1,600.00**

  18" l, 10½" w, hobstars sharply cut, clear blank **1,700.00**

Tumble Up, handled pitcher and matching tumbler, geometric and floral ... **410.00**

Tumbler

  Bristol Rose pattern, Mount Washington, set of three **210.00**

  Clear Button Russian pattern **95.00**

  Harvard, rayed base, set of three ... **120.00**

  Hobstars **35.00**

  Hobstars, strawberry diamonds, fans, hobstar cluster and base, set of six **330.00**

  Notched prism, hobstar, cane **55.00**

  Panel, sgd "Hawkes," rare **400.00**

  Russian Button pattern, set of nine .. **315.00**

  Star of David pattern, 4" h, set of four **260.00**

Umbrella Stand, 24" h, hobstar chain around top, middle, and base with vertical notched prism bars between **1,600.00**

Vase

  4½" h, bud, trumpet shape, daisy, sgd "Sinclaire," pr **170.00**

  5" h, Brazilian pattern, trumpet, Hawkes **155.00**

Vase, brilliant cutting, vertical panels of bars and circles above and below hobstars, American Brilliant period, 14½" h, $330.00. Photograph courtesy of Skinner, Inc.

8" h, trumpet, intaglio cut poppy, Tuthill 165.00

8¾" h, oval, intaglio cut, frosted rose blossoms, buds, leaves, and thorny branches, minor rim chips 220.00

8¾" h, 9" d, flared, pointed diamond pattern, Brilliant Period, chased sterling silver rim marked "Bailey Banks & Biddle Co," monogrammed 675.00

11" h, urn, Vintage cutting, two handles, Brilliant Period, Tuthill 475.00

11¾" h, cylindrical, knob stem, spreading cylindrical foot, cut and etched garlands of flowers, Hawkes, Gravic mark 260.00

12"
Corset shape, cosmos and cane .. 75.00
Russian and Pillar pattern 900.00
Trumpet, punty, hobstar, and strawberry diamond 75.00

12" h, 4", Queens pattern, cylindrical, sgd "Hawkes" 825.00

12" h, 5" d, trumpet, notched vertical prism and sq cutting, starred buttons, 24 point rayed base, sgd "J Hoare & Co" 275.00

12¾" h, flared trumpet, Kalana Poppy, intaglio poppy blossoms, ornate curvilinear stems, center Assyrian pattern, sgd "Sinclaire" 1,300.00

14" h, trumpet, Queens pattern, sgd "Hawkes" 825.00

14" h, 5" d
Assyrian pattern, sgd "Sinclaire" 1,300.00
Lotus pattern, rayed base, sgd "Eginton" 395.00

14½" h, vertical panels of bars and circles above and below hobstars, Brilliant Period, minimal roughness 330.00

15" h, Queens pattern, facet cut knob, hobstar base, slight glass tint, sgd "Hawkes" 1,000.00

16" h, trumpet, Teutonic pattern, sgd "Hawkes" 500.00

Violet Vase
Fancy notched prism bowl, rayed base 190.00
Hobstars and strawberry diamonds . 225.00
Hobstars and zipper 80.00

Wall Placket, 9" l, Mums pattern, sgd "Hawkes Gravic" 150.00

Water Carafe
7½" h, Arcadia pattern, cut ring neck 165.00
8" h, Russian pattern panels separated by notched prism stripes, pr ... 660.00
14" h, trumpet, deep burgundy cut to clear, deep cut strawberry diamond and fans, cross–cutting, clear star cut base 415.00

Water Pitcher
9½" h
Brilliant Period cutting, sgd "Fry" 250.00
Harvard pattern panels and intaglio cut sprays of flowers and foliage 275.00
Panels of hobstars, cane, and cross–cut diamonds 350.00

10" h
Copper wheel cut leaves and butterfly, sgd "Libbey" in circle ... 150.00
Keystone Rose pattern 135.00

11" h, Harvard pattern, rayed base, double punty handle, sgd "Hawkes" 315.00

Water Set
9" h pitcher and six tumblers, hobstars, rose hatching 250.00

10" h pitcher and five tumblers, columns of large hobstars with fans, sawtooth rim, notched handle, Brilliant Period 275.00

10½" h pitcher, six 4⅛" tumblers, Brilliant Period, Fortuna type pattern, fans at top 650.00

10¾" pitcher, six 4" tumblers, Brilliant Period
Buzz stars separated by horizontal bands, diamond center and fans 500.00
Floral and butterfly, attributed to Niland 470.00

Whiskey Decanter, pr
11" h, panel cut, orig stopper 250.00
13" h, handle, panel cut, lapidary knob, sgd "Clair" 770.00

Whiskey Jug
Hob and Lace pattern, Dorflinger ... 365.00
Swirled bands of strawberry diamond and cane, hobstar chain, fans, 8½" h 500.00

Whiskey Shot Glass
Hobstar chain and cane, 3½" h, 2½"
d rim **125.00**
Russian pattern, Brilliant Period **75.00**
Wine
4½" h, Russian pattern, Brilliant Period, overlaid in color, four green,
three yellow–amber, three red,
some wear and roughness, set of
ten **3,600.00**
5" h
Brazilian pattern, teardrop stem,
fully cut foot, Hawkes **330.00**
Burgess pattern, teardrop knob
through stem **385.00**
Cranberry cut to clear, fields of
cross diamonds and fans, Dorflinger, set of four **400.00**
7" h, green cut to clear, engraved
roses and vines, Hawkes, set of four **310.00**
8½" h, green cut to clear, hobstars,
fan, and cane, quintuple flute cut
stem, double teardrop, hobstar
base **175.00**

CUT VELVET

History: Several glass manufacturers made cut
velvet during the late Victorian era, c1870–1900.
An outer layer of pastel color was applied over
a white casing. The layers were fused and blown
into a mold. The piece then was molded or cut
in a ribbed or diamond shape in high relief,
exposing portions of the casing. The pieces were
usually acid finished, which gives the piece a
satin velvety feel, hence the name "cut velvet."
Some glossy pieces have been found.

This exquisite glassware was made in many
forms. Bowls, ewers, pitchers, and vases are the
most common. Ruffled edges, rigaree, and applied clear handles are sometimes added to enhance the beauty or usefulness of a piece. Although two-toned bodies have been found, most
are single colors, shaded by the shape and technique. Colors include amethyst, apple green,
apricot, blue, butterscotch, pink, tan, turquoise,
and yellow with white linings.

Celery Vase, 6½" h, raised diamond
quilted pattern, deep blue body, white
lining, box pleated top **725.00**
Creamer, 5¼" h, raised ribbed pattern,
butterscotch body, white lining **150.00**
Rose Bowl, 3¼" d, 3¾" h, egg shape,
raised diamond quilted pattern, rose
body, white lining, six crimp top ... **185.00**
Vase
5¼" h, blue body, quatrefoil top ... **125.00**
6¼" h, opaque white body, pale pink
lining, ribbon candy rim **125.00**

Vase, blue, bottle neck, 6" h, $225.00.

6½" h, stick type, raised diamond
quilted pattern, rose body, white
lining **225.00**
6¾" h, bulbous, raised diamond
quilted pattern, pink body, ruffled
rim **200.00**
7⅛" h, 2⅞" d, bulbous base, tall
neck, deeply ruffled rim, raised
ribbed pattern, rich blue body,
white lining **195.00**
7¾" h, 3" d, squared bulbous, raised
ribbed pattern, rose body, white lining **185.00**
8⅜" h, bulbous, raised diamond
quilted pattern, pale blue body ... **250.00**
9" h, cylindrical, raised diamond
quilted pattern, blue body, ruffled
rim **245.00**
13½" h, 6" d base, double gourd, long
pumpkin stem neck, pale gold, diamond quilted pattern **650.00**

CZECHOSLOVAKIAN ITEMS

History: Objects marked "Made in Czechoslovakia" were produced after 1918 when the country claimed its independence from the Austro–
Hungarian Empire. The people became more
cosmopolitan, liberated, and expanded their
scope of life. Their porcelains, pottery, and glassware reflect many influences.

A specific manufacturer's mark may be identified as being much earlier than 1918, but this
only indicates the factory existed in the Bohemian or Austro–Hungarian Empire period.

Czechoslovakian glassware can range from exquisite cut glass to Art Deco designs executed in
bright colors. Vivid color combinations of orange, blue, and black with white are common.
Spatter-type wares and bright streaks of color are
also readily found. Modern Czechoslovakian
craftsmen are producing some lovely pieces
which should be included in any collection of
Czechoslovakian glassware. The mass-produced
bowls, perfume bottles, vases and other types of

items are starting to command high prices as collectors seek these colorful pieces of glassware.

References: Dale and Diane Barta and Helen M. Rose, *Czechoslovakian Glass & Collectibles*, Collector Books, 1992; Ruth A. Forsythe, *Made in Czechoslovakia*, Richardson Printing Corp., 1982; Jacquelyne Y. Jones–North, *Czechoslovakian Perfume Bottles and Boudoir Accessories*, Antique Publications, 1990.

Candlestick, tortoise glass, brown and white, marked "Made in Czechoslovakia," 7¾" h, $100.00.

Basket
6½" h, 3⅞" d, end of day lavender, pink, and white spatter overlay, white lining, emb raindrop pattern, ruffled edge, cobalt blue twisted handle **80.00**
6½" h, 5" d, clear, red and yellow spangle, applied clear handle **65.00**
Bowl, cased, black exterior, yellow lining, polished pontil, sgd **48.00**
Box, cov, 4" d, 3" h, cut glass, engraved **45.00**
Decanter Set, figural owl decanter, four matching cups, blue ground, painted eyes **175.00**
Flask, 12½" h, Burmese type ground, birds perched on stems, foliage, moon, sgd "Tischer #426" **500.00**
Inkwell, 3¼" h, clear, figural, sitting Scottie dog, silver plated collar, marked **65.00**
Jack-In-The-Pulpit Vase, 7⅛" h, orange, black sponged design, marked **60.00**
Jar, cov, 7¼" h, 3½" d, pink spatter overlay, darker pink stripes, white lining, knob finial, applied black glass feet **50.00**
Lamp, mushroom shape, frosted glass shade, glass base with silhouette of lady and gentleman, raised small roses and beading on shade **350.00**

Necklace
Caramel, beveled glass, chrome links, Art Deco **45.00**
Green, cut cubes, 15", marked **65.00**
Perfume Bottle
2¼" h, 2" d, reticulated ormolu enameled florals, studded blue stones, screw on jeweled top, long dabber **65.00**
5½" h, cut, pink, frosted floral stopper **70.00**
8½" h, cut, amber, eight panels, waisted, amber stopper **110.00**
Powder Box, cov, round, yellow ground, black knob **60.00**
Vase
5¼" h, triple gourd shape, flared undulating rim, dappled irid gold, three clear ball feet, attributed by Dagobert Peche, stamped "Czechoslavakia" **500.00**
6" h, cased, blue ground, white lining, red ruffled top, marked **145.00**
8" h, yellow ground, applied black snake, ruffled top **175.00**

1895–1942

DAUM NANCY

History: Daum Nancy glassware originates in the Nancy, France, region and most pieces are attributed to members of the Daum family. Also known as Cristalleries de Nancy, the glassworks operated from 1875 to the present.

Daum family members include the founder, Jean Daum (1825–85), Jean–Louis Auguste Daum (1853–1909), Jean–Antonin Daum (1864–1930), Paul (1890–1944), Henri Daum (1894–1930), Michel Daum (b1900), and Jacques Daum (b1919). Both Jean–Louis Auguste and Jean–Antonin were greatly influenced by Emile Gallé.

Cameo glass wares were carefully crafted in addition to production of colored glassware with enameled decoration, etch glass, cased glass, and several other techniques. Crystal glassware and pate–de–verre was reintroduced into the firm's lines during the late 1960s.

All items made are marked with an engraved signature which varies from artist to artist.

References: Victor Arwas, *Glass Art Nouveau To Art Deco*, Rizzoli International Publications, Inc.; Harold Newman, *An Illustrated Dictionary of Glass*, Thames and Hudson, 1977; Wolf

Uecker, *Art Nouveau and Art Deco Lamps and Candlesticks*, Abbeville Press, 1987.

Manufacturer/Distributor: Daum Inc., 41 Madison Ave, 9th Floor, New York, NY 10010.

Reproduction Alert: Examples of period Daum Nancy items have been copied and reproduced. Most lack the details and exquisite cutting of the originals.

Bottle, 4½" h, cameo, romboid shape, short, narrow cylindrical neck, everted rim, mottled and streaked green and white, dark red splashes on base, green and gray overlay, cut pendant leafy branches and stems of deep orange berries, sgd in cameo, c1900 . **1,980.00**
Bowl
  5½" h, 14⅛" l, navette form, interrupted rim, domed circular foot, shading from mottled orange to raspberry at base of bowl and foot, inscribed "Daum Nancy" with cross of Lorraine on edge of foot, c1910 .... **700.00**
  5¾" d, 2¼" h, cameo, circular, inverted quatrefoliate mouth, mottled yellow and tangerine ground, cut and enameled winter scene of snowy field, bare trees, shaded black and white, rosy orange sky, black enameled trees in distance, base inscribed "Daum Nancy" with cross of Lorraine, c1900 .... **2,475.00**
  6" d, quatrefoil rim, etched and gilt mistletoe branches, white enameled berries, gilt sgd **450.00**
  9½" h, trumpet form, shaped sq foot, taupe ground, deeply etched Art Deco horizontal bands, engraved "Daum Nancy France" with cross of Lorraine **1,750.00**
  11¾" d, 5½" h, wide flaring rim, ftd, green, vertical etched ribs, engraved "Daum Nancy France" with cross of Lorraine **1,750.00**
Chandelier, 15" d, hemispherical, everted rim, streaked and mottled fuchsia and shades of mustard, satin finish, pierced with three mounting hooks, attached sockets and chains with central mount, suspended by single chain, wheel engraved "Daum/ Nancy" with crois de Lorraine, c1900 **700.00**
Compote, 7½" h, Berluze, wide conical vessel, serrated trefoil rim, mottled green and blue glass, hydrofluoric acid highlights, raised circular foot, etched "Daum Nancy" **1,200.00**
Creamer, 3⅛" h, 3" d, cameo, squared bulbous, round mouth, mottled gold shading to mottled brown frosted

ground, enameled green leaves and brown berries, single acid cutting, cameo sgd **1,650.00**
Cruet, 7¼" h, green ground, stylized foliate branch with white enamel berries, gold enamel accents, applied brushed gold highlights, sterling silver edged matching flat sided stopper, orig silver holder with cut out edge, gold enamel sgd "Daum Nancy," cross of Lorraine **1,750.00**
Egg, 5" h, fiery opalescent egg shaped oval, acid etched eggshell texture, shallow cameo cut ducks in groups of three, sgd on glass base, mounted to gilt metal beaded pedestal foot **1,500.00**

Lamp Base, 18½" vase form, shaped cylindrical vase, blue, orange, and yellow, elaborate wrought iron stand with floral and bird motifs, sgd "Daum Nancy Majorelle," $2,600.00. Photograph courtesy of William Doyle Galleries.

Lamp, table
  17" h, mottled orange and brown shade, three arm wrought iron base, sq foot, hammered texture, shade engraved "Daum Nancy" with cross of Lorraine **1,210.00**
  25" h, 13⅞" d dome shade, mottled orange, held by six wrought iron arms, openwork trefoil foot with wrought curling vines and leaves **4,620.00**
  26½" h, 14" d mushroom dome shade, mottled yellow glass with green and red shadings, shade layered in green and black cameo cut and wheel finished broad seascape with sailing vessels, conforming baluster shaft base with full length cameo floral design, sgd "Daum Nancy" with cross of Lorraine in

cameo, two smoothed areas on shade 15,000.00
Liqueur Shot Glass, 2" h, ovoid, clear glass mottled with yellow, overlaid and enameled winter forest scene of bare trees in snowy field, brown, black, and white, sgd "Daum Nancy" and cross of Lorraine in black, c1910 ....1,100.00
Ornament, clear and frosted, inscribed "Daum France," orig label
16" l, Cadillac, 1951 model 500.00
16¾" l, Bugatti Limousine Imperiale, black slate rect plinth 850.00
17" l, racing boat, fitted tinted aqua and blue pate de verre base 800.00
Pitcher, 3¾" h, mottled orange, green, and purple glass, etched pendent branches, leaves, and berries, black and red enamel highlights, three applied glass berries, applied green glass handle, etched "Daum Nancy" 3,100.00
Salt, 2" l, 1" h, oval, mottled yellow and red–brown ground, shallow acid etched floral dec, enameled green and red–orange, sgd "Daum Nancy" in design, pr 1,000.00
Sculpture, 8¼" h, clear and frosted, designed by Folon, #81 of limited edition of 300, etched "Folon Daum France 81/300" 150.00
Toothpick Holder, 2¼" h, 4½" l, oval, vertical grooving on inside cased layer, orig paper label, c1960 ...... 100.00
Vase
1⅛" h, cabinet, oval, opalescent, etched, gray enameled scene of

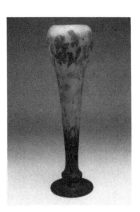

Vase, cameo and wheel carved, trumpet, everted rim, mottled green, blue, and white ground, blue, green, and rust–maroon overlay, bright blue blossoms, green yellow foliage, engraved mark, 18¾" h, $5,225.00. Photograph courtesy of Skinner, Inc.

sailboats and windmill, faint gilt sgd 450.00
3¼" h, cabinet, mottled and shaded yellow and orange ground, shallow acid etched poppy dec, enameled green, yellow, and orange, sgd "Daum Nancy" at side 1,100.00
4½" h, pillow shape, opalescent, etched, enameled summer scene of trees in meadow, enamel sgd 1,650.00
4¾" h, cabinet
Tapered cylinder, striated amber and pink, etched and enameled thistle blossoms, gilt sgd 450.00
Waisted diamond section, pale green, etched and gilt ivy leaves, gilt sgd 425.00
4⅞" h, cylindrical, mottled purple ground, etched and enameled green, pink, and purple columbines, sgd in cameo 2,000.00
5¼" h, 4⅝" d, flared cylinder, circular foot, body and foot joined by five applied purple handles, mottled purple ground, etched and enameled purple and green violets, curvilinear gilt border, gilt highlights, gilt sgd 32,000.00
5¾" h, 2¼" w, 1¼" d, single acid cutting, flattened body, anemones, gold highlights, amethyst ground . 565.00
6" h, 8" d, Art Nouveau, encased clear glass with tiny air bubbles, applied rope dec around top and middle, sgd "Daum Nancy, France" with cross of Lorraine ...2,200.00
6½" h, cameo cut and applied, mottled yellow, orange, and green layered in shades of green cut with berries and leafy branches, three applied cabochons over foil backing, two cut as insects, engraved name and cross mark 6,600.00
7¼" h, ovoid, everted rim, pink and gray flecks, vertical stripe etched surface, engraved "Daum Nancy France" with cross of Lorraine ... 700.00
7⅜" h, cylindrical, everted rim, cushion foot, double overlay, cameo cut and carved, mottled orange overlaid in orange and brown, carved riverside scene, sgd in cameo ...1,650.00
7½" h
Baluster, everted rim, ftd, green shading to orange, etched and enameled persimmon branches, sgd in cameo 1,000.00
Pear shape, everted rim, icy blue, irregular vertical striped etching, engraved "Daum Nancy France"3,000.00
8⅛" h, 11¾" d, flared cylinder, black flecked clear ground, orange over-

laid flecks, deeply carved Art Deco stylized flower branch, engraved "Daum Nancy France" with cross of Lorraine 5,000.00

8¼" h, shouldered cylindrical, internally dec, white and brown pulled diagonal stripes ground, enameled birch trees in foreground, bushy trees in background, browns, green, gray, and white, sgd "Daum/Nancy" with cross of Lorraine . . .2,200.00

9½" h, tapering cylinder, high shoulders, short neck, mottled orange and green in cream, overlaid light and dark green, cut landscape scene, trees in foreground, small islands with trees reflected in lake, cameo sgd "Daum/Nancy" with cross of Lorraine, c1900 . . . . .5,000.00

10½" h, high shouldered waisted ovoid, short neck, applied flat handles, frosted blue ground, seven rows of regularly spaced gilt fleur–de–lis overlay, one side with trailing banner inscribed "La Gloire des Lys," sgd in gilt "Daum Nancy" and cross of Lorraine 3,850.00

12" h, spherical, long slender neck, Solifleur, etched and enameled black scene, figure walking through grove of bare trees, orange and gilt thorny leaves and vines, gilt sgd . 1,000.00

12⅛" h, tapering cylindrical, everted rim, ftd, applied bright pink handle snaking down side, multicolored mottled glass, etched wild grape clusters, applied berries, engraved "Daum Nancy" with cross of Lorraine, crack to foot 2,860.00

13" h, ovoid, cameo, Art Deco, sapphire blue, alternating frosted, textured, and polished panels, imp mark at lower rim 1,650.00

13½" h, flared, mottled yellow ground shaded to red and maroon at bulbed base, brick–red, maroon, and black overlay, cameo cut and wheel carved foxgloves and tall leafy stalks, sgd "Daum Nancy" with cross in central design 3,900.00

Wall Sconce, 5½" l shade, 2" d fitter rim, bell form shade, mottled yellow and orange, orange stripes, wrought iron mount with grapes and grape leaves, shade sgd 530.00

DEGENHART GLASS

History: John (1884–1964) and Elizabeth (1889–1978) Degenhart operated the Crystal Art Glass factory of Cambridge, Ohio, from 1947 to 1978.

The factory specialized in reproduction pressed glass novelties and paperweights. Over 50 molds were worked by this factory including ten toothpick holders, five salts, and six animal covered dishes of various sizes.

Degenhart pressed glass novelties are collected by mold (Forget–Me–Not toothpick holders or all Degenhart toothpick holders), by individual colors (Rubina or Bloody Mary), or by group colors (opaque, iridescent, crystal, or slag).

Correct color identification is the key to full enjoyment of collecting Degenhart glass. Because of the slight variations in the hundreds of colors produced at the Degenhart Crystal Art Glass factory from 1947 to 1978, it is important for beginning collectors to acquire the eye for distinguishing Degenhart colors, particularly the green and blue variations. A knowledgeable collector or dealer should be sought for guidance. Side by side color comparison is extremely helpful.

Later glass produced by the factory can be distinguished by the trademark of a "D" in a heart or only a "D" on certain molds where space prohibited the full mark. Use of this mark began around 1972 and by late 1977 most of the molds had been marked. Prior to this time, c1947–1972, no glass was marked with the exception of the owl, and occasionally other pieces that were identified by hand-stamping a block letter "D" to the object as it came out of the mold. This hand-stamping was started and continued during the period 1967 to 1972.

Collecting unmarked Degenhart glass made from 1947 to c1970 poses no problem once a collector becomes familiar with molds and colors being worked during that period. Some of the most sought after colors such as Amethyst & White Slag, Amethyst Carnival, and Custard Slag are unmarked, yet are the most desirable. Keep in mind that some colors such as Custard (opaque yellow), Heliotrope (opaque purple), and Tomato (opaque orange red) were repeated and can be found marked and unmarked depending on production date.

When the factory ceased operation, many of the molds were purchased by Boyd Crystal Art Glass, Cambridge, Ohio. Boyd has issued pieces in many new colors. All are marked with a "B" in a diamond.

Reference: Gene Florence, *Degenhart Glass and Paperweights: A Collector's Guide To Colors And Values,* Degenhart Paperweight and Glass Museum, 1982.

Collectors' Club: The Friends of Degenhart, Degenhart Paperweight and Glass Museum, Inc., P. O. Box 186, Cambridge, OH 43725.

Museum: The Degenhart Paperweight and Glass Museum, Inc., Cambridge, OH. The museum covers all types of Ohio valley glass.

Reproduction Alert: Although most of the Degenhart molds were reproductions themselves, there are contemporary pieces that can be confusing, such as Kanawha's bird salt and bow slipper; L. G. Wright's mini–slipper, daisy & button salt, and 5" robin covered dish; and many other contemporary American pieces. The 3" bird salt and mini–pitcher also are made by an unknown glassmaker in Taiwan.

Animal Dish, covered
  Hen
    3", intro 1967, marked 1973

Champagne	35.00
Dark Green	25.00
Mint Green	20.00
Pigeon Blood	48.00
Sapphire Blue	20.00

    5", intro 1971, marked 1972

Bittersweet	65.00
Crown Tuscan	60.00
Sapphire Blue	60.00

  Lamb, intro 1961, marked 1972

Cobalt	40.00
Emerald Green	35.00

  Robin, intro 1960, marked 1972

Bloody Mary	90.00
Fawn	55.00
Taffeta	50.00

  Turkey, intro 1971, marked 1972

Amber	35.00
Amethyst	50.00
Custard	80.00
Slag, gray	80.00
Tomato	100.00

Bicentennial Bell, intro 1974, marked 1974

Amethyst	4.00
Elizabeth's Lime Ice	15.00
Ivorene	12.00
Peach	9.00
Seafoam	10.00

Boot
  Daisy and Button, high, intro 1952, marked 1972, Peach Blo 25.00
  Skate, intro 1961, marked 1972, Sapphire Dark 30.00
  Texas, intro 1974, marked 1974

Baby Green	15.00
Peach (clear)	12.00

Candy Dish, cov, Wildflower pattern, intro 1971, marked 1972

Apple Green	30.00
Twilight Blue	25.00

Child's Mug, Stork and Peacock pattern, intro 1971, marked 1972

Baby Green	20.00
Smokey Heather	25.00

Coaster, intro 1974, marked 1975

Crystal	8.00
Shamrock	6.00

Creamer and Sugar
  Daisy and Button, intro 1970, marked 1972, Cambridge Pink 75.00
  Texas, intro 1962, marked 1972

Cobalt Carnival	125.00
Pine Green	45.00

Cup Plate
  Heart and Lyre, intro 1965, marked c1977

Aqua	10.00
Cobalt Blue	12.00
Gold	9.00
Mulberry	15.00

  Seal Of Ohio, intro 1971, marked c1977

Opalescent	15.00
Sunset	10.00

Hat, Daisy and Button pattern, intro 1974, marked 1972

Crown Tuscan	20.00
Custard	20.00
Milk Blue	12.00
Vaseline	15.00

Jewel Box, Heart, Nile Green, marked 1972, $30.00.

Jewel Box, Heart, intro 1964, marked 1972

Blue Jay	25.00
Heliotrope	35.00

Owl, intro 1967, marked 1967, over 200 colors made

Amberina	35.00
Bluebell	30.00
Canary	35.00
Crown Tuscan	40.00
Frosty Jade	45.00
Ivory, Light	30.00
Lavender Blue	50.00
Misty Green	40.00
Nile Green Opal	45.00
Seafoam	36.00
Shell	40.00
Sunset	25.00
Willow Blue	48.00

Paperweight
  Crystal Art Glass, Zack and Bernard

Boyd, Rollin Braden, Gus Theret
and William Degenhart
Hand painted plate weight 75.00
Marble 150.00
Multicolored 75.00
Red Flower 65.00
Single–colored window weight ... 200.00
Paperweight by John or Charles De-
genhart
Morning Glories 80.00
Name weight 35.00
Star Flower 70.00
Pitcher, Mini, intro 1973, marked 1973,
Jade 20.00
Pooch, intro 1976, marked 1976, ap-
proximately 110 colors made
Canary 15.00
Heatherbloom 30.00
Mauve 12.00
Smokey Blue 12.00
Portrait Plate, Degenhart, intro 1974,
marked 1974, Crystal 35.00

Priscilla, ivory, marked 1976, $65.00.

Priscilla, intro 1976, marked 1976, only
40 colors made
Amber 75.00
Daffodil 100.00
Periwinkle 75.00
Salt
Bird, 1½", intro 1966, marked 1972
Amber 12.00
Orchid 15.00
Daisy and Button, intro 1970, marked
1972
Amberina 15.00
Rose Marie 12.00
Pottie, intro 1971, marked 1972
Chocolate Creme Slag 15.00
Milk White 10.00
Star and Dew Drop, intro 1952,
marked 1972
Forest Green 12.00

Lemon Opal 20.00
Salt and Pepper Shakers, pr, Bird, intro
1958, marked 1973
Baby Green 35.00
Ruby 50.00
Slipper
Daisy and Button or Bow
Blue Marble Slag 25.00
Taffeta 20.00
Kat, intro 1947, marked 1972
Frosty Jade 25.00
Sapphire 15.00
Miniature, intro 1965, marked 1972
Emerald Green 12.00
Vaseline 15.00
Tomahawk, intro 1947, marked c1975,
Custard Maverick 55.00
Toothpick Holder
Baby or Tramp Shoe, intro 1962,
marked 1972
Gold 8.00
Lemon Custard 20.00
Pigeon Blood 25.00
Basket, intro 1963, marked c1974
Milk White 20.00
Sparrow Slag 15.00
Beaded Oval, intro 1967, marked
1972
Bittersweet 30.00
Tomato 45.00
Bird, intro 1959, marked 1972
Dichromatic 30.00
Persimmon 15.00
Colonial Drape and Heart, intro
1961, marked 1972
Amethyst, Light 12.00
Ruby 20.00
Daisy and Button, intro 1970, marked
1972
Apple Green 15.00
Fawn 12.00
Peach Blo 15.00
Elephant Head, intro c1957, marked
1972
Amber 20.00
Jade 50.00
Forget–me–not, intro 1965, marked
1972, made in over 150 colors
April Green #1 .... 15.00
Bloody Mary #2 .... 40.00
Cambridge Pink 25.00
Grape 15.00
Zach Boyd Slag 40.00
Gypsy Pot, intro 1962, marked 1972
Bittersweet 30.00
Blue Fire 15.00
Elizabeth's Lime Ice 25.00
Red 30.00
Tray, hand shape, intro 1949, marked
c1975
Bittersweet 15.00
Taffeta 12.00

Wine
    Buzz Saw, intro 1967, marked 1973
        Honey Amber **15.00**
        Pistachio **20.00**
        Taffeta **40.00**
    Daisy and Button, intro 1969, marked
        1972, Sunset **20.00**

DEPRESSION GLASS

History: Depression glass is a glassware made during the period of 1920–40. It was an inexpensive machine–made glass produced by several companies in various patterns and colors. The number of pieces within a pattern also varied.

Depression glass was sold through variety stores, given as premiums, or packaged with certain products. Movie houses gave it away from 1935 until well into the 1940s.

Like Pattern glass, knowing the proper name of a pattern is the key to collecting. Collectors should be prepared to do research. Also like pattern glass, color plays a large factor in the pricing of Depression glass. The listing below does not list every piece made or every color known for patterns. It is a sampling of the present Depression glass market.

References: Gene Florence, *The Collector's Encyclopedia of Depression Glass, Tenth Edition,* Collector Books, 1992; Gene Florence, *Elegant Glassware of the Depression Era, Fourth Edition,* Collector Books, 1991; Gene Florence, *Very Rare Glassware Of The Depression Years,* Collector Books, 1987, 1990 value update; Gene Florence, *Very Rare Glassware of the Depression Years, Second Series,* Collector Books, 1991; Carl F. Luckey and Mary Burris, *An Identification & Value Guide to Depression Era Glassware, Second Edition,* Books Americana, 1986; Mark Schliesmann, *Price Survey, Second Edition,* Park Avenue Publications, Ltd., 1984; Hazel Marie Weatherman, *1984 Supplement & Price Trends for Colored Glassware Of The Depression Era, Book 1,* published by author, 1984.

Periodical: *The Daze,* Box 57, Otisville, MI 48463.

Collectors' Club: National Depression Glass Association, Inc., P.O. Box 69843, Odessa, TX 79769.

Reproduction Alert: Send a self addressed stamped business envelope to *The Daze* and request a copy of their glass reproduction list. It is one of the best bargains in the antiques business. Patterns listed below with an asterisk are known to have been reproduced. In some cases, the entire pattern has been reproduced, in other cases only specific pieces represent problems. Now that importers are reproducing the modern reproductions, careful attention must be paid to those patterns which have already been copied.

Note: The examples listed below are only a small sampling of the patterns and variety of objects found in this large collecting area. Please refer to one of the reference books mentioned above for more detailed listings of a particular pattern or manufacturer.

Adam, Jeannette Glass Co., 1932–34*
Ashtray, green **18.00**
Bowl, 7¾" d
    Green **15.00**
    Pink **17.50**
Butter Dish, cov
    Green **295.00**
    Pink **75.00**
Cake Plate, green, ftd **22.00**
Candlesticks, pr, 4" h
    Green **80.00**
    Pink **60.00**
Candy Jar, cov, 2½" h
    Green **75.00**
    Pink **60.00**
Cereal Bowl, green **40.00**
Creamer
    Green **15.00**
    Pink **12.50**
Coaster, pink **20.00**
Compote, pink **18.00**
Cup
    Green **17.00**
    Pink **18.50**
Fruit Bowl, clear, oval, 10" l **10.00**
Goblet, clear **17.50**
Iced Tea Tumbler, green, 5½" h **40.00**
Juice Goblet, pink, 4¾" h **65.00**
Pitcher, 8" h, 32 oz
    Green **35.00**
    Pink **32.50**
Plate
    Bread and Butter, 6" d
        Green **6.00**
        Pink **5.00**
    Dinner, 9" sq
        Green **17.50**
        Pink **18.00**
    Grill, 10¼" d
        Clear **7.50**
        Pink **16.00**
    Salad, 7¾" sq
        Green **8.50**
        Pink **8.00**
Platter, green, oval **17.50**
Relish, pink, four sections **16.00**
Salt and Pepper Shakers, pr, pink ... **45.00**
Saucer, 6" sq
    Green **5.00**
    Pink **4.00**
Sherbet
    Green **32.00**

Pink 20.00
Sugar
  Green 15.00
  Pink 12.50
Tumbler, green, 4¼" h 18.00
American Sweetheart, MacBeth–Evans
Glass Co., 1930–1936
Berry Bowl
  Cremax 8.50
  Pink, 9" d 34.00
Cereal Bowl, pink 11.00
Chop Plate, monax, 11" d 9.50
Console Bowl, blue, 18" d 85.00
Cream Soup, 4½" d
  Monax 42.50
  Pink 32.50
Creamer
  Blue 75.00
  Monax 7.50
  Pink 8.00
Cup
  Monax 7.50
  Pink 10.00
  Red 65.00
Plate
  Bread and Butter, 6"
    Monax 2.00
    Pink 2.50
    Smoke 15.00
  Dinner, 9" d
    Monax 9.00
    Pink 17.50
    Smoke 50.00
  Luncheon, smoke, 9" d 30.00
Platter, monax 48.00
Salt and Pepper Shakers, pr, monax . 250.00
Salver, red, 12" d 150.00
Saucer
  Monax 1.50
  Pink 2.50
Sherbet, ftd, 4¼" h
  Monax 13.00
  Pink 12.00
Sugar
  Monax, cov 155.00
  Pink, open, ftd 8.50
  Red 120.00
Tidbit Server, monax, two tiers, 8"
  and 12" 95.00
Tumbler
  Monax, 3½" h, 5 oz 48.00
  Pink, 4½" h, 9 oz 55.00
Anniversary, Jeannette Glass Co.,
1947–49
Bowl, 9" d
  Clear 7.00
  Pink 12.00
Butter Dish, cov, pink 45.00
Cake Plate, clear 6.00
Creamer
  Clear 3.50
  Pink 7.50

Cup
  Clear 2.75
  Pink 4.75
Plate
  Dinner, 9" d
    Clear 3.50
    Pink 5.50
  Sherbet, 6¼" d
    Clear 1.25
    Pink 2.00
Saucer
  Clear 1.00
  Pink 1.50
Sherbet
  Clear 2.50
  Pink 4.50
Soup Bowl
  Clear 4.75
  Pink 7.50
Sugar
  Clear 2.50
  Pink 5.00
Aunt Polly, U.S. Glass Co., late 1920s
Berry Bowl, blue, 7⅞" d 30.00
Butter Dish, cov, green 210.00
Candy, cov, irid 50.00
Compote, blue, handle 32.50
Creamer
  Blue 35.00
  Green 22.00
Pitcher, blue, 8" h 170.00
Plate
  Luncheon, blue, 8" d 15.00
  Sherbet, green, 6" d 4.00
Sherbet, ftd
  Blue 9.00
  Green 7.50
Sugar
  Blue 32.50
  Irid 35.00
Tumbler, blue 20.00
Avocado, (No. 601), Indiana Glass Co.,
1923–1933*
Bowl, green, 7½" d 45.00
Creamer
  Green 27.50
  Pink 25.00
Cup
  Green 27.50
  Pink 25.00
Plate
  Luncheon, 8¼" d
    Green 15.00
    Pink 14.00
  Sherbet, 6⅜" d
    Green 12.50
    Pink 10.00
Salad Bowl, 7½" d
  Green 40.00
  Pink 30.00
Saucer
  Green 20.00

Pink **18.00**
Sherbet
  Green **47.50**
  Pink **45.00**
Sugar, ftd
  Green **27.50**
  Pink **25.00**
Tumbler
  Green **150.00**
  Pink **100.00**
Block Optic, (Block), Hocking Glass Co., 1929–1933
Bowl, 4¼" d
  Green **6.00**
  Pink **5.00**
Candlesticks, pr, pink, 1¾" h **75.00**
Candy Jar, cov, 2¼" h
  Green **35.00**
  Pink **35.00**
  Yellow **45.00**
Cereal Bowl, green, 5¼" d **12.00**
Creamer
  Green **10.00**
  Pink **10.00**
  Yellow **10.00**
Cup
  Green, flared **5.00**
  Pink **5.00**
  Yellow **10.00**
Goblet, 5¾" h, 9 oz
  Green **17.00**
  Pink **20.00**
Ice Bucket, green **30.00**
Pitcher, 7⅝" h, 68 oz
  Green **60.00**
  Pink **55.00**
Plate
  Dinner, 9" d
    Green **13.50**
    Pink **20.00**
    Yellow **30.00**
  Grill, 9" d
    Green **8.50**
    Pink **12.00**
    Yellow **28.00**
  Luncheon, 8" d
    Green **3.00**
    Pink **2.75**
    Yellow **3.75**
Salad Bowl, green **17.50**
Saucer
  Green **7.50**
  Pink **6.50**
Sherbet, 3¼" h
  Green **4.50**
  Pink **6.50**
  Yellow **7.50**
Sugar
  Green **9.00**
  Pink **8.50**
  Yellow **9.50**

Tumbler, 9 oz, ftd
  Green **13.50**
  Pink **12.00**
  Yellow **18.00**
Bubble, (Bullseye, Provincial), Anchor Hocking Glass Co., 1934–1965
Bowl, blue, 4½" d **9.00**
Cereal Bowl, dark green **7.50**
Creamer
  Blue **25.00**
  Dark Green **7.50**
Cup
  Blue **2.50**
  Dark Green **3.00**
  Red **4.00**
Plate
  Bread and Butter, 6¾" d
    Blue **2.00**
    Dark Green **1.50**
  Dinner, 9⅜" d
    Blue **5.00**
    Dark Green **5.00**
    Red **5.50**
Platter, blue **10.75**
Saucer, blue **2.00**
Sugar
  Blue **8.50**
  Dark Green **6.50**
Cameo, (Ballerina, Dancing Girl), Hocking Glass Co., 1930–34*
Berry Bowl, 8¼" d
  Green **25.00**
  Pink **125.00**
Butter Dish, cov, green **175.00**
Cake Plate, green, 10" d **15.00**
Candy Dish, cov, green, low **55.00**
Console Bowl, green, ftd **54.00**
Creamer, green, 3¼" h **20.00**
Cup
  Clear **5.00**
  Green **12.00**
  Pink **60.00**
  Yellow **6.50**
Goblet, 6" h
  Green **40.00**
  Pink **150.00**
Mayonnaise, green, ftd **25.00**
Plate
  Dinner, 9½" d
    Green **12.00**
    Pink **50.00**
    Yellow **6.00**
  Grill, 10½" d
    Green **7.50**
    Pink **38.00**
    Yellow **6.00**
  Luncheon, 8" d
    Clear **3.50**
    Green **7.50**
    Pink **25.00**
    Yellow **7.50**
Platter, green, closed handles, 12" l . **18.00**

Relish, green, four sections, ftd, 7½"
d 27.00
Salt and Pepper Shakers, pr, green .. 60.00
Salad Bowl, green, 7¼" d 50.00
Sandwich Plate, green, 10" d 10.00
Saucer
   Green 2.00
   Pink 72.00
   Yellow 2.00
Sherbet, green 20.00
Sugar, green, 4¼" h 20.00
Vase, green, 5¾" h 175.00
Cherry Blossom, Jeannette Glass Co.,
1930–1939*
Berry Bowl, green, 4¾" d 16.00
Bowl, pink, 10" d, ftd 65.00
Cereal Bowl, green 27.50
Creamer
   Delphite 19.00
   Green 18.00
   Pink 17.00
Cup
   Delphite 12.50
   Green 15.00
   Pink 16.00
Mug, pink, 7 oz 235.00
Pitcher, green, ftd, 8" h 45.00
Plate
   Dinner, 9" d
      Delphite 13.00
      Green 18.00
      Pink 15.00
   Grill, 9" d
      Green 16.50
      Pink 18.00
   Salad, 7" d
      Green 14.50
      Pink 17.00
Sandwich Plate, green, 10½" d 20.00
Sherbet
   Delphite 12.00
   Green 13.50
   Pink 12.00
Sugar
   Delphite 15.00
   Green 12.50
   Pink 10.00
Vegetable Bowl, pink, oval, 9" d ... 30.00
Colonial, (Knife and Fork), Hocking
Glass Co., 1934–1936
Berry Bowl, green, 9" d 23.00
Cocktail, green 18.00
Cream Soup
   Clear 42.00
   Green 40.00
   Pink 40.00
Creamer
   Clear 10.00
   Green 17.50
   Pink 15.00
Cup
   Clear 6.00

   Green 9.00
   Pink 9.00
Goblet, 5¾" h
   Clear 12.50
   Green 24.00
   Pink 30.00
Iced Tea Tumbler
   Clear 20.00
   Green 42.00
   Pink 35.00
Plate
   Dinner, green, 10" d 48.00
   Grill, pink 15.00
   Luncheon, pink 6.50
   Sherbet, clear 2.50
Saucer
   Clear 2.50
   Green 4.00
   Pink 3.50
Spooner, green 90.00
Sugar
   Clear 8.00
   Green 10.00
   Pink 18.00
Tumbler, 4" h, 9 oz
   Clear 10.00
   Green 16.00
   Pink 12.50
Columbia, Federal Glass Co., 1938–
1942
Bowl, clear, ruffled edge 10½" d ... 16.00
Butter Dish, cov
   Clear 15.00
   Ruby Flashed 18.00
Cereal Bowl, clear, 5" d 10.00
Cup
   Clear 4.50
   Pink 15.00
Plate
   Bread and Butter, 6" d
      Clear 2.00
      Pink 8.00
   Luncheon, 9½" d
      Clear 5.00
      Pink 20.00
Saucer
   Clear 2.00
   Pink 5.00
Snack Plate, clear 30.00
Tumbler, clear, 9 oz 14.00
Coronation, (Banded Rib, Saxon),
Hocking Glass Co., 1936–1940
Berry Bowl, 4½" d
   Pink 3.50
   Ruby 4.50
Cup
   Pink 3.50
   Ruby 4.50
Nappy
   Pink 4.00
   Ruby 9.00

Plate
Grill, pink, 8½" d 7.00
Luncheon, 8½" d
  Green 25.00
  Pink 3.50
  Ruby 6.50
Sherbet, pink, 6" d 1.75
Saucer, pink 1.75
Sherbet
  Green 37.50
  Pink 15.00
Tumbler, 10 oz, ftd
  Green 72.00
  Pink 17.50
Cube, (Cubist), Jeannette Glass Co.,
1929–1933
Bowl, pink, 4½" d 4.50
Butter Dish, cov, green 40.00
Candy Dish, cov, green 21.00
Coaster
  Green 4.50
  Pink 3.50
Creamer, 3" h
  Green 7.50
  Pink 5.50
Cup
  Green 7.00
  Pink 5.00
Pitcher, 8¾" h
  Green 175.00
  Pink 150.00
Plate
Luncheon, 8" d
  Green 5.00
  Pink 3.00
Sherbet, 6" d
  Green 2.50
  Pink 1.50
Powder Jar, cov
  Green 17.50
  Pink 16.00
Salad Bowl, green, 6½" d 13.00
Saucer
  Green 1.50
  Pink 1.25
Sherbet
  Green 6.00
  Pink 4.50
Sugar, 3" d
  Green 10.00
  Pink 8.00
Tumbler, 9 oz
  Green 45.00
  Pink 40.00
Daisy, (No. 620), Indiana Glass Co.,
production dates vary according to
color
Berry Bowl, amber, 7⅜" d 14.00
Creamer, amber, ftd 7.50
Cream Soup, 4½" d
  Clear 3.00
  Green 3.00

Red 7.50
Cup
  Amber 4.50
  Clear 2.50
  Green 2.50
  Red 4.50
Plate
Dinner, 9⅜" d
  Amber 7.25
  Clear 3.50
  Green 3.50
  Red 7.00
Luncheon, 8⅜" d
  Amber 5.00
  Clear 2.00
  Green 2.00
  Red 5.50
Salad, 7⅜" d
  Amber 5.50
  Clear 2.50
  Green 2.50
  Red 6.00
Platter, amber, 10¾" l 10.00
Relish, amber, three sections 21.00
Saucer
  Amber 1.50
  Clear 1.00
  Green 1.00
  Red 1.50
Sugar, ftd
  Amber 7.50
  Clear 3.50
  Green 3.50
  Red 7.00
Vegetable Bowl, amber, oval, 10" d .   16.50
Diana, Federal Glass Co., 1937–1941
Ashtray
  Clear 2.00
  Green 3.00
  Pink 3.00
Cereal Bowl, 5" d
  Amber 8.50
  Clear 3.50
  Pink 4.50
Candy Jar, cov
  Amber 25.00
  Clear 12.00
  Pink 20.00
Console Bowl, amber, 11" d 9.00
Creamer
  Amber 7.50
  Clear 3.50
  Pink 5.50
Cup
  Amber 7.00
  Clear 4.00
  Pink 5.50
Demitasse Cup and Saucer
  Clear 8.50
  Pink 18.00
Plate
Bread and Butter, 6" d

Amber	1.75
Clear	1.00
Pink	1.5⌐
Dinner, 9½″ d	
Amber	7.50
Clear	5.00
Pink	6.50
Platter, amber	12.00
Salt and Pepper Shakers, pr	
Amber	85.00
Clear	20.00
Pink	50.00
Sandwich Plate, amber, 11¾″ d	7.00
Saucer	
Amber	1.50
Clear	1.00
Pink	1.50
Sugar, open, oval	
Amber	4.50
Clear	3.00
Pink	4.50

Dogwood, tumbler, pink, 5″ h, $35.00.

Dogwood, (Apple Blossom, Wild Rose), Mac–Beth Evans Glass Co., 1929–1932

Berry Bowl, 8½″ d	
Cremax	2.00
Green	20.00
Pink	18.00
Cake Plate, pink, 11″ d	200.00
Creamer	
Green	13.00
Pink	14.00
Cup	
Cremax	32.00
Green	20.00
Monax	30.00
Pink	15.00
Pitcher, pink	140.00
Plate	
Bread and Butter, 6″ d	
Cremax	20.00
Green	6.00
Pink	5.00

Grill, 10½″ d	
Green	17.50
Pink	17.50
Luncheon, 8″ d	
Green	6.00
Pink	5.00
Saucer	
Cremax	15.00
Green	5.00
Monax	15.00
Pink	4.50
Sugar, thin	
Green	35.00
Pink	15.00
Tumbler, 10 oz, dec	
Green	65.00
Pink	35.00

Doric, Jeannette Glass Co., 1935–1938

Berry Bowl, 4½″ d	
Delphite	25.00
Green	5.50
Pink	5.00
Butter Dish, cov	
Green	75.00
Pink	60.00
Cake Plate	
Green	14.00
Pink	14.00
Candy Dish, cov, pink, 8″ d	27.50
Creamer, 4″ h	
Green	9.00
Pink	8.00
Cup	
Green	7.50
Pink	6.50
Pitcher, green, 6″ h, 36 oz	40.00
Plate	
Dinner, 9″ d	
Green	12.00
Pink	9.00
Grill, 9″ d	
Green	15.00
Pink	10.00
Salad, 7″ d	
Green	13.50
Pink	12.50
Relish, 4 x 8″	
Green	10.00
Pink	7.50
Saucer	
Green	2.50
Pink	2.00
Sugar	
Green	10.00
Pink	8.00
Tray, 8 x 8″	
Green	12.00
Pink	10.00

Floragold, (Louisa), Jeannette Glass Co., 1950s

Bowl, irid, 9½″ d	6.50
Butter Dish, cov, irid, oblong	20.00

Candlesticks, double branch, pr, irid   40.00
Coaster, irid 4.50
Creamer and Sugar, irid 14.00
Cup and Sugar, irid 15.00
Pitcher, irid, 64 oz 25.00
Plate, irid
  Dinner, 8½" d 20.00
  Sherbet, 5¼" d 8.00
Platter, irid, 11¼" l 15.00
Tumbler, irid, ftd 12.00
Floral, (Poinsettia), Jeannette Glass Co.,
1931–1935*
Berry Bowl, 4" d
  Delphite 25.00
  Green 12.00
  Pink 12.00
Candlesticks, pr, green, 4" h 69.00
Candy Jar, cov
  Green 35.00
  Pink 30.00
Creamer
  Cremax 50.00
  Delphite 65.00
  Green 12.00
  Pink 10.00
Cup
  Green 9.50
  Pink 8.50
Juice Tumbler, ftd, 4" h
  Green 17.50
  Pink 15.00
Pitcher, green, 32 oz, ftd, 8" h 32.00
Plate
  Dinner, 9" d
    Delphite 110.00
    Green 14.00
    Pink 12.00
  Grill, green, 9" d 148.00
  Salad, 8" d
    Green 8.50
    Pink 7.50
Platter, green, oval, 10¾" l 15.00
Relish, green, two sections 11.00
Salt and Pepper Shakers, pr, green, ftd   35.00
Saucer
  Green 8.50
  Pink 7.50
Sugar
  Cremax 50.00
  Delphite 55.00
  Green 24.50
  Pink 20.00
Florentine #1, (Old Florentine, Poppy
No. 1), Hazel Atlas, 1932–1935
Ashtray, 5½" d
  Clear 20.00
  Green 20.00
  Pink 25.00
  Yellow 25.00
Berry Bowl, green 7.00
Cereal Bowl, 6" d
  Clear 17.50

Green 17.50
Pink 15.00
Yellow 18.00
Creamer, ruffled
  Clear 18.00
  Pink 30.00
Cup
  Blue 65.00
  Clear 7.50
  Green 7.00
  Pink 6.50
  Yellow 8.00
Iced Tea Tumbler, 5¼" h
  Green 20.00
  Pink 25.00
  Yellow 25.00
Juice Tumbler, yellow, ftd 18.00
Pitcher, green, 36 oz, ftd, 6½" h ... 38.00
Plate
  Dinner, 10" d
    Clear 10.00
    Green 10.00
    Pink 17.50
    Yellow 18.00
  Salad, 8½" d
    Clear 6.00
    Green 6.00
    Pink 9.00
    Yellow 10.00
Platter, clear, oval, 11½" l 12.00
Saucer
  Clear 2.50
  Green 2.50
  Pink 4.50
  Yellow 4.50
Sherbet
  Clear 6.50
  Green 6.50
  Pink 7.50
  Yellow 8.50
Sugar
  Clear 8.00
  Green 8.00
  Pink 10.00
  Yellow 12.00
Florentine #2, (Poppy No. 2), Hazel
Atlas
Berry Bowl, pink, 8" d 25.00
Condiment Set, yellow, tray, salt and
  pepper shakers, sugar and creamer 200.00
Creamer and Sugar
  Green 12.50
  Yellow 18.00
Cup and Saucer
  Amber 65.00
  Green 8.00
  Yellow 10.00
Custard Cup
  Green 50.00
  Yellow 65.00
Parfait, yellow 50.00

Plate
  Dinner, 10" d
    Green 10.00
    Pink 12.00
    Yellow 12.00
  Grill, 10¼" d
    Green 7.50
    Yellow 8.50
Relish, pink, three sections 24.00
Tumbler, green 11.00
Vegetable Bowl
  Green 40.00
  Yellow 55.00
Holiday, (Buttons and Bows), Jeannette
Glass Co., 1947–49
Berry Bowl, pink, 5⅛" d 8.00
Butter Dish, cov, pink 30.00
Candlesticks, pr, pink 75.00
Console Bowl, pink, 10½" d 100.00
Creamer, pink 8.00
Cup, pink 5.00
Pitcher, pink
  4¾" h 45.00
  6¾" h 25.00
Plate, pink
  Dinner, 9" d 12.00
  Sherbet, 6" d 3.50
Saucer, pink 4.00
Sherbet, pink 5.00
Sugar, pink 22.00
Tumbler, ftd, pink, 4" h 28.00
Homespun, (Fine Rib), Jeannette Glass
Co., 1939–1949
Ashtray, clear 6.50
Bowl, 4½" d
  Clear 4.50
  Pink 5.00
Butter Dish, cov, pink 62.00
Creamer, ftd, pink 7.50
Cup, clear 4.50
Plate
  Dinner, 9¼" d
    Clear 10.00
    Pink 10.00
  Sherbet, 6" d
    Clear 2.50
    Pink 2.50
Saucer, pink 2.00
Sherbet, pink 12.00
Sugar, pink, ftd 10.00
Tumbler, pink, 4" h 6.00
Iris, (Iris and Herringbone), Jeannette
Glass Co., 1928–1932, 1950s, 1970s
Berry Bowl, clear, beaded edge, 8" d 75.00
Bowl, clear
  9½" d, ruffled 10.00
  11" d, straight edge 45.00
Butter Dish, cov, clear 40.00
Cocktail, clear 17.50
Creamer, irid, ftd 10.00
Cup
  Clear 9.00

Irid 8.50
Demitasse Cup 20.00
Goblet, 4¼" h 15.00
Nut Set, clear 38.50
Plate
  Dinner, irid, 9" d 38.50
  Sandwich Plate, irid, 11¾" d 22.00
  Saucer, clear 6.50
Sherbet, low, ftd 16.00
Tumbler, irid, 6" h 14.00
Wine, clear 15.00
Lace Edge, (Open Lace), Hocking Glass
Co., 1935–1938
Bowl, clear, 8¼" d 12.00
Butter Dish, cov, pink 58.50
Candlesticks, pr, pink 150.00
Candy Jar, cov, ribbed, pink 35.00
Compote, pink, 7" d 22.00
Cookie Jar, cov, pink 55.00
Creamer, pink 17.50
Cup and Saucer, pink 25.00
Fish Bowl, clear 18.50
Plate, pink
  Dinner, 10½" d 20.00
  Grill, 10½" d 15.00
  Salad, 8¼" d 14.00
Sugar, pink 15.00
Lorain, (Basket, No. 615), Indiana Glass
Co., 1929–32
Bowl, yellow, 8" d 160.00
Creamer, ftd, green 12.50
Cup, yellow 10.00
Plate
  Dinner, green, 10¼" d 30.00
  Luncheon, yellow, 7¾" d 10.00
Relish, yellow, four parts 25.00
Sandwich Plate, yellow, 7¼" d 51.00
Sherbet, ftd, clear 15.00
Saucer, green 3.50
Sugar, yellow, ftd 16.00
Tumbler, yellow, ftd, 9 oz 10.00
Manhattan, (Horizontal Ribbed), An-
chor Hocking Glass Co., 1938–43
Ashtray, clear, 4" d 9.00
Bowl, clear, closed handles, 8" d ... 12.00
Compote, clear 30.00
Creamer, pink 8.00
Cup, clear 17.00
Pitcher, clear, 24 oz 20.00
Plate, clear
  Dinner, 10¼" d 12.00
  Salad, 8½" d 9.00
Relish, clear, four sections, 14" d ... 17.00
Salt and Pepper Shakers, pr, pink ... 30.00
Saucer, clear 3.75
Sugar, pink 7.50
Mayfair, (Open Rose), Hocking Glass
Co., 1931–37
Bowl, cov, pink, 10 " d 100.00
Butter Dish, cov, blue 230.00
Cake Plate, green, ftd, 10" d 85.00
Celery Dish, pink 25.00

Cereal Bowl, blue 35.00
Cookie Jar, cov, yellow 165.00
Cup and Saucer, pink 45.00
Decanter, orig stopper, pink 100.00
Goblet, pink, 5¾" h 48.00
Iced Tea Tumbler, pink 35.00
Plate
    Dinner, pink, 9½" d 35.00
    Luncheon, green, 8½" d 60.00
Platter, pink 18.00
Relish, pink, four sections, 8⅜" d .. 24.00
Sandwich Server, center handle
    Blue 45.00
    Pink 30.00
    Yellow 95.00
Sugar
    Blue 50.00
    Yellow 165.00
Tumbler, pink, 4¼" h 22.00
Vegetable Bowl, blue, oval, 9½" d . 50.00
Miss America, (Diamond Pattern),
    Hocking Glass Co., 1935–37*
Bowl, clear, 6¼" d 6.00
Cake Plate, pink 38.00
Candy Dish, cov, pink 105.00
Celery, pink, 10½" l 18.00
Coaster, clear, 5¾" d 12.00
Creamer, pink 13.00
Cup and Saucer, clear 10.00
Goblet, pink 35.00
Iced Tea Tumbler, clear 20.00
Pitcher, ice lip, clear, 8½" h 60.00
Plate
    Dinner, pink, 10¼" d 18.00
    Salad, clear, 8½" d 5.00
Platter, pink 18.50
Relish, round, four sections, clear,
    8¾" d 16.00
Salt and Pepper Shakers, pr, clear .. 30.00
Tumbler, green 15.00
Wine, pink 50.00

Moderntone, plate, blue, 6″ d, $5.00.

Newport, (Hairpin), Hazel Atlas Co.,
1936–40
Cereal Bowl, cobalt blue 14.00

Creamer, amethyst 13.00
Cream Soup, amethyst 12.00
Plate, luncheon, cobalt blue, 8½" d   8.00
Salt and Pepper Shakers, pr, cobalt
    blue 55.00
Sandwich Plate, cobalt blue, 11½" d 25.00
Saucer, amethyst 3.00
Sugar, amethyst 12.00
Tumbler, amethyst, 4½" h, 9 oz 28.00
Patrician, (Spoke), Federal Glass Co.,
1933–37
Berry Bowl, pink, 8½" d 39.00
Butter Dish, cov
    Green 80.00
    Pink 225.00
Cereal Bowl, green 20.00
Creamer, pink, ftd 10.00
Cream Soup, amber 12.00
Cup, clear 7.00
Pitcher, amber, molded handle, 8" h,
    75 oz 95.00
Plate
    Dinner, amber, 10½" d 4.50
    Grill, pink, 10½" d 9.50
Platter, amber, oval 24.00
Salt and Pepper Shakers, pr, pink ... 125.00
Saucer, green 5.00
Sherbet, clear 8.50
Tumbler, amber, 8 oz, ftd, 5¼" h ... 35.00
Vegetable Bowl, green, oval, 10" d . 24.00

Pretzel, creamer, clear, 4″ h, $4.00.

Princess, Hocking Glass Co., 1931–35
Ashtray, green, 4½" d 65.00
Berry Bowl, pink 22.00
Bowl, green, hat shape 35.00
Butter Dish, cov, green 80.00
Cake Plate, green 15.00
Candy Dish, cov, pink 45.00
Cereal Bowl, pink 25.00
Creamer and Sugar, green 25.00
Cup, pink 6.00
Juice Pitcher, pink 50.00
Juice Tumbler, green 22.00
Plate
    Dinner, topaz, 9" d 12.50
    Salad, green, 8" d 9.50

Salt and Pepper Shakers, pr, pink ...   40.00
Sandwich Plate, green, handle, 11" d   17.00
Saucer, pink 3.50
Spice Shakers, pr, green 35.00
Tumbler, green, ftd, 5¼" h 25.00
Queen Mary, (Prismatic Line, Vertical Ribbed), Hocking Glass Co., 1936–1949
Ashtray, clear, oval 2.00
Bowl, pink, 5½" d 5.00
Candlesticks, pr, pink, round, 6" h .   30.00
Creamer and Sugar, clear 30.00
Cup, pink 5.00
Plate
  Dinner, pink, 9¾" d 40.00
  Salad, clear, 8¾" d 4.00
Punch Cup, pink 6.00
Relish, three sections, clear 10.00
Saucer, clear 1.50
Tumbler, pink, ftd 30.00
Rosemary, (Dutch Rose), Federal Glass Co., 1935–37
Creamer, amber 6.50
Cream Soup, pink 15.00
Cup and Saucer, green 13.50
Plate, dinner, pink 12.00
Platter, pink 24.00
Sugar, ftd, green 10.00
Tumbler, amber 22.50
Royal Lace, Hazel Atlas Co., 1934–1941
Berry Bowl, green 22.00
Butter Dish, cov, blue 520.00
Candy Dish, cov, blue 40.00
Creamer, clear 18.00
Cream Soup, green 20.00
Cup and Saucer, clear 7.50
Pitcher, clear, 8" h 50.00
Plate
  Dinner, pink, 9⅞" d 14.50
  Luncheon, green, 8½" d 10.00
Salt and Pepper Shakers, pr, green ..   110.00
Sherbet, metal holder, blue 22.00
Sugar, clear 15.00
Sharon, (Cabbage Rose), Federal Glass Co., 1935–39*
Berry Bowl, pink 7.50

Spiral, sherbet, ultramarine, 2⅞" h, 4⅛" d, $8.50.

Butter Dish, cov, amber 45.00
Cake Plate, amber, 11½" d 22.00
Cheese Dish, cov, amber 168.00
Creamer, amber, ftd 12.00
Cup and Saucer, amber 12.00
Fruit Bowl, pink 25.00
Pitcher, pink, 80 oz, ice lip 130.00
Plate
  Dinner, green, 9½" d 13.40
  Salad, amber, 7½" d 12.00
Platter, amber, 12½" d 12.00
Salt and Pepper Shakers, pr, pink ...   35.00
Soup Bowl, amber, 7½" d 40.00
Sugar, pink 10.00
Vegetable Bowl, green, oval, 9½" d   22.50
Strawberry, U.S. Glass Co., early 1930s
Berry Bowl, irid 5.00
Compote, green, 5¾" d 22.00
Creamer and Sugar, large, pink 65.00
Pickle Dish, clear 7.00
Pitcher, green, 7¾" h 210.00
Sherbet, pink 6.50

Sunflower, ashtray, pink, 5⅛" d, $7.00.

Tearoom, Indiana Glass Co., 1926–31
Banana Split, green 65.00
Candlesticks, pr, green 65.00
Creamer and Sugar, matching tray, pink 50.00
Cup and Saucer, pink 55.00
Ice Bucket, green 78.00
Parfait, green 50.00
Salt and Pepper Shakers, pr, green ..   60.00
Sundae, pink, ruffled top 60.00
Tumbler, green 24.00
Vase, clear, 9½" h 15.00
Victory, Diamond Glass–Ware Co., 1929–1932
Bon Bon, amber 9.00
Cereal, black 20.00
Creamer and Sugar, amber 20.00
Cup, pink 9.00
Plate, dinner, green, 9" d 15.00
Sandwich Plate, pink, center handle   28.00
Saucer, green 2.00
Vegetable Bowl, green 25.00
Waterford, (Waffle), Hocking Glass Co., 1936–44
Ashtray, clear, 4" d 6.00

Waterford, dinner plate, clear, 9½″ d, $5.00.

Bowl, clear, 8¼″ d	10.00
Butter Dish, cov, clear	25.00
Cake Plate, clear, handle, 10¼″ d	7.00
Cereal Bowl, clear, 5½″ d	18.50
Creamer and Sugar, pink	15.00
Cup and Saucer, clear	5.00
Goblet, Miss America style, clear	25.00
Juice Pitcher, tilted, clear	17.50
Juice Tumbler, Miss America style, pink	48.00

Plate
Dinner, clear, 9⅝″ d	5.00
Sherbet, pink, 6″ d	3.50
Relish, five sections, clear	13.75
Sandwich Plate, clear, 13¾″ d	9.50
Sherbet, clear, ftd, scalloped base	5.00

Windsor, (Windsor Diamond), Jeannette Glass Co., 1936–46

Ashtray
Delphite, 5¾″ d	55.00
Green, 5¾″ d	46.50
Bowl, clear, pointed edge, 4¾″ d	7.00
Butter Dish, cov, pink	45.00
Cake Plate, pink, closed handle, 10″ d	135.00
Candy Jar, cov, clear	15.00
Console Bowl, pink, 12½″ d	75.00
Creamer, pink	7.50
Cup, green	9.00
Pitcher, green, 6¾″ h	40.00

Plate
Chop, green, 13⅝″ d	30.00
Dinner, clear, 9″ d	3.50
Salad, pink, 7″ d	9.00
Sherbet, clear, 6″ d	1.50
Salt and Pepper Shakers, pr, green	44.00
Sandwich Plate, clear, handle, 10¼″ d	8.00
Sherbet, clear, ftd	6.00
Saucer, pink	2.50
Sugar, green	25.00

Tray, clear, handles
4″ sq	2.50
4⅛ x 9″	10.00
Tumbler, pink, 5″ h	20.00

DUNCAN AND MILLER

History: George Duncan, Harry B. and James B., his sons, and Augustus Heisey, his son–in–law, formed George Duncan & Sons in Pittsburgh, Pennsylvania, in 1865. The factory was located just two blocks from the Monongahela River, providing easy and cheap access by barge for materials needed to produce glass. The men, from Pittsburgh's southside, were descendants of generations of skilled glassmakers.

The plant burned to the ground in 1892. James E. Duncan, Sr., selected a site for a new factory in Washington, Pennsylvania, where operations began on February 9, 1893. The plant prospered, producing fine glassware and table services for many years.

John E. Miller, one of the stockholders, was responsible for designing many fine patterns, the most famous being "Three Face." The firm incorporated, using the name The Duncan and Miller Glass Company until its plant closed in 1955. The company's slogan was "The Loveliest Glassware in America." The U. S. Glass Co. purchased the molds, equipment, and machinery in 1956.

References: Gail Krause, *The Encyclopedia Of Duncan Glass*, published by author, 1984; Gail Krause, *A Pictorial History Of Duncan & Miller Glass*, published by author, 1976; Gail Krause, *The Years Of Duncan*, published by author, 1980.

Collectors' Club: National Duncan Glass Society, P.O. Box 965, Washington, PA 15301.

Vase, blue, opal rim, 4¼″ h, $20.00.

Animal Figurine
Duck, crystal	55.00

Swan
10″ h, Pall Mall, crystal, leaf cutting	75.00
12″ h, ruby	50.00
13″ h, Pall Mall, red	110.00

Arliss
Mug, crystal, green, cobalt blue, amber, or red handle	20.00

Astair
Tumbler, ruby, 10 oz 15.00
Canterbury
Candy Box, cov 40.00
Celery Tray, 11" l, clear 20.00
Champagne, blue 15.00
Cheese Compote, clear 20.00
Claret, blue, 5" h 17.50
Creamer and Sugar, clear 20.00
Cup and Saucer, clear 15.00
Goblet, 6" h 17.50
Tumbler, 6¼" h, clear 12.00
Vase, 7¼" h, inverted candle type .. 110.00
Caribbean
Bowl
3½" d, blue 100.00
8½" d, blue 45.00
Cheese Dish, cov, blue 32.00
Epergne, 9½" h, blue 90.00
Punch Bowl Set, punch bowl, base,
twelve cups, clear, ruby handles . 225.00
Vase, 9" h, blue, flared 125.00
Deauville, crystal
Champagne 15.00
Cordial 16.00
Goblet 20.00
Wine 20.00
Early American
Basket, loop handle, 11½" h, clear . 110.00
Cake Stand, 13" d, clear 60.00
Goblet 20.00
Top Hat, 2½" h, crystal 16.00
First Love
Bowl
5½" d, handle 38.00
11" d, round 40.00
Candlesticks, pr, 5¾" h, two lite, clear 60.00
Creamer and Sugar, matching tray, in-
dividual size 35.00
Cup and Saucer 20.00
Goblet, three ball stem 18.00
Ice Bucket, orig handle 75.00
Martini Pitcher 145.00
Relish, 9" l, two handles, four part,
#111 .... 40.00
Vase, 10" h, cylinder 70.00
Hobnail
Bowl, 12" d, blue, crimped rim 65.00
Candlesticks, pr, 4" h, blue opales-
cent 55.00
Champagne, pink 20.00
Cologne Bottle, pink opalescent 35.00
Cruet, orig stopper, amber 50.00
Cup and Saucer, blue opalescent ... 20.00
Flip Jug, crystal, half gallon 60.00
Hat, blue opalescent, 2½" h 25.00
Plate, 8½" d, pink 30.00
Passion Flower
Bowl, 12½" d 27.50
Plate, 14½" d 30.00
Patio
Cigarette Box, cov, green 40.00

Puritan
Bowl, 4¾" d, ftd, green 8.50
Compote, green 18.00
Console Bowl, clear, rolled edge, cut-
ting 30.00
Creamer, green 4.50
Sugar, green 5.00
Sandwich
Basket, 7" l, shallow 115.00
Bowl, 12" d, flared 45.00
Cake Salver, 13" d, pedestal 85.00
Candlesticks, pr, 4" 25.50
Celery Tray, 10" l 28.00
Champagne, 5¼" h, 5 oz 20.00
Cheese Dish, cov 110.00
Cigarette Box, cov 36.00
Coaster 10.00
Cocktail 12.00
Creamer and Sugar, individual,
matching tray, crystal 25.00
Cruet, oil, matching tray 50.00
Cup, tea, 6 oz 10.00
Deviled Egg Plate, 12" d, crystal ... 70.00
Epergne, 12" h, three part 250.00
Fruit Bowl, 11½" d, crimped 38.00
Goblet, 5¼", 9 oz 12.00
Ice Cream, 4¼" d, 5 oz 6.50
Juice Tumbler 11.00
Mayonnaise, 5" d 19.00
Nappy, 5" d 5.50
Parfait 22.00
Pickle Dish, 7" l 20.00
Pitcher, 8" h, ice lip 115.00
Plate
6" d 7.50
7" d 9.00
8" d 9.50
Relish, three part, 12", crystal 40.00
Salad Bowl, 10" d 60.00
Salt and Pepper Shakers, pr 20.00
Serving Plate, 13½" d, round 35.00
Sherbet 10.00
Sugar, cov, ftd, 3¼", 9 oz 7.00
Sugar Shaker 70.00
Tumbler, 3¾" h, ftd 8.50
Vase, 10" h, ftd 75.00
Sanibel
Bowl
8" d, blue opalescent 75.00
14" d, yellow opalescent 75.00
Celery Tray, 13" l, three part, pink
opalescent 42.00
Floating Garden Bowl, 13½" l, pink
opalescent 50.00
Mint Tray, 7" l, blue opalescent 25.00
Plate, 8" d, pink opalescent 28.00
Relish, two part, blue opalescent ... 28.00
Salad Plate, 8½" d
Blue Opalescent 25.00
Yellow Opalescent 25.00
Spiral Flutes
Bowl, 6¾" d, flange, green 7.50

Chocolate Box, cov, amber	210.00
Compote, 6" d, amber	18.00
Cup and Saucer, amber	8.00
Demitasse Cup and Saucer, green	20.00
Finger Bowl, green	7.50
Nut Bowl, individual, green	20.00
Parfait, green	18.00
Sherbet, 4¾" h	
Green	10.00
Pink	10.00
Tumbler, 5" h, ftd, green	20.00

Sylvan

Box, cov, 7½" w, crystal, cobalt blue handle	38.00
Candy Dish, cov, 7½" d, blue opalescent	24.00

Teardrop

Ashtray, 3", individual, clear	3.75
Bowl, 11½", flared, clear	28.00
Candy Dish, 7½", heart shape, clear	12.50
Champagne, 6⅛", bead stem, clear	9.00
Condiment Set, clear, five pcs	70.00
Cruet, 3 oz, clear, orig stopper	15.00
Mayonnaise, underplate	18.00
Nut Dish, two part, clear	5.25
Plate, 7½", clear	3.75
Sherbet, low, ftd	5.00

Terrace

Bon Bon, rolled up handles, cobalt blue	18.00
Tumbler, ftd, 4½" h, cobalt blue	30.00

Willow

Goblet, cut dec	8.00
Plate, 8¾" d	12.00

DURAND

History: Victor Durand (1870–1931), born in Baccarat, France, apprenticed at the Baccarat glass works where several generations of his family worked. In 1884 Victor came to America to join his father at Whitall–Tatum & Co. in New Jersey. In 1897 father and son leased the Vineland Glass Manufacturing Company in Vineland, New Jersey. Products included inexpensive bottles, jars, and glass for scientific and medical purposes. By 1920 four separate companies existed.

When Quezal Art Glass and Decorating Company failed, Victor Durand recruited Martin Bach, Jr., Emil J. Larsen, William Wiedebine, and other Quezal men and opened an art glass shop at Vineland in December, 1924. Quezal-style iridescent pieces were made. New innovations included cameo and intaglio designs, geometric Art Deco shapes, Venetian Lace, and oriental-style pieces. In 1928 crackled glass, called Moorish Crackle and Egyptian Crackle, was made.

Much of Durand glass is not marked. Some bear a sticker labeled "Durand Art Glass," some have the name "Durand" scratched on the pon-

til, and some have "Durand" inside a large "V." Etched numbers may be part of the marking.

Durand died in 1931. The Vineland Flint Glass Works was merged with Kimble Glass Company a year later, and the art glass line was discontinued.

Ashtray, 5" d, irid blue and green ground, match holder center	750.00
Bowl, 8" d, 6½" h, orange cased to opal, irid green leaf and vine dec, sgd "Durand" in "V"	1,400.00
Box, cov, 3½" d, green luster ground, gold luster King Tut dec	950.00
Candlesticks, pr	
9¼" h, clear amber baluster, pulled blue tip feathers, etched wheat and leaves on flanged rim	295.00
10" h, baluster, irid blue, sgd	425.00
Charger, 14½" d, transparent ambergris plate, narrow emerald green border at outer edge, ten ribs, sgd "Durand"	150.00
Compote	
5½" d, 4½" h, irid gold and opal, King Tut, sgd	250.00
8" d, white feather design in center, blue ground, pale green stem and foot	725.00
Dessert Set, ten white rimmed ruby ftd bowls, seven plates, 15" d center bowl, pr ruby with topaz candlesticks	770.00
Ginger Jar, cov, 10½" h, gold and green, King Tut dec	1,850.00
Goblet, 5½" h, irid ruby ground, pale yellow stem and base, sgd	450.00
Lamp	
Boudoir, 17" h, all over threading, butterscotch ground, matching metal leaf dec shade	1,100.00
Floor, 70" h, 12" d shade, tripartite swan cage, gold threaded vasiform shade, gilt metal twisted shaft, three leaf and scroll dec feet	1,000.00
Table, 14" h, shade with gold and green hearts and vines, irid opal ground, applied heavy gold threading, yellow lining, bronze tree form base	2,100.00
Torchere, 15½" h, flared trumpet form, Moorish Crackle, transparent amber, vertical red stripes, heavily iridized, gilt metal lamp base	470.00
Plate	
7¾" d, cobalt blue ground, opal pulled feather, cross hatched pontil, sgd	500.00
8½" d, ruby, paneled, ten sided, hand blown, sgd	200.00
8⅝" d, feather pattern, blue, opal, and clear, cross hatched cut center	200.00
Rose Bowl, 5½" d, blue ground, gold threads, gold foot, sgd	375.00

Vase, purple on irid gold, 14⅜" h, $975.00.

Sherbet, 3⅜" h, ruby and opal, feather
   pattern 165.00
Vase
   7⅛" h, baluster, ftd, King Tut, pale
      green ground, gold swirling dec,
      sgd "Durand" 715.00
   7½" h, flared ovoid, King Tut, brilliant
      blue, coiled and swirled white dec,
      blown and dec by Emil J Larson and
      Harry Bretton 880.00
   8" h, tooled beehive, brilliant blue irid
      ambergris, silver signature 990.00
   9" h, flared bulbous, pattern molded,
      sixteen ribs, transparent Royal Pur-
      ple 330.00
   9¼" h, cobalt blue iridized, vertical
      gold heart and vine motif, purple
      shading, incised signature 1,210.00
   16¼" h, ftd oval, flared lip, colorless
      crystal, cased in brilliant ruby, cut
      alternating vertical rows of circles
      and faceted panels, attributed to
      Charles Link 365.00

EARLY AMERICAN GLASS

History: Early American glass covers glass made
in America from the colonial period through the
mid–19th century. As such it includes the early
pressed glass and lacy glass made between 1827
and 1840.
   Major glass producing centers prior to 1850
were Massachusetts with the New England Glass
Company and the Boston and Sandwich Glass
Company; South Jersey; Pennsylvania with Stiegel's Manheim factory and Pittsburgh; and Ohio
with Kent, Mantua, and Zanesville.
   Early American glass was collected heavily
during the 1920 to 1950 period. It has now re-
gained some of its earlier popularity. Leading
sources for the sale of early American glass are
the auctions of Richard A. Bourne, Early Auction
Company, Garth's, and Skinners.

References: William E. Covill, *Ink Bottles and
Inkwells*, 1971; Lowell Inness, *Pittsburgh Glass:
1797–1891*, Houghton Mifflin Company, 1976;
George and Helen McKearin, *American Glass*,
Crown, 1975; George and Helen McKearin, *Two
Hundred Years of American Blown Glass*, Dou-
bleday and Company, 1950; Helen McKearin
and Kenneth Wilson, *American Bottles And
Flasks*, Crown, 1978; Adeline Pepper, *Glass Gaf-
fers of New Jersey*, Scribners, 1971; Jane S. Spill-
man, *American and European Pressed Glass*,
Corning Museum of Glass, 1981; Kenneth Wilson, *New England Glass And Glassmaking*,
Crowell, 1972.

Periodicals: *Antique Glass Quarterly*, Rudi Pub-
lishing, P. O. Box 1364, Iowa City, IA 52244;
Glass Collector's Digest, Antique Publications,
P. O. Box 553, Marietta, OH 45750–0553.

Collectors' Club: The National Early American
Glass Club, P. O. Box 8489, Silver Spring, MD
20987.

Museums: Historical Glass Museum, Redlands,
CA; New Bedford Glass Museum, New Bedford,
MA; The Bennington Museum, Bennington, VT;
The Chrysler Museum, Norfolk, VA; The Corning
Museum of Glass, Corning, NY; The Toledo Mu-
seum of Art, Toledo, OH; Wheaton Historical
Village Association Museum of Glass, Millville,
NJ.

**Zanesville, flask, brilliant amber, ex-
panded vertical ribbing, 24 rib mold, 8¼"
h, 6⅞" w, $1,200.00.**

ENGRAVED, UNKNOWN MAKERS

Celery Vase, 5⅛" d, 8½" h, clear, elaborate pattern of festoons, small flowers, and leaf band, twenty gadrooned
   ribs, applied foot with knob stem,
   early 19th C, slight crazing 225.00
Goblet, 7" h, clear, applied foot, hollow
   hourglass stem and bowl, copper-

wheel engraved ivy and B.D.C., at-
tributed to NE Glass Co **100.00**
Mug, clear
  3¾" h, handled, twenty four wide
  ribs, applied strap handle with curl,
  copperwheel engraved tendrils,
  and letter P **125.00**
  5½" h, applied foot and handle, Stie-
  gel type copperwheel engraved tu-
  lip **125.00**
Tumbler, 6¾" h, copper wheel engraved
  floral design **90.00**
Wine, 5⅛" h, clear, blown, Pittsburgh
  type engraved foliage, tapered stem
  and bowl, applied foot **50.00**
Wine Funnel, 3⅜ x 5¾", clear, en-
  graved border of leaves and flowers,
  eight cut flutes continue down stem **75.00**

FREE BLOWN, UNKNOWN MAKERS

Bowl
  4⅞" d, 2⅞" h, puce, sixteen vertical
  ribs, broken swirl to right, ftd, pon-
  til, inward folded rim **250.00**
  8½" h, cov, matching underplate, cut
  diamond point and panel design on
  facet cut finials, minor wear, pr . . **300.00**
Candlestick
  7⅜" h, clear, flint, Spillman plate 889,
  minor roughness **85.00**
  9⅞" h, clear, dolphin, minor rough-
  age to base **175.00**
Creamer, 4⅜" h, clear, applied chain
  design around waist, large rim chip . **250.00**
Cup, octagonal, light yellow green,
  scrolled handle, ovals in panels, chip
  in foot caused by broken bubble . . . **350.00**
Decanter, quart, clear, three applied
  pouring rings, pontil **50.00**
Flat Iron, miniature, light green, one
  shallow chip, several small flakes at
  base, handle check **450.00**
Hat, 9⅛" h, emerald green, slightly
  rolled brim, pontil **125.00**
Jar
  4½ x 6⅜", golden amber, cylindrical,
  wide flat folded rim, tubular pontil **300.00**
  8" h, clear, two horizontal ribs,
  domed dov, airtrip finial **150.00**
Lamp, sparking, 4⅜" h, free blown font,
  lacy pressed base, minor roughness to
  base **250.00**
Pitcher, 8⅜" h, helmet shape, circular
  foot, heavy horizontal mid rib, fine
  applied handle, c1830 . . . . **400.00**
Sand Shaker, opaque blue **250.00**
Vase
  7¾" h, sq pressed foot, blown bowl,
  chips on base, pr **210.00**
  9¾" h, trumpet, applied foot, folded
  edge, tear drop stem **100.00**

  9⅞" h, applied flared foot, folded rim **250.00**
  12⅝" h, amethyst, trumpet, applied
  foot, hollow stem, folded rim **200.00**
Wine
  7½" h, panel cut flared bowl, baluster
  stem, applied foot, pr **130.00**
  7¾" h, air twist stem, wear and
  scratches **45.00**

LACY AND PRESSED PATTERNS

Amelung (New Bremen Glass)
Salt, 2½ x 2¾", cobalt blue, pattern
  molded, checkered diamond, ap-
  plied solid foot **850.00**
Wine, 6⅜" h, clear, blown, applied
  dome foot, folded rim, hollow
  stem, small bubble in thick solid
  base of bowl, attributed to Amelung **250.00**
Bakewell
Lamp, fluid, 11¾" h, clear, blown
  pear shaped font, typical cut Pittsburgh pattern, large bulbous knops,
  heavy pressed ftd base, pewter col-
  lar **600.00**
Window Pane, 6⅞" h, 4⅞" w, clear,
  church, gothic arch design, sgd
  "Bakewell" on reverse, Innes Fig
  303–2 . . . . **2,000.00**
Boston and Sandwich Glass Co
Sugar Bowl, cov
  5¼" h, canary yellow, octagonal,
  Acanthus Leaf pattern, slight
  roughness to under cover edge,
  one tiny vertical flake on top
  edge of bowl **2,700.00**
  5⅜" h, canary yellow, Gothic Arch
  pattern, c1840–50, very slight
  rim roughness to edge of lid and
  bowl **1,900.00**
Tumbler, 3¼" h, Eye and Scale pat-
  tern, pillar flute motifs, listed as first
  pressed glass tumbler, 1827 . . . . . **750.00**
Ellenville, NY
Creamer, 3¾" h, brilliant yellow am-
  ber, blown, Jacob Relyea **500.00**
Keene Glassworks, Keene, NH
Decanter, 7¼" h, deep amber, pint,
  blown three mold, bubbles in neck,
  c1820 . . . . **350.00**
Ink Bottle, 2⅜" h, olive amber, octag-
  onal **75.00**
Inkwell, 2½" d, olive–amber, blown
  three mold, McKearin GIII–29 . . . **145.00**
Kent, OH
Bottle, 7⅛" h, aqua, tapered, twenty
  molded ribs, slightly swirled to the
  right, flanged lip, pontilled base . . **100.00**
Smelling Salts Bottle, 3" h, peacock
  blue, ovoid, twenty–six vertical
  molded ribs, sheared mouth and
  pontil **225.00**

Lockport, NY
Creamer, 4⅞" h, blue, free blown, solid applied handle and foot, folded rim, wide flaring mouth, pontil **600.00**
Salt, 3½" h, bluish aqua brown, applied foot, knop stem **200.00**
Tumbler, 3⅜ x 4⅛", blue, free blown, cylindrical, plain lip, pontil **175.00**
Vase, 3½" d, 7⅛" h, blue, free blown, three part vase, flared mouth, round base set onto solid baluster stem, thick solid circular foot, 5¼" d witch ball cov **600.00**

Mantua
Flask, blown, chestnut
4⅛" h, amber, 16 vertical ribs, terminal ring, attributed to Mantua or Kent **300.00**
6" h, blown chestnut, pale green, sixteen swirled ribs **150.00**
Pan
5¼" d, 1¾" h, light green, blown, fifteen diamonds, folded rim, attributed to Mantua by Henry Hall White **2,000.00**
5½" d, 1½" h, brilliant aqua, free blown, 15 diamond, folded in rim, minor flakes at pontil **3,850.00**
6" d, pale green, blown, sixteen ribs, folded over rim **375.00**
Toilet Bottle, 4½" h, one–quarter pint, deep purple–amethyst, flared, flanged lip, pontiled base **450.00**

Marlboro Street Glassworks, Keene, NH
Flask, GIV–1, emb masonic emblem and American eagle, "IP" in oval, clear bluish–green, open pontil .. **250.00**
Smelling Salts Bottle, 1⅞" h, deep amethyst, flattened globular body, applied side quilling, sheared mouth, pontilled base, c1815–20**1,350.00**

Midwestern
Bottle, globular, pale green
5¼" h, thirty swirled ribs **225.00**
6⅞" h, eighteen swirled ribs, minor sickness in base **100.00**
Bowl, 5⅝" d, 3⅞" h, cobalt blue, lacy period, ftd, c1830, one moderate chip under rim, small rim chips and roughness **900.00**
Candlesticks, pr, 7⅛" h, clear, free blown sockets, lacy hairpin pattern base **5,250.00**
Compote, 6" d, 3⅞" h, pressed Roman Rosette bowl, blown stem and base **150.00**
Creamer and Sugar, 3½" h, medium sapphire blue, blown, seventeen swirled ribs, drawn base, hollow foot, flared, folded rim, applied handle **425.00**

Flask, pitkin, olive green, half pint, thirty–six broken swirled ribs, five bubbles, c1790–1830 .... **200.00**
Plate, 5" d, eagle, six scallops damaged **575.00**
Sugar, cov, clear, lacy, Peacock Feather pattern, one foot scallop chipped **500.00**

Mount Vernon Glassworks, New York, c1840
Bowl, 5½ x 2⅜", geometric, clear, gray tint **700.00**
Decanter, clear, quart, GI–29, narrow flanged mouth, heavy int. haze .. **75.00**
Lamp, fluid, 6⁷⁄₁₆" h, clear, blown three mold, cylindrical font, patterned from half pint decanter mold, mounted with wafer to heavy pressed base of two lion's paws on stepped and scalloped flat oval base **1,200.00**
Pitcher
McKearin GI–29, clear, geometric, ribbed barrel design, large handle **1,100.00**
McKearin GIII–2, Type 1, 7¼" h, light aquamarine, blown three mold, quart **7,750.00**

New England Glass Company
Celery, 7½" h, deep fuschia, Venetian Diamond pattern, ground pontil .. **435.00**
Compote
4¼" h, 6½" d, lacy, Heart and Shield pattern, small rim chip .. **750.00**
7¼ x 4⅜", clear, free blown, engraved with grapes and leaves, mounted on a serpentine three tiered pressed standard, minor chips under folded rim of bowl **65.00**
Cuspidor, 8⅝" d, blown, translucent, powder blue **225.00**
Flip, 5⅜" h, clear, blown, panel molded **100.00**
Goblet
Ellipse pattern, cobalt blue **300.00**
Paneled, light blue, chip on foot . **150.00**
Lamp, fluid, whale oil
6¾" h, blown and patterned, deep cobalt blue inverted cone shaped font, sixteen swirl ribbed pattern, slightly domed clear cup plate base (Lee–Rose 43), rough overfill on base **11,000.00**
7⅝" h, opaque white, McKearin 196–7, chipped base **475.00**
9" h, opaque white, monumental base, several base chips, open bubble imperfections on font .. **400.00**
9⅛" h, clear, blown font with frosted cut grape design, baluster stem, reeded and stepped

pressed base, shallow chips on
base **115.00**
10⅞" h, cut and pressed, panel cut
conical font, faceted blown knop
stem, pressed stepped base, minor foot chips **300.00**
19⅜" h, pressed and cut, clear,
frosted and cut matching shades,
minor roughness and small
chips, pr **900.00**
Miniature, Wash Bowl and Pitcher,
paneled, cobalt blue **1,100.00**
Tumbler, bar type, Pineapple pattern,
clear, set of 10 .... **350.00**
Vase, Loop and Ellipse, hexagonal,
amethyst, gauffered rim, McKearin
205–51, large annealing check on
base **250.00**
Whiskey Taster
Fluted, opalescent blue, minor
roughness **75.00**
Nine Paneled, apple green **110.00**
Paneled, canary yellow **90.00**
Ten Paneled, electric blue, handled **150.00**
Thumbprint, sapphire blue, small
bruise in upper rim **70.00**
New Geneva, PA
Bottle, 5⅞" h, chestnut, elongated
and flattened, blue green, sixteen
vertical ribs, c1800–20 .... **175.00**
Tumbler, 3⅛ x 4½", yellow–green,
plain sheared rim, large polished
pontil **275.00**
New Jersey, South
Bank, 10⅜" h, clear, blown, applied
rigaree and prunts, arch of four applied struts, applied chicken finial,
solid ball stem attached to thick
round base **1,200.00**
Bottle
7" h, amethyst, triangular, heavy
annealing marks, late 19th C .. **125.00**
11⅜" h, clear, blown, powder horn
form, opaque white loopings, cobalt blue bands **225.00**
11⅝" h, clear, blown, powder horn
form, opaque white loopings,
cranberry bands **225.00**
Bowl, 5¾" h, clear, blown, opaque
white loopings **175.00**
Cane, 32½" l, clear, amber center,
four applied opaque swirled ribs . **125.00**
Creamer
4⅛" h, cobalt blue, applied foot,
handle, ring, and gadrooning,
threaded lip **575.00**
5⅞" h, cobalt blue, applied
crimped foot and solid curled
handle, tooled rim, int. spall on
side of spout **650.00**
Miniature
Compote, 2" d, 1⅞" h, brilliant

green, circular, straight sides,
hollow knop stem, applied circular foot, McKearin Plate 75,
No. 20 .... **450.00**
Creamer, 1⅜" h, aquamarine, free
blown, baluster shaped bowl,
applied circular flat foot, applied
solid ear shaped handle, lower
end turned back **500.00**
Pitcher, 7⅝" h, aquamarine, opaque
white loopings, double ribbed applied handle crimped at base,
tooled lip, heavy circular applied
foot **650.00**
Wine, 4⅜" h, clear, smoky cast, thick
applied base, iron pontil **75.00**
New York
Bowl, 14" d, 4¼" h, aqua, folded rim,
wear, star in flared rim **225.00**
Compote
6⅜" d, 6¼" h, free blown, clear,
thick applied base, polished pontil **50.00**
8¼" d, tilted 4 to 4¾" h, bluish–
aqua, applied lily pad dec, wide
folded rim, heavy applied base **1,200.00**
Plate, 6⅝" d, ¾" h, cobalt blue, free
blown, attributed to Lancaster **85.00**
Vase, 4½" h, 5½" w, urn shape, yellow–green, rolled rim, large faint
pontil **125.00**
Philadelphia, PA
Pomade jar, opaque blue, figural,
bear, molded mark on base "J
Hauel & Co, Phila," 3¾" h, one
large chip to cov **700.00**
Pittsburgh, PA
Bar Bottle, 10½" h, medium amethyst, heavy applied lip, polished
pontil **650.00**
Bowl
4⅜" d, 3⅞" h, cobalt blue, clear
foot, wide flaring rim, rough pontil **600.00**
4⅞" d, 2⅝" h, pattern molded, broken swirl, sixteen ribs to the
right, folded rim, tooled foot,
lead glass, sapphire blue, pontil
scar **335.00**
Candlestick
6¾" h, dolphin, clambroth base,
opaque blue socket, McKearin
196–6, minute roughness **700.00**
7" h, canary yellow, dolphin, minute roughness on bases, annealing lines in one socket, McKearin
196–6, pr **850.00**
9" h, olive green, blown socket
with bulbous base, pr **1,800.00**
9½" h, clear, hexagonal, minor
roughness **50.00**

9⅝" h, clear, hexagonal, chip in socket, several other chips **30.00**

10⅛" h, clear, blown, wide foot, hollow pillar molded stem, bulbous socket, pewter insert **725.00**

10¼" h, clear, free blown, large hollow socket, heavy shaft, thick round base, white, amethyst red, and translucent blue green air twist ribbons in shaft **1,200.00**

Celery Vase, 8¼" h, 5¼" d, clear, gadrooned base, copper wheel engraved swags, flowers, and leaves, flared mouth, solid wine glass stem, thick solid base **450.00**

Compote, cov, 6½" d, 7" h, lacy, Hairpin pattern, two large rim chips **2,750.00**

Compote, open
8 x 7½", clear, ftd, copper wheel engraving, swags, acorn–like tassels, solid knop stem **275.00**

8¾ x 5¼", cranberry cased bowl, clear solid knop stem, thick heavy base, c1850 . . . . **435.00**

10 x 8¾" h, clear, flint, blown, bowl with folded rim, baluster stem, applied foot, broken blister on int. of bowl **175.00**

10½ x 8¼" h, clear, flint, blown, pillar molded, bowl and baluster stem with unusual serrated rim, applied foot **415.00**

Creamer
4½" h, deep sapphire blue, applied solid handle, heavy crimped end, McKearin Plate 52, No. 3 **1,300.00**

5⅛" h, opalescent blue, 8 rib pillar molded, short circular stem, circular foot, applied handle **4,500.00**

5½" h, clear, flint, blown, pillar molded, ribbed body, wafer stem, applied foot, applied handle poorly attached, minor roughness **220.00**

Creamer and Sugar, 3⅝" h, clear, blown, blue applied rim, 12 panel bowl, flared foot, folded rim, applied handle **900.00**

Decanter
8⅜" h, clear, flint, blown, fifteen vertical ribs, applied collar, applied foot and handle, pewter cap missing **100.00**

10¼" h, clear, flint, blown, pillar molded, applied collar and lip, wear **175.00**

10⅞" h, clear, flint, blown, pillar molded, applied ring collar, flared lip minor int. stain **95.00**

Ewer, 7¼" h, clear, flint, blown, applied foot and handle, hollow stopper **95.00**

Inkwell, 5½" h, clear, free blown, egg shaped body, two reservoirs, applied rounded well, small cup for seals, short knop stem, circular foot, nine applied rosettes **1,000.00**

Lamp, 12¼" h, clear, pressed base, blown hollow stem and font, wafers, cut foliage, panels, strawberry diamonds, and fans, pewter collar, minor chips on base **575.00**

Pitcher
7¼" h, clear, flint, blown, pillar molded, applied hollow handle **160.00**

8" h, eight pillar molded, blown, applied handle **350.00**

8¼" h, clear, flint, blown, pillar molded, applied handle, ground pontil **95.00**

9½" h, clear, flint, Cleat pattern, applied handle and ring, minor wear and scratches **100.00**

Plate
5¹⁵⁄₁₆" d, octagonal, clear, lacy, steamboat, Lee 170–3, minute roughness on upper rim **1,800.00**

6⅛" d, octagonal, clear, lacy, Constitution "Union," Lee 170–4, small rim flakes **1,400.00**

7" d, lacy, octagonal, clear, Basket of Flowers pattern, R. B. Curling & Sons, Pittsburgh, several small chips and edge roughness **300.00**

Powder Horn, 11¼" l, blown, clear applied foot and two applied rings, red loopings, minor sickness **250.00**

Salt, master, Neal OL–20a, clear, minor roughness **45.00**

Sugar, cov
7¼", deep sapphire blue, patterned in 12 rib mold and expanded, foot not pattern molded, McKearin Plate 52, No. 2 . . . . . . **2,500.00**

9⅞" h, clear, applied domed foot with blue rim, blue looping on bowl and domed cov, clear finial, shallow flake on foot **1,150.00**

Sweetmeat, 5¾" h, 4⅝" d, pillar molded, clear, ftd, flared folded rim, solid attached stem and base, eight pronounced ribs, large pontil scar **575.00**

Tumbler, 3¼" h
Clear, blown, cut flutes, strawberry point band, copperwheel engraving of flowers and seated greyhound **2,250.00**

Sapphire blue, eight panel **50.00**

Vase, 7⅞" h, panel and roundel cut bowls, knop stem, applied foot, pr **510.00**

Providence Flint Glass Works
Salt, master, Neal OG–10, clear, minor roughness **50.00**
Sugar Bowl, cov, clear, lacy, Rose, Plate X, No. 145, one minute rim roughness **1,800.00**
Redwood or Redford Glass Works, NY
Bowl, 14" d, 5 7/16 to 5 7/8" h, brilliant aquamarine, wide flaring rim, heavy out folded edge, applied circular foot, superimposed lily pad dec, similar to McKearin Plate 15, c1831–50 . . . . **4,000.00**
Compote, 9" d, 4 1/2" h, brilliant aquamarine, blown, circular bowl flaring to wide out folding rim, short cylindrical stem, circular stepped foot, superimposed gather of lily pad dec **9,000.00**
Pitcher, 10 1/4" h, light aquamarine, free blown, globular body, broad cylindrical neck with fine wide spaced applied threading extending to slightly flaring rim, tiny pinched lip, applied ear shaped aquamarine handle, applied circular foot, superimposed gather tooled swooping lily pad dec, McKearin Plate 20, No. 8 . . . . **19,000.00**
Vase, 4 3/4" h, free blown, brilliant aquamarine, urn form, two applied miniature handles **700.00**
Saratoga, NY
Compote, 4 1/8" h, 3 3/4" d, amber, blown, one piece, hollow bulbous base and stem, flared bowl with folded in rim, very minor sickness and some residue in hollow foot . **175.00**
Creamer, 4" h, olive–green, yellow tones, applied solid handle and foot, attributed to Morris Holmes . **575.00**
Miniature, pitcher, 1 13/16" h, deep green, blown, applied handle crimped at base, McKearin Plate 69, No. 3 . . . . **700.00**
Sugar Bowl, cov, 7 5/8" h, flaring lip, applied threading extending to mid body, thick strap handles, large medial ribs, blown ball shaped cov, green–aqua, pontil scar, two small pieces of threading missing, McKearin Plate 69, lower right **2,900.00**
South Boston
Bowl, 8" d, 3 3/8" h, clear, flint, applied rings **90.00**
Decanter
9" h, clear, free blown, two bands of chain dec around bodies and two around necks, period stopper, pr **700.00**
Quart, clear, free blown, four rows of chain dec, orig mercurial stopper, made by Thomas Caines at South Boston or Phoenix Glass Works, light stains inside stopper **900.00**
Pitcher, 7 7/8" h, rings, applied handle **200.00**
Sugar, cov, 5 7/8" h, clear, free blown, galleried rim, one band of applied chain dec on base and one on cover **3,250.00**
Stourbridge Flint Glass Works
Salt, dark blue, lacy, Innes Color Plate 6 . . . . **1,200.00**
Wheeling
Compote, 7 1/4" d, 4 1/4" h, octagonal, Oak Leaf pattern, bull's eye rim, Roman Rosette pattern base **1,200.00**
Window Pane, 7" h, 5" w, clear, portrait of steamboat in center with name "J & C Ritchie" above, c1833 **5,000.00**
Whitney Works, Glassboro, NJ
Pitcher, 6 15/16" h, medium sapphire blue, free flown, horizontal threading around neck, folded rim, small pinched lip, heavy circular applied foot, solid applied handle crimped at lower end, Joel Duffield, South Jersey c1835–40, McKearin Plate 60, No. 6 . . . . **1,300.00**
Zanesville
Bottle
4 1/2" h, chestnut, pale green, blown, twenty four vertical ribs, minor ext. scratches **100.00**
5" h, chestnut, aqua, twenty four vertical flattened ribs, pint, attributed to Zanesville, OH, c1800–35 . . . . **75.00**
7 3/8" h, globular, citron, blown, twenty four swirled ribs, minor traces of int. sickness **550.00**
8 1/4" h, deep golden amber, blown, globular, twenty four swirled ribs **550.00**
9" h, globular, amber, blown, twenty four swirled ribs **600.00**
Bowl, 8 1/2" d, 3 3/4" h, amber, blown, folded rim, minor broken blisters . **450.00**
Cruet, 6 3/8" h, purple–blue, taper shape, twenty four molded ribs, swirled to the left, slightly flared, rolled lip **2,300.00**
Flask, McKearin GIV–32, emb Masonic arch and farmer's arms, American eagle and "Zanesville, Ohio J Shepard & Co.," reddish–amber, pint, open pontil, c1820 . . **750.00**
Flip, 4 1/8" d, 4 5/8" h, blue–green, twenty four ribs, broken swirl to left **350.00**
Pan, 6 5/8" d, light green, blown, faint impression of twenty four ribs, folded rim **250.00**
Salt, 2 1/2 x 3 1/8", ftd, blue–green, twenty four vertical ribs, applied ir-

regular solid foot, pontil, slightly
ground rim .1,200.00
Scent Bottle, clear, twenty four ribs,
swirled to the right, rolled over col-
lar–pontil 225.00

PATTERN MOLDED, UNKNOWN MAKERS

Bar Bottle, clear, Divided Diamond,
pint, heavy applied lip, polished pon-
til 100.00
Cup Plate, 2⅜" d, lacy, sapphire blue .   35.00
Creamer, 5¼" h, cobalt blue, sixteen
vertical ribs, ftd, applied solid handle,
curl ending, folded rim, attributed to
Pittsburgh 400.00
Goblet, 6⅜" h, canary, Ringed Framed
Ovals pattern 85.00
Plate, 8" d, vaseline, Scotch Plaid pat-
tern, several rim chips and roughness,
McKearin 150–2 . . . . 175.00
Salt, master, lacy
   Neal BF–1b, opalescent, chips,
   roughness to edge 100.00
   Neal BT–9, opalescent, chip to keel,
   other minor chips 150.00
   Neal CN-1, clear, small chips and
   roughness to extreme edges 25.00
   Neal EE–2, clear, small chips and
   roughness to extreme edges 40.00
   Neal GA–4, clear, several large chips
   on upper edges, minor nicks 80.00
   Neal OG–11, clear, small chips and
   roughness to extreme edges 25.00
   Neal OP–20, clear, chip to top edge,
   minor roughness 70.00
Vase, 9¼" h, sapphire blue, Loop pat-
tern, gauffered rim, sq base 850.00
Whiskey Taster, 1⅞" d, clear, double
loop type pattern, polished base 25.00
Wine, 4" h, clear, twelve panel pattern,
applied base, pontil 40.00

PILLAR MOLDED, UNKNOWN MAKERS

Bar Bottle, 10⅛" h, clear, triangular,
eight heavy ribs, heavy applied lip
and pouring ring 100.00
Celery Vase, 5⅛ x 8¾", clear, twelve
swirled to right ribs, solid applied
stem, polished pontil 125.00
Creamer, 6" h, clear, eight ribs, solid
stem, thick applied base, solid applied handle with curl, polished pon-
til 200.00
Decanter, 8½" h, clear, eight blue ribs,
thick sloping lip and pouring ring, po-
lished pontil 1,200.00
Salt, 2½ x 1¼", twelve wide ribs, pontil   65.00

Sugar, 5⅜ x 4⅛", clear, eight ribs,
folded rim, solid stem, thick applied
base, polished pontil 200.00

EUROPEAN GLASS

History: European glassmakers have been creating utilitarian and decorative glassware items
for centuries. The necessity of food and beverage
storage vessels created a demand for early
pieces. Other items, such as wine goblets and
other types of stemware, exist today as fine examples of the many craftsmen who worked all
across Europe.

Because of the variation in raw materials from
one region to another, differences in techniques
and colors exist. These differences provide clues
to scholars and collectors when determining the
origin of a piece. The existing examples also
reflect the political and religious views of the
periods. It was not unusual for a reigning monarch to shelter and encourage a glassblower. Unfortunately, wars and changes in monarchs
caused shortages of money and materials for
glassmakers. During some periods, production
halted and it was often years before techniques
were reinstated or developed by later craftsmen.

Brilliant colors, exquisite detailed cuttings, and
engravings are frequently found on European
glassware. The addition of enamel and gilt decorations further enhanced the glassware. Utilitarian pieces, such as bowls and bottles, were
frequently left plain. Most pieces are unmarked.
Glass composition, design, and texture are the
most important keys to identifying regions and
periods.

Today, European craftsmen are beginning to
capture international markets with innovative
and colorful glassware. Leading auction houses,
such as Skinner's and William Doyle Galleries,
Inc. include these examples and are finding they
do quite well with today's collectors.

References: Charles R. Hajdamach, *British
Glass, 1800–1914*, Antique Collectors' Club,
1991; Brigitte Klesse and Hans Mayr, *European
Glass from 1500–1800, The Ernesto Wolf Collection*, Kremayr & Scheriau, 1987.

Museum: Corning Museum of Glass, Corning,
NY.

Beaker, 4½" h, German, engraved,
seven irate women fighting over pair
of trousers and verse 825.00
Bowl
   3¾" h, French, heavily walled, conical, translucent amber ground,
   etched graduated depths with descending, overlapping squares,
   etched artist's monogram of Jean
   Luca, c1925 . . . . 800.00

4¾" h, Austrian, lobed spherical form, undulating rim, purple irid ground, applied pink and white trailing and two floriform spirals . . **225.00**

Compote, 3¾" h, Austrian, conical lime green body, circular black glass foot, everted circular rim, black enamel lattice dec, attributed to Wiener Werkstaette, early 20th C **200.00**

Cordial Service, colorless faceted 8" h decanter, eight wines, 11¼" d conforming serving tray, polychrome enamel floral swag and scroll dec, center garden portrait reserves, Lobmeyr manner **825.00**

Cup, cov, Austrian, colorless stemmed blown glass bowl, conforming cov, orange, amber, and white designs, initialed, attributed to Wiener Werkstatte, manufacturing imperfections . **165.00**

Candelabra, Regency, crystal and gilt bronze, early 19th C, 18" h, pr, $21,000.00. Photograph courtesy of William Doyle Galleries.

Figure
8⅛" h, French, opalescent, nude female, arms outstretched holding drape around shoulders, molded "Etling France," c1930 . . . . **550.00**
10½" h, French, opalescent, nude maiden, diaphanous cloak, carrying lamb on shoulders, molded "Etling France 142," c1930 . . . . . . **800.00**

Goblet, 8" h, Austrian, irid pale green **275.00**

Lamp
Boudoir, 19" h, acid cut and enameled, repeating dec of violet blossoms and leaves, white latticework, gilt metal griffin socket and shade mounts **500.00**
Table, 13" h, Austrian, 10" d amber irid shade with pink trailing, sq silvered metal base with spreading foot cast with lotus blossoms **1,650.00**

Liqueur Set, 3½" d x 10¾" h decanter,

six matching 1¼" d x 4½" h stemmed liqueur glasses, cobalt blue ground, encrusted gold, pink and blue enamel flowers, matching serving tray **345.00**

Marble, 1⅝" d, German, end of day, blue, red, white, and yellow streaks, mica flecks, 1880–1915 . . . . **415.00**

Night Light (Veilleuse), French, 5½" h, bulbous mottled green and blue glass shade, patinated wrought iron mount surrounded by three curling tendrils, inscribed "Robj, Paris," c1920 . . . . . **600.00**

Pokal, cov
10¾" h, clear lead glass, engraved acanthus leaf dec, bowl engraved with man on horseback with dog chasing stag, pontil scar, engraved in Germany **325.00**
11¾" h, clear lead glass, hollow silesian stem on goblet and cov finial, goblet finely engraved with falconers and coat of arms, German inscription translates as "Let your allegiance soar as the falcons fly," small chip on cov finial base, blown and engraved in Germany late 19th C **1,900.00**

Toothpick Holder, 2¾" h, cameo, shaded yellow–orange ground, orange and black overlay, cameo cut and carved sunset riverside landscape scene, sgd "Weis" in cameo **275.00**

Tumbler, 4½" h, vertically faceted, gilt dec, genre scenes, six graduated glasses fit together, orig composition cylinder box **330.00**

Vase
3¼" h, Austrian, compressed spherical form, ruffled neck, blue irid ground, gilt curling vines, jeweled butterflies **475.00**
4⅛" h, Austrian, spherical, lobed sides, everted rim, pale irid gold ground, amber spots **350.00**
6" h
Austrian, cylinder, mottled blue, green, and orange ground, bronze overlay of oak branch with acorns, bronze rim and foot **450.00**
Federzeichnung, MOP, brown ground, maze of pearl air traps, gold enamel, pink lining, base engraved "Rd 76057" **2,125.00**
6½" h, Austrian
Baluster, three handles, tangerine ground, dark amethyst applied rim and handles, attributed to Michael Powolny **385.00**
Pear shaped, everted rim, lobed sides, irid gold ground, speckled green **250.00**
6⅜" h, Burgun and Schverer, rect,

amber ground, etched and enameled, one side dec with polychrome roundel of Grecian man playing lute, other dec panels of Grecian maidens and mythological beasts, ground of symbols and blossoms, floral bordered rim, gilt trim gilt mark on base **2,350.00**

6⅝" h, Austrian, bulbous, cylindrical neck, silver rim, pale green irid ground, applied snake **225.00**

6⅞" h, Austrian, tulip form, circular base, three leaves, green base and stem, silver and green spotted golden irid flower **1,650.00**

7⅞" h, Austrian, conch shell shape, irid golden shell, green seaweed foot **375.00**

8¼" h, Federzeichung, MOP, cased, flared shaped tricorn rim, brown oval body, internal swirled dec, gilt surface enameling, small rim chip   **600.00**

9" h, Escalier de Cristal, sq, flaring neck, everted rim, intalgio carved bird in flight diving after insect, engraved "Escalier de Cristal" **1,540.00**

9¾" h, Austrian, cylinder, inverted scalloping rim, irid citron yellow, bright orange dappling around base   **465.00**

10⅛" h, Austrian, cylinder, ruffled rim, green, pink, and purple irid ground, surface dec, three arm brass mounting, Secessionist style openwork foliate base **900.00**

10¼" h, 5¼" d, Federzeichnung, mother of pearl, gloss finish, brown ground, gold band around top edge, white lining **1,700.00**

10⅜" h, Austrian, swelled cylinder, ruffled rim, purple striated irid ground, open curvilinear silver overlay **800.00**

12" h, Austrian, tapered cylinder, bulbous shoulder, everted rim, pale irid yellow, golden wave dec **450.00**

12½" h, vasiform, cut overlay, colorless ground, white and amethyst overlay, cut stylized branches, broad leaves, and cherries, faceted rim, two small rim chips **330.00**

13" h, German, engraved, shouldered angled form, engraved flower filled baskets flanked by flowerheads and foliage scrolls, scattered sprigs, waisted neck **200.00**

Wine Glass

Cotton Stem, 6" h, English, opaque white eight ply spiral band surround a pair of spirals, fluting and wrythen pattern at base of ogee bowl, clear lead glass, pontil scar   **250.00**

Enameled, colorless faceted 8" h de-

canter and eight wine glasses, conforming 11¼" d serving tray, polychrome enamel floral swag and scroll dec, center garden portrait reserves, Lobmeyr manner **825.00**

Engraved

6½" h, engraved "De Vereen De Staaten," (the union of states,) lance and rope joining American and Austrian flags, clear lead glass, pontil scar, blowing attributed to England, engraving attributed to Europe, late 19th or early 20th C **4,500.00**

Engraved Cotton Stem, English

5" h, two sets of four opaque bands surround a spiral gauze, engraved leaves, grapes, and birds, clear lead glass, pontil scar, c1770 . . . . **175.00**

6½" h, four opaque white bands surround mesh, ogee bowl engraved with flowers and leaves, clear lead glass, pontil scar **50.00**

Twist Stem

Air Twist, attributed to England

5⅜" h, red, white, and blue stem twist, clear lead glaze, polished pontil **175.00**

6" h, unusual knop, clear lead glass, pontil scar, 1740–50 . . **300.00**

6½" h, flaring bowl, clear lead glass, pontil scar **80.00**

6⅝" h, bell bowl, unusual knop treatment, clear lead glass, pontil scar **275.00**

6¾" h, corkscrew type pattern, waisted bucket bowl, clear lead glass, pontil scar, c1760   **350.00**

7⅜" h, heavy, early trumpet bowl, clear lead glass, pontil scar, c1750 . . . . **350.00**

Opaque Twist

5" h, four opaque white bands surround gauze spiral, clear non–lead glass with grayish cast, pontil scar, attributed to Continental Europe, c1770 . . . . **150.00**

6" h, opaque white spirals, four band spiral around fine mesh, slightly domed foot, clear non–lead glass with grayish cast, pontil scar, attributed to Continental Europe, c1770 . . . . **100.00**

6" h, English, two white spirals surround corkscrew gauze, clear lead glass, pontil scar **200.00**

6" h, English, two white spirals surround fine mesh, ogee bowl, clear lead glass, pontil scar **175.00**

6½" h, English, opaque white bands, four ply spiral surrounds

multiply cork screw, straight
sided bowl, clear lead glass, pontil scar, c1760 .... **165.00**

FAIRY LAMPS

History: Fairy lamps, originating in England in
the 1840s, are candle burning night lamps. They
were used in nurseries, hallways, and dim corners of the home.

Two leading candle manufacturers, the Price
Candle Company and the Samuel Clarke Company, promoted fairy lamps as a means to sell
candles. Both contracted with other manufacturers of glass, porcelain, and metal to produce the
needed shades and cups. For example, Clarke
used Worcester Royal Porcelain Company, Stuart
& Sons, and Red House Glass Works in England,
plus firms in France and Germany. Clarke's trademark was a small fairy with a wand surrounded
by the words "Clarke Fairy Pyramid, Trade
Mark."

Fittings were produced in a wide variety of
styles. Shades ranged from pressed to cut glass,
from Burmese to Nailsea. Cups are found in
glass, porcelain, brass, nickel, and silver plate.

American firms selling fairy lamps included
Diamond Candle Company of Brooklyn, Blue
Cross Safety Candle Co., and Hobbs–Brockunier
of Wheeling, West Virginia.

Fairy lamps are found in two pieces (cup and
shade) and three pieces (cup with matching
shade and saucer). Married pieces are common.

References: John F. Solverson, *Those Fascinating
Little Lamps,* Antique Publications, 1988; John F.
Solverson (comp.), *Those Fascinating Little
Lamps, Miniature Lamps Value Guide,* Antique
Publications, 1988.

Reproduction Alert: Reproductions abound.

3" h, 3¾" d, overshot, pyramid, green
   overshot shade, clear marked Clarke
   base **110.00**
3½" h, 2⅞" d
Satin, Diamond Quilted pattern,
   MOP, rose, white lining, clear
   marked Clarke base **175.00**
Vaseline, ribbed vaseline dome,
   green pressed Clarke base **165.00**
3⅝" h, 2⅞" d
Overshot, opaque yellow, embossed
   swirl, pyramid size, clear marked
   Clarke base **95.00**
Satin, deep pink, Diamond Quilted
   pattern, MOP, white lining, pyramid size, clear marked Clarke base **145.00**
3⅝" h, 3" d, amber, pyramid, white opal
   swirl glass shade, clear marked Clarke
   base **100.00**
3¾" h, Peachblow, green leaves dec,

Overshot, "Crown," blue, Clarke base,
$145.00.

clear marked Clarke base, Thomas
   Webb & Sons **400.00**
3¾" h, 2⅞" d
Cranberry, frosted ground, opaque
   white arboresque like pattern, pyramid size, clear marked Clarke
   base **110.00**
Opalescent, blue emb rib, pyramid,
   clear marked Clarke base, shade re-
   gistrar #130643 .... **85.00**
4" h
Amber, diamond point shade, matching base marked Clarke Pyramid . **195.00**
Burmese, salmon pink shading to yellow, acid finish, matching base
   marked Clarke Pyramid **500.00**
4⅛" h, 4" d, Nailsea type, cranberry
   ground, opaque white looping on
   shade, clear marked Clarke base ... **150.00**
4½" h
Burmese, clear pressed base, shade
   marked "S. Clarke's Patent, Trademark, Fairy" **325.00**
Nailsea type, blue ground, clear
   marked Clarke Cricklite base **375.00**
4½" h, 2⅞" d, clear, opalescent overshot, crown shaped, pyramid size,
   clear marked Clarke base, made for
   Queen Victoria's 1887 Jubilee **165.00**
4½" h, 3" d, crown shaped cranberry
   overshot shade, clear marked Clarke
   base **200.00**
4½ h, 3⅞" d, Stevens and Williams,
   pink and white swirled striped, clear
   marked Clarke base **175.00**
4⅝" h, 3⅞" d
Sapphire blue, Diamond Quilted pattern, melon ribbed, clear marked
   Clarke **175.00**
Satin, chartreuse green, melon ribbed
   overlay, white lining, clear marked
   Clarke base **210.00**
4¾" h, Nailsea type citron ground,
   marked Clarke Cricklite crystal base **175.00**
5" h, Nailsea type pink and white, clear
   marked Clarke Cricklite base **190.00**

5¼" h, Peachblow, Mt Washington, clear glass candle cup **250.00**
5¼" h, 4" d, Baccarat, Rose Tiente, Sunburst pattern, saucer base **235.00**
5½" h, satin
Diamond Quilted pattern, MOP, pink, clear marked Clarke base **200.00**
Swirled pattern, rainbow stripes, crimped top, clear marked "S. Clarke" base **450.00**
5½" h, 6½" d, cranberry, frosted verre moire dome shade, matching ruffled base, clear marked Clarke insert, clear candle cup **500.00**
6" h, Burmese candle insert, marked "S. Clarke, Fairy" sgd "Thos. Webb & Sons–Queen's Burmese" **1,550.00**
6" h, 5¼" d, Stevens and Williams, blue, white, and crystal stripes, turned down edge, matching ruffled base, clear marked Clarke candle cup **825.00**
6⅜" h, peachblow shade and base with blue, white, brown and green enamel dec, white int., clear marked Clarke Cricklite base **410.00**
7" h, 5⅜" d, Burmese, Webb, acid finish, dome shade, matching reversible ruffled base, marked Clarke candle cup and insert cup **550.00**
10" h, Pairpoint, puffy shade, grapes and butterflies dec, turned mahogany base **500.00**
14" h, 4" d, Swirl pattern shade, gold, white, and pink spatter, white int., clear marked Clarke glass peg base, brass candlestick **425.00**
17" h, opaline, French blue, four large faceted purple and dark blue jewels, filigree brass mountings **275.00**
17¾" h, 13¾" d, double, emb ribbed overlay spatter shades, silver plated Cricklite base **450.00**

FENTON GLASS

History: The Fenton Art Glass Company began as a cutting shop in Martins Ferry, Ohio, in 1905. In 1906 Frank L. Fenton started to build a plant in Williamstown, West Virginia, and produced the first piece of glass in 1907. Early production included carnival, chocolate, custard, and pressed plus mold blown opalescent glass. In the 1920s stretch glass, Fenton dolphins, jade green, ruby, and art glass were added.

In the 1930s boudoir lamps, "Dancing Ladies," and various slags were produced. The 1940s saw crests of different colors being added to each piece by hand. Hobnail, opalescent, and two–color overlay pieces were popular items. Handles were added to different shapes, making the baskets they created as popular today as then.

Through the years Fenton has added beauty to their glass by decorating it with hand painting, acid etching, color staining, and copper wheel cutting. Several different paper labels have been used. In 1970 an oval raised trademark also was adopted.

References: Shirley Griffith, *A Pictorial Review Of Fenton White Hobnail Milk Glass*, published by author, 1984; William Heacock, *Fenton Glass: The First Twenty–Five Years*, O–Val Advertising Corp, 1978; William Heacock, *Fenton Glass: The Second Twenty–Five Years*, O–Val Advertising Corp, 1980; William Heacock, *Fenton Glass: The Third Twenty–Five Years*, O–Val Advertising Corp., 1989.

Collectors' Club: Fenton Art Glass Collectors Of America, Inc., P. O. Box 384, Williamstown, WV 26187.

Bell, Rosaline, orig paper label, 7" h, 1969–71, $30.00.

Ashtray
Hobnail Opalescent pattern, French, 5" w, fan **35.00**
Jade, ftd **10.00**
Banana Bowl, Silver Crest pattern, low, ftd **55.00**
Barber Bottle
Ribbed Optic pattern, vaseline opalescent, 7½" h **75.00**
Spanish Lace pattern, vaseline opalescent **109.00**
Basket
4" h
Hobnail Opalescent pattern
Blue **42.00**
Cranberry **85.00**
Yellow **85.00**
Water Lily and Cattails pattern, amethyst opalescent **28.00**
7" d, Silver Crest pattern **35.00**
7" d, 3" h, Dot Optic pattern, cranberry opalescent **45.00**
7" d, 5" h, Peach Crest pattern, overlay, peach handle **95.00**
7" h, Hobnail Opalescent, blue **50.00**

10½" d, 5" h, Big Cookies pattern,
Mandarin Red, hat shape, c1933 . **95.00**
13" h, Silver Crest pattern, handled . **70.00**
Bon Bon
Dolphin pattern, green, 6¼" l **32.00**
Hobnail Opalescent pattern
Cranberry, 6" d **20.00**
Yellow, 4" sq, two handles **40.00**
Strawberry pattern, amberina **250.00**
Stretch, Paneled pattern (No. 643),
Celeste blue, cov, ftd **25.00**
Swan, green **20.00**
Water Lily pattern, Peking blue **25.00**
Bone Dish, crescent, Hobnail Opalescent pattern, yellow **35.00**
Bowl
5½" d, 4½" h, Hobnail Opalescent
pattern, cranberry, ruffled rim,
c1941–77 .... **30.00**
6½" d, Blackberry Spray pattern, custard, red staining **50.00**
7" d, Walking Lion pattern, custard,
ruffled rim **65.00**
9" d, Open Edge Basketweave pattern, Mandarin Red **75.00**
9" octagonal bowl, 15" d underplate,
Ming Green, c1935 .... **350.00**
9¼" d, Coin Dot pattern, cranberry
opalescent **55.00**
10" d, Flame, rolled rim **95.00**
10½" d, Silver Crest pattern, ruffled . **40.00**
12" d, 6" h, Crystal Crest pattern, orig
paper label **50.00**
Cake Plate, 13" d
Aqua Crest pattern, ftd **95.00**
Emerald Crest pattern, pedestal base **65.00**
Hobnail Opalescent pattern, yellow,
ftd **135.00**
Silver Crest pattern, ftd **45.00**
Cake Stand
Silver Crest pattern, 13" d **40.00**
Spanish Lace pattern, green pastel .. **40.00**
Candlesticks, pr
6" h, Hobnail Opalescent pattern,
blue, cornucopia **45.00**
8" h
Flame pattern, baluster, round
base, yellow–orange, c1924 ... **70.00**
Venetian pattern, yellow–orange . **135.00**
Candy Dish, 4" h, Diamond Optic pattern, dolphin handles, ftd, green ... **55.00**
Cologne Bottle, Moonstone pattern,
ebony stopper **24.00**
Compote
7" d, Silver Crest, Violet in Snow ... **30.00**
8" d, 3½", Hobnail Opalescent pattern, deep cranberry, ftd **75.00**
Console Set, Ming Rose, cornucopia
candlesticks, 12" oval bowl **115.00**
Creamer
Dot Optic pattern, cranberry opalescent **25.00**

Emerald green overlay, melon,
beaded **55.00**
Creamer and Sugar, Hobnail Opalescent
pattern, blue **45.00**
Cruet
4" h, Hobnail Opalescent pattern,
blue **32.00**
6" h, Coin Dot pattern, cranberry opalescent **85.00**
Decanter, Hobnail pattern, mulberry,
crystal stopper **250.00**
Dresser Set, Silver Crest, melon shaped
cologne and powder jar **50.00**
Egg
Ebony ground, white flowers **50.00**
White satin ground, flowers and butterfly **40.00**

Epergne, Diamond Lace, French opalescent, applied aqua rim, three lily vases, 9½" h, 12" d, $165.00.

Epergne
Diamond Lace Pattern, 9½" h, blue
opalescent **165.00**
Hobnail Opalescent pattern, French **125.00**
Silver Crest pattern, four pcs **145.00**
Fruit Bowl
Hobnail Opalescent pattern, yellow,
12" d, ftd, dec **110.00**
Silver Crest pattern, sq, ftd **70.00**
Ginger Jar, cov, Mandarin Red, black
cover and base, c1934 .... **220.00**
Hurricane Lamp, Hobnail Opalescent,
French **225.00**
Ivy Ball, 9" h, Polka Dot pattern, cranberry opalescent, pr **150.00**
Jug
Hobnail Opalescent pattern
4½" h, French **45.00**
5½" h, blue, reed clear handle ... **55.00**
9" h, Peach Crest **48.00**
Kettle, Hobnail, milk glass **10.00**
Lavabo, Wild Rose pattern, white milk
glass hobnail **300.00**

Marmalade, Hobnail Opalescent pattern, blue, four pcs 75.00
Mayonnaise, three pcs
   Hobnail Opalescent pattern, blue .. 65.00
   Snow Crest, emerald green, heart shaped, orig spoon 65.00
Mustard, Hobnail Opalescent pattern, blue, three pcs 30.00
Nut Compote, Silver Crest pattern, ftd . 20.00
Paperweight, Patriot Eagle, red 25.00
Perfume Bottle, 4½" h, Hobnail Opalescent pattern, blue, orig stopper 55.00
Pitcher
  4" h
   Hobnail Opalescent pattern, blue, clear handle 55.00
   Jacqueline pattern, milk glass 20.00
  5½" h, Hobnail Opalescent pattern, blue, clear handle, squatty 48.00
  6½" h, Coin Dot pattern, cranberry opalescent, applied clear handle . 80.00
Plate
  7" sq, 1639 Cobalt pattern, floral leaf wheel cutting 25.00
  7½" d, Horse Medallion pattern, pink satin 120.00
  8½" d, Emerald Crest 25.00
Plate
  9" d
   Dot Optic pattern, cranberry opalescent 125.00
   Leaf pattern, French opalescent .. 30.00
  12" d, Silver Crest 32.00
Rose Bowl
  3½" d base, 3¾" w, Polka Dot pattern, cranberry, pinched top 75.00
  4½" h, 4" d, Hobnail Opalescent pattern, green 75.00
  5" d, 4" h, Snow Crest pattern, deep cranberry, spiral optic molding ... 75.00
Salt and Pepper Shakers, pr
  Hobnail Opalescent pattern, French
   Flat 35.00
   Footed 80.00
  Silver Crest pattern 65.00
Sherbet, 1639 Cobalt pattern, floral leaf wheel cutting 25.00
Slipper, Hobnail Opalescent pattern, blue 23.00
Tidbit Server, 2 tiers, Silver Crest pattern 45.00
Top Hat
  Hobnail Opalescent pattern, blue .. 24.00
  Ivory Crest, ruffled brim, 3½" d base 55.00
  Rib Optic pattern, French Opalescent, 10" h 235.00
  Ruby Overlay, 4" h 65.00
Tray, 10½" w, Hobnail Opalescent pattern, yellow, fan shape 40.00
Tumbler
  Coin Dot pattern
   Cranberry opalescent, 9 oz 45.00
   Honeysuckle opalescent 30.00

Colonial pattern, blue 15.00
Hobnail Opalescent pattern, French, 15 oz, 6" h, ftd 35.00
1639 Cobalt pattern, floral leaf wheel cutting, 12 oz 45.00
1800 Sheffield pattern, amethyst, 4" h 18.00
Vase
  4" h, Hobnail Opalescent pattern, yellow, tricorn 40.00
  4½" h
   Hobnail Opalescent pattern, lime green, flared 30.00
   Dot Optic pattern, cranberry opalescent 35.00
  5" h, Hobnail Opalescent pattern, French, cupped, flared, spiral 75.00
  6" h, fan, ftd
   Hobnail Opalescent pattern, blue 34.00
   Periwinkle 70.00
  7" h, Dot Optic pattern, cranberry opalescent 35.00
  7¾" h, Polka Dot pattern, cranberry opalescent, hand painted dec 110.00
  8" h, Hobnail Opalescent pattern, yellow, hand painted dec 65.00
  8½" h, emerald green overlay, hand painted dec 68.00
  8¾" h, Snow Crest pattern, emerald green, spiral optic ribbing 90.00
  9" h, emerald green overlay, beaded, melon 45.00
  11" h
   Bubble Optic pattern, honey amber 150.00
   Snow Crest, amber spiral optic ... 75.00
Water Set, pitcher, six tumblers, Ming pattern, rose 225.00

FINDLAY ONYX GLASS

History: Findlay onyx glass, produced by Dalzell, Gilmore & Leighton Company, Findlay, Ohio, was patented in 1889 for the firm by George W. Leighton. Due to high production costs resulting from a complex manufacturing process, the glass was made only for a short time.

Layers of glass were plated to a bulb of opalescent glass through repeated dippings into a glass pot. Each layer was cooled and reheated to develop opalescent qualities. A pattern mold then was used to produce raised decorations of flowers and leaves. A second mold gave the glass bulb its full shape and form.

A platinum luster paint, producing pieces identified as silver or platinum onyx, was applied to the raised decorations. The color was fixed in a muffle kiln. Other colors such as cinnamon, cranberry, cream, raspberry, and rose were achieved by using an outer glass plating which reacted strongly to reheating. For example, a purple or orchid color came from the addition of manganese and cobalt to the glass mixture.

Reference: James Measell and Don E. Smith, *Findlay Glass: The Glass Tableware Manufacturers, 1886–1902*, Antique Publications, 1986.

Collectors' Club: Collectors of Findlay Glass, P. O. Box 256, Findlay, OH 45839–0256.

Jar, creamy white, gold dec, 3⅞" d, $310.00.

Bowl
7" d, 2¾" h, silver onyx 300.00
7½" d
  Cream onyx 375.00
  Raspberry onyx 425.00
Butter Dish, cov, 5½" d, silver onyx .. 800.00
Celery, 6¼" h, cream onyx 250.00
Creamer, 4½" h
  Cream onyx 525.00
  Raspberry onyx 275.00
Dresser Box, cov, 5" d, cream onyx,
  round 650.00
Mustard, cov, 3" h, hinged metal cov,
  orig spoon marked "Sterling"
  Cream onyx 275.00
  Raspberry onyx 550.00
Pitcher
  7½" h, cream onyx, applied opales-
    cent handle, polished chip on rim 800.00
  8" h, cream onyx, amber florals and
    handle, minor bubbles in inner
    liner 660.00
Salt and Pepper Shakers, pr, 3" h, plat-
  inum onyx 550.00
Spooner, 4¼" h
  Platinum blossoms, rough edge 245.00
  Raspberry onyx 600.00
Sugar, cov, 5½" h
  Cream onyx 400.00
  Raspberry onyx 650.00
Sugar Shaker, 6" h
  Raspberry onyx 350.00
  Silver onyx 300.00
Syrup, cov, 7" h, silver onyx, silver
  plated lid marked "Pat. March 28,
  82", lid finial missing 400.00
Toothpick Holder, 2½" h
  Cinnamon onyx 400.00
  Cream onyx 375.00

Tumbler, Floradine pattern, raspberry
onyx 785.00

FIRE-KING

History: Fire-King dinnerware and kitchenware was made by the Anchor Hocking Glass Corporation. Production began in the early 1940s and continued into the early 1970s. Dinnerware patterns include Alice, Charm, Fleurette, Game Bird, Honeysuckle, Jane Ray, Laurel, Primrose, Turquoise Blue, Swirl, and Wheat. Utilitarian kitchen items and ovenware patterns were also produced. Anchor Hocking's Fire-King was a contemporary to Pyrex and other "oven proof" glasswares.

Housewives eagerly purchased Fire-King sets and could assemble large sets of matching dinnerware and ovenware patterns. Advertising encouraged consumers to purchase prepacked sets of Anchor Hocking dinnerware sets, starter sets, luncheon sets, and snackware sets, as well as casseroles and baking sets.

Oven glassware items include almost everything needed to completely stock the kitchen, from bakers to roasters to skillets.

Fire-King patterns are found in azurite, forest green, gray, ivory, jadite, peach luster, pink, plain white, ruby red, sapphire blue, opaque turquoise, white with different rim colors, and even decaled wares. Collectors tend to focus on the older patterns and colors as well as ovenware items.

Anchor Hocking used a molded mark for Fire-King as well as oval foil paper labels.

References: Gene Florence, *Collectible Glassware From The 40's, 50's, 60's, An Illustrated Value Guide*, Collector Books, 1992; Gene Florence, *Kitchen Glassware of the Depression Years, Fourth Edition*, Collector Books, 1990; Garry and Dale Kilgo and Jerry and Gale Wilkins, *A Collectors Guide to Anchor Hocking's Fire-King Glassware, 1st Ed.*, K & W Collectibles Publisher, 1991; Glyndon Shirley, *The Miracle In Grandmother's Kitchen*, published by author, 1983; April M. Tvorak, *History & Price Guide To Fire–King*, published by author, 1991.

Periodical: *The Daze*, Depression Glass Daze, 275 State Rd, Box 57, Otisville, MI 48463–0057.

Collectors' Club: The National Depression Glass Association, P. O. Box 69843, Odessa, TX 79769.

Mug, Jadite, Restaurant Ware, 7 oz, $5.00.

DINNERWARE

Alice, 1940–1950s

Cup	
Jadite	1.75
White, blue trim	5.00
Plate, 9½" d, dinner	
Jadite	10.00
White, blue trim	12.00
Saucer	
Jadite	1.00
White, blue trim	3.00

Jane Ray, 1940–1950s, jadite

Bowl, 4⅞" d	2.50
Creamer and Sugar, cov	10.00
Cup and Saucer	2.00
Demitasse Cup and Saucer	20.00
Oatmeal Bowl, 5⅞" d	2.50
Plate	
7¾" d, salad	3.00
9" d, dinner	3.50
Platter, oval, 12" l, 9" w	9.00
Soup Plate	8.00
Vegetable Bowl, 8¼" l	6.75

Plain Jane

Bowl, 6½" d, turquoise	12.00
Creamer, turquoise	4.50
Cup	
Turquoise	3.50
White, floral decal	2.50
Custard, 3¾" d, white	2.00
Mixing Bowl, turquoise	
6¾" d, 1 qt	10.00
7½" d, 2 qt	8.00
Plate	
7" d, fired–on dark green	2.00
7¼" d, white	2.00
Snack Plate, turquoise, gold trim	4.00

Swirl, 1955–1960s

Bowl, 4⅞" d, white with brushed gold	2.50
Creamer	
Blue	3.00
Jadite	5.00
Pink	6.00
Creamer and Sugar	
Azurite	10.00

White with brushed gold	5.00
Cup and Saucer	
Custard	2.25
Pink	3.50
White	2.00
White with brushed gold	3.00
Plate	
7⅝" d, white with brushed gold	2.50
9" d	
Blue	4.00
White	2.00
White with brushed gold	3.25
10" d, white	3.00
Platter, ivory	3.50
Saucer, ivory with red trim	1.00
Soup Plate	
Blue	6.00
White	2.50
White with brushed gold	2.75
Sugar, open, ivory with red trim	3.00

Turquoise Blue, 1950s

Ashtray	6.50
Batter Bowl	30.00
Berry Bowl, 4⅞" d	4.25
Cereal Bowl, 5" d	4.75
Creamer	4.00
Cup	2.50
Egg Plate	10.00
Mixing Bowl, 3 qt	6.00
Mug	7.50
Plate	
6" d, salad	3.75
7" d, luncheon	5.00
9" d, dinner	4.75
10" d, dinner	15.00
Relish, three part	8.50
Salad Bowl, 6⅝" d	10.00
Saucer	.75
Sugar	4.00
Vegetable Bowl, 8" d	9.50

KITCHENWARE

Batter Bowl, jadite	13.00
Bowl, 4¾" d	
Ivory	2.50
White	2.50
Cereal Bowl, jadite, heavy walls	3.00
Chili Bowl, 5" d	
Custard	3.50
White	3.50
Hot Plate, clear	6.00
Measuring Bowl, pouring spout, 16 oz, sapphire blue	18.00
Mixing Bowl, 7" d, jadite, swirl	7.00
Mug	
Jadite, oval handle	5.00
White	
Plain	3.75
Tiger decal	4.50
Pie Plate, 9" d, dark amber	14.00

OVENWARE

Baker, 1 qt, sapphire blue	**5.00**
Bowl, 8" d, orange	**4.00**
Casserole, sapphire blue	
Individual	**12.00**
Pint	**10.00**
Custard, 5 oz, sapphire blue, orig paper	
label	**3.00**
Deep Dish Pie Plate, 5⅜" d, sapphire	
blue	**11.00**
Loaf Pan, 9" l, 5" w, sapphire blue ...	**15.00**
Mug, sapphire blue	**20.00**
Percolator Top, 2⅛" h	**3.50**
Pie Plate, sapphire blue	
8⅜" d	**7.00**
9⅛" d	**7.50**
Platter, 11" l, orange	**6.00**
Refrigerator Dish, cov, 5 x 9", sapphire	
blue	**25.00**
Roaster, 8¾" l, sapphire blue	**15.00**
Utility Bowl, 10⅛" d, sapphire blue ..	**18.00**

FOSTORIA GLASS

History: Fostoria Glass Co. began operations at Fostoria, Ohio, in 1887, and moved to Moundsville, West Virginia, its present location, in 1891. By 1925 Fostoria had five furnaces and a variety of special shops. In 1924 a line of colored tableware was introduced. Fostoria was purchased by Lancaster Colony in 1983, and continues to operate under the Fostoria name.

Fostoria was known for tableware and stemware of high quality. These fine wares included clear, colored, etched, gilded, lustered, and pressed items. Fostoria reacted to the market and the times by actively competing with their contemporaries, such as Cambridge, Heisey, and Westmoreland. Some of the Fostoria patterns and colors were designed to directly compete with these companies. Careful study of their patterns will show the similarities in design and color. Fostoria's Azure blue compares to Cambridge's blue. Etched patterns such as June or Navarre compare to Cambridge's Rose Point and Heisey's Orchid pattern.

Fostoria produced patterns with a wide range of items, allowing a bride to set her table with everything from ashtrays to vases. Plates of every size and use complimented the stemware. She could use a different piece of stemware to serve grapefruit, oysters, parfaits, and sherbets, as well as water and wine.

One of the most popular patterns ever produced by Fostoria is American. It's production began in 1915 and continued until the merger with Lancaster Glass in 1983. Most production was in clear glass, although some color pieces were made. This pattern was very popular with World War II brides and was made in many forms. Over fifty different sizes of bowls were made for use as serving pieces.

References: Gene Florence, *Elegant Glassware Of The Depression Era, Fourth Edition,* Collector Books, 1991; Robert E. Foster, *Fostoria American Pattern,* published by author, 1984; JoAnn Schliesmann, *Price Guide To Fostoria, The Popular Years, Third Edition,* Park Avenue Publications, Ltd.; Sidney P. Seligson, *Fostoria American, A Complete Guide,* published by author, 1992; Hazel M. Weatherman, *Fostoria, Its First Fifty Years,* published by author, c1972.

Collectors' Club: Fostoria Glass Society of America, P.O. Box 826, Moundsville, WV 26041.

Museum: Huntington Galleries, Huntington, WV.

Animal	
Deer, standing, milk glass	**37.50**
Owl, ebony, pr	**350.00**
Squirrel, amber	**35.00**
Bell, Christmas, 1977, sgd	**40.00**
Bookends, pr, Mandarin Lady, ebony .	**350.00**
Figure	
Madonna, frosted	**67.50**
Mermaid, crystal	**125.00**

PATTERNS

American Pattern

Almond Bowl, 3¾" d	**8.50**
Appetizer Set	**245.00**
Ashtray	
2⅞" w sq	**6.00**
5½" l oval	**9.00**
Basket, reed handle	
7" d, 9" h	**90.00**
10" h	**55.00**
Bell	**25.00**
Bitters Bottle, 5¾" h	**35.00**
Boat, 12" l	**12.00**
Bon Bon, 6¾" d, three small feet ...	**8.00**
Bowl	
9" d, oval, float	**35.00**
10½" d, three foot	**14.00**
11" d, tricorner	**25.00**
11¾" l, oval	**45.00**
Butter Dish, cov, round	**50.00**
Cake Plate, 10" d, pedestal	
Round	**75.00**
Square	**100.00**
Candlesticks, pr	
3" h	**20.00**
6" h	**50.00**
Candy Box, three part	**50.00**
Catsup Bottle, orig stopper	**110.00**
Celery Tray, 10" l	**12.00**
Cheese and Cracker Set	**45.00**
Cigarette Box, cov	**32.00**
Cocktail, ftd	**12.50**

Cologne Bottle, 4½ oz **25.00**
Compote, 9½" d **28.00**
Condiment Bottle, orig stopper **125.00**
Cream Soup **39.00**
Creamer
   9 oz **9.00**
   9½ oz, 4" h **8.00**
Cruet, orig stopper **25.00**
Cup and Saucer **8.50**
Decanter, orig stopper
   Cordial **130.00**
   Rye/Scotch, chrome holder **325.00**
Dessert, 4½ oz **7.00**
Finger Bowl, handled **16.00**
Fruit Bowl, 13" d, shallow **45.00**
Glove Box, cov, 9½" l **28.00**
Goblet
   6⅞" h, hex foot **10.00**
   9 oz, round foot **8.00**
   10 oz **12.00**
Hairpin Box, cov, 3½" w **20.00**
Hat, top, 3" h **28.00**
Hurricane Lamp **70.00**
Ice Tub **45.00**
Iced Tea Tumbler, ftd **13.00**
Jelly, cov, 6¾" h **28.00**
Juice Tumbler, ftd **10.00**
Lemon Bowl, cov, 5½" d **24.00**
Marmalade, cov, orig spoon, ftd **45.00**
Mayonnaise and liner **25.00**
Mug **50.00**
Mustard, cov **25.00**
Muffin Tray, two handles **20.00**
Napkin Ring **4.50**
Nappy
   4½" d **8.75**
   6" d **10.00**
Nut, master, oval, 4" l **25.00**
Old Fashioned **11.00**
Pickle **11.00**
Picture Frame **10.00**
Pitcher, half gallon, 8" h **55.00**
Plate
   7¾" d, salad **7.00**
   8½" d, luncheon **11.00**
   9½" d, dinner **16.00**
   9⅞" d, dinner **12.00**
Platter, 12" l, oval **45.00**
Punch Bowl, matching base and un-
   derplate **250.00**
Punch Cup, flared **6.00**
Relish
   Three part **25.00**
   Four part, 11" sq **65.00**
Rose Bowl, 3½" d **18.00**
Salt, open, individual **9.00**
Salt and Pepper Shakers, pr, individ-
   ual, matching tray **18.00**
Sandwich Server, 12" d **32.00**
Sauce Boat, liner **45.00**
Sherbet, 5½ oz **9.00**
Shrimp Bowl **400.00**

Straw Jar, cov **255.00**
Sugar, 3¼" h **6.00**
Sugar, cov, two handles **15.00**
Sundae **8.00**
Syrup, glass lid, liner **110.00**
Sweet Pea Vase **75.00**
Tidbit, 7" d, three toes **22.00**
Tom and Jerry Bowl **160.00**
Toothpick **20.00**
Torte Plate, 13" l, oval **40.00**
Tray, 12" d **175.00**
Trophy, two handles **35.00**
Tumbler, 3⅞" h **15.00**
Urn, 6" h, sq **24.00**
Vase
   5" h, flared **10.00**
   6" h, flared **30.00**
   6½" h, urn shape **20.00**
   7" h, flared **50.00**
   8" h, straight **50.00**
   8½" h, bud, flared **18.00**
   9" h, sq, ftd **40.00**
   9½" h, flared **75.00**
   9¾" h, sq, ftd **37.00**
   10" h, cupped **150.00**
   12" h **95.00**
Wedding Bowl, cov **85.00**
Whiskey, 2½" h **9.00**
Wine, 2½" h, hexagon ftd **10.00**
Youth Set, bowl, mug, 6" d plate . . .   **45.00**

**Candy Dish, Baroque, marigold, 4¾" h,
5½" d, $25.00.**

Baroque
Bowl
   4" d, sq, topaz, handle **12.00**
   6" d, sq, crystal **6.00**
   6½" d, sq, divided, topaz **12.00**
   12" d, flared, blue tint **28.00**
Butter Dish, blue **275.00**
Cake Plate, 10" d, crystal **8.75**
Candlesticks, pr
   Crystal, 7¾" h, lusters **85.00**
   Topaz **16.00**

Candy Dish, cov
Blue, 9½" h, ftd 70.00
Crystal, Meadow Rose etch 90.00
Compote, 4¾" h, crystal 7.00
Creamer and Sugar, crystal 15.00
Cream Soup Bowl, crystal 8.50
Cruet, stopper, crystal 55.00
Cup and Saucer
Blue 20.00
Crystal 9.00
Yellow 16.00
Goblet, 9 oz
Crystal 10.00
Yellow 22.00
Ice Bucket
Blue 70.00
Crystal 30.00
Iced Tea Tumbler, 6" h, blue 75.00
Jelly, cov, crystal 40.00
Mayonnaise, liner, crystal 22.00
Mint Tray, 4¼" d, yellow, ftd 18.00
Mustard, cov, crystal 20.00
Pitcher, water, crystal 125.00
Plate
6" d, blue 5.50
7" d, yellow 7.50
8" d, crystal 17.50
9" d, blue 25.00
14" d, Meadow Rose etch, crystal 45.00
Platter, 12" l, oval, clear 15.00
Punch Bowl, crystal 400.00
Relish
6" d, sq, two part, blue 35.00
10" l, three part, topaz 22.00
Rose Bowl, 3¾" d, crystal 34.00
Salt and Pepper Shakers, pr, individ-
ual size, crystal 25.00
Serving Dish, 8½" d, crystal, handle 10.00
Sherbet, crystal 7.00
Tray, 8" l, blue 65.00
Tumbler, 5¾" h, crystal 6.50
Vase, 7" h, blue 25.00

Bellwether
Champagne, flute, 10½" h, crystal .. 10.00
Goblet, 8½" h, crystal 10.00

Bouquet
Bowl, tricorn, three toes 18.00
Goblet 21.00
Pickle Dish, 8½" l 18.00
Pitcher, 6⅛" h 75.00
Salt and Pepper Shakers, pr 22.00

Buttercup
Bowl, 10" d, handle 45.00
Celery 35.00
Mayonnaise, liner, ladle 55.00
Pickle Dish 25.00
Vase, 7" h, ftd 135.00
Wine, 3½ oz 29.50

Camillia
Candy Jar, cov, 7" h 65.00
Claret, 3½ oz 15.00

Creamer and Sugar Set, matching tray,
individual size 45.00
Parfait, 5½ oz 16.00
Century
Bowl, 5" d, handled 8.00
Candlesticks, pr, crystal 55.00
Candy Dish, cov, ftd 40.00
Compote, crystal 18.00
Creamer and Sugar Set, creamer, cov
sugar, matching tray 30.00
Mayonnaise, orig liner 24.00
Pitcher, cereal 50.00
Salt and Pepper Shakers, pr, individ-
ual, crystal, matching tray 18.00
Chintz
Bon Bon, three legs 20.00
Bowl
5" d, handled, ftd 17.00
10" d, two handles 55.00
12" d, flared 65.00
Cake Plate, 10" d, two handles 40.00
Candlesticks, pr, 4" h 30.00
Candy, cov, three part 85.00
Champagne 22.50
Cocktail 18.00
Compote, 5½" d 35.00
Cordial 42.00
Creamer 14.00
Creamer and Sugar, matching tray, in-
dividual size 67.00
Goblet, 9 oz 24.00
Iced Tea Tumbler, ftd 21.00
Juice Tumbler, ftd 17.50
Mayonnaise, ladle, liner 50.00
Plate
9½" d, dinner 45.00
12½" d 39.00
Sandwich Plate, 14" d 50.00
Sherbet, tall 17.00
Tidbit, three toes 31.00
Tumbler, ftd, 13 oz 22.50
Wine 40.00
Coin
Ashtray
5" d, light blue frost 20.00
7" d, blue 45.00
7½" d
Amber 18.00
Crystal 20.00
Bowl, 8" d
Amber 25.00
Crystal 28.00
Red 40.00
Candlesticks, pr, 4½" h
Amber 25.00
Crystal, 7" h 75.00
Emerald Green 85.00
Olive 28.00
Red, 8" h 125.00
Candy Box, cov, red 45.00
Candy Dish, cov
Olive 28.00

Red, tall 60.00
Compote, 8½" h, emerald green ... 125.00
Creamer and Sugar, cov, crystal 35.00
Cruet, orig stopper, crystal 75.00
Fruit Bowl, 10" d, olive green, pedestal 85.00
Jelly
  Blue 25.00
  Crystal 18.00
Lamp
  Coach, oil, amber 120.00
  Electric, patio, emerald green 225.00
  Oil, 9¾" h, amber 125.00
Nappy, 5" d, handle
  Amber 15.00
  Crystal 18.00
  Red 20.00
Pitcher, olive green 45.00
Salt and Pepper Shakers, pr
  Blue 45.00
  Crystal 40.00
  Red 60.00
Tumbler, 3¾" h, crystal 30.00
Urn, cov, 12¾" h, red 95.00
Vase, bud
  Amber 25.00
  Crystal 15.00
Wedding Bowl, cov
  Emerald Green 150.00
  Red 95.00

Colony
Bon Bon, two small feet, crystal 15.00
Bowl, 10½" d, low, crystal, ftd 65.00
Butter, cov, ¼ lb
  Crystal 42.00
  Milk Glass 45.00
Cake Plate, 10" d, handles, crystal .. 18.00
Candlesticks, pr, two lights, crystal . 35.00
Candy Box, cov, low, crystal 35.00
Cheese Compote, crystal 15.00
Cocktail, crystal, ftd 9.00
Compote, cov, low
  Crystal 32.00
  Milk Glass 45.00
Creamer and Sugar, crystal 15.00
Cruet, oil, stopper, crystal 35.00
Cup and Saucer, crystal 10.00
Goblet, 9 oz, crystal 10.00
Ice Jug, 2 quart, crystal 90.00
Iced Tea Tumbler, ftd, crystal 12.00
Juice Tumbler, ftd, 5 oz, crystal 9.00
Luncheon Tray, handles, crystal 27.00
Mayonnaise, 3 pcs, crystal 32.50
Muffin Tray, handles, crystal 27.00
Olive Dish, cupped, 5½" d, crystal . 20.00
Oyster Cocktail, crystal 8.00
Plate, crystal
  7½" d, salad 7.00
  9" d, dinner 24.00
Relish, three part, crystal 24.00
Salad Bowl, 9" d, crystal 30.00

Salt and Pepper Shakers, pr, crystal, gold tops 32.00
Serving Dish, 8½" d, handle, crystal 17.00
Sherbet, crystal 6.50
Sweetmeat, 5" h, crystal 9.00
Tumbler, 9 oz, crystal 10.00
Vase
  6" h, bud, crystal 14.00
  7" h, crystal 45.00
  7½" h, flared, crystal 30.00
  7¾" h, flared, crystal 32.00
Vegetable Bowl, oval, crystal 24.00
Wine, crystal 19.00
Fairfax
Ashtray, azure blue 25.00
Bowl, 5" d, azure blue 9.00
Butter Dish, cov
  Orchid 350.00
  Yellow 50.00
Cake Plate, 10" d, handle, blue 37.50
Candy, cov, 1/2 lb, azure blue 90.00
Champagne, orchid 25.00
Cocktail, yellow 22.00
Compote, 8" d, #2350, azure blue . 60.00
Cordial, orchid 55.00
Cream Soup, green 7.00
Creamer, individual size, azure blue 15.00
Creamer and Sugar, tea size
  Green 15.00
  Yellow 18.00
Creamer and Sugar, dinner size, azure
  blue 30.00
Cruet, orig stopper
  Azure blue 225.00
  Pink 125.00
Cup and Saucer, dinner size
  Blue 12.50
  Green 9.25
  Topaz 9.25
Demitasse Cup and Saucer, azure
  blue 35.00
Goblet
  Azure blue 25.00
  Blue 25.00
  Yellow 25.00
Grapefruit, liner, orchid 75.00
Ice Bucket, yellow 45.00
Lemon Dish
  Azure blue 12.00
  Blue 20.00
  Green 8.00
Parfait, blue 31.00
Pickle Tray, rose 10.00
Plate
  6" d
    Azure blue 2.00
    Green 2.00
  7½" d
    Azure blue 4.00
    Green 3.00
  9½" d, yellow 12.50
Relish, oval, azure blue 18.50

Salt and Pepper Shakers, pr, azure
blue **95.00**
Sandwich Server
   Azure blue **32.00**
   Topaz **13.00**
Saucer, yellow **2.00**
Sweetmeat, two handles, blue **22.50**
Sugar, individual
   Azure blue **15.00**
   Green **6.00**
Tray, azure blue, center handle **18.00**
Tumbler, ftd, 2½ oz, azure blue **15.00**
Vegetable Bowl, 9" d, blue **18.00**
Water, 5¼" h, topaz **11.00**
Whipped Cream Bowl, azure blue .. **20.00**
Whiskey, orchid **30.00**
Wine, 5½" h, topaz **16.00**

Fascination
Goblet
   Burgundy **20.00**
   Red **35.00**
Tumbler, 13 oz, burgundy **22.00**
Wine, burgundy **20.00**

Heather
Bowl, 10¾" d, flared, ftd **45.00**
Candlesticks, pr, 4½" h **35.00**
Mayonnaise, underplate **35.00**

Heirloom
Bon Bon, green opalescent **16.00**
Bowl, 13" d, green opalescent **40.00**
Vase, 11" h, blue opalescent **40.00**

Hermitage
Cruet, topaz **85.00**
Ice Cream Dish, azure blue **15.00**
Pitcher, 3 pint, topaz **125.00**

Jamestown
Goblet, 9½ oz
   Blue **14.00**
   Green **6.00**
   Red **16.00**
Iced Tea Tumbler
   Amethyst **11.00**
   Blue **19.00**
Juice Tumbler, ftd, 5 oz, amethyst .. **6.00**
Pitcher, amethyst **95.00**
Plate, 8" d, blue **12.00**
Salt Shaker, pink **25.00**
Sauce Dish, cov, blue **40.00**
Sherbet, 6½ oz
   Amethyst **8.00**
   Blue **15.00**
Tumbler, ftd, 12 oz
   Amber **8.00**
   Blue **19.00**
Wine, 4 oz
   Blue **12.50**
   Crystal **6.00**

June
Ashtray, pink **60.00**
Baker, oval, pink, 9" l **85.00**
Bon Bon, pink **32.50**

Candlesticks, pr
   Blue **50.00**
   Pink, #2375 .... **60.00**
Cocktail, pink **45.00**
Compote, 7" d **75.00**
Console Set, yellow, 11½" d bowl, 2"
   h candlesticks **65.00**
Creamer and Sugar
   Blue **50.00**
   Pink **60.00**
   Yellow **30.00**
Cream Soup, liner, yellow **50.00**
Cup, pink **30.00**
Cup and Saucer, azure blue **37.50**
Demitasse Cup, crystal **20.00**
Goblet, 8¼" h, 10 oz
   Blue **32.00**
   Crystal **22.50**
   Pink **40.00**
Ice Bucket, orig tongs
   Azure blue **135.00**
   Pink **145.00**
Iced Tea Tumbler, pink **50.00**
Oyster Cocktail
   Crystal **18.00**
   Pink **35.00**
Parfait, yellow **55.00**
Pitcher
   Azure blue **500.00**
   Crystal **300.00**
   Pink **525.00**
Plate
   6" d
      Pink **14.00**
      Yellow **5.50**
   7½" d, crystal **7.00**
   8¾" d, pink **20.00**
   9½" d, yellow **22.00**
   10¼" d, pink **80.00**
Platter, 10½" l, pink **125.00**
Salt and Pepper Shakers, pr, pink ... **175.00**
Sherbet
   High, crystal, 6 oz **17.50**
   Low, pink **25.00**
Wine, pink **80.00**

Lafayette
Ashtray, 4" d **30.00**
Candlesticks, pr, 2" h, wisteria **65.00**
Cordial, wisteria **150.00**
Juice Tumbler, wisteria **37.50**
Tumbler, wisteria **35.00**

Mayfair
Ashtray, red **20.00**
Demitasse Cup and Saucer, yellow . **20.00**

Meadow Rose
Compote **25.00**
Creamer and Sugar, crystal **30.00**
Cup and Saucer **22.50**
Salt and Pepper Shakers, pr **40.00**
Water, ftd **22.00**

Navarre
Bell

Blue	65.00
Crystal	45.00
Celery	
9" l	25.00
11½" l	35.00
Champagne	20.00
Cheese Compote	20.00
Cocktail	22.00
Cordial, 1 oz	50.00
Cracker Plate	35.00
Creamer, 4¼" h, ftd	19.00
Cup and Saucer	24.00
Goblet, 9 oz	
Blue	18.00
Crystal	25.00
Mayonnaise, two part, #2498	35.00
Oyster Cocktail	26.00
Plate	
7½" d	15.00
8" d, ftd	25.00
9½" d	35.00
Salt and Pepper Shakers, pr, blue	
Flat	45.00
Footed	60.00
Sugar, 3⅝" h, ftd	17.50
Tray, 8" l, oblong	30.00
Tumbler, blue	20.00
Wine	22.00

Oak Leaf

Bowl, 12" d, pink	65.00
Cake Plate, green, handles	125.00
Candlesticks, pr, 3" h, black	85.00

Rogene

Champagne, saucer, 5 oz	15.00
Goblet, 9 oz	15.00

Romance

Oyster Cocktail	22.50
Server, center handle	35.00
Sherbet, crystal, low	14.00
Tumbler, 6" h	25.00
Water Goblet, crystal	18.00

Royal

Sauce Boat, green, liner	45.00
Sherbet, amber	14.00
Tumbler, 6" h, amber, ftd, 12 oz	18.00

Trojan

Bowl, 12" d, ftd	40.00
Cream Soup and Liner, topaz	28.00
Finger Bowl, topaz	20.00
Goblet, topaz	25.00
Pitcher, topaz	325.00
Relish, round, three part	40.00
Sauce Boat and Liner, topaz	95.00
Sugar Pail, topaz	110.00
Vegetable Bowl, topaz, oval	55.00

Versailles

Baker, 9" l, oval, yellow	60.00
Bowl	
5½" d, yellow	20.00
10" d, blue, scroll	60.00
Candlesticks, pr, 3" h, blue	50.00

Cheese and Cracker Set, yellow, #2375	75.00
Cocktail, pink	25.00
Console Set, azure blue, scroll bowl	145.00
Cordial, green	80.00
Cream Soup, orig liner, blue	37.50
Creamer, green	18.00
Creamer and Sugar, yellow	35.00
Cup and Saucer, green	22.00
Finger Bowl, blue	30.00
Goblet, blue	40.00
Grapefruit, pink	35.00
Ice Bucket, metal handle	
Blue	100.00
Yellow	75.00
Pitcher	
Green	360.00
Pink	335.00
Plate	
Dinner, pink	75.00
Salad, 7½" d, yellow	9.00
Salt and Pepper Shakers, pr, pink	150.00
Sherbet, low, 6 oz	
Green	17.00
Yellow	22.00
Tumbler, ftd	
2½ oz, blue	45.00
5¼" h, pink	20.00
Vase, yellow, 6" d	15.00

Vesper

Candlesticks, pr, amber	32.00
Compote, 8" d, amber	45.00
Console Bowl, amber, rolled edge	28.00
Cream Soup, handle, amber	10.00
Demitasse Cup, amber	22.00

Virginia

Candlesticks, pr, 6" h, blue	20.00
Oyster Cocktail, etched	5.00

Willowmere

Champagne	13.00
Cheese and Cracker Set	60.00
Cocktail	22.50
Creamer and Sugar, 4" h, pr	25.00
Cup and Saucer	12.50
Goblet	24.00
Relish, three part	32.50
Sandwich Server	42.00
Sugar, cov	12.50
Sweetmeat	22.50
Torte Plate, 14" d	37.50

FRUIT JARS

History: Fruit jars are canning jars used to preserve food. Thomas W. Dyott, one of Philadelphia's earliest and most innovative glassmakers, was promoting his glass canning jars in 1829. John Landis Mason patented his screw–type canning jar on November 30, 1858. This date refers to the patent date, not the age of the jar. There are thousands of types of jars in many colors, types of closures, sizes, and embossings.

References: Alice M. Creswick, *The Red Book of Fruit Jars No. 6*, published by author, 1990; Dick Roller, *The Standard Fruit Jar Reference*, Acorn Press, 1983; Bill Schroeder, *1000 Fruit Jars: Priced And Illustrated, Revised 5th Edition*, Collector Books, 1987.

Atlas, E–Z seal, blue, raised letters, glass lid, wire bail, 1 quart, $5.00.

ABGA Mason Perfect, aqua, qt 28.00
Acme, pt, shield with stars and stripes   4.00
AGWL, aqua, qt, handmade, wax seal   20.00
Air–Tight, amber, pt, handmade, zinc lid 50.00
Allen's, aqua, pat June 1871 . . . .   130.00
American Fruit Jar, light green, qt, handmade, glass lid, wire bail 100.00
Anchor Hocking, clear, qt, machine made, glass lid, wire bail, anchor emb on side, H superimposed on anchor 5.00
Atlas E–Z Seal, cornflower blue, pt . . .   10.00
Atlas Mason, aqua, qt, handmade, zinc lid 25.00
Ball
  Aqua, qt, handmade, glass lid, ground top, emb in script "The Ball, Pat. Apl'd For" 45.00
  Green, pt, handmade, zinc lid, ground lip, emb in script "Ball Mason's Patent 1858" 3.25
  Yellow–green, qt, Standard 70.00
Baltimore Glass Works, aqua, qt, handmade, applied lid 175.00
Banner, clear, qt, machine made, glass lid, wire bail, emb "Trade Mark Banner Warranted" 10.00
Beehive, qt, emb bees and hive 125.00
Blue Ribbon, clear, qt, glass lid, wire clip 7.50

Boldt Mason Jar, blue, pt, zinc lid 15.00
Bosco Double Seal, clear, qt, glass lid   5.00
Brockway Clear–Vu M, pt 10.00
Buckeye No 1, aqua, half gal, metal yoke 140.00
Canadian King, clear, qt, machine made, glass lid, wide mouth 20.00
Champion Syrup and Refining Co, aqua, qt 25.00
Clark Fruit Jar Co, blue, qt, handmade, glass lid emb "Clark Fruit Jar Cleveland" 48.00
Clyde Improved Mason, green, qt, glass lid, metal band 15.00
Columbia, aqua, pt, handmade, glass lid, wire clip 25.00
Conserve, clear, qt, handmade, glass lid, wire bail 7.50
Crystal Jar, amethyst, qt, handmade, glass lid 35.00
Dalbey's Fruit Jar, green, qt, handmade, metal lid, thumbscrews, emb "Dalbey's Fruit Jar, Pat Nov 16, 1858" . .   560.00
Doolittle, aqua, qt, handmade, glass lid, emb "Doolittle The Self Sealer" 60.00
Double Safety, clear, pt, machine made, glass lid, wire bail 4.00
Drey Ever Seal, clear, half pt, glass lid, wire bail 4.00
Eagle, green, qt, handmade wax seal .   75.00
Eclipse, light green, qt, handmade, threaded glass lid, name emb on side   175.00
Economy, amber, pt, metal lid, spring clip 5.00
E I, Newark, Ohio, yellow green, half gal, c1860 . . . .   85.00
Empire, aqua, qt, handmade, stopper neck, name emb in arch 215.00
Eureka, script, aqua, pt 10.00
Favorite, aqua, pt, handmade, zinc lid, name emb in script 18.00
Faxon, blue, qt, handmade, zinc lid . .   8.00
Flickinger, aqua, qt, handmade, glass lid, wire bail 18.00
Garden Queen, qt 4.00
Gem, Wallaceburg, clear, qt, glass lid, screw band 8.00
Glassboro, aqua, qt, handmade, glass lid, screw band, emb "Glassboro Trade Mark Improved" 14.00
Good House Keepers, clear, 2 qt, machine made, zinc lid 2.00
Green Mountain Co, aqua, pt, slug plate   10.00
H & S, aqua, qt, handmade, metal stopper, emb monogram 375.00
Halle, green, qt, handmade, wax seal .   50.00
Hamilton, clear, qt, handmade, glass lid, metal clip 45.00
Harvest Mason, half gal, beaded neck   10.00
Hoosier, aqua, qt, handmade, threaded glass lid, emb "Hoosier Jar" 315.00
Howe, Scranton, half gal 75.00

Independent, aqua, qt, handmade, glass
screw lid **40.00**
Inker, qt, Mason patent **30.00**
Ivanhoe, clear, qt, metal lid, name on
bottom **5.00**
Kilner Jar, clear, pt, machine made,
glass lid, screw band, emb "The Kil-
ner Jar" **5.00**
King, Kant Krack Lid, pt, side clips ... **10.00**
Knowlton Vacuum, Star, aqua, qt **20.00**
L'Ideale, green, pt, glass lid, wire clip . **18.00**
Mallinger, clear, qt, machine made,
zinc lid **4.00**
Mansfield, light green, pt, machine
made, glass lid, screw band, emb
"Mansfield Improved Mason" **15.00**
Marion Jar, aqua, pt, Mason's Pat Nov
30th, 1858 .... **35.00**
Mason's
Fruit Jar, qt, three lines **8.00**
Improved, Cross, light green, qt **15.00**
Patent, 1868, green yellow **110.00**
McDonald Perfect Seal, clear, pt, ma-
chine made, glass lid, wire bail, emb
"McDonald Perfect Seal" **5.00**
Mission, bell, trademark, clear, qt, zinc
lid **15.00**
My Choice, amber, half gal **200.00**
Ohio, clear, 2 qt, handmade, zinc lid,
emb "Ohio Quality Mason" **12.00**
Pansy, aqua, qt, handmade, 20 panels,
emb "Pansy" **125.00**
Penn, The, green, qt, handmade glass
lid, zinc band **25.00**
Pine Deluxe Jar, clear, pt, machine
made, glass lid, wire bail, emb **5.00**
Potter & Bodine, Philadelphia, aqua, qt,
name emb in script **85.00**
Protector, aqua, qt, recessed panel ... **40.00**
Rau's Improved Grove Ring Jar, aqua,
pt, handmade, wax seal **25.00**
Regal, clear, qt, handmade, glass lid,
emb "Regal" in oval **3.00**
Reverse Ball, script, aqua, qt **5.00**
Royal, deep aqua, qt, emb "Royal of
1876" **60.00**
Samco, clear, qt, zinc lid, emb in script
"SAMCO/SUPER JAR" **3.00**
Schram Automatic Sealer, aqua, qt, flag **5.00**
Sealtite, aqua, qt, glass lid, wire bail .. **3.00**
Selco Surety Seal, blue, pt **4.00**
Smalley's Royal Trademark Nu–Seal, pt,
double helix **10.00**
Star, aqua, qt, handmade, glass lid, zinc
band, star emb over name **75.00**
Stevens, aqua, half gal, handmade, wax
seal **75.00**
Sun, aqua, half gal, circle with radiating
rays **50.00**
Sure, aqua, qt, handmade, glass lid,
spring wire clip, emb **220.00**
Texas Mason, clear, qt, zinc lid **15.00**

Tropical, clear, qt, machine made, zinc
lid, name emb in script **2.75**
Tropical Canners, pt **5.00**
Universal, aqua, qt, zinc lid, name emb
upside down **10.00**
Valve Jar Co, Philadelphia, aqua, qt, 8"
h **125.00**
Victory, qt, milk glass lid with shield .. **10.00**
Weideman Boy Brand, Cleveland, qt .. **6.00**
White Crown Mason, milk glass, aqua,
pt **10.00**
Winslow Jar, aqua, qt, handmade, glass
lid, wire clip, emb **45.00**
Woodbury Improved, aqua, pt, hand-
made, glass lid, metal clip **25.00**
Worcester, aqua, qt, handmade, tapered
stopper, emb **85.00**
Yeoman's Fruit Bottle, aqua, half gal .. **20.00**

FRY GLASS

History: The H. C. Fry Glass Co. of Rochester,
Pennsylvania, began operating in 1901 and continued until 1933. Their first products were brilliant period cut glass. They later produced
Depression tablewares. In 1922 they patented
heat resisting ovenware in an opalescent color.
This "Pearl Oven Glass" was produced in a variety of oven and table pieces including casseroles, meat trays, pie and cake pans, etc. Most
of these pieces are marked "Fry" with model
numbers and sizes.

Fry's beautiful art line, Foval, was produced
only in 1926–27. It is pearly opalescent, with
jade green or delft blue trim. It is rarely signed,
except for occasional silver overlay pieces
marked "Rockwell." Foval is always evenly opalescent, never striped like Fenton's opalescent
line.

Reference: Fry Glass Society, *Collector's Encyclopedia of Fry Glass*, Collector Books, 1989,
1990 value update.

Collectors' Club: H. C. Fry Glass Society, P.O.
Box 41, Beaver, PA 15009.

Reproduction Alert: In the 1970s, reproductions
of Foval were made in abundance in Murano,
Italy. These pieces, including candlesticks, toothpicks, etc., have teal blue transparent trim.

ART AND CUT GLASS

Bowl, 8" d, cut, pineapple design,
wheel cutting, sgd **125.00**
Candleholder, Azure blue **20.00**
Creamer, 4" h, yellow, pinched top,
three blue–green loops, applied deep
blue handle **150.00**
Ice Cream Tray, 14" l, 7" w, cut, Nelson
pattern variation, all over cutting, sgd **275.00**

Pitcher, 6¼" d, 9¼" h, Diamond Optic
pattern, chrome green, ground pontil   **75.00**
Punch Cup, Crackle, clear crackle finish
cup, deep blue handle **28.50**
Sherbet, 4" h, cut, Chicago pattern . . .   **75.00**
Tumbler, 5¼" h, Crackle, green handle   **75.00**
Vase, 12" h, opal, pink loopings **200.00**

Tumbler, Foval, waisted, 3⅞" h, $32.00.

OVENWARE

Bean Pot, 1 qt **35.00**
Butter Dish, cov, marked "Pearl Oven
Ware" **70.00**
Casserole, cov, round, marked "Pearl
Oven Ware" **25.00**
Custard Cup, 3¼" marked "Pearl Oven
Ware" **7.00**
Plate, 10½" d, grill, marked "Pearl
Oven Ware" **30.00**
Platter, etched rim, marked "Pearl Oven
Ware" **25.00**

**Goblet, Foval, cobalt blue stem, 5¾" h,
$75.00.**

FOVAL

Bouillon Cup and Saucer, two blue han-
dles **70.00**
Canape Plate, 6¼" d, 4" h, cobalt blue
center handle **175.00**
Compote, 8¾" d, 6¾" h, pale blue loop-
ings, opalescent bowl, blue foot **175.00**
Creamer, blue tinted loopings, applied
Delft blue handle **165.00**
Cruet, pedestal base, cobalt blue han-
dle, orig stopper **250.00**
Cup and Saucer
Delft blue handle **70.00**
Green handle **50.00**
Decanter, 9" h, ftd, applied Delft blue
handle **175.00**
Goblet, fiery opalescent bowl, pink
loopings **85.00**
Jack-In-The-Pulpit, 10½" h, 3½" w top,
jade green trim **785.00**
Lemonade Tumbler
Icicle pattern, 6¼" h, green handle .   **60.00**
Pearl Ware, 6" h, Delft blue handle .   **125.00**
Parfait, 6½" h, Delft blue stem **175.00**
Plate, 9½" d, Delft blue rim **72.00**
Tea Set, Opalware, teapot, six matching
cups and saucers, transparent opal
ground, applied green handles, spout,
and finial **500.00**
Toothpick Holder, Delft blue handle . .   **70.00**
Vase, 9" h, trumpet, jade green base . .   **375.00**
Water Set, tankard pitcher, six glasses,
Delft blue base and handles, 7 pcs .   **265.00**
Wine, Delft blue stem **150.00**

1867–1904

GALLÉ

History: Emile Gallé was one of the most famous
glassmakers and designers from Nancy, France.
Born in 1846, he learned the art of glassmaking
from his father and further studies in Art at Wei-
mar, and through frequent travel to Paris and
London to study glass and glass techniques.

Gallé opened his own glasshouse in 1867 and
began production of art glass in 1874 with his
father. This Nancy factory did very well and soon
expanded into cameo and cased glass wares.
Gallé was a leading exponent in the Art Nouveau
movement in glassmaking, furniture, and other
decorative arts.

Complicated cameo cutting techniques allowed intricate glasswares to be crafted to Gallé's
exacting standards. One of the more common
techniques of the factory was the production of
cameo ware with detailed floral patterns on an
opaque white background. Opaque backgrounds

of many other colors were also used. Much like his contemporary, Louis Tiffany, Gallé was a designer who left much of the actual crafting to others. The lovely glass creations he designed were influenced by the Art Nouveau movement, as well as the increasing interest in Japanese and other Oriental-style decoration.

Examples of Gallé's wares were exhibited at the Paris Expositions of 1878 and 1884. They were also exhibited there in 1889 and 1900 and received wide acclaim for their beauty. Gallé's influence on other glass houses, such as De Verre, in the Nancy region were felt as the "School of Nancy" grew around his factory.

After Gallé's death in 1904, the factory continued production until 1931. Most pieces of Gallé glass were signed. Cameo glasswares have the bold signature cameo carved into the piece. Pieces made after Gallé's death are sgd with the classic signature and a star.

References: Victor Arwas, *Glass Art Nouveau to Art Deco*, Rizzoli International Publications, Inc., 1977; Tim Newark, *Emile Gallé*, The Apple Press, 1989; Harold Newman, *An Illustrated Dictionary of Glass*, Thames and Hudson, 1977; Albert C. Revi, *Nineteenth Century Glass*, reprint, Schiffer Publishing, 1981.

Museums: Bergstrom–Mahler Museum, Neenah, WI; The Chrysler Museum, Norfolk, VA; The Corning Museum of Glass, Corning, NY; The Toledo Museum of Art, Toledo, OH.

Bottle, 10¾" h, elongated baluster shape, pale yellow ground, multicolored wildflower and foliage dec, long stopper **5,800.00**
Bowl
    4¾" d, hemispherical, green ground, brown and green overlay, cut fern with leafy stalks and unfurling tendrils, fire polished, shaved, chip to foot ring, sgd in cameo "Gallé" with star, c1910 ....**1,650.00**
    11¾" l, 3½" h, shaded lemon ground, dark red overlay, cut bleeding heart flowers, scrolling leafy vines, sgd in cameo, under surface circular stamp "Made In France," c1900 . **4,400.00**
Box, cov, 4⅜" d, compressed spherical shape, flat lid, amber ground, purple overlay, carved stalk of starflowers, lid and base sgd in cameo, lid cracked . **125.00**
Brush Pot, 5½" h, sq, dark yellow ground, overlay small trumpet flowers and leaves, enameled white, green, and maroon, gilt highlights, sgd in cameo, c1900 ....**3,300.00**
Canoe, 6⅞" l, frosted glass ground, violet and green overlay, cut hydrangea and stem on exterior, pink single blossoms interior, sgd in cameo, c1900 **2,475.00**

Creamer, 3¼" h, 2¼" d, frosted peach ground, red berries and leaves, two acid cuttings, applied frosted handle, sgd **1,500.00**
Dish, 10¼" l, circular, scalloped, molded as lily pad, two sides curing to form tray, interior green overlay, salmon pink exterior cut with spider mums, sgd in cameo, c1900 ......**3,575.00**
Ewer, 9¼" h, compressed spherical body and spout, applied handle and vines, clear, wheel carved lines simulating opening calla lily, sgd "E Gallé, En Sol Cristallerie A Nancy" **3,500.00**
Sherbet, 3" h, faceted circular bowl, short stem, circular stepped foot, enameled red, green, and white, three cherries and leafy branches, gilt band, engraved "E Gallé" on base, c1900 .... **550.00**
Tumbler
    2¾" h, frosted colorless and pink opal ground, white, blue, and green overlay cut in four petaled blossoms and leaves, sgd in cameo .. **600.00**
    4½" h, faceted, slightly tapering cylinder, enameled French peasant woman holding umbrella in the rain, two acanthus leaves, inscription on reverse, blue, yellow, red, and white, enameled "Emile Gallé Depose," c1870 ....**1,550.00**

Vase, ovoid, fiery amber ground, green, olive, and mauve overlay, cameo cut and carved fruited prunus branches, 21⅜" h, estimated $12,000–15,000. Photograph courtesy of Skinner, Inc.

Vase
    2½" h, cabinet, frosted glass, orange overlay, carved nasturtiums, sgd in cameo **350.00**

2¾″ h, cabinet, squatty baluster, frosted glass, purple overlay, carved leafy vines and berries, sgd in cameo, pr **600.00**

3″ h, cabinet, bulbous, frosted clear ground, lavender and amethyst overlay, cameo cut spring blossoms and broad leaves, sgd in cameo .. **660.00,**

3¼″ h, cabinet, candlestick shape, frosted clear ground, purple overlay, carved wisteria, sgd in cameo   **385.00**

3½″ h, cabinet
Baluster, ftd, dusty rose ground, purple overlay, carved violets, sgd in cameo **715.00**

Violet, bulbous, mottled yellow, amethyst, pale green, and amber overlay, cameo cut and carved violet blossoms, buds, and leaves, sgd in cameo **1,430.00**

3½″ h, 3½″ d, cabinet, colorless frosted and mottled amethyst ground, amber and purple overlay, cameo cut iris blossom, bud, and leaf stalks, overall glossy polished surface, sgd in cameo **1,980.00**

3¾″ h, cabinet, tapered cylinder, pale gray ground, purple overlay, carved morning glories, sgd in cameo ... **350.00**

4½″ h, cabinet, baluster, pink ground cased in clear, lavender and green overlay, carved pendant wisteria branches, sgd in cameo **1,150.00**

5″ h, compressed baluster, pale gray ground, purple overlay, deeply carved Japanese iris, fire polished surface, engraved "Cristallerie de Gallé, modele et decor deposes"   **2,450.00**

5¼″ h, tapered cylinder, everted rim, amber ground, lavender overlay, carved buttercup, incised "Gallé"   **600.00**

5¾″ h, bulbous, trumpet neck, pale pink ground, green and brown overlay, carved oak branches and acorns, sgd in cameo **800.00**

6″ h, flask, frosted pink ground, purple overlay, cameo etched sinuous stems, leaves, and large blossom, sgd in cameo **1,200.00**

6½″ h
Baluster, frosted ground, deep purple overlay, etched pendent branches, berries, and leaves, sgd in cameo **1,000.00**

Banjo shape, pink tinted ground, purple and green overlay, carved hydrangea, sgd in cameo **1,150.00**

Pear form, conical neck, slender foot, yellow ground, brown overlay, carved hydrangea, sgd in cameo **665.00**

Stick, elongated, mottled pink

shaded to amethyst ground, blue and green overlay, cameo cut four petaled blossoms and leafy stems, sgd in cameo at side ... **1,045.00**

6⅝″ h, banjo, pink tinted ground, white, pale green, and dark green overlay, carved maple leaves and pods, sgd in cameo **950.00**

7½″ h
Cylindrical, circular foot, frosted salmon ground, amber overlay, etched blossoms, stems, and large leaves, sgd "Gallé" in cameo and in Chinese manner . **900.00**

Trumpet, cupped mouth, mottled pale pink ground, lower half splashed with yellow, yellow streaked and mottled orange overlay, cut umbel rising over scrolled overlapping stems and leaves, orange and yellow cased base, sgd in cameo, c1900 .... **1,100.00**

8″ h, ovoid, everted rim, shading from green rim to pink, yellow and blue mottled pink base, browns and greens overlay, cut orchids, sgd "Gallé" in cameo with star, c1910 **4,125.00**

8¼″ h, 5½″ w, baluster, yellow ground, dark lotus flower, foliage, and band carved dec **5,800.00**

8½″ h, slender trumpet neck, spreading circular base, pale amber ground, cherry red overlay, carved carnations, sgd in cameo **1,320.00**

9⅛″ h, candlestick shape, pale blue ground, amber and green overlay, carved honeysuckle vines, sgd in cameo **1,450.00**

9¼″ h, flat sided pear form, long neck, everted rim, tangerine ground, orange overlay, carved crab apple branches, sgd in cameo **1,650.00**

9⅝″ h, oviform, circular collar neck and foot, frosted lemon yellow ground, purple overlay, etched and molded clematis blossoms, stems, and leaves, sgd in cameo **11,500.00**

9¾″ h
Elongated neck over bulbous base, fiery opalescent yellow shaded ground, amethyst overlay, cameo cut decumbent blossoms and leafy branches, selective polishing, sgd in cameo at side **2,750.00**

Narrow tapering ovoid, colorless frosted ground, apricot shallow cut blossoms and leafy stems, sgd at side **1,210.00**

9⅞″ h, narrow tapering ovoid, everted mouth, peach tinted ground, brown and green overlay, landscape scene, tall trees in fore-

ground, bushy trees in distance, sgd
"Gallé" in intaglio, c1910 ......**3,850.00**
11½" h, spherical, short neck, everted
rim, short foot, frosted ground,
tinted orange and neck and base,
maroon overlay, cut branches of
full blown roses and buds, sgd in
cameo on side **19,800.00**
12½" h, baluster, frosted colorless
ground, pink and maroon overlay,
cut wild roses and leafy stems, intaglio butterfly carved on pedestal
foot, sgd in cameo on side **1,600.00**
13" h, swelled cylinder, tapering to
circular foot, cantaloupe ground,
brown overlay, carved snapdragon
stalks, sgd in cameo **1,200.00**
13¼" h, candlestick shape, pink
tinted ground, green and brown overlay, etched leaves and berries,
sgd in cameo **1,450.00**
13½" h, candlestick shape, pink
tinted ground, white and green overlay, carved pendant maple leaves
and pods, sgd in cameo **1,650.00**
13¾" h, ovoid, knopped, circular
base, frosted clear ground, green
and brown overlay, carved scene of
boats, tree lined lake, sgd in cameo **6,675.00**
14" h, 10⅜" d, for 1889 Exposition
Universelle Internationale in Paris,
ftd cylinder, martele ground, dark
brown overlay, carved entrelac design, rim carved "En Deuil Jusqua
Ce Que," pontil sgd "Emile Gallé
Nancy 1889, Exposition, Paris"
and "E. G." within vase, base
cracked **9,000.00**
15" h, slender stem, slightly bulbous
body, circular foot, frosted and
lemon yellow ground, deep red overlay, etched primrose, buds,
stems, and leaves, sgd in cameo .**3,600.00**
16¼" h, ovoid, everted rim, pale yellow, cherry red and burgundy overlay, carved hydrangea, sgd in
cameo **17,600.00**
22⅞" h, tall tapering ovoid, deep amber tinged glass mouth and base,
long leafy fuchsia branch overlay,
purple flowers and buds, sgd in
cameo, c1900 ....**12,100.00**
27¼" h, trumpet, circular foot, frosted
ground, green overlay, etched ferns
and florals, sgd in cameo **3,800.00**

GOOFUS GLASS

History: Goofus glass, also known as Mexican
Ware, Hooligan glass, and Pickle glass, is a
pressed glass with relief designs. The back or
front was painted. The designs are usually in red
and green with a metallic gold ground. It was
popular from 1890 to 1920 and was used as a
premium at carnivals.

Goofus glass was produced by several companies: Cresent Glass Company, Wellsburg, West
Virginia; Imperial Glass Corporation, Bellaire,
Ohio; La Belle Glass Works, Bridgeport, Ohio;
and Northwood Glass Co., Indiana, Pennsylvania, Wheeling, West Virginia, and Bridgeport,
Ohio. Northwood marks include "N," "N" in
one circle, "N" in two circles, and one or two
circles without the "N."

Goofus glass lost its popularity when people
found the paint tarnished or scaled off after repeated washings and wear. No record of its manufacture has been found after 1920.

Reference: Carolyn McKinley, *Goofus Glass,*
Collector Books, 1984.

**Oil Lamp, raised floral design, yellow
ground, red flowers, green highlights,
$10.00.**

Ashtray, red rose dec, emb adv	**8.00**
Basket, 5" h, strawberry dec	**45.00**
Bon Bon Dish, 4" d, Strawberry pattern, gold, red, and green dec	**35.00**
Bowl	
4½" d, red roses dec, gold trim	**15.00**
5½" d, La Belle Rose pattern, sq ...	**30.00**
6½" d, Grape and Lattice pattern, red grapes, gold ground, ruffled rim ..	**35.00**
7" d	
Iris pattern, gold and red	**25.00**
Thistle and scrolling leaves, red dec, gold ground, ruffled rim ..	**20.00**
8½" d, floral, red dec, gold ground .	**20.00**
8¾" d, fluted, beaded rim, relief molded, teardrops and red hearts .	**35.00**
9" d	
Carnation pattern, red flowers, re-lief molded	**25.00**
Cherries pattern, red dec, gold ground	**20.00**
Red roses dec, ruffled, relief molded	**20.00**

9½" d, relief molded

Carnation pattern, red flowers	35.00
Strawberry pattern, red berries . . .	40.00

10" d

Dahlias, scalloped	50.00
Pears and apples dec	30.00

10½" d

Red roses, relief molded, gold ground	35.00
Water Lily dec	50.00

11" d, ruffled, relief molded, red cherries **25.00**

Bread Plate, 7" w, 11" l, The Last Supper pattern, red and gold, grapes and foliage border **60.00**

Cake Plate

11" d, Dahlia and Fan pattern, red dec, gold ground	32.00
12" d, red roses dec, gold ground . .	15.00

Candle Holder, red and gold **18.00**

Candy Dish, 8½" d, figure eight design, serrated rim, dome footed **55.00**

Coaster, 3" d, floral, red dec, gold ground **10.00**

Compote

4" d, Grape and Cable pattern	30.00
6" d, jelly, Strawberry pattern, strawberries and foliage, ruffled	28.00
6½" d, Poppy pattern, red flowers, gold foliage, green ground, sgd "Northwood"	32.00

9½" d

Floral and foliage dec, red and gold dec, green ground, crimped and fluted rim, pedestal foot, sgd "Northwood"	30.00
Strawberry pattern, strawberries and leaves, red and green dec, gold ground, ruffled	45.00

10¼" d, relief molded, red fruits . . . **65.00**

Decanter

La Belle Rose pattern, orig stopper . .	50.00
Single Rose pattern, basketweave ground, rose emb stopper	45.00

Dish

7¼" l, fluted, green, floral dec	12.00
11" l, chrysanthemum sprays, red and gold, scalloped rim	70.00

Dresser Tray, 6" l, Cabbage Rose pattern, red roses dec, gold foliage, clear ground **28.00**

Fairy Lamp, roses dec, green trim, clear candle cup **25.00**

Flask, Zig–zag pattern, milk glass ground, gold paint, metal screw top **45.00**

Jar, cov, butterflies, red and gold **20.00**

Jewel Box, 4" d, 2" h, basketweave, rose dec **40.00**

Miniature Lamp, 12" h, Cabbage Rose pattern **42.00**

Mug, Cabbage Rose pattern, gold ground **30.00**

Nappy, 6½" d

Cherries pattern, red cherries, gold foliage, clear ground **35.00**

Strawberry pattern, red strawberries and green leaves, molded applied ring handle **12.00**

Perfume Bottle, 3½" h, pink tulips dec **15.00**

Pickle Jar, aqua, relief molded, gold, blue, and red painted floral design . **25.00**

Pin Dish, 6½" l, oval, red and black florals **15.00**

Pitcher, red rose bud dec, gold leaves . **48.00**

Plate

6" d, relief molded

Rose and Lattice pattern	18.00
Sunflower pattern, red dec center	8.00

7½" d, apples, red dec, gold ground **18.00**

7¾" d, Carnation pattern, red carnations, gold ground **18.00**

8" d, relief molded

Red apples	15.00
Red poppies, gold ground	25.00

8½" d

Gibson cameo, red and gold	40.00
Red apples, relief molded, gold ground	20.00

10½" d, grapes dec, gold ground, irid pink edge **25.00**

11" d

Dahlia pattern, red and gold	35.00
Roses dec, deep red and gold, scalloped rim	22.00

Platter, 18" l, red rose dec, gold ground **65.00**

Powder Jar, cov

3" d, puffy, rose dec, red and gold . . **35.00**

4½" d, Cabbage Rose pattern, relief molded, white cabbage rose **20.00**

Rose Bowl, 4" d, red roses dec, gold ground **20.00**

Salt and Pepper Shakers, pr

Grape and Leaf pattern, 4" h	40.00
Poppy pattern	35.00

Syrup, relief molded

Red roses dec, lattice work ground, orig top **45.00**

Strawberry pattern **32.50**

Toothpick Holder, red rose and foliage dec, gold ground **20.00**

Tray, 8¼" w, 11" l, red chrysanthemum dec, gold ground **35.00**

Tumbler, 6", red rose dec, gold ground **25.00**

Vase, relief molded

6" h, Cabbage Rose pattern, red dec, gold ground **40.00**

6½" h, Grape and Rose pattern, crackle glass, red and gold **10.00**

7" h, Cabbage Rose pattern, white . . **45.00**

7¼" h, Grapes pattern, purple dec . . **25.00**

7½" h, red bird, brown ground **18.00**

8" h

Grapes pattern, purple dec	20.00
Red roses, molded, gold ground . .	15.00

9" h
Bird sitting on grape vine, red and
gold on satin glass 15.00
Poppies pattern, blue and red dec,
gold ground 25.00
10½" h, Peacock pattern 75.00
12" h
Parrot pattern, red and blue bird,
molded foliage 70.00
Red roses, relief molded, gold
ground 40.00

GREENTOWN GLASS

History: The Indiana Tumbler and Goblet Co.,
Greentown, Indiana, produced its first clear,
pressed glass table and bar wares in late 1894.
Initial success led to a doubling of plant size in
1895 and other subsequent expansions, one in
1897 to allow for the manufacture of colored
glass. In 1899 the firm joined the combine
known as the National Glass Company.

In 1900, just before arriving in Greentown,
Jacob Rosenthal developed an opaque brown
glass, called "chocolate," which ranged in color
from a dark, rich chocolate to a lighter "cream"
coffee hue. Production of chocolate glass saved
the financially pressed Indiana Tumbler and
Goblet Works. The Cactus and Leaf Bracket patterns were made almost exclusively in chocolate
glass. Other popular chocolate patterns are Austrian, Dewey, Shuttle, and Teardrop and Tassel.
In 1902 National Glass Company bought Rosenthal's chocolate glass formula so other plants in
the combine could use the color.

In 1902 Rosenthal developed the Golden Agate and Rose Agate colors. Golden Agate was
the color used for the Holly Amber pattern, designed by Frank Jackson, in January of 1903.
Over thirty forms were developed for this pattern
which featured a gold colored body with a marbleized onyx color on raised design elements.
All work ceased on June 13, 1903, when a fire
of suspicious origin destroyed the Indiana Tumbler and Goblet Company Works.

After the fire, other companies, e.g., McKee
and Brothers, produced chocolate glass in the
same pattern designs used in Greentown. Later
reproductions also have taken place, with Cactus
among the most heavily copied pattern.

References: Brenda Measell and James Measell,
A Guide To Reproductions of Greentown Glass,
2nd ed., The Printing Press, 1974; James Measell, *Greentown Glass, The Indiana Tumbler &
Goblet Co.*, Grand Rapids Public Museum, 1979.

Collectors' Club: National Greentown Glass Association, 19596 Glendale Ave, South Bend, IN
46637.

Museums: Greentown Glass Museum, Green-

town, IN; Grand Rapids Public Museum, Ruth
Herrick Greentown Glass Collection, MI.

Animal Dish, cov
Cat, hamper base
Chocolate, chip on base 200.00
Red Agate 350.00
Dolphin, chocolate, beaded rim, fish
finial 315.00
Rabbit, dome top, amber 250.00
Robin, nest base, milk glass 200.00
Berry Set, Leaf Bracket, chocolate, 7 pcs   235.00
Bowl
Cactus, 6½" d, chocolate 75.00
Dewey, 8" d, amber, ftd 30.00
Herringbone Buttress, 7¼" d, green .   135.00
Holly Amber
7½" l, 4½" w, 2" h, oval 360.00
8" d 450.00
8½" d, berry 375.00
Pattern No. 11, 6¼" d, blue, gold trim   125.00
Six Fluted, chocolate 150.00

**Left, Syrup, Geneva, chocolate, orig tin
top, $625.00; right, Cruet, Leaf Bracket,
chocolate, 5½" h, $275.00.**

Butter Dish, cov
Cactus, chocolate 200.00
Cupid, chocolate 575.00
Daisy, milk glass 70.00
Herringbone Buttress, green 200.00
Holly Amber, 7¼" d, 6¼" h 1,200.00
Leaf Bracket, chocolate 175.00
Overall Lattice, clear 65.00
Cake Stand, Holly Amber 2,000.00
Celery Vase, Beaded Panel, clear 90.00
Compote, cov, Holly Amber, 8½" h, 12"
d 1,800.00
Compote, jelly, Cactus, chocolate 100.00
Cookie Jar, Cactus, chocolate 250.00
Cordial
Austrian, canary–yellow 125.00
Overall Lattice 35.00
Shuttle 35.00
Creamer
Cactus, chocolate 110.00

Cord Drapery, blue	90.00
Cupid, Nile green	400.00
Holly Amber, 4½" h	600.00
Indian Head, Nile green	475.00
Indoor Drinking Scene, 5½" h, chocolate	185.00
Shuttle, tankard, clear	45.00

Cruet
Cactus, chocolate	295.00
Chrysanthemum Leaf, chocolate	850.00
Dewey, vaseline	175.00
Geneva, chocolate 1,000.00
Holly Amber, 6½" h 2,100.00
Leaf Bracket, chocolate	275.00
Wild Rose & Bowknot, chocolate ..	300.00

Dresser Tray, Wild Rose and Bowknot,
chocolate 310.00

Goblet
Beehive	60.00
Diamond Prisms	65.00
Overall Lattice	35.00
Honey, cov, Holly Amber	750.00
Lemonade Tumbler, Cactus, chocolate	75.00
Match Holder, Holly Amber	400.00

Mug
Elf, green	95.00
Herringbone Buttress	65.00
Holly Amber, 4½" h, ring handle ...	535.00
Overall Lattice	40.00
Troubadour, 6½" h, milk glass, cov .	60.00
Mustard, cov, Daisy, opaque white ...	75.00

Nappy
Holly Amber	375.00
Leaf Bracket, chocolate, triangular ..	50.00
Masonic, chocolate	95.00
Parfait, Holly Amber	575.00

Pitcher, water
Cord Drapery, clear	65.00
Fleur–De–Lis, clear	85.00
Racing Deer and Doe, clear	175.00
Ruffled Eye, chocolate	500.00
Squirrel, clear	175.00
Teardrop and Tassel, cobalt blue ...	175.00
Plate, Serenade, chocolate	160.00

Punch Cup
Cord Drapery, clear	18.00
Shuttle, clear	10.00

Relish
Cord Drapery, amber	90.00
Holly Amber, oval	275.00
Leaf Bracket, 8" l, chocolate	70.00
Rose Bowl, Austrian, small	30.00

Salt and Pepper Shakers, pr
Cactus, chocolate	145.00
Holly Amber	500.00

Sauce
Cactus, chocolate, ftd	50.00
Holly Amber	225.00
Leaf Bracket, chocolate	25.00
Six Fluted, chocolate	225.00
Water Lily and Cattail, chocolate ...	90.00
Wild Rose and Bowknot, chocolate .	75.00

Spooner
Austrian, clear	45.00
Cupid, clear	145.00
Holly Amber	425.00
Wild Rose and Bowknot, chocolate .	135.00
Stein, Serenade, clear	25.00

Sugar, cov
Cupid, opaque white	110.00
Dewey, cobalt blue	135.00
Sugar, open, Holly Amber	425.00

Syrup
Cord Drapery, chocolate	225.00
Holly Amber, 5¾" h, silver plated hinged lid 2,000.00
Indian Feather, green	175.00
Toothpick Holder, Cactus, golden agate	125.00

Tray
Dewey, serpentine, canary–yellow yellow	60.00
Holly Amber, water, round	600.00
Venetian, 4 x 5", chocolate	275.00

Tumbler
Cactus, chocolate	55.00
Cord Drapery, chocolate	225.00
Dewey, canary–yellow	70.00
Geneva, chocolate	95.00
Holly Amber	385.00
Icicle, chocolate	125.00
Leaf Bracket, chocolate	125.00
Shuttle	75.00
Teardrop and Tassel, cobalt blue ...	65.00
Wildflower, amber	40.00
Vase, Holly Amber, 6" h	425.00

Wine
Cord Drapery	75.00
Shuttle, clear	12.00

1900–58

HEISEY GLASS

History: The A. H. Heisey Glass Co. began producing glasswares in April, 1896, in Newark, Ohio. Heisey was not a newcomer to the field, having been associated with the craft since his youth.

Many blown and molded patterns were produced in crystal, colored, milk (opalescent), and Ivorina Verde (custard) glass. Decorative techniques of cutting, etching, and silver deposit were employed. Glass figurines were introduced in 1933 and continued until 1957 when the factory ceased production.

All Heisey glass is notable for its clarity. Popular patterns were widely sold through stores and today's collectors delight in finding Heisey glass advertisements in women's magazines of the era. Most Heisey glassware is marked with the familiar "H" within a diamond; however not every piece was marked. Some pieces were simply marked with paper labels.

Heisey colors include rainbow hues of alexandrite, amber, black, blue, cobalt blue, dawn, emerald green, flamingo (pink), helitrope, marigold (deep amber–yellow), moongleam (green), red, sahara (yellow), tangerine, vaseline, and zircon.

References: Neila Bredehoft, *The Collector's Encyclopedia of Heisey Glass, 1925–1938,* Collector Books, 1986, 1991 value update; Mary Louise Burns, *Heisey's Glassware of Distinction,* 2nd edition, published by author, 1983; Lyle Conder, *Collector's Guide To Heisey's Glassware for Your Table,* L–W Books, 1984; Tom Felt and Bob O'Grady, *Heisey Candlesticks, Candelabra, and Lamps,* Heisey Collectors of America, Inc, 1984; Frank L. Hahn and Paul Kikeli, *Collector's Guide to Heisey and Heisey by Imperial Glass Animals,* Golden Era Publications, 1991; Sandra Stoudt, *Heisey On Parade,* Wallace–Homestead, 1985.

Collectors' Club: Heisey Collectors of America, 169 W. Church St., Newark, OH, 43055.

Museum: National Heisey Glass Museum, Newark, OH.

Reproduction Alert: Some Heisey molds were sold to Imperial Glass of Bellaire, Ohio, and certain items were reissued. These pieces may be mistaken for the original Heisey. Some of the reproductions were produced in colors which were never made by Heisey and have become collectible in their own right.

Examples include: the Colt family in Crystal, Carmel Slag, Ultra Blue, and Horizon Blue; the mallard with wings up in Carmel Slag; Whirlpool (Provincial) in crystal and colors; and, Waverly, 7" oval footed compote in Carmel Slag.

Animal	
Cygnet	**125.00**
Giraffe, head back	**150.00**
Goose, wings half up	**90.00**
Mallard	**150.00**

Salt, open, clear, individual, "H" in diamond mark, $25.00.

Pony, standing	**65.00**
Ringneck Pheasant	**110.00**
Rooster, fighting stance	**110.00**
Scottie Dog	**90.00**
Sparrow	**75.00**
Tropical Fish, frosted	**850.00**
Bookends, pr	
Fish	**150.00**
Horse Heads, frosted	**120.00**
Box, cov, horse head, 4" l	**110.00**
Candlesticks, pr	
Petticoat Dolphin, 6" h, Flamingo pink	**300.00**
Sandwich Dolphin, 10" h, cobalt blue	**2,250.00**
Candy Dish, cov, seahorse, tall, ftd, handles	**150.00**
Cocktail Shaker, rooster stopper	**90.00**
Flower Frog, Kingfisher, Flamingo pink	**200.00**
Stemware, cocktail, figural stems	
Bantam Rooster	**40.00**
Goose	**200.00**
Seahorse	**140.00**

PATTERNS

Acorn
Plate, 9" d, Hawthorne etching, clear	**12.50**
Sherbet, Flamingo pink	**16.00**

Banded Flute
Claret, clear	**24.00**
Punch Set, punch bowl, 14" d, high base, five cups, crystal	**275.00**

Chintz, 1931–38
Celery Tray, 10" l, clear	**18.00**
Champagne, clear	**12.00**
Claret, clear	**18.00**
Cocktail, Sahara	**35.00**
Creamer, Sahara	**40.00**
Grapefruit, clear	**20.00**
Finger Bowl, Sahara	**14.00**
Mint Dish, Sahara	**30.00**
Nasturtium Bowl, 7½" d, clear	**18.00**
Pickle and Olive Bowl, 13" d, two sections, clear	**17.50**
Pitcher, three pint, dolphin foot, Sahara	**150.00**
Plate, 8" sq, luncheon, clear	**10.00**
Platter, 14" l, oval, clear	**25.00**
Preserve Bowl, handle, clear	**15.00**
Sandwich Tray, center handle, 12" sq, clear	**35.00**
Sugar, Sahara	**40.00**
Tumbler, 10 oz, Sahara	**24.00**
Vase, 9" h, dolphin foot, clear	**65.00**

Colonial
Candy Dish, cov	**55.00**
Champagne, clear	**14.00**
Claret	**14.00**
Cordial	**12.00**

Coaster 10.00
Cruet, Flamingo pink, octagonal stop-
per 600.00
Custard, Colonial 5.00
Goblet 14.00
Jug, one pint 155.00
Plate, 4½" d 8.00
Punch Bowl, matching base, 13" d,
clear 155.00
Sherry, Colonial, 2 oz 10.00

Powder Box, cov, Crystolite, 5" d, $50.00.

Crystolite
Ashtray, zircon 60.00
Basket, 6" h, clear 165.00
Bowl
11½" d, clear 30.00
12" d, clear 30.00
Cake Plate 325.00
Candle Block, sq 10.00
Candlesticks, pr, three branches,
clear 48.00
Candy Dish, cov, 7" d, brass and glass 50.00
Cigarette Lighter 12.00
Coaster, 3½" d
Clear 6.00
Sahara 32.50
Zircon 42.50
Creamer, individual 12.00
Cruet, orig stopper 47.00
Goblet, Arcadia cutting 20.00
Hurricane Block, sq 25.00
Ladle 25.00
Mustard Jar, cov, amber, orig spoon 125.00
Plate, 7" d 7.00
Relish
Four sections, four leaf clover
shape 35.00
Five sections, round, 10" d 40.00
Salt and Pepper Shakers, pr 25.00
Sugar, individual 12.00
Tumbler, 10 oz 15.00
Urn, 7" h 15.00
Empress
Ashtray
Alexandrite 140.00
Sahara 85.00

Bowl
6" d, dolphin foot, Moongleam
green 40.00
7½" d, dolphin foot, Sahara 50.00
9" d, rolled edge, Sahara 35.00
11" d, dolphin foot, Sahara 70.00
Candlesticks, pr, 6" h, dolphin foot,
pink 170.00
Candy Dish, cov, silver overlay, ftd . 60.00
Celery, 13" l, Sahara 22.00
Cheese Dish, etched, pink, 6" d 15.00
Compote, 6" h, ftd, Sahara 50.00
Cream Soup, Sahara 25.00
Cream Soup Set, matching sq under-
plate, Alexandrite 180.00
Creamer, dolphin foot, Sahara 36.00
Creamer and Sugar Set, Moongleam
green, matching tray 195.00
Cruet, Moongleam green foot and
stopper 250.00
Cup and Saucer, sq
Alexandrite 110.00
Moongleam green 40.00
Sahara 42.00
Demitasse Cup, pink 28.00
Grapefruit, 6" sq, Sahara 14.00
Jelly Compote, Sahara, 6" h 30.00
Lemon Dish, dolphin handles 75.00
Mint Dish, etched, pink, 6" d 15.00
Nut Cup, clear 8.00
Oyster Cocktail 22.00
Plate
4½" d, Sahara 12.00
6" w, sq, Sahara 18.00
7½" d, Alexandrite 40.00
8" d
Alexandrite, round 75.00
Sahara, square 25.00
Preserves Bowl, Sahara, two handles,
5" d 30.00
Relish, three sections, center handle,
Sahara 45.00
Saucer, Sahara 12.00
Salt and Pepper Shakers, pr, Sahara . 70.00
Sugar, dolphin foot, three handles,
Sahara 22.50
Tray, center handle, 12" sq, Sahara . 55.00
Vegetable, 10" d, oval, Sahara 42.50
Fern
Bon Bon, 6" d, handle, zircon 60.00
Candlesticks, pr, clear, two branches,
bobeches and prisms 75.00
Greek Key
Almond Dish, individual 35.00
Banana Split Dish, 9" l, ftd 20.00
Butter Dish, cov 160.00
Candy Dish, cov, ftd 55.00
Celery Tray, 12" l 40.00
Compote, jelly, handled 21.00
Creamer and Sugar, hotel size, oval 50.00
Egg Cup 45.00
Finger Bowl 15.00

Horseradish, cov 60.00
Ice Tub, cov 55.00
Jug, three pints 175.00
Nappy 8.50
Orange Bowl, 14" d, flared rim 60.00
Pitcher, jug, three pint 200.00
Plate
   4½" d 10.00
   6" d 12.00
   7" d 14.00
   8" d 15.00
   9" d 18.50
Punch Cup
   Clear 15.00
   Flamingo pink 45.00
Sherbet, 4½ oz, ftd, flared rim 12.00
Spooner 60.00
Straw Jar, open 60.00
Tankard, quart 60.00
Tray, 13" l, oblong 55.00
Tumbler, 12 oz, flared rim 28.00
Water Bottle 200.00

Heisey Minuet
Champagne, saucer 22.00
Goblet 35.00
Iced Tea Tumbler 42.50
Plate, 8" d 20.00
Wine 68.50

Heisey Rose
Butter Dish, cov, etched 175.00
Candlesticks, pr, three branches,
   #142 .... 175.00
Cheese and Cracker Set, 12" d 150.00
Compote, 6" h 45.00
Mayonnaise, liner, Rose 85.00
Sauce Boat, two pcs, Rose 50.00
Tray, 14" d, dolphin center handle .. 175.00

Ipswich
Candle Vases, clear candle insert, co-
   balt blue vase, pr 425.00
Centerpiece Vase, 7½" h, clear, ftd . 90.00
Champagne, clear 10.00
Cocktail Shaker, clear 275.00
Creamer, clear 17.50
Finger Bowl, underplate, Moongleam
   green 40.00
Mantel Lusters, pr, cobalt blue,
   prisms, orig inserts 990.00
Plate
   7" sq, Flamingo pink 24.00
   8" sq, Sahara 28.00
Sherbet, Sahara 30.00
Sugar, Flamingo pink 28.00
Tumbler, 10 oz, cupped rim, Moon-
   gleam green 32.00

Jamestown
Champagne, clear, Narcissus etching,
   6 oz 24.00
Cocktail, Barcelona etching, clear, 3
   oz 25.00
Cordial, Rosalie etching 75.00
Sherbet, Barcelona etching, clear ... 15.00

King Arthur
Celery Tray, diamond optic, hand
   dec, 11" l 24.00
Server, center handle, diamond optic,
   hand dec 40.00
Water Set, diamond optic, hand dec, ftd
   pitcher, six matching goblets 225.00

Lariat
Ashtray
   3½" d, round 12.00
   4" d 12.00
Bon Bon, hand painted dec, 7½" d . 95.00
Bowl
   8½" d 35.00
   9" d, 4" h, flared 40.00
   11" d, floral etching 45.00
Candy Basket, Moonglo cutting 45.00
Celery Tray, 10" l 25.00
Centerpiece Bowl, crimped, 11" d .. 30.00
Champagne 15.00
Coaster 5.00
Cocktail, Moonglo cutting 18.00
Creamer and Sugar 20.00
Cruet, loop stopper and handle, orig
   label, 4 oz 65.00
Deviled Egg Plate, 13" d 125.00
Ice Tub 50.00
Iced Tea Tumbler, 12 oz 15.00
Juice Tumbler, ftd, 5 oz 7.50
Mayonnaise, orig liner 40.00
Plate
   7" d 8.00
   8" d 9.00
   14" d 22.00
Relish, three sections 45.00
Salt and Pepper Shakers, pr 150.00
Sherbet, Moonglo cutting 18.00
Wine 10.00

Narrow Flute
Goblet, clear 25.00
Jug, three pint 70.00
Mustard, cov 35.00

Octagon
Basket, 5" h, Hawthorne etching ... 115.00
Bon Bon, sides up, crystal 8.00
Celery Dish, Moongleam green 35.00
Creamer and Sugar, Moongleam
   green 70.00
Cup and Saucer, after dinner, Flam-
   ingo pink 18.00
Hors D'oeuvre Plate, 13" d, Flamingo
   pink 24.00
Ice Tub, Hawthorne etching 65.00
Muffin Plate, 10" d, Flamingo pink . 20.00
Nut Dish, individual, Flamingo pink . 12.00
Plate, 8" d, luncheon, Moongleam
   green 15.00
Salad Bowl, 12½" d, Sahara 24.00
Soup Plate, 9" d, Sahara 18.50
Vegetable Bowl, 9" d, Flamingo pink 18.00
Old Dominion, 1930–39
Bar Tumbler, Moongleam green 28.00

Bouillon Cup, two handles, ftd, Flamingo pink 18.00
Cigarette Holder, clear 15.00
Creamer and Sugar, cov, etched, Sahara 65.00
Cup and Saucer, Flamingo pink 35.00
Grapefruit, 6" d, Moongleam green . 37.50
Nappy, 8" d, Sahara 40.00
Plate
  6" d, round, Sahara 7.50
  7" w, square, Flamingo pink 15.00
  9" d, round, clear 15.00
  10½" w, square, Moongleam green 65.00
Oyster Cocktail, clear 10.00
Sandwich Plate, center handle, 12" d, Flamingo pink 50.00
Tumbler, 8 oz, clear 10.00
Wine, Sahara, set of 7 .... 150.00

Old Sandwich
Beer Mug, Sahara 130.00
Bowl, 11" d, oval, ftd, Moongleam green 120.00
Catsup Bottle, clear 30.00
Creamer and Sugar, oval, Flamingo pink 45.00
Decanter, Moongleam green 175.00
Goblet, 10 oz 18.00
Iced Tea Tumbler, ftd, 12 oz, clear . 12.00
Parfait, clear 12.00
Plate, 7" w, sq, Flamingo pink 14.00
Popcorn Bowl, cupped, Moongleam green 70.00
Sherbet, Moongleam green 15.00
Sundae Dish, Sahara 18.00

Orchid, 1940–57
Ashtray, 3" sq 28.00
Bowl, 12" d 60.00
Butter Dish, cov 180.00
Cake Plate, 13½" d, ftd 239.00
Candlesticks, pr, three branches 145.00
Celery Tray, 11" l 45.00
Champagne 30.00
Cheese and Cracker Set, 12" d 125.00
Cocktail, 4 oz 35.00
Condiment Bottle, orig stopper 250.00
Cordial 110.00
Creamer, individual size 27.50
Creamer and Sugar 50.00
Cup and Saucer 50.00
Goblet 38.00
Iced Tea Tumbler 45.00
Juice Tumbler, ftd 40.00
Mayonnaise, liner, orig spoon, ftd .. 150.00
Pickle Dish 35.00
Pitcher, 64 oz, ice lid 500.00
Relish, 7" d, three sections 40.00
Sherbet 19.00
Sugar 26.00
Torte Plate, 14" d, rolled edge 48.00
Tumbler 50.00
Wine 48.00

Plantation
Cake Plate, ftd, 12½" d 75.00
Candle Blocks, pr, pineapple shape . 75.00
Compote 25.00
Creamer and Sugar 30.00
Cruet 125.00
Fruit Bowl, 9" d 145.00
Gardenia Bowl, 13" d 30.00
Honey, 6½" d, ftd, cupped 25.00
Marmalade Jar, pineapple shape, cov, sgd spoon 95.00
Mayonnaise, liner, matching underplate, etched 110.00
Plate, 8½" d 24.00
Relish, three sections, 11" l 35.00
Salt and Pepper Shakers, pr, orig tops, clear 48.00
Sherbet 18.00
Sugar Shaker, clear 115.00
Syrup Pitcher, orig top, clear 70.00
Tumbler, 10 oz 27.50
Vase, 5" h, ftd 25.00
Wine 25.00

Pleat and Panel
Bread Plate, 7" d, clear 5.00
Champagne, Moongleam green 14.00
Cheese and Cracker Set, 10½" d, matching tray, Flamingo pink 32.00
Compote, cov, 7" h, Flamingo pink, gold trim 65.00
Creamer and Sugar, hotel size, clear 18.00
Cruet, Moongleam green 95.00
Iced Tea Tumbler, Flamingo pink ... 15.00
Lemon Dish, cov, 5" l, Flamingo pink, sgd 45.00
Marmalade Jar, ftd, clear 20.00
Sandwich Plate, 14" d, Moongleam green 30.00
Spice Tray, 10" d, Flamingo pink ... 28.00

Prince of Wales
Creamer and Sugar, ruby stained ... 115.00
Punch Bowl Set, punch bowl, base, twelve cups, clear 245.00
Tankard, clear, gold trim, half gallon 100.00
Toothpick Holder, clear, gold trim .. 135.00

Provincial
Butter Dish, cov 80.00
Cruet 45.00
Mustard 45.00
Nut Bowl, 5" d 14.00
Oil Bottle, 4 oz 10.00
Oyster Cocktail 15.00
Plate, 18" d 35.00
Snack Plate, 7" d, two handles 12.00
Violet Vase, 3½" h, Moongleam green 60.00

Queen Anne
Bowl, 9" d, shallow, Orchid etching 70.00
Creamer and Sugar, cov, dolphin foot, Minuet etching, clear 75.00
Nappy, 9" d, crimped, clear 60.00

Ridgeleigh
Ashtray, club shape 10.00

Candlesticks, pr, 2" h, sq 42.00
Candle Vase, Sahara 65.00
Celery Dish, 12" l 25.00
Claret, 4 oz 25.00
Coaster, 3½" d, Sahara 12.00
Creamer and Sugar, oval 40.00
Cruet 45.00
Decanter, pint 60.00
Goblet, luncheon 14.50
Old Fashioned Tumbler, 8 oz 15.00
Pitcher, half gallon, ice lip 60.00
Plate
  7" w, square 7.50
  8" d, round 7.00
Salt and Pepper Shakers, pr 22.00
Sherbet 10.00
Torte Plate, 13½" d, ftd 24.00
Vase, 8" h, Sahara 125.00
Wine 20.00

Thumbprint and Panel
Candlesticks, pr, two branches
  Cobalt Blue 400.00
  Yellow 100.00
Console Bowl, ftd, yellow 60.00

Twist
Baker, Moongleam green 24.00
Bowl, 9" d, Flamingo pink 30.00
Candleholders, pr, 2" h, Flamingo
  pink 20.00
Celery Dish, Sahara 35.00
Console Bowl, 12½" d, Moongleam
  green, gold bird border 60.00
Creamer, zigzag handles, ftd, Sahara 50.00
Cup, zigzag handles, Flamingo pink 17.50
Ice Tub, silver handles, Moongleam
  green 70.00
Nasturtium Bowl, 8" l, oval, Moon-
  gleam green 35.00
Nut Dish, individual, Moongleam
  green 25.00
Plate, 9" d, marigold 20.00
Platter, 12" l, Flamingo pink 30.00
Relish, two sections, cut dec, Sahara 65.00
Saucer, Flamingo pink 20.00
Sugar, ftd, clear 15.00

Sherbet, Victorian, clear, ftd, sgd, $18.00.

Tumbler, 8 oz, Sahara 32.00
Victorian
Champagne, clear 35.00
Claret, clear, two ball stem, 4 oz ... 18.00
Cologne Bottle, orig stopper 50.00
Creamer and Sugar, clear 24.00
Juice Tumbler, clear, 5 oz 7.50
Punch Bowl Set, 15" d bowl, twelve
  cups 300.00
Wine 20.00
Wabash
Oyster Cocktail, Frontenac etching,
  clear 12.00
Wine 18.00
Wampum
Ashtray, clear 20.00
Cigarette Set, cigarette box and four
  ashtrays, clear 95.00
Plate, 12" d, clear 35.00
Warwick
Candlesticks, pr, two branch
  Crystal 32.50
  Sahara 48.00
Vase, 9" h, cornucopia shape, cobalt
  blue 175.00
Waverly
Bowl
  10" d, crimped, Rose etching 75.00
  12" d, flared 55.00
  13" d
    Clear, flat, orig label 36.00
    Tea Rose 70.00
Box, cov, 5" l 30.00
Butter Dish, cov, Rose etching 175.00
Candy Box, cov, 6" l, bow tie knob . 25.00
Compote, jelly, 6½" d, clear 40.00
Creamer and Sugar, Rose etching ... 80.00
Cup and Saucer 9.50
Honey Dish, 6½" d, ftd 7.50
Mayonnaise, 5½", 3 ftd, Rose etching 52.00
Plate
  7" d 5.00
  8" d, Narcissus etching, clear 18.00
  11" d 15.00
Salt and Pepper Shakers, pr 28.00
Sherbet 15.00
Vegetable Bowl, 9" d 32.00
Whirlpool
Candlesticks, pr, clear, two branches 115.00
Mustard, cov 40.00
Nut Dish, individual, clear 10.00
Plate, 12½" d 25.00
Punch Bowl Set, punch bowl, ten
  cups 185.00
Yeoman
Banana Split Dish, Moongleam green,
  ftd 35.00
Bon Bon, 6½" d, Flamingo pink 30.00
Celery, 13" d, green 40.00
Cream Soup, Moongleam green 18.00
Creamer and Sugar, Hawthorne etch-
  ing 55.00

Cruet, orig stopper	
Flamingo pink	45.00
Moongleam green, 4 oz	85.00
Sahara, 2 oz	65.00
Cup and Saucer, Flamingo pink	20.00
Egg Cup, Flamingo pink	24.00
Gravy, underplate, Moongleam green	30.00
Parfait, clear	10.00
Plate	
6″ d, Flamingo pink	15.00
8″ d, clear	10.00
10½″ d, clear	12.50
Relish, three sections, Moongleam green, handle	55.00
Salt, open, Flamingo pink	8.50
Sherbet, Flamingo pink	10.00
Soda Tumbler, 4½ oz, Flamingo pink	6.50
Sugar Shaker, Moongleam green ...	62.00
Tray, 11″ d, three sections, clear ...	18.00
Tumbler, 10 oz, straight sides, Flamingo pink	17.50
Whiskey, 2½ oz, Sahara	9.50

HOBBS, BROCKUNIER

History: The Hobbs Glass Company was located in Wheeling, West Virginia, from 1845 until 1891. Their principal production was brilliant cut glass. John L. Hobbs and James B. Barnes founded the firm after leaving the New England Glass Company. Their sons, John H. Hobbs, and James F. Barnes, soon joined the business. In 1863, the name was changed to Hobbs, Brockunier & Co. to reflect changes in management by John L. Hobbs, John H. Hobb, and Charles Brockunier. Brockunier was formerly a superintendent at the New England Glass Company. William Leighton, Sr., was in charge of production.

William Leighton devised a formula for soda lime glass in 1864. Leighton's formula was responsible for production of a cheaper, but also clear type of glassware and revolutionized the glass industry.

By the 1880s, the firm was producing fine art glass, including amberina, spangled, and several opalescent patterns. It is generally these colored wares that are considered when the name Hobbs, Brockunier is mentioned.

Barber Bottle, Francesware Hobnail pattern, frosted ground, amber stain ...	125.00
Basket, Leaf and Flower pattern, clear with ruby stain, scalloped, pressed-rope handle	40.00
Berry Bowl	
Francesware Swirl pattern, clear, master	85.00
Hexagon Block pattern	
7″ d, clear, deep, pointed scalloped rim	20.00

8″ d, clear with amber stain, shallow, scalloped rim	35.00
9″ d, clear with ruby stain, deep, pointed scalloped rim	40.00
Berry Set, Leaf and Flower pattern, clear and frosted, amber stain flowers, 8″ d deep master bowl, twelve sauces ...	325.00
Bowl	
Francesware Hobnail pattern, clear, 7″ l, oval	35.00
Francesware Hobnail pattern, clear and frosted ground, 7½″ d, sq ...	75.00
Satin, plush velvety finish, soft pink ground, applied yellow edge, thirty crimps, 8″ d, 4″ h	425.00
Bride's Basket, Francesware Hobnail pattern, clear and frosted ground, orig silver plated holder	130.00
Butter Dish, cov	
Francesware Hobnail pattern, frosted ground, amber stain rim	
Flanged rim	75.00
Plain rim	100.00
Hexagon Block pattern, clear with ruby stain, flanged base	125.00
Hobbs' Block pattern, clear	35.00
Butter Pat, Daisy and Button pattern, amberina, deep fuchsia to honey amber, set of six	650.00
Castor Set, Francesware Swirl pattern, salt and pepper shakers, oil and vinegar cruets, orig silver plated holder	600.00
Celery Tray	
Francesware Swirl pattern, clear	65.00
Hobbs' Block pattern, clear, boat shape	25.00
Celery Vase	
Francesware Hobnail pattern, clear and frosted ground	55.00
Hexagon Block pattern, clear, ftd ...	25.00
Compote, Hexagon Block pattern, clear with amber stain, high standard,	

Cruet, Herringbone, opalescent white stripes on cranberry ground, clear faceted stopper, $350.00.

pointed scalloped rim, deep bowl, 7"
d 48.00
Creamer, applied handle
 Francesware Hobnail pattern, clear
  and frosted ground 42.00
 Francesware Swirl pattern, clear 50.00
 Hexagon Block pattern, clear, ftd . . . 25.00
 Hobbs' Block pattern, clear 30.00
 Hobnail pattern, clear and frosted . . 35.00
 Leaf and Flower pattern, clear with
  amber stain 40.00
Cruet
 Francesware Hobnail pattern, frosted
  ground, amber stain, orig faceted
  stopper 250.00
 Francesware Swirl pattern, clear, orig
  faceted stopper 200.00
 Inverted Thumbprint pattern, Rubena
  Verde, cranberry shading to vase-
  line, petticoat shape, orig cut vase-
  line stopper, 6" h, 4" w 400.00
 Spangle, crystal ground with hint of
  blue at base, silver mica flakes, profuse random white mottling, clear
  faceted stopper 235.00
Custard Cup, Hexagon Block pattern,
 clear, applied handle, ftd 15.00
Finger Bowl
 Francesware Hobnail pattern, frosted
  ground, amber stain rim, 4" d 50.00
 Hexagon Block pattern, clear, ruby
  stain, pointed scalloped rim 40.00
 Leaf and Flower pattern, clear, ruby
  stain, scalloped rim 25.00
Goblet
 Hexagon Block pattern, clear with
  amber stain 40.00
 Hobbs' Block pattern, clear with am-
  ber stain 95.00
Lamp Shade, Francesware Swirl pattern,
 clear, bulbous 90.00
Lemonade Set, Francesware Hobnail
 pattern, frosted ground, amber stain
 rim 350.00
Miniature Lamp, Francesware Swirl pat-
 tern, clear, orig shade, burner, and
 chimney 400.00
Mustard, cov, Francesware Swirl pat-
 tern, clear 80.00
Pickle Jar, cov, Hexagon Block pattern,
 clear with ruby stain, ftd, smooth rim 85.00
Pitcher
 Francesware Hobnail pattern, frosted
  ground, amber stain rim, 8½" h . . 150.00
 Francesware Swirl pattern, clear,
  ovoid, applied handle, half gallon 150.00
 Hexagon Block pattern, clear, applied
  handle 75.00
 Hobnail pattern, frosted rubena, 7¼"
  h, applied handle 295.00
 Spangle, light gold ground, diamond
  quilted body, gold mica flecks,

Pitcher, tankard, Poinsettia, blue ground,
13⅜" h, $225.00.

 white lining, applied amber shell
  reeded handle, 5" h, 5" w, 3" sq top 275.00
Salt and Pepper Shakers, pr
 Francesware Hobnail pattern, clear
  and frosted ground, orig tops 90.00
 Francesware Swirl pattern, clear 90.00
 Hexagon Block pattern, clear, ftd . . . 35.00
Sauce
 Francesware Hobnail pattern, frosted
  ground, amber stain, ruffled rim . . 30.00
 Francesware Swirl pattern, clear,
  oval, deep 24.00
 Hexagon Block pattern, clear with
  amber stain, pointed scalloped rim 20.00
 Hobbs' Block pattern, clear, scal-
  loped rim 10.00
Spooner
 Francesware Hobnail pattern, frosted
  ground, amber stain 50.00
 Francesware Swirl pattern, clear 45.00
 Hexagon Block pattern, clear 20.00
 Hobbs' Block pattern, clear with am-
  ber stain 30.00
 Leaf and Flower pattern, clear, scal-
  loped 25.00
Sugar, cov
 Francesware Hobnail pattern, frosted
  ground, amber stain 85.00
 Francesware Swirl pattern, clear, fac-
  eted knob finial 85.00
 Hexagon Block pattern, clear with
  amber stain, ftd 90.00
 Hobbs' Block pattern, frosted with
  amber stain 55.00
 Leaf and Flower pattern, clear with
  ruby stain 135.00
Sugar Shaker
 Inverted Thumbprint pattern, frosted,
  amber top 110.00
 Venetian Diamond pattern, cranberry 110.00
Syrup, cranberry ground, opalescent

hobnails, orig pewter top marked
"Pat. Mar 20 83" **385.00**
Toothpick Holder
Francesware Hobnail pattern, frosted
  ground, amber stain rim, hobs with
  silky opalescence, 2½" h **50.00**
Francesware Swirl pattern, clear, ruf-
  fled rim **140.00**
Hobnail pattern, blue **35.00**
Tumbler
Francesware Swirl pattern, clear **40.00**
Hexagon Block pattern, clear with
  ruby stain **35.00**
Hobbs' Block pattern, clear **17.50**
Vase
Inverted Thumbprint pattern, honey
  amber, reeded swirled ruffled top,
  two handles, 12" h **125.00**
Morgan, Wheeling peachblow, shiny
  finish, deep fuchsia shading to
  honey amber, orig glass griffin
  holder, two griffins with repairs . .**1,650.00**
Waste Bowl, Francesware Hobnail pat-
  tern, frosted ground, amber stain rim,
  4" d **50.00**
Water Bottle, Hobbs' Block pattern,
  clear **45.00**
Water Tray, Francesware Hobnail pattern, frosted ground, amber stain, leaf
  shape, 12" l **125.00**

lectibility of this pattern, it is listed in a separate category. It is one of those patterns known by the pattern name first, and the manufacturer second. Imperial produced many other patterns, including Cape Cod and Crystolite, but these never achieved the success of the Candlewick line.

Imperial has acquired the molds and equipment of several other glass companies—Central, Cambridge and Heisey. Many of the "retired" molds of these companies are once again in use. The resulting reissues are marked to distinguish them from the originals.

References: Margaret and Douglas Archer, *Imperial Glass*, Collector Books, 1978, value update 1990; Myrna and Bob Garrison, *Imperial Cape Cod Tradition To Treasure*, printed by author, 1982; Frank L. Hahn and Paul Kikeli, *Collector's Guide to Heisey and Heisey by Imperial Glass Animals*, Golden Era Publications, 1991; National Imperial Glass Collector's Society, *Imperial Glass 1966 Catalog*, reprint, 1991 price guide, Antique Publications.

Collectors' Club: National Imperial Glass Collectors Society, P.O. Box 534, Bellaire, OH 43906.

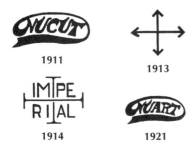

1911

1913

1914

1921

Ivy Ball, Hobnail pattern, blue opalescent, 6⅛" h, 1940s, $35.00.

IMPERIAL GLASS

History: Imperial Glass Co., Bellaire, Ohio, was organized in 1901. Its primary product was pattern (pressed) glass. Soon other lines were added including carnival glass, NUART, NUCUT, and NEAR CUT. In 1916 the company introduced "Free–Hand," a lustered art glass line, and "Imperial Jewels," an iridescent stretch glass that carried the Imperial cross trademark. In the 1930s the company was reorganized into the Imperial Glass Corporation and continues to produce a great variety of wares.

Probably the most well-known Imperial Glass pattern is Candlewick. Because of the high col-

ENGRAVED OR HAND CUT

Bowl
6½" d, clear, flower and leaf dec,
  molded star base **20.00**
9" d, berry, Design No. 114, clear,
  five hand cut daisy like flowers .. **24.00**
9½" d, clear, three sprays with flowers, molded star base **30.00**
Candlesticks, pr, Amelia, 7" h, clear .. **35.00**
Celery Vase, clear, three side stars, cut
  star base **25.00**
Nut Dish, Design No. 112, 5½" d, clear **20.00**

Pitcher, 6" h, clear, daisies, molded star
base **40.00**
Plate, Design No. 12, clear, 5½" d ... **15.00**
Sherbet, Design No. 300, clear, engraved stars, ftd **12.00**
Syrup, Design No. 112, clear, silver
plated top **35.00**
Table Set, cov butter, creamer, cov
sugar, and spooner, Design No. 4, cut
star pattern, clear **200.00**
Tankard, Design No. 110, clear, flow-
ers, foliage, and butterfly cutting ... **50.00**
Tumbler, clear, buzz star dec **18.00**

JEWELS

Bowl
6¼" d, pearl green luster, purple,
marked **75.00**
9" d, 4" h, irid amber **75.00**
Candlesticks, pr, blue luster **50.00**
Candy Dish, cov, pink **40.00**
Compote, 7½" d, irid teal blue **50.00**
Creamer
Amethyst, pearl, and green luster ... **65.00**
Yellow luster **40.00**
Plate
8" d, irid pale green **45.00**
9" d, white luster **65.00**
Rose Bowl, amethyst, green irid **75.00**
Vase
6" h, irid pearl green and purple luster **135.00**
8" h, irid silver, mulberry ground,
flared rim **120.00**

LUSTERED (FREE HAND)

Candlesticks, pr, 10¾" h, cobalt, white
vine and leaf dec **325.00**
Center Bowl, 14¾" d, 13½" h, shallow,
flared, irid gold, stretched irid, sgd
"Lustre Art 114," verdigris metal standard with three caryatids of nude men **700.00**
Hat, 9" w, ruffled rim, cobalt blue
ground, embedded irid white vines
and leaves **115.00**
Lamp, hall, elaborate scrolled gilt metal
platform and chain design, center
gold, white, and green irid shade, sgd
"Lustre Art" on top rim **500.00**
Lamp Shade, 5" l, Art Nouveau, irid
ivory, gold, and green feather pattern,
colored threading, sgd **175.00**
Pitcher, 10" h, pale yellow luster, white
pulled loops, applied clear handle .. **225.00**
Rose Bowl, 6" h, irid orange, white floral cutting **65.00**
Vase
5" h, flared, blue and gold
ground, textured irid finish **115.00**

6" h
Opal ground, pulled blue and
green leaf pad and random vine
design, orange lining, flared rim,
partial paper label **325.00**
Oyster white ground, embedded
green hearts and vines, deep orange luster lining **250.00**
White opal ground, ovoid, tapering
to short neck, flattened flared
rim, pulled blue and green leaf
pads on vine, orange irid int.,
partial paper label **360.00**
6¾" h, flared cylindrical, scalloped
rim, dark blue and orange ground,
white heart and vine dec **225.00**
7" h, all over swirls, blue and white
ground, white int. **150.00**
8" h, irid red ground, ruffled trumpet
top, irid brown stretched throat,
verre de soie foot **230.00**
8¼" h, King Tut, deep irid blue
ground, white loopings **315.00**
8½" h, butterscotch ground, orange
luster throat **115.00**
8¾" h, white ground, yellow loops,
orange luster lining **115.00**
9" h, slender hourglass shape, pearl
luster ground, green hearts and
vines **145.00**
9½" h, bright green ground, leaf and
vine dec, orange luster lining **300.00**
10" h
Blue and ruby irid ground, leaves
and veins dec, cobalt blue foot **175.00**
White irid ground, gold luster neck,
light green hearts and vines dec **300.00**
10¾" h, baluster, blue ground, orange
trailing heart and vine dec **335.00**
11" h, irid emerald green ground,
embedded white hearts and vines,
orange luster throat, orig paper label **300.00**
11¼" h, baluster, triangular pull–ups
at mouth, opal opaque white
ground, embedded irid blue trailing
vines, orig paper label **335.00**
11½" h, applied black rim, white and
yellow luster ground, blue and gray
veined large leaves and vines **300.00**

NUART

Ashtray, marked "Nuart" **20.00**
Lamp Shade
Crystal, frosted int., cluster electric
type, flower etching, marked
"Nuart" **25.00**
Marigold **50.00**
Pearl ruby, fan and star etching,
marked "Nuart" **35.00**

Vase, 7" h, bulbous, irid green, marked
"Nuart" **125.00**

NUCUT

Berry Bowl
4½" d, tab handles, marked "Nucut"   **15.00**
7½" d, marked "Nucut" **20.00**
Bowl, 8½" d, Rose Marie, pink, ftd,
marked "Nucut" **40.00**
Celery Tray, 11" l, marked "Nucut" .. **18.00**
Compote, 5½" d, marked "Nucut" ... **22.00**
Creamer, marked "Nucut" **12.00**
Fern Dish, 8" l, brass lining, ftd, marked
"Nucut" **35.00**
Nappy, 6" w, heart shape, marked "Nu-
cut" **20.00**
Orange Bowl, 12" d, Rose Marie,
marked "Nucut" **48.00**
Punch Bowl Set, 13" d punch bowl, six
cups, Rose Marie, marked "Nucut" . **175.00**
Salad Bowl, 10¾" d, marked "Nucut" **32.00**
Sauce, 4½" d, handles, marked "Nu-
cut" **15.00**
Tumbler, flared rim, molded star,
marked "Nucut" **15.00**

PRESSED

Animal
Bulldog, clear **30.00**
Scottie, clear **45.00**
Swan, amethyst, 4¾" h **18.00**
Terrier, caramel slag **125.00**
Tiger, jade green **15.00**
Animal Dish, cov Chicken on nest, ame-
thyst slag **100.00**
Rabbit on nest, white milk glass, 4½"
h **45.00**
Rooster, lacy basket base, amethyst
slag **125.00**
Ashtray, Cathay, jade **65.00**
Basket, 10½" h **30.00**
Birthday Cake Plate, Cape Cod **50.00**
Bitters Bottle, Cape Cod, 6 oz **38.00**
Bon Bon, D'Angelo, green, ring handle,
5¼" d **18.00**
Bookends, pr, Cathay, jade **100.00**
Bowl
8" d, Empress, blue **22.00**
9" d, Roses, milk glass **12.50**
10" d, Cape Cod, flared, ftd **80.00**
11" d, Cape Cod, two part, oval ... **45.00**
13" d, Cape Cod **35.00**
Butter Dish, cov
Cape Cod, round handle **27.00**
Fancy Colonial, rose **50.00**
Cake Plate, Molly, opalescent green, 12"
d **48.00**
Cake Salver, Cape Cod, 10" d **40.00**
Candlesticks, pr, dolphin, blue **28.00**
Celery, Cape Cod, 10½" l, oval **45.00**

Cheese Dish, cov, Monticello **35.00**
Cocktail, Cape Cod **5.00**
Cologne Bottle, Hobnail, milk glass,
blue, ruffled, stopper, pr **24.00**
Compote, cov
Cape Cod, tall **60.00**
Red slag, satin, herringbone design . **15.00**
Condiment Set, Cape Cod, five pc set . **100.00**
Cordial
Cape Cod **15.00**
Park Lane
Amber **4.50**
Crystal **3.75**
Riviera, blue **4.00**
Wakefield, amber **12.00**
Creamer and Sugar
Cape Cod, clear **20.00**
Flora, rose **15.00**
Cruet
Cape Cod, 4 oz **15.00**
Fancy Colonial, pink **30.00**
Figurine, Cathay, Junk, sgd **145.00**
Goblet
Cape Cod, red **20.00**
Park Lane, amber **5.00**
Tradition, 5½" h, crystal **10.00**
Hot Sauce, Cape Cod, ceramic tube .. **50.00**
Iced Tea Tumbler, Cape Cod, 5" h, flat
foot **10.00**
Juice Tumbler, Cape Cod **12.00**
Marmalade Jar, cov, Cape Cod **10.00**
Martini Mixer, Big Shot series, red **75.00**
Mayonnaise, underplate, orig spoon,
Monaco, amber **25.00**
Mug, red slag, robin **16.00**
Old Fashioned Tumbler, Cape Cod ... **23.00**
Parfait, Cape Cod **10.00**
Peanut Butter Jar, cov, Cape Cod, han-
dle **65.00**
Pepper Mill, Cape Cod **35.00**
Pitcher, red slag, windmill design, pint **40.00**
Plate, Fancy Colonial, 7½" d, pink ... **9.00**
Platter, Cape Cod, 13½" l, oval **65.00**
Punch Bowl Set, Cape Cod, 15 pcs ... **160.00**
Relish, Cape Cod, 11" l, five sections . **70.00**
Rose Bowl, Lace Edge, amber opal, oval **25.00**
Salt and Pepper Shakers, pr
Cape Cod, ftd **10.00**
Huckabee, aluminum tops **25.00**
Sandwich Tray, black handle **25.00**
Server, multi, Cape Cod **105.00**
Sherbet
Mt Vernon, ruby **5.00**
Park Lane, amber **7.50**
Sugar, cov, Lace Edge, green opal **18.00**
Sweet Pea Vase, 4" h **15.00**
Tea Cup and Saucer, Cape Cod **10.00**
Tom and Jerry Mug **32.00**
Toothpick Holder, ivory, orig paper la-
bel **18.00**
Tumbler, Cape Cod **17.50**
Vase, Cape Cod, 11" h, ftd **55.00**

Vegetable Dish, Cape Cod, 10" l, oval   **80.00**
Wine
  Cape Cod, 3 oz **5.00**
  Park Lane, amber **4.00**

JACK-IN-THE-PULPIT VASES

History: Jack-in-the-Pulpit glass vases, made in the trumpet form, were in vogue during the late 19th and early 20th centuries. The vases were made in a wide variety of patterns, colors, and sizes by many manufacturers.

The form imitates the wildflower, known as Jack-in-the-Pulpit. These vases are generally found with a bulbous base, slender stem, and a flaring throat which develops into a lovely diamond shaped back. Art glass examples provide collectors with lovely shaded and colorful additions to their glassware collections.

Opaline, white, ruby red ruffles, pleated and dimpled, 9¼" h, $165.00.

4" h, squatty, blossom form, white satin ground, emerald green lining, seven applied and frosted feet **65.00**
4½" h, opaque jade green, ruffled, emb ribbed base, enameled small white flowers, gold trim **75.00**
5" h, opaline, ruffled purple top **90.00**
5⅜" h, opalescent, flower petal top, pink and yellow stripes **85.00**
5¾" h, spangle, white ground, pink lining, ruffled rim, clear edging, mica flecks **120.00**
6" h, Steuben, bright gold Aurene, strong irid, sgd "Aurene 2699" **1,300.00**
6" h, 6" w, cased, white ground, shaded maroon lining, ruffled top **110.00**
6½" h, Loetz type, gold luster, pinched body **175.00**
6¾" h, Mt Washington
  Burmese, trumpet **300.00**

Satin, pale violet blue, pink ruffled rim **275.00**
7⅛" h, orange, sponged black dec, marked "Czechoslovakia" **48.00**
7¼" h
  Cased, creamy opaque ground, white and yellow flowers, green leaves, gold trim, deep rose pink lining, amber edge, ormolu leaf feet **125.00**
  Rubina Verde, ruffled **135.00**
  Spatter, green, peach, yellow and white spatter at top, green diamond quilted pattern body **55.00**

Transparent pink and light green, ruffled, pontil mark, $150.00.

7½" h
  Nailsea, frosted chartreuse green ground, white loopings, applied frosted feet **145.00**
  Silver overlay, ruffled, shaded purple   **100.00**
8" h, 7" w scalloped rim, Pairpoint, Burmese, applied base **725.00**
9⅜" h, Stevens and Williams, ruffled, chartreuse and white stripes **135.00**
9¾" h, Burmese, acid finish, crimped edge **450.00**
10" h, cranberry, applied crystal rigaree and feet **200.00**
10" h, 5" w, Mt Washington, deep rose shading to pink satin finish, white lining, tightly crimped top **475.00**
10¼" h, Imperial, stretch, irid purple .   **90.00**
11¾" h, Loetz, flower form, lusterous stretched and swirled irid amethyst .   **300.00**
12" h, Loetz type, green ground, silver–blue irid spots, c1900 ....   **450.00**
12½" h, Mt Washington, trumpet, satin, white, lavender and white flowers, green leaves, ruffled rim **325.00**
13¼" h, New England Glass Co, Inverted Thumbprint pattern, amberina   **300.00**
15¾" h, cased, blue, white lining, ruffled, applied crystal spiral trim, clear foot with scalloped shell trim **210.00**

KITCHEN GLASSWARE

History: The Depression era brought inexpensive kitchen and table products to center stage. Hocking, Hazel Atlas, McKee, U. S. Glass, and Westmoreland were companies which led in the production of these items.

Kitchen glassware complemented Depression Glass. Many items were produced in the same color and style. Because the glass was molded, added decorative elements included ribs, fluting, arches and thumbprint patterns. Kitchen glassware was thick to achieve durability. The result were forms which were difficult to handle at times and often awkward aesthetically. After World War II, aluminum products began to replace kitchen glassware. Will the age of the microwave bring back kitchen glassware-type items?

Kitchen glassware was made in large numbers. Although collectors do tolerate signs of use, they will not accept pieces with heavy damage. Many of the products contain applied decals; these should be in good condition. A collection can be built inexpensively by concentrating on one form such as canister sets, measuring cups, etc.

References: Gene Florence, *Kitchen Glassware of the Depression Years, Fourth Edition*, Collector Books, 1990, value update 1992; Glyndon, Shirley, *The Miracle in Grandmother's Kitchen*, privately printed, 1983.

Allspice Shaker, Jeannette, light jadite, round, black metal lid, horizontal ribs, black label **25.00**
Ashtray, Jeannette, delphite, adv, cowboy, marked "Delphite by Jeannette"   **95.00**
Batter Bowl, Anchor Hocking, clear, vertical ribs **18.00**
Bowl
 6" d
  Custard, McKee, red Dots pattern . .   **18.00**
  Delphite, Jeannette, vertical ribs . .   **85.00**
  Green Transparent, Hocking, rolled rim, vertical ribs, square base . .   **9.00**
  Light Jadite, Jeannette, vertical ribs   **18.00**
 6⅝" d, 7⅝" d, 8⅝" d, and 9⅝" d, cobalt blue, nesting, flared rim, vertical ribs, squared base, set of four **80.00**
 7½" d, light jadite, horizontal ribs . .   **25.00**
 7¾" d, Jeannette, delphite, vertical ribs **80.00**
 7⅜" d, McKee, black **32.00**
 8" d, custard, flanged rim with spout
  Plain **18.00**
  Red Stripe **24.00**
 9" d, light jadite
  Jeannette, vertical ribs **22.00**
  McKee, plain **20.00**
 9½" d, light jadite, horizontal ribs . .   **48.00**

Bucket Reamer, Jeannette, green transparent, Hex Optic pattern, metal frame **45.00**
Bud Vase
 Delphite **25.00**
 Jadite, Jeannette, horizontal ribs **10.00**

Butter Dish, opaque light blue, $30.00.

Butter Dish, cov, one pound
 Amber, Federal, vertical ribs, tab handles **52.00**
 Chalaine, plain, no handles **350.00**
 White
  Hazel Atlas, top emb "Butter Cover" **40.00**
 McKee, tab handles
  Plain **35.00**
  Red Ship design **40.00**
Cake Stand, dark amber, scalloped edge, pedestal base **18.00**
Canister, cov
 Clear, Hazel Atlas, round, paneled .   **30.00**
 Custard, McKee, 20 oz, round **35.00**
 Green Transparent
  Round, Hazel Atlas, paneled **95.00**
  Square, metal threaded lid, smooth sides
   8 oz **15.00**
   20 oz **30.00**
Cereal Canister, cov
 Light Green Opaque, Hocking, ball finial, vertical ribs on paneled sides, black and silver label **40.00**
 White, McKee, round, black script lettering **55.00**
Cocktail Shaker, green transparent, metal lid, etched design **25.00**
Coffee Canister, cov
 Clear, metal threaded lid, round, paneled, emb "Coffee" **30.00**
 Clear, metal threaded lid, round, emb "Coffee," zipper–type design **30.00**
 Dark Jadite, Jeannette
  40 oz, round, metal threaded lid, horizontal ribs, black lettering .   **90.00**
  48 oz, square, glass cov, Floral pattern inside cov, black lettering, 5½" h **55.00**
 Delphite, Jeannette, 40 oz, round, horizontal ribs, black lettering . . .   **485.00**

Coffeepot, Glasbake, clear **20.00**
Cookie Canister, cov, Hocking, green transparent, 64 oz, square, metal threaded lid, vertical ribs, silver and black paper label **45.00**
Cookie Jar, cov
  Green Transparent, L E Smith, finial, barrel shaped, etched, tab handles **95.00**
  Pink, horizontal ribs, handles, etched design **70.00**
Crock, cov, Jeannette, light jadite, 40 oz, round, recessed handle **40.00**
Cruet, stopper
  Dark Green, US Glass, clear stopper **30.00**
  Green Transparent, Hocking **18.00**
Cruet Set, 2 cruets and oval tray, US Glass, green transparent, faceted stoppers **95.00**
Decanter, jadite, pinched, stopper **155.00**
Dispenser, cov, McKee, Skokie green, emb design **112.00**
Drippings Jar, cov
  Light Jadite, Jeannette, round, horizontal ribs, recessed handle, black lettering **50.00**
  White, McKee, round, 8 oz, red Ships pattern **25.00**
Egg Cup, Chalaine **25.00**
Flour Canister, cov, Owens–Illinois, forest green, 40 oz, square, metal threaded lid, diagonal ridged, silver paper label **32.00**
Flour Shaker, Jeannette, dark jadite, 8 oz, round, metal threaded lid, horizontal ribs, black lettering **22.00**
Funnel, clear, canning **10.00**
Ginger Shaker, Jeannette, light jadite, round, black metal lid, horizontal ribs, silver label **20.00**
Gravy, underliner, Cambridge, amber . **45.00**
Ice Bucket, Hocking
  Frosted Green, round, tab handles, horizontal bands, marked "Frigidaire Ice Server" **12.00**
  Red Transparent, fluted sides, metal bail handle **30.00**
Ice Tub, Paden City, green, Party Line, horizontal ribs **22.00**
Mailbox, clear, metal holders, emb "Visible" **85.00**
Match Holder, Jeannette, delphite, round
  Black Lettering, "Matches" **90.00**
  No Lettering **45.00**
Measuring Cup
  1 Cup
    Clear, Armour's Extractor, adv, side spout **30.00**
    Green Transparent, side spout ... **45.00**
    Light Green Opaque **170.00**
    White, Hazel Atlas, green ring at top and bottom, three spouts .. **65.00**

2 Cup, McKee
  Clear, Glasbake **32.00**
  Custard, red stripe **30.00**
Measuring Pitcher, McKee, custard, red trim, 2 cup **22.00**
Measuring Jar, clear, 4 cup, no handle, emb "Family Measuring Jar" **40.00**
Mixer, clear, 1 quart, red handle **7.00**
Mug
  Custard, McKee, Tom and Jerry, black lettering **10.00**
  Red Transparent, New Martinsville, polka dot–type pattern **15.00**

Ribbon, mixing bowl, green, 8⅞" d, 3¾" h, $6.00.

Napkin Holder, Nar–O–Fold, white, marked "Property of trade Nar–O–Fold mark Napkin Company, Chicago, reg. U.S.A." **50.00**
Nutmeg Canister, cov, Jeannette, light jadite, 3" h, square, black lettering . **60.00**
Paprika Shaker, Jeannette, delphite, 8 oz, round, metal threaded lid, horizontal ribs, black lettering **160.00**
Pitcher
  2 Cup
    Delphite
      Jeannette, sunflower bottom ... **75.00**
      McKee **155.00**
      Skokie Green, McKee **18.00**
  4 Cup
    Skokie Green, McKee **40.00**
    White **20.00**
Provision Jar, cov, green transparent, 8 oz, round finial **15.00**
Radium Emanator Filter, McKee, vaseline, two bottles, marked "Radium Emanator Filter Co. Inc. North Haledonn, NJ," 21" h, orig box **350.00**
Reamer
  Chalaine, McKee, emb "Sunkist," large **185.00**
  Dark Delphite, Jeannette, small **85.00**
  Green Transparent, Jeannette, large, side pour, tab handle, 5⅞" d **15.00**

Light Delphite, Jeannette, large 22.00
Light Jadite, McKee, emb "Sunkist,"
  large 25.00
Pink
  Cambridge, large, ftd base 185.00
  McKee, emb "Sunkist," large 50.00
Seville Yellow, McKee, emb "Sunk-
  ist," large 40.00
White, McKee, small, emb "McK,"
  ftd base 15.00
Reamer Pitcher
  Amber, US Glass, 2 cup, loop handle 285.00
  Light Jadite, Jeannette, 2 cup 40.00
  Pink, US Glass, cov, horizontal
    bands, 4½" d, 3 piece set 165.00
  Transparent Green, Hocking, Circle
    pattern 60.00
Refrigerator Dish, cov
  Amber, Federal
    4 x 4", vertical ribs 8.00
    4 x 8", vertical ribs 12.00
  Chalaine, 4 x 5" 95.00
  Clear, Hocking, 4½" d, round, verti-
    cal ribs 3.00
  Cobalt Blue, Hazel Atlas, 4½ x 5",
    stacking, recessed handle 45.00
  Delphite, Jeannette, 32 oz, round, re-
    cessed handle 55.00
  Light Jadite, Jeannette, 32 oz, round,
    recessed handle 28.00
  Pink, Jeannette, 4½ x 9", Jennyware   22.00
Rice Canister, cov, Owens–Illinois, for-
  est green, 20 oz, square, metal
  threaded lid, diagonal ridged, silver
  paper label 25.00
Salad Set, fork and spoon
  Amber, rounded, ribbed handle 30.00
  Clear, diamond design handle 8.00
Salt and Pepper Shakers, pr
  Cobalt, Hazel Atlas, round, metal
    threaded lid, ringed 40.00
  Custard, square, metal threaded lid,
    black lettering 25.00
  Delphite, Jeannette
    Round, 8 oz, metal threaded lid,
      horizontal ribs, black lettering .   95.00
    Square, metal threaded lid, black
      lettering 175.00
  Green Transparent, round, metal
    threaded lid, silver and black paper
    label 45.00
  White
    Hocking, Red Circle, red metal
      threaded lid, range 30.00
    McKee, square, metal threaded lid,
      Roman arch side panels, black
      lettering 35.00
Spice Canister, cov, Jeannette, light jad-
  ite, square, "Ginger," black lettering,
  3" h 55.00
Sugar Canister, cov
  Clear, 20 oz, square, metal threaded

lid, black and silver paper label
  "Sugar Jar" 40.00
Dark Jadite, Jeannette, 40 oz, round,
  metal threaded lid, horizontal ribs,
  black lettering 90.00
Green Transparent, Hocking, 40 oz,
  square, metal threaded lid, vertical
  ribs, black and silver paper label .   55.00
White, McKee, round, clear glass lid,
  black script lettering 55.00
Sugar Shaker
  Light Jadite, Jeannette, square, metal
    threaded lid, black lettering 25.00
  White, McKee, large, square, metal
    threaded lid, black lettering 60.00
Tea Canister, cov
  Clear, black metal threaded lid, ver-
    tical ribs, black label 25.00
  Clear, metal snap lid, paneled, raised
    dots 20.00
  Delphite, Jeannette
    20 oz, round, metal threaded lid,
      horizontal ribs, black lettering . 260.00
    29 oz, square, recessed handle,
      black lettering, 5" h 285.00
  Light Jadite, Jeannette
    16 oz, round, metal threaded lid,
      horizontal ribs, black lettering .   45.00
    29 oz, square, glass cov, recessed
      handle, black lettering 40.00
Tom and Jerry Bowl, McKee, custard,
  black lettering 60.00
Tom and Jerry Set, bowl and 12 cups,
  McKee, custard, black lettering 65.00
Tumbler, McKee, Skokie green, ftd . . .   12.00
Vegetable Dish, Corning, blue, Pyrex,
  oval, divided 15.00

LALIQUE

History: Rene Lalique (1860–1945) first gained
prominence as a jewelry designer. Around 1900
he began experimenting with molded glass
brooches and pendants, often embellishing them
with semiprecious stones. By 1905 he was de-
voting himself exclusively to the manufacture of
glass articles.

In 1908 Lalique began designing packaging for
the French cosmetic houses. He also produced
many objects, especially vases, bowls, and figurines, in the Art Noveau style in the 1910s. The
full scope of Lalique's genius was seen at the
1925 Paris International Exhibition of Decorative
Arts. He later moved to the Art Deco form.

The mark "R. LALIQUE FRANCE" in block
letters is found on pressed articles, tableware,

vases, paperweights, and mascots. The script signature, with or without "France," is found on hand blown objects. Occasionally a design number is included. The word "France" in any form indicates a piece made after 1926.

The post–1945 mark is "Lalique France" without the "R"; there are exceptions to this rule.

References: Katherine Morrison McClinton, *Introduction to Lalique Glass*, Wallace-Homestead, 1978; Tony L. Mortimer, *Lalique*, Chartwell Books, 1989.

Collectors' Club: Lalique Society of America, Jacques Jugeat Co., 11 East 26th St., New York, NY 10010.

Reproduction Alert: Much faking of the Lalique signature occurs, the most common being the addition of an "R" to the post–1945 mark.

Animal
  Fish, 7" l, sgd "Lalique, France," orig paper label **500.00**
  Fox, 2¾" h, frosted, circular, engraved script sgd "R Lalique France" **525.00**
  Rooster, 9" h, numbered, sgd "R Lalique, France," orig paper label .. **2,000.00**
Ashtray
  5¾" d, lion, molded gargoyle form rim, extended mane ridges, engraved script sgd **165.00**
  6" l, oval, Medicis, tiny blossoms and nude figures at each end, etched "R Lalique France No 280" and molded "R Lalique" **350.00**
  8" d, frosted cherubs, orig paper label **150.00**
Atomizer, cylindrical
  2½" h, Epines, clear, molded thorny bramble design, lavender patina, raised molded sgd, gilt metal atomizer fittings, damage to orig bulb and net **300.00**
  3¾" h, relief molded frieze of six nude maidens, holding floral garland, waisted gilt metal mount, Le Provencal fragrance, molded "R Lalique, Made In France" **250.00**
  4¾" h, relief molded frieze of six nude maidens, holding floral garland, waisted gilt metal mount chased with ribbon tied floral festoons, stamped "LE Parisiene BteS G. D. G. Made in France/O/F," base low relief molded "R. Lalique Made In France" **880.00**
Auto Mascot
  5¼" h, 6¼" l, Chrysis, nude woman, frosted, clear, chromed radiator cap, marked "R Lalique France" . **3,700.00**
  6¼" h, falcon, molded, polished and frosted, circular platform base,

raised molded mark, numbered on base **935.00**
  8¼" h, rooster, molded, polished and frosted, ruffled tail feathers, low disk base, etched block mark, numbered on base **660.00**

Beverage Set (center), frosted and clear crystal, Setubal pattern, leaf and berry design, six flared tumblers, matching 18" l tray, $770.00; Luncheon Service (left and right), opalescent crystal, 5¼" d bowl, 7¾" d plate, block signatures, service for six, $1,430.00. Photograph courtesy of Skinner, Inc.

Beverage Service, crystal, octagonal faceted bases, pitcher, decanter, three sizes of wine and cordial glasses, each script engraved "Lalique France," minor chips, 45 pcs **525.00**
Bookends, pr
  6¼" h, floral, birds, sgd **475.00**
  7⅛" h, frosted, three molded putti bearing garlands, stenciled "Lalique France" **600.00**
Bottle, display, 8¾" h, Imprudence, clear, acid stamped "R Lalique France" **415.00**
Bowl
  5¼" d, Coquilles, opalescent, scallop shell molded ext. design, etched reverse signature "R. Lalique France N. 3204" **175.00**
  8" d, 3½" h, Gui, molded, clear, imp mistletoe leaves and stems, gray patina, berry clusters in relief form feet, raised block letter mark **300.00**
  8¼" d, Ondine Ouverte, opalescent, half round, molded six nude swimming water sprites, raised molded mark, etched "France" **1,430.00**
  8½" d, Volubilis, opalescent, molded entwined triparte design forms three feet, raised black mark, etched "France" **880.00**
  9" d, Actina, clear and frosted, blue opalescence **400.00**
  9½" d, Chicoree, clear and frosted, molded Verrerie d'Alsace mark ... **375.00**
  10" d, Nemours, dark gray frosted,

molded intaglio blossoms, eleven rows of stylized flowerheads in graduated sizes, int. center sgd in cameo "R Lalique/France," 1930 **3,100.00**

Box, cov, circular 2¹⁵⁄₁₆" d, opalescent, Coquilles, molded stylized shells, engraved "R Lalique France" **330.00**

3" d, female masks hiding among bunches of roses, turquoise patina, sgd "R Lalique" **350.00**

Brooch, 1¾" d, moths, clear and frosted glass roundel, four flying moths, bright blue foil backing, gilt metal frame stamped "Lalique," sq "RL" trademark **1,200.00**

Candlestick, 3½" h, sgd "R Lalique" . . **600.00**

Carafe, 7¾" h, clear, indented and molded large blossoms, brown patina in recesses, inscribed "R Lalique" . . **400.00**

Castor Set, 5½" h, two bottles, frosted, matching frosted glass holder, engraved script sgd **220.00**

Centerpiece Bowl
14" d, daisy, broad molded rim, clear, brown patina on floral border **450.00**

18" l, frosted oak leaves, clear base . **700.00**

Champagne, 6½" h, clear, engraved "R Lalique, France" **880.00**

Chandelier, 20⅞" d, hemispherical dome, twelve curved plaques, each with three tiers of rosebuds, enameled tan ground, enclosed in squares, chrome rings, suspended by six rope twist cords, conical frosted glass ceiling cov, c1925 . . . . **10,000.00**

Charger
11½" d, Fish Assiette, transparent, opalescent, molded swirl of fish on ext., central bubbles, raised molded mark "R. Lalique" **990.00**

14¼" d, Malines, opalescent, molded mark "R Lalique," wheel carved "France" **2,970.00**

14½" d, Martigues, opalescent, deeply molded swimming fish, molded mark "R Lalique" **2,700.00**

Cigarette Box, 5½" l, rect, hinged top, trimmed in silver, lid molded with heads of wheat, inscribed "Lalique, France" **2,200.00**

Clock
8½ l, 6" h, demilune, circular matt finished silvered metal face, stylized dahlia encircled by polished Arabic numerals, arching frosted glass case, relief molded pairs of finches among flowering vines, inscribed in block letters "R Lalique France," dial inscribed "ATO" and impressed "Made In France," c1930 . . . .**2,750.00**

14" w, 14" h, frosted and clear crystal arched frame, two recessed molded women in diaphanous gowns, center clock insert, luminar base, gilt metal, clock and light need restoration **9,900.00**

Dish, 11⅝" d, Gazelles, clear and frosted **375.00**

Figure
5½" h, Pan, dancing with wood nymph, c1950 . . . . **325.00**

6" h, nude with goose, sgd "Lalique," orig paper label **500.00**

Jardiniere, 18¼" l, 5⅛" h, Saint Hubert, frosted elliptical bowl, ends spreading to form reticulated ear shaped handle, molded relief of leaping antelope among clear leafy branches, wheel cut block letters "R Lalique/France," incised script "No. 3461," c1932 . .**3,300.00**

Liqueur Glass, 2¼" h, frosted cherubs, clear ground, sgd "R Lalique" **110.00**

Luminiere, 11⅛" h, Thasis, clear and frosted, nude female holding drapery, cast bronze electrified base, inscribed "R Lalique" **5,750.00**

Old Fashioned Glass
Femmes Antiques, molded frieze of classical maidens, set of 15 . . . . .**1,200.00**

Shene, clear and frosted, set of 12 . . **700.00**

Paperweight, Tete D'Aigle, eagle head, clear and frosted, clear, sgd in mold at side "R Lalique" **1,100.00**

Pendant, 2⅛" d, oval, clear and frosted, molded with two female nudes, engraved "R Lalique" **770.00**

Perfume Bottle
4" h
Blue sphere, star design, quarter moon stopper, marked "Sans La Nuit" **360.00**

Frosted urn, four faces molded at corners, marked "Guerlain Masques," orig black case **550.00**

5¼" h, Ambre D'Orsay, clear and frosted, molded "Lalique" and "Ambre D'Orsay" **2,200.00**

5½" h, Perles, frosted, three rows of graduated strings of pearls, domical stopper, small chip on base, stopper chipped and ground, marked . **200.00**

Place Card Holder, 1⅝" h, demilune form, clear and frosted, molded baskets of flowers and fruit, engraved "R Lalique," set of 8 . . . . **800.00**

Plate
9¼" d, Coquilles, four stylized shells, molded cameo mark, set of six . . . **700.00**

11¾" d, Assiette Plate Ondine, opalescent, mermaids among bubbles, inscribed "R Lalique France" **1,400.00**

13½" d, Felix, clear and frosted, stylized petals, stenciled "R Lalique France" **250.00**

Powder Box, cov
3¼" d, round, four moths on cov, pale green patina, molded trees base, sgd **825.00**
4" d, circular, Emilane, clear and frosted, floral molded lid, molded "R Lalique France" **300.00**

Scent Bottle
3⅜" h, Epines, molded briars, green patina in recesses, engraved "R Lalique France" and molded "R Lalique" **550.00**
3¾" h, Coeurs, frosted, clear, four hearts, gilt screw cap, molded mark "R Lalique France," orig hand stitched red leather sheath **175.00**
4½" h, Palerme, clear, molded "R Lalique" engraved "France" **725.00**
5½" h, Helene, four panels of classical maidens, brown patina, etched "Lalique, France" **750.00**

Toothpick Holder, 3½" h, sgd "R Lalique" **600.00**

Tray, 10½" d, pale blue opalescent, all over shell pattern, sgd "R Lalique" . **250.00**

Vase
4¾" h, Tournesol, clear and frosted, engraved "R Lailque, France, No. 1007" **660.00**
4⅞" h, Malines, opalescent, engraved "R Lalique France, No. 957," later silver rim **450.00**
5" h, Dahlias, enameled, molded "R Lalique" **2,530.00**
5½" h
Camaret, frosted, engraved "R Lalique France, No. 1010" **800.00**
Montlhery, clear and frosted molded design, traces of brown patina, scrolling deeply recessed repeating motif, base marked "R Lalique France" **425.00**
5¾" h, Avallon, clear and frosted, birds among berried branches, traces of amber patina, wheel carved "R Lalique, France," engraved "No. 986" **600.00**
5¾" h, 9¼" l, Caudebec, clear and frosted textured body, broad oval handles, molded blossom and leaf design on handles, traces of blue patina, sgd on base **700.00**
6" h, Boulouris, flared cylinder, opalescent band of sparrows on shoulders, vertical ribbing, stamped "R Lalique" **1,760.00**
6¼" h
Meander, clear and frosted, c1935, engraved "R Lalique, France" . **1,145.00**

Raisins, opalescent, engraved "R Lalique France No. 3878" **825.00**
6⅝" h, Ormeaux, clear and frosted, engraved "R Lalique France No. 984" **385.00**
6¾" h
Formose, clear and frosted glass, molded "R Lalique" **1,325.00**
Gui
Cased, opalescent, engraved "R Lalique No. 948" **660.00**
Cased, yellow, molded "R Lalique" **2,200.00**
7" h
Druides
Blue patina, engraved and molded marks **990.00**
Cased opalescent, molded "R Lalique" **1,320.00**
Clear and frosted, molded "R Lalique," engraved "France" ... **770.00**
Saint Francois, opalescent, stamped "R Lalique France" ... **900.00**
Satyrs, cylindrical, clear and frosted, traces of blue patina, center band of satyrs among ivy leaves, acid etched "R Lalique, France" **1,100.00**
7⅛" h, Mossi, flared cylinder, molded all over with hemispherical bosses, acid stamped "R Lalique France" **1,870.00**
7⅜" h, Chardons, butterscotch cased over opal, molded "R Lalique," engraved "France" **2,860.00**
7½" h
Coquilles, blue patina, molded marks **900.00**
Dentele, gray, engraved "R Lalique, France, No. 943" **1,100.00**
Patinated, flared cylinder, green patinated clear ground, molded leaves and curling tendrilled vines, acid stamped "R Lalique, France" **1,550.00**
8⅛" h, Tristan, clear and frosted, wheel carved "R Lalique, France" **3,200.00**
8½" h, Escargot, frosted fiery opalescent, molded as snail shell, strong blue–green patina, sgd and numbered on base **2,200.00**
9¼" h, Monnaie Du Pape, clear and frosted, traces of amber patina, molded "R Lalique," engraved "France" **1,760.00**
9½" h, Ceylon, fiery opalescent, molded, four pairs of lovebirds, sgd "R Lalique France No. 905" **3,500.00**
10" h, 10" d, Sophora, flat extended rim, molded sphere, frosted, clear polished, and green patinated levels, repeating leaf design, recessed "R Lalique" mark, chips at top rim edge **1,320.00**

10⅛" h, Sauterelles, oviform, red,
heavily molded grasshoppers
perched on thick blades of grass,
inscribed "R Lalique France" **3,400.00**
10¼" h
Archers, clear and frosted, engraved "R Lalique France No.
893" **3,000.00**
Perruches, oviform, clear and
frosted, molded pairs of parak-
eets perched on floral laden
branches, charcoal washed re-
cesses, inscribed "R Lalique" .. **4,250.00**
10¾" h, Antelopes, bulbous, short
waisted neck, flaring rim, molded
shallow relief, black enameled,
four rows of antelopes, abstract foliate forms ground, each animal
leaving over large convex molded
sphere, inscribed "R Lalique,"
c1925 .... **15,500.00**
Wall Sconce, 14¾" w, 21¼" h, convex
kite shaped wall light, four triangular
molded Lalique frosted glass panels,
nickel plated mounts, c1925, pr ... **1,550.00**

LAMPS AND LIGHTING

History: Lighting devices have evolved from simple Stone Age oil lamps to the popular electrified
models of today. Aim Argand patented the first
oil lamp in 1784. Around 1850 kerosene became
a popular lamp burning fluid, replacing whale
oil and other fluids. In 1879 Thomas A. Edison
invented the electric light bulb, causing fluid
lamps to lose favor and creating a new field for
lamp manufacturers to develop. Companies like
Tiffany and Handel developed skills in the manufacture of electric lamps, having their decorators produce beautiful aesthetic bases and
shades.

References: James Edward Black, ed., *Electric
Lighting of the 20s & 30s, Volume 2 with Price
Guide,* L–W Book Sales, 1991; J. W. Courter,
Aladdin, The Magic Name in Lamps, Wallace–
Homestead, 1980; J. W. Courter, *Aladdin Col-
lectors Manual & Price Guide #13,* published by
author, 1990; J. W. Courter, *Aladdin Electric
Lamps,* published by author, 1987; Robert De
Falco, Carole Goldman Hibel, John Hibel, *Han-
del Lamps,* H & D Press, Inc., 1986; Larry Free-
man, *New Light on Old Lamps,* American Life
Foundation, 1984; Edward and Sheila Malakoff,
Pairpoint Lamps, Schiffer Publishing, 1990;
Nadja Maril, *American Lighting: 1840–1940,*
Schiffer Publishing, 1989; Leland & Crystal Pay-
ton, *Turned On: Decorative Lamps of the 'Fifties,*
Abbeville Press, 1989; Jo Ann Thomas, *Early
Twentieth Century Lighting Fixtures,* Collector

Books, 1980; Catherine M. V. Thuro, *Oil Lamps,*
Wallace–Homestead, 1976; Catherine M. V.
Thuro, *Oil Lamps II,* Thorncliffe House, Inc.,
1983; Catherine M. V. Thuro, *Oil Lamps: The
Kerosene Era In North America, Updated Prices,*
Wallace–Homestead, 1992; Wolf Ueker, *Art
Nouveau and Art Deco Lamps and Candlesticks*
Abbeville Press, 1987.

Collectors' Clubs: Aladdin Knights of the Mystic
Light, Route 1, Simpson, IL 62985; Historical
Lighting Society of Canada, P.O. Box 561, Postal
Station R, Toronto, ON M4G 4E1; Rushlight
Club, Old Academy Library, 150 Main Street,
Wethersfield, CT 06109.

Museum: Winchester Center Kerosene Lamp
Museum, Winchester Center, CT.

Additional Listings: See specific makers and Pattern Glass.

ALADDIN

Boudoir, 14½" h, 8" d reverse painted
bell shade, pine border, floral molded
polychromed metal base **200.00**
G–16, Alacite **550.00**
G–130, Opalique, figure only **750.00**
G–163, Opalique **1,200.00**
No. 1250, 60" h, 18" d shade **325.00**

BOUDOIR

Handel
13" h, 6¾" d flared reverse painted
shade, moonlit marine scene of
sailing vessels and moorings, mon-
ochromatic gray and black, pale
apricot ground, marked and initialed "Handel 6450 PV," ribbed
and floral molded bronzed Handel
base, brown–green patina **1,650.00**
14" h, 7" d reverse painted floral swag
dome shade, metal base, sgd and
numbered, stripped finish **660.00**
14" h, 8" d shade, hexagonal ribbed
textured reverse painted shade,
multicolored tropical landscape,
green and mauve palm trees,
moonlit ocean, blue sky background, bronzed metal base with
molded forest scene, sgd and numbered, several chips on lower inside rim **2,310.00**
14¾" h, torchere, daffodil motif
painted on ribbed and molded
flared shade, sgd "Handel #3180,"
bronzed metal base, open fretwork
design, molded Handel mark **660.00**
Loetz, 12¼" h, white metal base, adjustable irid amber spotted and purple
lined shades, pr **1,350.00**
Tiffany Studios, 18" h, candle lamp, ten

ribbed opal glass shade, five gold and green pulled feather dec, fitted to bobeche ring, trifid bronze base, green glass blown–out shaft, shade sgd "L. C. T." roughness at collet rim **1,760.00**

Unknown Maker, 14" h, 10" d dome reverse painted shade, expansive landscape, amber rolling hills, clusters of green trees, blue skies shading to pale sunset orange, numbered 2700 at lower edge, single socket quatraform molded metal base, green patina **880.00**

Victorian, blue, pink, yellow, and white mother of pearl satin glass shade, diamond quilted pattern, ruffled, silver plate and brass base **2,550.00**

Desk, Tiffany Studios, shell shaped shade, shaded green Favrile glass, stamped mark, bronze base with monogram of Tiffany Glass and Decorating Company, 13" h, $5,500.00.

DESK

Handel
6½" d, leaded glass green shade, bronze base, overhanging style, sgd **2,000.00**
15" h, 8" l reverse painted cylinder shade, pastel colored pastoral scenes, sgd "Handel 6768G," adjustable weighted Handel base, flat chip on side edge **880.00**
17" h, paneled amber and red glass cylinder piano shade, adjustable carved bronze base, threaded label **825.00**

Tiffany Studios
7½" h, 11" l, adjustable hinged dark gold dore cylinder lamp, three irid gold turtleback tiles, oval base imp "Tiffany Studios New York 413" . **1,760.00**
14" h, two gold irid turtleback tiles,

orange beaded bronze single socket shade, molded platform base with curvilinear design, sixteen inserted glass jewels, imp "Tiffany Studios New York" and "Glass & Decorating Company" trademark, minor bead damage, bent frame **3,100.00**

16½" h, 10" d abalone shade, twelve frosted colorless linenfold panels, fabrique segmented border, gilt bronze shaft, octagonal platform with abalone shell inserts, orig base, shade and base sgd "Tiffany Studios New York" **6,500.00**

17½" h, 7" d, ribbed emerald green favrile cased to opal glass shade, gold horizontal linear dec above repeating wavy border design, sgd "L.C.T. Favrile," adjustable bronze harp frame, ribbed cushion base, five ball feet, base imp "Tiffany Studios New York 424," flat chip at collet edge under rim **3,300.00**

FLOOR

Bradley and Hubbard, 56" h, 7" d small domed leaded glass shade, green slag glass, gold key border, open framework, adjustable standard, domed circular foot **365.00**

Durand, 69" h, flared oval amber, opal, white, and blue crackle glass shade, gilt metal, onyx, and brass standard **675.00**

Handel, 61" h, 20" d leaded glass shade, double standard base **3,600.00**

Tiffany Studios
46" h, assembled leaded glass panels of white apple blossoms, yellow centers, green leaves, telescoping bronze base, single socket lamp shaft, five arched spade feet, one imp "Tiffany Studios New York 429A" **3,300.00**
53" h, 10" d irid green cased to opal white ripple striped shade, sgd at collet rim, five ftd shaped shaft, worn patina, counterbalance threading stripped **4,750.00**
55" h, ball shade of green glass turtleback jewels, dark purple–blue irid, bronze shaft, four splayed pad feet, imp mark **8,000.00**

FLUID

Adams & Co, 12" h, flower display under glass center with orig label, clear and frosted font, clear and stippled four column base **900.00**

Atterbury & Co
7½" h, Gem pattern, clear font, am-

ber pressed base, textured match striker panels on stem **145.00**

8¼" h, Chapman pattern, clear **75.00**

9¼" h, Wave pattern, panel base, clear, marked "October 7th 1873" **65.00**

Beaumont Glass Works, Bellaire, OH, 8⅞" h, Optic pattern, silver stained band, frosted leaves and flowers . . . **285.00**

Boston and Sandwich, 8" h, Blackberry pattern **225.00**

Central Glass Co, 9½" h, Columbian Coin pattern, milk glass **125.00**

Dalzell, Gilmore & Leighton, Findlay, OH, 8" h, Queen Heart pattern, clear font, medium green base **265.00**

Hobb's Glass Co, 2⅞" h, hand type, Snowflake pattern, cranberry ground, white opalescent pattern, applied clear handle **550.00**

Lacemaker's

10" h, free blown, clear, cut circles ring font **325.00**

16" h, cranberry overshot shade, polished brass base **375.00**

New England Glass Co, 9½" h, Acorn and Drapery pattern, cut and frosted free blown font, three ring knob, pewter collar, stepped pressed base **250.00**

Richards and Hartley, 8½" h, Three Panel pattern, apple green **195.00**

Ripley

13¾" h, candle, baptismal font, medium blue with cross and "I.H.S.," marked "Ripley & Co. Pat Pending," pewter connector and sockets, no lid, minor dents **300.00**

14½" h, marriage, opaque white and blue, double fonts **475.00**

Satin, 16½" h, 9½" d shade, gold mother of pearl satin base, shade with brass inset and feet, diamonds pattern, stylized flower in each diamond **750.00**

Sandwich Glass

11" h, Acanthus Leaf pattern, opaque blue and white, whale oil burner, sandy finish **700.00**

13" h, Onion pattern, opaque white, c1840 . . . . **650.00**

South Jersey, 10¾" h, blown glass, large pear shaped amethyst font, mounted on clear standard and base, late **125.00**

12⅛" h, Tulip pattern, clambroth colored semi opaque ground, brass stem, presentation floral dec, marble base, chip on font **75.00**

HANGING AND CHANDELIERS

Bradley and Hubbard, 52" h, store type, opaque white shade, brass font, filler cap **575.00**

Cameo, 23" d, etched glass, intaglio sgd "Daum Nancy," c1925 . . . . **900.00**

Handel

16¼" d, 19" h, gold bronze tassel and foliage emb fixture, satin finished dec shade with foliage dec **225.00**

27¾" l, brown angular strapwork design, verdigris finish, four cylindrical textured glass shades, marked "Handel 3410" **1,100.00**

Mount Washington, 15" l, peachblow, hobnail shade, prisms, brass font and fittings **1,000.00**

Muller Freres, 24" h, 24" w sq black painted wrought iron frame with scrolling floral vines, pierced ceiling plate, inset mottled purple, pink, green, and orange circular bowl, acid etched "Muller Freres, Luneville," four candle branches with ovoid mottled glass shades, electrified, c1925 **1,650.00**

Tiffany Studios

12" d, hanging favrile glass ball shade, opal ground, glossy gold irid all over lily pad and vine motif, rim marked "L. C. T.," bronze collar, three scrolled arms, three chains suspended from ceiling fixture . . . **3,850.00**

19" d, 17" drop, half round dome, amber and white striated ripple glass segments, border bands of sq emerald green turtleback tiles, apex dome with gold irid turtleback disk, bronze wire twists, swag beading, and ball drops **13,200.00**

20" d, half round dome, translucent red amber leaded glass segments, geometric symmetrical rows, four pronged bronze hanger imp "Tiffany Studios New York" **5,500.00**

Unknown Early American Maker, 15" l, aqua, blown bell shaped globe, flared rim, applied knobs in tin crown frame, tooling, cut scallops, punching, traces of red paint **675.00**

TABLE

Adams & Co, 12⅞" h, Bradford pattern, clear and frosted font, black glass base, foliage engraved panels, c1880 **420.00**

Argand, 31½" h, clear cut and frosted shade, prisms, flat spherical font, reeded column, brass, stepped scalloped base **275.00**

Astral, cut glass globe, gold ormolu stem, marble base, dated 1870 . . . . . **425.00**

Bradley and Hubbard

23½" h, 18¼" d flattened domical shade, cylindrical border, eight radiating panels of light yellow etched glass, blue border, mounted

Table, Dufner and Kimberly, domed stained glass shade with lotus flower border, 24″ h, 21½″ d shade, c1910, $2,600.00. Photograph courtesy of William Doyle Galleries.

in gilt metal ribbed frame, pierced paneled border of foliate and scrollwork, red and green enameled center quatrefoil, fluted column gilt metal standard, circular base with fluting, beading, and relief quatrefoils, early 20th C **1,875.00**
24″ h, 18″ d octagonal shade, green and gold amber glass panels, gilt metal frame of tropical island scene, two socket telescoping vasiform metal base with triangular B & H trademark, metallic finish worn **450.00**
Cameo, Daum Nancy, 14″ h, 5″ d conical shade, trumpet base of translucent white mottled glass with blue, green–brown overlay, ten opal wheel carved flower heads, lighted base and shade, wrought iron shade supports, sgd **3,750.00**
Durand, 29½″, blue glass standard, opaque white and clear feather pattern, brass standard **250.00**
Handel
19½″ h, 14″ d textured dome shade, colorful border of pink and maroon blossoms with yellow centers, green leaves, rosy–beige ground, sgd at edge "Handel 7983″, two socket copper colored base imp "Handel" **1,320.00**
21½″ h, reverse painted hemispherical shade, serene lake and swan scene, stylized stems and leaves on cast base **1,300.00**
22″ h, 18″ d reverse painted dome shade, Bird of Paradise, exotic col-

ored bird, blue blossoms, pink roses, yellow forsythia, vertically striped background with green leafy vines, sgd at edge "Handel 7125″ and monogrammed, flared three socket Art Nouveau ebonized metal Handel base **13,475.00**
23″ h, 17¾″ d reverse painted shade, Teroma style, road scene, painted brown, green, and orange trees, golden sky, numbered "6230," sgd "WR," urn shaped base **13,750.00**
23″ h, 18″ d shade
Leaded glass caramel slag panels over green, pine needle border, three socket bronzed base, sgd **1,540.00**
Reverse painted Elephantine Island landscape, four robed people, columned buildings, palm trees, blue sky, sgd "Handel 6825 John Bailey," three socket urn form bronzed base sgd "Handel" ... **7,425.00**
Reverse painted shade, grove of orange and green maple trees, golden ground, emb tree trunks and branches on slender base, orig patina, metal collar marked "Handel Lamps Patent Number 979664," bronze base die stamped "Handel" **8,800.00**
24″ h, 18″ d, textured, reverse painted, riverside clusters of tall trees, mountainous horizon, dramatic clouded skies, green, brown, orange–amber, and lavender, bronzed metal baluster form Oriental influenced base, incised "John Bailey/Handel 7031″ **7,150.00**
27″ h, 18″ d conical glass shade
Daffodils, sand textured surface, realistic painted daffodil blossoms, spiked leaves, massive leaf molded bronze base marked "Handel" **4,250.00**
Treasure Island, textured, reverse painted, blue and green tropical moonlit coastline scene, boats in lagoon and in background, sgd "Handel 6391," three socket Handel base **10,175.00**
Jefferson
20″ h, 14″ d shaped dome shade, reverse painted mountainous landscape, sgd "2906 Jefferson OC," two socket metal base, green patina, small edge bruise on shade . **825.00**
20½″ h, 16″ d smooth dome shade, reverse painted band of blossoms, earth tone faux marble background, metal rim imp "Jefferson," baluster form metal base painted to simulate marble **1,210.00**

21" h, 16" d reverse painted smooth dome shade, red–orange poppy blossoms, brown centers, leaves, and border grasses, orange–amber ground, numbered, imp mark on metal rim, two socket molded metal weighted base 1,210.00

21" h, reverse painted 16⅛" d shade with florals and leaves, apricot ground, black finished metal base, sgd 650.00

23" h, 18" d conical reverse painted shade, yellow Black–Eyed Susans, reddish–brown shaded ground, sgd "1841–R," imp "Jefferson" on metal rim, two socket baluster base, gold and black painted metal 1,760.00

Miller, 26" h, 16" quatraform filigreed metal shade, bent panels of green, pink, and white slag glass, metal base with green patina 1,100.00

Pairpoint

17¾" h, 13¾" d puffy border shade, shaped circular shade with ribbed horizontal top, outwardly tapering sides, relief molded flowerheads and two hummingbirds, interior purple, blue, and yellow enameling, sponged purple ground, green and yellow birds, silvered metal knopped baluster form standard, molded lozenge mark, impressed "Pairpoint/E3032" 9,500.00

20" h, seascape, 15" d, flared Exeter glass shade, four ocean scenes, scallop shell and dolphin panels, artist sgd "Ona M" and "Pairpoint Corp," two socket urn shaped metal base, green–bronze patina, base sgd "Pairpoint," two chips on shade 1,400.00

20½" h, puffy, 14" d quatraform blown–out glass dome, four butterfly and blossom repeats, red, pink, blue, orange, yellow, and green, white lining, gold exterior highlights, sgd "Pairpoint Corp," drilled and mounted to gilt metal petal–molded base sgd "Pairpoint" with trademark 5,200.00

21½" h, 18" d flared Exeter shade, hand painted, New Bedford harbor scene, fishermen with nets, sailboats, tall ships, and lighthouse, bright full moon, church spires in background, marked "The Pairpoint Corp'n," mounted on three socket bronzed metal Pairpoint base 3,960.00

22" h, reverse painted conical shade with six painted glass panels of

Grecian ruin in forest, patinated base stamped "Pairpoint Made in USA" 1,200.00

22" h, 17½" d conical reverse painted Carlisle shade, three colorful cockatoos among jungle foliage and blossoms, bronzed metal urn form columnar Pairpoint base 3,300.00

22" h, 18" d flared Exeter glass shade, broad apron of stylized pink, blue, beige, and amber blossoms, bright yellow–green ground, two socket gilt metal raised urn columnar base, sgd "Pairpoint," small imperfection at inner rim 1,600.00

25" h, 20" flared domed Berkeley reverse painted shade, broad after–glow border of waterfront city and pastoral landscape background, deep honey amber ground, greens, orange, and earth colors, sgd "Pairpoint Corp'n Ambero," three socket urn form bronzed metal Pairpoint base 1,540.00

Pittsburgh

18" h, 14" d scenic textured glass dome, hp tropical trees and plants, blue sky, gilt metal two socket base 715.00

23" h, 17" d pebble textured dome shade, reverse painted snowy landscape, cottages, and tall trees, lavender sky, copper colored two socket base, some restoration 935.00

23¼" h, 16" d reverse painted dome shade, continuous mountain lake and landscape, green, brown, and red highlights, deep blue water shading to violet, brown patinated metal standard cast with two loop handles and pendant rose garlands, spreading circular base with foliate bands, early 20th C 1,325.00

Tiffany Studios

13" h, gold blossom shades, tripartite upright bronze stems, circular fluted platform base, imp mark ..2,600.00

22½" h, 16" shade

Apple Blossom, domed shade, transparent green segmented background, yellow centered pink and white blossoms, brown apple tree branches, imp tag "Tiffany Studios New York," bronze spider arms over ribbed shaft, cushion base, five ball feet, imp mark on base 11,000.00

Dragonflies, conical shade, seven mesh winged dragonflies, blue bodies, jewel eyes, blue and green mottled and striated glass segments, rim sgd "Tiffany Studios New York 1462–3," bronze

urn form oval shaft, tripod and squared platform base, imp mark **22,000.00**
23½" h, 16" d dome shade, smooth "stones" arranged as flowers, pink and red favrile glass jewels set as five petaled cherry blossoms, green, blue, and opalescent white centers, gilt metal bronze baluster shaft, molded organic sworls, masks, feathers, and claw–foot devices, six pronged spade foot platform base, unsgd, descended from Arthur J. Nash **40,700.00**
24" h, 16" d shade, nineteen irid green turtleback tiles, bordered above and below by mottled green sq and rect favrile glass segments, sgd "Tiffany Studios New York," orig matching urn form bronze base, medial band of twelve green turtleback tiles, tripartite cage and platform, sgd "Tiffany Studios New York 7812," imp "TS" trademark **23,000.00**
24" h, 19" d shaped dome shade, leaded glass segments, twelve green swirling swags over repeating green border, white and mottled yellow background, bronze oil lamp base with green favrile glass blown–out body, ball feet, fuel canister imp "Tiffany Glass & Decoration Company" and "Tiffany Studios New York D506 S1261," rim restored, some bronze scrolls detached on one foot **44,000.00**
24½" h, 19" d linenfold shade, twelve sided angular gilt bronze shade with amber fabrique glass panels, matching drapery glass above and below, rim imp "Tiffany Studios New York 1927 Pat. Appld. for," conforming amber glass paneled heat cap, complimentary textured gilt bronze vasiform base imp "Tiffany Studios New York 676" . . .**12,100.00**
Wilkerson
20" h, 16" d leaded shade, white clematis blossoms with amber centers, two socket black and gilt metal base **325.00**
21½" h, 18" d leaded shade, green and amber slag glass segments in geometric pattern, red jewel accent squares, diamonds, and triangles at apron, single socket ribbed and beaded metal base **825.00**
23" h, 18" d stained glass tulip border shade, twenty four narrow radiating amber and white striated and mottled slag glass panels, three narrow

bands of rect blue and amber tiles, meandering vine with yellow shaded red tulips, green leaves, scalloped rim, gilt and turquoise patinated metal baluster form standard, foliate cast forms, spreading circular base with egg and dart band, early 20th C **1,325.00**
29" h, 21½" d leaded conical shade, red, yellow, orange, and pink blossoms and buds, green leaves, white and tan slag glass segments, curved at apron, embellished with scalloped yellow border, floral molded bronze base, fine dark patina **5,775.00**

SPARKING

3⅝" h, clear, free blown font, tin burner **525.00**
3⅞" h, clear, free blown font, pressed cup plate base, applied handle, tin burner, minor nicks and roughness, tool mark at end of handle **850.00**
4⅜" h, clear, free blown font, lacy pressed base, minor roughness to base **250.00**

WHALE OIL

6⅞" h, free blown teardrop font, stepped cloverleaf base, chip on base, tiny nick on top rim of font **70.00**
8" h, free blown font, heavy pressed molded base, minor roughness to base **75.00**
9" h
Free blown teardrop font, heavy pressed 8–sided stepped base, small chips to base **110.00**
Star and Punty pattern, clear, fluted brass stem, marble base **65.00**
9⅛" h, frosted cut blown font, heavy stepped pressed base, chips on base corners **70.00**
9¼" h
Free blown teardrop font, pressed stepped base **75.00**
Loop pattern, flint, clear, slight roughness to base **85.00**
10⅝" h, Waffle and Thumbprint pattern, flint, clear, several small nicks **10.00**
11¾" h, Sawtooth pattern, flint, clear, several small chips to font, normal base roughness **150.00**
12" h, Acanthus Leaf, jade green font, double stepped clambroth colored semi opaque base, minor roughness, several small base chips **1,900.00**

LAMP SHADES

History: Lamp shades were made to diffuse the harsh light produced by early gas lighting fixtures. These early shades were made by popular Art Nouveau manufacturers including Durand, Quezal, Steuben, Tiffany, and others. Many shades are not marked.

Lamp shades offer a glass collector exciting shapes and colors. Many of the art glass and decorated shades make lovely cabinet pieces. Preservationists also seek period lamp shades as replacements for antique lighting fixtures.

References: Dr. Larry Freeman, *New Lights on Old Lamps*, American Life Foundation, 1984; Denys Peter Myers, *Gaslighting In America: A Pictorial Survey, 1815–1910*, Dover Publications, Inc., 1978; Jo Ann Thomas, *Early Twentieth Century Lighting Fixtures*, Collector Books, 1980.

Reproduction Alert: Lamp shades have been widely reproduced.

Luster Art, opal, blue pulled double hooked feather, gold border, gold irid interior, acid etched signature, 5″ h, 2¼″ d fitter, $385.00.

Bigelow Kennard, 18″ d, 4¼″ aperture, leaded glass, ridged jewel–toned mottled red, blue, green, and purple segments above and below acorn patterned belt, sgd tags at rim read ''Bigelow Studios/Bigelow Kennard Co, Boston'' **2,970.00**
Bradley and Hubbard, 18″ d, leaded glass, geometric mottled green pattern **350.00**
Burmese, 8¾″ d, birds, butterflies, and flowers dec, gas fitter ring **275.00**
Cameo Glass, 8⅜″ d, 5″ h, 3⅞″ d fitter ring, white leaves, yellow ground, . . **225.00**
Cased Glass, 6⅞″ d, 6⅜″ h, shaded rose to pink, mushroom shape, emb swirl design, ruffled top **225.00**

Custard Glass, 2″ d fitter ring, brown nutmeg stain **35.00**
Durand
8″ d, opal ground, iridescent threads, lily, sgd **250.00**
9½″ d, Egyptian Crackle, gold ground, blue and white overlay, bulbous, ruffled rim, sgd **175.00**
Fenton, 4″ d, blue ground, white opal hobnails **85.00**
Fostoria
5″ d, white luster ground, gold, green leaves, and vines **150.00**
5½″ d, Zipper pattern, green pulled dec, opal ground, gold lining **175.00**
Galle, 6½″ d, cameo glass, milky sides overlaid with orange and olive, fire polished, floriform, sgd in cameo . . . **475.00**
Handel, 22″ d, ceiling light bowl of white panels, fitted gilt metal grid work forms decorative border, green diamond accents, sgd ''Handel,'' mounted with four hanging hooks, electrical fittings **550.00**
Imperial
Luster Art
4¾″ h, iridescent gold, pulled opal feathering **100.00**
5″ h, opalescent ground
Band of gold waves **185.00**
Blue short hooked feathering, gold borders, gold lining **275.00**
Nu Art, Carnival glass, marigold, pr **125.00**
Lalique, sgd
12″ d, amber, molded shells **560.00**
13″ d, crystal, molded ivy, green stain **750.00**
Leaded Glass, unmarked
18″ d, mottled green slag, hexagonal **300.00**
22″ d, purple and green grapes, green leaves, greenish amber ground . . . **850.00**
Loetz, 8½″ d, iridescent, green oil spotting, ribbon work over white glass int., c1900 . . . . **225.00**
Lutz, 7½ to 8″ sq, 6¼″ h, 2½″ d fitter ring, opaque white looping, applied cranberry threading, ribbon edge, sq top **150.00**
Muller Freres, 6″ d, satin frosted white top, cobalt blue base, yellow highlights **90.00**
Pairpoint
7″ h, puffy, flower basket, reverse painted pink and yellow poppies and roses **400.00**
14″ d, quatraform blown–out dome, red and pink roses, bright yellow centers, green leafy branches, four multicolored butterflies, sgd at rim ''The Pairpoint Corp,'' drilled and mounted with socket and chain, several chips at lower edge **2,860.00**

Quezal

5½" d, dark green, platinum feathering, gold lining 650.00

6½" d, opalescent ground, pulled green feathering outlined in gold, irid gold lining 190.00

6⅞" d, opalescent ground, iridescent gold trellis design, gold lining, ruffled rim 765.00

Iridescent gold ground
King Tut, white pattern, gold lining 165.00
Opal fishnet design 175.00
Opal snakeskin top, irid gold and green snakeskin base, corset shape, pr 275.00

Rubena, 7¼" d, 7⅝" h, 3⅞" d fitter ring, cranberry shading to clear, frosted and clear etched flowers and leaves, ruffled 175.00

Steuben
Aurene
Iridescent blue, platinum leaf and vine motif 850.00
Iridescent brown, platinum applied border 425.00
Iridescent gold, tulip shape 175.00
Calcite, etched dec, acorn shape ... 225.00

Tiffany Studios
1⅝" top d, 1½" base d, 3" h, iridescent blue ground, soft blue, yellow pulled feather dec, scalloped rim . 250.00
4⅞" h, iridescent gold ground, hexagonal, matched set of six 1,500.00
5¼" h, iridescent gold ground, bell shape, matched set of four 1,000.00
7" d, 2¼" d top rim, desk type, ten rib molded green dome cased to opalescent, gold horizontal damascene wavy design, bright irid luster, unsgd, descended from Arthur J Nash, chips at collet rim 2,750.00
9½" d, octagonal form, leaded panels, experimental blue–green glass, irid to brilliant silver–blue, crackled surface, matching rect border panels, unsgd, descended from Arthur J Nash, two panels cracked 935.00
22" d, 23" l, leaded glass dome, drop raised rim, shaped beaded apron, rippled amber, dichroic green, and yellow segments, autumn leaf motif, bronze cap and hanging chain, six socket fixture 9,350.00

Verlys, 3⅝" d, 5¾" h, 1⅝" d fitter ring, raised birds and fish dec 275.00

Williamson & Co
9" d, ball shape, white ground, yellow spots, red pulled feathers 175.00
7" l, stalacite shape, blue and green ground, blue loops 135.00

LIBBEY GLASS

History: In 1888 Edward Libbey established the Libbey Glass Company in Toledo, Ohio, after the closing of the New England Glass Works of W. L. Libbey and Son in East Cambridge, Massachusetts. The new Libbey company produced quality cut glass for the "Brilliant Period."

In 1930 Libbey's interest in art glass production was renewed. A. Douglas Nash was employed as a designer in 1931.

The factory continues production today as Libbey Glass Co.

Reference: Carl U. Fauster, *Libbey Glass Since 1818—Pictorial History & Collector's Guide,* Len Beach Press, 1979.

Manufacturer: Libbey Glass, One Sea Gate, Toledo, OH 43666.

Additional Listings: Amberina Glass and Cut Glass.

Berry Bowl, Maize pattern **115.00**
Bon Bon, 7" d, 1½" h, amberina, six pointed 1½" w fuchsia rim, shallow pale amber bowl **600.00**

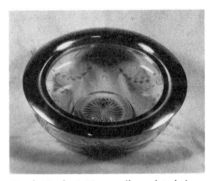

Bowl, Hardy & Hayes, silver-plated rim, sgd Libbey in circle, 14" d, 4½" h, $375.00.

Bowl
7" d, 1¾" h, amberina, ruffled turned out rim, sgd **375.00**
8¼" d, scalloped rim, turned over ruby border, amberina body, Wave pattern, three applied amber feet, acid stamped "Libbey" in circle, c1900 .... **450.00**
10" d, 4" h, amberina, fold down rim, sgd **825.00**
Butter Dish, cov, 7¼" d, 6" h, Maize pattern, pale green kernels of corn, gold trimmed husks **485.00**

Candlesticks, pr, Silhouette pattern, clear candle cup, opalescent figural camel stem 350.00
Celery Vase, 7" h, Maize pattern, amber stained kernels of corn, blue stained husks 550.00
Champagne, 6½" h, twisted stem, thin green concentric circles, sgd 145.00
Cocktail, Silhouette pattern, clear bowl, black silhouette of kangaroo in stem 145.00
Compote
10½" d, clear foot, clear ribbed crystal with pink optic swirl bowl, sgd 215.00
11" d, 7½" h, clear crystal bowl, fiery opalescent figural elephant stem and platform base, Libbey trademark, designed by Douglas Nash . 550.00

Condiment Set, Maize, clear, salt and pepper shakers and mustard, glass base, 5¾" h, 6" w, $195.00.

Cordial
American Prestige pattern, c1930 ... 45.00
Concord pattern, clear, sgd 48.00
Embassy pattern, clear, sgd 75.00
Cruet, cut glass, all over cutting, sgd .. 195.00
Goblet, 7" h, Silhouette pattern, clear bowl, opalescent silhouette of cat in stem, sgd 150.00
Pickle Castor, amberina, Swirled Rib pattern, ftd Meriden frame 465.00
Pitcher, 8¾" h, 5½" d, Maize pattern, barrel shaped, creamy opaque kernels of corn, green husks, applied strap handle 575.00
Plate, 7" d
Cut Glass, border of strawberry diamonds and fans, sunburst center, sgd 65.00
Optic Swirl pattern, green, sgd, set of four 165.00
Punch Bowl, 14" d, cut glass, American Brilliant Period, stenciled "Libbey" . 700.00
Punch Cup, Moravignian pattern, red pulled design, sgd 135.00

Salt Shaker, Maize pattern, creamy opaque kernels of corn, yellow husks, orig top 100.00
Spooner, Maize pattern, creamy opaque kernels of corn, gold trimmed blue husks 185.00
Sherbet
Cut Glass, matching underplate, American Brilliant Period, set of 12 900.00
Silhouette pattern, clear bowl, black silhouette of rabbit in stem 65.00
Sherry, 5" h, Silhouette pattern, clear bowl, black silhouette of monkey in stem 95.00
Sugar Bowl, cov, 2¾" h, Optic Rib pattern, pale blue opalescent, satin finish, gold enameled "World's Fair 1893" 170.00
Sugar Shaker, Maize pattern, creamy opaque kernels of corn, gold trimmed blue husks, orig top 225.00
Toothpick Holder, Maize pattern, creamy opaque kernels of corn, blue husks 300.00
Tumbler, Maize pattern, creamy opaque kernels of corn, yellow husks 125.00
Vase
8¼" h, tapered, optic fern and pink threaded design, clear foot, sgd .. 315.00
9" h
Cylindrical, slightly flaring, light vertical ribbing, blue threaded dec, opal ground, c1933 ...... 265.00
Lily, vertical ribbing design, amber shading to fuchsia 400.00
11¼" h, 4" d, deep red ball shaped bowl, 7½" l hollow amber stem, 4" d circular base, sgd 1,000.00
12" h, trumpet
Amberina, fuchsia base, vertical ribbing 415.00
Cut glass, floral pattern, flutes and horizontal ladder, precise cutting, clear blank, 1906–19 trademark 295.00
15" h, floriform, amberina, c1917 .. 950.00
Water Carafe, Maize pattern, creamy opaque kernels of corn, yellow husks outlined in gold 325.00
Wine, 7" h, Silhouette pattern, clear bowl, black silhouette of cat in stem, sgd 125.00

LOETZ

History: Loetz is a type of iridescent art glass made in Austria by J. Loetz Witwe in the late 1890s. Loetz was a contemporary of L. C. Tiffany and worked in the Tiffany factory before establishing his own operation; therefore, much of the wares are similar in appearance to Tiffany. Some pieces are signed "Loetz," "Loetz, Austria," or "Austria." The Loetz factory also produced ware with fine cameos on cased glass.

Bottle, 11¾" h, bulbous, extended neck, everted rim, four upturned handles, rose gold irid ground, rainbow irid oil spot dec **19,800.00**

Bowl, irid green, unsgd, 6½" d, 3½" h, $185.00.

Bowl
  5½" d, 3¾" h, silver and emerald green layered between crystal, center opal layer, polished pontil ...**1,800.00**
  6½" d, shallow, thumbprint molded sides, wavy rim, amber–blue irid ground, salmon pink molded irregularly placed circles, c1900 .....**1,250.00**
  10½" d, 4" h, fluted rim, honeycomb, rainbow irid oil spot dec, green glass ground, ground pontil **400.00**
  12" d, ruffled, rim, irid deep cranberry shading to mottled green to clear, sgd **475.00**
  14" d, deep, internally dec with large green, white, and claret blossom, claret border, c1930 ....**2,000.00**
Bride's Basket, irid blue, silver threading, molded coin spots, brass holder **425.00**
Candlesticks, pr
  7¼" h, opal, amber streaks ground, irid threading on base, sterling silver rim **650.00**
  15⅜" h, cobalt blue ground, annulated round tapering stem, stepped cushion foot, bell form nozzle, conical drip pan, rainbow irid oil spot dec **2,100.00**
Chalice, 5½" h, blue–green irid ground, tear drop motif, engraved "Loetz, Austria," c1900 ....**2,425.00**
Compote
  10" d, ruffled, silver base, glass scarabs, sgd **650.00**
  10⅝" d, 5¼" h, wide flaring rim, deep black exterior, bright orange lining, three ball feet, c1920 .... **350.00**

Cracker jar, 7¾" h, irid green–blue, brown oil spots, blown–out teardrops, silverplate lid and mountings **625.00**
Dish, 12½" l, leaf shape, channel molded, S–curved form, pinched, ruffled rim, honeycomb textured exterior, yellow with pink irid ground, sgd "Loetz/Austria," c1900 .... **900.00**
Inkwell, 4½" w, 2½" h, rainbow irid, pinched corners, hammered brass lid **300.00**
Pendant, 1½" l, ovoid, irid turquoise and yellow **175.00**
Rose Bowl, 6½" d, ruffled, purple irid raindrop dec **250.00**
Sweetmeat Jar, cov, 5¼" h, 4¾" d, green ground, maroon threading, sterling silver top, sq handle, sgd "Loetz, Austria" **300.00**
Urn, 9¼" h, ovoid, two handles, irid, three colors, blue oil spot dec, inscribed "Loetz, Austria" **1,500.00**

Vase, floral pattern, orange glass with silver irid waves highlighted by gold threading, silver overlay, unsgd, 4" h, $285.00.

Vase
  4½" h, double gourd shape
    Bright blue ground, rough surface finish **225.00**
    Gold ground, rough surface finish **225.00**
  5" h, bud, stick, irid ground, platinum and black pulled feather dec, slender stem, small lip **725.00**
  5½" h, tooled quatrefoil lip, layered with metallic green and silver–blue, cased orange int. **1,045.00**
  6" h, frosted camphor, stork in rushes dec, minor roughness on base ... **550.00**
  6" h, 2¼" w, triangular, two applied shells, rippled free form drips on each side and ends, textured ground **500.00**
  6¾" h, triangular, pinched and everted rim, all over random lozenge form indentations, blue silver irid over emerald green ground .. **750.00**

7″ h
Gourd, four dimples, tobacco ground, silvery turquoise oil spots **1,750.00**
Oval, yellow–green, pulled horizontal green striped flowing motif, random Papillon irid drops, overlaid silver cut in scrolling floral elements, hallmarked at border, numbered **3,600.00**
7¼″ h, flared, Art Deco, cased, orange ground, black vertical stripes, border, and knop, attributed to Michael Powolny **660.00**
7½″ h, folded lip, four sectioned bowl base, amber and maroon swirled and coiled irid dec, mounted in Art Nouveau bronze metal frame, some int. water stains **550.00**
8″ h, tapering cylindrical, swelling to bulbous base, mottled and striated deep blue, green, and copper tones, copper overlay strapwork, two inset semiprecious irid green cabochons **1,750.00**
11¼″ h, oval, ftd, dark red, four silver–blue pulled feather elements, sgd "Austria" with circular arrow mark **2,750.00**
12″ h, baluster, deep ruby red, four silver–blue irid pulled feather dec, sgd on base with circular crossed arrow and star mark and "Austria" **2,600.00**
12″ h, 12″ w, flared fan, red–orange satin finish rim shading to opal and mottled green, gold irid spotted surface dec **1,650.00**
13¼″ h, translucent salmon ground, silver irid feather pulls, inscribed "Loetz, Austria" **5,000.00**

LUTZ-TYPE GLASS

History: Lutz-type glass is an art glass attributed to Nicholas Lutz. He made this type of glass while at the Boston and Sandwich Glass Co. from 1869 until 1888. Since Lutz-type glass was popular, copied by many capable glassmakers, and unsigned, it is nearly impossible to distinguish genuine Lutz products.

Lutz is believed to have made two distinct types of glass, striped and threaded glass. This style often is confused with a similar style Venetian glass. The striped glass was made by using threaded glass rods in the Venetian manner. Threaded glass was blown and decorated by winding threads of glass around the piece.

Barber Bottle, 8″ h, clear ground, multicolored threaded latticino and opaque stripes **220.00**

Finger Bowl, clear, aquamarine twist bands, gold borders, 4½″ d, 2¾″ h, 6¾″ d underplate, $125.00.

Beverage Set, nine pieces, 7½″ h tankard pitcher, four lemonade tumblers, four large tumblers, clear ground, cranberry threading, engraved pattern of water plants and Great Blue Heron on pitcher **450.00**
Bowl, 3¼″ d, 3″ h, clear ground, white, amethyst, and yellow latticino, goldstone border **45.00**
Cake Stand, threaded, clear ground, white threads **115.00**
Compote
6½″ h, 8⅞″ d, Diamond Quilted pattern, threaded, amberina ground, clear hollow stem **500.00**
7″ h, clear ground, lavender, pink, and opalescent swirls, entwined serpent stem **265.00**
Dish, 12″ w, leaf shape, clear ground, white latticino, goldstone and white waves **140.00**
Epergne, three pieces, clear ground, pink threads **250.00**
Finger Bowl
4½″ d, 2¾″ h, matching underplate, clear ground, aquamarine twist bands, gold borders **125.00**
5″ d, 2⅜″ h, clear ground, white latticino, red rim, clear applied baby face handles **275.00**
7″ d, ruffled edge, clear ground, amber swirls, amethyst latticino, gold metallic borders, matching underplate **150.00**
Lamp Shade, 8″ sq, 6¼″ h, 2½″ fitter, sq top, clear ground, opaque white loopings, applied cranberry threading, clear ribbon edge **175.00**
Lemonade Tumbler, 5½″ d, clear ground, cranberry threading, engraved dec, applied clear handle ... **125.00**
Marble
1¾″ d, clear ground, green, red, white, and blue treaded twists, minor bruises, some roughness **30.00**

2⅛" d, clear ground, cranberry and white swirl **90.00**

2⅜" d, multicolored, minor roughness and bruises **100.00**

Pitcher, 10" h, clear ground, pink threading **175.00**

Plate, 6¼" d, threaded, rose shaded to amber body, goldstone dec, ruffled . **115.00**

Punch Cup, 3" d, 2⅝" h, clear ground, cranberry threading, circular foot, applied clear handle **85.00**

Scent Bottle, figural, sea horse
2⅛" l, blown, clear ground, opaque white spiral ribs, applied blue rigaree **95.00**
2¾" l, opaque white ground ribbed . **75.00**

Syrup Pitcher, blue ground, white stripes, frosted handle **175.00**

Tea Service, seven pieces, creamer, cov sugar, two cups and saucers, clear ground, light pink, blue, and white latticino **250.00**

Tumbler
3" h, clear ground, gold and white latticino, threaded, six applied strawberries, ftd **95.00**
3½" h, clear ground, white, green, and orange latticino **115.00**
3¾" h, clear ground, white and amethyst latticino, goldstone highlights **75.00**

Vase
7" h, cylindrical, clear ground, cranberry threading **90.00**
8" h, bulbous, clear ground, white latticino, applied clear handle **140.00**

Whimsey, 6⅜" h, tiny Frozen Charlotte doll in clear glass tube, latticino rings dec, bulbous finial, knob stem, clear foot **350.00**

MARY GREGORY-TYPE GLASS

History: The use of enameled decoration on glass, an inexpensive imitation of cameo glass, developed in Bohemia in the late 19th century. The Boston and Sandwich Glass Co. copied this process in the late 1880s.

Mary Gregory (1856–1908) was employed for two years at the Boston and Sandwich Glass Co. factory when the enameled decorated glass was being manufactured. Some collectors argue that Gregory was inspired to paint her white enamel figures on glass by the work of Kate Greenaway and a desire to imitate pate–sur–pate. However, evidence for these assertions is very weak. Further, a question can be raised whether or not Mary Gregory even decorated glass as part of her job at Sandwich.

The result is that "Mary Gregory-Type" is a better term to describe this glass. Collectors should recognize that most examples are either European or modern reproductions.

Barber Bottle
7½" h, cobalt blue ground, white enameled boy and girl playing badminton **120.00**
7⅝" h, deep amethyst ground, white enameled young girl, landscape setting, pr **295.00**

Beverage Set, pitcher and six tumblers, clear ground, white enameled girl, garden setting **275.00**

Box, cov, hinged lid
3⅛" d, 2¾" h, round, cranberry ground, white enameled girl and floral sprays **265.00**
5¼" d, 4¾" h, sapphire blue ground, white enameled young girl holding basket of flowers on lid, multicolored enamel dec on base, fancy wire legs **630.00**

Cologne Bottle
7" h, amber ground, white enameled girl and foliage, white trim, bulbous, amber ball stopper **175.00**
9¼" h, cranberry ground, white enameled boy feeding birds, matching stopper **275.00**

Creamer, 2½" d, 3¾" h, green ground, white enameled girl, Inverted Thumbprint pattern, applied green handle . **145.00**

Cruet
8½" h, sapphire blue, ground, sq, dimpled sides, white enameled two girls facing each other, blue handle and orig stopper **485.00**
9½" h, amber ground, white enameled boy, applied clear handle, clear bubble stopper **275.00**

Decanter, 5" d, 10⅝" h, cranberry ground, white enameled young girl with hat by fence **365.00**

Dresser Set, cranberry ground, tray, two perfume bottles, powder box, ring tree, and pin tray, 6 pcs **1,100.00**

Dresser Tray, 10½" l, 8" w, oval, emerald green ground, white enameled boy and girl dancing while another girl plays the mandolin **275.00**

Ewer, 10" h, 3⅛" d, cranberry ground, white enameled girl in garden setting, applied clear handle **220.00**

Jewel Box, cov
3" h, 3½" d, cranberry ground, hinged lid **400.00**
10" l, 4" w, blue ground, white enameled boy and girl pulling cart, girl astride huge bottle, boy carrying goblet, floral garlands, silver plated

edges, base, and feet, sgd "Middletown Plate Co" **850.00**
Liqueur Glass, 3⅜" h, 1¼" d, lime green ground, clear stem, white enameled girl **50.00**
Mug
   3" h, 2⅛" d, cranberry ground, white enameled boy, applied clear handle **80.00**
   3" h, 2¼" d, cranberry ground, white enameled girl, applied clear handle **75.00**
   3⅞" h, 2¼" d, amber ground, applied amber handles, white enameled boy on one, girl on other, pr **135.00**
   4½" h, amber ground, white enameled girl praying, ribbed body, applied handle **55.00**
Patch Box, cov, 3" h, 3¾" d, lift off cov, green ground, white enameled girl, melon ribbed body, emb scrolls **150.00**
Perfume Bottle
   4" h, sq, blue ground, white enameled boy on one, girl on other, cut glass stoppers, pr **250.00**
   4⅝" h, 2" d, cranberry ground, white enameled little girl dec, clear ball stopper **165.00**
   5¾" h, 3" d, sapphire blue ground, white enameled boy chasing butterfly, tinted facial features, blue ball stopper **195.00**
Pin Basket, 3⅜" d, 3¾" h, ruby ground, white enameled girl and flowers, ormolu mounts, brass feet and handle **195.00**
Pitcher
   3¼" h, 2¾" d, cranberry ground, white enameled boy, tankard shape, applied clear handle **185.00**
   6⅝" h, 4¼" d, lime green ground, bulbous, optic effect, round mouth, white enameled boy, applied green handle **125.00**

Vase in Victorian silver stand, cased, 9" h vase, 13½" overall height, $385.00.

9½" h, 7½" d, medium green ground, white enameled boy with bird and trees and girl with bowl and brush dec, pr **250.00**
10" h, medium blue ground, white enameled young girl, brown enameled hair, gold band around top, applied clear handle **265.00**
Plate, 6¼" d, cobalt blue ground, white enameled girl with butterfly net **125.00**
Rose Bowl, 3" h, 3¼" d, cranberry ground, white enameled young girl, crimped top **225.00**
Salt Shaker, 5" d, blue ground, white enameled girl in garden, paneled body, brass top **180.00**
Stein, 4" h, smoky amber ground, white enameled boy and girl, pewter and glass lids, matched pr **110.00**
Toothpick Holder
   Cranberry ground, white enameled boy looking at bird **65.00**
   Cranberry ground, white enameled girl and floral sprays **55.00**
Tumble–Up, cranberry ground, white enameled girl on carafe, boy on tumbler **400.00**
Tumbler
   2½" h, 1¾" d, cranberry ground, white enameled boy on one, girl on other, facing pr **100.00**
   4½" h, sapphire blue ground, white enameled boy, ribbed body **65.00**
   5" h, 2½" d, sapphire blue ground, white enameled girl carrying basket of flowers **85.00**
   5½" h, cobalt blue ground, white enameled girl picking flowers, narrow gold band at top **95.00**
   5¾" h, transparent light blue ground, white enameled boy, gold band at top, pedestal foot **135.00**
Urn, cov, 14¼" h, 5⅝" d, cobalt blue ground, white enameled girl carrying basket of flowers, white enameled dot borders **350.00**
Vase
   4¼" h, 1⅝" d, cranberry ground, clear pedestal foot, detailed white enameled girl **100.00**
   7" h, bud, sapphire blue ground, white enameled boy, pedestal foot **125.00**
   8" h, 2½" w, double ring shape, sapphire blue ground, white enameled girl offers bouquet of flowers to boy on matching vase, Mt Washington, pr **425.00**
   8⅞" h, 4" d, cranberry ground, white enameled young girls carrying watering cans, facing pair **400.00**
   9" h, 4" d, frosted emerald green

ground, white enameled girl holds
flowers in her apron and hand ... **150.00**
9⅞" h, cranberry ground, white
enameled boy running with butterfly net, girl with bouquet of flowers,
holding apron, clear pedestal foot,
facing pr **450.00**
10¾" h, 5¼" d, cobalt blue ground,
white enameled girl, scarf around
neck, long dress, facing pr **400.00**
11¼" h, 3⅞" d, cranberry ground,
white enameled young boy with
tam holding sprig, cut scalloped top **325.00**
12⅛" h, 4" d, cranberry ground, girl
reaching up into tree at bird and
bird's nest **295.00**
13" h, 6⅞" d, cranberry ground, white
enameled girl with flowers in her
apron, scalloped top, applied clear
reeded snail handles **400.00**
14" h, 5¾" d, cobalt blue ground,
white enameled boy with butter-
flies, pedestal base **225.00**
Wine Bottle, 9"h, 3⅛" d, cranberry
ground, white enameled girl holding
floral spray, orig clear bubble stopper **165.00**

McKEE GLASS

History: The McKee Glass Company was established in 1843 in Pittsburgh, Pennsylvania. In
1852 it opened a factory to produce pressed
glass. In 1888, the factory relocated to Jeannette,
Pennsylvania, and began to produce many types
of kitchenwares. The factory was among several
located there to make Depression era wares. The
factory continued until 1951 when it was sold to
the Thatcher Manufacturing Co.

The McKee Glass Company produced many
types of glass including glass window panes,
tumblers, tablewares, Depression glass, milk
glass, and bar and utility objects.

McKee named its colors Chalaine Blue, Custard, Seville Yellow, and Skokie Green. They pre-
ferred Skokie Green to jadite which was popular
with other manufacturers at the time. McKee also
made several patterns on these opaque colors,
including dots of red, green, and black and red
ships. A few items were decaled. Most of the
canisters and shakers were lettered in black to
indicate the purpose for which they were made.

References: Gene Florence, *Kitchen Glassware
of the Depression Years, Fourth Edition,* Collector
Books, 1990, value update 1992; Lowell Innes
and Jane Shadel Spillman, *M'Kee Victorian
Glass,* Dover Publications, 1981.

Animal Dish, cov
   Canary, nest base, milk glass **115.00**
   Cat, milk glass **185.00**

**Tumbler, "Bottoms–Up," caramel opales-
cent, marked "Patent No. 77726," 3¼"
h, $75.00.**

Dove, round base, beaded rim, vase-
   line, sgd **350.00**
Hen, milk glass, orig eyes **135.00**
Horse, milk glass **165.00**
Rabbit, milk glass **160.00**
Squirrel, split rib base, milk glass ... **125.00**
Basket, Queen pattern, apple green ... **125.00**
Berry Set, Hobnail with Fan pattern,
   blue, master bowl, eight serving
   bowls **165.00**
Bird House, gray body, red roof **150.00**
Bowl
   Autumn pattern, opaque green, ftd . **24.00**
   Eugenia pattern, heavy brilliant flint,
     cov **60.00**
   Eureka pattern, heavy brilliant flint, 8"
     l, oval **40.00**
   Flower Band pattern, 9½" d, Skokie
     Green **15.00**
   Laurel pattern, 9" d, Skokie Green .. **12.50**
   Prescut, flowers and fruit dec **100.00**
   Queen pattern, blue **55.00**
   Rock Crystal pattern, 5" d, ruby **24.00**
   Star Rosetted pattern, 8" d, clear ... **15.00**
   Strigil pattern, clear **20.00**
Bread Plate
   Queen pattern, canary yellow **35.00**
   Star Rosetted pattern, "A Good
     Mother Makes A Happy Home" .. **50.00**
Butter Dish, cov
   Eureka pattern, heavy brilliant flint . **65.00**
   Gothic pattern, clear, pyramid shaped
     finial **40.00**
   Queen pattern, canary yellow, domed
     lid **75.00**
   Star Rosetted pattern, clear **45.00**
   Strigil pattern, clear **35.00**
Cake Stand
   Queen pattern, amber **60.00**
   Rock Crystal, green, low **50.00**
Candlestick
   8½" h, Rock Crystal pattern, ruby,
     baluster **65.00**
   10" h, crucifix form, Christ figure and

"INRI" plaque, hexagonal base, clear **115.00**
Candy Dish, cov, 7¾" h, orange body, gold trim, gold finial, clear pedestal base **24.00**
Castor Bottle, Eugenia pattern, heavy brilliant flint **25.00**
Celery Vase
  Eugenia pattern, heavy brilliant flint **90.00**
  Gothic pattern, clear, ruby stained, scalloped **85.00**
  Strigil pattern, clear **15.00**
Champagne
  Eugenia pattern, heavy brilliant flint **85.00**
  Eureka pattern, heavy brilliant flint . **85.00**
Cheese and Cracker Set, Rock Crystal pattern, ruby **175.00**
Cheese Dish, cov, Queen pattern, blue **125.00**
Clock, Daisy and Button pattern, tambour shape, Skokie Green, 8" h, 7" w **65.00**
Compote, cov, high standard
  Eugenia pattern, heavy brilliant flint, 8" d **145.00**
  Eureka pattern, heavy brilliant flint, 7" d **80.00**
  Queen pattern, apple green **75.00**
  Star Rosetted pattern, 8½" d, clear .. **65.00**
Cookie Jar, Patrician pattern, clear **85.00**
Cordial
  Eugenia pattern, heavy brilliant flint **90.00**
  Eureka pattern, heavy brilliant flint . **40.00**
  Gothic pattern, clear **20.00**
  Rock Crystal, clear **22.50**
Creamer
  Comet pattern, clear **40.00**
  Eugenia pattern, heavy brilliant flint **170.00**
  Eureka pattern, heavy brilliant flint, ftd, applied handle **45.00**
  Gothic pattern, clear, ruby stained .. **45.00**
  Masonic pattern **20.00**
  Queen pattern, canary yellow **30.00**
  Star Rosetted pattern **35.00**
  Strigil pattern, clear **25.00**
Creamer and Sugar, Rock Crystal pattern, clear, ftd **38.00**
Cruet, orig stopper
  Rock Crystal pattern, amber **185.00**
  Strigil pattern, clear **25.00**
Decanter Set, decanter, six whiskey glasses, pink ground, ring dec **115.00**
Egg Cup
  Eugenia pattern, heavy brilliant flint, pedestal base **30.00**
  Strigil pattern, clear **20.00**
Fruit Bowl, Gothic pattern, clear, ruby stained **100.00**
Goblet
  Eugenia pattern, heavy brilliant flint **65.00**
  Eureka pattern, heavy brilliant flint . **35.00**
  French Ivory **30.00**
  Puritan pattern, pink stem **25.00**
  Queen pattern, amber **25.00**

Rock Crystal pattern, clear **16.00**
Star Rosetted pattern **35.00**
Strigil pattern, clear **40.00**
Grapefruit Bowl, Rock Crystal pattern, red **45.00**
Ice Bucket, cov, black **55.00**
Jelly Compote, Gothic pattern, clear, scalloped rim **15.00**
Juice Tumbler, Rock Crystal pattern, clear **15.00**
Kitchenware
  Baker, 7" l, 5" w, oval, Skokie Green **16.00**
  Butter Dish, cov, rect
    Chalaine Blue **75.00**
    Clear top, custard base **20.00**
    Custard **45.00**
    Seville Yellow **65.00**
    White, plain **38.00**
  Canister, 10 oz, round, custard **16.00**
  Coffee Canister, cov, Skokie Green . **28.00**
  Egg Beater Bowl, Skokie Green, pouring spout **10.00**
  Egg Cup, custard, ftd **15.00**
  Flour Shaker, Seville Yellow **20.00**
  Grease Jar, cov, Seville Yellow **37.50**
  Measuring Cup
    Clear, Glasbake, two cup **32.00**
    Custard, four cup **37.00**
    Fired On, red, two cup **20.00**
  Mixing Bowls, nested, Ships pattern, set of three **35.00**
  Reamer, juice
    Chalaine Blue **275.00**
    French Ivory **50.00**
    Seville Yellow **165.00**
  Refrigerator Dish, cov, 5" l, 4" w, custard **18.00**
  Refrigerator Water Dispenser, 11" l, 5" w, 4" h, Skokie Green **90.00**
  Rolling Pin, Seville Yellow **200.00**
  Salt and Pepper Shakers, pr, large, white **70.00**
  Spice Condiment Set, custard, jars labeled "Cinnamon, Ginger, Nutmeg," metal lids, orig rack **50.00**
  Sugar Canister, cov, French Ivory ... **18.00**
  Sugar Shaker, transparent green, bullet shape **85.00**
  Towel Bar, Jadite **25.00**
  Tumbler, 4¼" h, custard, ftd **8.00**
Lamp
  Dance de Lumierre, green **750.00**
  Eugenia pattern, heavy brilliant flint, whale oil burner **150.00**
  Ribbed Tulip pattern, 9½" h, clear font, milk glass base **125.00**
Mustard Bottle, Eugenia pattern, heavy brilliant flint **25.00**
Pepper Bottle, Eugenia pattern, heavy brilliant flint **25.00**
Pickle Dish
  Queen pattern, blue **20.00**

Star Rosetted pattern, clear, oval ... **15.00**
Pitcher
   Aztec pattern, 5" h, clear **17.50**
   Eureka pattern, heavy brilliant flint . **125.00**
   Gothic pattern, clear **65.00**
   Queen pattern, blue **55.00**
   Snowflake pattern, clear **45.00**
   Star Rosetted pattern **65.00**
   Strigil pattern, clear **40.00**
   Wild Rose and Bowknot pattern, frosted, gilt dec **48.00**
Plate
   Holly pattern, 8" d, Skokie Green .. **10.00**
   Laurel pattern, 9" d, Skokie Green .. **8.00**
   Rock Crystal pattern, 12" d, clear ... **17.50**
   Serenade pattern, 6⅜" d, opaque white **55.00**
   Star Rosetted pattern, 9" d, clear ... **25.00**
Punch Bowl, Rock Crystal pattern, clear **90.00**
Relish
   Gothic pattern, clear **15.00**
   Prescut, milk glass **20.00**
Ring Box, cov, Skokie Green **18.00**
Salt and Pepper Shakers, pr
   Gothic pattern, clear **30.00**
   Roman Arches pattern, opaque white **20.00**
Salt
   Eureka pattern, heavy brilliant flint, master, ftd, scalloped **30.00**
   Strigil pattern, clear, individual **5.00**
Sauce
   Eureka pattern, heavy brilliant flint . **10.00**
   Gothic pattern, clear **15.00**
   Queen pattern, clear, ftd **10.00**
   Star Rosetted pattern, 4" d, clear, ftd **15.00**
   Strigil pattern, clear **5.00**
Server, Rock Crystal pattern, ruby, center handle **125.00**
Sherbet
   Laurel pattern, Skokie Green **7.50**
   Rock Crystal pattern, clear **10.00**
Spooner
   Eureka pattern, heavy brilliant flint . **40.00**
   Queen pattern, amber **25.00**
   Star Rosetted pattern, clear **25.00**
   Strigil pattern, clear **15.00**
Sugar, cov
   Eugenia pattern, heavy brilliant flint, dolphin finial **200.00**
   Eureka pattern, heavy brilliant flint . **50.00**
   Laurel pattern, Skokie Green **9.00**
   Queen pattern, apple green **55.00**
   Rock Crystal pattern, clear **30.00**
   Star Rosetted pattern, clear **50.00**
   Strigil pattern, clear **30.00**
Tom and Jerry Set, serving bowl, twelve cups, white opal, red letters **95.00**
Toothbrush Holder, Skokie Green **18.00**
Toothpick Holder
   Aztec pattern **20.00**
   Figural, hat shape, vaseline **35.00**

Gothic pattern, clear, ruby stained, scalloped rim **85.00**
Rock Crystal pattern, clear **35.00**
Tumbler
   Eugenia pattern, heavy brilliant flint, ftd **40.00**
   Eureka pattern, heavy brilliant flint, ftd **25.00**
   Gladiator pattern
      Cobalt Blue, gold trim **48.00**
      Green, gold trim **32.00**
   Gothic pattern, clear **20.00**
   Queen pattern, blue **35.00**
   Ribbed Palm pattern **70.00**
   Rock Crystal pattern, clear, ftd **20.00**
   Strigil pattern, clear, ftd **20.00**
Vase
   8½" h, triangular, relief molded nude woman, latticework background, Skokie Green **135.00**
   11" h, Rock Crystal pattern, amber . **75.00**
Vinegar Bottle, Eugenia pattern, heavy brilliant flint **25.00**
Whiskey Tumbler, orig coaster, Bottoms Up
   Clear **110.00**
   French Ivory **120.00**
   Skokie Green **115.00**
Wine
   Colonial pattern, green **40.00**
   Eugenia pattern, heavy brilliant flint **35.00**
   Eureka pattern, heavy brilliant flint . **30.00**
   Gothic pattern, clear **15.00**
   Queen pattern, canary yellow **30.00**
   Rock Crystal pattern, clear **16.00**
   Star Rosetted pattern, clear **45.00**
   Strigil pattern, clear **20.00**
   Sunk Buttons pattern, blue **38.00**

MERCURY GLASS

History: Mercury glass is a light bodied, double walled glass that was "silvered" by applying a solution of silver nitrate to the inside of the object through a hole in the base of the formed object. F. Hale Thomas, London, patented the method in 1849. In 1855 the New England Glass Co. filed a patent for the same type of process. Other American glassmakers soon followed. The glass reached the height of its popularity in the early 20th century.

Atomizer, dec colored floral bud shaped glass stopper **48.00**
Bottle, 7½" h, 4¼" d, bulbous, flashed amber panel cut neck, etched grapes and leaves dec, corked metal stopper, c1840 .... **165.00**
Bowl
   4¾" d, enameled floral dec, gold luster interior **50.00**

6" d, enameled white floral dec 40.00

Cake Stand, 8" d, pedestal base, emb floral dec 75.00

Candlesticks, pr
4" d, plain 40.00
5½" d, enameled white floral dec, domed base 65.00
8" h, baluster 130.00
11" h, enameled floral dec 125.00
12¾" h, baluster, domed circular foot, amber, enameled floral sprigs 300.00

Candy Dish, cov, 8¼" h, 4¼" d, pedestal base, clear glass domed cov .. 40.00

Carafe, 12" h, 5½" d, mushroom stopper, dated 1909 .... 50.00

Christmas Ornament, 7" d ball, brass collar and hanger, c1890 .... 50.00

Compote, 7" h, 6½" d, enameled white floral dec, gold luster interior 65.00

Creamer
6" h, etched grapevine dec, applied clear handle 115.00
6½" h, etched ferns, applied clear handle, Sandwich 125.00

Cup and Saucer, etched floral dec 60.00

Garniture, 14" h, baluster, raised circular molded foot, everted rim, enameled foliate motif 215.00

Goblet
6⅞" h, silver, etched Vintage pattern, gold luster interior 50.00
7½" h, Ivy pattern, engraved grape leaves and grapes 145.00

Inkwell, two mercury wells, glass stand 75.00

Mug, 2⅞" h, silver, applied clear handle 30.00

Perfume Bottle, emerald green, cut and enamel dec, orig stopper 225.00

Pitcher
6" h, bulbous, etched fern dec, applied clear handle 150.00
9¾" h, 5½" d, bulbous, panel cut neck, engraved lacy florals and leaves, applied clear handle, c1840 200.00
12½" h, bulbous, applied clear handle 185.00

Rose Bowl
3¼" h, crimped edge, enamel floral dec 45.00
5" h, gold luster interior 60.00

Salt, master
1¼" h, 1¾" d, silver, three applied clear feet 35.00
2⅝" h, ftd, applied floral dec, gold luster interior 45.00
3" h, ftd, enameled floral dec 40.00

Spooner, Vintage pattern 72.00

Sugar, cov, 6¼" h, 4¼" d, low foot, enameled white foliage dec, knob finial 35.00

Sweetmeat Dish, cov, 4" d, 7½" h, pedestal base, clear cov 45.00

Tazza, 5¾" d, 2¾" h, etched birds and leaves dec 65.00

Tiebacks, pr
3¼" d, etched grapes, vines, and leaves, pewter shanks 65.00
4" d, etched budding iris and scrolls 90.00

Toothpick Holder
3½" h, gold, pedestal base 35.00
5" h, gold, pedestal base, etched ferns 45.00

Urn, 13" h, baluster shape, marked "Harnish & Co, London" 250.00

Candlestick, silver, hand painted floral dec, green leaves, white scroll, 8¼" h, $35.00.

Vase
4¾" h, silver, sanded foliage dec ... 45.00
8" h, cut to show emerald glass, marked "Harnish & Co, London, Pat" 95.00
8¾" h, emerald green, hand painted floral dec, c1890, pr 185.00
9½" h, floral bands, enameled scene of castle on front 65.00
9¾" h, cylindrical, raised circular foot, everted rim, bright enameled yellow, orange, and blue floral sprays and insects, pr 225.00
10¼" h, paneled sides, frosted palm trees, flowers, gold luster interior, pr 195.00
10½" h, cylindrical, hand painted floral and leaf band around center .. 110.00
12" h, ribbed, emerald green, enameled floral and bird dec 125.00
13" h, trumpet shape, enameled panel of orange, yellow, green, and blue floral clusters and butterflies 220.00

Wig Stand, 10¼" h, discolored stem .. 90.00

Wine, engraved Vintage dec, amber interior 100.00

Witch Ball, emerald green, attached base 185.00

MILK GLASS

History: Opaque white glass attained its greatest popularity at the end of the 19th century. American glass manufacturers made opaque white tablewares as a substitute for costly European china and glass. Other opaque colors, e.g., blue and green, were made. As the Edwardian era began, milk glass expanded into the novelty field.

The surge of popularity in milk glass subsided after World War I. However, milk glass continues to be made in the 20th century. Some modern products are reissues and reproductions of early forms. This presents a significant problem for collectors, although it is partially obviated by patent dates or company markings on the originals and by the telltale signs of age.

Collectors favor milk glass from the pre–World War I era, especially animal covered dishes. The most prolific manufacturers of these animal covers were Atterbury, Challinor–Taylor, Flaccus, and McKee.

References: E. McCamley Belknap, *Milk Glass,* Crown Publishers, 1949, out–of–print; Regis F. and Mary F. Ferson, *Yesterday's Milk Glass Today,* published by author, 1981; Regis F. and Mary F. Ferson, *Today's Prices For Yesterday's Milk Glass,* privately printed, 1985; S. T. Millard, *Opaque Glass,* Wallace–Homestead, 1975, 4th edition.

Collectors' Club: National Milk Glass Collectors Society, 1113 Birchwood Drive, Garland, TX, 75043.

Museum: Houston Antique Museum, Chattanooga, TN.

Notes: There are many so–called McKee animal covered dishes. Caution must be exercised in evaluating pieces because some authentic covers were not signed. Further, many factories have made, and many still are making, split rib bases with McKee–like animal covers or with different animal covers. There also is disagreement among collectors on the issue of flared vs. unflared bases. The prices for McKee pieces as given are for authentic items with either the cover or base signed.

Pieces are cross referenced to the Ferson's and Belknap's books by the (F—) or (B—) marking at the end of a listing.

Animal Dish, cov
  Collie, floral base, old gold paint, sgd "Vallerystahl" on base **265.00**
  Deer, fallen tree base, sgd "E. C. Flaccus Co, Wheeling, WV" (F34) ... **175.00**
  Fish, 8¾" l, walking, divided horizontally, five central fins support body, detailed scales, red glass eyes (B167b) **175.00**

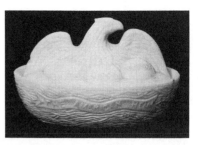

Animal Dish, cov, eagle on nest, white, banner embossed "The American Hen," eggs embossed "Porto Rica, Cuba, and Phillippines," $90.00.

Hen
  6¾" l, stand–up ribbing, lay down type scalloped edge, chain border on underside **100.00**
  7½" l, lacy base, head turned to left, marbleized white and deep blue, Atterbury (F8) **150.00**
Lamb, octagonal picket base, blue body, white head, Westmoreland (F87) **90.00**
Pintail Duck, basketweave base, traces of old paint, numbered **50.00**
Quail, scroll base **60.00**
Rabbit, patent date on base, Atterbury (F48) **150.00**
Robin with Berry (F217) **45.00**
Setter, white base, sgd "Flaccus," repair to tail **145.00**
Squirrel, acorn base (F15) **125.00**
Swan, closed neck, basketweave base (M278) **75.00**
Turkey, nest base (F62) **85.00**
Bon Bon, scoop shape, Eagle Glass Co, 1899 (F597) **35.00**
Bottle, figural
  Bear, 10¾" h, facing forward, sitting, forelegs folded across chest (F132) **120.00**
  Duck, 11½" h, vertical bill, head, and neck form flanged opening, rimmed oval for label, no closure, Atterbury (F433) **350.00**
Bowl
  Arch Border pattern, 8" d, alternating wide curved arches and interlocking narrow pointed arches, Challinor, Taylor (B100a) **45.00**
  Ball and Chain pattern, 8" d, openwork rim (B100b) **45.00**
  Cut Star pattern, 7¼" d, blue, scalloped edge, twelve rayed stars (F289) **75.00**
  King's Crown, 8" d, basketweave pattern, slanted sides, vertical bar pattern on base, eight triangular points forming crown (B1078b) **65.00**

Daisy pattern, 8¼" d, all over leaves and flower pattern, repeated on inner base, open scalloped edge (F165) **80.00**

Bread Tray, basketweave border, motto "Give Us This Day Our Daily Bread" inscribed on rim, Atterbury (F345) .. **65.00**

Butter Dish, cov

Crossed Fern pattern, 6" d, animal claw grasping ball feet and finial, scalloped edge, Atterbury (F232) . **65.00**

Gooseberry pattern, narrow beaded edges, band of fruit on cov and base, berry finial, Sandwich (F248) **90.00**

Roman Cross pattern, 4⅞" l, sq ftd base, curves outwards toward top, cube shape finial (F240) **50.00**

Calling Card Receiver, bird, back view, wings extended over fanned tail, head resting on leaf, detailed feather pattern (F669) **130.00**

Candlestick

3⅝" h, clown, bust rises from wide curved neck ruffle (F129) **65.00**

7¾" h, swirl, ribbing twists counterclockwise form base, column, cup, and wax guard (F522) **35.00**

Candy Container, figural, top hat, tin threaded lid (W12A) **40.00**

Celery Vase

Blackberry pattern, 6⅝" h, scalloped rim, plain band above vertical surface, low stem rising from circular base, Hobbs Brockunier (F317) ... **95.00**

Burred Hobnail pattern **40.00**

Children's Dish, cov butter dish, Versailles pattern, emb roses, raised scalloped draping, blue trim, Ditheridge, c1900, (F591) **150.00**

Compote

Atlas pattern, lacy edge, blue **180.00**

Blackberry pattern, 9" h, large figural blackberry finial on cov, Hobbs Brockunier (B121) **150.00**

Chick and Eggs, 11" h, pedestal, chick emerging from heaped eggs, finial cov, mounted on curved tripod, central support, rounded lacy edge base, emb Atterbury patent date, Aug 6, 1889 inside cov (F362) ... **175.00**

Lattice Edge pattern, 8½" d, floral dec, Daisy and Button type pattern pedestal base, Challinor, Taylor (M116a) **75.00**

Condiment Set, Forget–Me–Not pattern, salt and pepper, 5⅛" h cruet, trefoil tray, bulbous shape, six lobed, floral pattern, blue, Challinor, Taylor (F164) **190.00**

Conestoga Wagon, five rib type **100.00**

Creamer

Beaded Circle pattern, applied handle (F322) **55.00**

Blackberry pattern **40.00**

Burred Hobnail pattern **40.00**

Forget–Me–Not pattern **35.00**

Paneled Wheat pattern, 5⅞" h, Hobbs Brockunier (F255) **50.00**

Roman Cross pattern, 4⅝" h (F239) . **40.00**

Sunflower pattern (B82b) **40.00**

Dresser Box, cov, horseshoe, horse, floral dec **25.00**

Egg Cup, cov, 4¼" h, bird, round, fluted, Atterbury (F130) **130.00**

Fish Set, figural fish platter, four serving dishes, emb patent date, Atterbury .. **225.00**

Inkwell, horseshoe, circular inkwell in center, pen rests (F449) **35.00**

Jar, cov, 6½" h, figural, eagle, "Old Abe," rests upright, leafy base, "E Pluribus Unum" on encircled banner, gray (F568) **95.00**

Lamp

Columbian Coin, 8¼" h, six coin size medallions on base (F512) **275.00**

Goddess of Liberty, 11" h, bust, three stepped hexagonal base, clear and frosted font, brass screw connector, patent dated, Atterbury (F329) ... **200.00**

Match Holder

Indian Head (B219) **115.00**

Jolly Jester, 4¼" h, patent date on rear (F201) **85.00**

Minstrel Boy **125.00**

Trilby, patent date, reversed "9," small chip **100.00**

Match Safe, 4½" h, baby in hat, corrugated striker, black hat, (F534) **310.00**

Mug

Ivy in Snow pattern, 3" h **32.00**

Liberty Bell, Centennial dates emb between two bells (F674) **165.00**

Mustard, cov, bull's head (F14) **135.00**

Pickle Dish, 9⅝" l, fish, realistic detailed scales, head, and fins, tail handle, Atterbury patent date June 4, 72 (F360A) **25.00**

Pitcher

Birds on Branch pattern, trio of small birds on leafy branch, cold painted dec (F519) **72.00**

Dart and Bar pattern, 8" h, blue, rect handle, ftd (B85a) **95.00**

Fish, 7¼" h, finely detailed, Atterbury (F328) **165.00**

Plaque, Abraham Lincoln, 8¼" l, oval, Kemple (F560) **165.00**

Plate

Cats, 6" d, two cats form upper edge, bracketed dog head, open work swirled leaves, emb "He's all right" (B20d) **90.00**

Contrary Mule, 7½" d, mule pulling back on rein, Westmoreland (B271, row 5a) **35.00**

Eagle pattern, 8" d, stars border, Fenton **40.00**
Easter Ducks, 6¼" d, four ducks below work "Easter," patterned edge, Dithridge (B24d) **40.00**
Jefferson Davis, 9¼" d, center emb with bust of Davis facing left, backward "C" border, Civil War Centennial commemorative plate, LE Smith Glass Co (F554) **48.00**
Roger Williams Memorial, 7¼" d, Williams monument emb in center, flags, eagles, and fleur de lis border, patent date, Westmoreland (F639) **125.00**
Platter
 Blaine Logan Campaign, 13⅛" l, emb bust of Blaine faces Logan, notched border (F564) **350.00**
 Retriever 13¼" l, swimming dog pursuing duck through cattails, lily pad border (B53) **70.00**
Salt Shaker
 Atterbury Dredge, 3⅜" h, combination octagonal paneled salt and pepper shaker shaped as small cov stein, (F415) **75.00**
 Brownie, 2⅜" h, Palmer Cox Brownies in different poses on each of four vertical sides (F448) **90.00**
 Diamond Point and Leaf pattern, 2¾" h, blue (F489) **40.00**
Spooner
 Beaded Circle pattern, 5⅝" h, scalloped, ftd, flint, attributed to Sandwich (F321) **50.00**
 Monkey pattern, 5⅛" h, cylinder shape, scalloped top, seated monkeys molded around circumference (F275) **115.00**
 Paneled Flower, 4⅝" h, ribbing separates six diamond point panels, stylized floral dec, scalloped edges, Challinor, Taylor (F284) **40.00**
Sugar, cov
 Almond Thumbprint, 7½" h, large scalloped edges (F367) **115.00**

Sugar Castor, Panelled Sprig, 4½" h, $55.00.

Ceres pattern, 7¼" h, cameo profiles in beaded circles, leafy sprays, bust finial (B217) **75.00**
Nine Panel pattern, Ihmsen Glass Co, flared bowl, factory product on low feet panel, cov fits inside base edge (F670) **400.00**
Sunflower pattern (B82b) **50.00**
Trumpet Vine pattern, fire painted, sgd "SV" **65.00**
Sugar Shaker
 Netted Oak, 4¼" h, oak leaf centered on netted panels, green top band, Northwood (F495) **75.00**
 Royal Oak pattern **75.00**
Syrup
 Alba pattern, 6½" h, enameled floral sprays, Ditheridge (F139) **75.00**
 Beehive, 5⅝" h, emb beehive center, ribbed top and base, strap handle (F372) **145.00**
 Bellflower pattern, single vine, dated, Collins & Wright (F155) **225.00**
Toothpick Holder, Tramp Shoe (F194) . **45.00**
Tumbler, Royal Oak pattern, orig fired paint, green band **45.00**
Whimsey, rowboat, patent date, Atterbury **37.50**
Wine, Feather pattern **35.00**

MILLEFIORI

History: Millefiori (thousand flowers) is an ornamental glass composed of bundles of colored glass rods fused to become canes. The canes were pulled while still ductile to the desired length, sliced, arranged in a pattern and again fused together. The Egyptians developed this technique in the first century B.C.; it was revived in the 1880s.

Reproduction Alert: Millefiori items, such as paperweights, cruets, toothpicks, etc., are being made by many modern companies.

Bowl
 2" d, pink, green, and white canes, applied clear handles **45.00**
 4" d, blue and white canes, applied clear handles **80.00**
 8" d, 2½" h, tricorn, scalloped, folded sides, amethyst and silver deposit **125.00**
Box, cov, 3" d, multicolored **125.00**
Creamer
 4" h, white ground, scattered millefiori, applied handle **250.00**
 4¼" h, 3" d, white and cobalt blue canes, yellow centers, satin finish **100.00**
Cruet, bulbous, multicolored canes, applied camphor handle, matching stopper **100.00**

Cup and Saucer, white and cobalt blue
  canes, yellow centers, satin finish .. **85.00**
Dish, 5" d, octagonal, blue and white
  canes **125.00**
Door Knob, 2½" d, paperweight, center
  cane dated 1852, New England Glass
  Co **375.00**
Goblet, 7½" h, multicolored canes,
  clear stem and base **150.00**
Inkwell, 4½" h, sgd "Paul Ysart" **190.00**
Jug, 2¼" h, multicolored canes, applied
  clear handle **90.00**

**Miniature Lamp, 8½" to top of chimney,
$375.00.**

Miniature Lamp, 11" h, mushroom cap
  shade, matching glass lamp shaft, red,
  blue, and white, gilt metal "Bryant"
  electrical fittings **1,200.00**
Perfume Bottle, round body, seven portrait canes, orig metal mountings,
  Venetian, c1830–40 .... **425.00**
Pitcher, 6½" h, multicolored canes, applied candy cane handle **165.00**
Rose Bowl, 6" h, crimped top, cased,
  white lining **145.00**
Slipper, 5" l, multicolored canes, camphor ruffle and heel **135.00**
Sugar, cov, 4" h, 3½" d, white canes,
  yellow centers, satin finish **115.00**
Toothpick Holder, ruffled top, multicolored canes, c1890 .... **200.00**
Vase
  3½" h, cabinet, waisted, ruffled top,
    light blue, cobalt blue, medium
    blue, and white canes, four applied
    knob handles **35.00**
  4" h, multicolored canes, applied
    double handles **100.00**
  5½" h, purple bands, white oval lines
    and bands, red flowers, yellow cen-
    ters **165.00**
  8" h, ruffled rim, multicolored canes,
    applied clear handles **180.00**
  11" h, bulbous, yellow and green
    canes, red dots **125.00**

MINIATURE LAMPS

History: Miniature oil and kerosene lamps, often
called "night lamps," are diminutive replicas of
larger lamps. Simple and utilitarian in design,
miniature lamps found a place in the parlor (as
"courting" lamps), hallway, childrens' rooms,
and sickrooms.

Miniature lamps are found in many glass types
from amberina to satin glass. Miniature lamps
measure 2½ to 12 inches in height with the prin-
ciple parts being the base, collar, burner, chimney, and shade. In 1877 both L. J. Atwood and
L. H. Olmsted patented burners for miniature
lamps. Their burners made the lamps into a popular household accessory.

Study a lamp carefully to make certain all parts
are original; married pieces are common. Reproductions abound.

References: Ann Gilbert McDonald, *Evolution of
the Night Lamp*, Wallace–Homestead, 1979;
Frank R. & Ruth E. Smith, *Miniature Lamps,*
Schiffer Publishing Ltd., 1981, 6th printing; Ruth
E. Smith, *Miniature Lamps - II,* Schiffer Publishing
Ltd., 1982; John F. Solverson, *Those Fascinating
Little Lamps*, Antique Publications, 1988; John F.
Solverson (comp.), *"Those Fascinating Little
Lamps"/Miniature Lamps*, (includes prices for
Smith numbers) *Value Guide*, Antique Publica-
tions, 1988.

Note: The numbers given below refer to the figure numbers found in the Smith books.

Figure III–I, satin, red, Artichoke pattern, nutmeg burner **550.00**
Figure VII–II, satin, rainbow, Kosmos
  Brenner burner, 10½" h **2,700.00**
Figure VIII–I, cameo, white maidenhair
  fern and butterflies, citron ground ..**5,400.00**
Figure XVIII–II, overshot, frosted, house
  scene, 5½" **750.00**
Figure XXIX–II, satin, swirled emb
  ribbed rose shade, emb scene, sterling silver pedestal base, 13½" h ... **700.00**
#9–I, opaque white, Fire Fly, orig dated
  burner **225.00**
#11–I, milk glass pedestal base and
  shade, clear pressed font, Sandwich,
  6¾" h **245.00**
#20–II, blue glass shade, Aladdin type **265.00**
#25–II, cranberry, Berger Lamp **125.00**
#28–II, milk glass, Glow Lamp, melon
  ribbed **150.00**
#29–I, cobalt blue glass font, emb
  "Nutmeg," narrow brass band forming handle, nutmeg burner, clear glass
  chimney, 2¾" d base **100.00**
#30–I, green glass shade, tin holder,
  acorn burner **115.00**
#40–I, opalescent, cranberry, Spanish

Lace pattern, applied handle, hornet burner 315.00

#49–I, cobalt blue, Little Butter Cup, 2" h, pr 250.00

#49–II, Little Banner 85.00

#50–I, opaline, log cabin, hornet burner 725.00

#54–I, custard, emb brass band, iron ring handle, nutmeg burner 100.00

#59–II, clear, emb "Vienna" 125.00

#78–I, nickel plated, wall type, emb "Comet," blue glass beehive chimney shade, 7¼" h 75.00

#82–II, milk glass, Block pattern, matching globe, 6½" h 100.00

#86–I, brass, double student lamp,white bristol shades 435.00

#89–I, brass, double student lamp, orig opaque white shades, 9¾" h 500.00

#95–II, clear, applied handle 55.00

#98–II, clear, ribs, applied handle ... 100.00

#100–II, dark blue, emb star 110.00

#106–I, clear, block font and base, nutmeg burner missing 75.00

#109–I, green, Beaded Heart pattern, acorn burner, clear glass chimney, 5½" h 190.00

#112–I, amber, Bull's Eye pattern, nutmeg burner, clear glass chimney, 5" h 100.00

#116–I, amber, Fishscale pattern, nutmeg burner, clear glass chimney ... 135.00

#118–I, amber, Buckle pattern, 8½" h 125.00

#121–I, mercury glass, acorn shape, emb acorn cap base, acorn burner . 115.00

#125–I, milk glass, red paint, ball shaped shade, emb flowers and designs, acorn burner, clear glass chimney, 7¼" h 135.00

#143–I, frosted amber, Lincoln Drape pattern, acorn burner 125.00

#144–I, clear, Westmoreland, acorn burner 125.00

#156–I, milk glass, emb flower and scrolls, 8" h 115.00

#161–II, emb Prism pattern, Atterbury 125.00

#165–II, clear, fine ribbing, acorn burner, patent collar 100.00

#166–I, clear, Greek Key pattern, acorn burner 80.00

#184–I, milk glass, beaded and emb design, blue painted highlights on base and globe–chimney shade, hornet burner 200.00

#184–II, Swirl, orig reflector 45.00

#190–I, milk glass, Block and Dot pattern, 7¾" h 135.00

#192–I, clear, Block pattern, hand painted blue and green flowers, acorn burner, 6½" h 60.00

#193–I, good dec, all orig 165.00

#203–I, opaque white, Plume pattern, gilt dec, nutmeg burner, 8¼" h 115.00

#204–II, blue, camphor shade 100.00

#213–I, clear, ruby stain, Chrysanthemum and Swirl pattern base and globe, hornet burner, 9" h 425.00

#215–I, milk glass, emb beaded panels and boats, windmill and lighthouse on base, vertical roses of beading on globe–chimney shade, hornet burner, 7¾" h 325.00

Lamp, Consolidated Lamp and Glass Co, c1894, nutmeg burner 430.00

#221–I, milk glass, blue, emb floral dec, hornet burner 400.00

#230–I, milk glass, Acanthus pattern, fired on yellow dec, base marked "Buc. PA/1898," 8½" h 175.00

#231–I, satin, Drape pattern, globe shade, clear glass chimney, nutmeg burner, 8⅝" h

Green 315.00

Red 275.00

#250–I, milk glass, Diana pattern, painted dec, nutmeg burner 100.00

#267–II, Pairpoint, all orig, sgd "Dresden" on base 400.00

#276–I, milk glass, Pineapple in a Basket pattern, fired on green, nutmeg burner 330.00

#286–I, Cosmos pattern, 9" h, electrified 75.00

#287–I, overshot, apricot shaded to clear, tulip molded base and shade, clear glass chimney, nutmeg burner, 8½" h 650.00

529–I, cased, pink, white candy stripe, 7¾" h, $745.00.

#317–I, milk glass, pink and yellow flowers, shaded green ground 300.00

#368–I, spatter glass, molded Beaded Rib pattern, hornet burner 400.00

#368–II, milk glass, blue bands, pink flowers, green leaves, Dietz Night Light burner 460.00

#369–I, spatter glass, tortoiseshell coloring, 8¼" h 250.00

#390–I, cased glass, yellow, glossy finish, melon ribbed, nutmeg burner . . **500.00**
ribbing, hand painted pink, yellow, and green florals, clear glass chimney, nutmeg burner **285.00**
#393–II, peg, brass saucer, applied handle, milk glass font, nutmeg burner **70.00**
#394–I, satin, blue, puffy diamond quilted pattern base and umbrella shade, nutmeg burner, clear glass chimney, 8″ h **475.00**
#400–I, satin, pink, Gone with the Wind style shape, Beaded Drape pattern, 10″ h **385.00**
#403–I, opalescent, Beaded Drape pattern, nutmeg burner, 9½″ h
Cranberry **350.00**
Ruby **285.00**
#409–II, cranberry, threaded base **125.00**
#421–II, milk glass, banquet style shape, three tiers, brass pedestal base **550.00**
#428–II, Burmese shade and chimney, sterling silver sq pedestal ribbed base, Hinks & Son burner **925.00**
#439–I, Amberina glass, hornet burner **515.00**
#452–II, Bristol glass, black wrought iron pedestal holder **325.00**
#459–II, satin, red shaded to pink, emb scrolled leaves and swirl, 10″ h **1,650.00**
#460–I, cranberry, white enamel floral dec, 11⅝″ **450.00**
#477–I, sapphire blue, hobnail, 7¼″ h **375.00**
#482–I, Daisy and Cube pattern, nutmeg burner, 8″ h
Clear **225.00**
Vaseline **355.00**
#483–II, satin, light blue, enameled tulips and leaves, gold trim **425.00**
#488–II, amber, applied handle **75.00**
#508–I, opalescent, Spanish Lace pattern, nutmeg burner **350.00**
#538–I, Amberina glass, paneled, amber feet, 9¼″ h **1,500.00**
#546–I, blue, Swirl pattern, 8½″ h . . . **500.00**
#600–I, satin, Raindrop pattern, mother of pearl, four petal feet, 8¾″ **600.00**
#610–I, Burmese, Webb, brown and green foliage, red berries **4,000.00**

MONART GLASS

History: Monart glass is a heavy, simple shaped art glass in which colored enamels are suspended in the glass during the glass making process. This technique was originally developed by the Ysart family in Spain in 1923. John Moncrief, a Scottish glassmaker, discovered the glass while vacationing in Spain, recognized the beauty and

potential market, and began production in his Perth glassworks in 1924.

The name "Monart" is derived from the surnames Moncrief and Ysart. Two types of Monart were manufactured: a "commercial" line which incorporated colored enamels and a touch of aventurine in crystal, and the "art" line in which the suspended enamels formed designs such as feathers or scrolls. Monart glass, in most instances, is not marked. The factory used paper labels.

Collectors' Club: Monart & Vasart Collectors Club, 869 Cleveland St., Oakland, CA 94606.

Basket, brown to light tan opal vertical striations, Cluthra type **585.00**
Bowl
9″ d, Aventurine, blue, mottled brown, and goldstone, pebbled texture **145.00**
10½″ d, white, gray crackle, yellow and green flecks, oxblood red base and rim **165.00**
11½″ d, mottled orange and green . **185.00**
Candlestick, two shades of green, goldstone mica, paper label **95.00**
Lamp Shade, 6½″ d, white opal **85.00**

Vase, green rim shaded to clear to brown, green pedestal, 8½″ h, $195.00.

Vase
5⅞″ h, 5⅝″ d, mottled shades of blue, goldstone flecks, orig paper label . **195.00**
6½″ h, mottled shades of red and blue, white lining **190.00**
7″ h, 7″ d, gray, blue, and white swirls on dark red ground, orig paper label **195.00**
8½″ h, goldstone shading to clear, cylindrical, flaring rim, Scottish Cluthra **195.00**
8½″ h, 8″ d, blue, silver, mica, orange streaks, small bubbles **250.00**

11" h, mottled orange shades to deep orange at flared rim **250.00**
14" h, bulbous, tapered, extended neck, flared rim, blue shaded to pink, gold highlights, Cluthra **625.00**
14½" h, blue iridescent ground, treebark texture **195.00**
16" h, green, flecked neck, orange body, dark inclusions, gold Cluthra centers **450.00**

MONT JOYE GLASS

History: Mont Joye is a type of glass produced by Saint-Hilaire, Touvier, de Varreaux & Company at their glassworks in Pantin, France. Most pieces were lightly acid etched to give them a frosted appearance and decorated with enameled floral decorations. All pieces listed are frosted, unless otherwise noted.

Rose Bowl, acid etched, enameled purple violets, gold stems, gold dec, pinched sides, 3¾" h, 4¼" d, $175.00.

Bowl, 3¾" d, frosted ground, enameled floral dec, sgd **275.00**
Ewer, cov, cameo cutting, crystal, green and gold, brass spout and handle, removable cov, artist sgd "Cristalle Rie Depantin" **500.00**
Jar, cov, 7" h, cylindrical, crystal ground, etched, enameled iris, gilt leaves, crystal knop, gilt factory mark, c1900 .... **250.00**
Pitcher, 10" h, amethyst frosted ground, enameled aqua, blue, pink, and gold flowers, sgd **250.00**
Rose Bowl, 4¼" d, frosted ground, enameled purple violets, gold stems, gold dec, pinched sides **175.00**
Vase
5⅛" h, spherical, cylindrical neck and foot, frosted ground, etched and gilt

oak leaves and acorns, gilt signature **195.00**
5½" h, Nile green frosted ground, gold enameled leaves, enameled lilies of the valley floral dec **375.00**
5¾" h, green glitter body, gold leaf painted dec, applied opal glass spheres **375.00**
6½" h, green frosted ground, cut poppies, enameled in crimson and gilt, sgd **250.00**
7½" h, dark green satin ground, enameled pink iris dec **400.00**
8" h, light turquoise ground, etched iris dec, gold highlights, acid etched frosting, gold band around crimped edge **375.00**
8½" h, cameo, icy frosted ground, enameled leaves, deep red poppies, sgd **430.00**
9" h, frosted ground, enameled purple orchids, green leaves **145.00**
10" h
Amber ground, enameled silver and gold flowers **300.00**
Crystal ground, gold leaves, enameled purple violets **350.00**
Crystal shaded to opalescent green ground, bulbous, narrow neck, thistle dec in natural colors, highlighted in gold **275.00**
11" h, tomato red ground, lacy gold dec, enameled iris and foliage dec **245.00**
13¾" h, flattened ovoid shape, cameo, crystal ground, etched, molded and enameled iris, gilt leaves, c1900 .... **325.00**
18" h, green frosted ground, enameled purple flowers, gold leaves, sgd **250.00**
25¾" h, flaring waisted bottle form, green metallic flaked ground, overlaid foliate dec, MOP beads, base stamped "Mont Joye," c1910 ....**1,200.00**

MORGANTOWN GLASS WORKS

History: Morgantown Glass Works, Morgantown, West Virginia, was founded in the late 19th century. By 1903 it was reorganized and the name changed to the Economy Tumbler Company. The blown tumbler lines were expanded to include pressed, blown, cut, and etched patterns. Morgantown also sold blanks to other companies for finishing.

With the introduction of color in 1924, the name was changed to Economy Glass Company and its wares were marked under the "Old Morgantown" label. In 1939 the name Morgantown

Glass Works was revived. Additional reorganizations occurred after 1940. The factory, no longer bearing the Morgantown name, closed in the early 1980s.

Morgantown Glass Works produced glass in a wide range of colors during the 1920s and 1930s. Some distinctive color combinations were red and black, yellow and black, pink and magenta, rose and rose amber, and color and crystal. Popular items were beverage and liquor sets, tumblers, and stemware.

A distinctive characteristic of many stemware pieces is a decorative insert between the bowl and the base, e.g. a smooth or faceted ball or an open square or diamond. Other stem variations were branched, beautifully finished columns, or twists. Stemware often had clear bowls and colored stems or the reverse arrangement.

Reference: *Old Morgantown, Catalogue of Glassware, 1931,* catalog reprint available from Old Morgantown Glass Collectors' Guide.

Collectors' Club: Old Morgantown Glass Collectors' Guild, P. O. Box 894, Morgantown, WV 26507.

Bowl, Connoisseur pattern
Crystal, 10¼" d	15.00
Stiegel Green, 12" d, ftd, bubble stem	18.00

Candlestick
Sharon pattern, crystal	12.00
Steel pattern, burgundy, 8¾" h	40.00

Candy Jar, cov, Old English pattern,
crystal, ftd	20.00

Champagne
Cressey cut, crystal	10.00
Old English pattern, ruby	12.00

Cocktail
American Modern pattern, Russel
Wright, seafoam, 2½" h	22.00
Rooster stem, crystal, 3½ oz	12.00
Venetian pattern, red	22.00

Cordial
American Modern pattern, Russel
Wright, seafoam, 2" h	35.00
Cobalt blue, crystal wafer stem	14.00

Golf ball dec
Cobalt blue	28.00
Spanish red	30.00

Goblet
American Modern pattern, Russel Wright
Coral, 4" h	30.00
Seafoam	30.00
Art Moderne pattern, crystal bowl, black stem	35.00
Button pattern, crystal	15.00
Dancing Girl pattern, blue	48.00
Ducal pattern, crystal	18.50
Ebony pattern, crystal, octagonal ...	8.50
Fairwin pattern, crystal	18.00
Golf Ball dec, cobalt blue	32.00

Old English pattern, ruby	12.50
Palm Optic pattern, pink	8.50
San Tog pattern, crystal	15.00
Square pattern, crystal	12.00
Virginia Etch, crystal, 7½" h, set of 6	100.00
Willow pattern, crystal	12.00

Iced Tea Tumbler
American Modern pattern, Russel Wright, 5" h
Chartreuse	18.00
Seafoam	20.00
El Mexicano pattern, amethyst	15.00
Spanish Red, crystal wafer stem, ftd, 6¼" h	22.00

Ivy Ball
Crystal, cut dec, 4" d	15.00
Peacock Blue, golf ball, 6¾" d	65.00

Jug, Old Bristol pattern	25.00

Juice Tumbler
American Modern pattern, Russel
Wright, chartreuse, 4" h	15.00
El Mexicano pattern, amethyst	10.00

Liquor Set, decanter, six glasses
Little King pattern, Ritz blue	70.00
Sparta pattern, rose	65.00

Martini Set, 9¾" h shaker, three 3" h ftd
tumblers, amethyst	30.00
Parfait, Old English pattern, crystal ...	15.00

Pitcher
Connoisseur pattern, crystal	25.00
Crinkle Amy pattern, crystal, tankard	95.00
Crinkle Pink pattern, crystal	95.00
Old Bristol pattern, Ritz blue	40.00
Peacock Optic pattern, green	25.00
Somerset pattern, Stiegel green	25.00

Plate
Ebony, octagonal	7.50
Palm Optic pattern, pink	5.00
Primrose Lane pattern, pink	7.50

Sherbet
American Modern pattern, Russel Wright, 2½" h
Coral	24.00
Gray	20.00
Seafoam	20.00
Button pattern, crystal	12.00
Cobalt Blue, crystal wafer stem and base	22.00
Crinkle Amy pattern, crystal	7.00
El Mexicano pattern, light blue	7.00
Marilyn pattern, crystal	8.00
Old English pattern, red, crystal stem	8.00
Radiant Stem, cobalt blue, "v" shape stem, set of 12	265.00
Simplicity pattern, crystal	7.50

Tumbler
American Modern pattern, Russel
Wright, seafoam, 4½" h	17.00

Crinkle Red pattern
4⅛" h, 7 oz	12.50
4¼" h, 11 oz	16.00
5⅛" h, 12 oz	20.00

El Mexicano pattern, amethyst 12.00
Palm Optic pattern, green 10.00
Pineapple Optic pattern 6.00
Square 6.00
Zombie pattern, 15 oz, set of 8 different colors 160.00
Vase
5⅞" h, crystal, trellis etching 18.00
6" h, green, oval 45.00
Wine
American Modern pattern, Russel Wright, 3" h
Coral 25.00
Gray 25.00
Seafoam 25.00
Art Moderne pattern, crystal bowl, black stem, wide optic bowl 32.00
Witch Ball, side opening
3½" d, crystal 30.00
6" d, crystal, ebony base 40.00

c1940

c1940

MOSER GLASS

History: Ludwig Moser (1833–1916) founded his polishing and engraving workshop in 1857 in Karlsbad (Karlovy Vary), Czechoslovakia. He employed many famous glass designers, e.g., Johann Hoffmann, Josef Urban, and Rudolf Miller. In 1900 Moser and his sons, Rudolf and Gustav, incorporated Ludwig Moser & Söhne.

Moser art glass included clear pieces with inserted blobs of colored glass, cut colored glass with classical scenes, cameo glass, and intaglio cut. Many inexpensive enameled pieces also were made.

In 1922 Leo and Richard Moser bought Meyr's Neffe, their biggest Bohemian rival in art glass. Moser executed many pieces for the Wiener Workstätte in the 1920s. The Moser glass factory continues to produce new items.

References: Gary Baldwin and Lee Carno, *Moser–Artistry In Glass: 1857–1938,* Antique Publications, 1988; Mural K. Charon and John Mareska, *Ludvik Moser, King of Glass: A Treasure Chest of Photographs And History,* published by author, 1984.

Bowl, 7¼" d, 5⅝" h, opalescent pink shaded ground, multicolored enameled oak leaves and foliage, applied lustered acorns, sgd in gold on base **1,200.00**

Pitcher, green shading to clear, blue and white flowers on brown twig, green leaves, clear handle, gold rim, 6¾" h, 5¼" w, $210.00.

Box, cov
3⅜" h, circular, deep purple ground, gold enameled fauns and maidens, fitted cov, four ball feet, etched "Made in Czechoslovakia Moser Karlsbad" 1,200.00
3½" d, 4" h, black amethyst ground, relief etched classical design, faceted knob and sides 125.00
4½" d, amethyst ground, multicolored enameled flowers and gold trim, amber applied glass salamander on lid, three salamanders form feet 650.00
6" d, 3¾" h, cranberry ground, white enameled woman carrying cornucopia and grapes, gold enameled vine and berries 650.00
Calling Card Holder
Cranberry ground, turquoise jewels, gold prunts, four scrolled feet 350.00
Crystal ground, two multicolored enameled birds of paradise in center, bird on ruffled rim 180.00
Centerpiece, 11" d, oval bowl, intaglio, emerald green shading to clear ground, sgd 200.00
Chalice, cov, 9½" h, amber and colorless ground, faceted, central landscape frieze, elk and grape carved cov 225.00
Cologne Bottle, 10¾" h, cranberry ground, gold leaves outlined in white, gold and black dots, white dotted blossoms, neck, base, and orig stopper heavily gold encrusted 400.00
Compote
4" h, 8¼" d, hollow base, pale amber ground, electric blue rigaree and four applied dec, interior dec of twelve painted leaves, brown branches, gold leaves, white cherries, matching branch on base ... 645.00

6⅝″ h, 7″ d, purple ground, gilt alle-
gorical figures, unsigned **245.00**
9½″ h, quatraform, crystal ground,
gilt enameled heavy scrollwork reserves, matching dec on pedestal
foot, crystal stem, pr **385.00**
Cordial, 1⅜″ h, cranberry ground bowl,
clear stem, multicolored enameled
flowers, bee, and insect dec on base   **85.00**
Cruet, 13″ h, pigeon blood ground,
eleven raised acorns, raised enameled
tracery branches and dragonfly, trefoil
spout, applied handle, orig paper label **1,800.00**
Decanter, 12½″ h, amber ground, all
over etching **250.00**
Demitasse Cup and Saucer, cranberry
ground, gilt enameled flowers, fruits,
acorns, and cameos, set of three ... **375.00**
Ewer
5¾″ h, 2¾″ d, crystal shaded to gold
ground, multicolored enameled
flowers and green leaves, pedestal
base, unsigned **275.00**
9″ h, cov, horn shape, aquamarine
ground, all over gold leaves, vines,
and flowers, pedestal base **915.00**
10¾″ h, cranberry ground, gold oak
leaves, lacy gold foliage, small applied glass acorns, pedestal foot,
ruffled top, applied clear handle,
unsigned **750.00**
Finger Bowl
6″ d, matching 7″ d underplate, scalloped, shaded pink to lavender
ground, gold, silver, and blue
enameled Arabesque dec, white
petit–point dec **975.00**
6½″ d, Alexandrite, matching underplate, sgd **95.00**
6¾″ d, quatraform, crystal ground,
gilt enameled heavy scrollwork and
floral dec, conforming undertrays,
set of six **1,320.00**
Flask, 7½″ l, powder horn shape, deep
cranberry ground, multicolored
enameled fern dec, brass spigot, fittings and orig chain **775.00**
Goblet, 5¾″ h, deep amethyst ground,
gold figures dec, pr **175.00**
Ice Cream Set, master bowl and four
serving bowls, clear shading to gold
ground, mermaid relief, gilt highlights **385.00**
Jar, cov, 7″ h, 5″ d, cranberry ground,
panels, gold tracery dec **195.00**
Juice Tumbler, emerald green ground,
nine applied acorns, two multicolored enameled bees and oak leaves,
unsigned **200.00**
Liqueur, 2½″ h, cranberry ground,
multicolored applied acorns and
leaves, sgd **200.00**

Liqueur Set, 11¾″ h liqueur bottle, four
stemmed 2¾″ h liqueurs, matching
tray, cranberry ground, lacy gold
enamel dec, multicolored enameled
flowers and green leaves, crystal bubble stopper, sgd **1,100.00**
Mug, 3¼″ h, emerald green ground,
multicolored oak leaves and bee, applied acorns **300.00**
Perfume Bottle
5″ h, emerald green ground, all over
floral dec, orig stopper **265.00**
6½″ h, 4¼″ d, Malachite, molded bottle and stopper, slab polished sides
and top **275.00**
Pitcher
8½″ h, amber ground, multicolored
enameled florals **200.00**
9½″ h, sq top, blue ground, gold dec,
sgd **200.00**
11¾″ h, bright transparent blue
ground, heavy gilding, enameled
fern fronds, bird, and insects, applied salamander handle **2,300.00**
Plate, 7⅜″ d, amberina ground, gold
dec **125.00**
Scent Bottle
3″ h, purple ground, prism cutting,
orig stopper **200.00**
5″ h, emerald green ground, multicolored leaves and berries, ball stopper **165.00**
11″ h, cranberry ground, leaves,
white and gold dec **400.00**
Sherry, 4¼″ h, crystal ground, gold and
white beading, knobbed stem, wafer
base **200.00**
Sweetmeat Dish, round, cranberry
ground, engraved, gold band **225.00**
Tumbler
3½″ h, octagonal, ruby cut to clear
ground, gold dec **60.00**
3⅞″ h, thin, delicate crystal ground,
hand painted, medallion of mis-
chievous cupid teasing bashful
maiden **485.00**
4″ h, lavender ground, vines, leaves,
berries, and floral work, heavy gilting **175.00**
Vase
3″ h, cobalt blue ground, gold bands,
Oriental woman **150.00**
4⅛″ h, shaded opalescent apricot
ground, multicolored enameled
oak leaves, applied lustered glass
acorns, sgd **250.00**
6½″ h, amber ground, applied fish
dec **600.00**
7¾″ h, long neck shading from emerald green to clear ground, bulbous base, gold and platinum floral
dec, diamond point signature **350.00**

8" h, chocolate brown ground, jeweled, gold trim **225.00**
8¼" h, quatraform bulbous shape, crystal ground, heavy Baroque gilt enameled scrolling elements, delicate blue forget–me–nots and monogram, pr **990.00**
8½" h, cranberry ground, lady playing harp, heavy gold dec, handles **250.00**
8¾" h, Malachite, molded nude women, vineyard background, faceted borders **500.00**
9½" h, emerald green ground, multicolored florals, applied gold bees, sgd **475.00**

Vase, clear green glass, enamel floral dec, pinched top, 10" h, $215.00.

11" h, emerald green ground, intricately enameled fish, four applied pickerel, handles **900.00**
12" h, triangular baluster, ruby ground, gold enameled children dec **250.00**
15½" h, clear and frosted ground, deeply etched thistles, inscribed "Moser/Karlsbad" **400.00**
20" h, trumpet shaped, opalescent lavender–pink ground, central enameled painted nude woman, gilt floral borders, sgd and numbered on base **650.00**
Wine
Rainbow Glass, funnel shaped cup, Inverted Baby Thumbprint pattern, enameled grapes and leaves dec, applied row of gold knobs around top **350.00**
Turquoise shading to clear ground, all over gold leaf dec, heavy applied prunts **395.00**

MOUNT WASHINGTON GLASS COMPANY

History: In 1837 Deming Jarves, founder of the Boston and Sandwich Glass Company, established for George D. Jarves, his son, the Mount Washington Glass Company in Boston, Massachusetts. In the following years the leadership and the name of the company changed several times as George Jarves formed different associations.

In the 1860s the company was owned and operated by Timothy Howe and William L. Libbey. In 1869 Libbey bought a new factory in New Bedford, Massachusetts, where the Mount Washington Glass Company began operating under its original name. Henry Libbey became associated with the company early in 1871. He resigned in 1874 during the general depression, and the glass works was closed. William Libbey had resigned in 1872 to work for the New England Glass Company.

The Mount Washington Glass Company opened again in the fall of 1874 under the presidency of A. H. Seabury and the management of Frederick S. Shirley. In 1894 the glass works became a part of the Pairpoint Manufacturing Company.

Throughout its history the Mount Washington Glass Company made a great variety of glass including pressed glass, blown glass and art glass, lava glass, Napoli, cameo, cut glass, Albertine, and Verona.

References: George C. Avila, *The Pairpoint Glass Story,* Reynolds–DeWalt Printing, Inc., 1968; Leonard E. Padgett, *Pairpoint Glass,* Wallace–Homestead, 1979; John A. Shuman III, *The Collector's Encyclopedia of American Art Glass,* Collector Books, 1988, value update 1991.

Collectors Clubs: Mount Washington Art Glass Society, P.O. Box A2038, New Bedford, MA 02741; Mount Washington Art Glass Society, 13 Bellevue Drive, Treasure Island, FL 33706.

Museum: The New Bedford Glass Museum, New Bedford, MA.

Additional Listings: Burmese, Crown Milano, Peachblow, and Royal Flemish.

Biscuit Jar, cov, enameled pink and brown chrysanthemums, relief oak leaf on base, silver plated cov, rim, and bail handle, marked "M. W." .. **650.00**
Bowl
4½" d, satin, pink floral dec **85.00**
10½" d, blue satin interior, chrysanthemums and leaves dec on exterior, ruffled **240.00**

Cheese Dish, Lava glass, black ground, applied multicolored shards, 13¾" d base plate, 1880s, $1,250.00.

Box, cov, 7" h, blown—out floral dec, pink roses, light to dark green ground   **525.00**

Bride's Basket
8¼" h, sq, cased, deep rose and white exterior, white interior, dragon, floral, and leaf dec, ruffled edge **650.00**
10½" h, 8" sq crimped bowl, white cased to rose—red, cameo cut winged griffins, floral bouquets, and swags, silver plated metal stand with leaf and berry embellished handle marked "Pairpoint" **825.00**
11" d, pink exterior, peachblow interior, gold stylized flowers dec, ornate silver plated holder with aquatic marine motif, marked "Pairpoint Mfg Co" **875.00**

Candlestick, 12" h, pink and white, hand painted florals, ftd Pairpoint holder **200.00**

Castor Set, satin, multicolored enameled floral dec, silver plated Pairpoint holder, three pcs **245.00**

Center Bowl, 11½" h, 13" l, swan, cranberry, clear curved neck and head, polished beak **330.00**

Compote
6¼" d, 10" h, Napoli, crystal clear ground, pastel green chrysanthemum leaves on wafer base, stem forms pedestal, four golden yellow chrysanthemum blossoms on underside of flared bowl, flowers outlined in gold on interior **585.00**
11" d, 4½" h, Ambero, thick bowl with reverse painted enameled grapes and leaves, thin layer of lemon flashing on base and wafer foot, rolled over rim, sgd "Ambero C" **850.00**

Cookie Jar, satin, blown—out pulled drapery pattern, gold highlights, Burmese salmon pink interior, fancy cover, bail, and handle sgd "MW 4413" ..   **875.00**

Creamer, 3" h, melon ribbed, enameled leaf and floral dec, silver plated handle and spout **185.00**

Cruet, 5¾" h, amberina, Inverted Thumbprint pattern, applied amber handle, period amber stopper **325.00**

Dresser Jar, 3¼" h, Burmese colored ground, pansy and leaf dec, dec attributed to Timothy Canty, silver plated cov, marked "MW" **275.00**

Ewer
7¾" h, conical lusterless white ground, hand painted and enameled thistle blossoms and leaves, elongated pouring lip, applied reeded handle **175.00**
13" h, mother of pearl, shaded blue ground, white lining, applied frosted and twisted rope handle, white pedestal base **775.00**

Flower Frog, mushroom dec **250.00**

Jar, cov, apricot, white daisies dec, sgd "Pairpoint," 3" h, $165.00.

Jug, 6" h, 5½" w, Verona, yellow, gold, and purple spider mums and buds, green leaves dec **425.00**

Lamp Base, 8" d cameo base, pink ground, white overlay acid etched with ornate urn and bird design, brass and gilt metal lamp fittings **375.00**

Miniature Lamp
8½" h, Delft blue windmill dec, white opaque base and shade, Smith #276–II, sgd on base **585.00**
10½" h, white ground, multicolored floral dec, gold highlights, burner sgd "The A & H Mf'g Co. Acorn," sgd "Dresden" **845.00**

Perfume Bottle, 6" h, 2¼" w, sq, satin, woman in 1890s dress, script on back "Hout's Milk White March 19, 1894—50th Performance Boston Theatre Boston," orig threaded atomizer **135.00**

Pickle Castor, deep cranberry satin ground, Optic Diamond and Inverted Thumbprint pattern insert, gold spider chrysanthemum dec, ftd Simpson Hall frame, ornate engraved cov, orig silvering **685.00**

Pitcher
    5" h, 5" w, Verona, gold fish swimming among coral, rust, purple, and green sea plants, blue ground, green plants on handle, gold trim spout and rim 950.00
    5½" h, 3¼" d, Hobnail pattern, Burmese, deep salmon shading to bright yellow ground, acid finish, applied bright yellow handle 1,600.00
    8" h, Verona, bulbous, maiden hair fern dec, gold highlights, applied clear reeded handle 225.00
Plate
    7" d, country scene of stone bridge, cottage, and lake, factory dec, orig paper label 100.00
    12" d, twin cupids, leaf and floral border 115.00
Rose Bowl
    4½" d, 3½" h, satin, blue shaded to pale blue ground, mezzotint of cherub wearing bright blue cape, vines and leaves dec 175.00
    5½" d, pale blue ground, life–like pansy dec, numbered "617" on bottom 565.00
    5½" d, 5" h, lusterless white ground, eight crimp top, orig matte finish, c1870 .... 65.00

Salt Shaker, Pillar Rib, hand painted dec, 4" h, $125.00.

Salt and Pepper Shakers, pr
    Chicks, 2¼" h, 2½" l, egg shaped opal glass, hand painted floral dec, figural metal chicken head covers . 450.00
    Fig, enameled pansy dec, satin, orig prong top 225.00
    Melon, squatty, enameled daisy dec, satin, orig 2 pc top 115.00
Scent Bottle, lusterless white ground, reserve with couple, basket of flowers on reverse 100.00
Sugar Shaker
    4" h, 3¼" d, egg shape, pastel pansies, pronged top 585.00

5½" h, Inverted Thumbprint pattern, lighthouse shape, Bluerina, orig metal top 270.00
Toothpick Holder, satin glass, Brownie Policeman, billy club in hand, holding another Brownie by scruff of neck, sitting Brownie on back 550.00
Tumbler, peachblow, band of apple blossom pink shades to soft blue–gray 1,450.00
Vase
    3¾" h, classic shape, Lava, shiny jet black ground, inlaid chips of blue, green, and pink, two curl handles, gold dec 1,750.00
    8" h, 5" d, double gourd, four barn swallows, black, brown, blue, and white dec, yellow shading to pink half way down 1,200.00
    8¼" h, 4" d, satin, bulbous, ruffled top, shaded pale blue to white, c1880 .... 145.00
    8½" h, 5" d bulbous base, Napoli, eight vertical ribs on clear crystal, frog sitting in bullrushes, interior dec with turquoise, blue, green, and rust, exterior with gold outlines, minor interior paint loss ... 975.00
    10" h, Lava, black ground, blue, pink, green, and white inclusions, gold swirls and outlines, applied reeded handles, pr 2,530.00
    16" h, court jester and blossom dec, pink ground, sgd 750.00
    18⅜" h, Napoli, base sgd "Napoli/841" 1,400.00

MURANO GLASS

History: Murano, Italy, is the home of several interesting Italian glassmakers. The Barovier and Toso Studio and the Ermanno Nason Murano Studio are modern examples, having produced glassware in the 1950s. The Venini Glassworks was established in 1925 by Paolo Venini and is presently operated by his descendants.

Venini Glassworks revived several old Venetian glass techniques, such as millefiore, and has also developed several new distinctive styles.

Principal designers of Venini Glassworks include Ludovico Diaz De Santillana and Finnish designer Tapio Wirkkala, who served as art director of the firm for many years.

Modern Italian glassware is currently doing quite well in some of the major auction houses. Works by artists such as Ermanno Nason are realizing high prices.

Items made by the Barovier and Toso Studio are often identified by a signature which reads "Murano/Antica Vetreia/F 11: TOSO," and may even include a design or style number. Items made by Venini Glassworks may be engraved or acid stamped. Some are marked "Venini Murano, Made in Italy," or "Venini Murano, Italia."

Bowl
7" w, 9" l, 3¾" h, oval, cranberry, opalescent ribs, sgd "Murano" ... **100.00**
7¾" d, 3½" h, pointed oval, bubbled moss green, sgd "Venini Murano" **100.00**
Decanter, 14" h, blue and lavender casings, fine incised dec **900.00**
Figurine, 9" h, musician, long gown, opal, 1950, set of four **1,200.00**

Vase, brilliant cobalt blue vasiform, applied white swirling repeating elements evolving from rectangles to circles, designed by Erocle Barovier, base engraved "Barovier & Toso Murano," 8⅜" h, $1,210.00. Photograph courtesy of Skinner, Inc.

Vase
4¼" h, 6" l, squatty egg shape, horizontal layers of metallic gray, transparent amber, and opaque gray–white, two offset apertures at top, attributed to Thomas Stearns, sgd "Venini/Italia" **4,800.00**
6" h, handkerchief, white cased in clear, etched mark "Venini, Murano" **350.00**
8¼" h, slightly flattened oval, patchwork design, alternating sqs of red, blue, green, and clear, designed by Fulvio Bianconi, c1957, etched mark "Venini Murano Italia," minor wear, slight scratch on side **7,500.00**
9" h, pear shape, green, gray, and clear stripes, etched "Venini Italia" **395.00**
10" h, baluster, clear ground, white flecks, applied leaves **195.00**
12" h, 6" w, modified baluster shape, tulip shaped lip, deep cranberry casing, clear outer layer with inclusions of gold flecks in wide vertical swath, encased brown, yellow, and green, attributed to Ermanno Toso **300.00**

13" h, aqua ground, white net inclusions, etched mark "Venini Murano" **6,000.00**

NAILSEA-TYPE GLASS

History: Nailsea-type glass is characterized by swirls and loopings, usually white, on a clear or colored ground. One of the first areas where this glass was made was Nailsea, England, 1788–1873, hence the name. Several other glass houses, including American factories, made this type of glass.

Bottle
6½" h, medium gray–blue ground, white loopings, pewter threading, pontil scar, cap missing, attributed to Germany, mid 18th C **1,650.00**
7⅝" h, rect, beveled edges, medium sapphire blue ground, white loopings, pewter threads, pontil scar, attributed to Germany or Northern Europe, c1750 .... **1,210.00**
8½" h, clear ground, white loopings, sheared lip, pontil scar, 1860–80 . **135.00**
8¾" l, gemel, cranberry ground, white looping, applied rigaree ... **165.00**
10½" l, bellows, white ground, rose loopings, applied rigaree, stand .. **250.00**
Bowl, 4¼" d, 2¼" h, citron ground, narrow white looping, applied rigaree loop dec rim, ground pontil **120.00**
Candlestick, 10" h, clear ground, white loopings, folded socket rim, hollow blown socket drawn out to a double knop, bulb shaped stem, and two additional knops, inverted cone shaped base, early 19th C **375.00**
Cologne Bottle, 5⅜" h, opaque white body, blue and cranberry loopings, clear stopper with white, pink, and blue loopings, pontil scar, New England, 1840–60 .... **475.00**
Fairy Lamp
6" h, blue shade, matching ruffled trifold rim base, clear pressed insert **710.00**
6½" h, 5¾" d, Verre Moire, red satin ground, white loopings, dome shaped shade, bowl shaped base with six pinched pleats, clear Clarke insert marked "Clarke Fairy Patent Trade Mark" **845.00**
Finger Bowl, 4¼" d, ftd, clear ground, swirled streaks of deep blue and white, foot drawn from body, applied clear handles imp with cherub's face **60.00**
Flask
6¾" h, clear ground, white loopings, flattened round body, short sheared

lip, small rough pontil, attributed to South Jersey **150.00**

7¼" h, opaque white ground, pink loopings, sheared lip, pontil scar, attributed to England 1860–80 ... **160.00**

7¾" h, opaque white ground Large cranberry loopings, folded over lip, pontil scar, attributed to South Jersey, 1870–80 .... **180.00**

Pink loopings, incised creases in lip, pontil scar, attributed to England, 1860–80 .... **135.00**

8" l, clear ground, white loopings, sheared lip, pontil scar, 1860–80 . **100.00**

Fairy Lamp, rose, white loopings, frosted, sgd "S. Clarke," clear base, 4¾" h, 4" d, $325.00.

Lamp, 10" h, clear ground, white loopings, pear shaped font, swirl base stem, sq marble base **200.00**

Mug, 5¼" h, 3⅝" d, clear ground, white and blue loopings, cylindrical, tapering slightly to rim, applied clear solid handle, rough pontil **360.00**

Pipe, 18" l, white ground, red loopings, bulbous bowl, knopped stem **275.00**

Pitcher

6½" h, 4" d, clear ground, white loopings, ftd, solid applied base, triple ribbed solid handle with curled end, flaring formed mouth, attributed to South Jersey, c1840–60 .. **1,125.00**

9½" h, cranberry ground, thick white loopings, applied clear handle with five crimps, applied clear foot, pontil scar, attributed to South Jersey, 1840–50 .... **4,100.00**

Powder Horn

11" h, clear ground, blue and white loopings, tooled lip, pontil scar, ground lip, mid 19th C **90.00**

13" l, clear ground, white loopings and red stripes, stand **250.00**

Rolling Pin

16½" l, clear ground, deep ruby loopings, 1883 English coin trapped in-

side, attributed to Nailsea district, England, 1880s **385.00**

18" l, clear ground, pink and white loopings **250.00**

Salt, open, 3¼" d, 1¼" h, clear ground, white loopings, wide gauffered rolled rim, applied cobalt blue rim band, applied solid foot, polished pontil .. **425.00**

Tankard, 7" h, aqua ground, white loopings, applied solid aqua handle, pontil scar, crack at upper handle attachment, attributed to South Jersey, mid 19th C **412.50**

Tumbler, white ground, blue loopings . **115.00**

Vase

8" h, 5" d, cylindrical, flared mouth and base, clear ground, white loopings, plain sheared rim–pontil, attributed to South Jersey **175.00**

9¾" h, medium blue ground, white loopings, hollow knop stem containing 1842 dime, applied foot, pontil scar, stem previously broken off and re–glued, attributed to Pittsburgh or South Jersey, 1840–50 .. **605.00**

9⅞" h, bulbous, flaring neck, ftd, clear ground, spiraling white bands, applied clear swagging, applied clear baluster stem, thick round base, attributed to New England, 19th C **3,200.00**

Witch Ball

5¼" d, clear ground, opaque white casing, red loopings, attributed to Pittsburgh **250.00**

16" h, matching ball and vase stand, clear ground, white loopings, pontil scar, attributed to Pittsburgh or New Jersey, 1840–50 .... **1,210.00**

NASH GLASS

History: Nash glass is a type of art glass attributed to Arthur John Nash and his sons, Leslie H. and A. Douglas. Arthur John Nash, originally employed by Webb in Stourbridge, England, came to America and was employed in 1889 by Tiffany Furnaces at its Corona, Long Island, plant.

While managing the plant for Tiffany, Nash designed and produced iridescent glass. In 1928 A. Douglas Nash purchased the physical facilities of Tiffany Furnaces. The A. Douglas Nash Corporation firm remained in operation until 1931.

Bottle, 4½" h, squatty, pinched sides, amber iridescence, green and amber iridescent striated feather dec, inscribed "LCT B1," c1890 .... **1,150.00**

Bowl

5¾" d, inverted rim, leaf design, sgd **150.00**

7¾" d, 2½" h, Jewel pattern, gold
phantom luster **275.00**
13" d, Diamond Optic pattern, clear
ground, cranberry threads, wide
rim **275.00**
15½" d, Chintz pattern, amber, blue,
and green opalescent, turned down
rim **300.00**
Candlesticks, pr
4" h, ball stem, Chintz pattern, blood
red and silver dec, sgd **450.00**
4½" h, iridescent blue, sgd and num-
bered **500.00**
5" h, Chintz pattern, blood red and
silver dec **750.00**
Champagne, 5" h, pale iridescent am-
ber, shallow cup splitting to three
stems continuing to domed circular
base **750.00**

**Dish, irid gold, blue–green, etched grape
leaves and vines, marked "Nash 569 C–
1", 5⅜" d, ½" h, $290.00.**

Cologne Bottle
5" h, flaring bulbed base, Chintz pattern, wide pale green stripes separated by wide clear stripes with thin
blue centers, clear stopper with
controlled bubble, sgd "Nash/
1008/JJ" **500.00**
6" h, cylindrical, Chintz pattern, pap-
erweight stopper **225.00**
Compote, 6" d, 2 h", fold over rim,
Chintz pattern, green–blue bowl,
clear pedestal foot, sgd **175.00**
Cordial, 5½" h, Chintz pattern, green
and blue **75.00**
Creamer, 4¼" h, pale orchid and green
design, applied clear handle **325.00**
Finger Bowl, 4¾" d, matching under-
plate, opalescent rays, cranberry rim,
sgd **220.00**
Goblet
6½" h, Chintz pattern **85.00**
6¾" h, feathered leaf motif, gilt dec,
sgd **275.00**
Perfume Bottle
7½" h, bulbous bottle shape over

blown–in–mold apron, iridescent
gold, conforming stopper with 7" l
wand, sgd "Nash 523" **935.00**
7⅞" h, blue and lilac rays, pale blue
foot, silver–blue iridescence, orig
pointed amber stopper **750.00**
Plate
4½" d, iridescent amber, scalloped
edge, sgd and numbered **300.00**
6½" d, Spiral pattern, orchid and
clear spirals, sgd **175.00**
8" d, Chintz pattern, green and blue **175.00**
Salt, open, 4" d, 1¼" h, iridescent gold,
ruffled rim, sgd and numbered **350.00**
Sherbet, 3½" d, 2¼" h, vein textured,
gold rainbow iridescence, sgd **115.00**
Tumbler, 5" h, conical, Chintz pattern,
blue and silver, low pedestal foot, sgd **115.00**
Vase
4¾" h, blue–gold iridescence, pedestal base, inscribed "Nash 644" . **325.00**
5½" h, iridescent blue, marked
"R526" **600.00**
6¼" h, sq top, iridescent gold, sgd . **275.00**
6¼" h, 3½" d, trumpet shape, Chintz
pattern, sgd and numbered **365.00**
6½" h, bulbous, feathery blue strokes,
bubbly lime green streaks, sgd . . . **400.00**
7½" h, beaker, Chintz pattern, blood
red, sgd "Nash RD 1025" **450.00**
7¾" h, baluster, brilliant iridescent
pumpkin, lemon–yellow interior . **3,500.00**
8½" h, Chintz pattern, green, brown,
and gold flecks **295.00**
9" h, Chintz, blood red and gray, ball
shaped clear stem **475.00**
9½" h, green and gold iridescent
body, clear iridescent circular base **295.00**
12" h, trumpet shape, orange and yellow vertical stripes, inscribed
"Nash 62AA" **450.00**
Wine, 6" h, Chintz pattern, pink and
green **95.00**

NEW MARTINSVILLE VIKING

History: New Martinsville glass predating 1935
appears in a wide variety of colors. Later glass
was only made in crystal, blue, ruby, and pink.

Look for cocktail, beverage, liquor, vanity,
smoking and console sets. Amusing figures of
barnyard and sea animals, dogs, and bears were
produced. Both Rainbow Art Glass and Viking
glass are handmade and have a paper label.
Rainbow Art Glass pieces are beautifully colored
and the animal figures are more abstract in design

than New Martinsville. Viking makes plain, colored, cut and etched tableware, novelties, and gift items. Viking began making black glass in 1979.

The New Martinsville Glass Manufacturing Company, founded in 1901, took its name from its West Virginia location. Early products were opal glass decorative ware and utilitarian items. Later productions were pressed crystal tableware with flashed-on ruby or gold decorations. In the 1920s innovative color and designs made vanity, liquor, and smoker sets popular. Dinner sets in patterns such as Radiance, Moondrops, and Dancing Girl, as well as new colors, cuttings and etchings were produced. The 1940s brought black glass formed into perfume bottles, bowls with swan handles and flower bowls. In 1944 the company was sold and reorganized as the Viking Glass Company.

The Rainbow Art Glass Company, Huntington, West Virginia, was established in 1942 by Henry Manus, a Dutch immigrant. This company produced small, hand fashioned animals and decorative ware of opal, spatter, cased and crackle glass. Rainbow Art Glass also decorated for other companies. In the early 1970s, Viking acquired Rainbow Art Glass Company and continued the production of the small animals.

Reference: Hazel Marie Weatherman, *Colored Glassware of the Depression Era, Book 2,* Glassworks, Inc., 1982.

Animal	
Elephants, crystal, pr	175.00
Polar Bear	45.00
Rooster, large	80.00
Squirrel	45.00
Swan	
5¼" h, cobalt blue	32.00
10" h, crystal body, ruby neck	65.00
Tigers, crystal, pr	300.00
Ashtray	
4" d, Fish	10.00
5" d, Skillet	12.00
Basket	
8¾" h, 5" d, Radiance pattern, amber, ftd, 1937–68	25.00
14" h, crystal, sq	25.00
Bicentennial Plate	15.00
Bon Bon	
Janice pattern, crystal	18.50
Radiance pattern, amber	10.00
Bookends, pr, crystal	
Cornucopia, 5¾" h	45.00
Daddy Bear, 4½" h	100.00
Lady's heads	250.00
Nautilus Shell	35.00
Police Dog	55.00
Sailing Ships, 5¾" h, rect block background, c1940	90.00
Starfish	50.00

Wolfhound	55.00
Bowl	
5" d, Peach Blow, yellow–caramel shading to peach to beige, scalloped rim	50.00
5½" d, Meadow Wreath pattern	8.00
12" d	
Prelude etching, ftd	20.00
Radiance pattern, amber	40.00
13" d, Radiance pattern, ruby	65.00
Butter Dish	
Moondrops pattern, cobalt blue	300.00
Radiance pattern, crystal, sterling silver overlay	100.00
Cake Plate, 14" d	
Hostmaster, amber	24.00
Radiance pattern, light blue	35.00
Candlesticks, pr	
3" h, Moondrops pattern, amber, ruffled	24.00
6" h, #44531	38.00
8½" h, Hostmaster, cobalt blue, sterling silver trim	35.00
Candy Dish, cov, 8" h, orange, pedestal, orig Viking label	8.50
Celery Tray	
Janice pattern, crystal, 11" l	15.00
Meadow Wreath, 10" l	12.00
Cheese and Cracker Set, Prelude etching	85.00
Cigarette Holder, cart shape, crystal	12.00
Cocktail Shaker, Moondrops pattern, red, handle	70.00
Compote, 11" d, Radiance pattern, crystal, sterling base	70.00
Console Set, 10½" d swan shaped center bowl, 4½" h pr swan shaped candlesticks, amber bodies, crystal necks, c1940–60, three pc set	55.00
Cordial, Moondrops pattern	
Amethyst	10.00
Cobalt Blue	35.00
Creamer and Sugar	
Eagle pattern, crystal	20.00
Florentine pattern, crystal	24.00
Janice pattern, light blue	65.00
Cup and Saucer, Hostmaster, ruby	12.00
Decanter, 10" h, Moondrops pattern	
Amethyst	55.00
Pink	25.00
Fruit Bowl, 12" d, Janice pattern, apricot, ftd	35.00
Goblet	
Hostmaster, 6¼" h, cobalt blue	20.00
Mt Vernon pattern, cobalt blue	18.50
Prelude etching, crystal	22.00
Honey jar, cov, Radiance pattern, ruby	225.00
Ice Bowl, 5½" d, Hostmaster, ruby	40.00
Ice Bucket, Janice pattern, forest green	40.00
Iced Tea Tumbler, Prelude etching	10.00
Juice Tumbler, Moondrops pattern, cobalt blue, ftd	15.00
Luncheon Set, Janice pattern, blue,	

twelve luncheon plates, cups, and
saucers, two serving plates **245.00**
Marmalade, cov, Janice pattern, crystal **20.00**
Mayonnaise, cov, underplate, Radiance
pattern, amber **20.00**
Nut Dish, 5" d, Radiance pattern, am-
ber, two handles **8.50**
Perfume, triangular, green frosted, silver
trimmed dauber **40.00**
Powder Jar
  Cinderella Coach, crystal **25.00**
  Diamond, three toes, frosted, lavender celluloid lid **11.00**
  Triangular, green frosted **15.00**
Plate
  9" d, Florentine pattern **12.00**
  9½" d, Moondrops pattern
    Green **20.00**
    Pink **10.00**
  11" d
    Florentine pattern, crystal **12.00**
    Meadow Wreath pattern, crystal .. **15.00**
  11½" d, Prelude etching, crystal ... **15.00**
  14" d, Prelude etching **20.00**
Punch Bowl, 14" d, Radiance pattern,
  crystal **115.00**
Punch Cup, Radiance pattern, ice
  blue **12.00**
Relish, 8¼" l, 5" w, Radiance pattern,
  amber **20.00**
Salad Bowl, 11" d, Wild Rose etching,
  crystal **20.00**

**Salt and Pepper Shakers, pr, Muranese,
3½" h, $48.00.**

Salt and Pepper Shakers, pr, Radiance
  pattern, amber **48.00**
Sherbet, Moondrops pattern, cobalt
  blue **12.00**
Sugar, cov
  Florentine pattern **12.00**
  Meadow Wreath pattern **7.00**
Tray, Moondrops pattern, amethyst ... **15.00**
Tumbler
  Hostmaster, cobalt blue **8.50**
  Moondrops pattern, ruby **12.00**
Vanity Set, cov box, two jars, tray
  Geneva pattern **50.00**

Shining Star pattern **35.00**
Vase
  6" h, Cornucopia, crystal **20.00**
  9" h, Morning Dove pattern **42.00**
  10" h, Radiance pattern
    Amber, etched **55.00**
    Ruby **65.00**
Water Set, Oscar pattern, tankard
  pitcher and two tumblers, amber,
  c1930 .... **50.00**
Whiskey Shot Glass, Moondrops pattern, red, handle **15.00**

NORTHWOOD GLASS

History: The Northwood Glass Company was
incorporated in 1887 in Martin's Ferry, Belmont
County, West Virginia by Henry Helling, Henry
Floto, William Mann, Thomas Mears, and Harry
Northwood. Production started early in January
1888 with blown ware, consisting of lamp
shades, tablewares, water sets, and berry sets.
Harry Northwood was the designer and general
manager and surely used the years of experience
he had working with the former Hobbs, Brockunier, and La Belle Glass Works to develop new
glass techniques and patterns. The Northwood
Company soon became known for its numerous
patterns and items, as well as the vivid colors
and types of art glass it produced. Harry Northwood also was responsible for obtaining several
patents for glass manufacturing devices. In November of 1888, he obtained a patent for a
speckled type of glass ware. This technique was
often used with colored grounds, such as cranberry, and produced an innovative type of glassware, now known as spatter. Production reports
of many types of colorful wares can be found.
By April, 1889, however, the directors dissolved
the company and an attempt was made to settle
affairs. It appears from most written accounts,
that although the products were wonderful, the
sales force could not carry through. The Northwood Company reorganized as an Ohio corporation. Accomplished glassmakers continued to
produce quality products and added fine examples of cased, satin, and agate type wares. Skilled
patterns such as Royal Ivy were developed and
widely advertised.

By 1898, the Northwood Glass Company was
beginning to feel pressure from the giant United
States Glass conglomerate. Natural supplies were
becoming more expensive and Harry Northwood
even invested in a natural gas company in an
effort to keep prices low. Plans to relocate developed and in 1892 corporation papers were
filed in Pennsylvania. Lawsuits relating to the
business began to shake the foundations as the
company moved to Ellwood City, PA. By 1898,
the company was failing and closed late in the
year.

Harry Northwood went on to the Indiana Glass Company, Indiana, PA. His presence was quickly known as new products were developed, including some intricate pressed patterns to rival cut glass.

H. Northwood & Co. was founded in 1902 by Harry Northwood and Thomas Dugan in Wheeling, West Virginia. The first items the new company made were ornate tableware patterns as well as lemonade sets. Ironically, the company was located in the former Hobbs, Brockunier plant where young Englishman Harry Northwood held his first glass job.

By 1907, H. Northwood & Co. was established as one of American's finest glassware manufacturers. Novelties and pressed patterns were produced in opalescent colors, as well as solid green, amethyst, and blue, some of which featured gold decorations. Carnival glass production began in 1908, but continued only until 1915. Despite its popularity, it was discontinued due to hard financial times. H. Northwood & Co. continued to pioneer glass formulas and produced a fine line of custard patterns as well as an imitation marble-type glass.

Harry Northwood died in 1919 and the company reorganized. Several new patterns and colors were added. Competition from companies such as Westmoreland, Fenton, and Imperial was becoming fierce and the company began to falter. By 1925, the company ceased production and the plant was closed.

References: Marion T. Hartung, *Northwood Pattern Glass In Color, Clear, Colored, Custard, and Carnival,* privately printed, 1969; William Heacock, James Measell, Berry Wiggins, *Harry Northwood: The Early Years, 1881–1900,* Antique Publications, 1990; William Heacock, James Measell, Berry Wiggins, *Harry Northwood: The Wheeling Years, 1901–1925,* Antique Publications, 1992.

Museums: The Chrysler Museum, Norfolk, VA; The Corning Museum of Glass, Corning, NY; The Toledo Museum of Art, Toledo, OH.

Additional Listings: Carnival Glass, Custard Glass, Opalescent Glass, and Pattern Glass.

Basket, blue opalescent, 4½″ h, 4½″ d, $85.00.

Chrysanthemum Sprig pattern, custard, 11″ oval unsigned master, six sauces sgd "Northwood" script, seven pcs 675.00
Everglades pattern, custard 725.00
Grape and Cable pattern, custard, basketweave ext., nutmeg stain, 7½″ d 50.00
Leaf Medallion pattern, cobalt blue, gold trim 300.00
Memphis pattern, green 165.00
Bon Bon
  Grape and Cable pattern, carnival, blue 60.00
  Stippled Rays pattern, carnival, blue 40.00
  Three Fruits pattern, carnival, marigold 50.00
Bowl
  Coin Dot pattern, carnival, marigold, 7″ d 38.00
  Grape and Cable pattern, clear, gold leaves 65.00
  Nippon pattern, carnival, marigold, 9″ d 50.00
  Paneled Cherry pattern, clear, red stained cherries, gold leaves, 9½″ d 40.00
Butter Dish, cov
  Cherry Thumbprint pattern, clear ... 110.00
  Everglades pattern, custard 375.00
  Fan, Dugan 215.00
  Geneva pattern, custard, green and red trim 135.00
  Intaglio pattern, green, gold trim ... 60.00
  Leaf Umbrella pattern, cranberry ... 600.00
  Louis XV pattern, custard 120.00
  Maple Leaf pattern, custard 200.00
  Peach pattern, clear, gold and red trim 95.00
  Springtime pattern, carnival, purple . 210.00
  Strawberry and Cable pattern, clear . 100.00
Candlesticks, pr
  Chinese Red pattern, 10″ h 95.00
  Grape and Cable pattern, green 85.00
Candy Dish, cov, Beaded Cable pattern, carnival, marigold 45.00

Banana Boat, Grape & Thumbprint pattern, custard 375.00
Berry Bowl, master
  Argonaut Shell pattern, custard, gold dec, oval, marked "Northwood" . 245.00
  Beaded Circle pattern, custard 185.00
  Geneva pattern, custard, green trim, 8½″ l oval 95.00
Berry Set, master and six individual sauces
  Acorn Burrs pattern, carnival, marigold 215.00
  Cherry Thumbprint pattern, clear ... 135.00

Celery Vase
  Leaf Mold pattern, cranberry **135.00**
  Ribbed Pillar pattern, pink and white
    spatter **85.00**
Cologne Bottle, Leaf Umbrella pattern,
  mauve, cased, orig stopper **265.00**
Compote, Intaglio pattern, custard, ftd,
  9″ d **365.00**
Condiment Set, Chrysanthemum Sprig
  pattern, custard, cruet, pr salt and
  pepper shakers, tray **1,150.00**
Console Set, Chinese Red pattern, 9½″
  d ftd compote, matching candlesticks **135.00**

Creamer and Sugar, Argonaut Shell, custard, gold dec, $225.00.

Creamer
  Cherry and Plum pattern, clear, ruby
    and gold trim **75.00**
  Chrysanthemum Sprig pattern, custard type blue body, gold dec **385.00**
  Grape and Cable pattern, custard ... **100.00**
  Jackson pattern, custard **65.00**
  Leaf Umbrella pattern, cranberry,
    breakfast size **225.00**
  Lustre Flute pattern, carnival, green . **48.00**
  Peach pattern, clear, gold and red
    trim **50.00**
  Pods and Posies pattern, green, gold
    trim **60.00**
  Wild Bouquet pattern, custard **130.00**
Cruet, orig stopper
  Daisy and Fern pattern, opalescent,
    blue, Parian Swirl mold **110.00**
  Intaglio pattern, custard, green dec . **400.00**
  Inverted Fan & Feather pattern, custard **600.00**
  Wild Bouquet pattern, custard,
    enamel dec **550.00**
Dresser Tray
  Grape and Cable pattern, carnival,
    marigold **110.00**
  Northwood Grape pattern, custard .. **225.00**
Finger Bowl, Leaf Umbrella pattern,
  blue, cased **95.00**
Goblet
  Grape and Gothic Arches pattern,
    custard, nutmeg stain **65.00**
  Nearcut, clear **25.00**
  Strawberry and Cable pattern, clear . **35.00**

Ice Cream Bowl, Peacock and Urn pattern, custard **35.00**
Marmalade Jar, cov, Paneled Sprig pattern, cranberry, silver plate rim, cov,
  and bail handle **175.00**
Mug
  Dandelion pattern, carnival, purple . **275.00**
  Singing Birds pattern, carnival, purple **95.00**
Nappy
  Lustre Flute pattern, carnival, marigold **30.00**
  Northwood Grape pattern, custard .. **50.00**
Nut Bowl, Leaf and Beads pattern, carnival, purple **65.00**
Pitcher
  Beaded Circle pattern, custard **425.00**
  Cherry and Lattice pattern, clear, gold
    trim **85.00**
  Cherry and Plum pattern, clear, gold
    trim **150.00**
  Coin Dot pattern, carnival, marigold **165.00**
  Daisy and Fern pattern, cranberry,
    ball shape **150.00**
  Dandelion pattern, carnival, marigold **375.00**
  Everglades pattern, custard **600.00**
  Grape and Gothic Arches pattern,
    green, gold trim **100.00**
  Leaf Mold pattern, cranberry, white
    spatter **295.00**
  Louis XV pattern, custard **225.00**
  Memphis pattern, clear, gold trim .. **75.00**
  Paneled Holly pattern, green, gold
    trim **195.00**
  Peach pattern, clear, gold trim **125.00**
  Royal Ivy pattern, rainbow, cased .. **245.00**

Plate, Three Fruits, carnival, purple irid, marked, 9⅛″ d, $150.00.

Plate
  Good Luck pattern, carnival, purple,
    9″ d **300.00**
  Grape and Cable pattern
    Carnival, purple, sgd "Northwood," 9″ d **100.00**
    Custard, 8″ d **70.00**

Paneled Cherry pattern, red cherries, gold leaves, 10½" d **37.50**

Thistle pattern, clear, 10" d **30.00**

Three Fruits pattern, custard, 7½" d . **22.00**

Powder Jar, cov, Grape and Cable pattern, carnival, green **100.00**

Punch Bowl, Memphis pattern, carnival, marigold, 11½" d bowl, matching base **195.00**

Punch Cup

Cherry and Cable pattern, clear **25.00**

Grape and Cable pattern

Carnival, marigold **24.50**

Custard **48.00**

Singing Birds pattern, clear **20.00**

Rose Bowl

Beaded Cable pattern, carnival, aqua opalescent **285.00**

Grape and Gothic Arches pattern, custard **75.00**

Salt Shaker, Leaf mold, aqua, 2½" h, $95.00.

Salt and Pepper Shakers, pr, orig tops

Beaded Circle pattern, custard **255.00**

Bow and Tassel pattern, milk glass, orig tops **35.00**

Carnelian pattern, custard **450.00**

Heart pattern, custard **160.00**

Leaf Umbrella pattern, mauve, cased **125.00**

Maple Leaf pattern, custard **500.00**

Sauce

Everglades pattern, custard **65.00**

Geneva pattern, custard, oval **35.00**

Maple Leaf pattern, custard **80.00**

Wild Bouquet pattern, custard **50.00**

Spooner

Aurora pattern, pink satin ground, white spatter **70.00**

Cherry and Plum pattern, clear, ruby and gold trim **70.00**

Chrysanthemum Sprig pattern, custard type blue body, gold trim **220.00**

Grape and Cable pattern, custard, nutmeg stain **95.00**

Memphis pattern, green **65.00**

Singing Birds pattern, clear **65.00**

Springtime pattern, carnival, marigold **120.00**

Wild Bouquet pattern, custard **70.00**

Sugar, cov

Argonaut Shell pattern, custard **160.00**

Cherry and Plum pattern, clear, ruby and gold trim **75.00**

Everglades pattern, custard **150.00**

Intaglio pattern, custard **115.00**

Memphis pattern, green **72.00**

Peach pattern, clear, gold and red trim **70.00**

Springtime pattern, carnival, purple . **210.00**

Syrup, orig top

Geneva pattern, custard **250.00**

Leaf Umbrella pattern, cranberry, white spatter **250.00**

Table Set, cov butter, creamer, spooner, and cov sugar

Belladonna pattern, green, gold trim **285.00**

Nearcut, clear, gold trim **245.00**

Paneled Holly pattern, green, gold trim **450.00**

Regal pattern, green, gold trim **255.00**

Toothpick Holder

Argonaut Shell pattern, custard **275.00**

Inverted Fan & Feather pattern, custard **350.00**

Maple Leaf pattern, custard **550.00**

Memphis pattern, green **45.00**

Ribbed Optic pattern, rubena **50.00**

Threaded Swirl pattern, rubena **250.00**

Wild Bouquet pattern, custard type blue body, enameled dec **100.00**

Tumbler

Atlas pattern, opaque pink **24.00**

Coin Dot pattern, carnival, marigold **48.00**

Flower and Bud pattern, clear **48.00**

Geneva pattern, custard, red and gold trim, 3⅞" h, 3" d **50.00**

Grape and Gothic Arches pattern, opaque creamy ground, gold trim, carnival type finish **55.00**

Grape and Leaf pattern, white opaque **35.00**

Greek Key pattern, carnival, purple . **75.00**

Intaglio pattern, custard, green trim . **40.00**

Jackson pattern, custard **30.00**

Oriental Poppy pattern, clear, gold trim **20.00**

Paneled Holly pattern, clear **40.00**

Peach pattern, clear **40.00**

Strawberry and Cable pattern, clear . **20.00**

Wishbone pattern, carnival, green **125.00**

Vase, 8" h, 3¾" d, satin, rose bowl type five crimp top, rose, pink, and chartreuse pulled design, white ground, creamy lining **550.00**

Water Set, pitcher and six matching tumblers

Beaded Shell pattern, mint green, gold trim **425.00**

Cherry and Plum pattern, clear, gold trim **295.00**

Golden Peach pattern, green, gold
trim **500.00**
Oriental Poppy pattern, table size
pitcher **375.00**
Peacock At The Fountain pattern,
green, gold trim **885.00**
Whiskey Shot Glass, Threaded Swirl
pattern, rubena **65.00**

OPALESCENT GLASS

History: Opalescent glass is a clear or colored
glass with milky white decorations, which shows
a fiery or opalescent quality when held to light.
The effect was achieved by applying bone ash
chemicals to designated areas while a piece was
still hot and then refiring it at tremendous heat.

There are three basic categories of opalescent
glass: (1) Blown (or mold blown) patterns, e.g.,
Daisy & Fern and Spanish Lace; (2) Novelties,
pressed glass patterns made in limited pieces
which often included unusual shapes such as
Corn or Trough; and (3) Pattern (pressed) glass.

Opalescent glass was produced in England in
the 1870s. Northwood began the American production in 1897 at its Indiana, Pennsylvania,
plant. Jefferson, National Glass, Hobbs, and Fenton soon followed.

References: Charles R. Hajdamach, *British
Glass, 1800–1914*, Antique Collectors' Club,
1991; William Heacock, *Encyclopedia of Vic-
torian Colored Pattern Glass, Book II, Opalescent
Glass from A to Z, Second Edition*, Antique Pub-
lications, 1977; William Heacock and William
Gamble, *Encyclopedia of Victorian Colored Pat-
tern Glass, Book 9, Cranberry Opalescent from
A to Z*, Antique Publications, 1987; William
Heacock, James Measell and Berry Wiggins,
Harry Northwood: The Early Years 1881–1900,
Antique Publications, 1990; William Heacock,
James Measell and Berry Wiggins, *Harry North-
wood: The Wheeling Years 1901–1925*, Antique
Publications, 1991.

BLOWN

Barber Bottle, Stars and Stripes, cran-
berry **150.00**
Berry Set, Chrysanthemum Base Swirl,
cranberry, master bowl, six serving
bowls **325.00**
Biscuit Jar, Spanish Lace, vaseline **275.00**
Bottle, Bull's Eye, blue **115.00**
Bowl, Seaweed, 9" d, white **60.00**
Bride's Basket, Bubble Lattice, cran-
berry **165.00**
Butter Dish, cov, Spanish Lace, blue .. **250.00**
Celery Vase
Chrysanthemum Base Swirl, 6¾" h,
cranberry, satin finish **160.00**

**Bowl, Spanish Lace, vaseline, ruffled
edge, tricorner flared rim, twig design, 9"
d, $65.00.**

Consolidated Criss–Cross, Rubena,
satin finish **250.00**
Daffodils, blue **95.00**
Reverse Swirl, cranberry **175.00**
Ribbed Coin Spot, cranberry **150.00**
Spanish Lace, blue, ruffled rim **100.00**
Swirl, cranberry, ruffled rim **95.00**
Windows, Swirled, cranberry **95.00**
Cheese Dish, Hobb's Swirl, cranberry . **350.00**
Creamer, Reverse Swirl, blue **75.00**
Cruet, orig stopper
Daisy and Fern, Parian Swirl mold,
blue **110.00**
Hobb's Hobnail, orig faceted stopper
Blue **225.00**
Cranberry **300.00**
Paneled Sprig, clear **110.00**
Ribbed Opalescent Lattice, blue **235.00**
Seaweed, blue **145.00**
Spanish Lace
Canary Yellow **145.00**
Clear ground **85.00**
Stripe, blue, applied blue handle, cut
faceted blue stopper **145.00**
Windows, Plain, cranberry **375.00**
Windows, Swirled, cranberry **325.00**
Finger Bowl
Buckeye Lattice, cranberry **90.00**
Hobb's Hobnail, cranberry **60.00**
Hobb's Optic Diamond, cranberry .. **45.00**
Spanish Lace, blue **48.00**
Lamp, Reverse Swirl, cranberry, satin
base **425.00**
Miniature Lamp
Coin Spot, (Smith #510), 8¾" h **625.00**
Spanish Lace, 4" h, blue **225.00**
Mustard, Reverse Swirl, vaseline **50.00**
Pickle Castor, Daisy and Fern, cran-
berry, swirl mold body, ornate metal
frame and cov **365.00**
Pitcher, water
Arabian Nights, cranberry **325.00**
Buttons and Braids, blue **80.00**
Christmas Snowflake, cranberry **375.00**
Coin Dot, blue, three tier, Northwood **275.00**

Coin Spot, cranberry, star crimped
  top, applied clear handle 245.00
Daisy and Fern, cranberry, ball shape 150.00
Daisy in Criss–Cross, cranberry 600.00
Hobb's Hobnail, cranberry, heavy
  opalescent, opalescent handle ... 200.00
Paneled Sprig, cranberry 200.00
Poinsettia, 13" h, blue, tankard 200.00
Spanish Lace, ruffled rim, blue 250.00
Stripe and Swirl, sq top 285.00
Swirl, cranberry, sq ruffled top, ap-
  plied clear handle 275.00
Punch Cup, Chrysanthemum Base
  Swirl, cranberry 40.00
Rose Bowl, Daisy and Fern, blue 50.00
Salt Shaker
  Consolidated Criss–Cross, cranberry,
    orig top 85.00
  Daisy and Fern, cranberry, orig top,
    Northwood 85.00
  Reverse Swirl, blue 35.00
Stripe Opalescent
  Cranberry, 4½" h, replaced top .. 35.00
  Yellow, 2½" h, orig oxidized top . 40.00
Spooner
  Bubble Lattice, cranberry 135.00
  Consolidated Criss–Cross, cranberry 125.00
Sugar, cov
  Bubble Lattice, cranberry 150.00
  Reverse Swirl, blue 125.00
  Spanish Lace, blue 95.00
  Stripe, cranberry 80.00
Sugar Shaker, orig top
  Bubble Lattice
    Blue 135.00
    Rubena 250.00
  Fern, white 100.00
  Paneled Sprig, cranberry 185.00
  Poinsettia, blue 165.00
  Reverse Swirl, cranberry 150.00
  Windows, Swirled, blue 235.00
Syrup Pitcher, orig top
  Bubble Lattice, canary yellow 150.00
  Coin Spot, blue 150.00
  Coin Spot and Swirl, white 65.00
  Daisy in Criss–Cross, blue 250.00
  Poinsettia, blue 450.00
  Reverse Swirl
    Blue 150.00
    Vaseline 145.00
  Ribbed Opalescent Lattice, cranberry,
    silver plated spring lid, applied
    clear handle, marked "Pat Apr 28,
    81" and "Mar 28, 82" 275.00
  Spanish Lace
    Blue 225.00
    Vaseline 275.00
  Windows, Plain, blue 175.00
Toothpick Holder
  Paneled Sprig, clear ground 70.00
  Ribbed Opalescent Lattice, blue 145.00
  Swirl, blue 100.00

Windows, Swirled, cranberry 115.00
Tumbler
  Arabian Nights, blue 60.00
  Consolidated Criss–Cross, white 50.00
  Coin Spot, blue 40.00
  Daisy and Fern, cranberry 50.00
  Herringbone, cranberry 75.00
  Hobb's Hobnail, cranberry 115.00
  Poinsettia
    Blue 50.00
    Green 35.00
  Reverse Swirl, cranberry 60.00
  Spanish Lace, cranberry 45.00
  Swirl, blue 25.00
Water Set, water pitcher and six tum-
  blers, 7 pcs
  Arabian Nights, blue 400.00
  Buttons and Braids, blue 300.00
  Daffodils, blue 650.00
  Poinsettia, blue 250.00

**Pitcher, Coin Spot, white opalescent on
clear, fluted top, applied clear handle,
9½" h, $125.00.**

NOVELTIES

Basket, figural, bushel type shape, blue,
  Northwood 55.00
Bowl
  Astro, 8" d, ruffled
    Blue 45.00
    Green 90.00
  Blossoms and Web, ftd, clear ground,
    opaque white pattern, red goofus
    dec 25.00
  Cashews, blue, crimped 42.00
  Consolidated Criss–Cross, 8" d, cran-
    berry 150.00
  Greek Key and Ribs, 8" d, green ... 35.00
  Jolly Bear, white 75.00
  Leaf and Beads
    8" d, blue, fluted, twig feet 40.00
    8½" d, 3" h, green, twig feet 42.00
  Many Loops, blue, crimped, fluted . 45.00
  Meander, blue, 9" d, ftd, fluted 46.00

Poinsettia Lattice, white, 8½" d, ruf-
fled, ftd 48.00
Reflecting Diamonds, blue, 8¾" d .. 35.00
Rose Show, blue, ruffled 125.00
Ruffles and Rings, green, ftd 45.00
Compote
Dolphin, vaseline 85.00
Squirrel and Acorn, ruffled
Blue 150.00
Green 145.00
Curtain Tie Back, 5¾" d, fiery opalesc-
ence, lacy, young woman seated
holding straw hat, Boston and Sand-
wich Glass Co 150.00
Epergne, 9½" h, 19½" d, green, four
lilies, ruffled base, applied glass spiral
trim 325.00
Jack-In-The-Pulpit Vase
5¾" h, 6¼" d, Leaf Chalice, blue ... 45.00
8½" h, Squirrel and Acorn
Blue 145.00
Green 135.00
Vaseline, light 175.00
White 110.00
13½" h, blue, eight petal top, yellow
enameled inside of top and down
front 265.00
Mug, Singing Birds, blue 135.00
Plate, Wishbone and Drape, green ... 20.00
Pump and Trough, blue 115.00
Rose Bowl
Leaf Chalice, green pedestal 50.00
Open O's, blue 48.00
Palm and Scroll, green, three ftd ... 70.00
Pearls and Scales, blue, ftd 55.00
Vase
4" h, vaseline, melon ribbed body,
applied clear leaf feet, flower petal
top 65.00
6" h, Aurora Borealis, white 30.00
10" h, Piasa Bird, blue 50.00

PRESSED PATTERNS

Banana Boat, Jewel and Fan, green ... 110.00
Berry Bowl, master
Beatty Rib, white 45.00
Everglades, vaseline, gold trim, oval 195.00
Flora, canary yellow 85.00
Berry Set, master bowl, six matching
sauce dishes
Alaska, blue 385.00
Inverted Fan and Feather, white 245.00
Scroll with Acanthus, clear ground . 200.00
Bowl
Beaded Cable, 4½" d, blue, three ftd,
ruffled 40.00
Beaded Stars, low base, green 40.00
Beatty Rib, rect 35.00
Diamond Spearhead, 9" d, blue 35.00
Intaglio, blue, pedestal base 200.00
Iris with Meander, 8" d, vaseline ... 125.00

Jewel and Fan, blue 30.00
Jeweled Heart, 6" d, green, crimped 35.00
Peacock, 9" d, Northwood 135.00
Regal, green 60.00
Tokyo, 8" d, blue 40.00
Water Lily and Cattails, 9¼" d, white,
scrolled rim 45.00
Wild Bouquet, blue 125.00
Wreath and Shell, 8" d, vaseline ... 100.00
Butter Dish, cov
Argonaut Shell 275.00
Beatty Rib, white 75.00
Drapery, blue, gold trim 200.00
Flora, blue 225.00
Fluted Scrolls, 7" d, 6½" d, dec
Blue 145.00
Vaseline 165.00
Idyll, green 350.00
Jackson, blue 115.00
Jewel and Flower, blue 175.00
Regal, white, gold trim 85.00
Stippled Leaf and Basketweave, blue 240.00
Tokyo, blue 195.00
Candy Dish, cov, Jackson, canary yel-
low 45.00
Celery
Alaska, blue, dec 125.00
Diamond Spearhead, cobalt blue ... 115.00
Regal, blue 90.00
Wreath and Shell, vaseline 150.00
Creamer
Alaska, canary yellow 55.00
Argonaut Shell, blue, script sgd 75.00
Beatty Rib, white 25.00
Circled Scroll
Green 80.00
White 35.00
Flora, canary yellow 75.00
Intaglio 65.00
Jewel and Flower, vaseline 75.00
Palm Beach, blue 48.00
Paneled Holly, blue 75.00
Scroll with Acanthus, green 48.00
Shell, blue 75.00
Tokyo, blue 95.00
Wild Bouquet, blue 50.00
Wreath and Shell, vaseline 60.00
Cruet, orig stopper
Alaska, vaseline, enameled dec 265.00
Christmas Pearls 250.00
Everglades, vaseline 275.00
Fancy Fantails, blue 375.00
Intaglio, blue 175.00
Jackson, blue 150.00
Scroll with Acanthus, blue 185.00
Swag with Brackets, green 285.00
Wild Bouquet, white 115.00
Finger Bowl, Hobb's Hobnail, cranberry 50.00
Goblet, Diamond Spearhead, vaseline 115.00
Jar, cov, Beatty Rib
Blue 90.00
White 75.00

Jelly Compote
  Diamond Spearhead, vaseline **75.00**
  Everglades, blue, gold trim **85.00**
  Intaglio
    Blue **42.00**
    Canary Yellow **40.00**
  Iris with Meander
    Blue **95.00**
    Vaseline **90.00**
  Regal
    Blue **65.00**
    Green **60.00**
  Swag with Brackets, blue **50.00**
Lamp
  Christmas Snowflake, cranberry **300.00**
  Snowflake, cranberry, hand type . . .   **500.00**
Mug, Diamond Spearhead
  Cobalt Blue **72.00**
  Vaseline **40.00**
Pitcher
  Beatty Swirl, canary yellow **165.00**
  Diamond Spearhead, tankard
    Cobalt Blue, 7" h **235.00**
    Green **225.00**
  Fluted Scrolls, blue **175.00**
  Gonterman Swirl, amber top **365.00**
  Intaglio, blue **200.00**
  Iris with Meander, canary yellow . . .   **250.00**
  Jeweled Heart, blue **245.00**
  Swag with Brackets, vaseline **225.00**
  Water Lily and Cattails, amethyst . . .   **390.00**
Plate, Palm Beach, 10" d, blue, set of 6   **895.00**
Powder Jar, cov, Jackson, blue **55.00**
Rose Bowl
  Beaded Cable, ribbon candy edge
    Green **35.00**
    White **40.00**
  Fancy Fantails, cranberry, four clear
    applied feet **650.00**
  Fluted Scrolls, blue **125.00**
Salt, open
  Beatty Rib, white **24.00**
  Wreath and Shell, blue **165.00**
Salt Shaker, Swag with Brackets, vase-
  line **150.00**
Sauce
  Alaska, vaseline **45.00**
  Drapery, 4⅝" d, vaseline **20.00**
  Everglades, vaseline, gold trim **35.00**
  Gonterman Swirl
    Amber top **50.00**
    Blue top **45.00**
  Jewel and Flower, white **20.00**
  Regal, green **55.00**
  Water Lily and Cattails, white **30.00**
  Wild Bouquet, blue **38.00**
Spooner
  Drapery, blue **60.00**
  Flora, canary yellow **65.00**
  Fluted Scrolls
    Blue, dec **60.00**
    Vaseline **65.00**

Intaglio, white **40.00**
Iris with Meander, canary yellow . . .   **90.00**
Palm Beach, vaseline **95.00**
Paneled Holly, blue **120.00**
Scroll with Acanthus. vaseline **75.00**
Shell, green **85.00**
Tokyo, blue **85.00**
Wreath and Shell
  Blue **125.00**
  Vaseline **95.00**
Sugar, cov
  Circled Scroll, green **80.00**
  Flora, canary yellow **75.00**
  Fluted Scrolls
    Blue
      Decorated **125.00**
      Plain **95.00**
    Vaseline **110.00**
  Intaglio, blue **70.00**
  Jewel and Flower, vaseline **85.00**
  Scroll with Acanthus, green **50.00**
  Swag with Brackets, blue **95.00**
  Tokyo, blue, gold trim **115.00**
  Wreath and Shell, vaseline, enameled
    dec **175.00**

**Syrup, Swirl and Dot, blue, orig brass top,
6" h, $145.00.**

Syrup, Diamond Spearhead, green **350.00**
Table Set, cov butter, creamer, spooner,
  and cov sugar
  Drapery
    Blue, gold trim **425.00**
    White, gold trim **395.00**
  Everglades
    Clear **410.00**
    Vaseline **600.00**
  Fluted Scrolls, vaseline **295.00**
  Jeweled Heart, green **600.00**
  Palm Beach, blue **525.00**
  Shell, blue **875.00**
  Swag with Brackets
    Blue **475.00**
    Green **475.00**
  Wild Bouquet, white **325.00**
Toothpick Holder
  Diamond Spearhead, green **45.00**

Flora, white, gold trim	150.00
Gonterman Swirl, amber top	150.00
Iris with Meander, green	85.00
Wreath and Shell, blue	275.00

Tumbler

Beatty Rib, white	35.00
Beatty Swirl, white	45.00
Drapery, white	20.00

Fluted Scrolls

Blue	30.00
White	25.00
Intaglio, white	45.00
Iris with Meander, blue	35.00
Jewel and Flower, vaseline	65.00
Jeweled Heart, blue	75.00
Swag with Brackets, blue	75.00
Wild Bouquet, white	25.00
Wreath and Shell, blue	55.00

Water Set, water pitcher and six tumblers, 7 pcs

Alaska, vaseline	850.00
Everglades, blue	700.00

Iris with Meander

Blue	650.00
Vaseline	295.00
Jeweled Heart, blue	625.00
Regal, green	575.00
Swag with Brackets, vaseline	575.00
Tokyo, green	675.00
Wine, Palm Beach, canary yellow	345.00

OPALINE GLASS

History: Opaline glass was a popular mid to late 19th century European glass. The glass has a certain amount of translucency and often is found decorated in enamel designs and trimmed in gold.

Reference: Charles R. Hajdamach, *British Glass, 1800–1914*, Antique Collectors' Club, 1991.

Basket, white opaque body, deep blue dec, gold enamel	150.00

Box, 5½ x 3⅝ x 4¼", brass band, $125.00.

Biscuit Jar, white opaque body, hand painted, florals and bird dec, brass lid and bail handle	150.00
Bowl, 8" d, 2" h, rose opaque body	50.00
Box, cov, 5½" l, 3⅝" w, 4¼" h, white opaque body, brass fittings	125.00
Candlestick, 7¼" h, white opaque clam-broth–color body, rib molded	150.00
Chalice, white opaque body, Diamond Point pattern	25.00
Cheese Dish, cov, white opaque body, gold enamel dec	180.00
Clock, 6" d, white opaque body, hanging, circular frame, hand painted, Welch Company, Forestville, CT, clockworks, orig brass chain	275.00

Cologne Bottle

6" h, jade green opaque body, orig stopper	90.00
8¾" h, jade green opaque body, gold ring dec, orig stopper	85.00
Creamer, shaded yellow to white opaque body, pink roses and blue forget–me–nots, silver plated rim and handle	125.00
Creamer and Sugar, opaque shaded yellow to white body, hand painted pink roses, blue forget–me–nots, silver plated rims, handles, and cov	265.00
Cup Plate, Lee–Rose 258, white opaque clambroth–color body, minute rim roughage	70.00
Dresser Jar, 7½" l, 5½" w, 5½" h, egg shape, blue opaque body, heavy gold dec	200.00
Ewer, 13¼" h, white opaque body, Diamond Point pattern	125.00
Finger Bowl, matching underplate, powder blue opaque body	125.00
Jack-In-The-Pulpit Vase, 5½" h, robin's egg blue opaque body, applied amber feet	85.00

Lamp

Fluid, 12⅛" h, Tulip pattern, brass stem, presentation floral dec, white opaque clambroth–colored body, marble base, chip on font	75.00

Whale Oil

12¼" h, Tulip pattern, white opaque clambroth–colored body, minor roughness to base	400.00
13" h, Tulip pattern, white opaque clambroth–colored body, annealing checks and small bruises to bases, pr	1,500.00
Match Holder, 1⅜" h, blue opaque body, gold flowers and leaves	35.00
Miniature, wash bowl and pitcher, powder blue opaque body, gilt dec	75.00

Perfume Bottle

2¾" h, blue opaque body, gold flowers and leaves, matching stopper	50.00

4" h, blue opaque body, gold, white, and yellow dec, matching stopper **65.00**

Pitcher, 4¼" h, pink opaque body, applied white handle **70.00**

Posy Holder, 8" h, blue opaque body, figural hand holding small vase, ruffled rim **75.00**

Rose Bowl, 4" d, green opaque body, gilt strawberries, flowers, and leaves dec **50.00**

Salt, 3¾" h, jade green opaque body, marked "Turnbridge, England" **75.00**

Sugar, cov, shaded yellow to white opaque body, pink roses and blue for-get–me–nots, silver plated cover, rim, and handle **150.00**

Toothpick Holder, lavender opaque body, small ball feet **75.00**

Tumbler, white opaque body, enameled pink rose **25.00**

Tumble–Up, carafe, tumbler, and underplate, pale green opaque body, gold beading, black and white jeweled dec, three pcs **300.00**

Urn, 13" h, blue opaque body, enameled blue flowers, gilt trim, flared rim, pr **335.00**

Vase

5⅜" h, blue opaque body, heavy gold trim, enameled yellow dec **65.00**

8" h, hand holding vase with ruffled rim, blue opaque body, figural . . . **75.00**

13" h, blue opaque body, enameled blue floral dec, gilt trim, urn shape, flared rims, pr **335.00**

16¾" h, oviform, circular cushioned foot, parcel gilt, enameled, turquoise blue opaque body, gilt rimmed molded border and handles, oval panels with artists' portraits, one with Raphel, other Van Dyke, brown, claret, white, and flesh tones, gilt borders with scrolling foliate edges, French, 19th C, pr **2,475.00**

Violet Bowl, 3½" d, 3" h, Peachblow pink ground, blue and white enameled flowers, gray leaves and vines, base sgd, Mt Washington **275.00**

Whiskey Taster, white opaque clam-broth–colored body

Lacy, Sandwich, Lee, plate 150–5, minute rim nicks **40.00**

Ten Panel, handle, small chip on bottom **85.00**

ORREFORS

History: Orrefors Glasbruck, Sweden, was established in 1898. First production items were glass windows and ink bottles. New ownership in 1913 introduced more items. The firm now produces fine art glass and tablewares, as well as limited edition plates.

One of the most sought after types of Orrefors glass is Graal. Simon Gate, F. Hald, and Knut Bergqvist were all instrumental in the development of this line around 1917. Cased glasswares were developed by Simon Gate and Advard Hald around 1920. The Ariel line was developed in 1936 by Edvin Ohrstrom. Internally decorated wares were introduced by Jan Johansson, c1970.

Designers employed by Orrefors include: Knut Bergqvist (c1919), Gunnar Cyren (c1959), Simon Gate (c1915), Advard Hald (c1917), F. Hald, Jan Johansson (c1970), Nils Landberg (c1925), Vicke Lindstrand (c1928–41), Ingegorg Lundin (c1947), Edvin Ohrstrom (c1936), Sven Palmqvist (c1936), John Selbing (c1927), and Heinrich Wollman (c1919).

The marks used by Orrefors include the name engraved on the base, often including a design number, and the designer's name. A "U" in the mark indicates that the piece was machine fire polished. Finding an "A" after the mark indicates the piece is a hand worked piece of cut glass.

Manufacturer/Distributor: Orrefors Inc., 140 Bradford Drive, Berlin, NJ 08009.

Bottle, blue, fishnet dec, deep blue neck, sgd "Sven Palmquist Kraka" . . **750.00**

Bowl

6¼" h, 6½" d, 1000 Window, pedestal, sgd **325.00**

8½" h, Graal, internally tinted purple body, clear lattice work dec, inscribed "Orrefors Sweden/Graal nr S105/Edvard Hald" **600.00**

9⅝" l, hexagonal, flaring sides, clear, engraved semi–nude women with widely flaring long hair, geometric borders, starburst base, designed by Simon Gate, c1925 . . . . **2,100.00**

11" d, shallow, clear, molded balloons encircling center **75.00**

Candleholders, pr, clear, ball shaped . . **75.00**

Decanter, 11¾" h, clear, rect, rounded shoulder, short cylindrical neck, shaped rect stopper, engraved underwater fisherman, sgd, mid 20th C . . **150.00**

Finger Bowl, 5" h, 8¾" l underplate, clear, oval tapering bowl, finely engraved frieze of cavorting nude females, holding lengths of drapery and fringed festooned fabric, scalloped borders, designed by Simon Gate, c1926, sgd "OF F 109.26 C" **2,750.00**

Goblet, 8" h, heavy, clear crystal, etched frosted design on cup and part of stem, sgd "Orrefors Palmquest 3397 61.5" **550.00**

Limited Edition Collector's Plate, 1970, gold cathedral dec **125.00**

Perfume Bottle, 3¾" h, 2" w, bulbous, flat front and back, clear, engraved swan, ball stopper **80.00**

Rose Bowl, 5½" h, globular, layered, sgd "Orrefors H 7 48," c1948 . . . . .   **190.00**

Vase
4" h, teardrop shape, paperweight type, ruby with clear casing **90.00**
4½" h
Conical, tinted deep blue, etched running figures, animals, and horse–drawn cart, landscape with rain clouds etched at rim, designed by Edvard Hald, inscribed "Orrefors Hald" **900.00**
Paperweight type, Graal, internally dec with ten green fish, underwater plants, underwater type scene **575.00**
5" h, clear, engraved bird in flight, artist sgd **110.00**
5½" h, 3¾" sq mouth, clear, Art Deco style, four bulbous sides, thick engraved panel of woman holding baby above her head, polished pontil, artist sgd **100.00**
6¼" h, Ariel pattern, clear, straight sides with trapped air bubbles in various geometric shapes against olive–green ground, designed by Ingeborg Lundin, sgd, c1960 . . . .   **900.00**
6½" h, oblong, clear, engraved, two nude children carrying basket of flowers, designed by Sven Palmquist **350.00**
7" h, sgd "Kraka No. 340 Sven Palmquist" **300.00**
7¼" h, Graal, clear, pyriform, thick walls, internally dec with fish swimming among sea grasses, sgd "Edvard Hald," c1960 . . . .   **500.00**
8" h, bud, smoke with clear casing .   **100.00**
8¾" h, Graal, clear, internally decorated, amorphic figures playing games, designed by Edwin Ohrstrom, inscribed "Orrefors 1938 Graal" **6,500.00**
9½" h, carved nude Medusa–like woman beside fawn, sgd "Orrefors/Lindstrand" and numbered **200.00**
10¼" h, frosted slender nude female archer holding bow aloft, sgd "Orrefors/Lindstrand/1484/B1/SR," minor surface scratches **100.00**
10½" h, 5" w, heavy, clear crystal, flared rect shape, Art Nouveau style etched engraving of two dancing girls, sgd "Orrefors Palmquist 2941 A 9" **700.00**
11" h, heavy, clear crystal, two deep and large oval thumbprints, sgd "Orrefors DU 3322" **250.00**

OVERSHOT GLASS

History: Overshot glass was developed in the mid–1800s. A gather of molten glass was rolled over the marver upon which had been placed crushed glass to produce overshot glass. The piece then was blown into the desired shape. The finished effect was a glass that was frosted or iced in appearance.

Early pieces were mainly made in clear. As the demand for colored glass increased, color was added to the base piece and occasionally to the crushed glass.

Pieces of overshot generally are attributed to the Boston and Sandwich Glass Co., although many other companies also made it as it grew in popularity.

Basket
4½" d, 7" h, green ground, scalloped, applied yellow flower and leaf, applied clear handle **180.00**
6" d, 7½" h, octagonal, orange shaded to vaseline ground, emb prunts on sides, applied vaseline handle **215.00**
Bowl, blue ground, petal top **150.00**
Biscuit Jar, cov, 7" h, 5" d, clear ground, melon ribbed, applied cranberry coiled snake handle **250.00**
Bride's Bowl, 8⅝" d, 6⅝" h, shaded clear to blue ground, lobed, crimped edge, decorative brass holder **200.00**
Compote
6¾" h, 8⅜" d, cranberry shaded to clear bowl, applied clear scalloped and ruffled edge, fancy brass dome ftd pedestal base **115.00**
9" h, 8⅞" d, clear ground, applied gold dec cranberry serpent around stem **100.00**

Ice Bucket, clear, flint, silver-plated rim and bail handle, attributed to Sandwich, 5⅜" h to rim, 5⅛" d, $75.00.

12¾" h, 8½" d, rubena overshot
bowl, white metal bronze finished
figural standard **125.00**
14" h, 9" d, rubena overshot bowl,
white metal bronze finished figural
standard **150.00**
Custard Cup, pink ground, applied clear
handle, Sandwich **50.00**
Decanter, clear ground, ice bladder,
orig stopper **700.00**
Dish, 6¼" d, crimped edge, canary yel-
low ground, cranberry–red overshot **160.00**
Ewer, 13½" h, trefoil top, clear ground,
twisted rope handle, Sandwich **250.00**
Fairy Lamp, 6" h, yellow ground,
ribbed, sgd clear Clarke base **125.00**
Finger Bowl, pink ground, fluted and
swirled **100.00**
Ice Bucket, clear ground, silver rim and
handle **75.00**
Lamp Shade, 7⅞" d, 2⅞" d fitter ring,
sapphire blue shaded to clear ground,
ruffled **125.00**
Marmalade Jar, cov, matching under-
plate, green ground, gold snake entwined on cov, attributed to Boston
and Sandwich Glass Co **295.00**
Mug, 3" h, clear ground, applied clear
handle **20.00**
Pitcher
5½" h, clear ground, applied clear
reeded handle **95.00**
6" d, cranberry ground, bulbous, ap-
plied clear reeded handle **115.00**
7" h, clear ground, applied clear
reeded handle **120.00**
7½" d, clear ground, bulbous, ap-
plied clear reeded handle **100.00**
8" d
Bulbous, clear ground, heavy
enamel dec of white roses, blue
forget–me–nots, and green
leaves, applied clear handle . . . **125.00**
Ovoid, cranberry ground, swirled
melon ribbed body, cylindrical
neck, pinched spout, applied
clear reeded handle **225.00**
9" h, cranberry ground, tankard, ap-
plied clear shell handle **300.00**
9" h, 5¼" d, bulbous, cylindrical
neck, flared rim, cranberry ground,
applied clear wafer foot, applied
clear handle **275.00**
9¼" h, tankard, cranberry ground, ap-
plied clear reeded handle, hinged
metal cov and thumbpiece **225.00**
12½" h, clear ground, gilt rim on undulating tricorn top, applied rope
handle loops around neck, pontil
scar, Boston and Sandwich Glassworks, Sandwich, MA, 1870–87 . **475.00**
Punch Cup, pink ground, applied clear

**Pitcher, light blue ground, applied light
amber handle, attributed to Sandwich,
7¾" h, $275.00.**

handle, attributed to Boston and
Sandwich Glass Co, set of eight **275.00**
Rose Bowl
3¾" d, rubena ground, applied flow-
ers and pale green leaves **150.00**
6" d, cranberry ground **125.00**
Sweetmeat, 7⅛" h, cranberry ground,
melon ribbed, ornate silver plated
holder **150.00**
Tazza, 5¾" h, 7¾" d, clear ground, flint
glass **185.00**
Vase
7½" h, bulbous base, slender neck,
clear ground, gold overshot, silver
floral dec **95.00**
8½" h, opalescent pink ground,
fluted, applied clear handle **115.00**
11" h, cranberry ground, two applied
pink flowers, green branch and
leaves, clear ruffled edge, applied
amber feet **300.00**
Water Carafe, clear ground, iridescent
amber overshot, hand painted flow-
ers, ground pontil **100.00**

PADEN CITY

History: Paden City Glass Manufacturing Co.
was founded in 1916 in Paden City, West Virginia. David Fisher, formerly of the New Martinsville Glass Manufacturing Co., operated the
company until his death in 1933 when his son,
Samuel, became president. The additional financial burden placed on the company by the ac-
quisition of American Glass Co. in 1949 forced
Paden City to close in 1951.

All Paden City glass was handmade and unmarked. The early glassware was of non–descript
quality, but in the early 1930s quality improved
dramatically. The cuttings were unpolished "gray
cuttings," sometimes mistaken for etchings.

Paden City is noted for its colors: opal (opaque

white), ebony, mulberry, Cheriglo (delicate pink), yellow, dark green (forest), crystal, amber, primrose (reddish–amber), blue, rose, and the ever popular red. No free–blown or opalescent glass was produced. Quantities of blanks were sold to decorating companies for gold and silver overlay and for etching.

Reference: Jerry Barnett, *Paden City The Color Company*, published by author, 1978.

Candy Dish, amethyst, etched, dots and floral vine dec, stepped domed lid, button finial, 6⅝" h, $62.00.

Animal
  Cottontail Rabbit
    Blue 85.00
    Crystal 65.00
  Pheasant
    Blue, shaded, 14" l 125.00
    Crystal 55.00
  Pony, 11½" h 100.00
  Rooster, 9½" h 85.00
  Squirrel, log base 45.00
Bowl
  Largo pattern, 11¼" d, ruby, handled 25.00
  Orchid pattern, 8¾" d, cobalt blue . 30.00
  Sunset pattern, 9" d, amber, ftd, wide etching 35.00
Cake Stand
  Ardith pattern, 11½" d, yellow, cherry etch, ftd 60.00
  Black Forest pattern, 11" d, low 60.00
  Crow's Foot pattern, 12" d, ruby ... 75.00
  Peacock and Rose pattern, green, low, ftd 60.00
Candlesticks, pr
  Cheriglo, low 24.00
  Garret pattern, 8½" h, black 30.00
Candy, cov
  Ardith pattern, floral etching, topaz . 24.00
  Crow's Foot pattern, crystal, gold encrusted flowers 18.00
  Gazebo pattern, crystal, three part .. 35.00

Mrs B pattern, ruby, three sections, gold filigree trim 50.00
Centerpiece Bowl, blue bowl, crystal flower frog 18.50
Champagne, Popeye and Olive pattern, ruby 10.00
Cheese and Cracker Server
  Glades pattern, cobalt blue 45.00
  SS Dreamship pattern, blue, 12" d plate 60.00
Cocktail Set, Hotcha Glade etch, frosted ice bucket, four ftd glasses 50.00
Compote
  Ardith pattern, yellow, cherry etch .. 55.00
  Black Forest pattern, 7½" d, green .. 55.00
  Crow's Foot pattern
    5" sq, yellow 20.00
    6½" d, ruby 25.00
  Party Line, Marie cutting, 4½" d, pink, ftd, orig spoon 45.00
Console Bowl, Ardith pattern, 12" d, yellow 40.00
Console Set, Largo pattern, crystal, sterling trim 35.00
Cordial, Cupid pattern 12.00
Creamer
  Crow's Foot pattern, white milk glass 12.00
  Cupid pattern, ftd 25.00
  Orchid pattern, green 15.00
Cup, Penny Line, amethyst 6.00
Cup and Saucer, Largo pattern, dark green 10.00
Decanter, orig stopper, Ardith pattern, oval, 5¾" w 95.00
Gravy Boat and Underplate, pink, gold encrusted trim 40.00
Goblet
  Cupid pattern 15.00
  Penny Line 8.00
Ice Tub, Nora Bird pattern, 6" d 45.00
Mayonnaise Set
  Gadroon pattern, ruby, three pcs ... 20.00
  Secrets pattern, crystal, two pcs 15.00
Pitcher, Popeye and Olive pattern, green 25.00
Plate
  Black Forest pattern, 7½" d 50.00
  Crow's Foot pattern, 9" d, amber ... 9.00
  Cupid pattern, 10" d, green 15.00
  Largo pattern, 12" d, crystal, sterling trim 15.00
  Penny Line, 7½" d, amethyst 5.00
  Popeye and Olive pattern, 12" d, ruby 20.00
  Wotta Line, 8" d, ruby 7.00
Reamer, amber, shaker type, gold trim 48.00
Relish, three part, Sunset pattern, amber 20.00
Salt and Pepper Shakers, pr
  Party Line, ruby 45.00
  Penny Line, cobalt blue, flat base .. 50.00
Sandwich Tray
  Amy pattern, chrome handles 20.00
  Swan handle, crystal 30.00

Sherbet
    Peacock Reverse pattern **25.00**
    Penny Line, amethyst **5.00**
Sugar, cov
    Nora Bird pattern, Cheriglo **35.00**
    Peacock Reverse, 2¾" h, yellow ... **40.00**
    Wotta Line, ruby **8.00**
Tray
    Gothic Garden pattern, 9½" l, yellow,
      sq center **45.00**
    Popeye and Olive pattern, 10½" l,
      green **8.00**
Tumbler
    Nora Bird pattern, 4" h **25.00**
    Peacock Reverse pattern, ruby **35.00**
    Penny Line, amethyst, flat base
      3½" h **6.50**
      5¼" h **8.00**
Vase
    Black Forest pattern, 6½" h, pink ... **45.00**
    California Poppy pattern, 12" h **125.00**
    Crow's Foot pattern, 10" h, white milk
      glass, floral dec **65.00**
    Cupid pattern, 8¼" h, pink **50.00**
    Leia Bird pattern, 8¼" h, green, el-
      liptical **80.00**
    Orchid pattern, 10" h, yellow **35.00**
    Peacock and Wild Rose pattern, black **48.00**
    Utopia pattern, 10½" h, green **125.00**
Whiskey Glass, Penny Line, 2 oz, ruby **7.50**

PAIRPOINT

History: The Pairpoint Manufacturing Co. was organized in 1880 as a silverplating firm in New Bedford, Massachusetts. The company merged with Mount Washington Glass Co. in 1894 and became the Pairpoint Corporation. The new company produced speciality glass items, often accented with metal frames.

Pairpoint Corp. was sold in 1938 and Robert Gunderson became manager. He operated it as the Gunderson Glass Works until his death in 1952. From 1952 until the plant closed in 1956, operations were maintained under the name Gunderson–Pairpoint. Robert Bryden reopened the glass manufacturing business in 1970, moving it back to the New Bedford area.

References: Edward and Sheila Malakoff, *Pairpoint Lamps*, Schiffer Publishing, 1990; Leonard E. Padgett, *Pairpoint Glass*, Wallace–Homestead, 1979; John A. Shumann III, *The Collector's Encyclopedia of American Art Glass*, Collector Books, 1988, value update 1991.

Collectors' Club: Pairpoint Cup Plate Collectors, Box 52D, East Weymouth, MA 02189.

Manufacturer/Distributor: Pairpoint Glass Works, 851 Sandwich Rd., Sagamore, MA 02561.

Museum: New Bedford Glass Museum, New Bedford, MA.

Additional Listing: Lamps and Lighting.

Basket, 11" l, 9" w, 6" h, clear ground, intaglio cut grapes, cherries, and peaches **200.00**
Bell, 9¾" h, ruby base, crystal swirled handle **195.00**
Biscuit Jar
    5" h, squatty, shaded pink to yellow ground, floral and leaf dec, enameled flowers, ormolu molded base, sgd "P" in diamond on lid **275.00**
    7" h, 6" d, molded bulbous base, hand painted, daisy dec, apricot ground, silver plated rim, cov, and bail handle, sgd and numbered .. **300.00**
Bowl
    8" d, 6½" h, cov, raised gold chrysanthemum blossoms and foliage, eggshell white ground, gold striped handles, fish finial, sgd and numbered **550.00**
    8½" d, peppermint stick, satin, clear, overlay rose rim cut to clear stripes, engraved **125.00**
    8½" d, 3½" h, Ambero, heavy walls, textured exterior, interior painted with trailing vines, three pink lotus blossoms, lush green leaves floating on pool of lime green water, sgd "Ambero L" **745.00**
Box, cov
    2½" h, round, controlled bubbles in clear body, sterling silver hinged lid **245.00**
    7¼" l, 2¾" h, molded quatraform oval, opal ground, gold enameled floral dec, hinged metal rim fittings, sgd on base "PMC 9524" **470.00**
    7¼" w, 6" l, buff ground, enameled gold and silver iris and foliage, hinged lid, sgd **450.00**
Bride's Basket, pink and white, ornate ruffled edge **325.00**
Calling Card Receiver, 5" d, engraved floral dec, clear controlled bubble ball connector to saucer base **125.00**
Candlesticks, pr
    4" h, amethyst, clear controlled bubble ball connector **100.00**
    6" h, Blue Swirl pattern, clear controlled bubble ball connector **185.00**
    11" h, amethyst, blown, hollow stem, set of four **330.00**
Centerpiece, 12" h, 13" l, swan, ruby glass blown body, applied clear swan's neck and head **450.00**
Champagne, 5⅛" h, Flambo pattern, crystal **50.00**

Cologne Bottle
  7⅛" h, ribbed, pointed stopper, orig
    Gunderson label **95.00**
  8" h, applied vertical cranberry rib-
    bing, elaborate flower form cran-
    berry and clear stopper **100.00**
Compote
  6" d, amber, engraved florals **75.00**
  7½" d, 6" h, Camelia Swirl, thirteen
    swirls in pinwheel design, crystal
    ground, bubble ball connector,
    clear base, bell tone flint, attributed
    to Gunderson **475.00**
  9¼" d, cov, ruby, clear controlled
    bubble ball connector, ruby base,
    steeple bubble finial **125.00**
Cordial, amberina, Gunderson–Pair-
  point, set of ten **365.00**
Cornucopia, 8⅜" h, ruby, clear sq base,
  labeled "Pairpoint" **135.00**
Creamer, Delft, blue windmill and land-
  scape scene, birds in flight, reverse
  with five sailing ships, blown–out
  scrolls base with blue highlights, silver plated handle, rim, and spout, left
  handed, base numbered **325.00**
Decanter, 10" h, Old English pattern,
  quart, matching stopper **1,250.00**
Dresser Jar, cov, 4" h, clear green
  ground, cranberry cov, clear finial,
  orig label **120.00**
Goblet, Adelaide pattern, cobalt blue . **45.00**
Hat, 4¼" h, deep red ground, white
  spatter, controlled bubbles, orig paper
  label **75.00**
Inkwell, 4" d, clear, all over controlled
  bubbles, sterling silver cap **200.00**
Jack-In-The-Pulpit Vase, 7¾" h, ruby,
  enameled bird on pine bough **165.00**
Jewel Box, cov, robin's egg blue opal
  glass, six scalloped pink, yellow, and
  coral rose medallions with green
  leaves, brown traceries, painted gold
  trim, four ball feet, gold washed silver
  plated base, sgd and numbered **325.00**
Lamp
  Boudoir, 15" h, 8½" d shade, flat top,
    blown–out ribbed glass shade, re-
    verse painted pink and blue blos-
    som clusters, black accented bor-
    der band, four stylized green trees,
    yellow ground, two small rim
    chips, single socket gilt metal stan-
    dard, numbered, marked "Pair-
    point" in diamond **1,980.00**
  Table, 27" h, 16" d shade, black ac-
    cented multi–flowered shade
    marked "The Pairpoint Corp," tri-
    parte gilt metal three socket stand,
    sq black onyx base marked "Pair-
    point" **4,400.00**
  31" h, 15" d conical Carlisle reverse

Lamp, Exeter form reverse painted shade, four brightly colored birds, blue and white blossoms, leaves, stylized yellow and pink motifs, stamped mark "The Pairpoint Corp'n," silvered metal urn form tri–column Pairpoint base, 22½" h, 18" d shade, $4,125.00. Photograph courtesy of Skinner, Inc.

  painted shade, raspberry pink
  ground with Egyptian Garden of Al-
  lah scene, three pyramids, ruins,
  oasis city, camel, and kneeling
  man, tall palm trees in background,
  sgd by artist "C Durand" and "The
  Pairpoint Corp'n," orig Pairpoint
  two socket baluster base with
  molded Egyptian motif **2,200.00**
Lamp Shade, 8" sq, puffy, sq closed top
  molded, reverse painted with deep
  red roses and multicolored butterflies,
  gold accents, marked "The Pairpoint
  Corp" and "Patented July 9, 1907" **3,000.00**
Mantel Lusters, pr, 11" h, black–amethyst, clear controlled bubble stem,
  ten brilliant clear crystal prisms **295.00**
Perfume Bottle
  5½" h, heavy crystal, controlled bub-
    bles **60.00**
  6" h, octagonal, heavy crystal, ribbed
    stopper **125.00**
Pitcher, 8½" h, amberina, applied ruby
  handle **175.00**
Plate, 5⅛" d, enameled floral dec, artist
  sgd "P. Kiluk," "P" in diamond mark **125.00**
Punch Cup, cylindrical, flaring rim and
  low foot, vaseline, engraved grapes . **30.00**
Rose Bowl, 6½" h, egg shape, enameled
  blue windmill scene, white opaline
  ground, c1890 . . . . **575.00**
Salt, master, clear, controlled bubbles . **85.00**
Smoking Stand, three opal bowls, 3¾ x
  3½" h, 3 x 2" h, and 2¼ x 2¼" h,
  Delft dec, windmills, houses, people,
  trees, and sailing ships, brass rims,

shield shaped maple piece, fancy brass trim and feet, brass cigar holder **550.00**
Tumbler, 5¼" h, bubbly, clear ground, black and white polar bear dec **75.00**
Urn, cov, 14" h, Vintage Grape pattern, amethyst **225.00**

Vase, ruby trumpet, clear paperweight base, Gunderson/Pairpoint, 7" h, $75.00.

Vase
5½" h, bud, amethyst, clear controlled bubble ball connector, orig label **100.00**
8½" h, blood red, turned down collar, clear controlled bubbles in ball stem **200.00**
9" h, Ambero, interior painted with scene of couple strolling down country lane, textured finish **750.00**
15" h, winged cherub in flowing pink drape with tray of peonies, reverse with spray of multicolored poppies, gold borders, powder blue rim shading to cobalt blue ground, applied cobalt blue openwork handles **1,250.00**
Wine
5⅛" h, flambe, red bowl, black stem, Rockwell silver design **150.00**
12" h, trumpet shape, crystal bubble ball stem **175.00**

PAPERWEIGHTS

History: Although paperweights had their origin in ancient Egypt, it was in the mid–19th century that this art form reached its zenith. The classic period for paperweights was 1845–55 in France where the Clichy, Baccarat, and Saint Louis factories produced the finest examples of this art. Other weights made in England, Italy, and Bo-

hemia during this period rarely matched the quality of the French weights.

In the early 1850s New England Glass Co. in Cambridge, Massachusetts, and the Boston and Sandwich Glass Co. in Sandwich, Massachusetts, became the first American factories to make paperweights.

Popularity peaked during the classic period and faded toward the end of the 19th century. Paperweights were rediscovered nearly a century later in the mid–1900s. Contemporary weights still are made by Baccarat, Saint Louis, Perthshire, and by many studio craftsmen in the U.S. and Europe.

References: Paul Hollister, Jr., *The Encyclopedia of Glass Paperweights,* Paperweight Press, 1969; Sibylle Jargstorf, *Paperweights,* Schiffer Publishing Ltd, 1992; Leo Kaplan, *Paperweights,* published by author, 1985; George N. Kulles, *Identifying Antique Paperweights–Lampwork,* Paperweight Press, 1987; James Mackay, *Glass Paperweights,* Facts on File, 1973; Edith Mannoni, *Classic French Paperweights,* Paperweight Press, 1984; Lawrence H. Selman, *All About Paperweights,* Paperweight Press, 1992; L. H. Selman Ltd., *Collector's Paperweights: Price Guide and Catalogue,* Paperweight Press, 1986.

Collectors' Club: Paperweight Collectors Assoc. Inc., P.O. Box 1059, East Hampton, MA 01027.

Periodicals: *Paperweight Gaffer,* 35 Williamstown Circle, York, PA 17404; *Paperweight News,* 761 Chestnut Street, Santa Cruz, CA 95060.

ANTIQUE

Baccarat
Clematis, 2½" d, white center flower, single bud, five green leaves, encircled in ring of canes **600.00**
Double Cut Overlay, 2¾" d, ruby cut to clear, interlaced strings of fine green and white canes encircling center group of circular set up canes, star cut base, minute edge nicks **900.00**
Garland, 2⅞" d, blue, white, and red cane garland, white and green cane central circle, coral and green star center **650.00**
Millefiori, 3¼" d, close millefiori mushroom, two silhouette canes of horse and monkey, blue and white torsade, star cut base **700.00**
Pansy, 3" d, violet and yellow flower, stem with eleven leaves, star cut base **500.00**
Primrose, 3¼" d, white flower, red center cane, petals outlined in blue, green leaves and stem, star cut base **600.00**

Clichy

Daisy, 2¾" d, five pink petals, green stem, swirling latticino cushion, c1845 ....1,200.00

Millefiori, 2⅜" d, spaced millefiori, center rose cane, dark blue ground, minor scratches and wear 850.00

Miniature, 1¾" d, four concentric rings of various colors, surrounding sixteen star cane 365.00

Pansy, 2⅝" d, soft purple upper and lower petals shaded lighter at edges, lower with purple–striped yellow centers, nodding bird, clear ground 1,400.00

Rose

2⅛" d, green and white center cane encircled by eight roses, fifteen blue and white canes, clear ground 400.00

3¼" d, pink, white, and green rose center cane, meandering chain of blue and white canes, five red, white, and green canes around perimeter, white muslin ground 2,500.00

Sodden Snow, 3" d, multicolored pastry mold canes, opaque white ground 950.00

Swirl, 2" d, turquoise and white, predominately red central pastry mold cane 950.00

Millville, NJ, 11" h, mantel type, multicolored tree design, crystal cone shaped body, fancy knopped stems, late 19th C, pr 300.00

Mount Washington, 3½" d, poinsettia, pink petals, green leaves, multicolored swirled ground 225.00

New England Glass Company

Apple, 3" d, molded, deep red shading to yellow, clear 750.00

Clematis, 2⅞" d, double pink flowers with striated petals, white center, five green leaves, swirling white latticino 1,700.00

Floral, 2½" d, three yellow, red, and white flowers, air trap centers, three multicolored canes surrounding pink, blue, and white center cane, six green leaves, white latticino ground 1,400.00

Fruit, 3" d, five pears, four cherries, three green leaves, white latticino ground 475.00

Mushroom, concentric circles, 3³⁄₁₆" d, faceted with quatrefoils, multicolored, shamrocks, hearts, and millefiori canes, white torsade 325.00

Pear, 2⅜" h, orange and yellow, green stem, clear circular base 900.00

Poinsettia, 3⅜" d, ten petals, five pale

blue dots, and dew drops on petals, pebble ground 325.00

Pairpoint, 2¾" d, faceted, diamond cut, upright pink roses, green foliage 150.00

Pantin, 2⅝" d, Lilies of the Valley, pink spray, thin pale amber stems, green leaves, clear 6,000.00

Sandwich

Bouquet, 2½" d, red center flower, two flowers on either side, green leaves, clear ground, white torsade 900.00

Diamond Rows, 2¾" d, bubble indents, deep green over white 675.00

Floral and Fruit, 3⅞" d, red, white, and blue flowers, three pears, and two cherries, twenty green leaves, white latticino ground 13,000.00

Pansy, 3" d, clear, full bloom, two pink, two cobalt, and one white and blue striped petal encircling a blue, pink, and white center cane, three green leaves, single stem ... 250.00

Poinsettia, 2½" d, blue, ten petal blossom, five jeweled green leaves, white latticino ground 475.00

Wild Rose, 3" d, white, blue and pink striping, eight leaves on green stem 500.00

Saint Louis

Bouquet, 2⅞" d, three blue flowers with yellow centers surrounded by garland of multicolored canes, clear ground 2,500.00

Chrysanthemum, 2¾" d, pink with striped petals, four green leaves and stem, swirling white latticino 1,850.00

Crown, 2⅞" d, center animal silhouette cane dated 1825, red, blue, green, and white 1,150.00

Posy, 2⅝" d, five florets, pink, ochre, pale and dark blue, and white, five green leaves, strawberry cut base . 490.00

Venetian, 7" d, 4¼" h, hollow, scrambled latticino, ribbon, and millefiori, mica and gold inclusions 170.00

HISTORICAL

Abraham Lincoln, Lindsey #275 ..... 175.00

General John J Pershing, 3⅞" d, circular, bust, reverse painted gold, 1917 ... 175.00

Plymouth Rock, Lindsey #18 .... 90.00

The Grand Army of the Republic, 2½" d, white and clear 50.00

MODERN

Rick Ayotte

Cardinal, orange and white carnations, sgd and dated 1985 .... 195.00

Cockatoo, yellow sulfur crest, deep blue translucent ground 350.00

Hummingbird, 2" d, green, red throat,

white belly, orange trumpet flowers, sgd and dated 1985 .... **195.00**
Snow Owl, perched on pine branch, moon on midnight ground, sgd .. **400.00**
Baccarat
Andrew Jackson, 2¾" d, emerald base, sgd "M. Perry A Jackson, 1971" **200.00**
John F Kennedy, 2⅞" d, sulfide bust, black amethyst ground **190.00**
Mount Rushmore, 4⅛" d, sulfide, red over white overlay, clear blue base, dated 1976 .... **100.00**
Ray Banford
2½" d, iris, red, white, and blue, green foliage, faceted, sgd Ray Banford **600.00**
2⅞" d, faceted, pink rose, leaves, and buds, star cut base, sgd, c1980 .. **500.00**
Harold J Hacker, 2¾" d, green salamander, black feet, color flecked gray–green ground **365.00**
Jokelson, Cristal d'Albret, Albert Schweitzer, sulphide, faceted, limited edition **200.00**

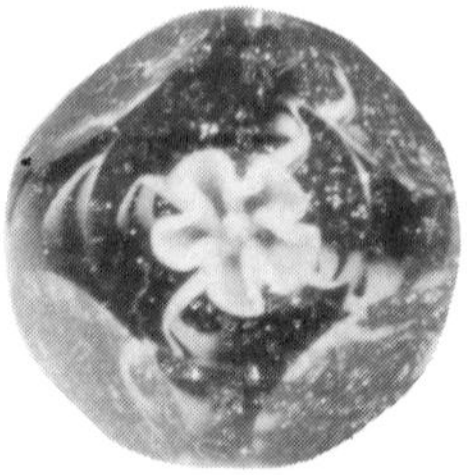

Modern, Kaziun, pink flower center, cobalt blue ground, sgd, $325.00.

Charles Kaziun
Button, ⅞" d, one red, one yellow, and one blue rose, green swirls separated by three gathering goldstones ground, encircled "K" signature cane **285.00**
Cameo, 1⅜" d, silhouette of lady, black and white, surrounded by six green, white, and pink floral canes, pink ground, six side facets, circular facet on top, sgd gold "K" **600.00**
Faceted, 2½" d, single pink and yellow flowers, star cut base, signature cane in center of three green leaves **1,950.00**
Millefiori, 2" d, seven multicolored millefiori canes with fish, turtle, duck, and heart silhouettes, white filigree with "K" initial, light green ground shot with gold, sgd "K" on base **500.00**

Miniature
1¼" d, 2" h, pedestal, single yellow and red flower, four green and white leaves, lavender ground shot with gold, sgd with gold "K" on base **250.00**
1⅞" d, set up canes in center, surrounded by pink and white spiral ring, cobalt ground shot with gold **800.00**
Overlay
2¼" d, double cut overlay, plum cut to white cut to clear, six side windows, single window on top, multicolored center cane with "K" signature surrounded by two concentric circles of green, red, and white canes, raised black ground **1,200.00**
2⅜" d, triple cut overlay, blood red to white to clear **4,500.00**
Pedestal, 2⅛" d, red rose, seven red heart canes surrounded by leaves and signature cane, c1960 ...... **750.00**
Millefiori, five petaled blossom, mottled red and green ground, controlled bubble bed, labeled "Birks 806" ... **50.00**
Lundberg Studios
Butterfly, 2¹¹⁄₁₆" d, flowers, lavender and orange, tan and green swirled iridescent ground, sgd and dated "1980, Buzzini 3186" **145.00**
Spider, 2¾" d, black, yellow outline, iridescent gold and smoky blue ground, sgd and dated "1980 Buzzini S675" **225.00**
Perthshire
Crocus, 2¾" d, lavender, upright pistil **150.00**
Dahlia, 3¼" d, pink flower, faceted, sgd and dated "P 1972" **450.00**
Dragonfly, 3⅜" d, three flowers with yellow ribbon, etched cross hatch base, dated 1974 .... **500.00**
Penguin in hollow bubble, ice blue flash overlay **350.00**
St Louis
Faceted, 3" d, bust, Queen Elizabeth encircled in pink and white ring, green and white alternating setup canes, sgd, dated 2/6/53 .... **100.00**
Pansy, 3" d, faceted, white muslin ground, sgd S.L./1980 in red cane on back **250.00**
Paul Stankard
Cactus, two yellow flowers and buds, stem, translucent dark blue ground **950.00**
Cayenne Pepper Plate, 2⅛" d, red and black peppers, pistachio ground, signature cane, inscribed "50/50 1974 C B617" **700.00**
Floral, 3⅛" d, mixed bouquet of multicolored flowers, buds and

green leaves, "Natures Splendors,"
red signature cane with black "S,"
numbered A 210, dated 1978 ... **1,800.00**
Orchid, 2⁹⁄₁₆" d, pink, opaque emerald green ground, faceted, sgd and
dated 1974 .... **285.00**
Violets, bouquet, purple and white
flowers, green leaves and stem,
clear ground **1,000.00**
Debbie Taristano, 3¼" d, blue flowers, three pussy willow sprigs, star
cut base, signature cane, c1984 .. **600.00**
Francis Whitefriars
Clematis, 2⅜" d, blue flower, white
jack–in–the pulpit, yellow flower
sprig, transparent wine ground ... **250.00**
Inkwell, concentric millefiori base,
matching stopper, chip at top rim
of stopper **250.00**
Millefiori, close concentric, pale
blue, white, olive green, and pink,
six facets around sides, one on top,
clear **200.00**
Sunflower, 2⅜" d, blue and white
flower, faceted, transparent wine
ground **265.00**
F. D. Whittemore
Rose, pedestal base
2¾" d, pink, four green leaves, yellow and black signature cane .. **150.00**
3⅛" h, powder blue, four green
leaves, yellow and black signature cane **175.00**

**Modern, Paul Ysart, Dahlia, purple
flower, circle of red and white canes, cobalt carpet, sgd, orig paper label,
$375.00.**

Paul Ysart
Butterfly, 3" d, single blue flower with
white center, long green stem, eight
leaves, mottled pink and white
ground **250.00**
Dragonfly, 3" d, ruby, green wings,
latticino stave basket, signature
cane, c1960 .... **275.00**

Flower, 3" d, yellow and white,
brown stem, three green leaves,
setup pink and white canes, deep
amethyst ground **450.00**

PATE–DE–VERRE

History: Pate–de–Verre can be translated simply
as glass paste. It is manufactured by grinding lead
glass into a powder or crystal form, making it
into a paste by adding a 2% or 3% solution of
sodium silicate, molding, firing, and carving. The
Egyptians discovered the process as early as 1500
B.C.

In the late 19th century, the process was rediscovered by a group of French glassmakers.
Amalric Walter, Henri Cros, Georges Despret,
and the Daum brothers were leading manufacturers.

Contemporary sculptors are creating a second
renaissance, lead by the technical research of
Jacques Daum.

**Tray, molded oval, green, darker green
figural fish with fanned gill fins, naturalistic detail, sgd "A. Walter Nancy," 9¼"
l, 5½" w, $2,200.00. Photograph courtesy
of Skinner, Inc.**

Ashtray
3½" sq, mottled turquoise and midnight blue, two rect compartments,
molded bumblebee with black and
orange body, green wings, deep
brown head, molded signature "A
Walter/Nancy" and Berge/SC,"
c1925 .... **800.00**
5" d, circular, brown beetle surmount,
Almeric Walter **1,200.00**
6¼" l, 3½" w, center medallion with
Egyptian head, molded in reds and

purples, small flower buds around edge, raised lattice work on bottom **1,600.00**
Atomizer, 5¾" h, red berries, green leaves, molded signature "H Berge" **1,000.00**
Bookend, 5¾" h, yellow fox leaping from leaf molded green ground to trellis hung with green and purple grapes and foliage, molded signature "A Walter Nancy," c1925 . . . . **850.00**
Bowl
2¾" d, molded sprays of red berries, green–brown branches, molded body lightly streaked with purple, c1920 . . . . **850.00**
4¾" h, tapering sides, two integral flattened handles molded in low and medium relief, olive–green, ochre, and brown berry laden leafy branches, lemon yellow shaded to mustard ground, molded signature "AWalter–Nancy," and "HBerge–Sc," c1925 . . . . **3,850.00**
10¼" d, ftd, molded with concentric blossoms, long necked birds rim, gray sides streaked with lavender and rose **4,000.00**
Clock, 4½" sq, stars within pentagon and tapered sheaves motif, molded in orange and black, molded signature "G Argy–Rousseau," clockworks by J E Caldwell **2,650.00**
Jewelry, pendant
2½" d, circular, molded high relief, stylized bouquet of orange flowers, black and purple centers, gray ground, molded signature "G.A.R.," (G. Argy–Rousseau,) c1925, replaced silk cord, orig burst air bubble on edge **1,550.00**
2⅝" d, circular, molded green mistletoe leaves encircling purple berried center, amethyst translucent ground trimmed in blue, green knotted silk cord and hanging tassel **600.00**
3" l, ovoid, molded high relief, cicada with black body and green wings, mottled rose and lemon yellow ground, molded signature "A. Walter/Nancy/H. Berge Sc," c1925 . . **1,450.00**
Paperweight
1¾" d, cast, speckled emerald green and black reptile, circular mustard and gray streaked ground, molded signature "A Walter–Nancy," c1920 . . . . **2,400.00**
3" l, molded in full relief, snail slithering over berried branch, shaded mustard ground with sienna, green, and brown highlights, molded signature "A Walter–Nancy," c1920 **3,575.00**
Plaque, 11" l, La Danse, oval, molded high relief, cloaked female, molded

in warm speckled brown, lemon yellow chiffon ground, molded title and "Daum L," c1950 . . . . **1,750.00**
Sculpture
3¾" h, Pan, seated young god playing pipes, molded in deep lemon yellow and lime green, modeled by Henri Mercer, molded signature "AWalter–Nancy" and "h. Mercer," c1925 . . . . **1,750.00**
4" h, baby blue jay, molded in dark turquoise, designed by Henri Berge, molded signature "A Walter, Nancy" **1,250.00**
7⅞" h, Danuese, woman, standing, draped in flowing robes, molded in emerald green shading to white, molded signature "A Walter/Nancy," c1920 . . . . **2,250.00**
12" h, Loie Fuller, dancer, molded in shades of blue, molded signature "A Walter" **5,750.00**
Tray, 8" l, 6" w, molded apple green ground, figural green and yellow duck with orange beak at one end, molded signature "Walter, Nancy" **750.00**
Vase
7" h, mottled gray sides molded in low relief with blue Australian bush babies hiding among grasses, molded signature "G Argy Rousseau–France" **6,000.00**
9" h, tapered cylindrical, rose faun, satyr, girl among amber waves, framed by purple morning glories, green ground **3,600.00**
9¾" h, baluster shape, aquamarine, purple streaked translucent ground, cobalt and sea–green geometric and stylized floral design, molded signature "G Argy–Rousseau–France" **2,500.00**

PATTERN GLASS

History: Pattern glass is clear or colored glass pressed into one of hundreds of patterns. Deming Jarves of the Boston and Sandwich Glass Co. invented the first successful pressing machine in 1828. By the 1860s glass pressing machinery had been improved, and mass production of good quality matched tableware sets began. The idea of a matched glassware table service (including goblets, tumblers, creamers, sugars, compotes, cruets, etc.) quickly caught on in America. Many pattern glass table services had numerous accessory pieces among which were banana stands, molasses cans, water bottles, etc.

Early pattern glass (flint) was made with a lead formula, giving it a ringing quality. During the Civil War lead became too valuable to be used in glass manufacturing. In 1864 Hobbs, Brockunier & Co., West Virginia, developed a soda lime (non–flint) formula. Pattern glass also was produced in colors, milk glass, opalescent glass, slag glass, and custard glass.

The hundreds of companies which produced pattern glass have histories of development, expansions, personnel problems, material and supply demands, fires, and mergers. In 1899 the National Glass Co. was formed as a combine of nineteen glass companies in Pennsylvania, Ohio, Indiana, West Virginia, and Maryland. U. S. Glass, another consortium, was founded in 1891. These combines resulted as attempts to save small companies by pooling talents, resources, and patterns. Because of this pooling, the same pattern can be attributed to several companies.

Sometimes the pattern name of a piece was changed from one company to the next to reflect current fashion trends. U. S. Glass created the States series by issuing patterns named for a particular state. Several of these patterns were new issues, others were former patterns renamed.

References: E. M. Belnap, *Milk Glass,* Crown Publishers, Inc., 1949; Regis F. and Mary F. Ferson, *Yesterday's Milk Glass Today,* published by author, 1981; William Heacock, *Toothpick Holders from A to Z, Book 1, Encyclopedia of Victorian Colored Pattern Glass,* Antique Publications, 1981; William Heacock, *Opalescent Glass from A to Z, Book 2,* Antique Publications, 1981; William Heacock, *Syrups, Sugar Shakers & Cruets, Book 3,* Antique Publications, 1981; William Heacock, *Custard Glass From A to Z, Book 4,* Antique Publications, 1980; William Heacock, *U. S. Glass From A to Z, Book 5,* Antique Publications, Inc., 1980; William Heacock, *Oil Cruets From A to Z, Book 6,* Antique Publications, 1981; William Heacock, *Ruby Stained Glass From A To Z, Book 7,* Antique Publications, Inc., 1986; William Heacock, *More Ruby Stained Glass, Book 8,* Antique Publications, 1987; William Heacock and William Gamble, *Cranberry Opalescent From A to Z, Book 9,* Antique Publications, 1987; William Heacock, *Old Pattern Glass,* Antique Publications, 1981; William Heacock, *1000 Toothpick Holders: A Collector's Guide,* Antique Publications, 1977; William Heacock, *Rare and Unlisted Toothpick Holders,* Antique Publications, 1984.

Bill Jenks and Jerry Luna, *Early American Pattern Glass—1850 to 1910: Major Collectible Table Settings with Prices,* Wallace–Homestead Book Co., 1990; Minnie Watson Kamm, *Pattern Glass Pitchers, Books 1 through 8,* published by author, 1970, 4th printing; Ruth Webb Lee, *Early American Pressed Glass,* Lee Publications, 1966, 36th edition; Ruth Webb Lee, *Victorian Glass,* Lee Publications, 1944, 13th edition; Bessie M.

Lindsey, *American Historical Glass,* Charles E. Tuttle Co., 1967; Robert Irwin Lucas, *Tarentum Pattern Glass,* privately printed, 1981; Mollie H. McCain, *Pattern Glass Primer,* Lamplighter Books, 1979; Mollie H. McCain, *The Collector's Encyclopedia of Pattern Glass,* Collector Books, 1982, value update 1990; George P. and Helen McKearin, *American Glass,* Crown Publishers, 1941; James Measell, *Greentown Glass,* Grand Rapids Public Museum Association, 1979; James Measell and Don E. Smith, *Findlay Glass: The Glass Tableware Manufacturers, 1886–1902,* Antique Publications, Inc., 1986; Alice Hulett Metz, *Early American Pattern Glass,* published by author, 1958; Alice Hulett Metz, *Much More Early American Pattern Glass,* published by author, 1965.

Dori Miles and Robert W. Miller, *Wallace–Homestead Price Guide To Pattern Glass, 11th Edition,* Wallace–Homestead, 1986; S. T. Millard, *Goblets I,* privately printed, 1938, reprinted Wallace–Homestead, 1975; S. T. Millard, *Goblets II,* privately printed, 1940, reprinted Wallace–Homestead, 1975; Arthur G. Peterson, *Glass Salt Shakers: 1,000 Patterns,* Wallace–Homestead, 1970; Jane Shadel Spillman, *American and European Pressed Glass in the Corning Museum of Glass,* Corning Museum of Glass, 1981; Jane Shadel Spillman, *The Knopf Collectors Guides to American Antiques, Glass Volumes 1 and 2,* Alfred A. Knopf, Inc., 1982, 1983; Doris and Peter Unitt, *American and Canadian Goblets,* Clock House, 1970; Doris and Peter Unitt, *Treasury of Canadian Glass,* Clock House, 1969, 2nd edition; Peter Unitt and Anne Worrall, *Canadian Handbook, Pressed Glass Tableware,* Clock House Productions, 1983; Dina von Zweck, *The Woman's Day Dictionary of Glass,* The Main Street Press, 1983.

Museums: Historical Glass Museum, Redlands, CA; National Museum of Man, Ottawa, Ontario, Canada; Schminck Memorial Museum, Lakeview, OR; The Chrysler Museum, Norfolk, VA; The Corning Museum of Glass, Corning, NY; The Toledo Museum of Art, Toledo, OH; Wheaton Historical Village Association Museum of Glass, Millville, NJ.

Periodicals: *Antique Glass Quarterly,* Rudi Publishing, P. O. Box 1364, Iowa City, IA 52244; *Glass Collector's Digest,* Richardson Printing Corp., P. O. Box 663, Marietta, OH 45750; *Glass Shards,* National Early American Glass Club, P. O. Box 8489, Silver Spring, MD 20907.

Additional Listings: Bread Plates, Children's Toy Dishes, Cruets, Custard Glass, Milk Glass, Ruby Stained Glass, Toothpicks Holders, and specific companies.

Reproduction Alert: Pattern glass has been widely reproduced. Collectors are urged to learn what pieces were originally made, what colors they were made in, etc. Careful attention to details is the best way to determine a reproduced piece of pattern glass.

Note: The examples listed below are only a small sampling of the patterns and variety of objects found in this large glass collecting area. Please refer to one of the reference books mentioned above for more detailed listings of a particular pattern or manufacturer.

Adonis pattern, plate, $15.00.

Ale Glass
Ashburton, flint, 5" h	**90.00**
Dancing Goat, frosted goat	**55.00**
Honeycomb, flint	**50.00**

Banana Boat
Amazon (Sawtooth Band), etched . .	**95.00**
Delaware (Four Petal Flower), rose, gold trim	**65.00**
Eyewinker (Cannon Ball, Crystal Ball, Winking Eye), flat	**80.00**
Feather (Doric), emerald green	**175.00**
Heart with Thumbprint (Bull's Eye in Heart)	**75.00**
Maryland (Inverted Loop and Fan; Loop and Diamond), ruby stained	**85.00**

Banana Stand, high standard
Arched Fleur–De–Lis	**35.00**
Beautiful Lady	**30.00**
Chandelier (Crown Jewel)	**100.00**
Eyewinker (Cannon Ball, Crystal Ball, Winking Eye)	**100.00**
Kansas (Jewel with Dewdrop)	**90.00**
Moon and Star (Palace)	**90.00**
Reverse Torpedo (Bull's Eye and Diamond Point)	**100.00**
Snail (Compact, Idaho, Double Snail)	**145.00**
Wisconsin (Beaded Dewdrop)	**75.00**

Bar Bottle
Ashburton, flint, bulbous lip, pewter dispenser cap, 10½" h	**125.00**
Horn of Plenty, flint, pewter spout . .	**135.00**

Argus pattern, celery vase (left), $80.00; champagne (right), $50.00.

Massachusetts (Geneva #2), metal shot glass cov	**75.00**

Barber Bottle
Heart with Thumbprint (Bull's Eye in Heart)	**115.00**
Honeycomb, flint	**45.00**

Basket
Broken Column (Irish Column, Notched Rib, Rattan), applied handle, 15" l	**125.00**
Dakota (Baby Thumbprint, Thumbprint Band), etched	**250.00**
Paneled Thistle (Delta)	**65.00**
Portland, gold trim	**85.00**
Snail (Compact, Idaho, Double Snail)	**85.00**
Vermont (Honeycomb with Flower Rim, Inverted Thumbprint with Daisy Band), gold trim	**30.00**

Berry Bowl, master
Adonis (Pleat and Tuck, Washboard), canary–yellow	**15.00**
Alabama (Beaded Bull's Eye and Drape)	**30.00**
Dakota (Baby Thumbprint, Thumbprint Band)	**30.00**
Jacob's Ladder (Maltese), ornate SP holder, ftd	**125.00**
Mardi Gras (Duncan and Miller #42, Paneled English Hobnail with Prisms)	**18.00**
Missouri (Palm and Scroll), emerald green	**35.00**
O'Hara Diamond (Sawtooth and Star)	**25.00**
Shell and Tassel (Duncan No. 555, Shell and Spike)	**35.00**
Tennessee (Jewel and Crescent, Jeweled Rosettes), colored jewels	**30.00**
Vermont (Honeycomb with Flower Rim, Inverted Thumbprint with Daisy Band), emerald green, gold trim	**45.00**

Berry Set, master and sauces
Atlas (Bullet, Cannon Ball, Crystal Ball), 9" d master bowl, four sauces	**45.00**

Canadian, 8" d cov master bowl, six
sauces **150.00**
Colorado (Lacy Medallion), 10" d ruf-
fled master bowl, five sauces, green **160.00**
Delaware (Four Petal Flower), boat
shaped bowl, five sauces, green .. **150.00**
Dolphin, high standard open shell, six
sauces **190.00**
Florida (Emerald Green Herringhone,
Paneled Herringbone), master, six
sauces, emerald green **110.00**
Flower with Cane, Maiden's Blush,
gold trim, master, six sauces **125.00**
Grape and Gothic Arches, 8½" d mas-
ter, five sauces **70.00**
King's Crown, ruby stained, etched
boat shaped master, six sauces ... **125.00**
Louis XV, master bowl, five sauces,
custard **300.00**

Biscuit Jar, cov
All–Over Diamond (Diamond Block,
Diamond Splendor) **60.00**
Broken Column (Irish Column,
Notched Rib, Rattan) **85.00**
Minnesota, ruby stained **150.00**
Pennsylvania (Balder), emerald green **100.00**
Reverse Torpedo (Bull's Eye and Dia-
mond Point) **135.00**
Three Face **300.00**

Bitters Bottle
Cabbage Rose, 6½" h **125.00**
Diamond Thumbprint, orig pewter
pourer, applied lip, polished pontil,
flint **450.00**

Bon Bon, Georgia (Peacock Feather) .. **25.00**

Bowl
All–Over Diamond (Diamond Block,
Diamond Splendor), 7" d **20.00**
Bird and Strawberry (Bluebird), col-
ored, 9½" d, ftd **85.00**
Buckle (Early Buckle), flint, 10" d ... **65.00**
Classic Medallion (Cameo)
6" d, ftd **30.00**
8" d, ftd **40.00**
Daisy and Button, blue, triangular .. **45.00**
Finecut and Panel (Russian, Button
and Oval Medallion, Nailhead and
Panel), amber, 7" d **28.00**
King's #500, Dewey Blue, gold trim,
7" d **30.00**
New Hampshire (Bent Buckle, Mod-
iste), gold trim, flared, 8½" d **15.00**
Pavonia (Pineapple Stem), 9" d **20.00**
Princess Feather (Rochelle), oval, 7" **20.00**
Scroll Cane Band, amber stained ... **43.00**
Shell and Tassel (Duncan No. 555,
Shell and Spike), shell feet **55.00**
Snail (Compact, Idaho, Double Snail),
ruby stained, 7" d **45.00**
Thousand Eye, blue **85.00**
Utah (Frost Flower, Twinkle Star) ... **18.00**

Wisconsin (Beaded Dewdrop), cov, 6"
l oval **40.00**
Zipper (Cobb, Late Sawtooth), 7" ... **15.00**

Bread Plate
Basketweave, canary–yellow **35.00**
Beautiful Lady **15.00**
Cape Cod **45.00**
Deer and Pine Tree (Deer and Doe),
blue **125.00**
Kansas (Jewel with Dewdrop) **45.00**
Lion (Frosted Lion) **90.00**
New Jersey (Loops and Drops, Red
Loop and Finecut), ruby stained .. **100.00**
Tennessee (Jewel and Crescent, Jew-
eled Rosettes) **40.00**
U. S. Coin (American Coin), frosted **325.00**
Wildflower, amber, 8" sq **25.00**

Breakfast Set, Heart with Thumbprint
(Bull's Eye in Heart), small creamer
and sugar, rect tray **55.00**

Bride's Basket, Delaware (Four Petal
Flower), green, gold trim, SP frame . **115.00**

Butter, cov
Actress (Theatrical) **75.00**
Adonis (Pleat and Tuck, Washboard),
blue **20.00**
Aegis (Bead and Bar Medallion,
Swiss) **35.00**
Baltimore Pear (Gipsy) **60.00**
Banded Portland (Virginia #1, Maid-
en's Blush) **50.00**
Beaded Acorn Medallion (Beaded
Acorn), acorn finial **65.00**
Bleeding Heart **48.00**
Colorado (Lacy Medallion) **60.00**
Croesus (Riverside's #484), green,
gold trim **135.00**
Daisy and Button With V Ornament
(Van Dyke), blue **95.00**
Esther (Tooth and Claw), green **100.00**
Holly **150.00**
Lion (Frosted Lion), lion's head finial **90.00**
Maryland (Inverted Loop and Fan;
Loop and Diamond), gold trim ... **65.00**
Nestor, amethyst, dec **125.00**
Oregon #1 (Beaded Loop), flanged . **50.00**
Pavonia (Pineapple Stem), ruby
stained **125.00**
Queen Anne (Bearded Man) **75.00**
Rose In Snow (Bryce #125, Rose), sq **45.00**
Sawtooth (Diamond Point, Mitre Dia-
mond), flint **75.00**
Thousand Eye, vaseline **90.00**
Utah (Frost Flower, Twinkle Star) ... **35.00**
Yale (Crow–Foot, Turkey Track) **45.00**
Zipper (Cobb, Late Sawtooth) **40.00**

Butter Pat, Horn of Plenty, flint **20.00**

Buttermilk Goblet
Hops Band **40.00**
Lily of the Valley **35.00**
Open Rose (Moss Rose) **15.00**

Cake Dome, Dakota (Baby Thumbprint, Thumbprint Band), etched, 8" **300.00**

Cake Plate

Adonis (Pleat and Tuck, Washboard), deep blue **35.00**

Feather (Doric) **65.00**

Kansas (Jewel with Dewdrop) **45.00**

Cake Stand

Arched Fleur–De–Lis **35.00**

Atlanta (Square Lion, Clear Lion Head), 10" d, frosted **110.00**

Bird and Strawberry (Bluebird) **65.00**

Bull's Eye and Fan **35.00**

Dakota (Baby Thumbprint, Thumbprint Band), etched, 10" d **50.00**

Finecut and Panel (Russian, Button and Oval Medallion, Nailhead and Panel), blue **75.00**

Hand (Pennsylvania #2) **55.00**

Horseshoe (Good Luck, Prayer Rug), 8" d **60.00**

Ivanhoe, 9" d **42.00**

Mardi Gras, (Duncan and Miller #42, Paneled English Hobnail with Prisms) 10½" d **65.00**

Missouri (Palm and Scroll) **35.00**

Paneled Thistle (Delta) **35.00**

Reverse Torpedo (Bull's Eye and Diamond Point) **85.00**

Thousand Eye, amber **50.00**

Utah (Frost Flower, Twinkle Star) ... **30.00**

Wisconsin (Beaded Dewdrop) **45.00**

Wyoming (Engima), 8½" d **50.00**

Yale (Crow–Foot, Turkey Track) **60.00**

Calling Card Tray

Colorado (Lacy Medallion), blue ... **45.00**

Heart with Thumbprint (Bull's Eye in Heart), folded **20.00**

Candelabrum, All–Over Diamond (Diamond Block, Diamond Splendor), four branches, orig lusters **175.00**

Candlestick, Excelsior **125.00**

Canoe, Daisy and Button, amber, 12" l **60.00**

Carafe

Bull's Eye **45.00**

Galloway, rose stained **85.00**

Minnesota **35.00**

New Hampshire (Bent Buckle, Modiste), gold trim **60.00**

Pennsylvania (Balder) **40.00**

Castor Set

Alabama (Beaded Bull's Eye and Drape), four bottles, glass frame .. **125.00**

Bellflower, five bottles, pewter stand **225.00**

Daisy and Button, vaseline, four bottles, glass stand **75.00**

Jacob's Ladder (Maltese), four bottles **100.00**

Celery Tray

Broken Column (Irish Column, Notched Rib, Rattan) **35.00**

California (Beaded Grape), emerald green **45.00**

Dakota (Baby Thumbprint, Thumbprint Band) **25.00**

Paneled Thistle (Delta) **20.00**

The States (Cane and Star Medallion), gold trim **20.00**

U. S. Coin (American Coin) **200.00**

Wisconsin (Beaded Dewdrop) **40.00**

Celery Vase

Almond Thumbprint (Almond, Finger Print), flint **50.00**

Banded Star **30.00**

Beaded Swirl (Swirled Column), emerald green **55.00**

Cupid and Venus, stemmed **45.00**

Daisy and Button with Crossbar, amber **35.00**

Diamond Thumbprint, flint, scalloped top **185.00**

Eyewinker (Cannon Ball, Crystal Ball, Winking Eye) **55.00**

Florida (Emerald Green Herringhone, Paneled Herringbone) **30.00**

Honeycomb, flint **45.00**

Kansas (Jewel with Dewdrop) **45.00**

Magnet and Grape (Magnet and Grape with Stippled Leaf), flint, frosted leaf **150.00**

Moon and Star (Palace) **35.00**

Pennsylvania (Balder) **15.00**

Queen Anne (Bearded Man)

Amber **60.00**

Clear **40.00**

Red Block (Late Block), ruby stained **85.00**

Snail (Compact, Idaho, Double Snail) **35.00**

Utah (Frost Flower, Twinkle Star) ... **20.00**

Viking (Bearded Head) **40.00**

Wildflower, vaseline **55.00**

Zipper (Cobb, Late Sawtooth) **25.00**

Champagne

Almond Thumbprint (Almond, Finger Print), flint **65.00**

Atlas (Bullet, Cannon Ball, Crystal Ball) **22.00**

Broken Column (Irish Column, Notched Rib, Rattan) **100.00**

Diamond Point, flint **85.00**

Horn of Plenty, flint **145.00**

Paneled Thistle (Delta) **40.00**

Sawtooth (Diamond Point, Mitre Diamond), flint **65.00**

Cheese Dish, cov

Actress (Theatrical) **235.00**

Flamingo Habitat **110.00**

Horseshoe (Good Luck, Prayer Rug) **215.00**

Lion (Frosted Lion), rampant lion finial **400.00**

Magnet and Grape (Magnet and Grape with Stippled Leaf), non–flint, stippled leaf **45.00**

Snail (Compact, Idaho, Double Snail) **95.00**

Zipper (Cobb, Late Sawtooth) **55.00**

Claret

Broken Column (Irish Column, Notched Rib, Rattan) 75.00

Diamond Point, flint 90.00

Mardi Gras (Duncan and Miller #42, Paneled English Hobnail with Prisms) 35.00

Three Face 100.00

Claret Jug

All–Over Diamond (Diamond Block, Diamond Splendor) 50.00

Delaware (Four Petal Flower), rose, gold trim, tankard 200.00

Cocktail, The States (Cane and Star Medallion) 25.00

Cologne Bottle

Bull's Eye, flint, orig stopper 45.00

Massachusetts (Geneva #2) 37.50

Thousand Eye, apple green 100.00

Compote, cov

Actress (Theatrical), 9″ h, 8″ d 160.00

Bellflower, 8″ d, high standard, single vine, fine ribbed 375.00

Boy with Basket 265.00

Cupid and Venus, 10″ d 70.00

Cupid's Hunt, 8″ d 165.00

Daisy Button, amber, 11½″ h, 8″ d . 105.00

Diamond Point, flint, high standard, 8″ d 135.00

Flamingo Habitat, 6″ d 55.00

Jacob's Ladder (Maltese), high standard, 9½″ d 125.00

Lion (Frosted Lion), high standard, rampant lion finial, 7″ d 150.00

Portland, gold trim, high standard, 6″ d 60.00

Reverse Torpedo (Bull's Eye and Diamond Point), high standard, 7″ d . 80.00

Snail (Compact, Idaho, Double Snail), cov, high standard, 8″ d 80.00

Three Face, high standard, 8″ d 175.00

Zipper (Cobb, Late Sawtooth), low standard, 8″ d 45.00

Compote, open

Aegis (Bead and Bar Medallion, Swiss), high standard 25.00

Austrian (Finecut Medallion), low standard, canary–yellow 150.00

Cupid and Venus, 7½″ d 25.00

Dakota (Baby Thumbprint, Thumbprint Band), etched

6″ d 35.00

8″ d 50.00

Deer and Pine Tree (Deer and Doe), high standard, 9″ d 55.00

Diamond Thumbprint, flint, low standard, 8″ d 50.00

Eyewinker (Cannon Ball, Crystal Ball, Winking Eye), high standard, 7″ d 60.00

Kansas (Jewel with Dewdrop), low standard, 6½″ d 45.00

Moon and Star (Palace), high standard, 9″ d 35.00

Oregon #1 (Beaded Loop), high standard, 8″ d 50.00

Sawtooth (Diamond Point, Mitre Diamond), flint, open, low standard, sawtooth edge, 8″ d 50.00

Shell and Tassel (Duncan No. 555, Shell and Spike), 7″ h, sgd "Duncan and Sons" 95.00

The States (Cane and Star Medallion), high standard, 9″ d 40.00

U. S. Coin (American Coin), high standard, quarters and dimes, 7″ d 200.00

Condensed Milk Jar, cov, All–Over Diamond (Diamond Block, Diamond Splendor) 25.00

Condiment Set, cruet, salt and pepper shakers, tray

Georgia (Peacock Feather) 75.00

O'Hara Diamond (Sawtooth and Star), ruby stained 250.00

S Repeat, sapphire blue 190.00

Wisconsin (Beaded Dewdrop) 100.00

Condiment Tray, Croesus (Riverside's #484), clear 25.00

Cordial

All–Over Diamond (Diamond Block, Diamond Splendor) 35.00

Almond Thumbprint (Almond, Finger Print), flint 45.00

Austrian (Finecut Medallion), emerald green 150.00

Basketweave, apple green 40.00

Bellflower, single vine, fine ribbed, knob stem, rayed base, barrel shape 115.00

Feather (Doric) 95.00

King's Crown 45.00

Mardi Gras (Duncan and Miller #42, Paneled English Hobnail with Prisms) 30.00

Sawtooth (Diamond Point, Mitre Diamond), flint 50.00

Thousand Eye, blue 40.00

Cracker Jar, cov

Esther (Tooth and Claw), ruby stained 200.00

Snail (Compact, Idaho, Double Snail) 85.00

Creamer

Actress (Theatrical) 70.00

Adonis (Pleat and Tuck, Washboard), canary–yellow 30.00

All–Over Diamond (Diamond Block, Diamond Splendor) 20.00

Almond Thumbprint (Almond, Finger Print), flint, applied handle, chip on foot, 5⅜″ h 95.00

Arched Fleur–De–Lis 30.00

Ashburton, flint, applied handle, roughness at base of handle, 6¾″ h 135.00

Atlanta (Square Lion, Clear Lion Head) 50.00

Baltimore Pear (Gipsy) 45.00
Blazing Cornucopia 30.00
Bow Tie 25.00
Broken Column (Irish Column,
  Notched Rib, Rattan) 42.50
Cardinal 40.00
Chair with Star 20.00
Cupid and Venus 55.00
Diamond Point, flint, applied handle 115.00
Diamond Thumbprint 195.00
Egyptian 30.00
Gibson Girl 65.00
Hand (Pennsylvania #2) 40.00
Heart with Thumbprint (Bull's Eye in
  Heart), small 22.00
Holly, applied handle 125.00
Homestead 18.00
Horn of Plenty, flint, applied handle,
  7" h 175.00
Iowa (Paneled Zipper) 30.00
Ivanhoe 25.00
King's Crown, ruby stained 30.00
Liberty 18.00
Log Cabin 100.00
Magnet and Grape (Magnet and
  Grape with Stippled Leaf), non-
  flint, stippled leaf 40.00
Maryland (Inverted Loop and Fan;
  Loop and Diamond), gold trim ... 25.00
Minerva 45.00
Minnesota, individual 20.00
New Hampshire (Bent Buckle, Mod-
  iste), rose stained 45.00
Ohio, etched 35.00
Paneled Grape, vine 30.00
Paneled Thistle (Delta), bee mark ... 45.00
Pennsylvania (Balder), emerald green 50.00
Picket 25.00
Psyche and Cupid 40.00
Queen Anne (Bearded Man) 50.00
Red Block (Late Block), ruby stained,
  individual 45.00
Reverse 44, gold trim 30.00
Shell and Jewel 20.00
Shell and Tassel (Duncan No. 555,
  Shell and Spike) 25.00
The States (Cane and Star Medallion),
  gold trim 26.00
Thousand Eye, amber, 4" h 32.00
Three Face 135.00
U. S. Coin (American Coin) 350.00
Utah (Frost Flower, Twinkle Star) ... 30.00
Vermont (Honeycomb with Flower
  Rim, Inverted Thumbprint with
  Daisy Band), gold trim 30.00
Wisconsin (Beaded Dewdrop) 50.00
Yale (Crow–Foot, Turkey Track) 35.00
Zipper (Cobb, Late Sawtooth) 35.00
Cruet, orig stopper
Almond Thumbprint (Almond, Finger
  Print), flint 55.00
California (Beaded Grape) 65.00

Empress, green, gold trim 325.00
Mardi Gras (Duncan and Miller #42,
  Paneled English Hobnail with
  Prisms) 45.00
Massachusetts (Geneva #2) 45.00
Riverside's Ransom, vaseline, gold
  trim 225.00
Snail (Compact, Idaho, Double Snail) 65.00
Three Panel, sapphire blue 155.00
Torpedo 37.50
U. S. Coin (American Coin) 375.00
Wildflower, vaseline 48.00
Wisconsin (Beaded Dewdrop) 80.00
Zipper (Cobb, Late Sawtooth) 45.00

Crystal Wedding pattern, cov compote, plain, $65.00.

Cup and Saucer
Basketweave, blue 35.00
Cornell, green, gold trim 25.00
Currier and Ives 30.00
King's Crown 55.00
O'Hara Diamond (Sawtooth and Star) 40.00
Star and Ivy 32.00
Stippled Forget–Me–Not 30.00
Wisconsin (Beaded Dewdrop) 50.00
Custard Cup
Bull's Eye and Fan 10.00
New Hampshire (Bent Buckle, Mod-
  iste), rose stained 10.00
Snail (Compact, Idaho, Double Snail) 30.00
Decanter
Almond Thumbprint (Almond, Finger
  Print), flint 70.00
Banded Portland (Virginia #1, Maid-
  en's Blush) 50.00
Cable, quart, ground stopper 295.00
Diamond Thumbprint, flint, quart,
  orig stopper 225.00
Georgia (Peacock Feather) 70.00
Magnet and Grape (Magnet and
  Grape with Stippled Leaf), flint,
  frosted leaf, pint 150.00
Pennsylvania (Balder), gold trim 100.00
Red Block (Late Block), ruby stained 175.00

Dresser Tray, Banded Portland (Virginia
#1, Maiden's Blush) 50.00
Doughnut Stand
Horseshoe (Good Luck, Prayer Rug)   75.00
Paneled Thistle (Delta) 25.00
Egg Cup
Aegis (Bead and Bar Medallion,
Swiss) 25.00
All–Over Diamond (Diamond Block,
Diamond Splendor) 20.00
Almond Thumbprint (Almond, Finger
Print), flint 45.00
Amazon (Sawtooth Band) 14.00
Atlanta (Square Lion, Clear Lion
Head), frosted 30.00
Basketweave, vaseline 25.00
Dahlia, apple green 65.00
Galloway 35.00
Lily of the Valley 40.00
Thousand Eye, vaseline 90.00
Egg Rack, cov, Bleeding Heart, three
eggs 350.00

Eyewinker pattern, cake stand, $70.00.

Finger Bowl
Block and Fan 55.00
Chandelier (Crown Jewel), etched .. 40.00
Daisy and Button With V Ornament
(Van Dyke), vaseline 55.00
Heart with Thumbprint (Bull's Eye in
Heart) 45.00
Mardi Gras (Duncan and Miller #42,
Paneled English Hobnail with
Prisms) 25.00
Snail (Compact, Idaho, Double Snail) 50.00
Goblet
Aegis (Bead and Bar Medallion,
Swiss) 30.00
All–Over Diamond (Diamond Block,
Diamond Splendor) 25.00
Argus, flint, cut type 20.00
Banded Portland (Virginia #1, Maid-
en's Blush), rose stained 47.00
Basketweave, canary–yellow 28.00
Beautiful Lady 35.00
Beaded Dart Band, ruby stained 75.00
Bismarc 18.00
Buckle (Early Buckle), flint 40.00

Bull's Eye and Fan, sapphire blue
stain 45.00
Buzz Star 18.00
Cardinal 20.00
Currier and Ives 30.00
Dakota (Baby Thumbprint, Thumb-
print Band), etched 35.00
Diamond Thumbprint, flint 350.00
Egg In Sand 25.00
Finecut and Panel (Russian, Button
and Oval Medallion, Nailhead and
Panel), vaseline 35.00
Fishscale 20.00
Frosted Polar Bear 95.00
Galloway 65.00
Greek Key, buttermilk 45.00
Hand (Pennsylvania #2) 45.00
Herringbone 45.00
Holly 100.00
Horn of Plenty, flint 65.00
King's Crown, ruby stained 45.00
Lacy Spiral 38.00
Loop with Dewdrops 35.00
Magnet and Grape (Magnet and
Grape with Stippled Leaf), flint,
frosted leaf, American shield 300.00
Maryland (Inverted Loop and Fan;
Loop and Diamond) 40.00
Michigan, excellent gold trim 32.00
Mitred Diamond Point 28.00
New Hampshire (Bent Buckle, Mod-
iste), gold trim 32.00
New Jersey (Loops and Drops, Red
Loop and Finecut), gold trim 40.00
Oregon #1 (Beaded Loop) 35.00
Oswego Waffle 7.50
Paneled Cherry 35.00
Paneled Diamond Cross 34.00
Paneled Sage Brush, Iowa City Glass
Co 125.00
Pavonia (Pineapple Stem), etched .. 40.00
Pendant 18.00
Pennsylvania (Balder) 20.00
Pleat and Panel 35.00
Plume
Clear 35.00
Frosted 65.00
Polar Bear 125.00
Portland, gold trim 35.00
Rosette and Palms 30.00
Seneca Loop 32.00
Snail (Compact, Idaho, Double Snail),
ruby stained 95.00
Swag Block Goblet, ruby stained ... 75.00
Texas Bull's Eye 28.00
The States (Cane and Star Medallion),
gold trim 38.00
U. S. Coin (American Coin), frosted   400.00
Utah (Frost Flower, Twinkle Star) ...   25.00
Westward Ho! (Pioneer) 95.00
Wisconsin (Beaded Dewdrop) 65.00
Yale (Crow–Foot, Turkey Track) 35.00

Zig–Zag	27.50
Zipper (Cobb, Late Sawtooth)	20.00

Hair Receiver

Heart with Thumbprint (Bull's Eye in Heart)	60.00
Minnesota	30.00

Hat

Daisy and Button, blue	40.00
Thousand Eye, vaseline	45.00

Honey Dish

Alabama (Beaded Bull's Eye and Drape), cov	60.00
Beaded Grape Medallion, open, 3½" d	10.00
Diamond Thumbprint, flint	25.00
Lily of the Valley	10.00
Oregon #1 (Beaded Loop)	10.00

Horseradish, Duncan Block #331, ground stopper 35.00

Ice Cream Tray, Block and Fan, rect .. 75.00

Ice Tub

All–Over Diamond (Diamond Block, Diamond Splendor)	35.00
Block and Fan	45.00

Inkwell

Chandelier (Crown Jewel)	85.00
Daisy and Button, apple green	50.00
Thousand Eye, blue	75.00

Jelly Compote

Feather (Doric)	100.00
Flamingo Habitat	35.00
Jewel and Dewdrop, ftd	30.00
New Jersey (Loops and Drops, Red Loop and Finecut), gold trim	45.00
Pennsylvania (Balder), gold trim	50.00
Tennessee (Jewel and Crescent, Jeweled Rosettes)	40.00
Utah (Frost Flower, Twinkle Star)	18.00

Juice Tumbler

Cut Log (Ethol, Cat's Eye and Block)	35.00
Massachusetts (Geneva #2)	15.00
Pennsylvania (Balder), gold trim	16.00

Lamp

Bellflower, single vine, fine ribbed, brass stem, marble base	175.00
Cable, glass base	135.00
Empress #2, green	200.00
Excelsior, hand	95.00
Moon and Star (Palace)	140.00
O'Hara Diamond (Sawtooth and Star)	50.00
Thousand Eye, amber, 12" h	120.00

Lamp Shade

Delaware (Four Petal Flower), rose, gold trim	100.00
Mardi Gras (Duncan and Miller #42, Paneled English Hobnail with Prisms)	35.00

Lemonade Pitcher

Bull's Eye and Fan	55.00
Pavonia (Pineapple Stem)	125.00

Lemonade Tumbler

Honeycomb, flint	40.00

Plume	28.00

Marmalade Jar

Actress (Theatrical)	95.00
Atlanta (Square Lion, Clear Lion Head)	75.00
Bow Tie, pewter lid	70.00
Butterfly with Spray	78.00
Deer and Pine Tree (Deer and Doe)	90.00
Jacob's Ladder (Maltese)	75.00
Log Cabin	275.00
Snail (Compact, Idaho, Double Snail)	90.00
Three Face	200.00
Viking (Bearded Head), ground stopper	175.00
Wisconsin (Beaded Dewdrop)	125.00

Miniature, bride's basket, Delaware (Four Petal Flower), green, gold trim 135.00

Mug

Arched Fleur–De–Lis, ruby stained	30.00
Basketweave, apple green	40.00
Beaded Swirl (Swirled Column)	10.00
Bird and Owl	80.00
Butterfly with Spray	25.00
Cupid and Venus	25.00
Daisy and Button With V Ornament (Van Dyke), amber	20.00
Georgia (Peacock Feather)	22.50
Kansas (Jewel with Dewdrop)	45.00
Lyre with Bird on Nest, 3" h	25.00
Massachusetts (Geneva #2)	15.00
Minnesota	15.00
Thousand Eye, apple green, 2½"	30.00
U. S. Coin (American Coin)	185.00

Mustard, cov, underplate

Button Arches, ruby stained	100.00
Florida (Emerald Green Herringhone, Paneled Herringbone)	25.00

Nappy

Bird and Strawberry (Bluebird), colored	65.00
Colorado (Lacy Medallion), emerald green	35.00
Galloway, rose stained	50.00
Lily of the Valley	20.00

Olive

Arched Fleur–De–Lis	15.00
California (Beaded Grape)	20.00
Illinois	18.00
Kentucky	25.00
Maryland (Inverted Loop and Fan; Loop and Diamond), gold trim	15.00
Thousand Eye, amber, 6" d	40.00

Orange Bowl, Block and Fan 50.00

Pepper Sauce Bottle, Horn of Plenty, pewter top 200.00

Pickle

Aegis (Bead and Bar Medallion, Swiss)	18.00
Barberry (Berry)	25.00
Lily of the Valley, scoop shape	20.00
Maryland (Inverted Loop and Fan; Loop and Diamond)	15.00

Pennsylvania pattern, syrup pitcher, $65.00.

Missouri (Palm and Scroll) **18.00**
U. S. Coin (American Coin) **200.00**
Utah (Frost Flower, Twinkle Star) . . .   **15.00**
Pickle Castor, SP frame
  Broken Column (Irish Column,
    Notched Rib, Rattan) **150.00**
  Daisy and Button With V Ornament
    (Van Dyke), vaseline **100.00**
  Feather (Doric) **145.00**
  Flamingo Habitat **130.00**
Pin Tray, Delaware (Four Petal Flower),
  green, gold trim **55.00**
Pitcher, milk
  Cane Horseshoe **35.00**
  Cape Cod **65.00**
  Cupid and Venus **95.00**
  Dahlia, vaseline **70.00**
  Eyewinker (Cannon Ball, Crystal Ball,
    Winking Eye) **70.00**
  Maryland (Inverted Loop and Fan;
    Loop and Diamond), ruby stained   **135.00**
  Paneled Thistle (Delta) **60.00**
  Tennessee (Jewel and Crescent, Jew-
    eled Rosettes) **55.00**
Pitcher, water
  Adonis (Pleat and Tuck, Washboard)   **35.00**

Picket pattern, pitcher, $90.00.

Alabama (Beaded Bull's Eye and
  Drape) **72.00**
Beaded Band, applied strap handle .   **75.00**
Bird and Strawberry (Bluebird) **235.00**
Bow Tie **140.00**
Cardinal **150.00**
Colorado (Lacy Medallion) **95.00**
Cottage **50.00**
Cupid and Venus **75.00**
Currier and Ives, amber **175.00**
Dahlia **55.00**
Daisy and Button with Crossbar, am-
  ber **65.00**
Deer and Dog, applied handle **155.00**
Dewey **75.00**
Diamond with Double Fans **50.00**
Esther (Tooth and Claw) **65.00**
Fan with Acanthus **55.00**
Galloway, tall **45.00**
Garden of Eden, with serpent **70.00**
Gridley (Spanish American) **120.00**
Heart with Thumbprint (Bull's Eye in
  Heart) **200.00**
Holly, applied handle **225.00**
Horseshoe Curve **30.00**
Illinois, squatty **75.00**
Jacob's Ladder (Maltese) **150.00**
Klondike, clear **50.00**
Log Cabin **300.00**
Michigan **50.00**
Minerva **200.00**
Mitred Diamonds, vaseline **65.00**
Oriental Poppy **60.00**
Plume, bulbous, ruby **210.00**
Princess Feather (Rochelle) **75.00**
Queen Anne (Bearded Man) **75.00**
Shell and Jewel, emerald green **60.00**
Star in Honeycomb **58.00**
Stippled Butterfly **80.00**
Teardrop and Tassel **65.00**
Thousand Eye, blue **95.00**
U. S. Coin (American Coin), frosted,
  dollars **800.00**
Wisconsin (Beaded Dewdrop) **70.00**
Yale (Crow–Foot, Turkey Track) **60.00**
Zipper (Cobb, Late Sawtooth) **40.00**
Plate
  Arched Fleur–De–Lis, 7" sq **15.00**
  Beautiful Lady, 8" d **18.00**
  Bird and Strawberry (Bluebird), 12" d   **125.00**
  California (Beaded Grape), 8¼" sq . .   **28.00**
  Cupid and Venus, handles, 10½" d .   **40.00**
  Diamond Point, flint, 8" d **65.00**
  Dog, Findlay **75.00**
  Illinois, 7" sq **25.00**
  Maryland (Inverted Loop and Fan;
    Loop and Diamond), gold trim, 7"
    d **25.00**
  O'Hara Diamond (Sawtooth and
    Star), 8" d **30.00**
  Snail (Compact, Idaho, Double Snail),
    5" d **35.00**

Star Rosette, amber, 7" d **45.00**
Wildflower, vaseline, 10" sq **30.00**
Platter
Actress (Theatrical), Miss Nielson . . .   **60.00**
Cape Cod **45.00**
Frosted Stork, frosted center, 101 pat-
tern border, Iowa City Glass Co . .   **65.00**
Shell and Tassel (Duncan No. 555,
Shell and Spike) **45.00**
Wildflower, apple green **45.00**
Pomade Jar, cov
Delaware (Four Petal Flower), small-
est size, clear, rose and gold trim .   **75.00**
Honeycomb, flint **45.00**
Sawtooth (Diamond Point, Mitre Dia-
mond), flint **45.00**
Powder Jar, Heart with Thumbprint
(Bull's Eye in Heart), SP cov **65.00**
Punch Bowl
All–Over Diamond (Diamond Block,
Diamond Splendor) **50.00**
Galloway **160.00**
Pennsylvania (Balder), gold trim **175.00**
Punch Bowl Set, The States (Cane and
Star Medallion), bowl, eight cups . . .   **120.00**
Punch Cup
Button Panels **7.00**
Fandango, Heisey **12.00**
Homestead, Duncan and Miller **7.00**
Galloway **8.00**
Kentucky **7.00**
King Arthur **7.00**
Louise **6.00**
Memphis **8.00**
Paneled Thistle (Delta) **20.00**
Pennsylvania (Balder) **8.00**
Snail (Compact, Idaho, Double Snail)   **35.00**
The Prize, ruby stained **20.00**
Wisconsin (Beaded Dewdrop) **10.00**
Relish
Actress (Theatrical) **30.00**
Amazon (Sawtooth Band), etched . .   **28.00**
Arched Fleur–De–Lis **15.00**
Beaded Acorn Medallion (Beaded
Acorn) **15.00**
Bird and Strawberry (Bluebird) **20.00**
Bleeding Heart, oval **35.00**
Bull's Eye and Fan, pink stain **20.00**
Currier and Ives **18.00**
King's #500, Dewey Blue, gold trim   **30.00**
Magnet and Grape (Magnet and
Grape with Stippled Leaf), non–
flint, stippled leaf **15.00**
New Hampshire (Bent Buckle, Mod-
iste), rose stained, diamond shape   **20.00**
Oregon #1 (Beaded Loop) **15.00**
Princess Feather (Rochelle) **20.00**
Tennessee (Jewel and Crescent, Jew-
eled Rosettes) **20.00**
Wisconsin (Beaded Dewdrop) **25.00**
Zipper (Cobb, Late Sawtooth) **15.00**

Ring Holder, Banded Portland (Virginia
#1, Maiden's Blush) **75.00**
Rose Bowl
Austrian (Finecut Medallion), canary–
yellow **150.00**
Galloway **25.00**
Heart with Thumbprint (Bull's Eye in
Heart) **30.00**
Paneled Thistle (Delta) **50.00**
Red Block (Late Block), ruby stained   **75.00**
Snail (Compact, Idaho, Double Snail),
5" h **45.00**
Rum Jug, Massachusetts (Geneva #2) .   **110.00**
Salt, individual
Atlanta (Square Lion, Clear Lion
Head), frosted **40.00**
Button Arches **15.00**
Illinois **15.00**
Moon and Star (Palace) **10.00**
Snail (Compact, Idaho, Double Snail)   **35.00**
Thousand Eye, blue **90.00**
Zipper (Cobb, Late Sawtooth) **5.00**
Salt, master
Amazon (Sawtooth Band) **18.00**
Argus **30.00**
Cabbage Rose, ftd **25.00**
Eureka, flint **18.00**
Excelsior, flint **30.00**
Jacob's Ladder (Maltese) **20.00**
Lily of the Valley, cov **125.00**
Snail (Compact, Idaho, Double Snail),
ruby stained **75.00**
Salt Shaker
Adonis (Pleat and Tuck, Washboard),
canary–yellow **24.00**
Banded Portland (Virginia #1, Maid-
en's Blush) **25.00**
California (Beaded Grape) **24.00**
Dakota (Baby Thumbprint, Thumb-
print Band) **50.00**
Galloway **20.00**
Missouri (Palm and Scroll), emerald
green **45.00**
Snail (Compact, Idaho, Double Snail),
bulbous **65.00**
Wildflower, vaseline **45.00**
Sardine Box, Banded Portland (Virginia
#1, Maiden's Blush) **55.00**
Sauce
Acorn, 5" d **15.00**
Actress (Theatrical), 4" d, ftd **20.00**
Adonis (Pleat and Tuck, Washboard),
4" d **10.00**
Arched Fleur–De–Lis, ruby stained .   **20.00**
Bleeding Heart, flat **15.00**
Colorado (Lacy Medallion), ruffled . .   **15.00**
Croesus (Riverside's #484), green . .   **25.00**
Cupid and Venus, ftd **15.00**
Feather (Doric) **12.00**
King's #500, Dewey Blue, gold trim   **35.00**
Maryland (Inverted Loop and Fan;
Loop and Diamond), gold trim . . .   **10.00**

Minnesota, ruby stained, boat shape	28.50
Reverse Torpedo (Bull's Eye and Diamond Point)	10.00
Shell and Tassel (Duncan No. 555, Shell and Spike)	8.00
Vermont (Honeycomb with Flower Rim, Inverted Thumbprint with Daisy Band), emerald green, gold trim	20.00
Zipper (Cobb, Late Sawtooth), ftd	12.00

Shell & Jewel pattern, pitcher (left), $45.00; creamer (right), $20.00.

Sherbet, Galloway	25.00
Shot Glass	
Horn of Plenty, flint, 3" h	100.00
Pennsylvania (Balder)	17.00
Spill Holder	
Buckle with Star	55.00
Diamond Point, flint	45.00
Honeycomb, flint	24.00
Sponge Dish, Chandelier (Crown Jewel)	30.00
Spooner	
Actress (Theatrical)	60.00
Adonis (Pleat and Tuck, Washboard), canary–yellow	38.00
Aegis (Bead and Bar Medallion, Swiss)	15.00
Basketweave, vaseline	30.00
Bow Tie	35.00
Broken Column (Irish Column, Notched Rib, Rattan)	35.00
Cable, flint	30.00
Cupid and Venus	30.00
Deer and Pine Tree (Deer and Doe)	65.00
Flamingo Habitat	25.00
Horn of Plenty, flint	45.00
King's Crown, ruby stained	35.00
Leaf Medallion, amethyst	75.00
Log Cabin	120.00
Magnet and Grape (Magnet and Grape with Stippled Leaf), non–flint, stippled leaf	30.00
Ohio, etched	40.00

Paneled Grape	25.00
Paneled Thistle (Delta)	25.00
Plume	32.00
Queen Anne (Bearded Man)	40.00
Shell and Tassel (Duncan No. 555, Shell and Spike)	35.00
Snail (Compact, Idaho, Double Snail)	45.00
Tennessee (Jewel and Crescent, Jeweled Rosettes)	35.00
Three Face	55.00
Wildflower, vaseline	40.00
Yale (Crow–Foot, Turkey Track)	25.00
Zipper (Cobb, Late Sawtooth)	25.00
Straw Holder, Illinois, horizontal	100.00
Sugar, cov	
Actress (Theatrical)	90.00
Adonis (Pleat and Tuck, Washboard), blue	50.00
Aegis (Bead and Bar Medallion, Swiss)	35.00
Almond Thumbprint (Almond, Finger Print), flint	20.00
Art (Job's Tears)	45.00
Baltimore Pear (Gipsy)	60.00
Beaded Acorn Medallion (Beaded Acorn)	45.00
Bird and Strawberry (Bluebird), colored	45.00
Cupid and Venus	70.00
Daisy and Button with Crossbar, amber	40.00
Diamond Point, flint, small edge chips, check in finial, 8⅛" h	40.00
Finecut and Panel (Russian, Button and Oval Medallion, Nailhead and Panel), blue	42.50
Heart with Thumbprint (Bull's Eye in Heart)	85.00
Hops Band	40.00
Iowa (Paneled Zipper)	30.00
Kentucky	30.00
Leaf Medallion, amethyst	175.00
Lion (Frosted Lion), lion's head finial	90.00
Nestor, amethyst	75.00
New Hampshire (Bent Buckle, Modiste), gold trim	45.00
Oregon #1 (Beaded Loop), ftd	30.00
Snail (Compact, Idaho, Double Snail), individual	50.00
Three Face	125.00
U. S. Coin (American Coin)	225.00
Wildflower, vaseline	45.00
Wisconsin (Beaded Dewdrop)	55.00
Zipper (Cobb, Late Sawtooth)	35.00
Sugar Shaker	
California (Beaded Grape), emerald green	85.00
O'Hara Diamond (Sawtooth and Star)	20.00
Reverse Torpedo (Bull's Eye and Diamond Point)	85.00
Snail (Compact, Idaho, Double Snail)	85.00
Wisconsin (Beaded Dewdrop)	90.00

Sweetmeat, cov
Almond Thumbprint (Almond, Finger
  Print), flint **65.00**
Bellflower, single vine, 6″ h, high
  standard **300.00**
New Jersey (Loops and Drops, Red
  Loop and Finecut), gold trim **45.00**
Ohio, etched **25.00**
Wisconsin (Beaded Dewdrop) **40.00**

Syrup
Adonis (Pleat and Tuck, Washboard),
  canary–yellow **150.00**
Currier and Ives **75.00**
Dahlia, amber **75.00**
Double Scroll **55.00**
Findley Dewdrop **85.00**
Inverted Baby Thumbprint, emerald
  green **125.00**
Knobby Bull's Eye, lid dented **35.00**
Magnet and Grape (Magnet and
  Grape with Stippled Leaf), flint,
  frosted leaf **125.00**
Patee Cross **38.00**
Reverse Torpedo (Bull's Eye and Dia-
  mond Point) **165.00**
U. S. Coin (American Coin), frosted **525.00**
Wisconsin (Beaded Dewdrop) **110.00**

Table Set, 4 pcs
Banded Star **135.00**
Beaded Swag, milk glass, pink flow-
  ers, Heisey **365.00**
Classic Medallion (Cameo) **130.00**
Clear Block **125.00**
Florida (Emerald Green Herringbone,
  Paneled Herringbone), emerald
  green **185.00**
Liberty Bell **355.00**
Three Panel, sapphire blue **175.00**
Winged Scroll, green, gold dec **325.00**

Tankard
Cut Log (Ethol, Cat's Eye and Block) **70.00**
Mardi Gras (Duncan and Miller #42,
  Paneled English Hobnail with
  Prisms), thumbprints **75.00**
New Hampshire (Bent Buckle, Mod-
  iste), gold trim, rose stained **90.00**
Priscilla **95.00**
Reverse Torpedo (Bull's Eye and Dia-
  mond Point) **160.00**
Snail (Compact, Idaho, Double Snail),
  milk **100.00**

Toothpick Holder
Arched Ovals **12.00**
Bull's Eye and Fan, emerald green .. **35.00**
Colorado (Lacy Medallion), emerald
  green **45.00**
Continental, Heisey **85.00**
Delaware (Four Petal Flower) **35.00**
Flower with Cane, amethyst, gold
  trim **85.00**
Galloway, rose stained **55.00**
Mardi Gras (Duncan and Miller #42,

Paneled English Hobnail with
  Prisms), ruby stained **125.00**
Paneled Cherry **18.00**
The States (Cane and Star Medallion),
  rect, curled lip, gold trim **45.00**
U. S. Coin (American Coin) **180.00**
Vermont (Honeycomb with Flower
  Rim, Inverted Thumbprint with
  Daisy Band), gold trim **30.00**
Wisconsin (Beaded Dewdrop) **55.00**

Tumbler
Adonis (Pleat and Tuck, Washboard),
  deep blue **20.00**
Almond Thumbprint (Almond, Finger
  Print), flint **48.00**
Barberry (Berry) **25.00**
Beveled Star **18.00**
Bird and Strawberry (Bluebird) **45.00**
Boxed Star **18.00**
Box–In–Box, etched **23.00**
Chandelier (Crown Jewel) **40.00**
Daisy and Button with Crossbar, am-
  ber **15.00**
Dewey, canary–yellow **55.00**
Diamond Block with Fan **12.00**
Diamond Thumbprint, flint **125.00**
Flamingo Habitat **20.00**
Fleur de Lis and Drape **20.00**
Georgia (Peacock Feather) **35.00**
Hand (Pennsylvania #2) **50.00**
Illinois, emerald green **40.00**
Kansas (Jewel with Dewdrop) **45.00**
Klondike, clear **25.00**
Mardi Gras (Duncan and Miller #42,
  Paneled English Hobnail with
  Prisms) **28.00**
Michigan **35.00**
New Hampshire (Bent Buckle, Mod-
  iste) **20.00**
Paneled Thistle (Delta) **30.00**
Pavonia (Pineapple Stem), etched .. **30.00**
Pennsylvania (Balder) **20.00**
Portland **25.00**
Reverse Torpedo (Bull's Eye and Dia-
  mond Point) **30.00**
Shell and Jewel
  Blue **25.00**
  Clear **15.00**
Snail (Compact, Idaho, Double Snail) **55.00**
Wildflower, vaseline **35.00**
Wreath and Shell, blue **42.50**
Tumble–Up, Bull's Eye **125.00**

Vase
Colorado (Lacy Medallion), blue, 12″
  h **85.00**
Heart with Thumbprint (Bull's Eye in
  Heart), emerald green, 6″ h **65.00**
Illinois, 6″ h, sq **18.00**
Michigan, bud **15.00**
New Hampshire (Bent Buckle, Mod-
  iste), rose stained **25.00**
Paneled Thistle (Delta), 9¼″ h **25.00**

Snail (Compact, Idaho, Double Snail) **50.00**
Vegetable Bowl
Beaded Grape Medallion, cov, ftd .. **75.00**
Broken Column (Irish Column, Notched Rib, Rattan), cov **90.00**
Eyewinker (Cannon Ball, Crystal Ball, Winking Eye), 6½" l **25.00**
Horseshoe (Good Luck, Prayer Rug) **35.00**
Lily of the Valley **30.00**
Violet Bowl
Chandelier (Crown Jewel) **40.00**
Snail (Compact, Idaho, Double Snail) **50.00**
Wall Pocket, Daisy and Button, amber **125.00**
Waste Bowl
Block and Fan **30.00**
Dakota (Baby Thumbprint, Thumbprint Band), etched **75.00**
Pavonia (Pineapple Stem) **60.00**
U. S. Coin (American Coin) **225.00**
Water Set, pitcher, six tumblers
Beaded Swag, milk glass, pink flowers, Heisey **365.00**
Red Block (Late Block), ruby stained **285.00**
Shell and Jewel, sapphire blue **235.00**
Water Tray
Basketweave, amber, 12" d **40.00**
Chandelier (Crown Jewel), etched .. **70.00**
Daisy and Button With V Ornament (Van Dyke), blue **65.00**
Thousand Eye, amber, 14" l, oval .. **65.00**
U. S. Coin (American Coin) **275.00**
Whiskey
Argus, applied handle **75.00**
Bellflower, single vine, fine ribbed, 3½" h **150.00**
Bull's Eye **70.00**
Diamond Point, flint, applied handle **85.00**
Wine
Almond Thumbprint (Almond, Finger Print), flint **30.00**
Arched Ovals **12.00**
Austrian (Finecut Medallion) **175.00**
Beaded Acorn Medallion (Beaded Acorn) **45.00**
Beveled Windows **18.00**
Bleeding Heart, knob stem **150.00**
Checkerboard **15.00**
Currier and Ives **24.00**
Dakota (Baby Thumbprint, Thumbprint Band) **20.00**
Dew and Raindrop **12.00**
Esther (Tooth and Claw) **35.00**
Flamingo Habitat **25.00**
Flower with Cane **23.00**
Holly **125.00**
Iowa (Paneled Zipper) **30.00**
Lady Hamilton **24.00**
Mardi Gras (Duncan and Miller #42, Paneled English Hobnail with Prisms) **25.00**
Maryland (Inverted Loop and Fan; Loop and Diamond) **35.00**

McKee's Rainbow **22.00**
Missouri (Palm and Scroll) **40.00**
Opposing Pyramids **18.00**
Paneled Dewdrop **19.00**
Paneled Thistle (Delta) **30.00**
Peerless **24.00**
Pennsylvania (Balder) **16.00**
Plain Panels **12.00**
Rosette and Palms **25.00**
Sawtooth (Diamond Point, Mitre Diamond) **12.00**
Serrated Spear Point **18.00**
Short Ribs **24.00**
Snail (Compact, Idaho, Double Snail) **65.00**
The States (Cane and Star Medallion) **32.00**
Teardrop and Thumbprint, etched .. **25.00**
Three Face **150.00**
U. S. Coin (American Coin) **225.00**
Wisconsin (Beaded Dewdrop) **75.00**
Wyoming (Enigma) **85.00**

PEACHBLOW

History: Peachblow, an art glass which derives its name from a fine Chinese glazed porcelain, resembles a peach or crushed strawberries in color. Three American glass manufacturers and two English firms produced peachblow glass in the late 1880s. A fourth American firm renewed the process in the 1950s. The glass from each firm has its own identifying characteristics.

Hobbs, Brockunier & Co., Wheeling peachblow: Opalescent glass, plated or cased with a transparent amber glass; shading from yellow at the base to a deep red at top; glossy or satin finish.

Mt. Washington "Peach Blow": A homogeneous glass, shading from a pale gray–blue to a soft rose color. Pieces may be enhanced with glass appliqués, enameling, and gilting.

New England Glass Works, New England peachblow [advertised as "Wild Rose," but called "Peach Blow" at the plant]: Translucent, shading from rose to white; acid or glossy finish. Some pieces enameled and gilted.

Thomas Webb & Sons and Stevens and Williams, England: Around 1888 these two firms made a peachblow style art glass marked "Peach Blow" or "Peach Bloom." A cased glass, shading from yellow to red. Occasionally found with cameo–type designs in relief.

Gunderson Glass Co.: About 1950 produced peachblow-type art glass to order; shades from an opaque faint tint of pink, which is almost white, to a deep rose.

Reference: John A. Shuman III, *The Collector's Encyclopedia of American Glass*, Collector Books, 1988, value update 1991.

Museum: New Bedford Glass Museum, New Bedford, MA.

GUNDERSON–PAIRPOINT

Butter Dish, cov, 9" d, 5" h, satin finish, scalloped edge, applied finial, c1960 **400.00**
Candlesticks, pr, 8" h, 3½" d, acid finish, Morning Glory, deep pink shading to white **1,450.00**
Compote, 5½" w, 5" h, acid finish, Morning Glory, pink shading to pale lavender to white baluster stem, c1940 . . . . **375.00**
Creamer and Sugar, 3½" h, 5¾" d, acid finish, deep pink, vertical stripes, applied reeded handles **485.00**
Cruet, glossy finish, orig stopper **265.00**
Cup and Saucer, 3½" w, 2¾" h cup, 5" d saucer, acid finish, deep pink shading to white, applied white reeded handle, applied foot, c1940 . . **265.00**
Goblet, acid finish, deep raspberry, applied Peachblow foot **275.00**
Hat, 3¼" h, satin finish, Diamond Quilted pattern **150.00**
Mug, satin finish, decorated, orig paper label, c1970 . . . . **125.00**
Puff Box, hinged cov, 7" d, 5½" h, satin finish, large finial, emb brass bindings **250.00**
Toothpick Holder, satin finish, fluted rim **165.00**
Tumbler, 5" h, satin finish **95.00**
Vase
  5½" h, satin finish, applied ribbon and acorn at neck **250.00**
  6½" h, 3¾" d at shoulder, satin finish, rose pink band at shoulder, pink to white rim shading, c1940 . . . . **145.00**
  7½" h, 4" d, satin finish, crimped rim, polished pontil **185.00**
  9" h, 3¼" w at base, acid finish, lily, deep color **425.00**
Wine, 4⅛" h, satin finish, trumpet shaped flared body, round foot **90.00**

MOUNT WASHINGTON

Biscuit Jar, cov, 7¼" h, satin finish, enameled and jeweled dec, sgd **675.00**
Bride's Basket, 11" d, pink exterior, peachblow interior, gold stylized flowers dec, ornate silver plated holder with aquatic marine motif, marked "Pairpoint Mfg Co" **875.00**
Condiment Set, 3" h salt and pepper shakers, mustard pot, acid finish, ribbed barrel form, enameled blue and white forget–me–nots, delicate green leaves and tracery, orig silver plated tops, replated silver plated stand marked "Pairpoint Mfg Co New Bedford Mass 705" **3,850.00**
Creamer, 3¾" h, satin finish, bulbous ovoid body, applied handle **1,550.00**

Perfume Bottle, 5" h, satin finish, enameled sprays of dainty white flowers, orig matching faceted cut stopper . . **650.00**
Pitcher, 5¾" h, satin finish, tankard, molded Hobnail pattern, applied handle **3,300.00**
Tumbler, satin finish, band of apple blossom pink shades to soft blue–gray **1,450.00**
Vase
  3¾" h, 3" d, acid finish, flower shape **900.00**
  7" h, satin finish, trumpet, fold–over rim **550.00**
  8" h, satin finish, slender neck, bulbous body **1,325.00**
  12" h, satin finish, baluster, wide flaring rim **1,200.00**

NEW ENGLAND

Bowl, 4¼" d, 2¾" h, satin finish **450.00**
Celery Vase, 6½" h, satin finish, scalloped rim **300.00**
Creamer and Sugar, 2¾" h creamer, 3¼" h open sugar, satin finish, ribbed, applied white handles **450.00**
Darner, 6" l, 2½" w, glossy finish **185.00**
Lamp Shade, 4½" h, 6¼" w, glossy finish **385.00**
Pitcher, 6¼" h, satin finish, ten crimp top, applied white handle **1,200.00**
Punch Cup, satin finish, deep rose shading to white, applied white acid finished handle **425.00**
Rose Bowl
  2½" h, satin finish, gold lettering "World's Fair 1893" **225.00**
  4" h, 4" d, glossy finish, deep color shading **485.00**
Salt Shaker, 3¾" h, acid finish, deep color, orig silver plated top **525.00**
Toothpick Holder, 2¼" h, satin finish, cylindrical, tricorn rim **385.00**
Tumbler, 3¾" h, glossy finish, thin delicate walls **385.00**
Vase
  6" h, satin finish, lily, tricorn top, deep raspberry shading to white **875.00**
  6¼" h, 4" d ball shaped base, 3" long slender neck, fired glossy finish . . **465.00**
  8" h, satin finish, lily, tricorn top, deep raspberry pink shading to opaque white **650.00**

NEW MARTINSVILLE

Bowl, 5" d, scalloped rim, yellow–caramel shading to peach to beige **50.00**
Bride's Bowl, 11" d, wavy ruffled rim, cased interior **125.00**
Dish, 5" d, 2½" h, wavy ruffled rim . . **110.00**

WEBB

Basket, 6½" h, glossy finish, applied
  clear thorn handle 375.00
Biscuit Jar, cov, 6" h, 4½" d, acid finish,
  heavy gold prunus blossoms, pine
  needles and butterfly dec, rich
  creamy white lining, silver plated rim,
  lid, and handle 895.00
Bowl, 8" sq, glossy finish 225.00
Celery Vase, 6½" h, acid finish 195.00
Creamer, 3½" h, 2⅜" d, satin finish, rich
  rose shading to pink exterior, creamy
  white lining, applied clear handle . . 300.00
Mustard Jar, 2½" h, satin finish, hand
  painted prunus dec, gold trim 415.00
Plate, 8¾" d, glossy finish, crimped
  edge, gold enameled butterfly and
  blossoming prunus branches 450.00
Punch Cup, glossy finish, creamy white
  lining 125.00
Rose Bowl, 3" h, 3¼" d, acid finish,
  eight crimp top, creamy white lining 245.00
Scent Bottle, 3⅞" h, 2¾" d, satin finish,
  dainty blue, white, and yellow enameled flowers, green leaves, monarch
  butterfly, creamy white lining, hallmarked sterling silver top 700.00
Vase
  8½" h, glossy finish, gold dec of hang-
    ing star shaped raised blossoms,
    two color gold leaves, gold bird in
    flight, gold band at top and base . 675.00
  8½" h, 5½" w at shoulder, satin finish,
    butterfly hovering at prunus
    branch, seven full bloom flowers,
    over one hundred gold buds, deep
    pink shading to white, creamy
    white lining, numbered on base . . 785.00

WHEELING

Bowl, 3¾" d, satin finish, ground rim,
  minute rim chips 175.00
Bride's Basket, satin finish, mahogany
  red shaded to light pink bowl, applied
  ribbon edge, silver plated frame
  marked "Pairpoint" 950.00
Carafe, glossy finish 725.00
Cream Pitcher, 4" h, glossy finish, sq
  top, name etched on shoulder 700.00
Cruet, 6¾" h, acid finish, faceted amber
  stopper, reeded amber handle 825.00
Decanter, 9⅛" h, satin finish, applied
  amber twisted handle, orig stopper . 1,200.00
Lemonade Tumbler, 5⅛" h, glossy finish, cylindrical, oyster white lining,
  polished pontil, pinpoint interior rim
  flake 225.00
Mustard Jar, 3" h, satin finish, ball

Vase, bulbous bottom, extended neck, Wheeling, 10" h, $975.00.

  shape, opal lining, orig pewter rim,
  cov, and attached handle 365.00
Pear, 6¾" l, 1¾" stem, 2½" w base, satin
  finish, red and amber, white lining . 485.00
Pitcher, 7¼" h, satin finish, bulbous
  body, sq rim, applied amber handle,
  minor interior staining 1,400.00
Punch Cup, 3⅝" d, 2½" h, satin finish,
  creamy white lining, applied amber
  ring handle 275.00
Salt and Pepper Shakers, pr, 2¾" h, satin
  finish, ball shape, opal lining, orig flat
  tops 725.00
Sugar Shaker, 5½" h, satin finish, orig
  metal top 700.00
Tumbler, cylindrical
  3¾" h, satin finish, oyster white lining 285.00
  3¾" h, 2¾" d, acid finish, creamy
    white lining 300.00
Vase
  7" h, glossy finish, Drape pattern, ruf-
    fled top 600.00
  8" h, satin finish, Morgan, cased opal
    lining, stand missing 615.00
  15¾" h, satin finish, bottle shaped,
    long slender neck, shading from
    peach–yellow to cherry red to fuch-
    sia 800.00

PEKING GLASS

History: Peking glass is a type of cameo glass of
Chinese origin. Its production began in the 1700s
and continued well into the 19th century. The
background color of Peking glass may be a delicate shade of yellow, green, or white. One style
of white background is so delicate and transparent that it often is referred to as the "snowflake"
ground. The overlay colors include a rich garnet
red, deep blue, and emerald green.

Bottle, 10" h, opaque yellow ground, carved birds in flight and orchid plants **400.00**

Bowl

4½" d, translucent opaque white ground, green prunus and rockwork dec **295.00**

6" d

Cobalt blue ground, two etched lotus reserves, diaper border **165.00**

Opaque white ground, blue overlay, carved figures of warriors and dragons in landscape setting **850.00**

6¼" d, opaque white ground, yellow overlay, bell form, inset ring foot, deeply carved with chrysanthemum branch and long tailed bird, prunus branch and two song birds on reverse, pr **4,125.00**

7" d, opaque white ground, blue overlay, deeply carved flowers, butterfly, and foliage, teakwood stand **250.00**

Cup, 3" d, opaque white ground, blue overlay, flaring, everted rim, engraved, dragon and cloud motif, silver holder, 19th C **225.00**

Jar, cov

5⅛" h, opaque white ground, red overlay, globular, four shaped medallions containing flower sprigs, ruyi band on shoulders, floriform knops, late 19th C, pr **800.00**

5¾" h, opaque white ground, cobalt blue geometric pattern, urn shape **600.00**

Snuff Bottle, pastel colored leaves, green jade top, 2⅜" h, $185.00.

Snuff Bottle

1⅞" l, opaque white ground, five color overlay, floral dec, flattened pear shape, blue glass stopper, late 19th C **185.00**

2½" l, camphor ground, blue overlay, horses dec, flattened ovoid body, blue glass stopper with aventurine **175.00**

3" h, camphor ground, six color overlay floral dec, floral form, green glass stopper, late 19th C .. **200.00**

Vase, opaque white ground, baluster form, yellow overlay cut with exotic fish, pond, lilies, pads, and aquatic grasses, 12" h, pr, $605.00. Photograph courtesy of Skinner, Inc.

Vase

4" h, opaque white ground, blue overlay, lotus leaves and flowers dec **150.00**

8" h, opaque white ground, red overlay floral and leaf dec, baluster, red rim, early 20th C **220.00**

8½" h, 5½" d, opaque white ground, cameo carved Chinese red dec of Peking ducks and lotus blossoms, bulbous, flaring top, double ring neck, pr **600.00**

9" h

Cased, emerald green exterior, opal glass interior, Bird's Eye pattern **45.00**

Opaque white ground, Chinese red cameo, deep cut leaves and berries, baluster, c1900 .... **550.00**

10" h, opaque white ground, baluster

Carved red overlay, goldfish and water lily dec, pr **650.00**

Carved yellow overlay, monkey and pine tree dec, early 20th C, pr **500.00**

12" h, opaque white ground, yellow overlay cut with exotic fish, pond, lilies, pads, and aquatic grasses, baluster, pr **605.00**

13" h, opaque white ground, Chinese red tropical fish, green lotus and pond dec, c1900 .... **850.00**

PELOTON

History: Wilhelm Kralik of Bohemia patented Peloton art glass in 1880. Later it was also patented in America and England.

Peloton glass is found with both transparent and opaque grounds with opaque being more common. Opaque colored glass filaments (strings) are applied by dipping or rolling the hot glass. Generally, the filaments (threads) are pink, blue, yellow, and white (rainbow colors) or a single color. Items also may have a satin finish and enamel decorations.

Cruet, clear with multicolored filaments, clear stopper, 7″ h, $275.00.

Basket, 7″ d, 6½″ h, blue ground, white filaments, applied looped briar type handle **220.00**
Biscuit Jar, cov
  5¼″ h, cased, clear ground, multicolored filaments, white lining, melon ribbed body, silver plated top **575.00**
  6¾″ h, pale blue ground, multicolored filaments, white lining, melon ribbed body, silver plated rim, cover, and bail handle **500.00**
Bowl, 3½″ d, 2½″ h, pinched top, ribbed sides, clear ground, white, pink, blue, and olive green filaments, fiery opal pastel orchid lining **175.00**
Cruet, 7″ h, light blue ground, pastel filaments, clear stopper **285.00**
Fairy Lamp, white ground, pastel filaments, undulating ruffled saucer base, clear Clarke insert **350.00**
Finger Bowl, clear ground, multicolored filaments **65.00**
Pitcher
  7″ h, cranberry ground, multicolored filaments, swirled body, applied clear reeded handle **375.00**
  8″ h, clear ground, blue filaments, yellow enameled floral dec, applied clear handle **395.00**
  9¾″ h, clear ground, red, yellow, and white filaments, swirled body, applied clear reeded handle **275.00**
  11″ h, amber ground, multicolored filaments, applied clear reeded handle **550.00**

Plate, 7¾″ d, clear ground, blue strings, enamel floral dec **115.00**
Punch Cup, turquoise ground, multicolored filaments, enameled florals, set of six **300.00**
Rose Bowl
  2½″ d, pale pink cased ground, multicolored filaments, applied crystal rigaree feet **295.00**
  2½″ d, 2¼″ h, crimped top, opaque white ground, pink, yellow, blue, and white filaments **250.00**
Sweetmeat Jar, cov, 4½″ h, opaque white ground, multicolored filaments, squatty, finely ribbed, silver plated top and mountings **600.00**
Toothpick Holder
  2½″ h, clear ground, green filaments **100.00**
  3″ h, clear ground, white filaments . **125.00**
Tumbler, 3¾″ h, clear ground, yellow, pink, red, light blue, and white filaments **125.00**
Vase
  3¼″ h, fiery lavender gray opalescent ground, multicolored filaments, bulbous, ruffled flared rim **225.00**
  3¼″ h, 3″ d, orchid pink ground, blue, pink, yellow and white filaments, ball shape, flared ruffled top **175.00**
  4″ h, white cased ground, blue, rose, yellow, and white filaments, melon ribbed body, clear curled rigaree base **145.00**
  4¼″ h, satin ground, yellow, red, and blue filaments, fan shape, frosted floral base **125.00**
  4¼″ h, 4¾″ d, tricorn folded down rim, clear ground, rose, yellow, blue and white filaments, white lining, squatty, melon ribbed body . . **300.00**
  4¾″ h, yellow–green ground blood red, yellow, green, and white filaments **175.00**
  6″ h, 4½″ d, shaded lavender to off–white opaque ground, cased in crystal, all over pink, white, yellow, blue, and red filaments, corset type shape, vertical ribs, tightly crimped top **450.00**
  6½″ h, 4″ d, white ground, pink, yellow, and blue filaments, vertical ribs, ruffled top, five wishbone feet **450.00**
  6¾″ h, 3″ d, yellow ground, white, rose, blue, and yellow filaments, white lining, stick type shape **225.00**
  7″ h, clear ground, cranberry red strings, bulbous **265.00**
  9″ h, sapphire blue ground, white filaments, baluster, double applied handles **225.00**
Water Set, blown water pitcher, polished pontil, five tumblers, light yel-

low amber ground, multicolored filaments **650.00**

PERFUME, COLOGNE, AND SCENT BOTTLES

History: Decorative bottles to hold scents have been made in various shapes and sizes. They reached a "golden age" during the second half of the 19th century.

An atomizer is a perfume bottle with a spray mechanism. Cologne bottles usually are larger and have stoppers which also may be used as applicators. A perfume bottle has a stopper that often is elongated and designed as an applicator.

Scent bottles are small bottles used to hold a scent or smelling salts. A vinaigrette is an ornamental box or bottle with a perforated top used to hold aromatic vinegars or smelling salts. Fashionable women of the late 18th and 19th centuries carried them in purses or slipped them into gloves in case of a sudden fainting spell.

References: Hazel Martin, *A Collection Of Figural Perfume & Scent Bottles*, published by author, 1982; Jacquelyne Jones–North, *Commercial Perfume Bottles,* Schiffer Publishing, 1987; Jacquelyne Jones–North, *Czechoslovakian Perfume Bottles & Boudoir Accessories*, Antique Publications, 1990; Jacquelyne North, *Perfume, Cologne, and Scent Bottles*, Schiffer Publishing, 1987; Jean Sloan, *Perfume and Scent Bottle Collecting With Prices, Second Edition,* Wallace–Homestead, 1989.

Collectors' Club: Perfume and Scent Bottle Collectors, 2022 East Charleston Blvd., Las Vegas, NV 89104.

Atomizer, Baccarat, amethyst panels, daisy clear cuts, conical, black cord, acid etched Baccarat in base, 5⅞" h, $100.00.

ATOMIZERS

Art Deco
  3" h, opaque black ground, gold dec   **65.00**

3¾" h, sq, yellow painted panels, stylized flowers and stars **50.00**
Baccarat
  6" h, amberina, swirled body **75.00**
  7" h, Rose Tiente, swirl patterned body **75.00**
Czechoslovakian, 8" h, cobalt blue, large enameled and faceted crystal stopper finial, c1930 . . . .   **85.00**
D'Argental, pear shape, double overlay cameo, amber translucent ground, overlay red flowers, brown grape leaf trellis, sgd "Marney France" **365.00**
DeVilbiss
  Black amethyst ground, goldstone spiderweb dec, bulb missing **80.00**
  Cranberry ground, gold dec, 10" h .   **250.00**
  Egyptian motif, gold leaf dec, orig label "DeVilbiss/Toledo" **250.00**
Moser, 4½" h, melon ribbed body, sapphire blue, tiny gold florals, leaves, and swirls, orig gold top and bulb . .   **250.00**
Steuben, 7" h, Aurene, gold **360.00**

COLOGNE BOTTLES

Apple Green, 5¼" h, hexagonal, cut bull's eyes and punty dec, ground stopper **525.00**
Aurene, blue irid, three lug feet, unsigned Steuben **800.00**
Cameo Glass, English
  3⅜" h, 2½" d, round body, frosted vaseline ground, white florals and butterfly, hallmarked silver hinged cap **800.00**
  5¾" h, raisin colored ground, white florals and butterfly, hallmarked silver hinged cap **1,350.00**
Canary Yellow, 5" h, hexagonal, cut stopper **195.00**
Cranberry, floral dec, gold trim, clear stopper **200.00**
Cut Glass, 7" h, 3½" d, slim cut neck, bulbous body, Cane pattern, pointed stopper **100.00**
Malachite, 6½" h, sgd "Moser" **250.00**
Paperweight Type
  5½" h, clear body, pink, blue, yellow, and white flowers with bubble centers, green ground, marked "St Clair Glass Works, Elwood, IN" . .   **65.00**
  7½" h, clear body, brass filigree ftd frame, brass cap, crystal stopper .   **125.00**
Ruby, 6¾" h, sanded gold, enameled green foliage, pink roses, three opal jewels, orig ruby ball stopper **125.00**

PERFUME BOTTLES

Amber, applied grapes, gold enameled insect dec **335.00**

Perfume, milk glass, clear ruffled neck, gold ribs on melon base, rose floral motif, clear fluted stopper with gold knob finial, label on base "Carlton/hand decorated 4188," 7¼" h, $62.00.

Amberina, stamped "Libbey," orig yellow stopper, c1920 .... **295.00**

Black Glass, 1¾" h, bell shape, cork stopper, marked "Made in France" . **35.00**

Cameo, 1⅞" h, 1¼" d, morning glory blossom, white cut to deep blue to powder blue body, white lining, hallmarked sterling silver top, English .. **700.00**

Cased Glass, 4⅛" h, 2½" d, pink, gold bands, enameled gold florals and flower garlands, orig clear ball stopper **100.00**

Cranberry

3¾" h, 2⅜" d, bulbous, enameled blue and gray flowers, blue, orange, and white leaves, clear flattened ball stopper **90.00**

4½" h, 2¾" d, melon ribbed body, emb, lacy gold enameled fern leaves, clear cut faceted stopper .. **150.00**

5¼" d, 2" d, gold bands, small blue and white florals, gold ball stopper **120.00**

Cut Glass

6½" h, Button and Star pattern, rayed base, faceted stopper, Brilliant period, American **100.00**

8½" h, amber, cut panels and designs, matching stopper **180.00**

Czechoslovakian, 2½" h, 1¾" d, all over filigree florals and mesh, white enameled florals, blue mirrored faceted stones, jeweled screw on cap and dauber **50.00**

Lalique, 4½" h, Je Reviens Eau de Cologne, globe shape, stars, coin shaped stopper, base sgd "Made in France by Lalique" **100.00**

Pairpoint, 5½" h, heavy crystal, controlled bubbles **60.00**

Quezal, 5" h, flattened teardrop form, iridescent multicolored ground, foliate mounts, bulbous stopper, c1915 **625.00**

Satin Glass, 6" l, MOP, Diamond Quilted pattern, shading yellow to white, lay down horn shape **400.00**

Steuben

8" h, Jade, green body, long tapering alabaster stopper **350.00**

8¼" h, all over cut facets, Cintra, hexagonal stopper with tapering tester, acid stamped mark, c1925 .....**3,300.00**

10½" h, Oriental Poppy, opalescent, rose, c1925 ....**1,250.00**

Stevens and Williams, 5" h, moss rose cased glass, silver mounts, sterling silver monogrammed cap, c1895 ..... **750.00**

Webb, 2½" h, cameo, blue ground, white cameo carved ferns, gilt sterling hinged top, crystal stopper, English hallmarks, c1900 .... **675.00**

Scent Bottle, clear, elongated point, cut effect, glass stopper, floral motif on sterling silver cap, 3½" h, $130.00.

SCENTS

Amethyst, 3⅜" h, pewter top **85.00**

Blue ground, 2½" h, flattened pear shape, faceted, rococo overlay ornament, inscribed "Armour Sans Fin" . **500.00**

Burmese, 4¾" h, 3⅜" d, acid finish, salmon pink to yellow, heavy gold leaves and birds, silver gilt screw-on top, hallmarked **825.00**

Cut Glass, 3⅞" l, sterling silver overlay, cobalt glass, yellow flashing, emb sterling silver cap **125.00**

Czechoslovakian, lay down, multicolored jewels, enameled top **100.00**

Enameled flowers, 3" l, pale blue body, hinged metal cap, finger ring, c1900 **65.00**

Lalique, 2¾" h, frosted and clear, sienna patina, circular, molded flowerheads, marked "R Lalique for Jay Thorpe Co, NY" **325.00**

Opalescent, 2⅝" h, sapphire blue, white opalescent swirls, pewter cap . **250.00**

Opaque white ground, 2⅜" h, Gothic paneled shape, pewter cap **95.00**

Ruby Glass, cylindrical, sterling silver cap dated 1884 .... **90.00**

Webb, 7" l, opaque white body, covered with stylized bamboo plant dec, burnished gold, lush tropical foliage of palm trees, ferns, and cacti, long neck with gold bamboo like dec on dark green ground, hallmarked "JG & S" sterling silver top, sterling silver chain **485.00**

PHOENIX GLASS

History: Phoenix Glass Company, Beaver, Pennsylvania, was established in 1880. Known primarily for commercial glassware, the firm also produced a molded, sculptured, cameo–type line from the 1930s until the 1950s.

Reference: Jack D. Wilson, *Phoenix & Consolidated Art Glass, 1926–1980,* Antique Publications, 1989.

Ashtray, white ground, relief molded praying mantis, triangular **45.00**
Basket, 4½" h, pink ground, relief molded dogwood dec **50.00**
Bowl
  9" d, frosted and clear, sculptured nudes **100.00**
  9½" d, 5½" h, white ground, relief molded bittersweet **150.00**
Candlesticks, pr
  3¼" h, blue ground, bubbles and swirls **55.00**
  4" h, blue ground, frosted **45.00**
Canoe
  8" l, white ground, sculptured green lemons and foliage **90.00**
  13½" l, opal ground, sculptured blue lovebirds **325.00**
Centerpiece Bowl, 14" d, opaque white ground, sculptured diving nudes, three colors **225.00**
Charger, blue ground
  14" d, relief molded white daffodils . **95.00**
  18" d, relief molded white dancing nudes **525.00**
Cigarette Box, cov, 4½" d, 3½" h, blue ground, sculptured white flowers . . . **75.00**
Compote, 8½" d, butterscotch ground, relief molded dragonflies and water lilies dec **80.00**
Console Bowl, white ground, relief molded diving ladies, blue figures . . **235.00**
Creamer and Sugar, yellow ground, Catalonia pattern **48.00**
Dish, cov, 8½" l, oval, amber ground, sculptured lotus blossoms and dragonfiles **95.00**
Ginger Jar, cov, frosted ground, bird finial **75.00**
Lamp, table
  17½" h, iridescent blue ground, green peacock feather pattern, sgd

"Phoenix Studios, Tom Arnold, #197" **185.00**
20" h, ivory ground, relief molded red cardinals on tree branches, green berries **225.00**
28" h, Gone with the Wind style, double oil burner, cameo cut, green opalescent ground, raised orchid design, brass mounts, sgd "Phoenix," converted to electric **3,000.00**
Planter, 8½" l, 3¼" h, white ground, relief molded green lion **90.00**
Plate
  6¾" d, frosted and clear ground, relief molded dancing nudes **38.00**
  8¼" d, yellow ground, relief molded dancing nudes **65.00**
  8½" d, frosted and clear ground, relief molded cherries **55.00**
Powder Box, cov
  6¾" d, lavender ground, sculptured roses and hummingbird **125.00**
  7¼" d, pale lavender ground, sculptured white violets **100.00**
Rose Bowl, rose pink ground, relief molded starflowers and white bands **145.00**
Tumbler, yellow ground, relief molded dancing nudes **40.00**

Vase, Flying Geese, blue pastel ground, orig paper label, 9½" h, 11½" w, $200.00.

Vase
  6" h, cream color ground, relief molded pink owls **95.00**
  6½" h, rect, white ground, opal sculptured lovebirds on branch **100.00**
  7½" h, salmon pink ground, blown–out pearlized white fern fronds and narrow leaves, orig label **250.00**
  8⅜" h, fan shape, pale blue–gray ground, sculptured praying mantis, foliage, pearlized and frosted **150.00**
  9" h, pastel blue ground, relief molded Canada geese in flight, opal white birds, remnants of paper label **165.00**
  9½" h, white ground, relief molded heavily gilted roses **125.00**

10" h, white ground, relief molded dogwood with blue tinted highlights, partial paper label **80.00**

10¼" h, blue ground, Madonna, sculptured head, white irid **240.00**

11" h, white ground, sculptured, coral, green, and brown dogwoods **275.00**

12" h, gray ground, relief molded pearlized dancing nymphs **575.00**

18" h, blue ground, relief molded pearlized white thistles, orig paper label **495.00**

PICKLE CASTORS

History: A pickle castor is a table accessory used to serve pickles. It generally consists of a silver-plated frame fitted with a glass insert, matching silver-plated lid, and matching tongs. Pickle castors were very popular during the Victorian era. Inserts are found in pattern glass and colored art glass.

Mount Washington, textured insert, hand painted pansy dec, 9½" h, $525.00.

Amber, Inverted Thumbprint pattern, silver plated frame **265.00**

Amethyst, applied floral dec, silver plated frame and lid **275.00**

Blue, 11" h, Inverted Thumbprint pattern insert, white enamel flowers, orig tongs **250.00**

Cranberry

Barrel shaped insert, multicolored enamel flowers, figural frame with acorns and dog's paw feet **400.00**

Inverted Thumbprint pattern

12" h, gold leaves and plums on one side, green leaves and pear on other, ornate frame, marked "Wilcox 4648" **800.00**

13" h, enameled daisies, twig feet, elaborate floral cut–out sides, top and tongs **325.00**

Craquelle, gargoyles on top, satin pewter silvery Pairpoint frame, acorn finial on engraved lid **250.00**

Crown Milano, 3¾" d, 4½" h creamy white diamond quilted body, swags of pastel pink and white blossoms, resilvered floral emb lid and 9" h holder, sgd on base "Pairpoint Mfg Co, New Bedford Quadruple Plate 661" **845.00**

Crystal

9" h, double, marked "Forbes No. 25," two matching forks **350.00**

10" h, Swirl pattern insert, begging dog finial, orig tongs, marked "Hartford Quadplate" **200.00**

11¾" h, acid etched octagonal insert with floral and bird medallion, frame marked "Meriden Co. 182," orig tongs **245.00**

Emerald Green, paneled insert with enameled florals, ornate silver plated frame **225.00**

Mount Washington, 8½" h, Albertine, pink shaded to white ground, tiny pink and white flowers, four–pointed star rim, orig silver plated frame ...**1,120.00**

New England Glass Co, Pomona pattern, second grind, blue cornflower dec, orig silver plated frame, cov, and tongs **500.00**

Northwood, 12" h, Netted Apple Blossom pattern, opaque white insert, ornate silver plated ftd frame marked "Western Silver Plate, Northwood Glass Co" **475.00**

Opalescent

Coinspot, 14⅜" h, cranberry ground, polychrome enameled flowers, opalescent spots, silver plated frame with lion and shield finial .. **215.00**

Daisy and Fern pattern, blue apple blossom mold insert, ornate ftd silver plated frame, orig tongs **265.00**

Pattern Glass

Beaded Dart pattern, sapphire blue insert, resilvered ftd Meriden frame and tongs **250.00**

Cupid and Venus pattern, clear insert, ftd Pairpoint frame, stylized swan head tongs **85.00**

Currier and Ives pattern, blue insert, orig silver plated frame **165.00**

Daisy and Button pattern, blue insert, silver plated Wilcox frame, lid and tongs **235.00**

Sprig pattern, blue, ornate Reed and Barton frame, orig fork and fancy lid **175.00**

Pigeon Blood, Beaded Drape pattern insert, Consolidated Glass Co, orig cov and frame **425.00**

Rubena, vertical optic pattern insert, or-

nate ftd Pairpoint fretwork frame and
bail handle **225.00**
Satin
 Cranberry, Optic Diamond and Inverted Thumbprint pattern insert,
 gold spider chrysanthemum dec,
 ftd Simpson hall frame, ornate en-
 graved cov, orig silvering **600.00**
 Pink, swirled body, ornate ftd Pair-
 point frame **235.00**
 Yellow barrel shaped insert, flowers
 and butterfly dec, cherubs on front
 and back corners of frame, marked
 "Rogers" **735.00**
Vaseline, white opalescent design, po-
 lished pontil, orig ruffled cov shaped
 as emb flower, stem finial, ornate ftd
 frame **450.00**

PIGEON BLOOD GLASS

History: Pigeon blood refers to the deep orange-
red colored glassware produced around the turn
of the century. Do not confuse it with the many
other red glasswares of that period. Pigeon blood
has a very definite orange glow.

Biscuit Jar
 Melon ribbed body, silver plated fit-
 tings **185.00**
 Torquay pattern, silver plated rim,
 cover, and handles **275.00**
Bowl
 8½" d, ornate silver plated rim **95.00**
 9" d, Torquay pattern, silver plated
 rim, master berry **110.00**
 12½" d, three applied clear lion head
 prunts on front, applied clear feet
 and handles **250.00**
Bride's Basket, 9½" d, enameled floral
 dec, silver plated holder **200.00**
Butter Dish, cov, Venecia pattern,
 enameled dec **350.00**
Candlesticks, pr, 7½" h, twisted stem . **165.00**
Celery Vase, 6" h, Torquay pattern, sil-
 ver plated rim **225.00**
Compote, 7" h, scalloped edge **185.00**
Creamer
 Torquay pattern, silver plated rim and
 handle **125.00**
 Venecia pattern, enameled dec **125.00**
Cruet, orig clear stopper
 Inverted Thumbprint pattern **225.00**
 Valencia pattern **700.00**
Decanter, 9½" h, orig stopper **75.00**
Goblet, bucket shaped bowl, cushioned
 stem, enameled medallion with land-
 scape and country scenes, heavy gold
 swirls, beads, and feathers, marked

"facon de Venise," German, early
 19th C **200.00**
Hand Cooler, 6" l, two sections, silver
 plated hinged covers, London hall-
 marks for 1888–89 . . . . **150.00**
Oil Lamp, clear chimney, orig burner . **245.00**
Perfume Bottle, 9" h, white enameled
 dec and jewels, orig stopper **95.00**
Pickle Castor
 Beaded Drape pattern insert, silver
 plated cov and frame, Consolidated
 Glass Co **425.00**
 Bulging Loops pattern, 8" h silver
 plated ftd frame, marked "Empire
 Mfg Co" **285.00**
 Torquay pattern, orig silver plated cov **125.00**
Pitcher, water
 Bulbous, gold aventurine ruffled, ap-
 plied clear ribbed handle, pontil
 mark **220.00**
 Diamond Quilted pattern, 10½", tan-
 kard shape **185.00**
 Melon ribbed, 9" h, applied clear
 handle **225.00**
 Torquay pattern, silver plated trim . . **325.00**
Plate, 7½" d **25.00**

**Salt Shaker, Consolidated Glass Co., 2½"
h, $90.00.**

Salt and Pepper Shakers, pr
 Bulging Loops pattern, orig tops **145.00**
 Bead and Scroll pattern **120.00**
 Flower Band pattern **150.00**
 Periwinkle pattern **135.00**
Sugar, cov, Torquay pattern, silver
 plated rim and cover **165.00**
Sugar Shaker
 Bulging Loops pattern, orig top **150.00**
 Torquay pattern, orig silver plated top **250.00**
Syrup
 Beaded Drape pattern, Consolidated
 Glass Co, orig hinged lid **245.00**
 Scroll and Net pattern, satin finish,
 applied frosted handle, orig top . . **575.00**
Toothpick Holder, Bulging Loops pat-
 tern **125.00**
Tumbler
 3¼" h, alternating panel and rib **75.00**
 3¾" h, hand painted floral dec **85.00**
Vase
 6" h, gourd shape, cased, gold leaf

dec, applied elephant head handles, Webb, pr 375.00
6½" h, enameled floral dec 150.00
7¼" h, enameled floral and jeweled dec 165.00
10½" h, enameled flowers dec 185.00
12" h, pedestal, applied clear glass rigaree 250.00

PINK SLAG

History: True pink slag is found only in the molded Inverted Fan and Feather pattern. Quality pieces shade from pink at the top to white at the bottom.

Reproduction Alert: Recently, pieces of pink slag, made from molds of the now defunct Cambridge Glass Company, have been found in the Inverted Strawberry and Inverted Thistle pattern. This is not considered "true" pink slag and brings only a fraction of the Inverted Fan and Feather pattern prices.

Tumbler, Inverted Fan and Feather, 4″ h, $450.00.

Bowl, 9″ d, ftd 500.00
Butter, cov 650.00
Compote, jelly 375.00
Creamer 450.00
Cruet, 6¾″ h 950.00
Marmalade Jar 875.00
Pitcher, water 750.00
Punch Cup, 2½″ h, ftd 275.00
Salt Shaker 300.00
Sauce Dish, 4½″ w, 2½″ h, four ball feet 285.00
Spooner 350.00
Sugar, cov 550.00
Toothpick Holder 400.00
Tumbler, 4″ h 450.00

POMONA GLASS

History: Pomona glass, produced only by the New England Glass Works and named for the Roman goddess of fruit and trees, was patented in 1885 by Joseph Locke. It is a delicate lead, blown art glass which has a pale, soft beige ground and a top one–inch band of honey amber.

There are two distinct types of backgrounds. First ground, made only from late 1884 to June 1886, was produced by fine cuttings through a wax coating followed by an acid bath. Second ground was made by rolling the piece in acid-resisting particles and acid etching. Second ground was made in Cambridge until 1888 and until the early 1900s in Toledo where Libbey moved the firm after purchasing New England Glass works. Both methods produced a soft frosted appearance, with fine curlicue lines more visible on first ground pieces. Designs are used on some pieces, which were etched and then stained in color. The most familiar design is blue cornflowers.

Do not confuse Pomona with "Midwestern Pomona," a pressed glass with a frosted body and amber band.

Reference: Joseph and Jane Locke, *Locke Art Glass: A Guide For Collectors,* Dover Publications, 1987.

Beverage Set, 8½″ h tankard pitcher, six glasses, Cornflower pattern, second grind, diamond quilted design 600.00
Bowl
4½″ d, 3″ h, first grind, dark amber stain 275.00
5″ d, Rivulet pattern, second grind, fluted, blue stain 90.00
5¼″ d, Cornflower pattern, second grind, fluted 35.00
10″ d, Cornflower pattern 650.00
Carafe, Cornflower pattern, second grind 200.00
Celery Vase, 6½″ h, Cornflower pattern, first grind 300.00
Creamer
Cornflower pattern, second grind,

Pitcher, Cornflower, light amber stain, first grind, 4½″ h, $450.00.

blue flower, ruffled top, applied
crystal crimped base, 3" h, 6" w .. **225.00**
Daisy and Butterfly pattern, second
grind, applied clear handle, three
applied clear feet **275.00**
Creamer and Sugar, first grind, 6½" l x
4" h creamer with applied loop handle, 5" w x 4" h open sugar, wishbone
feet, ten crimps on each top **675.00**
Cruet
Blueberry pattern, first grind, 5½" h,
gold leaves, applied clear handle,
clear ball stopper **285.00**
Pansy and Butterfly pattern, second
grind, 7¼" h, unstained dec and
handle, iridescent amber stopper . **476.00**
Finger Bowl, 5½" d, 3" h
Cornflower pattern, second grind, ruf-
fled rim, applied base **165.00**
Trailing Vines, second grind **95.00**
Lemonade Mug, 5¾" h
Cornflower pattern, first grind, blue
flowers **275.00**
Optic Diamond Quilt pattern, first
grind, iridescent, clear handle and
upper border **165.00**
Mustard, Flower and Pleat pattern, 3⅛"
h, light stain, silver plated top **50.00**
Nappy, 5¼" d, Cornflower pattern, first
grind, blue flowers, applied handle . **125.00**
Pitcher
First Grind
Acanthus leaf dec, 8¾" h, 4½" w,
5" l neck, bulbous, deep amber
stain **450.00**
Cornflower pattern, 6¼" h, sq top **400.00**
Thumbprint pattern, 4½" h, sq top,
stained rim and handle **350.00**
Second Grind
Blueberry pattern, milk pitcher size **200.00**
Cornflower pattern, sq top, milk
pitcher size **225.00**
Diamond Quilted pattern, 12" h,
slightly tapering cylindrical body,
amber stain at top and applied
handle, polished pontil **165.00**
Punch Cup
Cornflower pattern
First grind, blue flowers **100.00**
Second grind **90.00**
Rivulet pattern, second grind, amber
stained rim **175.00**
Spooner, 5" h, Inverted Thumbprint pat-
tern, second grind, red stemmed blue-
berry dec, crimped base **125.00**
Toothpick Holder, Cornflower pattern,
first grind **245.00**
Tumbler
Cornflower pattern
First grind, 3⅝", blue flowers **200.00**
Second grind, 4" h, blue flowers,
diamond quilted design **95.00**

Oak Leaf Band pattern, second grind **95.00**
Pansy and Butterfly pattern, first grind **135.00**
Vase
2½" h, 4" w, fan shape, first grind,
applied amber scalloped rim, applied amber scalloped base **350.00**
5" h, 2¾" w, Blueberry pattern, second grind, ruffled top, applied
crimped base **550.00**
7" h, Cornflower pattern, second
grind **175.00**
10⅞" h, lily form, second grind **400.00**

PURPLE SLAG (MARBLE GLASS)

History: Challinor, Taylor & Co., Tarantum,
Pennsylvania, c1870s–80s, was the largest producer of purple slag in the United States. Since
the quality of pieces varies considerably, there is
no doubt other American firms made it as well.

Purple slag also was made in England. English
pieces are marked with British Registry marks.

Other color combinations, such as blue,
green, or orange, were made but are rarely
found.

Additional Listings: Greentown Glass (chocolate
slag) and Pink Slag.

Reproduction Alert: Purple slag has been heavily
reproduced over the years and still is reproduced
at present.

Animal Dish, cov, rabbit **275.00**
Bowl
6" d, Beaded Rib pattern, cov **70.00**
7" d, 5" h, three lobes, relief molded
flowers and leaves, three fish
shaped feet, English **200.00**
8" d
Dart and Bar pattern **50.00**
Heart and Vine pattern **40.00**
9" d, Open Rose pattern **38.00**
10¾" d, scalloped, hand painted or-
ange and gold flowers **50.00**
Butter Dish, cov
Paneled Grape pattern **60.00**
Plain paneled sides, cow shaped finial **40.00**
Cake Stand
Flute pattern **75.00**
Plain, pedestal base **55.00**
Candlesticks, pr
Dolphin, figural **245.00**
Shell and Leaf pattern, 3¾" d, irreg-
ular purple and pale blue streaks . **195.00**
Celery Tray, 12" l, 4⅛" w, 2½" h, row-
boat shape, Daisy Block pattern **135.00**
Celery Vase
Blackberry pattern, 6⅝" h, scalloped
rim, plain band above vertical sur-

Celery Vase, Fluted Rib, Challinor, 8¼" h, 4¼" d, $95.00.

face, low stem rising from circular base, Hobbs Brockunier	95.00
Flute pattern	80.00
Jewel pattern	95.00
Compote	
Beaded Hearts pattern, 5" d	75.00
Openwork lattice edge, 8" d, 8" h	75.00
Scroll with Acanthus pattern, Fostoria	40.00
Thread pattern	65.00
Creamer	
Crossbar and Flute pattern	80.00
Figural, fish shape	90.00
Flower and Panel pattern	85.00
Flute pattern	80.00
Oak Leaf pattern	45.00
Scroll with Acanthus pattern, Fostoria	75.00
Cruet, 7" h, intricate pressed pattern, Imperial Glass	45.00
Goblet, Flute pattern	40.00
Jack-In-The-Pulpit Vase, 6" h	35.00
Jar, cov, figural, bull's head, Westmoreland	30.00
Match Holder	
Daisy and Button pattern	40.00
Figural, dolphin head, 5" h	65.00
Mug, rabbit	65.00
Pickle Castor, patterned insert, silvered ftd frame marked "Tufts"	150.00
Pitcher, Fan and Basketweave pattern	225.00
Plate	
10" d, lattice edge	100.00
10½" d, closed lattice edge	100.00
Salt, 2½" d, 4" h	50.00
Spooner	
Crossbar and Flute pattern	70.00
Flower Panel pattern	70.00
Flute pattern	70.00
Scroll with Acanthus pattern, Fostoria	65.00
Sugar, cov	
Crossbar and Flute pattern	85.00
Flower Panel pattern	85.00
Flute pattern	200.00
Scroll with Acanthus pattern, Fostoria	95.00

Toothpick Holder, Scroll with Acanthus pattern, Fostoria	115.00
Tray, Fishscale pattern, emb flower border, notched rim, 13" l, oval	80.00
Tumbler	
Flute pattern, 3¼" h	48.00
Ribbed pattern, 4½" h	45.00
Souvenir, "A Present From the Bristol Exhibition, 1893"	50.00
Vase, 10" h, wispy purple swirls against frosted and clear body	110.00
Whimsey, figural	
Cowboy Boot, stirrup and spur, 3¼" h	50.00
Kettle, three short legs, wire bail handle	40.00
Lady's Shoe, high button style, beaded diamond shaped base, 6" h	65.00

Quezal
1901–25

QUEZAL

History: The Quezal Art Glass Decorating Company, named for the "quetzal," a bird with brilliantly colored feathers, was organized in 1901 in Brooklyn, New York, by two disgruntled Tiffany workers, Martin Bach and Thomas Johnson. They soon hired two more Tiffany workers, Percy Britton and William Wiedebine.

The first products, unmarked, were exact Tiffany imitations. In 1902 the "Quezal" trademark was first used. Quezal pieces differ from Tiffany pieces in that they are more defined and the decorations more visible and brightly colored. No new techniques came from Quezal.

Johnson left in 1905. T. Conrad Vahlsing, Bach's son–in–law, joined the firm in 1918, but left with Paul Frank in 1920 to form Lustre Art Glass Company which copied Quezal pieces. Martin Bach died in 1924 and by 1925 Quezal had ceased operations.

Wares are signed "Quezal" on the base of vases and bowls and rims of shades. The acid-etched or engraved letters vary in size and may be found in amber, black, or gold. A printed label of a quetzal bird was used briefly in 1907.

Automobile Vase, 10½" h, irid gold amber ground, folded rim, elongated conical form, marked "Quezal"	145.00
Bowl	
5½" d, irid gold ground, flared rim	275.00
7½" d, irid butterscotch ground, ftd, sgd	325.00
9½" d, gold calcite ground, stretch rim, pedestal foot, sgd "Quezal"	800.00
12" d, peacock blue ground, ham-	

Cruet, pulled green feather, white opalescent ground, clear yellow handle and stopper, 6½" h, $2,350.00.

mered silver base, marked "Oscar
B Bach, NY" **465.00**
Candlesticks, pr
  6½" h, white opal ground, orange–
  green King Tut irid dec, flared bobeche rim, ringed hollow baluster,
  sgd **950.00**
  7¾" h, irid blue ground, sgd **550.00**
Cologne Bottle, 7½" h, irid gold ground,
  Art Deco design, sgd "Q" and
  "Melba" **245.00**
Compote
  4¾" h, pale pastel blue ground, pedestal foot, sgd and numbered **500.00**
  6" h, yellow irid ground, wide flaring
  bowl, slender pedestal, round foot,
  sgd **385.00**
  6¾" h, 6¼" d, irid gold ground, green
  irid swirls, deep shaped bowl with
  gold interior, gold stem and foot sgd **750.00**
Creamer, 2½" h, irid gold ground, applied lip and handle **550.00**
Cruet, white opal ground, green pulled
  feather design, clear yellow stopper
  and applied handle **2,350.00**
Cup and Saucer, irid gold interior, opal
  hooked feather pattern, sgd and numbered **1,045.00**
Cuspidor, 3⅜" h, 6¾" d, irid gold
  ground, gold and green feather pattern at base rising to white and green
  dec, lavender highlights, sgd "Quezal
  S804" **1,350.00**
Finger Bowl, 6" d, irid gold ground,
  opal, and gold pulled feathers,
  shaped bowls, matching opal and
  gold irid underplates, Martin Bach design, sgd and numbered, two matching prs, 4 pcs **1,200.00**
Flask, 8½" h, brilliant irid rainbow
  ground, finely chased silver overlay
  carnations, inscribed "Quezal," Alvin
  Corp mark stamped on silver **1,200.00**
Jack-In-The-Pulpit Vase
  11½" h, ivory ground, irid gold face,

stem, and back, gold and green leaf
  pulls and hooked waves, sgd "Quezal R 84" **6,000.00**
  14¾" h, irid deep amber ground,
  green and pink highlights, silvery
  blue and amber loopings and trail-
  ings, wide flaring turned up rim,
  cylindrical standard, circular
  domed foot, c1905–20 .... **2,400.00**
Knife Rest, 3½" l, irid gold ground, two
  sq ends, twisted bar, polished pontil
  with signature **120.00**
Lamp
  Chandelier, 23" d, six branches, six
  gold irid and opal sixteen–rib
  shades, gilt metal chain, suspended
  fixture, emb florals, drop pineapple
  finial, sgd on each shade, one
  shade with slight damage **1,210.00**
  Table
  20" h, twelve lily shades, irid gold
  ribbed blossom shades, slender
  stems rising from bronze leaf pad
  base, green patina, each shade
  sgd at outer collet, six shades are
  cased, six are single layer, unmarked base, wiring worn, some
  stems separated from leaves ... **4,800.00**
  22" h, 11¾" d shade, flared shade
  with eighteen molded ribs, five
  opal, gold, and green pulled
  feathers, irid gold interior, sgd
  "Quezal" on raised collet rim,
  turned mahogany urn form base **990.00**
Lamp Shade
  Floriform, 4" h, bright irid amber
  ground, ribbed, waisted, and everted edge, sgd "Quezal," pr **275.00**
  Pulled Feather, 5" h, white opal
  ground, irid gold interior, applied
  webbing **175.00**
  Ribbed, irid gold ground, sgd,
  matched set of three **225.00**
Miniature, 2" h, dish, irid gold ground,
  applied silver overlay carved in scrolling floral design, flared pinched rim,
  sgd "Quezal 334" **1,100.00**
Nut Dish, irid gold ground, triangular
  rim, gently rounded body, inscribed
  "Quezal" **125.00**
Perfume Bottle, 5" h, irid gold ground,
  flattened teardrop shape, bulbous
  stopper, Gorham sterling silver monogrammed foliate mounts **585.00**
Plate
  5⅞" d, irid gold ground, scalloped
  rim, sgd on pontil **185.00**
  8" d, irid gold ground, scalloped ... **250.00**
  10¾" d, fiery irid stretched orange–
  gold ground, ambergris dec, sgd
  "Quezal" across polished pontil,
  set of six **1,450.00**

Salt
  2½" h, 1⅛" d, gold luster satin
    ground, pink and blue highlights,
    sgd **225.00**
  2¾" h, irid gold ground, ribbed **175.00**
Toasting Goblet, 4" h, white opal
  ground, fiery irid gold interior, gold
  and green pulled feather dec, gold
  chain border, sgd "Quezal" inside
  applied hollow stem pedestal, pr ... **1,600.00**
Toothpick, 2¼" h, irid blue ground,
  green, purple, and gold highlights,
  melon ribbed, pinched sides, sgd ... **185.00**
Vase
  4" h, irid gold ground, fold–over top,
    thatched and lily pad dec **995.00**
  4" h, 3½" d, irid gold ground, gold
    hooked feather dec at base rising to
    opal top, squatty, narrow top **995.00**
  4¼" h, irid gold ground, green and
    gold threads, slender body, circular
    foot, folded back surface, sgd
    "Quezal 167" **1,000.00**
  4½" h, white opal ground, large green
    petals, flower form, sgd "Quezal S
    854" **1,500.00**
  5½" h, cased ivory over amber
    ground, lavender and yellow swirl
    dec, bulbous amphora shape, in-
    scribed name and number **495.00**
  6" h, bulbous, flared rim
    Hearts and Vines, irid opal ground,
      gold lining, decorated shoulders **500.00**
    King Tut **1,200.00**
  6⅜" h, irid gold neck, white body, irid
    gold feather pulled dec, green zig-
    zag band around shoulder, squatty,
    sgd "Quezal 861" **900.00**
  6⅝" h, irid ivory and green ground,
    platinum pulled feather design, sgd
    "Quezal 739" **1,100.00**
  6⅞" h, irid blue ground, abstract gold
    threading, opaque white hearts, sgd **500.00**
  7" h, white opal ground
    Five detailed green pulled feather
      leaf forms, gold outlines, bright
      irid gold interior, flared trumpet
      floriform, inscribed "Quezal S
      206" **1,045.00**
    King Tut pattern, pulled irid gold
      swirling dec, sgd **770.00**
  7¼" h, 5" d, white opal ground, gold
    and green feathered leaves, flower
    form top, sgd **1,695.00**
  7½" h, irid butterscotch ground, all
    over gold scalloped lines, brown
    swirl dec at top **990.00**
  8¼" h, classic ambergris body, irid
    blue luster, gold horizontal high-
    lights, sgd **475.00**
  9" h, white opal and irid gold ground,
    green pulled feather design, gold

    chain of hearts under rim, bright
    irid orange–gold interior, Martin
    Bach design, sgd "Quezal 6" ... **1,100.00**
  9½" h, white opal ground
    Irid gold dec, green pulled feather
      dec, gold heart–chain under rim,
      brilliant stretched irid gold inte-
      rior, Martin Bach design, sgd
      "Quezal 6" **1,500.00**
    Reverse pulled irid gold feathers
      above symmetrical spider web
      criss–cross designs, elongated
      bottle form, sgd "Quezal C 369" **1,320.00**
  9¾" h, ivory ground, gold and green
    hooked feather dec, waisted cylin-
    der, inscribed "Quezal A384" ... **1,600.00**
Wall Sconce, 14" h, irid floriform shade,
  white opal ground, gold pulled
  feather design, gold interior, molded
  brass sconce, foliage and mirror dec,
  sgd at base of shade **175.00**
Whimsey, pipe, 12" l, irid gold ground,
  floral and leaf design on bowl, pulled
  feather dec on stem **1,395.00**

ROSE BOWLS

History: Rose bowls gained popularity in the late
Victorian area. These decorative bowls were intended to hold rose petals or fragrant potpourri.
Practically every glass manufacturer made rose
bowls in a variety of patterns and glass types,
including fine art glass, carnival glass, and even
pattern glass.

Rose Bowls usually have a small opening
which may be crimped, pinched, scalloped, or
even petaled like a flower. Most rose bowls are
round in shape, although a few examples can be
found in an egg shape.

Reference: John Mebane, *Collecting Bride's Baskets And Other Glass Fancies*, Wallace–Homestead, 1976.

Reproduction Alert: Rose bowls have been reproduced in many glass types.

Amber, 3" h, white spatter tortoiseshell
  type dec, applied gold dec **130.00**
Amberina
  6" h, Hobnail pattern **275.00**
  6" h, 5" d, ribbed, cranberry shaded
    to olive–amber, enameled white
    and pink blossoms, tan branches . **245.00**
Amethyst, squatty, enameled dec, fluted
  top **95.00**
Cameo, 4⅜" h, 4¼" d, frosted blue
  ground, opaque white overlay, cameo
  carved flowers and scrolling design,
  cut scalloped top **425.00**
Cased Glass, 6" h, robin's egg blue exterior, white interior, applied crystal

Opalescent Swirl, Fenton, green, 5½" h, 4½" d, $85.00.

swag trim, crystal rosettes and scroll feet 265.00
Cranberry
  3¼" h, 4¼" d, Arboresque pattern, opaque white design, crackle finish, tightly crimped top 125.00
  4½" h, 5" d, Coin Spot pattern, eight loops top 185.00
Cut Glass, 3½" h, 4" d, cut hobs, strawberry diamond, fan, and single star, hobs base 195.00
Cut Velvet, 3¾" h, 3⅜" d, rose ground, Diamond Quilted pattern, white lining 175.00
Daum Nancy, 3" h, 3¼" d, mottled gold ground, acid cut river's edge landscape, enameled highlights, three petal top 650.00
Fenton, 5½" h, Hobnail pattern, opalescent cranberry 148.00
Northwood, 3⅛" h, 4½" d, satin, light tan ground, mauve pulled feather dec, robin's egg blue lining, tightly crimped top 1,000.00
Opalescent
  Beaded Drape pattern, green 45.00
  Fancy Fantails pattern, cranberry . . . 60.00
  Opalescent Open pattern, blue, pedestal base 48.00
  Opalescent Stripe pattern
    Blue 90.00
    Cranberry, enameled forget—me—nots dec 75.00
Pattern Glass
  Champion pattern, McKee & Brothers, dec by Beaumont Glass Works, clear, amber stain 40.00
  Eureka pattern, National Glass Co, clear, ruby stained 80.00
  Heart with Thumbprint pattern, Tarentum Glass Co, clear, ruby stained 95.00
  Red Block pattern, clear, ruby stained 75.00
  Scalloped Six Points pattern, George Duncan Sons & Co, clear 45.00
  Torpedo pattern, Thompson Glass Co, clear 85.00

Peach Blow
  2⅜" h, 2½" d, Diamond Quilted pattern, MOP, deep red shaded to amber—pink, eight crimp top, Webb . 325.00
  3¼" h, 4" d, Wild Rose, deep raspberry shading to white, matte acid finish, eight crimp top, elaborate lettering and scroll dec, made by Mt Washington for 1893 World's Fair 675.00
Peloton
  2½" h, 2¼" d, white opaque ground, pink, yellow, blue, and white filaments, crimped top 250.00
  3⅞" h, 3½" d, white opaque cased ribbed ground, multicolored filaments, pulled to four points on top 350.00
Rubena, 3⅝" h, 4¼" d, overshot type dec, eight crimps 100.00
Satin Glass
  2¼" h, rose, gold enameled flower and bee dec, ruffled top, Webb . . 165.00
  3¼" h, Rainbow, Diamond Quilted pattern, MOP, alternating pink, yellow, and narrow blue stripes, white lining, white enamel blossoms, small blemish at side 225.00
  3½" h, 4" h, blue, Herringbone pattern, MOP, white lining, six crimp top 235.00
  3½" h, 4¼" d, Rainbow, Diamond Quilted pattern, MOP, deep pink, yellow, and blue stripes, applied clear feet, applied berry pontil, marked "Patent" 1,400.00
  4" h, 5⅜" d, rose ground, white lining, multicolored petit point enamel, gold dots 350.00
Spangle Glass, 4" h, yellow ground, multicolored spangle with mica flecks, egg shape, satin finish 65.00
Stevens and Williams
  3" h, satin, pink ground, white lining, vertical ribs, pinched tricorn top . 375.00
  3½" h, 4½" d, satin, blue opalescent lining, emb swirls, box pleated top 200.00
Webb, 3" h, 3⅛" d, deep red shaded to warm pink–amber, acid finish, cream lining, eight crimp top 235.00

1892

ROYAL FLEMISH

History: Royal Flemish was produced by the Mount Washington Glass Company, New Bedford, Massachusetts. The process was patented by Albert Steffin in 1894. Royal Flemish was only produced for a limited time as the technique involved was labor intensive and therefore costly.

Royal Flemish has heavy, raised gold enamel lines on frosted transparent glass which has an acid finish. The raised gold enamel lines separate into sections, often colored in russet tones of tan, brown, and maroon. It gives the appearance of stained glass windows with elaborate floral or coin medallions in the design. Coats of arms, Guba ducks, rampant lions, and scrolls are other design elements found in this artistic glassware.

Royal Flemish wares were not all signed, although a round paper label is found on some pieces. A red enameled mark was also used.

Reference: John A. Shuman III, *The Collector's Encyclopedia of American Art Glass,* Collector Books, 1988, 1991 value update.

Museum: New Bedford Museum, New Bedford, MA.

Bowl, 10½" d, 4" h, enameled chrysanthemum dec, gold outlined panels . **1,750.00**
Box, cov, 3¾" h, 5½" d, swirled body,
gold outlined swirls, gold tracery
blossoms, enameled blossom on lid
with jeweled center **1,400.00**
Cologne Bottle, 5½" h, clear, frosted
body, enameled butterfly and daisy
dec, heavy gold tracery, dark maroon
enameled neck and stopper **4,000.00**
Cracker Jar, 7½" d, raised gold dec of
mythical figures, silver plated lid, and
bail handle **2,400.00**
Ewer
9½" h, Cupid slaying dragon, raised
gold, mythological fish in medallions, pastel blue and violet blossoms within side panels, gold tracery on extended neck, applied
twisted rope handle **4,500.00**
12" h, gold and silver rampant lion
and shield, raised gold borders,
pastel blue cross with raised gold
borders on reverse, applied twisted
rope handle **3,750.00**
Pitcher, 9¼" h, raised gold florals, tan
panels, six colorful shields surround-
ing neck, rope handle **4,200.00**
Rose Bowl, eight scalloped top, pale
brown shading to clear frosted, white
and blue asters, brown and green
stems and leaves, pontil with purple
number **1,285.00**
Rose Jar, cov
9" h, bright panels, Roman coins on
obverse, raised gold florals on re-
verse, finial with old repair **2,000.00**
10½" h, profuse gold dec, fire—
breathing dragon, orig lid **5,250.00**

**Vase, gilt green and brown scrolling de-
signs of winged dragons, shaded yellow
lusterless body, unsigned, 10½" h,
$2,530.00. Photograph courtesy of Skin-
ner, Inc.**

Sugar, 6¼" d, 2½" h, pink and yellow
apple blossoms, gilt enameled dec,
applied reeded handles **412.00**
Vase
7½" h
Bulbed body, spiral neck, frosted,
hand painted enameled roses,
gold outlines, applied leaf han-
dles, faint mark **2,200.00**
Gilt and green raised enamel dec,
winged dragons, simulated
stained glass partitions **2,860.00**
8" h, 6¾" d, tan and brown, raised
gold winged gargoyle, stylized flo-
rals **2,500.00**
8½" h, globular, tapered neck, shaped
rim turned out with two scroll handles, puce, pink, and blue enameling with gilt highlights, shaded
branches of blossoming fruit tree
with pendant leaves and applied
jeweled berries, frosted gray
ground, diagonal inscribed sq and
number mark, late 19th C **1,200.00**
11½" h, raised gold, chrysanthemum
blossoms, foliage, circles of dark
blue, light blue crosses, cerise
ground, lower panels of alternating
pale blue and tan **4,475.00**

RUBENA GLASS

History: Rubena crystal is a transparent blown glass which shades from clear to red. It also is found as the background for frosted and overshot glass. It was made in the late 1800s by several glass companies, including Northwood and Hobbs, Brockunier & Co. of Wheeling, West Virginia.

Rubena was used for several patterns of pattern glass including Royal Ivy and Royal Oak.

Vase, bud, enameled floral dec, 6″ h, $45.00.

Basket, applied clear thorn handle **125.00**
Biscuit Jar, cov, 7¼″ h, 6¼″ d, Diamond
 Quilted pattern, squatty bulbous
 body, ornate silver plated rim, domed
 cov, and scrolling bail handle, resilvered **375.00**
Bowl
 4½″ d, Daisy and Scroll pattern **60.00**
 9″ d, berry, Royal Ivy pattern, Northwood, frosted **125.00**
Butter Dish, cov
 Royal Ivy pattern, Northwood **175.00**
 Royal Oak pattern, Northwood,
 frosted **225.00**
Castor Set, Venecia pattern, salt and
 pepper shakers with orig tops, cov
 mustard jar, cruet, orig stopper, glass
 handled frame **250.00**
Celery Vase, threaded, Northwood ... **72.00**
Cologne Bottle
 5⅝″ h, 2¼″ sq, cut, clear faceted stopper **125.00**
 6¾″ h, 2¾″ d, gold bands, overall
 stippling, orig clear cut faceted
 stopper with gold trim, St Louis .. **135.00**
Compote
 12¾″ h, 8½″ d, rubena overshot
 bowl, white metal bronze finished
 figural standard **125.00**
 14″ h, 9″ d, rubena overshot bowl,
 white metal bronze finished figural
 standard **150.00**
Creamer, applied clear handle
 Medallion Sprig pattern **160.00**
 Royal Ivy pattern, Northwood, frosted **200.00**
 Royal Oak pattern, Northwood,
 frosted **200.00**
Cruet
 Medallion Sprig pattern, orig stopper **250.00**
 Royal Ivy pattern, Northwood,
 frosted, applied clear handle **350.00**

Royal Oak pattern, Northwood **350.00**
Decanter, 9″ h, bulbous base, narrow
 neck, applied clear handle **140.00**
Finger Bowl, Royal Ivy pattern, North-
 wood **45.00**
Marmalade Jar, cov, enamel dec, sgd
 "Moser" **315.00**
Miniature Lamp, Royal Ivy pattern,
 Northwood **250.00**
Perfume Bottle, 3¼″ h, silver plated top
 rim, cranberry cut stopper **125.00**
Pickle Castor, vertical optic insert, fancy
 fretwork on ftd Pairpoint silver plated
 frame **225.00**
Pitcher
 8″ h, Thumbprint pattern, applied
 clear handle **150.00**
 9¼″ h, tankard, enameled floral dec,
 applied clear reeded handle **200.00**
Rose Bowl, 4¾″ h, 4″ d, Royal Ivy pat-
 tern, Northwood, bulbous, swirled
 ribs **95.00**
Salt Shaker, orig top
 Royal Ivy pattern, Northwood,
 frosted, applied clear handle **45.00**
 Royal Oak pattern, Northwood **65.00**
Sauce
 Royal Ivy pattern, Northwood, frosted **35.00**
 Royal Oak pattern, Northwood,
 frosted **30.00**
Spooner
 Royal Ivy pattern, Northwood **65.00**
 Royal Oak pattern, Northwood,
 frosted **100.00**
Sugar, cov
 Royal Ivy pattern, Northwood, frosted **135.00**
 Royal Oak pattern, Northwood, acorn
 finial **150.00**
Sugar Shaker, 6½″ h, sq, cut diagonal
 stripes, Georgian style silver plated
 top **140.00**
Syrup, orig top, applied handle
 Royal Ivy pattern, Northwood, frosted **365.00**
 Royal Oak pattern, Northwood **250.00**
Sweetmeat jar, 5″ h, 6½″ d, applied
 threading, applied double row of
 vaseline ruffles, closely crimped top,
 silver plated basket, swing handle .. **150.00**
Toothpick Holder, 3″ h, ruffled rim,
 enameled orange flowers, gold trim,
 pedestal foot **350.00**
Tumbler
 Royal Ivy pattern, Northwood,
 frosted, 3¾″ h **48.00**
 Royal Oak pattern, Northwood,
 frosted **85.00**
Vase
 6″ h, bud, bank of cut diamonds,
 enameled floral dec **60.00**
 6″ h, 4½″ w, acid etched flowers and
 leaves, frosted, vertical ribbed int.,
 bell shaped top, Mt Washington .. **275.00**

9½" h, six crimp gold trim top, chrysanthemum dec, gold foliage, pr . **265.00**
10" h, trumpet, enameled gold dec . **125.00**
Water Set
Opalescent Hobnail pattern, pitcher,
applied clear handle, six matching
tumblers **750.00**
Opalescent Swirl pattern, pitcher, sq
ruffled mouth, four matching tumblers **350.00**

RUBENA VERDE GLASS

History: Rubena Verde, a transparent glass that shades from red in the upper section to yellow–green in the lower, was made by Hobbs, Brock-unier & Co., Wheeling, West Virginia, in the late 1880s. It often is found in the Inverted Thumb-print pattern, termed "Polka Dot" by Hobbs.

Modern glassblowers have tried to duplicate this technique and some new pieces do exist. The amount of labor involved to reheat the gather (molten or semi–molten state of glass) to create the color variations prohibits mass production of this glassware.

Biscuit Jar, crackle finish **135.00**
Bowl
9" d, ftd, rolled rim, Honeycomb pattern **100.00**
9½" d, Inverted Thumbprint pattern,
ruffled **175.00**
9¾" d, ruffled rim **185.00**
Butter Dish, cov, Thumbprint pattern
cov, Daisy and Button pattern type
base **225.00**
Celery Vase, 6¼" h, Inverted Thumbprint pattern **225.00**
Compote
6" h, Honeycomb pattern **125.00**
8" h, 8" d, Honeycomb pattern **125.00**
Creamer
5" h, Inverted Thumbprint pattern,
bulbous, applied reeded handle .. **265.00**
5½" h, Hobnail pattern, bulbous
base, sq mouth, applied handle .. **485.00**
Cruet, 6" h, Hobnail pattern, clear faceted stopper **250.00**
Finger Bowl, Inverted Thumbprint pattern **90.00**
Jack-In-The-Pulpit Vase, 13¾" h, applied crimped clear rigaree spirals
around stem, applied clear shells on
edge of base **275.00**
Pitcher
5½" h, Inverted Thumbprint pattern,
applied vaseline handle **300.00**
5¾" h, Hobnail pattern, applied handle **285.00**

7½" h, Hobnail pattern, bulbous
base, sq mouth, applied handle .. **400.00**
8" h, Reverse Thumbprint pattern, sq
top, applied vaseline handle **250.00**
8½" h, Inverted Thumbprint pattern,
applied vaseline handle **325.00**
Salt and Pepper Shakers, orig tops, pr . **200.00**
Sugar Shaker, enameled floral dec,
metal lid, Hobb's Coloratura pattern **295.00**
Syrup, 6¾" h, Inverted Thumbprint pattern, orig hinged pewter cov **300.00**
Toothpick Holder, 4" h, Hobnail pattern, opalescent hobs **125.00**

**Tumbler, paneled, 3¾" h, Hobbs Brock-
unier, $100.00.**

Tumbler
Hobnail pattern **140.00**
Paneled, 3¾" h **100.00**
Vase
4" h, threaded dec **225.00**
6½" h, melon shaped, ribbed, enameled flowers **215.00**
7" h, bulbous, scalloped rim, enameled floral dec **225.00**
7½" h, Hobnail pattern, ruffled top . **195.00**
10¼" h, applied clear edge, sq
mouth, clear rigaree band spiraling
from top to base, applied clear foot **195.00**
12⅛" h, 5¼" d, cranberry shading to
green, enameled flowers, green
leaves, lacy gold foliage, blue bow
ribbon accents **195.00**
13" h, trumpet, enameled gold scrolling, wafer connection to flaring
domed foot **100.00**

RUBY STAINED GLASS

History: Ruby stained glass was produced in the late 1880s and 1890s by several glass manufac-turers, primarily in the area of Pittsburgh, Penn-sylvania.

Ruby stained items were made from pressed

clear glass which was stained with a ruby red material. Pieces often were etched with the name of a person, place, date, or event and sold as souvenirs at fairs and expositions. Floral and other engravings were also added as decoration to ruby stained patterns.

In many cases one company produced the pressed glass blanks and a second company stained and etched them. In other cases, the pattern was originally made by one company only in clear glass, but when the pattern was later produced as a U. S. Glass Company Product, ruby staining was added.

Reference: William Heacock, *Encyclopedia of Victorian Colored Pattern Glass, Book 7: Ruby–Stained Glass From A to Z*, Antique Publications, Inc., 1986.

Reproduction Alert: Ruby staining is being added to many pieces through the use of modern stain glass coloring kits. Early ruby stained pieces will have a rich, deep color. Present fakers have difficulty in achieving the proper shade.

Toothpick Holder, Spearpoint Band, ruby stained top, frosted leaves, 2¼", $45.00.

Banana Stand
  Art pattern, US Glass Co, 10" d, high
    standard **150.00**
  Britannic pattern, McKee **100.00**
Biscuit Jar, cov
  Art pattern, US Glass Co **150.00**
  Block and Fan pattern **125.00**
  Broken Column pattern, US Glass Co **150.00**
Bowl
  Art pattern, US Glass Co, 8" d **55.00**
  Barred Ovals pattern, US Glass Co, 7"
    sq **35.00**
  Beveled Diamond and Star pattern,
    Tarentum Glass Co, 8" d **35.00**
  Block and Fan pattern, 6" d **35.00**
  Broken Column pattern, US Glass Co,
    8" d **125.00**
  Button Arches pattern, George Dun-
    can Sons & Co, 8" d **50.00**
  Crystal Wedding pattern, US Glass
    Co, 6" d, scalloped rim **65.00**
  Dakota pattern, US Glass Co **65.00**
  Heart with Thumbprint pattern, Tar-
    entum Glass Co, 6" h **65.00**

Locket on Chain pattern, Heisey, 8" d **125.00**
Red Block pattern, 9" d **75.00**
Ruby Thumbprint pattern, US Glass
  Co, 7" d **45.00**
Torpedo pattern, Thompson Glass Co **65.00**
Triple Triangle pattern, Doyle & Co,
  10" l, rect **45.00**
Truncated Cube pattern, Thompson
  Glass Co, 8" d **40.00**
Bread Plate
  Beveled Diamond and Star pattern,
    Tarentum Glass Co, 7" d **70.00**
  Broken Column pattern, US Glass Co **125.00**
  Triple Triangle pattern, Doyle & Co . **95.00**
Butter Dish, cov
  Art pattern, US Glass Co **100.00**
  Atlas pattern, US Glass Co, copper
    wheel engraving **95.00**
  Barred Ovals pattern, US Glass Co . **125.00**
  Beveled Diamond and Star pattern,
    Tarentum Glass Co **100.00**
  Britannic pattern, McKee **100.00**
  Broken Column pattern, US Glass Co **175.00**
  Crystal Wedding pattern, US Glass Co **125.00**
  Dakota pattern, US Glass Co, copper
    wheel engraved dec **145.00**
  Eureka pattern, National Glass Co .. **100.00**
  Locket on Chain pattern, Heisey ... **250.00**
  Ruby Thumbprint pattern, US Glass
    Co **125.00**
  Torpedo pattern, Thompson Glass Co **125.00**
  Triple Triangle pattern, Doyle & Co . **85.00**
  Truncated Cube pattern, Thompson
    Glass Co **80.00**
Cake Stand, high standard
  Atlas pattern, US Glass Co, 9" d **90.00**
  Barred Ovals pattern, US Glass Co,
    10" d **100.00**
  Beveled Diamond and Star pattern,
    Tarentum Glass Co, 9" d **90.00**
  Button Arches pattern, George Dun-
    can & Sons Co, 9" d **175.00**
  Red Block pattern **75.00**
  Ruby Thumbprint pattern, US Glass
    Co, 10" d **150.00**
Calling Card Tray, Heart with Thumb-
  print pattern, Tarentum Glass Co ... **45.00**
Carafe
  Barred Ovals pattern, US Glass Co . **85.00**
  Champion pattern, McKee, dec by
    Beaumont Glass Works **90.00**
  Heart with Thumbprint pattern, Tar-
    entum Glass Co **150.00**
Castor Set, Ruby Thumbprint pattern,
  US Glass Co, four bottles, orig stop-
  pers and frame **300.00**
Celery Tray
  Barred Ovals pattern, US Glass Co . **75.00**
  Britannic pattern, McKee **60.00**
  Broken Column pattern, US Glass Co **110.00**
  Red Block pattern **45.00**
  Triple Triangle pattern, Doyle & Co . **45.00**

Celery Vase
  Art pattern, US Glass Co, scalloped
    rim **60.00**
  Atlas pattern, US Glass Co **75.00**
  Beveled Diamond and Star pattern,
    Tarentum Glass Co **85.00**
  Champion pattern, McKee, dec by
    Beaumont Glass Works, scalloped **100.00**
  Eureka pattern, National Glass Co .. **65.00**
  Ivy in Snow pattern, Co–Operative
    Flint Glass Co **125.00**
  Locket on Chain pattern, Heisey ... **175.00**
  Ruby Thumbprint pattern, US Glass
    Co **85.00**
  Torpedo pattern, Thompson Glass Co **75.00**
  Truncated Cube pattern, Thompson
    Glass Co **50.00**

Champagne
  Broken Column pattern, US Glass Co **175.00**
  Ivy in Snow pattern, Co–Operative
    Flint Glass Co **55.00**
  Ruby Thumbprint pattern, US Glass
    Co **35.00**

Cheese Dish, cov
  Esther pattern, Riverside Glass Works,
    dec by Beaumont Glass Works ... **125.00**
  Red Block pattern **125.00**
  Ruby Thumbprint pattern, US Glass
    Co **225.00**

Cologne Bottle, orig stopper
  Britannic pattern, McKee **125.00**
  Eureka pattern, National Glass Co .. **85.00**

Compote, cov, high standard
  Art pattern, US Glass Co, 7" d **185.00**
  Atlas pattern, US Glass Co, 5" d **95.00**
  Broken Column pattern, US Glass Co,
    6" d **200.00**
  Ivy in Snow pattern, Co–Operative
    Flint Glass Co, 6" d **75.00**

Compote, open, high standard
  Barred Ovals pattern, US Glass Co, 8"
    d **90.00**
  Beveled Diamond and Star pattern,
    Tarentum Glass Co, 7" d, serrated
    rim **150.00**
  Crystal Wedding pattern, US Glass
    Co, 7" sq, scalloped rim **55.00**
  Ruby Thumbprint pattern, US Glass
    Co, 8" d **85.00**

Cordial
  Atlas pattern, US Glass Co **35.00**
  Red Block pattern **45.00**

Creamer
  Art pattern, US Glass Co
    Table size **50.00**
    Tankard **55.00**
  Atlas pattern, US Glass Co **60.00**
  Barred Ovals pattern, US Glass Co . **75.00**
  Beveled Diamond and Star pattern,
    Tarentum Glass Co, tankard **75.00**
  Block and Fan pattern, pressed handle **45.00**

Britannic pattern, McKee, tankard,
  applied handle **75.00**
Broken Column pattern, US Glass Co **124.00**
Button Arches pattern, George Dun-
  can & Sons Co
    Individual size, 2¾" h **45.00**
    Table size **85.00**
Champion pattern, McKee, dec by
  Beaumont Glass Works **60.00**
Crystal Wedding pattern, US Glass
  Co, applied handle **125.00**
Dakota pattern, US Glass Co **65.00**
Eureka pattern, National Glass Co .. **45.00**
Heart with Thumbprint pattern, Tar-
  entum Glass Co **90.00**
Ivy in Snow pattern, Co–Operative
  Flint Glass Co **75.00**
Locket on Chain pattern, Heisey ... **145.00**
Red Block pattern **55.00**
Ruby Thumbprint pattern, US Glass
  Co **55.00**
Torpedo pattern, Thompson Glass
  Co, tankard **65.00**
Triple Triangle pattern, Doyle & Co,
  pressed handle **55.00**
Truncated Cube pattern, Thompson
  Glass Co **55.00**
Cruet, applied handle, orig stopper
  Art pattern, US Glass Co **225.00**
  Barred Ovals pattern, US Glass Co . **220.00**
  Britannic pattern, McKee **150.00**
  Button Arches pattern, George Dun-
    can & Sons Co **175.00**
Cup and Saucer, Ruby Thumbprint pat-
  tern, US Glass Co **65.00**
Custard Cup
  Broken Column pattern, US Glass Co **40.00**
  Champion pattern, McKee, dec by
    Beaumont Glass Works **25.00**
  Ruby Thumbprint pattern, US Glass
    Co **25.00**
  Triple Triangle pattern, Doyle & Co . **25.00**
Decanter, orig stopper
  Aurora pattern, 11¾" h **45.00**
  Red Block pattern, 12" h **175.00**
  Torpedo pattern, Thompson Glass
    Co, 8" h **125.00**
  Truncated Cube pattern, Thompson
    Glass Co, 12" h **140.00**
Finger Bowl
  Atlas pattern, US Glass Co **50.00**
  Heart with Thumbprint pattern, Tar-
    entum Glass Co **65.00**
  Torpedo pattern, Thompson Glass Co **65.00**
Goblet
  Art pattern, US Glass Co **75.00**
  Atlas pattern, US Glass Co **35.00**
  Barred Ovals pattern, US Glass Co . **75.00**
  Beveled Diamond and Star pattern,
    Tarentum Glass Co **65.00**
  Britannic pattern, McKee **50.00**
  Broken Column pattern, US Glass Co **110.00**

Button Arches pattern, George Duncan & Sons Co **40.00**
Crystal Wedding pattern, US Glass Co **65.00**
Dakota pattern, US Glass Co **75.00**
Esther pattern, Riverside Glass Works, dec by Beaumont Glass Works ... **75.00**
Heart with Thumbprint pattern, Tarentum Glass Co **110.00**
Ivy in Snow pattern, Co–Operative Flint Glass Co **65.00**
Red Block pattern **45.00**
Ruby Thumbprint pattern, US Glass Co **45.00**
Torpedo pattern, Thompson Glass Co **85.00**
Triple Triangle pattern, Doyle & Co . **45.00**
Truncated Cube pattern, Thompson Glass Co **50.00**
Hair Receiver, Heart with Thumbprint pattern, Tarentum Glass Co, metal lid **95.00**
Honey Dish
Britannic pattern, McKee, cov, sq .. **185.00**
Broken Column pattern, US Glass Co, open, flat **25.00**
Dakota pattern, US Glass Co, open, ftd **30.00**
Ruby Thumbprint pattern, US Glass Co, cov, 8″ sq, tab handles **225.00**
Marmalade jar, cov
Atlas pattern, US Glass Co **110.00**
Esther pattern, Riverside Glass Works, dec by Beaumont Glass Works ... **75.00**
Ruby Thumbprint pattern, US Glass Co **185.00**
Mug
Atlas pattern, US Glass Co **30.00**
Britannic pattern, McKee **25.00**
Button Arches pattern, George Duncan & Sons Co **30.00**
Dakota pattern, US Glass Co **65.00**
Red Block pattern **40.00**
Mustard, cov, underplate
Button Arches pattern, George Duncan & Sons Co **100.00**
Ruby Thumbprint pattern, US Glass Co **100.00**
Nappy, Crystal Wedding pattern, US Glass Co, sq, handle **35.00**
Pickle Castor, patterned insert, silver plated frame
Broken Column pattern, US Glass Co **350.00**
Ruby Thumbprint pattern, US Glass Co **250.00**
Torpedo pattern, Thompson Glass Co **250.00**
Pickle Dish, rect
Art pattern, US Glass Co **48.00**
Barred Ovals pattern, US Glass Co . **35.00**
Beveled Diamond and Star pattern, Tarentum Glass Co **30.00**
Britannic pattern, McKee, crimped rim **40.00**
Eureka pattern, National Glass Co .. **45.00**
Locket on Chain pattern, Heisey ... **85.00**

Pitcher, milk, applied handle
Art pattern, US Glass Co **150.00**
Barred Ovals pattern, US Glass Co . **135.00**
Beveled Diamond and Star pattern, Tarentum Glass Co **135.00**
Button Arches pattern, George Duncan & Sons Co **85.00**
Dakota pattern, US Glass Co, tankard, pint **175.00**
Ruby Thumbprint pattern, US Glass Co **95.00**
Truncated Cube pattern, Thompson Glass Co **1100.00**
Pitcher, water
Art pattern, US Glass Co, bulbous, half gallon **175.00**
Barred Ovals pattern, US Glass Co . **185.00**
Beveled Diamond and Star pattern, Tarentum Glass Co, applied handle **150.00**
Britannic pattern, McKee, tankard, applied handle **175.00**
Broken Column pattern, US Glass Co, pressed handle **200.00**
Crystal Wedding pattern, US Glass Co **200.00**
Ruby Thumbprint pattern, US Glass Co, applied handle, serrated rim . **225.00**
Triple Triangle pattern, Doyle & Co, pressed handle **145.00**
Plate
Broken Column pattern, US Glass Co, 5″ d **50.00**
Button Arches pattern, George Duncan & Sons Co, 7″ d **25.00**
Heart with Thumbprint pattern, Tarentum Glass Co, 6″ d **35.00**
Punch Bowl, Ruby Thumbprint pattern, US Glass Co, 12″ d, serrated rim ... **300.00**
Punch Cup, Heart with Thumbprint pattern, Tarentum Glass Co **35.00**
Relish Tray
Art pattern, US Glass Co, rect **60.00**
Block and Fan pattern, oval **40.00**
Broken Column pattern, US Glass Co, 11″ l, oval **125.00**
Crystal Wedding pattern, US Glass Co **40.00**
Ivy in Snow pattern, Co–Operative Flint Glass Co **30.00**
Red Block pattern **45.00**
Rose Bowl
Eureka pattern, National Glass Co .. **80.00**
Heart with Thumbprint pattern, Tarentum Glass Co **95.00**
Red Block pattern **75.00**
Salt, open, master
Eureka pattern, National Glass Co .. **35.00**
Red Block pattern **60.00**
Ruby Thumbprint pattern, US Glass Co, sq **65.00**
Torpedo pattern, Thompson Glass Co **65.00**
Salt Shaker, orig top
Barred Ovals pattern, US Glass Co . **35.00**
Block and Fan pattern **35.00**

Broken Column pattern, US Glass Co   **85.00**
Crystal Wedding pattern, US Glass Co   **85.00**
Dakota pattern, US Glass Co **85.00**
Locket on Chain pattern, Heisey ...   **125.00**
Red Block pattern **60.00**
Torpedo pattern, Thompson Glass Co   **65.00**

Sauce
  Atlas pattern, US Glass Co, 4" d, ftd   **20.00**
  Barred Ovals pattern, US Glass Co,
    4½" d, flat **20.00**
  Beveled Diamond and Star pattern,
    Tarentum Glass Co, ftd **20.00**
  Button Arches pattern, George Dun-
    can & Sons Co, 4" d, flat **20.00**
  Crystal Wedding pattern, US Glass Co   **25.00**
  Dakota pattern, US Glass Co, copper
    wheel floral engraving, 4" d, flat .   **35.00**
  Eureka pattern, National Glass Co, 4"
    sq **20.00**
  Locket on Chain pattern, Heisey ...   **50.00**
  Red Block pattern, 5" d, ftd **25.00**
  Ruby Thumbprint pattern, US Glass
    Co, 4½" d **20.00**
  Torpedo pattern, Thompson Glass
    Co, 5½" d **25.00**
  Triple Triangle pattern, Doyle & Co,
    5" d **20.00**
  Truncated Cube pattern, Thompson
    Glass Co, 4" d **18.00**

Spooner
  Art pattern, US Glass Co, scalloped
    rim **55.00**
  Atlas pattern, US Glass Co **35.00**
  Barred Ovals pattern, US Glass Co .   **60.00**
  Beveled Diamond and Star pattern,
    Tarentum Glass Co **65.00**
  Block and Fan pattern **45.00**
  Britannic pattern, McKee **50.00**
  Broken Column pattern, US Glass Co   **85.00**
  Button Arches pattern, George Dun-
    can & Sons Co **45.00**
  Crystal Wedding pattern, US Glass Co   **65.00**
  Dakota pattern, US Glass Co **65.00**
  Eureka pattern, National Glass Co ..   **65.00**
  Heart with Thumbprint pattern, Tar-
    entum Glass Co **75.00**
  Locket on Chain pattern, Heisey ...   **145.00**
  Red Block pattern **45.00**
  Ruby Thumbprint pattern, US Glass
    Co **55.00**
  Torpedo pattern, Thompson Glass Co   **55.00**
  Triple Triangle pattern, Doyle & Co .   **65.00**
  Truncated Cube pattern, Thompson
    Glass Co **50.00**

Sugar, cov
  Art pattern, US Glass Co **55.00**
  Atlas pattern, US Glass Co **65.00**
  Barred Ovals pattern, US Glass Co .   **100.00**
  Beveled Diamond and Star pattern,
    Tarentum Glass Co **85.00**
  Block and Fan pattern **85.00**
  Britannic pattern, McKee **80.00**

Broken Column pattern, US Glass Co   **150.00**
Button Arches pattern, George Dun-
  can & Sons Co **75.00**
Crystal Wedding pattern, US Glass Co   **90.00**
Dakota pattern, US Glass Co **85.00**
Locket on Chain pattern, Heisey ...   **245.00**
Red Block pattern **75.00**
Ruby Thumbprint pattern, US Glass
  Co **95.00**
Torpedo pattern, Thompson Glass Co   **85.00**
Triple Triangle pattern, Doyle & Co .   **75.00**
Truncated Cube pattern, Thompson
  Glass Co **70.00**

Sugar Shaker, orig top
  Beveled Diamond and Star pattern,
    Tarentum Glass Co **110.00**
  Block and Fan pattern **125.00**

Syrup
  Beveled Diamond and Star pattern,
    Tarentum Glass Co, 7" h, orig metal
    top **160.00**
  Button Arches pattern, George Dun-
    can & Sons Co, orig glass top **175.00**
  Esther pattern, Riverside Glass Works,
    dec by Beaumont Glass Works ...   **195.00**

Toothpick Holder
  Atlas pattern, US Glass Co **45.00**
  Beveled Diamond and Star pattern,
    Tarentum Glass Co **80.00**
  Button Arches pattern, George Dun-
    can & Sons Co **35.00**
  Eureka pattern, National Glass Co ..   **65.00**
  Ruby Thumbprint pattern, US Glass
    Co **45.00**
  Truncated Cube pattern, Thompson
    Glass Co **45.00**

Tray
  Atlas pattern, US Glass Co **75.00**
  Truncated Cube pattern, Thompson
    Glass Co **40.00**

Tumbler
  Barred Ovals pattern, US Glass Co .   **40.00**
  Beveled Diamond and Star pattern,
    Tarentum Glass Co **35.00**
  Broken Column pattern, US Glass Co   **65.00**
  Crystal Wedding pattern, US Glass Co   **45.00**
  Dakota pattern, US Glass Co **45.00**
  Eureka pattern, National Glass Co ..   **40.00**
  Ivy in Snow pattern, Co–Operative
    Flint Glass Co **55.00**
  Red Block pattern, three rows of
    blocks **40.00**
  Ruby Thumbprint pattern, US Glass
    Co **35.00**
  Torpedo pattern, Thompson Glass Co   **50.00**
  Triple Triangle pattern, Doyle & Co .   **35.00**
  Truncated Cube pattern, Thompson
    Glass Co **35.00**

Vase
  Eureka pattern, National Glass Co, 9"
    h **40.00**

Heart with Thumbprint pattern, Tarentum Glass Co, 6" h **65.00**

Waste Bowl

Atlas pattern, US Glass Co **50.00**

Dakota pattern, US Glass Co **75.00**

Red Block pattern **45.00**

Whiskey Tumbler, Atlas pattern, US Glass Co **45.00**

Wine

Beveled Diamond and Star pattern, Tarentum Glass Co **45.00**

Britannic pattern, McKee **55.00**

Button Arches pattern, George Duncan & Sons Co **35.00**

Crystal Wedding pattern, US Glass Co **85.00**

Dakota pattern, US Glass Co **50.00**

Ivy in Snow pattern, Co–Operative Flint Glass Co **85.00**

Red Block pattern **40.00**

Ruby Thumbprint pattern, US Glass Co **45.00**

Torpedo pattern, Thompson Glass Co **115.00**

Triple Triangle pattern, Doyle & Co . **45.00**

Truncated Cube pattern, Thompson Glass Co **40.00**

SABINO GLASS

History: Sabino glass, named for its creator Ernest Marius Sabino, originated in France in the 1920s and is an art glass which was produced in a wide range of decorative glassware: frosted, clear, opalescent, and colored glass. Both blown and pressed moldings were used. Hand sculpted wooden molds that were cast in iron were used and are still in use at the present time.

In 1960 the company introduced a line of figurines, one to eight inches high, plus other items in a fiery opalescent glass in the Art Deco style. Gold was added to the batch to attain the fiery glow. These pieces are the Sabino that is most commonly found today. Sabino is marked with the name in the mold, an etched signature, or both.

Ashtray

Shell, 5½" l, 3½" w **30.00**

Violet, 4½" d **40.00**

Bird

Babies, 3" h, two chubby babies perched closed on twig with berries and leaves, oval molded base, relief molded "Sabino" **22.00**

Branch, 7 x 8", five birds perched on branch **1,200.00**

Cluster

Pair, 3½ x 4½" **225.00**

Trio, 5 x 5" **245.00**

Feeding, 1½ x 2" **85.00**

Fighting, 1½ x 2" **85.00**

Hopping, 1½ x 2" **85.00**

Jumping, 3¼ x 3½" **75.00**

Mocking, 6 x 4½" h **100.00**

Nesting, 1½ x 2" **85.00**

Perching **55.00**

Resting **50.00**

Shivering **65.00**

Teasing, 2½ x 3", wings up **75.00**

Blotter, rocker type, 6 x 3", crossed American and French flags **275.00**

Bowl

Beehive **145.00**

Berry, 5¾" d, relief molded **65.00**

Fish, 5" d **75.00**

Shell **45.00**

Box, cov, Petalia **125.00**

Butterfly

2¾" h, wings open **45.00**

6" h, relief molded "Sabino" **20.00**

Candlestick, two branches, relief molded grapes **145.00**

Cat

Napping, 2" h **20.00**

Sitting, 2¼" h **40.00**

Cherub, 2" h **35.00**

Chick

Drinking, wings down **45.00**

Standing, 3¾" h, wings up **60.00**

Dog

Collie, 2" h **50.00**

German Shepherd, 2" h **35.00**

Pekingese, sitting up, begging, 1¼" h, relief molded "Sabino" **30.00**

Poodle, 1¾" h **30.00**

Scottie, 1½ x 3 x 4" **90.00**

Dragonfly, 6" h, 5¾" l **125.00**

Elephant **25.00**

Fish, 4 x 4" **75.00**

Fox **25.00**

Gazelle **100.00**

Hand, left **200.00**

Hen **30.00**

Heron, 7½" h **115.00**

Knife Rest

Butterfly, 4" l **50.00**

Duck **20.00**

Lamp

Chandelier, 24" d, 25" h, central shaft, flared chrome corona, eight downswept arms in two registers, cylindrical shades, relief molded overlapping leaves, flanked by wings, c1925 .... **2,150.00**

Table, 7½" h, domed, three tiered shade, irregular edge, circular molded foot, fan shaped panels and triangles, shade molded "Sabino 4640 Paris Depose" **750.00**

Mouse, 3" **50.00**

Napkin Ring, birds, 2¼" h **45.00**

Owl, 4½" **65.00**

Panthers, 5¾ x 7¾", grouping	225.00
Pigeon, 6¼" h	125.00
Plate, 8½" d, sailing ships	245.00
Prism	75.00
Powder Box, cov, 3" d	40.00
Rabbit, 2" h	30.00
Rooster, large, 7" h	400.00

Rooster, 7⅜" h, 6½" w, $400.00.

Scent Bottle, orig stopper	
Nudes, 6" h, inscribed "Sabino, France"	125.00
Petalia	150.00
Pineapple, 5" h	175.00
Snail, 1 x 3", relief molded "Sabino"	38.00
Squirrel, 3½" h, eating acorn, oval molded base, relief molded "Sabino"	40.00
Statue	
Draped Nude, 7¼" h	425.00
Madonna, 5" h	95.00
Nudes	
6" h, woman, kneeling	250.00
6½" h, woman, long flowing hair	195.00
Venus de Milo, large	65.00
Stork, 7¼" h	135.00
Tray	
Butterfly, round	90.00
Shell, figural	45.00
Thistle, round	50.00
Turtle, small	30.00
Vase	
Art Deco	
11" h, 7" d, six lobes, geometric, royal blue patina, polished highlights, sgd	575.00
12" h, topaz patina, sgd	500.00
Beehive	250.00
Fish	125.00
Flowers, 8½" h, blown–out blossoms, eight panels	300.00
La Danse, 14" h, ovoid, flared rim, heavy walls, frosted, molded frieze of partially draped nude women, sgd "Sabino France," crack on base	500.00

Manta Ray	300.00
Zebra, 5½" l, 5½" h	150.00

SALT AND PEPPER SHAKERS

History: Collecting salt and pepper shakers, whether late 19th century glass forms or the contemporary figural and souvenir types, is becoming more and more popular. The supply and variety is practically unlimited; the price for most sets is within the budget of cost conscious young collectors. Finally, their size offers an opportunity to assemble a large collection in a small amount of space.

One can specialize in types, forms, or makers. Great art glass artisans such as Joseph Locke and Nicholas Kopp, designed salt and pepper shakers in the normal course of their work. Arthur Goodwin Peterson's *Glass Salt Shakers: 1,000 Patterns* provides the reference numbers given below. Peterson made a beginning; there are hundreds, perhaps thousands, of patterns still to be cataloged.

The clear colored and colored opaque sets command the highest prices—clear and white sets the lowest. Although some shakers, e.g., the tomato or fig, have a special patented top and need it to hold their value, it is not detrimental to the price to replace the top of a shaker.

The figural and souvenir type is often looked down upon by collectors. Sentiment and whimsy are prime collecting motivations. The large variety and current low prices indicate a potential for long-term price growth.

Generally older shakers are priced by the piece, and prices listed below are by the piece. All shakers are assumed to have original tops unless noted. Identification numbers are from Peterson's book.

References: Gideon Bosker, *Great Shakes: Salt and Pepper For All Tastes*, Abbeville Press, 1986; Melva Davern, *The Collector's Encyclopedia of Salt & Pepper Shakers: Figural And Novelty*, Collector Books, 1985, 1991 value update; Melva Davern, *The Collector's Encyclopedia of Salt and Pepper Shakers, Second Series*, Collector Books, 1990; Helene Guarnaccia, *Salt & Pepper Shakers*, Collector Books, 1984, value update 1990; Helene Guarnaccia, *Salt & Pepper Shakers III: Identification & Values*, Collector Books, 1991; Mildred and Ralph Lechner, *The World of Salt Shakers*, 2nd Edition, Collector Books, 1992; Arthur G. Peterson, *Glass Salt Shakers: 1000 Patterns*, Wallace–Homestead, 1970.

Collectors' Clubs: Antique and Art Glass Salt Shaker Collectors Society, 2832 Rapidan Trail, Maitland, FL 32751; Novelty Salt & Pepper Shakers Club, 581 Joy Road, Battle Creek, MI 49017.

Burmese glass, tomato, autumn shading, 1¾" h, $155.00.

ART GLASS

Consolidated Lamp and Glass Co
Apple Blossom, milk glass **25.00**
Cone, opaque pink **40.00**
Cord and Tassel, glossy pink mar-
bleized glass, round, orig top,
c1894, 157–M **40.00**
Guttate, opaque green **45.00**
Couderspot Glass Co
Creased Waist, opaque yellow, milk
glass **30.00**
Trailing Vine, opaque creamy yellow   **75.00**
Dithridge, Sunset, opaque white, 3" h,
40–U **30.00**
Heisey
Fluted Scrolls, custard **65.00**
Punty Band, custard **42.50**
Winged Scroll, custard **87.50**
Hobbs, Brockunier, Acorn, shaded
opaque pink to white, tin top, 3" h,
21–A **45.00**
Libbey, satin, egg, flat side, pewter top,
made for Columbian Exposition,
1893, 28–B **75.00**
Mount Washington
Burmese, satin finish, barrel, ribbed,
floral motif, two piece pewter top
with finial, 154–A **200.00**
Satin
Chick's head, egg body, silver
plated chick's head top, hand
painted florals, 2½" h, 24–T . . .   **225.00**
Fig, enameled pansy dec, orig
prong top **110.00**
Lobed Body, hand painted, enam-
eled orange floral spray, pewter
top with finial, 33–C **62.50**
Melon, squatty, hand painted,
enameled daisy dec, orig two
piece top **55.00**
New England Glass Co, amberina, In-
verted Thumbprint pattern, pewter
top **165.00**
Northwood
Carnelian, custard **225.00**
Everglades, purple slag, white, gold
highlights, pewter top, 160–K **70.00**

Inverted Fan and Feather, pink slag,
31–O **250.00**
Leaf Umbrella, cranberry matte finish,
cased, orig brass plated tin top, 3½"
h, 32–S **60.00**
Quilted Phlox, pale green, cased, orig
tin top, 3½" h, 36–H **55.00**
Royal Oak, frosted and clear rubena,
shading rose to white, orig brass
top, 171–E **65.00**
Pigeon Blood, Bulging Loop pattern, 3"
h, orig brass top, 37–C **65.00**
Rubena, enameled dec, orig pewter top,
175–O **200.00**
Satin
Erie Twist, white ground, hand
painted, delicate pink flowers,
shaded buff leaves, two piece pew-
ter top, patent date 1892, 28–B . .   **75.00**
Rainbow, MOP, royal blue shading,
pastel blue base **245.00**
Wheeling, Peachblow, orig top **300.00**

OPALESCENT GLASS

Argonaut Shell, Northwood, blue **55.00**
Beatty Honeycomb, white, 22–Q **35.00**
Circle Scroll, Northwood, blue, tin top,
5" h, 156–S **72.00**
Fluted Scrolls, Northwood, vaseline . .   **40.00**
Jewel and Flower, Northwood, blue,
164–J, replaced top **35.00**
Ribbed, white, brass top, 3" h, 36–W .   **42.50**
Ribbon Vertical **35.00**
Ribbons Short, cranberry **40.00**
Seaweed, Hobbs, cranberry **45.00**
Windows, Hobbs, blue, pewter top . . .   **45.00**

PATTERN GLASS

Actress, pewter top **40.00**
Banded Portland, maiden's blush stain   **35.00**
Barred Ovals, US Glass Co, ruby
stained, orig top **35.00**
Beautiful Lady, Bryce, Higbee and Co,
1905, clear **20.00**
Block and Fan, US Glass Co, 1891
Clear **15.00**
Ruby stained, orig top **35.00**
Broken Column, US Glass Co, ruby
stained, orig top **85.00**
Cane, Gillinder Glass Co, c1885, apple
green, non–flint **25.00**
Crown Jewel, O'Hara Glass Co, c1880,
etched **35.00**
Croesus, McKee Glass, 1899, amethyst,
gold trim **75.00**
Crystal Wedding, US Glass Co, ruby
stained, orig top **85.00**
Dakota, US Glass Co, ruby stained, orig
top **85.00**

Diamond Horseshoe, Brilliant Glass
Works, 1888, ruby stained **40.00**
Diamond Point, Boston and Sandwich
Glass Co, 1830–40, clear, flint **25.00**
Diamond Point and Leaf, blue milk
glass, diamond point ground broken
by compound leaf extending up side
of shaker 2¾" h, (F489) **35.00**
Double Deck, opaque green **35.00**
Eyewinker, orig top **65.00**
Feather, 28–N **20.00**
Francesware, Hobbs, Brockunier & Co,
c1880, hobnail, frosted, amber
stained **30.00**
Locket on Chain, Heisey, ruby stained,
orig top **125.00**
Maine, 22–M **20.00**
Mikado, Richards and Hartley, c1888,
vaseline, non–flint **20.00**
New Jersey, hotel size, 34–E **27.50**
O'Hara Diamond, ruby stained **35.00**
Paneled Sprig, milk glass, green dec .. **35.00**
Priscilla #2, emerald green, 169–G .. **35.00**
Red Block, ruby stained, orig top **60.00**
Scrolled Panel, opaque green **35.00**
Shell Triple **15.00**
Stars and Stripes, 173–S **20.00**
Thousand Eye, vaseline **30.00**
Torpedo, Thompson Glass Co, ruby
stained, orig top **65.00**
Wheat and Barley, blue **35.00**
Whirligig, US Glass Co, clear, tin top,
3½" h, 177–A **15.00**

SALTS, OPEN

History: When salt was first mined, the supply
was limited and expensive. The necessity for a
receptacle in which to serve the salt resulted in
the first open salt, a crude, hand-carved, wooden
trencher.

As time passed, salt receptacles were refined
in style and materials. In the 1500s both master
and individual salts existed. By the 1700s firms
such as Meissen, Waterford, and Wedgwood
were making glass, china, and porcelain salts.
Leading manufacturers in the 1800s included
Libbey Glass Co., Mount Washington, New England Glass Company, Smith Bros., Vallerystahl,
Wavecrest, Webb, and many outstanding silver-
smiths in England, France, and Germany.

Open salts were used as the only means of
serving salt until the appearance of the shaker in
the late 1800s. The ease of procuring salt from a
shaker greatly reduced the use and need for the
open salts.

References: William Heacock and Patricia Johnson, *5,000 Open Salts: A Collectors Guide*, Richardson Printing Corporation, 1982, 1989 value
update; L. W. and D. B. Neal, *Pressed Glass
Dishes Of The Lacy Period 1825–1850*, published by the author, 1962; Allan B. and Helen
B. Smith have authored and published ten books
on open salts beginning with *One Thousand Individual Open Salts Illustrated* (1972) and ending
with *1,334 Open Salts Illustrated: The Tenth
Book* (1984). Daniel Snyder did the master salt
sections in Volumes 8 and 9. In 1987 Mimi Rud-
nick compiled a revised price list for the ten
Smith Books.

Collectors' Club: New England Society of Open
Salt Collectors, 587 Dutton Road, Sudbury, MA
01776.

Note: The numbers in parentheses refer to plate
numbers in the Smith publications.

Cloudy, pedestal base, $32.50.

INDIVIDUALS

Baccarat, double salts, clear, pedestal,
paneled sides, one salt frosted panels,
sgd (395) **125.00**
Cameo Glass
Galle, green pedestal, enamel dec,
sgd, early (205) **275.00**
Webb, red ground, white lacy dec
around bowl, matching spoon
(137) **600.00**
Cranberry, ruffled salt held by rigaree in
wire holder, unmarked (373) **185.00**
Cut Glass
Hexagonal, twelve point star in bot-
tom, sgd "Libbey" (464) **48.00**
Octagonal, curved sides, polished cut
bottom (470) **20.00**
Pedestal
Faceted base (118) **50.00**
Hawkes, sgd with trefoil emblem
(86) **55.00**
Round, alternating zippered and
starred panels (361) **25.00**
Triangular, Star and Diamond, sgd
"Hawkes" (466) **65.00**
Tub, Diamond and Fan, tab handles
(361) **55.00**
Double, 3½" h, opaque blue, molded
rim form, several int. chips **175.00**

Moser, cobalt blue, Moser, pedestal, gold bands, applied flowers, sgd (380) **55.00**

Pressed Glass

American pattern, Fostoria, clear, round, gold rim, rayed bottom (465) **47.50**

Decagon pattern, Cambridge, amber, pedestal, (468) **32.50**

Hawaiian Lei pattern, Higbee clear, (477) **25.00**

Heisey Rose pattern, Heisey, diamond mark **25.00**

Liberty Bell, clear, oval **20.00**

Mt Vernon pattern, Cambridge clear, (80) **28.50**

Thumbprint pattern, double salts, octagonal, attributed to Sandwich (394) **75.00**

Quezal, irid gold (92) **200.00**

Ruby, dolphin in center (451) **85.00**

Sapphire Blue, white enamel stylized leaves, blossoms, and scrolls, touches of pink, green, blue, and yellow, gold rim and wafer foot, 3⅛" d, 1½" h .. **285.00**

Steuben, cobalt blue, pedestal (485) .. **245.00**

Vallerystahl, double, turquoise milk glass, sgd "Vallerystahl, Made in France" **35.00**

Jacob's Ladder, master, pressed glass, pedestal base, $35.00.

MASTERS

Aventurine, narrow base (316) **60.00**

Cranberry, geometrically cut to clear (384) **120.00**

Cut Glass, heart shape, alternating diamond and fan pattern (404) **65.00**

Green, light, dark green ruffled top, open pontil (449) **75.00**

Lacy

Basket of Flowers, opaque blue (BF1C:324) **350.00**

Double, clear, beaded rim and handles (329) **60.00**

Eagle

Clear (EE7b:327) **180.00**

Fiery milky opalescence, American eagle on corners, shield center, Sandwich Glassworks, c1840, 3" I **650.00**

Horn of Plenty, clear (329) **65.00**

Lafayette Boat, clear (BT6:329) **260.00**

Lyre, green (LE1:324) **225.00**

Mount Vernon, light citron (MV1a:324) **375.00**

Oblong Double, clear (OG12:326) . **70.00**

Oval Diamond on Pedestal, clear (OP3:407) **150.00**

Scrolled Heart, green (SC7:324) **275.00**

Staghorn, clear (SN1:328) **100.00**

Strawberry Diamond, yellow green (SD7:324) **280.00**

New England Glass Co, fiery opalescent, baskets of fruit and floral designs, emb "N. E. Glass Company Boston" on base, 2⅞" I **275.00**

Opalescent, blue, silver rim, Registry number "176566" (384) **110.00**

Pairpoint, raspberry ground, heavy, sq, (444) **65.00**

Pressed Glass

Bakewell Pears pattern, clear **20.00**

Barberry pattern, clear

Flat, oval berries **30.00**

Pedestal (344) **35.00**

Basketweave pattern, figural, sleigh (397) **110.00**

Eureka pattern, National Glass Co, ruby stained **35.00**

Eyewinker pattern, clear, pedestal (346) **82.50**

Gothic Arches variant, clear, pedestal, 2½" h, 2⅝" d, c1865 (3606) . **25.00**

Grasshopper pattern, clear **30.00**

Hamilton pattern, clear, pedestal (344) **35.00**

Hobnail pattern, clear, round (407) . **35.00**

Horizontal Framed Ovals pattern, clear **22.00**

Palmette pattern, clear (471) **60.00**

Paneled Diamond pattern, clear, pedestal (331) **47.50**

Red Block pattern, ruby stained **60.00**

Ruby Thumbprint pattern, US Glass Co, ruby stained, sq **65.00**

Sawtooth Circle pattern, clear **30.00**

Snail pattern, clear, ruby stained (348) **40.00**

Square Pillared pattern, clear (341) . **25.00**

Sunflower pattern, clear, pedestal (346) **35.00**

Toboggan pattern, clear (397) **175.00**

Torpedo pattern, Thompson Glass Co, ruby stained **65.00**

Viking pattern, clear **25.00**

Vintage pattern, clear (340) **30.00**

Purple Slag, Leaf and Flower pattern, (313) **60.00**

Satin Glass, tulip shaped, silver leaf holder (312) **80.00**

SANDWICH GLASS

History: In 1818 Deming Jarves was listed in the Boston Directory as a glass factory. The same year he was appointed general manager of the newly formed New England Glass Company. In 1824 Jarves toured the glassmaking factories in Pittsburgh, left New England Glass Company, and founded a glass factory in Sandwich.

Originally called the Sandwich Manufacturing Company, it was incorporated in April 1826 as the Boston & Sandwich Glass Company. From 1826 to 1858 Jarves served as general manager. The Boston & Sandwich Glass Company produced a wide variety and quality of wares. The factory used the free–blown, blown three–mold, and pressed glass manufacturing techniques. Clear and colored glass were both used.

Competition in the American glass industry in the mid–1850s forced a lowering of quality of the glasswares. Jarves left in 1858, founded the Cape Cod Glass Company, and tried to maintain the high quality of the earlier glass. At the Boston & Sandwich Glass Company emphasis was placed on mass production. The development of a lime glass (non–flint) led to lower costs for pressed glass. Some free–blown and blown and molded pieces, mostly in color, were made. Most of this Victorian era glass was enameled, painted, or acid etched.

By the 1880s the Boston & Sandwich Glass Company was operating at a loss. Labor difficulties finally resulted in the factory closing on January 1, 1888.

References: Raymond E. Barlow and Joan E. Kaiser, *The Glass Industry In Sandwich*, Vols. 2, 3 and 4, distributed by Schiffer Publishing, Ltd.; George S. and Helen McKearin, *American Glass*, Crown Publishers, Inc., 1941 and 1948; Ruth Webb Lee, *Sandwich Glass. The History Of The Sandwich Glass Company*, Charles E. Tuttle, 1966; Ruth Webb Lee, *Sandwich Glass Handbook*, Charles E. Tuttle, 1966; L. W. and D. B. Neal, *Pressed Glass Dishes Of The Lacy Period 1825–1850*, published by author, 1962; Catherine M. V. Thuro, *Oil Lamps II: Glass Kerosene Lamps*, Wallace–Homestead, 1983; Catherine M. V. Thuro, *Oil Lamps: The Kerosene Era In North America, Updated Prices*, Wallace–Homestead, 1992.

Museum: Sandwich Glass Museum, Sandwich, MA.

Additional Listings: Blown Three Mold, Cup Plates, Early American Glass, and Lamps and Lighting.

Bank, 12" h, clear, applied peacock blue rigaree, rooster finial, two silver US dimes dated 1835 within knop stem **7,775.00**

Bowl
 6¼" d
  Peacock Eye pattern, grape border, lacy, clear, ftd, shallow flake on foot **500.00**
  Tulip and Acanthus Leaf pattern, deep blue, Lee 131 .... **300.00**
 8½" d, Princess Feather pattern, medallion with heart, crossed swords center, herringbone and stippled ground **195.00**
 9¼" d, Gothic Arches pattern, lacy, clear, Lee 129 .... **150.00**
Butter Dish
 4⅞" h, Blurina, large, good enameling **675.00**
 5¼" h, 6" d, Horn of Plenty pattern, flint, bust of George Washington finial, small scallop chips **1,600.00**
Candlestick
 6½" h, translucent purple–blue, hexagonal, loop base, heat check in socket **250.00**
 7" h, opaque blue, hexagonal, ¼" annealing check in base **175.00**
 9" h, dolphin, clear, dolphins and shells on socket, McKearin 204–65 **800.00**
Celery Vase
 7¾" h, Excelsior pattern, clear, flint . **70.00**
 8½" h, Diamond Thumbprint pattern, clear, flint **125.00**
 11¼" h, Arch pattern, cobalt blue, cascade base **500.00**
Claret, 4½" h, Horn of Plenty pattern, flint, set of 8 .... **450.00**
Cologne Bottle, amber, gilded floral dec, orig gilded lily stopper **400.00**
Compote
 5" h, 7¼" d, Waffle pattern, clear, flint, minute under rim roughness **50.00**
 5⅞" h, 6" d, Horn of Plenty pattern bowl, Waffle pattern base, flint, minor chips and roughness, pr **100.00**
 6¼" h, 8½" d, Excelsior pattern, clear, flint **100.00**
 6½" h, 8" d, Horn of Plenty pattern, flint, minor roughness to base **80.00**
 7" h, 7" d, Horn of Plenty pattern, flint, minute roughness to base ... **90.00**
 8¼" h, 5" d, Acanthus Leaf pattern, clear, flint **225.00**
 12" h, 9" d, Sandwich Star pattern, electric blue **5,000.00**
Creamer
 Fish Scale pattern, lacy, clear **75.00**
 Gothic Arches pattern, lacy, deep purple–blue **800.00**
Cup and Saucer, lacy, clear **185.00**
Cup Plate, Lee–Rose 440–B, deep blue, heart **325.00**
Decanter, 12" h, Sandwich Star pattern,

canary yellow, period stopper, 1½–2
pint capacity, pr 3,300.00
Dessert Plates, 6⅜" d, Horn of Plenty
pattern, flint, set of 15, minor chips
and roughness **500.00**
Dish
   5¾" l, Rayed Peacock Eye pattern,
   clear, flint **150.00**
   6¼" l, Tulip and Acanthus Leaf pat-
   tern, lacy, clear **125.00**
   8" d, Scotch Plaid pattern, lacy, clear,
   deep, pontil mark **125.00**
   12" l, 9" w, 1¾" h, Peacock Eye pat-
   tern **800.00**
Egg Cup, 3¾" h, Horn of Plenty pattern,
flint, pr **85.00**
Flat Iron, amethyst, three minor flakes
on edges, handle check **650.00**
Goblet, 6" h, Horn of Plenty pattern,
flint, pr **50.00**
Goblet Mold, 7¼" h, carved wooden
prototype, Gothic Arch and Diamond
type pattern, mid 19th C **425.00**
Honey Dish, lacy, medium red–amber,
two scallops missing **100.00**
Jewel Casket, cov, 6½" l, oblong, lacy,
clear, Lee 162 . . . .**1,100.00**
Lamp
   4⅛" h, sparking, tin burner, clear,
   globular, minor roughness to base **300.00**
   9¾" h, whale oil, clear, blown teardrop font, heavy pressed triangular
   paw foot base, slight base rough-
   ness **1,200.00**
   10" h, whale oil, Horn of Plenty pat-
   tern, flint, clear, small nick on font **150.00**
   10⅛" h, fluid, Vine variant, clear,
   brass stem, marble base **125.00**
   10⅝" h, whale oil, free blown tear-
   drop shape font, triangular scrolled
   base, paw feet **700.00**
   11¼" h, Acanthus Leaf pattern, light
   peacock blue, sand finish, brass
   standard, brass collar, marble base,
   1850–60 . . . . **375.00**
   13" h, Tulip pattern, clambroth, an-
   nealing checks and small bruises on
   base, pr **1,500.00**
Lamp Shade, 8½" d, 5½" h, 3¾" fitter
ring, white, all over ruby threading,
4" ruby threaded floral band, ruffled
trim **250.00**
Marble
   1¾" d, spangled, green, red, white,
   and blue **140.00**
   2⅛" d
      Lutz–type, cranberry and white
      swirl, minor bruise **90.00**
      Spangled, multicolored, roughness
      and some nicks **140.00**
   2⅝" d, spangled, red, white, and blue **525.00**

Milk Pan, 7¼" d, 3" h, green, free
blown, folded rim, pinched lip **375.00**
Miniature
   Bowl, cov, 1⅝" d, pattern around
   base **100.00**
   Cup and Saucer, handleless, lacy,
   clear, Lee 80–7 . . . . **250.00**
   Flat Iron, blue–green **600.00**
   Plate, lacy, opalescent, Lee 81–5 . . . **150.00**
   Tray, 2¾" l, 2" w, oval, paneled **100.00**
   Tureen, cov, matching undertray,
   lacy, clear, Lee 180–12, minimal
   roughness **250.00**
   Wash Bowl and Pitcher, lacy, clear,
   Lee 80–3 . . . . **350.00**
Mustard Pot, cov, Peacock Eye pattern,
lacy, clear **375.00**
Ointment Jar, opaque white, orig pewter
lid, oval, concave panels, 3" d **125.00**
Pitcher
   8½" h, cranberry, applied crystal han-
   dle **325.00**
   12½" h, overshot, clear, gilt rim, rope
   handle, pontil scar, 1870–87 . . . . **475.00**
Plate
   6" d, Hairpin pattern, lacy, clear . . . **90.00**
   6¼" d, Heart border, lacy, clear **85.00**
   7⅛" d, Peacock Eye pattern, lacy,
   translucent moonstone, Lee 108–2 **150.00**
   8" d, Peacock Feather and Thistle pattern, lacy, clear, small rim chips
   and minor roughness **70.00**
   9½" d, Quatrefoil, lacy, clear **150.00**
Relish, 8⅛" l, Pipes of Pan pattern **250.00**

**Salt, Christmas, green leaves and brown
dec on yellow ground, top marked "Pat
Dec. 25. 1877.," 2¾" h, 1¾" d, $75.00.**

Salt
   Neal BF–1, lacy, lavender tint, one
   corner badly chipped **25.00**
   Neal BF–1c, lacy, clear, large chip to
   top edge, minor roughness **25.00**
   Neal BT–4D, boat, clear, Lafayette,
   small base chip **300.00**
   Neal CD–2, cov, lacy, clear, minor
   chips on underside of cov and one
   corner **400.00**
   Neal CT–1, silvery opaque blue, one

large chip on corner, several small
chips **150.00**
Neal EE–8A, lacy, clear, round, eagles
and ships **400.00**
Neal OP–12, lacy, opaque aqua, several annealing lines, open cracks in
the making, minor roughness **400.00**
Neal PO–4, lacy, clear, several small
chips to base, minor roughness .. **30.00**
Neal PR–1, lacy, clear, chip to base,
minor roughness **10.00**
Neal WN–1a, lacy, clear, chips and
roughness to corners and wheels . **120.00**
Sauce Bottle, 5⅞" h, Horn of Plenty,
flint, arched panel engraved "Hes-
wan," two small annealing lines at top **100.00**
Sauce Dish
Beaded Scale and Eye pattern, daisy
center, clear **75.00**
Horn of Plenty pattern, clear, flint
3¼" d **25.00**
4½" d **30.00**
5¼" d **35.00**
Peacock Eye pattern, clear **45.00**
Roman Rosette pattern, fiery opalescent **100.00**
Shell Medallion pattern, clear, octagonal **70.00**
Waffle pattern, clear, flint **45.00**
Scent Bottle
Deep emerald green, violin shape,
orig pewter screw top, McKearin
241–31 .... **225.00**
Medium purple–blue, McKearin 241–
55 .... **130.00**
Spillholder, 5" h, Sandwich Star pattern,
electric blue, several small chips on
base corners **800.00**
String Holder, 4" h, 3⅞" d, clear, cobalt
blue rim and ring around string hold **350.00**
Sugar, cov
Acanthus Leaf pattern, lacy, clear ... **350.00**
Gothic Arches pattern, Lee 158–4
Electric blue, slight roughness, two
minor upper rim flakes **1,500.00**
Fiery opalescent, minor damage .. **500.00**
Horn of Plenty pattern, 7½" h, flint,
minor flake on cov **185.00**
Sweetmeat, cov, Waffle pattern, clear,
flint, one scallop rim chipped **90.00**
Toddy Plate, 5⅞" d, star and fan border,
eight pointed star in center, raised sq
hobs **100.00**
Tray, 10" l, Butterfly pattern, lacy, clear,
Lee 95–3 .... **300.00**
Vase
7¼", Bull's Eye and Ellipse pattern,
dark emerald green, gauffered rims,
pr **3,000.00**
9½" h, tulip shape, amethyst, Mc-
Kearin 201–40, tiny flake under
point of one foot, pr **2,300.00**

9¾", tulip shape, honey amber, flint,
Lee 198–2, pr **2,000.00**
Vinegar Bottle, 6⅜" h, deep amethyst,
blown three mold, cobalt blue stopper **375.00**
Vegetable Dish
10½", lacy, clear, grape border, cov,
Lee 151–1 ....**5,500.00**
10¾" h, medium amethyst, thinly
blown bell, three printie block, expanded rim, heavy octagonal standard, sq base, c1845–60 ....**1,210.00**
11⅛" l, oval, Horn of Plenty pattern,
flint, small scallops chips **70.00**
Whiskey Taster
Hexagonal, deep cobalt blue, flint,
2⅜" h **225.00**
Lacy, clambroth, Lee plate 150–5,
minute rim nicks **40.00**
Wine, 5¼" h, Horn of Plenty pattern,
flint, set of 8 .... **650.00**

SATIN GLASS

History: Satin glass, produced in the late 19th
century, is an opaque art glass with a velvety
matte (satin) finish, achieved through treatment
with hydrofluoric acid. A large majority of the
pieces were cased or had a white lining.

While working at the Phoenix Glass Company,
Beaver, Pennsylvania, Joseph Webb perfected
Mother-of-Pearl (MOP) satin glass in 1885. Similar to plain satin glass in respect to casing, MOP
satin glass has a distinctive surface finish and an
integral or indented design, the most common
being diamond quilted (DQ).

The most common colors are yellow, rose, or
blue. Rainbow coloring is considered choice.
Satin glass, both plain and MOP, has been widely
reproduced.

Additional Listings: Cruets, Fairy Lamps, Miniature Lamps, and Rose Bowls.

Basket
8" d, white exterior, rose lining, applied scalloped camphor edges, applied camphor crossed branch handles **295.00**
8½" d, 9½" h, herringbone patterned
body, MOP, pink–salmon exterior,
tightly crimped edge, frosted clear
twisted thorn handle **635.00**
Biscuit jar, cov, 9" h, 5" d, diamond
quilted patterned body, MOP, shiny
finish, rainbow stripes, flared cylindrical base, silver plated bail handle
and cov, marked "Patent" **950.00**
Bowl
4½" d, 2¾" h, ribbed body, MOP,

shaded pink ground, very tightly
crimped ribbon edge **300.00**
5¼" d, 4¼" h, diamond quilted pat-
terned body, MOP, tricorn, blue
ground, crystal applique edge,
marked "Patent" **750.00**
6½" d, 2½" h, ribbed body, tricorn,
olive green ground, white lining,
edges dec with gold enamel flowering branches in Smith Bros man-
ner **200.00**
10½" d, 4½" h, squatty, MOP, gold,
amber, and red moire, lusterless
white lining, deeply crimped rim . **350.00**

**Rose Bowl, pink, vertical ribbed, pinched
tricorner top, water base, Stevens and
Williams, $385.00.**

Bride's Basket, 11" d, 15½" h, deep rose
exterior, MOP lining, enamel swan
and floral dec, heavy bronze holder
with birds perched at top **400.00**
Bride's Bowl, 12" d, 14¾" h, cream ex-
terior, MOP lining, enamel floral dec,
ruffled clear edge with gold trim . . . **450.00**
Celery Vase
6¾" h, 4¾" d, blue, pink and yellow
pastel stripes, white opalescent
honeycomb exterior **325.00**
8⅞" h, 5½" d, shaded yellow ground,
white lining, blue and white floral
dec, ruffled, frosted edge, silver
plate holder with ribbon bow han-
dle **250.00**
Cologne Bottle, 5½" h, globular, peach
ground, MOP, sterling silver top **250.00**
Creamer, 2½" h, elongated spot pat-
terned body, MOP, rainbow striped
ground, frosted handle **350.00**
Creamer, Sugar, and Spooner, diamond
quilted patterned bodies, MOP,
enameled large white flowers and
small blue flowers, green leaves,
white lining, ruffled tops, matched set **900.00**
Cruet, orig stopper
7" h, diamond quilted patterned body,

MOP, blue ground, applied clear
reeded handle, matching satin stop-
per **630.00**
8" h, diamond quilted patterned body,
MOP, rose ground, applied frosted
handle, clear faceted stopper **225.00**
Dish, 5¾" d, raspberry ground, ivory
ruffled rim **50.00**
Ewer
8½" h, swirl patterned body, MOP,
pink, blue, and yellow stripes,
white lining, applied glass rim and
handle **580.00**
9½" h, diamond quilted patterned
body, MOP, deep apricot shading
to light ground, applied clear thorn
handle **255.00**
11" h, herringbone patterned body,
MOP, white ground, wide bands of
yellow, blue, and pink, applied
thorn handle **2,675.00**
Finger Bowl and Underplate, 5" d, 2½"
h, diamond quilted patterned body,
MOP, white ground, rainbow stripes,
crimped top, marked "Patent" **675.00**
Hatpin Holder, 3¼" h, diamond quilted
patterned body, MOP, pink ground,
enameled floral dec **175.00**
Jar, cov, 6¼" h, diamond quilted pat-
terned body, MOP, salmon ground,
applied clear flower finial **325.00**
Jardiniere, 12½" d, 10¼" h, raised rim,
bulbous opal bowl, robin's egg blue
shaded ground, hand painted and
enameled bird and floral dec **350.00**
Marmalade, 4½" h, 3½" d, diamond
quilted patterned body, MOP, shaded
pink ground, black etched dec of bird
among berries and leaves, frosted applied shell ruffled top, silver plated
holder **250.00**
Mustard Pot, 3" h, diamond quilted pat-
terned body, MOP, apricot ground,
silver plated top **225.00**
Perfume Bottle
4" d, globular, ivory ground, sterling
silver top, gold dec **115.00**
4½" h, 4" d, Swirl pattern, MOP,
shaded pink ground, white and orange flowers dec, atomizer missing **160.00**
Pickle Jar, diamond quilted patterned
body, MOP, pink ground, large yellow rose and bud, yellow, brown, and
green enameled stem and leaves, silver plated stand, cov, and fork marked
"Rogers" **475.00**
Pitcher, bulbous
6" h, 4½" d, diamond quilted patterned body, MOP, shaded blue
ground, enameled pink and yellow
floral dec, green leaves, oval top,
applied handle **350.00**

7¾" h, 6" d, melon ribbed body, MOP, shaded pale pink to white ground, enameled white and gold coral dec, applied frosted handle . **750.00**

Rose Bowl
    3¼" h, diamond quilted patterned body, MOP, white ground, alternating pink, yellow, and narrow blue stripes, white enamel blossoms, small blemish at side **225.00**
    3½" h, 4¼" d, diamond quilted patterned body, MOP, white ground, deep pink, yellow, and blue stripes, applied clear feet, applied berry pontil, marked "Patent" **1,400.00**
    6" h, 5¼ d, diamond quilted patterned body, MOP, pale green ground, pink floral dec, green leaves **180.00**
    5" h, 5½" d, diamond quilted patterned body, MOP, shaded peach ground, white lining, eight crimp top, dimpled **275.00**

Scent Bottle, 4½" h, 3½" d, diamond quilted patterned body, MOP, ivory ground, enameled maroon leaves, hallmarked sterling silver top **275.00**

Sweetmeat Jar, 5½" h, 4¾" h, ribbed patterned body, MOP, pale blue ground, rainbow stripes, silver plated bail and cov with beehive finial **450.00**

Toothpick Holder, 2½" h, diamond quilted patterned body, MOP, yellow ground **150.00**

Tumbler, diamond quilted patterned body, MOP, deep blue to pearly white ground, heavy enameled pink blossoms, multicolored foliage **285.00**

Vase
    5" h, 3" d, diamond quilted patterned body, MOP, shaded apricot ground, ruffled top with frosted binding, five frosted applied wishbone feet **225.00**
    5½" h, hobnail patterned body, MOP, blue ground, folded in sq top **610.00**
    5½" h, 3" d, diamond quilted patterned body, peach ground, brown feather pull up dec, robin's egg blue lining, Northwood **750.00**
    9" h, swirl pattern body, MOP, chartreuse shading to blue ground, opal white lining **1,100.00**
    9¾" h, 4½" d, herringbone patterned body, MOP, blue ground, white lining, applied frosted thorny handles and feet, ruffled tops, pr **750.00**
    10" h, flattened oval, diamond quilted patterned body, MOP, shaded pink ground, enamel painted bluebird and gilt foliage dec, applied reeded camphor handles, English **360.00**

SCHNEIDER GLASS

History: Brothers Ernest and Charles Schneider, founded a glassworks at Epiney-sur-Seine, France, in 1913. Charles, the artistic designer, previously had worked for Daum and Galle.

Although Schneider art glass is best known, the firm also made table glass, stained glass, and lighting fixtures. The art glass exhibits simplicity of design; bubbles and streaking often are found in larger pieces. Other wares include cameo cut and hydrofluoric acid etched designs.

Schneider signed their pieces with a variety of script and block signatures, "Le Verre Francais," or "Charder." Robert, son of Charles, assumed art direction in 1948. Schneider moved to Loris in 1962.

Bowl
    6" d, amethyst, shallow, sgd **175.00**
    9¼" d, mottled, red and purple, sgd **175.00**

Centerpiece
    10" d, 4" h, red rim, mottled yellow ftd center, wrought iron handled holder with roses and leaves, sgd . **225.00**
    14¼" d, 7½" h, shallow mottled tortoiseshell brown shaded to orange center bowl, applied striped black and gray glass stem, wrought iron trifid base, applied metal leaves, three glass beads, sgd "Schneider" and "Ovington New York" **300.00**

Charger
    14" d, frosted glass ground, mottled orange overlay, cameo carved stylized fanning foliage, sgd in cameo **3,520.00**
    29¼" d, bowl shape, satin finish, opaque, rust–reds and browns, sgd "Schneider France, Ovington, NY" **625.00**

Compote
    8¼" d, deep amethyst, knobbed stem and pedestal, sgd **115.00**
    10⅜" d, 12½" h, large champagne

Compote, orange to dark blue, amethyst base with white ribbing, etched "Schneider," $280.00.

glass shape, pink opalescent bowl with mottled apple green, mottled cranberry foot and stem, sgd **375.00**

13½" d, 5½" h, orange shading to dark blue, amethyst base with white ribbing, etched "Schneider" **280.00**

15" d, 5" h, purple and red, sgd **275.00**

Dish, 13½" d, 5½" h, mottled orange and dark blue, amethyst with white ribbing pedestal base **260.00**

Ewer

6½" h, mottled blue and gray, applied black–amethyst handle **225.00**

12¼" h, ovoid, peaked spout, applied handle, mottled pink body, purple overlay, cameo carved stylized swags, cameo sgd "Charder" and "Le Verre Francais" **1,750.00**

Lamp Shade, 18" h, Art Deco style, sgd **1,050.00**

Night Light, 7⅜" h, tangerine ground, red overlay, cameo carved clusters of stylized blossoms and slender curled leaves, sgd "Charder" in cameo, engraved "Le Verre Francais," wrought iron base with three leaf form feet . .**1,450.00**

Pitcher

6" h, raspberry body, mottled handle and spout **350.00**

7½" h, maroon, white, and pink, sgd **325.00**

Plate, 4" d, mottled, deep pink **75.00**

Tray, 16" d, mottled orange, blue, and yellow, sgd **195.00**

Urn, 11" h, 9" w, two handles, flambe red shading from deep maroon to tomato red, internally dec in undulating waves, controlled bubbles, sgd **1,250.00**

Vase

5½" h, cased, blue, black, and clear, orange lining, wrought iron ftd base, c1925, sgd **250.00**

9½" h, round, handles, orange with lavender and lemon pulls at raised neck, sgd **325.00**

11¾" h, spherical body, cylindrical neck with two applied purple handles, mottled burgundy and tomato red, engraved "Schneider" **900.00**

12½" h, cameo, mottled yellow, white, and clear body, brown shaded to orange overlay, acid cut back, three stylized Art Deco blossoms, sgd "Schneider" and "Charder" **1,100.00**

14¼" h

Conical, clear walls, internally tinted orange glass, etched geometric band around top, three applied glass protrusions, dark black circular foot, etched "Schneider/France," c1920 . . . .**1,900.00**

Oviform, translucent, internally tinted

orange, applied deep orange glass handles, etched neck bands of squares and rectangles, stylized bowl of fruit on obverse, inscribed "Schneider," c1920 . . . .**4,000.00**

14⅞" h, hexagonal, knopped stem, circular foot, white ground, orange overlay, cameo carved stripes and rectangles, engraved "Charder, Le Verre Francais" **1,760.00**

15¾" h, heavy walled, mottled pink and white, yellow, orange, and lavender splotches, handles, sgd "Schneider" **990.00**

16½" h, baluster, cushion foot, pink and orange mottled ground, purple shading to lavender ground, cameo carved floral bowers and thorny vines, cameo sgd "Charder," engraved "Le Verre Francais" **1,750.00**

16¾" h, pear shape, everted rim, circular foot, jade green glass with multiple bubble inclusions, applied four vertical crimped glass stripes, acid stamped "Schneider" **1,550.00**

17" h, trumpet, ftd, clear with streaks of pink and raspberry, controlled bubbles, sgd **325.00**

23" h, cylinder, ftd, tangerine ground, bright orange shading to brown overlay, cameo carved three striped vertical panels enclosing stylized blossoms, cameo sgd "Charder," engraved "Le Verre Francais" . . .**2,420.00**

1904–28

SINCLAIRE GLASS COMPANY

History: H. P. Sinclaire and Company was founded in 1904 in Corning, NY. It was the twelfth glassworks to be located in the "Crystal City" of Corning. This factory never actually manufactered glass, instead it purchased blanks from other companies. The main supplier was the Corning Glass Works. H. P. Sinclaire and Company cut and engraved the blanks.

H. P. Sinclaire and Company is credited with producing some of the most beautiful glass of the American Brilliant Period. Many of the designs are naturalistic, including flowers, fruit, and foliage. Sinclaire approached these from an architectural viewpoint and the patterns reflected both a love of architecture and nature.

Unfortunately, H. P. Sinclaire and Company did not mark all their wares. However, a distinctive acid etched "S" in a wreath mark can be found. Other pieces are simply marked "Sinclaire."

Reference: Estelle Sinclaire Farrar, *H. P. Sinclaire, Jr., Glassmaker, Volume I,* Farrar Books, 1974.

Additional Listing: Cut Glass.

Bowl, deep cross miter and hobstar cutting, sgd with "S" in wreath and "Sinclaire," 9¼" d, 2¾" h, $165.00. Photograph courtesy of Skinner, Inc.

Berry Set, Pattern No. 8, 8½" d master
  bowl, six 6" d serving bowls, sgd ..**1,200.00**
Bowl
  8½" d, Assyrian pattern, sgd "Sin-
    claire" **300.00**
  9¼" d, 2¾" h, cut glass, heavy blank,
    deep cross miter and hobstar cut-
    ting, central sgd "S" in wreath
    mark, minor damage **165.00**
  9¾" h, hexagonal, engraved panels
    Floral dec, sgd **375.00**
    Intaglio cut fruit dec, sgd "Sinclaire
    & Co" **485.00**
  12" d, green, amber foot **195.00**
  13" d, canary yellow, etched florals . **185.00**
  13½" d, Pansy pattern, cut dec, sgd **400.00**
Box, cov, 3½" sq, intaglio cut grapes
  and bands **300.00**
Candlesticks, pr
  7" h, blue ground, cut dec, wide
    sweeping base, sgd **350.00**
  8½" h, crystal, engraved Steuben
    blanks **285.00**
  10" h, topaz, spiral stems **260.00**
Cocktail, 4¼" h, cut flowers, panels,
  and swags, sgd "Sinclaire" **75.00**
Cologne Bottle, 6" h, etched floral dec,
  sgd **190.00**
Compote, small, floral etching **75.00**
Console Set, etched dec
  Three pieces, amber, pr candlesticks,
    bowl, and 14" d center plate, cut
    dec, sgd "S" in wreath mark **325.00**
  Five pieces, green, four 3¼" h candle-

sticks, 14¼" d center bowl, sgd "S"
  in wreath mark **495.00**
Six pieces, amethyst, two 12" h
  candlesticks, 8½" d bowl, 9½" d
  bowl, two 7" h compotes **1,350.00**
Creamer and Sugar, Queen Louise pattern, sgd "S" in wreath mark **365.00**
Cruet, 8½" h, cut and engraved dec,
  orig stopper **195.00**
Goblet, engraved grapes and leaves .. **75.00**
Nappy, Adam II pattern **70.00**
Pitcher, 9" h, Pattern No. 4, pedestal
  base **1,200.00**
Plate
  8" d, amethyst, set of six **240.00**
  8½" d, green, sgd "Sinclaire" **65.00**
  10½" d, green, etched, ftd **90.00**
Relish, 11" l, 4½" w, Cane pattern, cut,
  sgd **250.00**
Rose Bowl, 5" d, Fan and Stars pattern,
  engraved florals **250.00**
Sandwich Tray, 11¾" l, 10" w, amber,
  etched, center handle **95.00**
Tray
  10" l, 8½" w, Silver Thread pattern,
    engraved medallions of roses, chry-
    santhemums, and asters, sgd **1,100.00**
  13" l, Georgian pattern **300.00**
  14½" l, 11½" w, oval, Plaid and This-
    tle pattern, cut and engraved, sgd
    "S" in wreath mark **4,200.00**
Tumbler, copper wheel engraved floral
  design **65.00**
Vase
  6½" h, Holly pattern, sgd **200.00**
  8" h, Grapes pattern, olive–green,
    copper wheel engraved dec, bul-
    bous, wafer foot, ring top **475.00**
  10½" h, Plateau pattern, Elfin green,
    fan shape **450.00**
  13½" h, Tulips pattern, etched, crys-
    tal body, sgd **295.00**
  14" h, cylindrical, intaglio cut flowers
    and leaves, crystal body **225.00**
  14¾" h, Silver Thread pattern, en-
    graved medallions of roses, chry-
    santhemums, and asters, sgd **1,200.00**

SMITH BROS. GLASS

History: After establishing a decorating department at the Mount Washington Glass Works in
1871, Alfred and Harry Smith struck out on their

own in 1875. Their New Bedford, Massachusetts, firm soon became known worldwide for its fine opalescent decorated wares, similar in style to those of Mt. Washington.

Their glass often is marked on the base with a red shield enclosing a rampant lion and the word "Trademark."

Reproduction Alert: Beware of examples marked "Smith Bros."

Atomizer, melon ribbed, creamy white satin ground, hand painted carnations outlined in gold, red rampant lion mark 595.00
Biscuit Jar, cov
   6¼" h, six sectioned opal glass body, gold enameled blossoming branches, silver plated rim, bail, and conforming cov, red rampant lion trade mark 350.00
   8" d, shaded pink satin ground, dainty blue florals and foliage, silver plated mountings 350.00
Bowl
   4¼" d, melon ribbed, creamy white satin ground, yellow daisies dec .. 235.00
   5½" d, creamy white satin ground, hand painted pansy dec, marked "Smith Bros" 195.00
   8¾" h, narrow ribbed body, creamy white satin ground, oak leaves and acorns outlined in gold, metal rim, marked 550.00
   9" d, melon ribbed, creamy white satin ground, large white flowers, green leaves, gold tracery, rampant lion mark 575.00
Box, cov, 4" d, melon ribbed, beige satin ground, blue florals, sgd 375.00
Creamer and Sugar
   2¾" h creamer, 3½" h, 3¼" d cov sugar, slightly ribbed creamy white satin ground, tiny yellow and orange flowers, silver plated trim, sugar marked 410.00
   3" h, 3" d creamer, silver plated handle and spout, 3½" h, 4" d sugar, silver plated bail and cov, cream ground, gold blossoms dec, raised gold edges, sgd "SB" on cov 475.00
Fernery
   10" d, orig insert, melon ribbed, creamy white shiny finished satin ground, hand painted violets and leaves, rampant lion mark, sgd "Smith Bros" 425.00
   10" d, 4" h, squatty, ten ribbed bulbous opal body, wild rose dec outlined in gold, raised edge, silver plated rim, red rampant lion mark 600.00
Jar, cov, 4½" h, squatty, melon ribbed,

creamy white satin ground, hand painted pansy dec, openwork silver top 275.00
Mayonnaise Dish, creamy white satin ground, floral dec, fancy silver plated top and handle, sgd 250.00

Mustard, cov, Sandwich Glass, 4½" h, $65.00.

Mustard Jar, cov, 2" h, melon ribbed, creamy white satin ground, gold prunus dec 300.00
Perfume, 5" h, creamy white satin ground, enameled floral dec, floral emb cap, rampant lion mark 450.00
Potpourri Vase, 10" h, creamy white satin ground, enameled chrysanthemums and leaves, gold outlines, sgd 950.00
Rose Bowl, 4¼" d, creamy white satin ground, pink and rose pansies, green leaves, sgd 300.00
Salt, open, melon ribbed, beaded rim, creamy white satin ground, hand painted florals 150.00
Salt and Pepper Shakers, pr, narrow ribbed body, mottled ground, orig pewter tops 175.00
Sugar Shaker, 6" h, narrow ribbed body, creamy white satin ground, heavy gold florals, orig metal top 250.00
Sweetmeat Jar, cov
   5¼" d, 5¼" h, melon ribbed body, creamy white satin ground, tiny blue flowers, silver plated collar and braided bail handle 625.00
   5½" d, 5" h, melon ribbed body, creamy white satin ground, enameled daisy spray, emb silver plated collar and bail, sgd 550.00
Tobacco Jar, 5" d, 6½" h, shaded pale lemon to deep peach satin ground, enameled pansies, gold trim, silver plated cov, crossed figural pipes finial, sgd on cov 350.00

Toothpick Holder, columned ribs, creamy white satin ground, pansies dec, blue enameled dots around rim **115.00**

Vase

4¼" h, narrow ribbed body, creamy white satin ground, enameled orange daisies, blue scroll work, rampant lion mark **350.00**

4½" h, creamy white satin ground, hand painted carnations, beaded enamel dot trim around top, sgd . **375.00**

5" h, 4" d, pinched, creamy white satin ground, hand painted florals, rampant lion mark **275.00**

6¾" h, bulbous swirled base, creamy white satin ground, hand painted blue flowers and gold dec, sgd ... **450.00**

7" h, bulbous swirled body, creamy white satin ground, pink flowers, green leaves, raised gold enameling, two beaded lines on top, red rampant lion mark **250.00**

7¼" h, 8" w, double, pilgrim, creamy white satin ground, lavender wisteria dec, traced in gold, gold beading on top **1,215.00**

8½" h, short stick neck, pedestal base, flat sides, creamy white satin ground, blue flowers, green leaf dec, raised gold enamel, beaded rim, red rampant lion mark **425.00**

8½" h, 6½" w, 1½" neck, canteen shape, pale pink shading to cream ground, purple wisteria dec, raised heavy gold leaves and branches, beaded top, sgd **1,250.00**

12" h, 7" d, creamy white satin ground, enameled birds, long branch, moon and sun overlapping behind birds **200.00**

L. E. SMITH GLASS COMPANY

History: L. E. Smith Glass Company was founded in 1907 in Mount Pleasant, Pennsylvania, by Lewis E. Smith. Although Smith left the company shortly after its establishment, it still bears his name. Early products were cooking articles and utilitarian objects such as glass percolator tops, fruit jars, sanitary sugar bowls, and reamers.

L. E. Smith glass is handmade and usually unmarked. Some older pieces bear a "C" in a circle with a tiny "S." Current glass has a paper label. The collector of older items should especially study black and Depression pieces. The Moon and Star pattern has been reproduced for many years. Smith glass of recent manufacture is found in house sales, flea markets, and gift and antiques shops.

In the 1920s, green, amber, canary, amethyst, and blue colors were introduced along with an extensive line of soda fountain wares. The company also made milk glass, console and dresser sets, and the always popular fish-shaped aquariums. During the 1930s, Smith became the largest producer of black glass. Popular dinner set lines were Homestead, Melba, Do–Si–Do, By Cracky, Romanesque, and Mount Pleasant.

L. E. Smith presently manufactures colored reproduction glass and interesting decorative objects. A factory outlet is available as well as factory tours. Contact the factory for specific times.

Reference: Hazel Marie Weatherman, *Colored Glassware of the Depression Era 2*, Glassbooks, Inc., 1982.

Animal

Cat, black, reclining, c1930, marked   **24.00**
Cow, black, reclining, c1930, marked   **20.00**
Goose, black, reclining, c1930, marked **20.00**

Horse, rearing

Blue **35.00**
Crystal **20.00**
Green **38.00**

Rooster, black, reclining, c1930, marked **20.00**
Scottie, black, reclining, c1930, marked **24.00**
Swan, opaque white **18.00**

Aquarium, 10" h, 15" l, green, King–Fish, c1920 .... **250.00**

Ashtray, elephant, black **35.00**

Bon Bon, ftd, handle

Cobalt blue **14.50**
Green **8.50**

Bookends, pr, rearing horse

Amber, 8" h, c1940 .... **42.00**
Cobalt blue, c1930 .... **60.00**
Crystal, c1930 .... **45.00**

Bowl

Amethyst, Pattern #77 .... **10.00**
Black, Pattern #515, 7" d, ftd **20.00**

Candlestick, Moon and Star Heritage Collection, yellow to red, 4¾" h, $8.00.

Melba Green, ruffled, 10½" d 12.00
Cake Plate, Do–Si–Do pattern, handles 15.00
Candlesticks, pr
  By Cracky, green 15.00
  Mt Pleasant, black 17.50
  Romanesque, pink 12.00
Casserole, cov, Melba pattern, 9½" l,
  oval 12.00
Compote, cov, Moon 'n' Star pattern,
  amberina 35.00
Cookie Jar, cov
  Black, floral dec 85.00
  Dark Amber, enameled dec 70.00
  Green, etched 100.00
Cordial Tray, #381
  Green 9.00
  Pink 9.00
Creamer
  Do–Si–Do pattern 4.50
  Homestead pattern, pink 6.00
  Moon 'n' Star pattern, amberina 10.00
Cruet, Moon 'n' Star pattern, ruby 30.00
Cup and Saucer
  Do–Si–Do pattern, pink, gold trim .. 7.50
  Homestead pattern, pink 6.00
  Melba, pink 6.50
Fairy Lamp, Moon 'n' Star pattern, ruby 30.00
Fern Dish, three small feet, 1930s
  Greek Key pattern
    Black opaque 18.00
    White opaque 10.00
  Kent pattern, white opaque 9.50
Flower Block, By Cracky, 3" h 4.00
Flower Pot, 4" h, silver floral dec, black
  ground 8.50
Goblet
  Do–Si–Do pattern 4.50
  Homestead pattern, pink 6.00
  Moon 'n' Star pattern, amberina 15.00
Mayonnaise, Kent pattern 6.75
Mug, crystal, 12 oz 5.00
Parfait
  Do–Si–Do pattern 4.50
  Homestead pattern, pink 6.00
  Soda Shop pattern 5.00
Planter, black–amethyst, nude dancers
  on sides, marked "L. E. Smith" 45.00
Plate
  Do–Si–Do pattern, 8" d 4.50
  Homestead pattern, pink
    8" d 6.00
    9" d, grill 7.50
  Melba pattern, amethyst, 6" d 5.00
  Mt Pleasant, pink, scalloped edge, 8"
    d 6.25
Rose Bowl, Mt Pleasant, cobalt blue,
  three small feet, rolled edges 18.50
Salt and Pepper Shakers, pr
  Dresden pattern, white 18.00
  Mt Pleasant pattern, cobalt blue 24.00
Sherbet
  Do–Si–Do pattern 4.50

Romanesque pattern, black 10.00
Slipper, Daisy and Button pattern, am-
  ber, 2½" h 5.00
Soda Glass
  Jumbo pattern, crystal, ribbed, ped-
    estal foot 7.00
  Soda Shop pattern, crystal 6.50
Sugar, cov
  Do–Si–Do pattern 6.50
  Homestead pattern, pink 8.00
  Kent pattern 6.50
  Melba pattern 7.00
  Moon 'n' Star pattern, amberina 12.00
Tray, 15" l, 6" w, oval
  Black 12.00
  Crystal 10.00
Vase
  6" h, black, silver bands 12.00
  7" h, Moon 'n' Star pattern, blue ... 8.50
  7½" h, Romanesque pattern, black,
    fan shape 12.00
Violet Bowl, Hobnail pattern, white
  opaque 8.60
Window Box, F. W. Woolworth 25.00
Wine
  Moon 'n' Star pattern, amberina 12.00
  Ruby body, crystal stem and foot ... 6.50

SOUVENIR AND HISTORICAL GLASSWARE

History: Souvenir and historical glassware has been produced to celebrate special events, places, and people.

Many localities issued plates, mugs, glasses, etc. for anniversary celebrations or to honor a local historical event. These items seem to have greater value when sold in the region from which they orginated.

World's fairs and expositions are another source of souvenir glassware. Beautiful examples have survived from the Chicago Columbian Exposition as well as others.

Historical glass includes several patterns of pressed glass which celebrate persons and events. Other types of historical glassware includes campaign and memorial items.

Souvenir and historical examples can be found mainly in clear, custard, and ruby stained glassware.

References: Bessie M. Lindsey, *American Historical Glass,* Charles E. Tuttle Company, Inc., 1967; George and Helen McKearin, *American Glass,* Crown Publishers, 1941; Jane Shadel Spillman, *White House Glassware,* The White House Historical Association, 1989.

Periodical: *Travel Collector,* P. O. Box 40, Manawa, WI 54949.

Reproduction Alert: Ruby stained souvenir toothpick holders have been cited. The ruby staining usually is of an inferior color and the etching poorly executed.

Additional Listings: Cup Plates, Custard Glass, and Pattern Glass.

Glass, commemorative, Admiral George Dewey, decal transfer, 3¾" h, 2¾" d, $35.00.

Basket, Clitherall, MN, clambroth–type opaque white ground **350.00**
Beer Mug, Chicago, Columbian World's Fair, 1893, eight pressed panels at bottom, marked "M Gordon, World's Fair, 1893," 3½" h **35.00**
Bell
  Chicago, Columbian Exposition, etched, frosted handle, 1893 .... **65.00**
  Elkhorn Fair, 1913, Button Arches pattern, ruby stained, clear paneled handle, 6½" h **65.00**
  St Louis, Louisiana Purchase Exposition, 1904, Liberty Bell replica, some gold **45.00**
Bottle
  Deadwood, SD **95.00**
  Dodge City **25.00**
  General Douglas MacArthur, aqua, 1942 .... **35.00**
Bowl, Centenary, M. E. Church, South Bonne, Terre, MO, scalloped edge, blue tint, 6" d **12.00**
Bread Plate
  Cape Cod, Triple Triangle pattern, ruby stained **65.00**
  Cleveland Reform, hobnail border, 10" d **35.00**
  President Taylor, Curtain Tieback pattern, 10½ x 7½" **50.00**
Butter Dish, Atlantic City, 1919, Button Arches pattern, ruby stained **75.00**
Candy Dish, cov, Columbia Exposition, 1893, ruby stained **65.00**

Creamer, Whitehall, MI, custard glass . **55.00**
Creamer and Sugar, Cambridge Springs, Georgia Gem pattern, breakfast size, custard glass **90.00**
Cup, Titusville, PA, ruby stained **35.00**
Goblet
  Centennial, draped roses **40.00**
  G. A. R., 21st Encampment, 1887 .. **95.00**
  Mother, Ruby Thumbprint pattern, ruby stained **30.00**
  1906, Triple Triangle pattern, ruby stained **30.00**
  Political, FDR, clear, three etched panels, one with spread wing eagle with "The New Deal," other with oval portrait of Roosevelt, dated 1933 and "Fiat" below, third with two doves and grapevine border which reads "Repeal of the 18th Amendment, Dec 7, 1933," upper edge inscribed "Franklin D. Roosevelt 32nd President of the United States of America Inaugurated March 4, 1933," inscribed on foot "Asst Sec of Navy 1913–20 Gov of New York State 1929–33 Presidential Glass 51," made by Vernay .. **800.00**
Hatchet
  Buffalo, Pan–American Exposition, 1901, Indian head on frosted blade, berries and leaves on handle **135.00**
  Hazelton, PA, white milk glass, red letters, 6" l **25.00**
  Washington, PA, Centennial 1810–1910, white milk glass **35.00**
Jelly Compote, Artesian, SD, ruby stained **35.00**
Jewelry Box, cov, Chicago, Columbian World's Fair, 1893, overview scene of fair, 3" sq **265.00**
Loving Cup, Oneonta, NY, ruby shading to clear, gold trim, two handles, 3½" h **45.00**
Mug
  Bermuda, Button Arches pattern, ruby stained **20.00**
  Charles Bray, Button Arches pattern, ruby stained **25.00**
  Dover, NH, custard glass **50.00**
  Hardwick, VT, custard glass, gold trim, 2⅜" h **24.00**
  Juneau, WI, Homecoming, 1914, clambroth–type opaque white ground **30.00**
  New Rockford, ND, custard glass .. **30.00**
  Ottawa, IL, Star and Punty Band pattern, green custard glass, gold grim, 3" h **35.00**
  Saratoga Springs, NY, frosted, weighted bottom, horses crossing finish line and spouting spring illus, 1950s, 5½" h **20.00**

White Rock, SD, custard glass **50.00**
World's Fair, 1904, Heart pattern,
ruby stained **20.00**
Napkin Ring, 1907, Diamond with Peg
pattern, ruby stained **85.00**
Paperweight
Apollo II, Venetian type glass, brass
back, limited edition, numbered
#1969/50,000, 4" d **45.00**
Brainard, MN, lake scene, 3" d **30.00**
Memorial Hall, 1776–1876, frosted,
mirror glass beneath, black opaque
glass base, 4⅜" w, 6⅛" h **175.00**
New Salem State Park, 2¾" d **30.00**
Old South Church, Boston, MA,
brown tone sepia photo scene, 4"
l, 2½" w **18.00**
Plymouth Rock, crystal, figural, 3¼"
h **75.00**
Pipe and Match Holder, Hot Springs,
AR, cobalt blue **22.50**
Pitcher
Bar Harbor, ME, custard glass, gold
trim, beaded base **24.00**
Confederate Civil War Officer, J H
Morgan, 1906, ruby stained, 4½" h **45.00**
Conneaut Lake, clear **52.00**
Dewey, cannonballs around portrait **85.00**
Pittsburgh, Button Arches pattern,
ruby stained, tankard **125.00**
Punch Cup, Chicago, Button Arches
pattern, ruby stained **20.00**
Rose Bowl, Chicago, Columbian
World's Fair, 1893, peachblow, Wild
Rose pattern, deep raspberry shading
to white, matte acid finish, elaborate
lettering and scroll dec, eight crimp
top, made by Mt Washington with
New England peachblow formula,
sold by Libbey, 3¼" h, 4" w **675.00**
Sauce Dish, Niagara Falls, Cathedral
pattern, ruby stained **18.00**
Shovel, Kearney, NE, gold scoop and
letters, clear handle, 6½" l **20.00**

**Tumbler, souvenir, ruby stained, marked
"William Frederick from F.W.C. 1909,"
3⅞" h, $50.00.**

Spooner, World's Fair
Chicago, 1893, Herringbone pattern,
ruby stained **45.00**
St Louis, 1904, custard glass, enam-
eled flowers **65.00**
Toothpick Holder
Atlantic City, 1899, King's Crown pat-
tern, ruby stained **25.00**
Coney Island, Shamrock pattern, ruby
stained **30.00**
Glen Ullen, ND, ruby stained, gold
trim **22.00**
Horse Island, ME, Quihote pattern,
custard glass, gold trim **28.00**
Lewiston, ME, Georgia Gem pattern,
custard glass, gold beaded trim .. **30.00**
Marshalltown, IA, ruby stained **18.00**
Providence, RI, Shamrock pattern,
ruby stained **20.00**
Tumbler
Deshler, OH, Inverted Strawberry pat-
tern, ruby stained **30.00**
Pearl Harbor **10.00**
Souvenir of Buffalo, sepia scenes ... **12.00**
World's Fair
Chicago, Century of Progress,
1933, clear, black and red in-
scriptions, silvered illus of Fort
Dearborn building, 5½" h **22.00**
Chicago, Columbian Exposition,
1893, Red Block pattern, ruby
stained **35.00**
New York, 1939, clear, multicol-
ored design, inscribed "Twen-
tieth Century Transportation"
and "Exhibits of Railroads and
Railroad Equipment Display–The
Transportation Bldg," 4½" h ... **38.00**
Vase
Parkers Prairie, MN, custard glass .. **75.00**
Red Wing, MN, 1920, multicolored
scene, custard glass, 6" h **40.00**
Whimsey, potty shape, Stratton, ME,
custard glass, gold trim **22.00**
Whiskey Glass, 1907, Ruby Thumbprint
pattern, ruby stained **25.00**
Wine
Asbury Park, NJ, ruby stained **35.00**
World's Fair, Button Arches pattern,
ruby stained **25.00**
Christmas, Triple Triangle pattern,
ruby stained **35.00**

SPANGLED GLASS

History: Spangled glass is a blown or blown
molded variegated art glass, similar to spatter
glass, with the addition of flakes of mica or metallic aventurine. Many pieces are cased with a
white or clear layer of glass. Spangled glass was

developed in the late 19th century and still is being manufactured.

Originally spangled glass was attributed only to the Vasa Murrhina Art Glass Company of Hartford, Connecticut, which distributed the glass for Dr. Flower of the Cape Cod Glassworks, Sandwich, Massachusetts. However, research has shown that many companies in Europe, England, and the United States made spangled glass, and attributing a piece to a specific source is very difficult.

Apothecary Jar, 6½" h, bulbous, pink and white, silver mica flakes, matching stopper **165.00**
Basket
  5" d, 6" h, bulbous, ruffled edge, mottled blue and white, silver mica flakes, applied clear twisted handle **175.00**
  6" l, 5" w, 6½" h, pink and gold, mica flaking, applied clear thorn handle **225.00**
  8½" d, amber ground, white casing, gold flakes, burgundy and opal ruffled rim, applied clear looped thorn handle **185.00**
  9" h, pleated, tan ground, gold mica flakes, white cased exterior, applied clear twisted handle **185.00**
Beverage Set, bulbous pitcher, six matching tumblers, rubena, opalescent mottling, silver flakes, attributed to Sandwich, c1850–60 .... **250.00**
Bowl, 4⅝" d, 2¼" h, rainbow, silver mica flakes, white lining **150.00**
Bride's Bowl, 10⅜" d, multicolored, ruby, cranberry, and green, ivory–yellow ground, silver flakes **100.00**
Candlesticks, pr
  8" h, green and maroon, gold mica flakes, white casing **115.00**
  8⅝" h, pink and white spatter, green Aventurine flakes, white casing ... **110.00**
Carafe, 8" h, 5" d, melon ribbed, dark blue, gold flakes **150.00**
Cologne Bottle, 6¾" h, blue, silver mica flakes, matching stopper **175.00**
Condiment Set, cranberry, green flakes, silver plated holder, three pieces ... **200.00**
Creamer and Sugar, cov, blue, gold mica flakes **225.00**
Cruet, Leaf mold pattern, cranberry, mica flakes, white casing, Northwood **450.00**
Ewer, 7⅞" h, 3¾" d, ruffled top, blue, silver mica flakes, white casing, applied clear thorn handle **125.00**
Fairy Lamp, 6⅜" h, multicolored, gold mica flakes, Clarke insert **200.00**
Finger Bowl, 4¼" d, 2½" h, ftd, swirled streaks of white, gold, and emerald green, clear body, foot drawn from body, applied clear handles imp with cherub's face **75.00**

Jack-In-The-Pulpit Vase, 5¾" h, white exterior, pink lining, silver mica flakes, ruffled clear edge **145.00**
Juice Tumbler, 3⅜" h, white ground, pink spatter, silver mica flakes, white casing **90.00**
Mug, amber, gold mica flakes **85.00**
Pitcher
  6¾" h, cobalt blue, gold mica flakes, applied amber handle with flakes . **245.00**
  7½" h, bulbous, four sided top, apricot, gold mica flakes form diamond pattern, white casing, pontil **165.00**
  8¾" h, bulbous, crimped rim with applied clear edge, deep rose, burgundy spatter, silver mica flakes, applied clear reeded handle **300.00**
  9¼" h, 3½" d, yellow, maroon, pink, white, and blue–green spatter, gold mica flakes, applied clear handle . **230.00**
  10" h, peach ground, ruby spatter, gold mica flakes, white casing, applied amber thorn handle **225.00**
Rose Bowl
  3¾" h, 3½" d, deep pink, silver mica flakes, white casing **175.00**
  4¼" h, 5⅜" d, shaded rose exterior, silver mica flakes, white casing, eight crimped top **150.00**
  5" h, 5¼" d, blue shading to white, silver mica flakes, white casing .. **125.00**
  6" d, lavender, silver veining, attributed to Cape Cod Glass Works ... **150.00**

Tumbler, rainbow spatter of pink, pale blue, butterscotch, green, beige, white, and silver spangles, case white interior, 3¾" h, $95.00.

Sugar Shaker, cranberry, mica flakes, white casing, Northwood **115.00**
Toothpick Holder, 2" h, blue, gold mica flakes **95.00**
Tumbler
  3½" h, pale blue and white spatter,

silver mica flakes form vertical paneled pattern, white casing **75.00**
3¾" h, yellow, maroon, pink, white, and blue, gold mica flakes, white casing **65.00**
4" h, pink, white, orange, red, yellow, and silver spangles **75.00**

Vase
7" h, pink, silver mica flakes, ribbon candy edge, applied clear thorn handles **125.00**
7⅞" h, pink and green, swirl pattern body, white casing, ruffled top ... **180.00**
8" h, modified baluster, tulip shaped lip, deep cranberry casing, clear casing with gold foil flakes in wide vertical swath, brown, green, yellow, and red spatter **225.00**
8" h, 4⅛" d, tan, beige, oxblood red and pink spatter, silver mica flakes, white casing **145.00**
8½" h, cased pink, ruffled crimped top, gold mica flakes, applied cherries and leaf rigaree, pr **550.00**
9¾" h, pink ground, silver mica flakes, white casing, applied vaseline rigaree shell trim, applied vaseline loop handles **145.00**
12" h, oviform, squatty circular base, amber, silver mica flakes, clear pinched neck **90.00**
12" h, 6" w, modified baluster shape, tulip shaped lip, deep cranberry casing, clear outer layer with inclusions of gold flecks in wide vertical swath, encased brown, yellow, and green, attributed to Ermanno Toso **300.00**
14½" h, melon ribbed, ruffled, pink, white, and green mica flakes **250.00**
Witch Ball, 8" h, tortoiseshell glass ball, attached to amber glass stem and foot **185.00**

SPATTER GLASS

History: Spatter glass is a variegated blown or blown molded art glass. It originally was called "End–of–Day" glass, based on the assumption that it was made from leftover batches of glass at the end of the day. However, spatter glass was found to be a standard production item for many glass factories.

Spatter glass was developed at the end of the 19th century and still is being produced. It was made in the United States and Europe. Companies like Northwood and Hobbs, Brockunier produced splendid examples of spatter glass. The Czechoslovakians used vivid color combinations creating some striking pieces of glassware.

References: William Heacock, James Measell and Berry Wiggins, *Harry Northwood: The Early Years 1881–1900*, Antique Publications, 1990; William Heacock, James Measell and Berry Wiggins, *Harry Northwood: The Wheeling Years 1901–1925*, Antique Publications, 1991.

Reproduction Alert: Many modern examples come from Czechoslovakia. Reproductions of Northwood pieces have also flooded the marketplace.

Syrup, cranberry, clear, and white, ring neck, applied clear handle, silver-plated top, $165.00.

Basket
4¾" w, 6½" h, pink, brown, and white, emb ribbing, white casing, ruffled, applied clear thorny handle **175.00**
5" w, 6½" h, aqua, brown, and white spatter, swirled ribbed body, ruffled edge, applied clear thorn handle . **240.00**
5½" w, 6" h, blue, white casing, applied clear thorn handle **185.00**
6" w, 7½" l, 8½" h, overlay, pink, blue, and gold, white casing, applied clear thorn handle and feet . **185.00**
Bottle, 11" h, rubena, opalescent spatter **125.00**
Bowl, red and yellow, white casing, pinched rim with clear edge, ground pontil **245.00**
Box, 7½" l, 4½" h, egg shaped, hinged, white casing, yellow and blue flowers, gold and white leaves, three applied clear feet **275.00**
Candlestick
7½" h, yellow, red, and white streaks, clear overlay, vertical swirled molding, smooth base, flanged socket . **50.00**
9¾" h, 4" d, pink and white spatter, clear ruffled base **85.00**
Cane, 30½" l, aqua, spiral twist at straight end of handle **145.00**
Cologne Bottle, 8½" h, etched adv "Rich Secker Sweet Cologne, New York," applied clear handles **60.00**

Creamer, 4¾" h, pink and white, applied clear handle, Northwood **45.00**

Cruet, orig stopper
Amber and white spatter, polished pontil **80.00**
Red and white spatter, applied clear handle, clear foot, clear ball stopper **125.00**

Darning Egg, multicolored, attributed to Sandwich Glass **125.00**

Fairy Lamp, 3¼" h, 2⅞" d, pyramid shape, pink, yellow, and white, white casing, clear base marked "Clarke" . **100.00**

Finger Lamp, 6¼ h, 4¼" d, peach ground, white and brown spatter, applied clear handle **135.00**

Jack-In-The-Pulpit Vase
9¼" h, ruffled, diamond quilted patterned body, white and peach spatter top, green base **100.00**
9⅜" h, 5½" d, green, white and peach spatter top, tiny diamond quilted patterned body, ruffled **125.00**

Jar, cov, 3¼" d, 6½" h, gold, maroon, white, and green, yellow casing, leaf finial **75.00**

Perfume, 4¾" h, yellow shaded to white ground, gold, blue, yellow, and white spatter **75.00**

Pitcher, pink and white, white casing, applied clear reeded handle **65.00**

Rose Bowl
3½" h, octagonal, crimped top, rose, white casing **95.00**
4½" d, pink and blue, pontil **40.00**

Salt, master, 3¼" h, 3" d, white, maroon, green, blue, and yellow, white casing, applied crystal rigaree and leaf dec **65.00**

Sugar Shaker, 4⅞" h, pink and white, silver plated on brass top **65.00**

Tumbler, 3¾" h, royal blue and white . **35.00**

Tumble–Up, bottle and matching tumbler, elongated thumbprint pattern, green, red, yellow, and pink, white casing, applied clear leaf feet **300.00**

Vase
7½" h, bulbous, ruffled rim, ruby, white spatter, gold butterflies, flowers, and foliage, etched mark, pr . **450.00**
10" h, pink, yellow, and tan swirls, white casing, cupped goblet type neck, pr **275.00**

Whimsey
3½" l, 1¾" h, figural, pig, vaseline exterior, red and white spatter interior **125.00**
3¾" h, 4½" l, figural, boot, pink and yellow, white casing, applied clear rigaree top, crystal applique leaf across top **75.00**

1903–32

STEUBEN GLASS

History: Frederick Carder, an Englishman, and Thomas G. Hawkes of Corning, New York, established the Steuben Glass Works in 1904. In 1918 the Corning Glass Co. purchased the Steuben Company. Carder remained with the firm and designed many of the pieces bearing the Steuben mark.

The most widely recognized wares are "Aurene," "Verre De Soie," and "Rosaline," but many other types were produced. Aurene is the name given to glassware which has an iridized golden sheen and may be found on amber, blue clear, or topaz colored glass. Examples of aurene with a red, green, or brown base are rare. Aurene was produced from 1904 through 1933. Verre de Soie is also an iridized type of glass. The silk-like texture is lightly frosted and should have a blue tint. Rosaline is a pink jade-type glass with a cloudy appearance. Rosaline pieces are commonly found with alabaster trim, feet, handles, and finials.

Steuben glassware can also be identified by the classic shapes and styles. Catalog reprints and other types of research materials have lead to identification of these distinctive shapes.

The firm continues operating, producing glass of exceptional quality.

References: Paul Gardner, *The Glass of Frederick Carder*, Crown Publishers, 1971; Paul Perrot, Paul Gardner, and James S. Plaut, *Steuben: Seventy Years Of American Glassmaking*, Praeger Publishers, 1974.

Manufacturer/Distributor: Steuben Glass, 5th Ave. at 56th St., New York, NY 10022.

Museums: The Corning Museum of Glass, Corning, NY; The Rockwell Museum, Corning, NY.

Reproduction Alert: Steuben pieces have been reproduced. The coloration can be duplicated, but the silky and iridized finishes originally produced by Steuben are not usually perfected on reproductions.

ACID CUT BACK

Bowl
8" d, 1¾" h, flared, alabaster, green jade overlay, cut swagged floral border, all over etched scrolling ground **300.00**
8" d, 7¼" h, green jade, cut chrysanthemums and leaves dec **600.00**

Candlesticks, pr, 14" h, black cut to clear, Poussin pattern, flowers and leaves **2,250.00**

Jar, cov, 5½" h, white ground, apple green leaves and flowers **800.00**

Lamp Base

7" h jade shaft, 22" h without shade, blue aurene cut to green jade, Fircone pattern, orig gilt bronze swan embellishment on platform base, two socket fittings **825.00**

13" h gold aurene shaft, cut to black amethyst, stylized sculptured pod dec, orig gilt bronze two socket fittings **1,320.00**

Lamp Shade, 9" d, globe, schoolhouse type, Ivorene, orig air brushed brass flush mounted fixture, ornate details, raised fleur–de–lis dec **345.00**

Vase

8" h, 10" d, shouldered oval, three layers, plum jade, dark amethyst to alabaster ground, double etched, acid cut back Chinese pattern, scrolled background, fleur–de–lis mark **3,100.00**

9" h, black, medieval pattern cameo dec, shape #2694, gold Steuben paper label **3,000.00**

9½" h

Baluster, green jade cut back to alabaster, Bird pattern, exotic birds, leafy flowering tree branches **1,045.00**

Urn shape, chartreuse, cased with green, scroll, fern, and classic medallion motif, sgd **1,300.00**

10¼" h, 3¾" d, heavy walled, cobalt blue Aurene ground, silver–blue irid, cut to dark cobalt, broad vintage frieze of grapes, leaves, and vines below shoulder dec of stylized leaves and berries, sgd "Steuben Aurene 2683" on base **4,000.00**

12" h, baluster, raised flared rim, triple layers, peach Cintra cased to alabaster, dark amethyst overlay, acid cut back Pagoda pattern, three repeats in shaped medallion windows with Canton landscapes, floral and fretwork borders, tiny rim chip **2,200.00**

13" h, flattened oval, rose quartz, chrysanthemums, Art Deco circle and triangle border, fleur–de–lis acid cut mark on lower side **2,860.00**

ANIMALS

Angel Fish, 10½" h, 10" l, lead crystal, hand polished, sgd on base, pr **800.00**

Dinosaur, 12¾" l, modeled by James Houston **600.00**

Elephant, 8½" h **350.00**

Fish, 6" h, lead crystal, perched on tail, applied tooled fins and eyes, sgd on base **350.00**

Penguin, 6½" h, numbered **175.00**

Rabbit, numbered **125.00**

Rooster, 10" h, modeled by Donald Pollard, inscribed "Steuben" **600.00**

Sea Horse, 9¼" h, modeled by Lloyd Atkins, numbered **265.00**

Songbird, 4½", numbered **185.00**

Squirrel, 5" h, modeled by Lloyd Atkins, inscribed "Steuben" **250.00**

Vase, alabaster glass, four green pulled leaf forms alternating with gold Aurene swirling feather dec, base inscribed "Aurene 598," 7¼" h, $6,160.00. Photograph courtesy of Skinner, Inc.

AURENE

Atomizer, 7" h, gold **360.00**

Basket

6" h, gold, mirror finish, sgd, #455 . **825.00**

14" h, gold glass basket, fancy ormolu frame and handle, sgd "Aurene, F Carder" **2,600.00**

Bowl

6¼" d, 7⅛" h, amber, goblet shape, tapered foot, irid purple neck and foldover lip **850.00**

8" d, 4" h, blue, irid finish with purple highlights, sgd "Steuben Aurene 2687" **825.00**

8" d, 4¼" h, blue irid with gold and purple luster, pedestal dish, four apertures for flower stems around central reservoir, sgd "Aurene 3080," partial label, crack around base edge **990.00**

9" d, low flat shape, sgd "Aurene," "LCT" signature on base **200.00**

10" d, 3¾" h, flaring rim, interior
heightened with pink, crackled rim,
low molded purple shaded foot, inscribed "Steuben Aurene/2851" .. **600.00**

Candlesticks, pr
3¾" h, everted rim tapering to stem
with applied glass protrusion, circular cushioned foot, all over brilliant peacock blue irid, inscribed
"Steuben Aurene L384" **800.00**
5¼" h, gold, sgd "Aurene 6637" ..**1,000.00**
8¼" h, gold, baluster, ring turned
shade, cupped pedestal foot,
marked "Aurene 3100" **700.00**

Cigarette Holder, 4¼" l, blue, ribbed . **350.00**

Compote
6" h, shallow circular cup, slender cylindrical stem, gold with pink shading, circular foot shading to purple
rim, inscribed "Aurene/2642," set
of 4 .... **800.00**
6" d, 8¼" h, gold, quarter round
bowl, elongated shaped stem, disk
pedestal foot, sgd "Steuben Aurene
2642" **500.00**
12" d, 5¾" h, circular dish, double
guard stem, circular foot, brilliant
peacock irid blue, inscribed "Aurene 6150" **550.00**

Console Set, 10" d scalloped ten–ribbed
bowl, bright orange toned irid, pr 8¼"
h rope twist candlesticks, sgd and
numbered, 3 pcs **900.00**

Decanter, 10¼" h, gold, dimpled body,
undulating rim, peaked stopper, engraved "Aurene" **660.00**

Finger Bowl and Underplate, millefiori,
irid gold, green vines and leaves, applied white flowers, sgd "Aurene/
Haviland & Co" **1,150.00**

Flower Frog, 4¾" h, irid blue, sgd "Aurene 2775" **300.00**

Lamp, 14" h, gold, faintly ribbed open
domed shade, amber ground, intense
gold irid with pink, blue, and metallic
luster, matching shaft with slightly
scalloped base, single socket metal
fittings **800.00**

Lamp Shade, green, platinum dec, gold
interior, sgd **750.00**

Nappy, gold, shaped tripartite rim, applied glass handle, inscribed "Aurene
F Carder" **400.00**

Nut Cup, 1¼" h, 3⅝" d, irid gold, fluted,
crackled edge, silver "Aurene & Haviland & Co" mark **225.00**

Perfume, 6" h, elongated vasiform body,
silvery blue irid, mirror base, sgd and
numbered, no stopper **210.00**

Plate, 8½" d, gold, sgd and numbered
3059 .... **220.00**

Powder Box, 4" d, copper wheel en-

graved dec, orig sterling silver enameled cov **1,250.00**

Rose Bowl, 6" d, 3" h, gold, ten ribs,
lustrous irid surface inside and out,
sgd "Aurene 565" **375.00**

Salad Bowl, 8½" d, shallow, flared,
gold, sgd "Aurene 3059," set of four **800.00**

Tumbler, 4⅛" h, 3¼" d, irid gold, flared
top, bronze highlights, sgd "Aurene" **225.00**

Vase
5" h
Baluster, ribbed, everted mouth,
round molded foot, blue, inscribed "Steuben," first quarter
20th C **300.00**
Tree Trunk, gold, ribbed and
nubbed, fine blue tinged luster,
top cut down **110.00**
5½" h, blue, ribbed and flared shape,
sgd **625.00**
5⅞" h, 5½" d, red, irid gold and
opaque white feather design, sgd
"Aurene/548" **3,900.00**
6" h, 4" d, elongated cuspidor shape,
gold, mirror brilliance, sgd "Steuben" **1,100.00**
8" h, baluster, short cylindrical neck
everted at rim, gold irid shaded
with pink on shoulder and base,
incised "Steuben Aurene 5687" .. **935.00**
8¼" h, bud, narrow cylinder, ringed
pedestal base, gold, sgd "Aurene
2556" **325.00**
10⅜" h, baluster, waisted neck, everted rim, blue, first quarter 20th C **660.00**
10½" h, baluster, brilliant green, gold
pulled heart and vine dec, cased
opal white lining, gold Aurene rim
and interior layer, base sgd "Aurene" **3,700.00**
12¼" h, cone, blue, applied pedestal
foot, sgd "Steuben Aurene 6034" **935.00**
14¼" h, floriform, flared cylindrical
body, ruffled rim, knopped stem,
circular foot, blue, silver printed
mark **825.00**

CALCITE

Bowl, 10" to 13¾" d, 3½" to 4¾" h,
gold Aurene interior, flared, small
disk platform base, graduated set of
four **450.00**

Centerpiece Bowl
10" d, 2¼" h, gold, flared shallow
bowl **250.00**
12" d, blue, sgd **500.00**

Compote
6⅛" d, matching underdish, gold Aurene interior **300.00**
8" d, baluster stemmed pedestal foot,
brilliant irid gold Aurene interior . **350.00**

9¾" d, 2¾" h, flared flattened rim,
bright gold irid Aurene bowl,
cupped calcite pedestal foot **275.00**
Console Set, 10¼" d centerpiece bowl,
blue aurene interior, trifid gilt metal
holder, pr 5½" blue candleholders,
white calcite sockets, sgd and numbered, bases ground at edge, surface
flaws, 3 pcs **800.00**
Goblet, 6" h, gold **250.00**
Lamp Shade, green leaf and vine **250.00**
Rose Bowl, 6½" d, 4" h, calcite exterior,
gold Aurene interior, Shape # 2687 **350.00**
Sherbet and Underplate, blue Aurene
lining **500.00**
Vase
6" h, 5" d, trumpet, slightly ruffled
rim, gold aurene interior **310.00**
6¼" h, 8" d, conical, blue Aurene
luster on flared flattened rim, disk
foot, Steuben triangular label on
base **900.00**
10" h, fine gold irid on flattened rim
and interior **660.00**

CLUTHRA

Bowl
7½" d, 5¾" h, bubbled and swirled
green jade, clear and white crystal **600.00**
15" d, 7½" h, heavy conical walls,
shaded black–gray to clear and
white crystal, irregular swirling
bubbles throughout **800.00**
Vase
6" h, shouldered ovoid, everted rim,
frothy mottled Pomona green, acid
stamped "Steuben" **200.00**
10½" h, shouldered ovoid, everted
rim, frothy mottled Pomona green,
acid stamped fleur–de–lis mark .. **625.00**
14½" h, flared cylindrical, shades of
rose, pink, and crystal, irregular
bubbles **375.00**

GROTESQUE

Bowl
5¼" h, quatrefoil freeform, Model
7090, sgd "Steuben" on base **330.00**
7" h, four ribbed freeform, creamy
ivory crystal **275.00**

IVORINE

Candlestick, 4" h, 3" d, foliate form, ftd **125.00**
Chandelier, 17" d, round, acid etched
floral swag and shield dec, white
painted metal ceiling mounts **475.00**
Lamp Shade, 5" h **75.00**
Vase
3" h, green edge trim **175.00**

Vase, Ivorine, flared flattened oval body, ten rib design, irid white aurene, partial paper label on base, 9½" h, 10½" w, $500.00. Photograph courtesy of Skinner, Inc.

4⅜" h, flaring, sgd "Steuben" **220.00**
10" h, jade handles **325.00**
12" h, triple, two lily form with center
trumpet vase, sgd "Steuben" **900.00**

JADE

Bowl, 12" d, jade bowl, alabaster base,
sgd **425.00**
Sherbet, green jade ground, engraved
flowers and festoons cut to alabaster,
alabaster stem and foot, matching
7¼" underplate **450.00**
Perfume, 5¾" h, green, internally ribbed
and tooled, white glass stopper, sgd
"F Carder–Steuben" **660.00**
Vase
7¼" h, quatreform, swirled, rib
molded, shaped corners **450.00**
9¼" h, classical vasiform, flared rim,
alabaster applied tooled handles . **800.00**
Wine, 7" h, jade bowl, alabaster stem,
set of six **550.00**

MISCELLANEOUS

Bottle, crystal, teardrop stopper **85.00**
Candlesticks, pr
4½" h, mushroom shape, green, sgd **135.00**
10¼" h, swirled milky glass baluster
stem, urn form nozzle, flat drip pan
highlighted with purple rim,
spreading deep purple circular foot,
first quarter 20th C **250.00**
12½" h, amethyst, ribbed design, sgd
on base **200.00**
Candy Jar, 7" h, Art Deco, black thread
dec and multifaceted lid, etched mark
base, c1920 .... **200.00**
Center Bowl
12½" d, 3½" h, Florentia, internal
green blossom center, shallow
flared bowl, applied pedestal foot,
sgd "Steuben" with fleur–de is on
base **2,750.00**

13" d, 3½" h, Silenium Red, flared flat
rim **275.00**
Champagne, 4⅝" h, opal striped pink
bowl and stem **100.00**
Cigarette Box, 4½" l, clear, Pan Am
Building on cov, sgd on base **120.00**
Cigarette Holder, 4½" l, Alabaster **190.00**
Cocktail Glass Set, 3¾" h, crystal, dou-
ble flared form, teardrop encased
within conical base, each sgd "Steu-
ben," orig case, set of twelve **650.00**
Compote, cov, 8¾" h, celeste blue, op-
tic rib, yellow to rose pear shaped
finial, green leaf, shape #3384 . . . . **900.00**
Decanter, 11" h, engraved Thistle pat-
tern, ring stopper **175.00**
Finger Bowl and Underplate, celeste
blue, shape #1820, fleur–de–lis mark **200.00**
Goblet
6" h, Celeste Blue, ribbed design,
crystal stems, fleur–de–lis mark,
two small chips, set of six **385.00**
8¼" h, opal striped pink bowl, green
stem and foot, sgd **300.00**
Lamp, torch, 15" h overall, 7" h agate
shade, Moss Agate, scalloped edge,
mottled and striated walls, amber,
gold, orange, burgundy, green, blue,
and bubbled variations, polychrome
metal electroilier lamp **1,430.00**
Luminor, 7" h, solid clear crystal sphere,
orig black glass sq light box
Florentia, internally dec, green five
petal blossom, controlled bubbles **825.00**
Internally dec, red and blue disks,
controlled bubbles **475.00**
Lemonade Set, pitcher and four glasses,
amethyst, blue applied handles,
ribbed design, sgd **550.00**
Pitcher, 8¾" h, clear, applied handle,
sgd on base **275.00**
Plate
8½" d, Cintra, opalescent body, blue
and red Cintra edge **175.00**
10" d, Zodiac, crystal, engraved,
"The Archer," Sagittarius, star filled
sky background, sgd **650.00**
Salt, translucent emerald green, sten-
ciled "Steuben" **40.00**
Urn, pr, 6⅞" h, clear, applied handles,
sgd on base **225.00**
Vase
6¼" h, swirled design, sgd on base . **170.00**
8½" h, vasiform, crystal, single gather
type, sgd, orig box **275.00**
9" h, urn shape, green, orig paper la-
bel **225.00**
10" h, green, etched tassels and
flower designs, sgd on base **275.00**
11½" h, baluster, flared rim, Rose
Quartz, splotched pink, crackled
interior, acid cut back sculptured

pattern of blossoms, mat–su–no–ke
leaves, etched trademark on lower
side **5,250.00**
12¼" h, cream, eight ribs, ruffled
edge **125.00**
Wine Goblet, 7½" h, green threaded de-
sign and airtraps, clear stems and
bases, set of three **65.00**

ORIENTAL POPPY

Champagne, green stem **375.00**
Compote, 7" h, twisted green stem . . . **700.00**
Cordial, green stem and foot, sgd **300.00**
Lamp, 7" h shaft, 18" h with silk shade,
ribbed green pastel glass shaft, gilt
bronze and matching green platform
base **1,100.00**
Perfume Bottle, 10 1 /2" h, opal, rose,
c1925 . . . . **1,150.00**
Sherbet, 4½" h **250.00**

ROSALINE

Centerpiece Set, low ftd bowl, pr 12" h
candlesticks, alabaster trim **700.00**
Compote, 10" d, 4½" h, flattened pink
jade bowl, applied alabaster stem and
foot **325.00**
Lemonade Mug, 5" h, alabaster applied
handles, set of four **275.00**
Nappy, 4½" w, 5½" l, alabaster handle,
shape #205, ground pontil **325.00**
Newel Post Ornament, 7½" h, bulbed
oblique, rosaline overlay, cut back
faceted roundels and star crest, applied faceted alabaster pedestal foot,
gilt metal mount **500.00**
Tumblers, 5" h, flared, set of four **200.00**
Vase, 7¼" h, flared ovoid, pink jade,
cupped alabaster pedestal foot, pr . . **850.00**

VERRE DE SOIE

Basket
1¾" d, 3½" h, applied handle with
prunts, ground pontil **465.00**
9½" d, 4½" h, engraved **225.00**
Champagne, 7" h, conical flute, bright
turquoise blue twisted stem and rim,
set of fourteen **1,400.00**
Cocktail Shaker, 10" h, turquoise prunts **300.00**
Compote, 10" d, 6" h, ruffled edge,
twisted stem **375.00**
Jardiniere, 8" h, 6" d, ten ribbed,
swirled, quatrefoil rim **250.00**
Nut Dish, 4" h, green rim **35.00**
Perfume Bottle, 5" h, melon ribbed, Ro-
saline Cintra dauber **525.00**
Plate
8" d, luncheon, applied opaque pink
rim, set of six **450.00**

8½" d, sgd "F Carder" **125.00**
Sherbet, 4" h, 6¼" d underplate, irid,
set of eight **550.00**
Tumbler, 5" h, sgd **75.00**
Vase
 7" h, aquamarine, turquoise band on
 rim, shape #938 .... **225.00**
 10" h, cylindrical, etched and wheel
 cut floral swags, silver rim, sgd,
 marked "Hawkes Sterling" **385.00**

19th C

STEVENS AND WILLIAMS

History: In 1824 Joseph Silvers and Joseph Stevens leased the Moor Lane Glass House at "Briar Lea Hill" (Brierley Hill), England, from the Honey–borne family. In 1847 William Stevens and Samuel Cox Williams took over, giving the firm its present name. In 1870 the firm moved to its Stourbridge plant. In the 1880s the firm employed such renowned glass artisans as Frederick C. Carder, John Northwood, other Northwood family members, James Hill, and Joshua Hodgetts.

Stevens and Williams made cameo glass. Hodgetts developed a more commercial version using thinner–walled blanks, acid etching, and the engraving wheel. Hodgetts, an amateur botanist, was noted for his brilliant floral designs.

Other glass products and designs manufactured by Stevens and Williams include intaglio ware, Peach Bloom (a form of peachblow), moss agate, threaded ware, "jewell" ware, tapestry ware, and Silveria. Stevens and Williams made glass pieces covering the full range of late Victorian fashion.

After World War I the firm concentrated on refining the production of lead crystal and achieving new glass colors. In 1932 Keith Murray came to Stevens and Williams as a designer. His work stressed the pure nature of the glass form. Murray stayed with Stevens and Williams until WWII and later followed a career in architecture.

References: Charles R. Hajdamach, *British Glass, 1800–1914*, Antique Collectors' Club, 1991; R.S. Williams–Thomas, *The Crystal Years*, Stevens and Williams Limited, England, Boerum Hill Books, 1983.

Additional Listing: Cameo Glass.

Basket, 9" l, 6" h, oblong, blue ground,
two sides folded in, enameled floral
dec, applied crimped amber edging,
arched open amber handles at sides,
slightly domed foot, sgd "S & W
Stourbridge" **250.00**
Biscuit Jar, 5½" d, 7¾" h, creamy
opaque ground, applied amber and
green leaves, deep pink lining, SP
rim, cov, and handle **275.00**
Bowl
 3¾" d, 3½" h, box pleated top, plain
 panels alternating with raised emb
 beaded panels, white shaded to
 cranberry ground, frosted cranberry
 lining, satin finish **175.00**
 6¾" d, 3¼" h, box pleated top, pink
 satin ground, MOP, Swirl pattern,
 cream lining **500.00**
 7⅜" d, 3¾" h, cloverleaf shape,
 closely ruffled edge, amber shaded
 to aqua satin ground, MOP exterior,
 robin's egg blue lining **895.00**
Calling Card Receiver, 10" l, applied
amber handle, rolled edge, translucent
opalescent ground, three applied
berries, blossoms, and green leaves,
three applied amber feet **725.00**
Cologne Bottle, 8" h, 3" d, green ground
cut to clear, intaglio dec, hallmarked
silver collar, matching green intaglio
cut stopper **275.00**
Cruet, 3½" d, 9½" h, amber, opaque
Arboresque pattern, applied amber
handle, amber pedestal foot, orig flattened
amber stopper **150.00**
Dresser Jar, cov, 3" h, rose alabaster .. **285.00**
Epergne, 13½" h, 10" w, clear crystal
ground, eight miniature baskets with
handles and berry prints, all hanging
from center vase **450.00**
Fairy Lamp, 6" h, 5¼" d, dome shade,
pink, white, and frosted alternating
swirling stripes, clear Clarke cup,
frosted ruffled base **600.00**
Finger Bowl, 6⅛" d, 2⅞" h, matching
8⅛" d underplate, royal blue ground
cut to clear, overall intaglio cut fruit
and foliage dec **295.00**
Jack-In-The-Pulpit Vase, 14" h, blue,
white, and clear striped ground, applied
clear spiraling from top to base,
applied clear base **235.00**
Jug, 9" h, cranberry ground cut to amber,
hinged cov **290.00**
Pitcher
 5½" h, bulbous, clear ground, blue
 and white swirled diagonal stripes,
 applied clear reeded handle **125.00**
 10½" h, applied green handle forms
 leaves and yellow flower, cranberry

overlay ground, blue lining, applied amber rim and feet **600.00**

Plate

4¾" d, ruffled shell shape, shaded pink to green satin ground, MOP, Swirl pattern **175.00**

10" l, 4½" h, rolled edges, translucent opalescent ground, applied amber berries and blossoms, applied green leaves and strawberries, applied amber handle and three applied feet **735.00**

Rose Bowl

3" h, rainbow ground, MOP, Diamond Quilted pattern, alternating stripes of pastel yellow, pink, and blue, imp "Stevens & Williams, Stourbridge Glass," crown logo, patent **1,045.00**

3¼" h, blue opalescent ground, applied glass strawberry, amber feet . **515.00**

3½" h, 4½" d, rose and pink swirled striped ground, 5¾" l attached pale green leaf tray **475.00**

Salt, irid gold ground, sterling silver basket, hanging spoon, English hallmarks **150.00**

Toothpick Holder, green ground cut to clear, hallmarked sterling silver rim . **350.00**

Toupee Stand, mushroom shape, rose alabaster **275.00**

Tumbler, butterscotch shading to white opalescent ground, white casing, applied florals **250.00**

Vase, cloudy to light green center, applied clear rose flower, leaves, and base fringe, 10¾" h, $195.00.

Vase

3¾" h, 3½" d, rich pink shaded exterior, white lining, applied amber branch and two applied amber plums **195.00**

4" h, ovoid, barrel shaped body, bright blue ground, white layer,

cameo cut and carved ferns, grasses, and wild thistle, sod border, circular mark "Stevens & Williams Art Glass Stourbridge" **1,320.00**

5¾", egg shape, opal and cranberry vertical stripes, gold and black floral dec, applied clear rigaree extends to three feet, pr **125.00**

5¾" h, 5" d, bulbous base, small ringed neck, white satin ground, MOP, alternating deep purple and lavender swirled pattern **1,000.00**

6" h, tapered ovoid body, flared, amethyst ground, white overlay, cameo cut and carved high relief nasturtium vines, blossoms, and buds, six legged beetle on side, sgd in script "Stevens & Williams" **3,520.00**

6¾" h, lily, swirled ribs, vibrant swirls of blue, pink, and yellow on white ground, trefoil crimped top, clear base **485.00**

7¼" h, cameo, peachblow ground, cut back floral designs, applied rigaree panels **615.00**

8¼" h, shaded pink ground, white lining, applied amber and green leaves and branches, applied soft blue and cream flowers, amber centers, applied amber loop feet . **300.00**

10" h, slender refined shape, six medallions of applied clear glass, trailing stems swirling to base, engraved ornate stylized petals and foliage, sgd in pontil "Frederick Carder," Stevens and Williams logo **745.00**

12" h, baluster, Silveria, green threading on shaded pink and white silver speckled ground, bright green lining **725.00**

12¼" h, cameo, classic shape, apricot ground, white overlay, cut and carved blossoming canterbury bells, butterflies, and medial border, marked "Stevens & Williams Art Glass Stourbridge," pinpoint border bubble **4,400.00**

Whimsey, 8¾" h, handled basket which hangs on stand made from inverted saucer base, white ground, intaglio cut pink overlay, applied clear thorn handle **965.00**

STIEGEL-TYPE GLASS

History: Baron Henry Stiegel founded America's first flint glass factory at Manheim, Pennsylvania, in the 1760s. Although clear glass was the most common color made, amethyst, blue (cobalt), and fiery opalescent are found. Products included bottles, creamers, flasks, flips, perfumes, salts, tumblers, and whiskeys. Prosperity was short-lived. Stiegel's extravagant living forced the factory to close.

It is very difficult to identify a Stiegel–made item. As a result the term "Stiegel-type" is used to identify glass made at that time period in the same shapes and colors.

Enamel decorated ware also is attributed to Stiegel. True Stiegel pieces are rare. An overwhelming majority is of European origin.

Reference: Frederick W. Hunter, *Stiegel Glass*, 1950, available in Dover reprint.

Reproduction Alert: Beware of modern reproductions, especially in enamel wares.

Additional Listings: Early American Glass, European Glass.

Bottle, Stiegel–type, red, yellow, blue, and white enameled floral dec, pewter rim, 6½" h, $325.00.

ENAMELED

Beaker, 5" h, blown peacock blue glass, six panels, enameled birds, dog, tiger, stag, fruit, and florals, loop design around base, polished pontil, c1840, slight lower crizzling **425.00**

Bride's Bottle

  4¾" h, blown clear glass, enameled polychrome dec, one side with white bird on red within yellow oval topped by blue, white, red, and yellow plumes, reverse with tulip, colored daisies on end panels, tooled, slightly flared mouth, pontil, slight interior deposit **600.00**

  5¾" h

    Blown clear glass, enameled sprays of flowers, red, yellow, white, green, and baby blue **250.00**

    Blown opalescent glass, enameled

floral dec, swirled ribbon dec on chamfered edges, orig pewter cap, European, 18th C **250.00**

6" h, blown clear glass, enameled red, white, yellow, and blue, long neck, rolled mouth, Carpenter's Arms, reverse inscribed "Vivat der Schreiner 1825" **200.00**

6½" h, blown clear glass, enameled bright colored floral dec, pewter collar **200.00**

6⅜" h, blown clear glass, enameled polychrome dec of birds and flowers, orig pewter collar, screw top missing, European, 18th C, ex–Corning Museum of Glass collection, slight chemical deposit in bottom **375.00**

6⅞" h, blown clear glass, enameled large spray of flowers, white, red, yellow, blue, and black, slight haze on bottom **275.00**

8⅜" h, blown clear glass, enameled bright colored dec, pewter collar . **225.00**

Cordial Bottle

  5½" h, blown clear glass, enameled florals and Germanic inscription, pewter top, pontil scar, European, mid 18th C **275.00**

  5⅝" h, blown clear glass, enameled floral dec, rect, beveled edges, pewter threaded lip, pontil scar, European, mid 18th C **255.00**

  6¾" h, blown clear glass, enameled florals and Germanic inscription, metal threads, pontil scar, inner stain, European, mid 18th C **180.00**

Flask, 5" h, blown clear glass, flattened oval, enameled Masonic dec, florals, and inscriptions, sheared lip, pontil scar, German, mid 18th C **275.00**

Flip

  3½" h, blown clear glass, enameled polychrome dec of birds and plants, ex–Corning Museum of Glass collection **400.00**

  6½" h, blown clear glass, enameled basket of flowers and leaves **375.00**

Humpen, 9¼" h, blown clear glass, enameled men smoking pipe, florals, and inscriptions, pontil scar, etched "FH 304/1" on base, European, late 19th C **250.00**

Mug, 3⅜" h, blown clear glass, enameled polychrome dec of birds, hearts, and flowers, applied strap handle, European, 18th C, ex–Corning Museum of Glass collection **375.00**

Pitcher, 9¾" h, blown aqua glass, twelve bands of threading around neck, enameled polychrome floral design, c1820–40 . . . . **1,980.00**

Tumbler
3⅛" h, blown clear glass, enameled polychrome dec of bird, heart, and foliage, minor enamel wear 350.00
3⅝" h, blown clear glass, enameled polychrome floral dec and phrase "We two will be true," minor enamel wear 600.00
Whiskey Tumbler, blown clear glass, enameled man on prancing horse .. 265.00

ENGRAVED

Bottle
7¾" h, blown clear glass, heavily engraved birds, heart, wreath, and florals, dated 1779, pewter threads, European, cap missing, pontil scar, crizzled 275.00
7⅞" h, blown clear glass, engraved large tulip on each side, monogram and date 1837, chemical deposit on bottom 150.00
9" h, blown clear glass, engraved floral dec 130.00
Firing Glass
4" h, blown clear glass, Masonic engraving, traces of gilding, pontil scar, European, late 19th C 175.00
4¼" h, blown clear glass, copper wheel engraving around rim, hollow stemmed, pontil scar, European, late 18th C 150.00
Flip
5¼" h, blown clear glass, engraved top border frieze of ovals, leaves, and berries beneath loop ribbon design 100.00
7¼" h, 6⅜" d, blown clear glass, engraved lovebirds in sunburst, frosted highlights 400.00
7¾" h, 6" d, blown clear glass, engraved Phoenix bird between two tulips 150.00
8" h, blown clear glass, engraved tulip and floral engravings, pontil scar, European, late 18th C, one with side crack, pr 300.00
8¼" h, blown clear glass, engraved tulip and floral design, pontil scar, European, late 18th C 235.00
Mug
5¼" h, blown clear glass, engraved floral design, pontil scar, applied strap handle with medial crease, Bohemia, mid 18th C 265.00
6" h, cov, blown clear glass, engraved floral motif, strap handle 400.00
6⅛" h, blown clear glass, elaborate frosted engraving, large applied strap handle 250.00
Tumbler, 4⅜" h, 3½" d, blown clear

glass, twenty two vertical flutes, engraved dec, cross–hatched ovals ... **45.00**
Vase, 9¾" h, blown clear glass, engraved hollyhocks and ferns dec, hollow base and stem, pontil 100.00

OTHER

Bottle, pocket
4⅞" h, amethyst, pattern molded, Daisy In Hexagon pattern, evidence of grinding on inside of neck and slight crack 4,750.00
5" h, amethyst, pattern molded, diamond over flute design, very strong impression 4,000.00
5⅛" h, amethyst, pattern molded, daisy diamond design 4,200.00
Bowl, miniature, amethyst, fifteen expanded diamond pattern 425.00
Christmas Light, 4" h, yellow–green, expanded diamond pattern, metal fixture 125.00
Creamer
3⅞" h, deep cobalt blue, twenty diamond mold, applied foot and handle, flake on bottom of handle, pinpoint rim flake 500.00
4⅛" h, cobalt blue, twenty expanded diamonds 300.00
Flask, 6" h, chestnut, blown clear glass, checkered diamond pattern, wear, sickness, pinpoint rim flake 725.00
Perfume Bottle, Daisy In Hexagon pattern, flake on neck 4,000.00
Salt
2⅝" h, blown blue glass, checkered diamond pattern 750.00
2¾" h, blown clear glass, ogee bowl, eighteen vertical ribs, applied petaled foot 200.00
3" h, blown deep violet–blue glass, eleven diamond mold, applied foot, minor pinpoint rim flakes ... 350.00
3⅛" h, blown deep violet–blue glass, twenty diamond mold, opalescent rim, applied foot ....:... 275.00
Sugar, cov, deep sapphire blue, eleven expanded diamond pattern **2,500.00**
Whiskey Tumbler, 2⅞" h, 2¼" d at mouth, blown cobalt blue glass, patterned molded, twelve ogival diamonds over twelve flutes design 500.00

STRETCH GLASS

History: Stretch glass was produced by many glass manufacturers in the United States between the early 1900s and the 1920s. The most prominent makers were Cambridge, Fenton (who probably manufactured more stretch glass than any of the others), Imperial, Northwood, and Steuben. Stretch glass can be identified by its iridescent, onionskin–like effect. Look for mold marks. Imported pieces are blown and show a pontil mark.

Reference: Berry Wiggins, *Stretch Glass*, Antique Publications, 1972, 1987 value update.

Collectors' Club: Stretch Glass Society, P.O. Box 770643, Lakewood, OH 44107.

Imperial, peacock, scalloped corners, 3″ h, 6½″ w, $125.00.

Ashtray, sapphire blue	15.00
Basket	
6″ h, blue, applied clear reeded handle	45.00
10¼″ d, white, applied clear handle	135.00
10½″ d, white ground, applied clear handle	135.00
Bobeches, vaseline, scalloped, pr	40.00
Bowl	
7½″ d, 3″ h, green, ftd	25.00
7½″ sq, orange, Imperial	60.00
9″ d, 4″ h, orange, flared, Imperial, cross mark	60.00
10″ d, 4½″ h, yellow irid, Imperial	85.00
12″ d, white, Fenton	40.00
13″ h, blue, wide rim, collared base	115.00
Cake Server, green, center handle	24.00
Candlesticks, pr	
8½″ h, Colonial Panels, olive–green	70.00
9½″ h, light green	50.00
10″ h, emerald green	60.00
10½″ h, vaseline	50.00
Candy Dish	
Colonial Panels pattern, 6″ d, yellow, cov	48.00
Pattern No. 636, topaz, Fenton	60.00
Cheese Dish, 4½″ d, 2½″ h, yellow ground, black edge, pedestal base, Northwood	40.00
Compote	
6″ d, 7″ h, purple	50.00
7⅝″ d, 4½″ h, green irid, clear stem, amber base	65.00
9½″ d, 5½″ h, vaseline, tree bark patterned stem, sgd "Northwood"	145.00
Console Bowl, 14″ d, red	175.00
Creamer and Sugar, Rings pattern, tangerine	75.00
Nappy, 7″ d, vaseline, Fenton	32.00
Lemonade Pitcher, celeste blue, applied cobalt handle	200.00
Nut Cup, yellow, Northwood	50.00
Pitcher, blue, applied cobalt blue handle	115.00
Plate	
6″ d, red, paneled, Imperial	50.00
8″ d, green, laurel leaf dec	20.00
8¼″ d, Aurene, gold	70.00
10″ d, brown and orange	25.00
Powder Jar, cov, ice blue	40.00
Ring Tree, 5″ d, yellow, enameled floral dec	35.00
Rose Bowl, 3½″ h, 5″ d, pink, melon ribbed	50.00
Salad Set, 14″ d bowl, six 8½″ plates, mayonnaise bowl with underplate, vaseline, c1920	115.00
Sherbet	
4″ h, red, melon ribbed	50.00
5½″ h, green, fluted	30.00
Tumbler, Colonial Panels pattern, red	95.00
Vase	
5½″ h, pink, Imperial	75.00
6″ h	
Cylindrical, rolled rim, clear ribbed interior, hand painted florals and leaves	40.00
Fan shape, ribbed, green	35.00
7″ h, vaseline, fan shape	35.00
10″ h, blue, vertical cut	50.00
11¾″ h, bud, pink	40.00

STUDIO ART

History: Studio Art of the 1990s may be the collectibles of the 21st Century. Collectors are becoming aware of some of the distinctive examples of studio glassware being currently produced. Many of the fine art glass examples we treasure today began as studio art in the preceding decades.

Collectors may decide to center their collections on specific types of glassware or a particular craftsman. Collectors should buy studio glass to be enjoyed as well as treasured. Careful documentation of additions to collections will be valuable as the collector's interests grow. Well-made, tastefully decorated glassware will surely increase in collectibility. Collectors of studio art often include paperweights in this collecting category as they are individual works of art. This is one of the most interesting and unexplored glass collecting categories in the antiques and collectibles field.

Periodical: *Glass Magazine,* New York Experimental Glass Workshop, Inc., 142 Mulberry St., New York, NY 10013.

Museums: The Chrysler Museum, Norfolk, VA; The Corning Museum of Glass, Corning, NY.

Additional Listings: Murano Glass and Paperweights.

Bell, St Clair, 6" h, yellow 60.00
Bowl
  6" d, Charles Lotton, Lansing, IL, cased, leaf and vine dec 450.00
  6¼" d, 5" h, Kosta, Swedish, heavy walled, colorless crystal, cased to green, internal dec of darker green and brown opaque random striations, sgd on base "Kosta 56675 V Lindstrand," etched on side "Kosta Sweden" 200.00
  8¼" d, 2½" h, Michael Higgins, speckled, green and aqua, three white and yellow circular designs, gold highlights 95.00
  10" d, Charles Lotton, Lansing, IL, cased, leaf and vine dec 750.00
Charger, 17" d, Michael Higgins, amethyst, chartreuse and blue geometric inclusions, sgd in gold 100.00
Lamp, 22" h, St Clair, paperweight type, white, matching paperweight finial .   145.00
Paperweight
  Charles Lotton, Lansing, IL, King Tut   90.00
  David Lotton, Lansing, IL, web design   75.00
  St Clair, green and white pulled ribbon pattern, marked "Joe St Clair"   68.00
Scent Bottle, Charles Lotton, Lansing, IL
  Multi–Flora, gold and ruby 700.00
  Sunset pattern 50.00

Sculpture, white, internal dec of black striping, applied black anthropomorphic arms, collar, and facial features, inscribed "Picasso" at side, base marked "Ermanno Nason–I.V.R. di Mazzesa–Murano," design attributed to Picasso, 11½" h, $1,210.00. Photograph courtesy of Skinner, Inc.

Sculpture, Roger Dane, volcanic glass
  16½" h, Frolicking Seal, diamond wheel carved abstract, brilliantly polished black obsidian, veins of amber striations, mounted on rect block of exotic hardwood **1,000.00**
  27" h, Nighthawk, stylized bird, cut, carved, and highly polished obsidian, flowing amber and silver–gray striations through black body, mounted on rect block of pao ferro hardwood, 1987 . . . .**2,000.00**
Vase
  4" h, Charles Lotton, Lansing, IL, web design 200.00
  5¼" h, Alton Manufacturing Co, Sandwich, MA, Trevaise, swirling irid pulled dec, double bulbed form, tooled tricon lip, crude surface, button pontil 715.00
  7" h, Charles Lotton, Lansing, IL, double multi–floral, cased **2,750.00**
  7½" h, Dorothy Thorpe, colorless, sandblasted and carved floral motif, sgd 200.00
  8" d, Charles Lotton, Lansing, IL, leaf and vine dec 250.00
  8¾" h, Leerdam, Dutch, heavy walled cylinder, colorless glass, cavities above cased in green, below cased in opal–amber, sgd "Leerdam UNKA Meydam" 100.00
  11" h, Beyers–Hudin, paperweight type, emerald green ground, three grasshoppers perched on elongated grass blades, sgd "Orient & Flume/Beyers–Hudin 1985–J35," orig label 335.00
  17" h, 19" w, Dale Chihuly Macchia Series, freeform, manipulated convoluted rim, bright yellow lip–wrap, opaque to translucent sky blue, molten state dec of horizontal stripes, random white spots, enhanced by yellow, blue, red, amber, and gold–infused green aventurine, engraved "Chihuly 1983"**6,050.00**

SWANKYSWIGS

History: Swankyswigs are decorated glass containers that were filled with Kraft Cheese Spreads. The first Swankyswigs date from the early 1930s. Production was discontinued during the last days of World War II because the paints were needed for the war effort. Production was resumed after the war ended. Several new patterns were introduced including Posy or Cornflower No. 2 (1947), Forget–Me–Not (1948), and Tulip No. 3 (1950). The last colored pattern was Bi–Centennial Tulip (1975).

In the mid–1970s, several copycat patterns emerged including: Wildlife Series (1975) and Sportsman Series (1976), most likely Canadian varieties; Rooster's Head, Cherry; Diamond over Triangle; and Circus. Kraft Cheese Spread is still available today, but in crystal–type glass.

Swankyswigs were very popular with economy minded ladies of the Depression era and used as tumblers and juice containers. They served as perfect companions to Depression glass table services and also helped to chase away the Depression blues.

The first designs were hand applied. When the popularity of Swankyswigs increased, new more and intricate machine–made patterns were introduced. Designs were test marketed. As a result of limited distribution, designs that failed are hard to identify and find.

The lack of adequate records about Swankyswigs makes it very difficult to completely identify all patterns. Since 1979, quite a few look–alikes have appeared. Although these glasses were similar, only Kraft glasses are considered Swankyswigs.

Collectors should select glasses whose pattern is clear and brightly colored. Rarer patterns include Carnival, Checkerboard, and Texas Centennial. Look–alike patterns from other manufacturers include the Rooster's Head, Cherry, Diamond over Triangle, and Circus pattern. The look–alike patterns date from the 1930s to the 1950s–60s.

References: M. D. Fountain, *Swankyswigs, Price Guide*, privately printed, 1979; Ian Warner, *Swankyswigs, A Pattern Guide Checklist*, Depression Glass Daze, 1982.

Kiddie Kup, chipmunk, brown, white trim, $2.00.

Antique
Black	2.00
Brown	2.00
Green	2.00
Orange	2.00
Band #2, red and black, 3⅜″	1.40

Bands, black and red	30.00
Bicentennial, 1938 type tulip, 1975	
Green	10.00
Red	10.00
Yellow	10.00
Bustling Betsy	
Blue	2.00
Brown	2.00
Green	2.00
Red	2.00
Carnival, fired on colors	
Dark Blue	3.00
Light Green	4.50
Orange	4.00
Red	3.00
Yellow	5.00
Checkerboard, red	25.00
Cornflower #1, light blue	2.00
Cornflower #2	
Dark Blue	1.75
Light Blue	1.75
Red	1.75
Yellow	1.40
Daisies, red daisies on top row, white in middle, green leaves	3.00
Dots and Circles	
Black	4.00
Blue	4.50
Green	3.75
Red	4.00
Forget–Me–Not	
Dark Blue	1.40
Light Blue	1.40
Red	1.40
Jonquil, yellow, green leaves	3.00
Kiddie Kup	
Black, pony and duck	1.90
Blue, pig and bear	1.90
Brown, deer and squirrel	1.90
Dark Blue, pig and bear	2.25
Green, kitten and rabbit	4.00
Orange, puppy and rooster	1.90
Red, elephant and bird	4.00
Posy	
Blue	3.00
Red	3.00
Yellow	3.00
Tulip #1	
Black	3.00
Green	3.00
Red	2.50
Tulip #2, 1938, dark and light blue	20.00
Tulip #3, yellow	2.75
Violets, blue flowers, green leaves	2.50

THREADED GLASS

History: Threaded glass is glass decorated with applied threads of glass. Before the English invention of a glass threading machine in 1876, threads were applied by hand. After this invention, threaded glass was produced in quantity by practically every major glass factory.

Threaded glass was revived by the art glass manufacturers, such as Durand and Steuben, and continues to be made today.

Bell, milk glass, red threads, brass clapper with faceted colored glass, 11" h, $75.00.

Basket, cranberry ground, ruffled top, applied clear thorn handle 175.00
Bowl, 16" d, clear ground, topaz threaded edge, controlled air bubbles, Steuben 125.00
Candlestick, 9⅞" h, clear ground, cut, flared base, bell nozzle with frosted floral and beaded dec, amethyst rim and threading in stem 175.00
Candy Jar, green ground, Steuben 80.00
Cheese Dish, cov, 7½" h, clear ground, light blue opalescent threading on upper half of bell shaped dome, faceted knob 125.00
Epergne, four purple lilies, white threading 375.00
Finger Bowl, matching underplate
  Clear ground, chartreuse threading, fluted edge, 5" d 65.00
  Cranberry ground, amber threading, 6" d, set of six, minor loss to threading 175.00
  Yellow–green opalescent ground, green threading, pr 75.00
Goblet, pink ground, threaded bowl, clear base and stem, Steuben 80.00
Honey Pot, cov, 5¾" h, 6½" w, satin finished crystal ground, pulled and twisted pattern of blue and white threads, twig finial on cov, twig–like metal frame 450.00
Lemonade Mug, 5⅜" h, clear ground, cranberry threading, Sandwich 125.00
Mayonnaise, underplate, cranberry ground, ground pontil scar 70.00
Perfume Bottle, 5½" h, clear ground, pink threading 175.00
Pitcher, 6" h, clear ground, red and clear

applied threading over entire body and neck, applied clear ruffles around base of neck, applied clear solid handle, polished pontil, attributed to Sandwich 150.00
Rose Bowl, 6" h, 5" d, clear ground, pink threading 48.00
Salt, 2¾" d, cranberry ground, opaque white threads, applied clear petal feet 75.00
Tumbler, 3⅛" h, opalescent ribbed ground, blue threads, Lutz type 25.00
Vase
  6" h, irid blue ground, gold threads . 300.00
  6½" h, cone shaped, amber ground, clear threading, three applied looped feet with strawberry pontils, English 85.00
  7" h, peacock blue ground, blue threading and white hearts, sgd "Quezal" 625.00
  7½" h, clear ground, Reeded Diamond pattern, Pomona green applied threads, Steuben fleur de lis mark 200.00
  8" h, petal top, cranberry ground, white threading, sgd "Stevens and Williams" 130.00
Wine, 7½" h, clear ground, green threads, clear stem and base, Steuben 25.00

TIFFANY

History: Louis Comfort Tiffany (1849–1934) established a glass house in 1878 primarily to make stained glass windows. There he developed a unique type of colored iridescent glass called Favrile. His Favrile glass differed from other art glass in manufacture as it was a composition of colored glass worked together while hot. The essential characteristic is that ornamentation is found within the glass. Favrile was never further decorated. Different effects were achieved by varying the amount and position of colors which project movement in form and shape.

In 1890, in order to utilize surplus materials at the plant, Tiffany began to design and produce "small glass" such as iridescent glass lamp shades, vases, and stemware and tableware in the Art Nouveau manner.

Commercial production began in 1896. Most Tiffany wares are signed with the name L. C. Tiffany or the initials L.C.T. Some pieces also carry the word "Favrile" as well as a number. A number of other marks can be found, e.g., "Tiffany Studios" and "Louis C. Tiffany Furnaces."

Louis Tiffany and the artists in his studio also are well-known for the fine work in other areas—bronzes, pottery, jewelry, silver and enamels.

References: Victor Arwas, *Glass, Art Nouveau and Art Deco*, Rizzoli International Publications, Inc., 1977; Vivienne Couldrey, *Tiffany: The Art of Louis Comfort*, Wellfleet Press, 1989; *The Art Work of Louis C. Tiffany*, Apollo Books, 1987; Robert Koch, *Louis C. Tiffany, Rebel In Glass*, Crown Publishers, Inc., 1966; John A. Shuman III, *The Collector's Encyclopedia of American Art Glass*, Collector Books, 1988, values updated 1991; Wolf Ueker, *Art Nouveau and Art Deco Lamps and Candlesticks*, Abbeville Press, 1987.

Periodicals: *Antique Glass Quarterly*, Rudi Publishing, P. O. Box 1364, Iowa City, IA 52244; *Glass Collector's Digest*, Antique Publications, P. O. Box 553, Marietta, OH 45750–0553; *Glass Magazine*, New York Experimental Glass Workshop, 142 Mulberry St., New York, NY 10013.

Museums: Bergstrom–Mahler Museum, Neenah, WI; Historical Glass Museum, Redlands, CA; The Chrysler Museum, Norfolk, VA; The Corning Museum of Glass, Corning, NY; The Toledo Museum of Art, Toledo, OH.

Bottle, 6½" h, sq, orange translucent Favrile glass, metallic blue, purple, and green swirled and pulled opaque bottom, sgd "L.C.T. T5224," small bubble burst hole on base **700.00**
Bowl
  4½" d, circular, pinched in, scalloping rim, Favrile, gold, engraved "L. C. T." **275.00**
  6" d, 1¾" h, diamond quilted patterned body, amber dish with opal white shading to deep blue rim dec, sgd "L.C.Tiffany Favrile 1264" .. **375.00**
  6" d, 2¼" h, flared blue and opal white, wheel cut grape leaves and vines inside base, sgd "L.C.Tiffany Favrile" **500.00**
  8" d, 2¾" h, flattened, flaring stretch rim of pastel lavender, opalescent reactive star pattern, marked "L. C. T. Favrile 1855" **670.00**
Candlesticks, pr, 4" h, urn form nozzle, downward curving drip pan, spherical standard, quilted circular foot, inscribed "L. C. Tiffany–Favrile 1846," orig paper label **1,800.00**
Candy Dish, 4" h, translucent foot and stem, shallow dish, widely flaring scalloped rim, white linear dec, crackled blue irid, inscribed "L. C. T. Favrile 1924" **950.00**
Centerpiece, 12¼" d, widely flaring circular rim, gently ribbed, raised leaves, all over crackled gold and mir-

ror irid, inscribed "1925 L. C. Tiffany–Favrile" **1,155.00**
Compote
  2¼" h, Favrile, pastel, white radiating stripes from center to mint green stretched rim, engraved "L. C. T. Favrile 1871" **385.00**
  2½" h, 7½" d, dark blue with blue, green, and purple irid stretched surface, wheel engraved forget–me–not blossom border, sgd "L. C. Tiffany Inc. Favrile W" **1,210.00**
  2¾" h, 4¼" d, ten ribbed gold irid bowl, baluster stem, raised foot, sgd "L.C.T. Favrile", stress marks at edge curve **300.00**
  3" h, 5⅛" d, pastel, flared, leaf design interior, stretched irid green surface, opal stem, disk foot, sgd "L. C. Tiffany Favrile 5–1700" ... **770.00**
  3¼" h, Favrile, pastel, white feather design radiating from center to mint green rim, engraved "L. C. T. Favrile 1700" **385.00**
  3¼" h, 5⅛" d, pastel, flared, irid aqua green, opal leaf dec interior, opalescent stem and disk foot, sgd "L. C. T. Favrile 1406" **440.00**
  3½" h, Favrile, gold, engraved "L. C. T.," set of six **1,100.00**
  3½" h, 6¼" d, purple irid, ribbed flared blue bowl, baluster stem, folded platform base, sgd "L.C.T. Favrile" **1,045.00**
  4¾" h, 5¼" d, floriform, stretched irid amber, green pulled feather dec, ruffled and flared rim, sgd "L. C. Tiffany–Favrile 7280C" **880.00**
  8¼" d, Favrile, gold, quilted pattern, knopped stem, circular foot, engraved "L. C. T. Favrile" **900.00**
Cordial, conical, etched frieze of grape clusters, vines, and leaves, slender stem, gold irid, inscribed "L. C. T.," set of seven **1,800.00**
Decanter Set, Moravignian pattern, 9" h peacock irid stoppered double gourd decanter, applied lily pads and tendrils dec, eleven matching gold irid globular cordials, each pc inscribed "L. C. T." **2,000.00**
Dish
  4¾" d, Favrile, gold, scalloped rim, engraved "L. C. T." **190.00**
  6" d, Favrile, pastel, silver rim, engraved "1898 L. C. Tiffany Favrile" **225.00**
Goblet
  6½" h, Favrile, gold, intaglio carved grapes, tendrils, and vines, engraved "L. C. T." **385.00**
  7¾" h, pastel, transparent, yellow, opalescent, ribbed, double bulbed

hollow stem, marked "L. C. Tiffany–Favrile" **440.00**
Humidor, cov, 9½" h, cylindrical, Favrile, gold, leafy green vine descending one side, gilt bronze inner cov and monogrammed lid, imp "Tiffany Studios, New York, 22504,6" **1,450.00**
Jack-In-The-Pulpit Vase, 19" h, irid gold, pink, blue, and lavender highlights, flared and ruffled flower blossom rim, narrow tapered stem, bulbed base, marked "L. C. T. Y4807" **9,900.00**
Juice Glass, applied lily pad and trailing stems, inscribed "L. C. T.," set of eleven **2,400.00**

Lamp, leaded shade of red, yellow, and orange poppies, shaded green ground, blue leaf border, stamped "Tiffany Studios New York 1531," gilt bronze base, 27" h, 20" d shade, $17,500.00. Photograph courtesy of William Doyle Galleries.

Lamp
  Candle, electrified
    12" h, blue irid, spiral twisted candlestick, matching Favrile glass and gilt metal insert supporting ruffled shade, sgd "L.C.T. Favrile" **2,310.00**
    17½" h, gold irid, tall spiral swirled candlestick, sgd "Gorham" silver and celluloid spring riser, ruffled Favrile glass shade, sgd "LCT," base labeled and star drilled for electricity **935.00**
  Chandelier, 9¼" h, 20½" d, Acorn, leaded Favrile glass, dome, early dichroic golden amber to green mottled glass segments, symmetrically repeating motif of opal gold stylized acorns, bronze beaded

rim, triple drop chains, six light central fixture **7,150.00**
Table
    22" h, 16" d Favrile leaded shade, Pomegranate pattern, mottled dichroic green–amber segments, stylized border of opal blue–green, green, and yellow, rim imp "Tiffany Studios New York 1457," bronze base imp "Tiffany Studios New York 533" **10,500.00**
    24½" h, 14" d shade, opaline glass dome shade, gilt metal twisted wire and swirled scrolling design casing, fluid reservoir with mercury–lined opal glass sphere, ornate classical columnar trifid base, electrified, small chips inside base rim **6,650.00**
Lamp Shade, 4½" l, lily, Favrile, pale gold, pink and white striations, Tiffany Studios **275.00**
Loving Cup, 7⅜" h, waisted cylindrical, Favrile, three scrolling handles, gold ground, green leaf and vine dec, engraved "471H, L. C. Tiffany–Favrile," small cracks **500.00**
Miniature
    Jardiniere, 2⅛" h, irid, gold, two pulled body handles, marked "L. C. T. W2375," circular paper label **467.50**
    Vase, Favrile, ovoid, opal white, five green double pulled and hooked feather dec, irid gold striations, marked "L. C. T. Y4747" **1,320.00**
Paperweight, 5¾" l, 4¾" w, turtleback, oval, gold irid tile mounted to conforming bronze frame, four disk feet, gold dore smooth finish, imp "Tiffany Studios New York 935" **935.00**
Perfume Bottle, 4¼" h, globular, short cylindrical neck, everted lip, ball shaped stopper, irid green trailing vine and ivy leaves dec, irid amber ground, shaded with pink, numbered, inscribed "L. C. Tiffany, Favrile," c1916 .... **1,000.00**
Salt, 1¼" h, 3¼" d, blue irid, ten ribs, crimped rim, sgd "L.C.T. Favrile" .. **525.00**
Serving Set, 9 pcs, 10" d serving bowl, four small bowls with matching undertrays, gold irid, marked "L. C. T." and/or "Favrile" **1,870.00**
Vase
    3" h, gold cased to opal, five green and gold pulled double feather designs, sgd "L.C.T. 5187D" **1,550.00**
    3½" h, classic oval, brilliant irid red Favrile, three gold and blue triple–pulled and hooked feather dec, sgd "L.C.T. 9356A" **4,500.00**
    3¾" h, freeform, irregularly rib

molded, amber irid, spotty pink–gold highlights, sgd and numbered, tiny rim rough spot **450.00**

4¼" h, Favrile, heavy walled double bulbed design, gold amber with five green leaf forms, gold pulled irid veins, marked "L. C. T. W8888" **2,090.00**

5" h, amber glass, swirled and coiled irid blue dec, button wafer, sgd "L.C.T. H1753" **1,430.00**

6" h, Favrile, gold, goblet form with eight dimpled ribs, conforming cupped disk foot, all over gold irid dec, marked "L. C. Tiffany–Favrile 3836C" **660.00**

6¼" h, gold irid body cased to opal white, medial band of green chain design, sgd "L.C.T. 2388B," orig label, minor orig imperfections in glass **1,200.00**

Sherbet, Favrile glass, wide ruffled rim, gold irid, green pulled feather design, inscribed "5689G L. C. Tiffany Favrile," 4½" h, $850.00. Photograph courtesy of William Doyle Galleries.

6½" h, Cypriote, green body overlaid with blue–black metallic irid glass, three lustrous gold leaf form decorations, all over crackled and pitted surface, sgd "LCT/K1476" **10,000.00**

7" h, Favrile, baluster shape, blue with silvery blue irid surface, sgd "L. C. Tiffany–Favrile 1145–5155W" **990.00**

7½" h, Favrile, ovoid, sq notched rim, green with vertical black and gold feathered stripes, intaglio rim border, engraved "L. C. T. R1605" . . **2,750.00**

8½" h, bud, elongated ten ribbed bulbed amber body, satin irid, sgd "L.C.T. 4970A," orig paper label . **700.00**

8¾" h, Egyptian form, amber body, internal dot and zipper dec, script sgd "L. C. T. A1802" **1,320.00**

9" h, baluster, irid amber–gold, green leaf and vine pulled dec, six leaves wheel cut in naturalistic finely de-

tailed cameo carving, two additional carved leaves at rim, sgd "L.C.Tiffany Favrile 6085," internal carbon specks in green leaf areas **3,100.00**

9¼" h

Bulbous double gourd shape, internally dec with swirling irid gold, amber, white, and brown striations, early signature "L.C.T. A1225" **2,300.00**

Floriform, irid gold, oval, fluted, green heart and vine dec, bulbed stem, ribbed folded foot, marked "L. C. Tiffany–Favrile 5060D" . **1,100.00**

10" h, bud, elongated conical body, dark cobalt blue, silvery blue irid, sgd "L.C.Tiffany Favrile X202" . . . **950.00**

10¼" h, Favrile, floriform, opalescent, five green and gold striated pulled leaf designs, bulbed stem, cupped ribbed pedestal foot, gold irid interior and under foot, marked "L. C. T. W4475" **3,850.00**

11½" h, floriform, transparent, aquamarine, ribbed, pale gold pulled petals below opalescent green border, bulbed stem, folded disk foot, marked "L. C. T. 1420," "T. G. D. Co." label **2,090.00**

11¾" h

Floriform, transparent, opal, gold and green ruffled flower blossoms form cupped pedestal disk, sgd "L.C.T. Q1858," interior water stain **1,210.00**

Trumpet, Favrile, cream ground, gold and green feather pull dec, engraved "LCT" on circular bronze foot, pineapple knop, imp "Tiffany Studios, New York 1043" **1,350.00**

12½" h, bud, twenty ribbed bulbous amber body, strong orange–gold irid, sgd "L.C.T. W2709" **1,300.00**

13½" h, trumpet, twelve ribbed flared amber flute, conforming cupped pedestal foot, outer edge marked "L.C.T. Favrile" **1,000.00**

14¼" h, Favrile, trumpet, pastel, pink and white stripes, pale yellow knopped stem, circular foot, engraved "1900 L. C. Tiffany Favrile" **1,650.00**

15" h, Favrile, floriform, white bowl, green stem, green feather pulls, gold lining, domed gold foot, engraved "L. C. T. R9722" **8,250.00**

25½" h, floor, flared gold irid glass cylinder, five green pulled leaves around lower half, sgd "L.C.T.," four ftd bronze cup on ribbed platform base, imp "Tiffany Studios New York 715" **2,500.00**

c1960

TIFFIN GLASS

History: A. J. Beatty & Sons built a glass manufacturing plant in Tiffin, Ohio, in 1888. On January 1, 1892, the firm joined the U. S. Glass Co. and was known as factory "R." Quality and production at this factory were very high and resulted in fine Depression era glass.

Beginning in 1916 wares were marked with a paper label. From 1923 to 1936, Tiffin produced a line of black glassware, called Black Satin. The company discontinued operation in 1980.

References: Fred Bickenheuser, *Tiffin Glassmasters, Book I,* Glassmasters Publications, 1979; Fred Bickenheuser, *Tiffin Glassmasters, Book II,* Glassmasters Publications, 1981; Fred W. Bickenheuser, *Tiffin Glassmasters, Book III,* Glassmasters Publications, 1985.

Collectors' Club: Tiffin Glass Collectors Club, P.O. Box 554, Tiffin, OH 44883.

Advertising
  Ashtray, Carnegie National Bank, 1902–1928, 6" d 30.00
  Jar, Heinz, crystal, 21" h 75.00
Basket, Black Satin 40.00
Cake Plate
  Flanders pattern, crystal, 10½" d, handle 50.00
  Shaggy Rose pattern 15.00
Candy Jar, cov, vaseline, frosted stripes 40.00
Center Bowl, Juno pattern, Mandarin yellow, 11" d, three toes 37.00
Center Piece, Canterbury pattern
  Flame and crystal, 7⅝" d 150.00
  Ruby and crystal, 6" d 150.00
Champagne
  Cadena pattern, Mandarin yellow .. 15.00
  Cherokee Rose pattern, crystal 18.00
  Empire pattern, rose 28.00
  Eternally Yours pattern, crystal 10.00
  Flanders pattern
    Crystal 14.00
    Topaz 25.00
  Fontaine pattern
    Green 30.00
    Pink 30.00
  Fuchsia pattern, crystal 18.00
  June Night pattern, crystal 18.00
  Persian Pheasant pattern, crystal 24.00
  Shawl Dancer pattern, crystal
    Plain stem 18.00
    Puffed stem 25.00

Cigarette Holder, Copen Blue pattern . 65.00
Claret
  Canterbury pattern, citron 17.50
  Cherokee Rose pattern, crystal 32.50
  June Night pattern, crystal 32.50
  Persian Pheasant pattern, crystal 30.00
Cocktail
  Cherokee Rose pattern, crystal 24.00
  Classic pattern, crystal 35.00
  Diana pattern, floral etched panel, crystal, ... 15.00
  Fuchsia pattern, crystal 18.00
  June Night pattern, crystal 25.00
  Persian Pheasant pattern, crystal 20.00
Compote, Palais Versailles pattern, gold 100.00
Console Bowl, amberina 70.00
Cordial
  Diana pattern, floral etched panel, crystal 24.00
  Flanders pattern, crystal 55.00
  Fuchsia pattern, crystal 45.00
  June Night pattern, crystal 40.00
  Killarny pattern, green 20.00
  Palais Versailles pattern, gold 40.00
  Persian Pheasant pattern, crystal 40.00
  Rambling Rose pattern, crystal 35.00
  Wisteria pattern, crystal 45.00
Cornucopia, Copen Blue pattern, 8¼" l vase 75.00
Creamer
  Cerice pattern, ftd 25.00
  June Night pattern, crystal 25.00
Creamer and Sugar
  Canterbury pattern, Twilight 75.00
  Flanders pattern, crystal 30.00
  June Night pattern, crystal 50.00
  Rosalind pattern, yellow 85.00
Creamer and Sugar, matching tray, Cerice pattern, crystal 95.00
Cup and Saucer
  Flanders pattern crystal 35.00
  Primo pattern, green 6.00
  Sylvan pattern, pink 35.00
Decanter, Cadena pattern, stopper, Mandarin yellow 225.00
Flower arranger, crystal, 2" h 85.00
Goblet
  Cerice pattern, crystal, pulled stem . 20.00
  Cherokee Rose pattern, crystal 22.00
  Empire pattern, rose 32.00
  Eternally Yours pattern, crystal 15.00
  Flanders pattern
    Crystal 17.75
    Pink 35.00
  Fontaine pattern
    Pink 40.00
    Twilight 47.50
  Fuchsia pattern, crystal, tall 24.00
  June Night pattern, crystal
    Crystal 22.00
    Crystal, gold trim 25.00
  La Fleur pattern, 8" h, topaz 32.00

Persian Pheasant pattern, crystal **24.00**
Rambling Rose pattern, crystal **23.00**
Shawl Dancer pattern, crystal, puffed
stem **20.00**
Wisteria pattern, crystal **25.00**
Iced Tea Tumbler
Byzantine pattern, crystal, black base **15.00**
Canterbury pattern, citron **15.00**
Cerice pattern, crystal, ftd **24.00**
Cherokee Rose pattern, crystal **24.00**
Classic pattern, crystal, green foot .. **45.00**
Flanders pattern
Topaz, ftd **22.50**
Yellow **24.00**
Fuchsia pattern, crystal, 15 oz **26.00**
June Night pattern, crystal, ftd **32.00**
Rambling Rose pattern, crystal **23.00**
Shawl Dancer pattern, crystal, cone
shape **20.00**
Jug, Shawl Dancer pattern, crystal **175.00**
Juice Tumbler
Cherokee Rose pattern, crystal, 5 oz **25.00**
Cordella pattern, Mandarin yellow,
.... **15.00**
Diana pattern, crystal, floral etched
panel, ftd **16.00**
Fontaine pattern, green **30.00**
Wisteria pattern, crystal **25.00**
Lamp, Torchere, Santa Maria pattern,
orange ground **295.00**
Marmalade Jar, cov, Jungle pattern,
green satin, painted parrots dec and
floral sprays, handles **100.00**
Mayonnaise, Cadena pattern, Mandarin
yellow, 3 pcs **40.00**
Oyster Cocktail, Fuchsia pattern, crystal **17.00**
Parfait
Flying Nun pattern, green **40.00**
Persian Pheasant pattern, crystal **24.00**
Perfume Bottle, Black Satin, hand
painted florals, tong applicator, 6" h **75.00**
Pitcher, La Fleur pattern, topaz **225.00**
Plate
Byzantine pattern, crystal, 10½" d .. **35.00**
Cadena pattern, Mandarin yellow,
dinner **30.00**
Cerice pattern, crystal, 12" d **45.00**
Empire pattern, Twilight, 8" d **17.50**
Flanders pattern
6" d
Crystal, ruffled **6.00**
Pink **12.50**
6¾" d, crystal **12.00**
8" d
Crystal, scratch **12.00**
Pink **17.50**
10½" d, yellow **35.00**
Fontaine pattern, 8" d
Green **15.00**
Pink **15.00**
June Night pattern, crystal, 8" d **16.50**
La Fleur pattern, yellow, 7½" d **12.50**

Othello Ebony pattern, 10¾" d, din-
ner **25.00**
Rosalind pattern, yellow, 10½" **35.00**
Shawl Dancer pattern, crystal, 7½" d **15.00**
Wisteria pattern, red, 8" d **16.00**
Relish
Cherokee Rose pattern, crystal, three
sections, 6¾" d **35.00**
Rambling Rose pattern, crystal,
round, three parts **17.50**
Saucer
Fontaine pattern, green **8.00**
Rosalind pattern, yellow **3.00**
Sherbet
Canterbury pattern, citron **12.50**
Diana pattern, floral etched panel,
crystal, low **12.00**
Flying Nun pattern, green **25.00**
Fuchsia pattern, crystal **15.00**
Rambling Rose pattern, crystal **16.00**
Sherry, Persian Pheasant pattern, crystal **20.00**
Sugar
Cherokee Rose pattern, crystal **22.50**
Flying Nun pattern, green **65.00**
Sundae
Cerice pattern, crystal **18.00**
Fontaine pattern, green **25.00**
Tankard, Swedish Modern pattern,
blown, crystal **60.00**
Tray, Birch Tree pattern, Deerwood
pink, center handle **45.00**
Tumbler
Byzantine pattern, Mandarin yellow,
ftd **20.00**
Cadena pattern, Mandarin yellow,
ftd, 5" h **20.00**
Cordella pattern, Mandarin yellow,
ftd **25.00**
Flanders pattern
Mandarin Yellow, 4¾" h, ftd **21.00**
Topaz, 9 oz, ftd **15.00**

**Vase, black ground, red coralene flowers,
6½" h, $55.00.**

Vase
Acid Cut Back, carnations, crystal, 6"
h **34.00**
Cerice pattern, crystal, bud, 10½" h **45.00**

Cherokee Rose pattern, crystal, bud
10¼" h, straight base **50.00**
10½" h **45.00**
Dahlia pattern, green satin, 10½" h .   **35.00**
Dawn pattern, lavender, 8½" h **135.00**
Empress pattern, smoke, 11¾" h . . .   **150.00**
Heliotrope pattern, 7¼" h **30.00**
Poppy pattern, pink **40.00**
Princess pattern, crystal, 4" h **22.50**
Swedish Modern pattern, blown,
crystal, 11½" h **55.00**
Teardrop pattern **110.00**
Whiskey
Flanders pattern, pink, ftd **65.00**
La Fleur pattern, topaz, ftd **12.50**
Wine
Cherokee Rose pattern **35.00**
Cordella pattern, crystal **14.50**
Eternally Yours pattern, crystal **14.75**
Flanders pattern, yellow **30.00**
Fuchsia pattern, crystal **35.00**
June Night pattern, crystal **35.00**
Psyche pattern, green **50.00**

TOOTHPICK HOLDERS

History: Toothpick holders, indispensable table accessories of the Victorian era, are small containers used to hold toothpicks.

They were made in a wide range of materials: china, glass (art, blown, cut, opalescent, pattern, etc.), and metals. Makers include both American and European firms.

Toothpick holders were used as souvenir items by applying decals or transfers. The same blank may contain several different location labels.

References: William Heacock, *Encyclopedia Of Victorian Colored Pattern Glass, Book I, Toothpick Holders From A To Z*, Antique Publications, 1981; William Heacock, *1,000 Toothpick Holders: A Collector's Guide*, Antique Publications, 1977; William Heacock, *Rare & Unlisted Toothpick Holders*, Antique Publications, 1984.

Collectors' Club: National Toothpick Collector's Society, P. O. Box 246, Sawyer, MI 49125.

Reproduction Alert: Reproduction toothpick holders abound. Carefully examining details on these small glass objects can be a challenge but often it is the best way to spot a reproduction.

ART GLASS AND COLORED GLASS

Alexandrite, Honeycomb pattern, shot
glass shape, straight rim, 2⅛" h **500.00**
Amberina
Daisy and Button pattern, intense
fuchsia pattern **385.00**

Cameo glass, Weis, shaded yellow–orange, layered orange and black, sunset riverside landscape, sgd "Weis" in cameo, 2¾" h, **$275.00.** Photograph courtesy of Skinner, Inc.

Venetian Diamond pattern, sq top,
round base **250.00**
Burmese, acid finish
Diamond Quilted pattern, tricorn . . .   **250.00**
Florals, berries, and oak leaf dec, hex-
agonal rim **350.00**
Carnival, Kitten pattern, amethyst, Fen-
ton **150.00**
Cranberry
Coin Spot pattern, pedestal **165.00**
Optic Thumbprint pattern **95.00**
Cut Glass, pedestal
Chain of hobstars **135.00**
Diamonds, fans, and cross–hatching,
rayed base **120.00**
Ovoid, blown blank, floral dec **75.00**
Depression Glass, Star, pattern, clear,
Federal Glass, c1910–14 . . . .   **45.00**
Greentown
Dog Head, frosted **125.00**
Wild Rose with Bowknot pattern,
chocolate **175.00**
Heisey
Fandango pattern **85.00**
Figural, urn **120.00**
Priscilla pattern **48.00**
Pomona, amber ruffled rim, clear body,
fan shaped, ftd **400.00**
Steuben, Grecian Urn, pedestal, applied
"M" shape handles, 2½" h **185.00**

FIGURAL

Alligator, milk glass, c1885 . . . .   **50.00**
Baby Bootie, amber, c1890–95 . . . . . .   **38.00**
Bird, yellow ground, opaque body . . .   **25.00**
Domino, clear **50.00**
Elephant, amber, c1890 . . . .   **65.00**
Kitten on pillow, clear **95.00**
Petticoat Hat, vaseline, gold trim **130.00**
Pig, pink **75.00**
Saddle over barrel, ruby stained **95.00**
Top Hat, fine cut, clear **45.00**
Tramp Shoe, white, milk glass **50.00**

OPAQUE GLASS

Custard
Bees on Basket pattern, sq, blue and
gold trim **85.00**
Chrysanthemum Sprig pattern, sgd
"Northwood" **150.00**
Diamond Peg pattern, hand painted
florals **75.00**
Tiny Thumbprint pattern **65.00**
Winged Scroll pattern, gold trim,
Heisey mark **165.00**
Milk Glass
Fern Heart pattern, gold trim **50.00**
Parrot and Top Hat pattern, c1895 . **28.00**
Rose Urn pattern, dec, two handles,
Fostoria Glass Co, c1905 .... **38.00**
Scroll pattern, claw foot, light pink
and blue dec, c1900 .... **40.00**
Sunset pattern **40.00**
Mount Washington, Ribbed pattern,
satin finish, white ground, hand
painted blue flowers **165.00**

OPALESCENT GLASS

Beatty Honeycomb, clear ground **45.00**
Chrysanthemum pattern, cranberry
ground, white opalescent stripes ... **145.00**
Diamond Spearhead pattern, vaseline . **85.00**
Reverse Swirl pattern, blue ground,
speckled **85.00**
Ribbed Lattice pattern, blue ground ... **145.00**
Windows pattern, blue ground **95.00**
Wreath and Shell pattern, blue ground **300.00**

PATTERN GLASS

Alabama, clear **60.00**
Arched Fleur–de–lis, clear **30.00**
Atlas, etched, clear **35.00**
Banded Portland, maiden's blush stain,
gold trim **45.00**
Beveled Diamond and Star, ruby stained **80.00**
Button Arches, ruby stained, souvenir of
Battleview, NJ **30.00**
California, green with gold **60.00**
Champion, clear **20.00**
Colorado, emerald green, gold trim ... **40.00**
Croesus, emerald green, trifid **85.00**
Eureka, ruby stained **65.00**
Florette, opaque, turquoise **100.00**
Intaglio Sunflower, clear **25.00**
Iris with Meander, light green **55.00**
Kansas, clear **45.00**
King's Crown, clear **40.00**
Ladders with Diamonds, clear **30.00**
Michigan, clear, yellow stain **175.00**
Minnesota, clear **35.00**
Monkey, clear, 3¾" h **45.00**
Pennsylvania, emerald green, gold trim **55.00**
Ruby Thumbprint, ruby stained **45.00**

Scalloped Six Point, clear, flared rim .. **35.00**
Scroll with Cane Band, ruby stained .. **90.00**
Shamrock, ruby stained, souvenir in-
scription **45.00**
Spearpoint Band, ruby stained **80.00**
Swag with Brackets, amethyst, gold dec **85.00**
Teardrop and Cracked Ice, clear,
c1900–03 .... **75.00**
Texas, clear, gold trim **27.00**
Three Face, clear **50.00**
Truncated Cube, ruby stained **45.00**
Twisted Hobnail, clear **50.00**
Vermont, green, gold dec **65.00**
Wisconsin, clear **40.00**

KEW-BLAS

1853

UNION GLASS COMPANY

History: Amory and Francis Houghton established the Union Glass Company, Somerville,
Massachusetts, in 1851. The company went
bankrupt in 1860, but was reorganized. Between
1870 and 1885 the Union Glass Company made
pressed glass and blanks for cut glass.

Art glass production began in 1893 under the
direction of William S. Blake and Julian de Cor-
dova. Two styles were introduced. A Venetian
style consisted of graceful shapes in colored
glass, often flecked with gold. An iridescent
glass, labeled Kew Blas, was made in plain and
decorated forms. The pieces are close in design
and form to Quezel products, but lack the sub-
tlety of Tiffany items.

The company ceased production in 1924.

Reference: John A. Shuman III, *The Collector's
Encyclopedia of American Art Glass,* Collector
Books, 1988, value update 1991.

**Bowl, green dec on cream ground, irid
interior, sgd, 4⅞" d, 4¼" h, $475.00.**

Bowl
5" d, irid gold ground, flared, ribbed **200.00**
14" d, red ground, pulled feather dec,
sgd **1,200.00**
Candlesticks, pr, 8½" h, irid gold
ground, twisted stems **725.00**
Compote, 7" h, irid gold ground, pink
highlights, twisted stem, ribbed bowl **375.00**
Creamer, 3¼" h, irid gold ground, ap-
plied handle **225.00**
Cuspidor, 5¾" d, 2½" h, amber ground,
irid gold dec, squatty, flattened flared
rim, sgd "Kew Blas" **275.00**
Decanter, 14" h, green–gold irid
ground, spherical long stemmed stop-
per, sgd **375.00**
Dish, 5½" d, irid gold ground, shaped
rim, shallow round bowl, sgd "Kew
Blas" on base **200.00**
Finger Bowl and Underplate, 5" d bowl,
6" d plate, metallic luster, gold and
platinum highlights ribbed, scalloped
border **465.00**
Goblet
4¾" h, irid gold ground, curved stem **200.00**
6" h, irid gold ground, knob stem . . **350.00**
Pitcher
4½" h, irid gold ground, green pulled
feather pattern, deep gold irid lining, applied swirl handle, sgd
"Kew–Blas" **800.00**
5" h, King Tut, white ground, green
and gold irid dec, irid blue lining,
blue handle, sgd **1,900.00**
Rose Bowl, 3½" h, butterscotch ground,
green and gold hooked dec, gold lin-
ing **525.00**
Salt, irid gold ground **200.00**
Sherbet, 5" h, irid gold ground **200.00**
Tumbler, 4" h, irid gold ground, pinched
sides, sgd **185.00**
Vase
4" h, ovoid, ivory ground, gold rim,
gold pulled feather dec, engraved
"Kew–Blas" **375.00**
4½" h, irid gold ground, green all
over snake skin pattern, scalloped
rim, sgd **650.00**
5" h, white ground, green and gold
pulled feather, spherical, rolled
gold rim, sgd **475.00**
6¼" h, pale orange ground, gold and
green swags, cylinder, rolled rim,
early 20th C, sgd, orig paper label **600.00**
7" h, irid butterscotch ground, pulled
feather dec, bulbous, flared, sgd**1,500.00**
7½" h
Baluster, white irid ground, amber
irid border, green pulled wave
pattern, scalloped everted
mouth, irid amber lining, in-
scribed "Kew Blas," early 20th C **375.00**

Flared, irid blue ground, sgd **900.00**
7¾" h, irid opalescent ground, pulled
green and gold Zipper pattern, sgd **950.00**
12½" h, irid gold ground, blue and
pink irid highlights, baluster, wa-
isted **750.00**
Wine Glass, 4¾" h, irid gold ground,
curving stem **185.00**

VALLERYSTAHL GLASS

History: Vallerystahl (Lorraine), France, has been
a glass producing center for centuries. In 1872
two major factories, Vallerystahl glassworks and
Portieux glassworks, merged and produced art
glass until 1898. Later, pressed glass covered animal dishes were introduced. The factory continues operation today.

**Salt, cobalt blue, ram's head dec, three
feet, 2½" d, 1½" h, marked, $45.00.**

Animal Dish, cov
Cow, 7" h, clear, pasture scene on cov **90.00**
Dog, patterned quilt top, raised flow-
ers on base, white milk glass, sgd **165.00**
Fish, white milk glass **90.00**
Hen, nest base, blue milk glass **90.00**
Rabbit, 6" h, white, frosted **60.00**
Robin, nest base, white milk glass . . **125.00**
Snail, figural strawberry base, white
milk glass, sgd **90.00**
Swan, blue milk glass **100.00**
Box, cov
3" h, 5" d, cameo, dark green ground,
applied and cut dec, sgd **950.00**
4" h, 3½" d, blue milk glass **85.00**
Breakfast Set, hen cov dish, six egg
cups, basket form master salt, and
tray, white milk glass, nine pcs **450.00**

Butter Dish, cov, figural
  Radish, white milk glass **95.00**
  Turtle, snail finial, white milk glass . **100.00**
Candlesticks, pr
  Baroque pattern, amber **75.00**
  Grecian Girl, frosted **90.00**
Candy Dish, 4⅛" d, white milk glass,
  basketweave base, rope handles and
  finial **90.00**
Compote, 6¼" d, 6¼" h, sq, blue milk
  glass **75.00**
Dish, cov, figural, lemon, white milk
  glass, sgd **65.00**
Goblet, blue milk glass, ftd **65.00**
Mustard, cov, swirled ribs, scalloped,
  matching cov with slot for spoon,
  blue milk glass **25.00**
Pitcher, Grape and Leaf pattern, vase-
  line, frosted **35.00**
Plate
  6" d, Thistle pattern, green **65.00**
  7½" d, floral dec, blue milk glass . .   **45.00**
  8" d, Thistle pattern, green **70.00**
Salt, cov, hen on nest, white opal **35.00**
Sugar, cov, 5" h, Strawberry pattern, salamander finial, white milk glass, gold
  trim **75.00**
Tumbler, 4" h, blue **40.00**
Vase
  8" h, cylindrical, Optic Diamond pat-
    tern, green, painted rose thistles,
    sgd **150.00**
  9¾" h, swelled cylindrical, scalloped
    rim, opalescent blue ground, cased
    in burgundy, intaglio carved cro-
    cus, engraved "Vallerystahl" **950.00**

1889

VAL SAINT-LAMBERT

History: Val Saint–Lambert, a twelfth century
Cistercian abbey, was located during different
historical periods in France, the Netherlands, and
Belgium (1930 to present). In 1822 Francois
Kemlin and Auguste Lelievre, along with a group
of financiers, bought the abbey and opened a
glassworks. In 1846 Val Saint–Lambert merged
with the Société Anonyme des Manufactures de
Glaces, Verres à Vitre, Cristaux et Gobeletaries.
The company bought many other glassworks.

Val Saint–Lambert developed a reputation for
technological progress in the glass industry. In
1879 Val Saint–Lambert became an independent
company employing 4,000 workers. Val Saint–
Lambert concentrated on the export market mak-

ing table glass, cut, engraved, etched, and
molded pieces, and chandeliers. Some pieces
were finished in other countries, e.g., silver
mounts added in the United States.

Val Saint–Lambert executed many special
commissions for the artists of the Art Nouveau
and Art Deco periods. The tradition continues.
The company also made cameo–etched vases,
covered boxes, and bowls. The firm celebrated
its 150th anniversary in 1975.

**Vase, pale yellow quatraform body, acid
etched fern leaf design, deep red overlay,
cut back poinsettia blossom design, attributed to Val St. Lambert, 7¾" h,
$440.00. Photo courtesy of Skinner, Inc.**

Ashtray, shell, gold label **5.00**
Bottle, 6⅞" h, green vines and flowers
  dec, clear acid finished ground, green
  cut to clear overlay edge, sgd "Val/St
  Lambert" **90.00**
Bowl
  6½" d, cov, deep cut purple florals,
    frosted ground, sgd "Val St Lam-
    bert" **750.00**
  8" d, floral swag dec, sgd **75.00**
Chest Set, crystal, clear crystal half,
  green and clear crystal remaining
  half, each pc labeled and sgd, 6½" h
  tallest pc **300.00**
Cologne Bottle, 6¾" h, frosted cranberry
  ground, fuchsia flowers and leaves,
  gold colored collar and screw stop-
  per, sgd "Cristaherie Le Gantin" . . . **450.00**
Dresser Jar, cov, 4¾" d, double cut, ruby
  cut to clear, sgd **100.00**
Dresser Set, atomizer and cov powder
  jar, cranberry cut to clear, sgd **175.00**
Goblet, 5⅜" h, clear, blown mold, ap-
  plied foot and stem **45.00**
Jar, cov, 5½" h, 3½" d, cranberry cut to
  clear, narrow cut panels, star cut
  base, multi-faceted knob **90.00**
Pitcher, clear, paneled, diamond shaped
  cuttings, sgd **85.00**
Plate, Van Dyck **65.00**
Sculpture, Madonna, solid crystal **90.00**
Tumbler, 6" h, blue cut to clear, gilt
  cameo classical band, set of six **350.00**

Vase, smoky opalescent flattened oval body, layered in green, yellow, red, and dark burgundy, tall trees centering a sail boat and distant shore, sgd "VSL" in cameo at side, 6¼" h, $1,100.00. Photograph courtesy of Skinner, Inc.

Vase
  6¼" h, cameo, flattened oval, smoky opalescent ground, green, yellow, red, and dark burgundy overlay, cameo cut scene, tall trees, center sail boat and distant shore, cameo sgd "VSL" at side **1,100.00**
  7¾" h, quatraform, pale yellow ground, acid etched ferns, deep red overlay cut poinsettia blossom, chip at base edge **440.00**
  8½" h, Art Deco style, gray **275.00**
  10" h
    Art Deco style, maroon and clear **650.00**
    Ribbed body, hand painted wine colored blossoms connected by gold branches of thorns, gold accents, ruffled top **200.00**
  23¾", slender neck, wide sloping foot, cameo, clear glass overlaid with white, brown, and green, c1900 .... **5,000.00**
Wine Glass, intaglio cut, ribbons, bows, and cranberry cameos, gold trimmed stems, set of 12 .... **480.00**

1970

VASART

History: Vasart is a contemporary art glass made in Scotland by the Streathearn Glass Co. The colors are mottled, and sometimes shade from one hue to another. It is readily identified by an engraved signature on the base.

Collectors' Club: Monart & Vasart Collectors Club, 869 Cleveland St., Oakland, CA 94606.

Ashtray, 4½" d, mottled blue shading to pink, sgd **60.00**
Basket
  5" l, 8¼" h, green shading to pink, applied clear handle **90.00**
  6" l, 4" h, mottled blue, applied clear handle **85.00**

Bowl, green–gray ground, goldstone flakes, 8" d, $75.00.

Bowl
  2" d, scalloped rim, mottled green .. **35.00**
  5" d, light green **35.00**
  6½" d, pierced handle, pink and green **70.00**
  8" d, gray–green, gold mica flakes .. **75.00**
Hat, mottled blue, sgd **45.00**
Mug
  Mottled blue and green **45.00**
  Mottled white and lavender **40.00**
Plate, 8" d, gray–green, gold mica flakes **75.00**
Rose Bowl
  Mottled white and green **50.00**
  Mottled white and lavender **60.00**
Tray, 12" l, mottled blue shading to green **75.00**
Vase
  7½" h, swelled cylinder, internal cluthra pink and green dec, pulled and hooked swirls dec **100.00**
  7¾" h, waisted cylinder, internal cluthra pink and green dec, pulled and hooked swirls dec, sgd "Vasart" **115.00**
  8½" h, mottled blue shading to pink **100.00**
  9" d, jade green, ftd, sgd **75.00**

VENETIAN GLASS

History: Venetian glass has been made on the island of Morano, near Venice, since the 13th century. Most of the wares are thin walled. Many types of decoration have been used: embedded gold dust, lace work, and applied fruits or flowers.

Reproduction Alert: Venetian glass continues to be made today.

Barber Bottle, green overlay, cut to clear **125.00**
Basket, 7¾" h, 6½" d, mauve shaded to pink, bulbous ribbing with controlled bubbles, gold dust in applied clear handle **65.00**
Bowl
  7" d, cov, red and white stripes **165.00**
  10¼" d, 4½" h, symmetrical spiraled wavy white, amethyst, and gold stripes, clear ground, rippled exterior, applied polished gold–dust foot **140.00**
Candleholders, pr, 3¾" h, flower form, aqua, opalescent, and clear, gold dec **80.00**

Candlestick, canary ground, opalescent ribbon twist stem, brass fittings, 5¼" d base, 11¼" h, $70.00.

Candlesticks, pr
  12" h, clear, gold dust **135.00**
  15¾" h, pink, clear glass shot with gold, dolphin standard **125.00**
Centerpiece, 13" l, 9" h, figural, swan, blue, flower frog **35.00**
Chalice, 9" h, diamond quilted patterned aqua bowl and pedestal, clear trim, gold handles and stem, gold interior, 19th C **135.00**
Champagne, Victorian couple, hand painted, gilt trim, hollow twisted stem **125.00**
Cologne Bottle, 10¾" h, pink, flower form stopper with long applicator, pr **125.00**
Compote
  6⅜" d, 7½" h, pink, clear glass, gold dec, dolphin standard **100.00**
  8½" h, blue bowl, gold flecked ball stem, applied gold leaf prunts **75.00**
  11" h, amethyst and clear shell form bowl, swan handles, applied seahorse handles on base, diamond quilted foot **125.00**

Cruet, lavender, double swirled, orig stopper **100.00**
Decanter
  13" h, sq bottle, silver speckled pale amber ground, random red, blue, and white star millefiore canes, conforming hollow ball stopper .. **360.00**
  19½" h, triangular bottle, repeating colored vertical bands, conforming conical stopper **275.00**
Flower Frog, 13" l, 9" h, swan, blue .. **35.00**
Goblet, 6¼" h, green, pink rigaree ... **40.00**
Jar, cov, 7" h, pink, applied gold dust bubble stem and finial, pedestal base **90.00**
Plate, 7" d, pink and white alternating latticino stripes **60.00**
Rose Bowl, ruffled, ftd, pink, gold flecks **100.00**
Salt, swan shape, pink, gold trim **35.00**
Sculpture, 26½" h, freeform, ornithological/botanical design, brilliant clear glass, frosted glass pedestal cylinder base, etched signature "Segauso A. V." **1,500.00**
Shot Glass, 2½" h, enameled figures, pr **140.00**
Sweetmeat, cov, pink and gold swirled ground, ftd **90.00**
Tumbler, 3¼" h, swirled opaque white and cobalt blue, gold dust dec **60.00**
Vase
  7" h, handkerchief, striped white and gold threaded latticino, pink, and colorless glass panels alternately arranged in folded bowl form **140.00**
  7¼" h, handkerchief, transparent green, cased creamy opaque lining, flat polished pontil **275.00**
  10½" h, ftd, goblet shape, quilted pattern, petals, stem, and applied berries, pale green, gold trim **48.00**
  11" h, ovoid, colorless, repeating pattern of eight white and one blue spiraling threads, applied opaque white lip and foot with gold speckles **275.00**

VERLYS GLASS

History: Verlys glass is an art glass originally made in France after 1930. For a period of a few months, Heisey Glass Co., Newark, Ohio, produced the identical glass, having obtained the rights and formula from the French factory.

The French-produced glass can be distinguished from the American product by the signature. The French is mold marked; the American is etched script signed.

Animal, pigeon, 4¼" h, frosted **265.00**
Ashtray
  3½" d, frosted, floral dec, script sgd   **40.00**
  4½" d, frosted doves, floral border,
    script mark **50.00**
  6" d, oval, frosted, duck perched on
    side, wave molded base **55.00**
Bowl
  6" d
    Cupids and Hearts pattern, clear . **45.00**
    Pinecone pattern, French blue ... **100.00**
  8½" d, Thistle pattern, three small feet **150.00**
  10" d, Chrysanthemum pattern, clear
    and frosted **125.00**
  13½" d, Poppy pattern, frosted **125.00**
  14" d, Dragonfly pattern, etched mark **150.00**
Box, cov
  6½" d, butterflies, script mark **100.00**
  6¾" d, relief molded bouquet of co-
    reopsis, molded "Verlys France" on
    lid and base **200.00**
Candy Dish, cov
  6" h, Pinecone pattern, frosted **40.00**
  6½" h, Lovebirds pattern, sgd **50.00**
  7" h, sculptured florals on cov, opal **375.00**
Candlesticks, pr, 5½" d, leaftip molded
  nozzle, spreading circular foot with
  molded nasturtiums, etched signature
  on base, minor chips on rim **90.00**
Centerpiece, 19¼" l, 4⅞" h, oval, high
  relief molded ext., four exotic fish
  with long swirling fins and tails, each
  molded with shaped handle formed
  by extended fan shaped tails, wavy
  ground scattered with bubbles, relief
  molded signature **350.00**
Charger, 13" d, Waterlily pattern **145.00**
Plate
  4⅞" h, Shells pattern, opal **145.00**
  5" d, fish, clear and frosted **60.00**
  6¼" h, Pinecone pattern, mold sgd . **65.00**
  11¾" d, bird dec **165.00**
Powder Box, lovebirds, frosted **65.00**
Vase
  4" h, Gems pattern, opal, ground base **85.00**

Vase, Lovebirds pattern, fan shape, script signature, 4½" h, 6½" w, $125.00.

8" d, Thistles pattern, dusty rose **275.00**
9" h, ovoid, flared flattened rim, topaz, frosted large blossoms and
  leaves, script sgd "Verlys" on base **600.00**
9¾" h, clear and frosted, high relief
  molded stalks of wheat, inscribed
  "Verlys" **150.00**

WATERFORD

History: Waterford crystal is quality flint glass commonly decorated with cuttings. The original factory was established at Waterford, Ireland, in 1729. Glass made before 1830 is darker than the brilliantly clear glass of later production. The factory closed in 1852. After 100 years it re-opened and continues in production.

Pitcher, ribbed, applied handle, 10½" h, $215.00.

Ashtray, 7" d **80.00**
Bowl, 9" d, leaf cut border over trellis
  work sides **100.00**
Candlesticks, pr, 7" h, pear shape, hollow center, horizontal oval cuts on
  wafers between fluted top and rayed
  base, looped cross cuttings in two
  sizes, downward spray with star cut **175.00**
Creamer and Sugar, diamond cut **50.00**
Cruet, 5" h, waisted body, short fluted
  neck, fluted rim, strawberry leaves
  and fan cutting, faceted stopper **100.00**

Decanter
　10" d, deep cut Sawtooth Rib pattern,
　　double rope ring neck, orig stopper **250.00**
　12" h, paneled neck, star cut base,
　　orig stopper **100.00**
　15" h, all over geometric cutting,
　　matching stopper **150.00**
Goblet
　Cameragh pattern **35.00**
　Glengarett pattern **45.00**
Jar, cov
　6" h, diamond cut body, triple sprig
　　chain bordering thumb cut rim and
　　star cut lid, faceted knob finial ... **100.00**
　7" h, fan and diamond cuttings **135.00**
Letter Opener **45.00**
Pitcher
　6¾" h, Lismore pattern, shaped spout,
　　applied strap handle **120.00**
　10" h, diamond cuttings, applied han-
　　dle **200.00**
Plate, 8" d, diamond cut center **100.00**
Rose Bowl, 5½" d, laurel border, spike
　diamond band **45.00**
Salt
　3" d, cut, star base **30.00**
　3⅞" d, oval, diamond cut **54.00**
Scent Bottle, 4½" l, diamond cut **75.00**
Sweetmeat, cov, pr, double dome cov,
　Fan pattern, scalloped rim, sq pedes-
　tal base **700.00**
Tumbler, all over cutting **72.00**
Vase
　7" h, fluted neck, flared rim, hobnail
　　cut, triple sprig chains, star cut cen-
　　tered base **85.00**
　7¼" h, bulbous, top to bottom vertical
　　cuts separated by horizontal slash
　　cuts, sgd **125.00**
Water Set, 6" h pitcher, six tumblers,
　diamond cut **600.00**
Wine Glass, diamond and flute cut, star
　base **25.00**

WAVE CREST WARE

c1892

WAVE CREST

History: The C. F. Monroe Company of Meriden,
Connecticut, produced the opal glassware
known as Wave Crest from 1898 until World War
I. The company bought the opaque, blown
molded glass blanks for decoration from the Pairpoint Manufacturing Co. of New Bedford, Massachusetts, and other glassmakers including European factories. Florals were the most common
decorative motif. Trade names used were "Wave
Crest Ware," "Kelva," and "Nakara."

References: Wilfred R. Cohen, *Wave Crest: The
Glass of C.F. Monroe*, Collector Books, 1987;
Elsa H. Grimmer, *Wave Crest Ware*, Wallace-
Homestead, 1979.

**Wall Pocket, hanging, opal ground, hand
painted florals, gilt metal and brass rims
and frame, sgd, 8″ h, $825.00. Photo-
graph courtesy of Skinner, Inc.**

Ashtray, attached matching cigarette
　holder, ftd, floral dec, marked **400.00**
Atomizer, white ground, pink roses,
　white dots, new atomizer **225.00**
Biscuit Jar, cov, pale pink ground,
　multicolored flowers, silver plated
　swing bail handle and lid **200.00**
Box, cov, hinged
　3¼" h, 5½" l, 4" w, oval, pink ground,
　　blue daisies, good condition orig
　　lining **540.00**
　6½" h
　　Beige shading to white ground,
　　　daisy dec, orig metal hardware . **600.00**
　　Pale blue–gray, five pink and white
　　　blossoms on top, green and
　　　brown leaves and stems, two
　　　flowers on base, orig brass hard-
　　　ware, sgd "Kelva" **600.00**
Cigar Box, 5" sq, hinged lid, white
　ground, pink daisies, raised scrolled
　panels and lid **625.00**
Creamer and Sugar, opal, enameled and
　gilt floral dec **225.00**
Dresser Box, 3" d, hinged cov, all over
　marbled style green band, large pink
　roses and buds, orig lining, sgd
　"Kelva" **300.00**
Dresser Tray, 6½" l, 4½" w, scalloped,
　emb, tiny pink roses, six ormolu feet,
　red banner mark **425.00**
Ewer, 17½" h, blue shaded to turquoise
　ground, floral dec, matched pr **300.00**
Fernery, 5¼" sq, creamy white ground,
　blue floral dec **345.00**
Glove Box, hinged cov, 9½" l, 5" w,
　creamy yellow ground, pink and

white roses, green leaves, emb design on top and base, ormolu feet, orig satin lining, marked **1,000.00**

Jar, 4½" d, 2¼" h, squatty, blue daisies, red–brown scrolled body, metal lid . **165.00**

Jewelry Box, 5¼" w, 3" h, oval, hinged cov, gold emb scroll around edge, creamy white ground, center with blue and white florals, pink sprays, green leaves, marked **275.00**

Pin Tray
3" d, circular, pink daisies, blue molded scrolls, double handled metal rim **115.00**
4½" d, emb rococo scrolls, handle, red banner mark **115.00**

Ring Box, 2½" h, hand painted cupids on lid **300.00**

Salt Shaker, Daisy mold, white, light blue flowers, 2" h, $165.00.

Salt and Pepper Shakers, pr
Helmschmeid Swirl, Erie Twist pattern, enamel blue asters dec, alternating white and beige swirls, pewter tops **185.00**
Hexagonal, blown–out dec, enameled florals **125.00**

Sugar, cov, Helmschmeid swirl, daisy dec **150.00**

Sweetmeat, cov, Helmschmeid swirl, hand painted, pink and lavender pansies, twisted handle, sgd **400.00**

Syrup, pale blue ground, enameled spray of pink wild roses, swirled body, silver plated top and handle **450.00**

Tray, 6½" l, 4¾" w, free form, raised scrolling, pink apple blossoms dec, ormolu feet **425.00**

Vase
9" h, white ground, wild roses dec, raised gold lines form panels connected with blue dots, blue collar with sepia circles, ormolu base . . **465.00**
10" h, tapered, white satin ground, pale blue daisies, pale green scrolls and leaves, four gold feet **550.00**

Whisk Broom Holder, 10½" l, 7¼" w, mauve holder with hand pained pastel flowers, bright, shiny ormolu holder, slightly frayed satin lining, red banner mark **985.00**

WEBB, THOMAS & SONS

History: Thomas Webb & Sons was established in 1837 in Stourbridge, England. The company probably is best known for its very beautiful English cameo glass. However, many other types of colored glass were produced including enameled glass, iridescent glass, pieces with heavy glass ornamentation, cased glass, and other art glass besides cameo.

References: Victor Arwas, *Glass Art Nouveau to Art Deco,* Rizzoli International Publications, Inc., 1977; Ray and Lee Grover, *English Cameo Glass,* Crown Publishers, Inc., 1980; Charles R. Hajdamach, *British Glass, 1800–1914,* Antique Collectors' Club, 1991; Albert C. Revi, *Nineteenth Century Glass,* reprint, Schiffer Publishing, 1981.

Additional Listings: Burmese, Cameo, and Peachblow.

Bowl, cameo glass, yellow half–round layered in white, carved trumpet blossoms and butterfly at reverse, hallmarked beaded silver rim, circular "Thos. Webb & Sons Cameo" mark, 8¼" d, 4¾" h, estimated $2,500–$3,000.

Bottle, 5¼" h, cameo, round cylindrical vial, yellow ground, white overlay, cameo cut and carved leafy spray of blossoms, two flying insects, double linear borders, hallmarked silver cover **750.00**

Bowl
3" d, 2½" h, tricorn, satin, shaded brown, gold prunus blossoms and butterfly dec, creamy interior, gold trim **325.00**
4⅞" d, 4¼" h, diamond quilted patterned body, MOP, satin, apple green, rich cream lining, six crimp top, applied frosted feet, frosted flower prunt **550.00**
10" d, butterscotch ground, gold floral dec, two handles **165.00**
10" d, 3¾" h, diamond quilted patterned body, MOP, satin, deep rose

shading to pink to white ground, box pleated top, applied solid frosted base 750.00

Bride's Basket, 10" d, diamond quilted patterned body, MOP, pink satin ground, ruffled edge, metal base, sgd 300.00

Claret Jug, opaque white body, brilliant gold palm trees and bamboo stalks, rust and dark green ferns and tropical foliage, silver plated flip top lid, collar, and handle, hallmarked and numbered 335.00

Cologne Bottle, 5½" h, globular, peach satin, sterling silver screw top 250.00

Creamer and Sugar, 3½" h creamer, 1¾" h x 4" d open sugar, cameo glass, Fish Scale pattern, white lining revealed through pink exterior, gold enamel butterfly and ivy dec, attributed to Thomas Webb, each pc sgd "G. L. F.," pr 485.00

Ewer, 9" h, 4" w, satin, shaded deep green to off white, gold enameled leaves and branches, three apples, applied ivory handle, base numbered 425.00

Flower Holder, 12½" l, 8¾" w, gold irid glass foot, brass leaves and branches, four irid gold ribbed flower shaped vases 500.00

Jar, 5" d, diamond quilted patterned body, MOP, blue, berries dec, silver plated hallmarked collar, lid, and bail handle 450.00

Perfume Bottle, 3½" h, globular, carved white blossoms, blue satin ground, sterling silver screw on cap 875.00

Relish Dish, 3" h, 5¾" d, 6½" h x 8" w silver plated tray, twin Burmese hat shaped bowls, pastel yellow crown, shading to blushed rolled rim, three butterflies and dragonfly dec on each, flattened brim with brilliant golden laden bittersweet blossoms, figural calla lily handle on silver plated handle 1,450.00

Rose Bowl
2½" d, 2⅜" h, shaded brown to ivory, satin, cream interior, eight crimp top 325.00

3⅛" d, 3" h, rose overlay, white interior, four crimp top, clear wafer foot, heavy gold flowers and branches, enameled "E" and spider web on base 265.00

3¾" d, blue swirled MOP satin glass bowl, green satin glass leaf shaped base 220.00

6¼" d, 5¼" h, satin, brown shading to yellow to cream, creamy white interior, box pleated top, six crimps 325.00

Salt, master, frosted, Adam and Eve, butterfly signature 65.00

Scent Bottle
1¼" h, 4¼" l, lay down, gold prunus blossoms, green shaded to yellow satin ground, hallmarked sterling silver domed monogrammed cap . 400.00

3½" h, black satin, white floral dec, small label reads "Lily of the Valley" 80.00

Toothpick Holder, Alexandrite, ruffled edge 1,000.00

Vase, cameo, four layer, elongated bottle form, crystal cased to bright red, yellow over white layers, cameo cut repeating Oriental pattern of stylized scrolling geometric and floral devices, stamped "Thomas Webb & Sons Gem Cameo," 7⅛" h, $8,250.00. Photograph courtesy of Skinner, Inc.

Vase
2½" h, cameo, red body, opal casing, white overlaid, cut rose and budding branches, butterfly, unsigned 1,100.00

5" h
Cameo, baluster, white honey suckle and leaves, red ground 1,400.00
Cameo, bulbous, white apple blossoms and leaves, red ground .. 1,275.00
Cameo, bulbous, red ground, white overlay, cameo cut and carved blossoms, buds, and twisting leafy stems, linear borders, marked "Thomas Webb & Sons Gem Cameo," two tiny base chips 2,400.00
Experimental, bulbous, crossed thorn design, ground top and rim chips 275.00

5¼" h, stick top, bulbous, blue satin glass 115.00

6" h, cameo, honey amber ground, white overlay, cameo cut leaves, grasses, and blossoms, marked "Thomas Webb & Sons Cameo" 1,100.00

6⅛" h, 3½" d, yellow satin, cream interior, gold prunus and butterfly dec **325.00**

6½" h, heat reactive amber to rose, cream lining, white overlay, cameo cut wild geraniums and grasses, top rim possibly ground, unsigned **1,100.00**

6⅞" h, peachblow, acid finish, deep cream lining, shaded rose to cream, heavy gold daisies and leaves, large gold dragonfly on back **650.00**

8" h, 4" w, satin finish, pink and white stripes, frilly top, bulbous base, c1885 .... **425.00**

8¼" h, 6¼" w at shoulder, satin, robin's egg blue shading to pale blue, bright yellow dec of bird in flight, prunus blossoms, berries, leaves, and large butterfly **425.00**

8¾" h, brown satin, fluted, elaborate gold filigree dec, blue and white enamel highlights, pr **600.00**

9" h, 4¼" d, deep coral red overlay, white lining, heavy gold flowers and branch dec **350.00**

10½" h, gourd shape, satin, bright yellow shading to pale yellow, creamy white interior, bleed thru pontil **285.00**

c1910

WESTMORELAND GLASS COMPANY

History: The Westmoreland Glass Company was founded in October, 1899, at Grapeville, Pennsylvania. From the beginning, Westmoreland made handcrafted high quality glassware. In early years the company processed mustard, baking powder, and condiments to fill its containers. During World War I candy–filled glass novelties were popular.

Although Westmoreland is famous for its milk glass, large amounts of other glass were produced. During the 1920s, Westmoreland made reproductions and decorated wares. Color and tableware appeared in the 1930s; but, as with other companies, 1935 saw the return to mainly crystal productions. In the 1940s to 1960s, black, ruby, and amber colors were made.

In May 1982 the factory closed. Reorganization brought a reopening in July, 1982. The Grapeville plant closed again in 1984.

The collector should become familiar with the many lines of tableware produced. English Hobnail made from the 1920s to 1960s is popular. Colonial designs were reproduced frequently, and accessories with dolphin pedestals are distinctive.

The trademark, an interwined "W" and "G," was imprinted on glass since 1949. After January, 1983, the full name "Westmoreland" is on all glass. Early molds were reintroduced. Numbered, signed, and dated "Limited Editions" were offered.

References: Lorraine Kovar, *Westmoreland Glass 1950–1984*, Antique Publications, 1991; Hazel Marie Weatherman, *Colored Glassware of the Depression Era, Book 2*, Glassbooks, Inc., 1982.

Collectors' Clubs: National Westmoreland Glass Collectors Club, P. O. Box 372, Export, PA 15632; Westmoreland Glass Collectors Club, P.O, Box 103, North Liberty, IA 52317.

Museum: Westmoreland Glass Museum, Port Vue, PA.

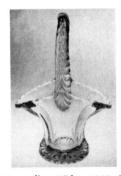

Basket, vaseline, 7" h, c1960, $20.00.

MISCELLANEOUS

Animal Covered Dish
Duck, cobalt blue, yellow glass eyes **65.00**
Hen
  1" h, frosted, pink, red trim **20.00**
  3½" h, milk glass **15.00**
Lovebirds on nest **45.00**
Bowl, 12" d, Lustre, crystal, three ball, bell shape **65.00**
Candy, cov, 8" d, #300, ruby **85.00**
Compote, cov, low, ftd, irid cobalt, sgd "#14 of 500," dated 1978 .... **80.00**
Egg Cup, chick **8.50**
Salt, Chick **15.00**
Toothpick Holder, owl **15.00**

PATTERNS

American Hobnail, Pattern #77, milk glass, white
Ashtray, 4½" d, round **5.00**

Bonbon, cov	25.00
Candleholders, pr, 5" h	30.00
Compote, 6" h, ftd	18.00
Creamer and Sugar	20.00
Mayonnaise, bell rim, ftd	17.00
Puff Box, cov	25.00
Rose Bowl, cupped, ftd	17.00

Beaded Edge, Pattern #22, milk glass, white

Nappy, 6" oval, painted strawberries	10.00

Plate

7" d, painted fruit	14.00
7¼" d, painted bird	6.00
10½" d, dinner	18.00
Tumbler, ftd, fruits dec	15.00

Beaded Grape, Pattern #1884, milk glass, white

Ashtray

4" d, roses dec	14.00
5" d	12.00
Candlesticks, pr	32.00
Candy, cov, 4" sq	15.00

Honey, cov

Plain	27.00
Roses dec	35.00
Sugar, 3½" h	10.00

Candy Dish, Beaded Grape, milk glass, sgd in lid, 1955, 5¾" h, $10.00.

Bramble/Maple Leaf, Pattern #1928, milk glass, white

Bowl, 4½" d

Round, ftd	25.00
Square, ftd	28.00
Compote, crimped, ftd	25.00
Creamer and Sugar	20.00
Rose Bowl, 4½" d, ftd	25.00

Della Robbia, Pattern #1058

Compote, 3¾" d, hand painted dark luster color	35.00
Creamer and Sugar, crystal	40.00
Nappy, 4¾" d, crystal, orig label	9.00
Punch Set, cupped punch bowl, 19" d liner, ladle, ten cups, hand painted dark luster color	650.00

Torte Plate, 14½" d, hand painted dark luster color	125.00
Water, 8 oz	10.00

English Hobnail

Cruet, large, milk glass	20.00
Goblet, milk glass	7.00
Nappy, 4" d, milk glass	4.00
Salt and Pepper Shakers, pr, barrel shape, milk glass	25.00

Old Quilt, Pattern #500, milk glass, white

Bowl

5" d, ftd, flared	30.00
6" d, ftd, bell shape	30.00
7½" d, ftd	35.00
Box, cov, sq	20.00
Butter, cov, round	35.00
Candlesticks, pr	40.00

Candy Dish, cov

4½" d, ftd	25.00
5" sq, ftd	18.00
Celery, ftd	20.00
Cheese, cov, round	35.00
Creamer, 3½" h	15.00
Creamer and Sugar, 4" h	35.00
Cruet, orig stopper	20.00
Fruit Bowl, 9" d, crimped skirt, ftd, orig label	48.00
Goblet	18.00
Honey, cov, 5" d	18.00
Iced Tea Tumbler, flat, 11 oz	20.00
Juice Tumbler	4.50
Nappy, 5½" d, bell shape	22.00
Salt and Pepper Shakers, pr	22.00
Spooner, ftd	20.00
Sweetmeat, cov, 6" h, ftd	30.00
Vase, 7" h, ftd, fan	18.00
Wine	25.00

Paneled Grape, Pattern #1881, milk glass, white

Appetizer Set, 9" d, 2 pcs	60.00
Basket, 6½" h, oval	22.50

Bowl

9" d, ftd	55.00
9¾" d, scalloped	50.00
12½" l, 6½" w, oblong	130.00
Butter, cov	30.00
Cake Salver, ftd, skirt	85.00
Candlesticks, pr, ftd	20.00
Canape Set, 13" d egg tray, 3½" h fruit compote, ladle	135.00
Candy, cov, three toes	35.00
Cheese, round	70.00
Chocolate Box, cov	38.00
Compote, ftd, piecrust, flared, roses dec	55.00

Creamer and Sugar

Individual size	45.00
Large, ftd	25.00
Cruet, orig stopper	22.00
Cup, coffee	9.00
Cup and Saucer	24.00

Decanter 200.00
Flower Pot 30.00
Goblet 18.00
Gravy, tray 55.00
Jardiniere, 6½" h, ftd 32.00
Jelly, oval 25.00
Jug
    Quart 35.00
    Pint 50.00
Mayonnaise, 3 pcs 30.00
Old Fashioned 18.00
Pitcher 30.00
Planter, oblong 35.00
Plate
    6½" d 20.00
    8½" d 24.00
Puff Box, cov 25.00
Punch Cup 12.50
Rose Bowl, 4" d, ftd 18.00
Salt and Pepper Shakers, pr, ftd 16.00
Sauceboat and tray 55.00
Toilet Bottle, orig stopper, 5 oz 45.00
Toothpick 35.00
Tray
    9" l, oval 75.00
    13½" l, oval 75.00
Vase
    6" h, scalloped ftd 15.00
    10" h, gold dec 45.00
Pineapple and Grape, milk glass, white,
  punch set, 15 pcs 375.00
Roses and Bows
  Wedding Bowl
    Large, "Best Wishes" dec 65.00
    Small 45.00
Three Fruits, punch set, bowl, twelve
  cups 250.00
Zodiac, platter, 16" l, Zodiac, blue, red,
  and gold 95.00

WHIMSIES

History: Glassworkers occasionally spent time during lunch or after completing their regular work schedule creating unusual glass objects, known as whimsies, e.g. candy striped canes, darners, hats, paperweights, pipes, witch balls, etc. Whimsies were taken home and given as gifts to family and friends.

Because of their uniqueness and infinite variety, whimsies can rarely be attributed to a specific glass house or glassworker. Whimsies occurred wherever glass was made, from New Jersey to Ohio and westward. Some have suggested that style and color can be used to pinpoint region or factory, but no one has yet developed an identification key that is adequate.

One of the most collectible types of whimsies is glass canes. Glass canes range from very short, under one foot, to lengths of ten feet and beyond. They come in both hollow and solid form. Hollow canes can have a bulb type handle or the rarer "C" or "L" shaped handle. Canes are found in many fascinating colors, with the candy striped being a regular favorite with collectors. Many canes are also filled with varied colored powders, gold, and white being the most common, and silver being harder to find. Sometimes they were even used as candy containers.

References: Joyce E. Blake, *Glasshouse Whimsies,* printed by author, 1984; Joyce E. Blake and Dale Murschell, *Glasshouse Whimsies: An Enhanced Reference,* printed by author, 1989.

Collectors' Club: The Whimsey Club, 4544 Cairo Drive, Whitehall, PA 18052.

Bellows Bottle
  8¾" l, clear, lead glass, threaded
    neck, body with multiple prunts,
    leaf, pinched, and quilled rigaree
    around edges, pontil scar, c1880,
    minor sections of threading missing **145.00**
  16½" h, ftd, clear neck and threading,
    clear quilled rigaree on each cor-
    ner, cranberry body, clear applied
    standard and foot, pontil scar **125.00**
Bird Feeder, 5¾" h, bottle green glass,
  emb bird and "Don't Forge to Feed
  Me" **135.00**
Bird Drinking Font, 4½" h, blown
  molded, applied cobalt blue ball top
  and rim **200.00**
Cane
  29" l, solid, aqua, round end, white
    threads, curved handle, 1860–80 . **95.00**
  30" l, solid, clear, looped end, white
    rod center **95.00**
  38" l, solid, aqua, bent handle, square
    shaft, center amber rod **85.00**
  48" l, blown, hollow, large ball on
    end, clear, red, white, and blue
    threadings, 1860–80 .... **330.00**
  50" l
    Blown, hollow, cranberry, white
      twist, 1860–80 .... **150.00**
    Solid, green–aqua, sq, twisted end
      and handle, 1860–80 .... **95.00**
  52" l, blown, hollow, clear, deep red,
    clambroth, light blue, and medium
    blue twists, 1860–80 .... **180.00**
Fly Catcher, 7" h, removable dome top,
  clear, 19th C **250.00**
Pen Holder, 3" h, 3½" paperweight
  base, blown spatter glass, cobalt blue,
  red, and white solid round sphere,
  pulled into six coils to hold pen **150.00**
Pipe, 26½" l, Nailsea type, opaque
  white ground, pink loopings, three
  separate pcs, bowl, stem, and connector, c1870 .... **175.00**

Witch Ball, Nailsea type, pale blue ground, white loopings, 4¼" d, $100.00.

Powder Horn
    6½" h, twenty–eight vertical ribs, ol-
        ive amber, applied ring and lip,
        pontil scar, New England, 1790–
        1830 .... **1,320.00**
    11" h, Nailsea type, ftd, clear ground,
        blue and white loopings, tooled
        ground lip, pontil scar, mid 19th C **100.00**
    14" h, cannon shaped, twisted neck,

clear, non–lead glass, blue and red
        loop pattern, pontil scar, American,
        mid 19th C **165.00**
Sword, clear, colored spirals in handles,
    attributed to Sandwich Glassworks,
    late 19th C, pr **360.00**
Witch Ball and Stand
    4" h, amber ground, white loopings,
        matching 4¾" h ribbed baluster
        form holder **400.00**
    8" h, tortoiseshell glass ball, attached
        to amber glass stem and foot **185.00**
    9½" h, free blown, deep sapphire
        blue, pontil scar, attributed to South
        Jersey, mid 19th C **1,200.00**
    12¼" h, golden amber, hollow feet,
        tooled lip, pontil scar, attributed to
        Whitney Glassworks, Glassboro,
        NJ, mid 19th C, pr **495.00**
    16" h, Nailsea type, clear, white loop-
        ings, pontil scar, attributed to Pitts-
        burgh or New Jersey glasshouse,
        1840–60 .... **1,210.00**

INDEX